Bloody Mary

Also by Carolly Erickson and published by Robson Books

To the Scaffold: The Life of Marie Antoinette
Bonnie Prince Charlie

Bloody Mary

The Life of Mary Tudor

CAROLLY ERICKSON

Robson Books

To Peter

This edition published in Great Britain in 1995 by Robson
Books Ltd, Bolsover House, 5-6 Clipstone Street, London
WIP 8LE

Copyright © 1978 Carolly Erickson
The right of Carolly Erickson to be identified as author of this
work has been asserted by her in accordance with the Copyright,
Designs and Patents Act 1988

British Library Cataloguing in Publication Data
A catalogue record for this title is available from the British
Library

ISBN 0 86051 976 7

Printed in Great Britain by St Edmundsbury Press Ltd, Bury St
Edmunds, Suffolk.

Contents

Preface

Preface

Mary Tudor has no monument in England. In her will she had asked that a memorial be raised to herself and her mother, "for a decent memory of us," but her request was ignored. The day of her death, November 17—the day of Elizabeth's accession—was a national holiday for two hundred years, and before the generation that remembered Mary as queen had died out the contrast between her "poor, short and despised" reign and the "glory, length and prosperity" of her sister's was becoming a historical commonplace. Succeeding generations called her Bloody Mary, and saw her reign through the pictures in Foxe's *Book of Martyrs* —pictures of Protestant prisoners fettered with leg irons, being beaten by their Catholic tormentors, praying as they awaited execution, their faces already touched with the ecstatic vision of heaven.

The memory of the martyrs still looms large in any appraisal of Mary's reign, but there were other themes in her story. Mary was a survivor. She outlasted an agonizing adolescence, illness, her mother's slow martyrdom and her father's whimsical tormenting. She lived through worse dangers in Edward's reign, and went on to win the throne when the odds were overwhelmingly against her. Contemporaries saw Mary's triumphant accession as nothing short of miraculous, and she herself had long since come to believe that she had a divinely appointed destiny to return England to Catholicism. As queen she endured mounting conflicts between her political status and her sexual status, enforced subordination to an indifferent husband, and the shattering disappointment of a false pregnancy.

Mary Tudor bore an extraordinary burden, yet she ruled with a full measure of the Tudor majesty, and met the challenges of severe economic crises, rebellion and religious upheaval capably and with courage. Her resiliency impressed itself on the men around her. In describing her character several of them hit on the same metaphor. She was a single candle, they wrote, which shone on even when battered about by great winds, and seemed to burn more resplendently in the midst of the storm.

In writing this account of Mary's life I have had help and support from Peter Dreyer, who stood by in friendship as the manuscript took shape, from Dennis Halac, who read the completed draft, and from Hal Erickson and Roberta Phillips, whose interest encouraged me as I went along. I want to thank Michael Ossias of Doubleday for his enthusiastic sponsorship and my research assistant, Martha Moore, for her cheerful and competent work over many months. And to Ron Erickson, who read each chapter as it was written and typed most of the manuscript, I owe a heartfelt debt.

Berkeley, California

Bloody Mary

Edinburgh

SCOTLAND • Flodden Field

• York

Hatfield•

E N G L A N D

Norwich
Peterborough
Ludlow • Kimbolton • Framlingham
Coventry•
Newmarket
W A L E S

Oxford• Maldon•
London Blackwater
Windsor•
Rochester• Dover Oostende
Folkestone• Calais• Brussels
Winchester• Guines•
Exeter Boulogne• St. Omer• FLANDERS

English Channel F R A N C E

PART ONE

The Princess

I

 Owre Royall Rose now reignyng, rede and whyte,
Sure grafted is on ground of nobylnes
In Harry the viij owr joye and our delyte
Subdewer of wronges mayntenar of rightwysnes
Fowntayne of honor exsampler of larges.
Our clypsyd [eclipsed] son now cleryd is from the darke
By Harry owr Kyng, the flowr of natewr's warke.

On a bright winter day in February of 1511 servants crowded the tiltyard of Henry VIII's palace at Westminster, readying the lists, carrying body armor and horse barbs, and covering the walls of the wooden spectators' pavilion with tapestries and hangings of cloth of gold. A solemn joust had been proclaimed, to celebrate the recent birth of Henry's heir, the infant Prince Henry, duke of Richmond and Somerset and chief hope of the Tudor dynasty.

Inside the pavilion the queen, Katherine of Aragon, took her place of honor under the small golden cloth of estate, concealing her plumpness in a dark gown with sleeves of gold and black. At her throat she wore her emblem, the pomegranate of Spain, suspended from a chain, and pomegranates had been painted on the wooden trim of the pavilion. Surrounded by her sumptuously dressed ladies, and by the nobles and court officials in their velvets and heavy gold chains of office, Katherine was the center of attention as a crowd of Londoners gathered to watch the spectacle. This was her first public appearance since her churching, and her usually pale face, smiling as always, flushed with pride. She had finally done what she was sent from Spain to do ten years earlier. She had produced an heir to the English throne.

The trumpeting of mounted heralds bearing the arms of England announced the opening of the jousts. At one end of the tiltyard—a long,

narrow stretch of ground divided along its length by a solid wooden barrier—the line of grooms and liveried guardsmen parted as a huge decorated pageant car rolled slowly into view. Nearly as wide as the tiltyard itself, and so tall it towered over the pavilion, it was like a large stage set
mounted on wheels, complete with scenery, actors and props. A forest
landscape with grass-covered hills, rocks and a variety of trees and
flowers had been fashioned from green damask and colored silks and
satins. In the foreground amid the trees were six foresters in Lincoln
green velvet, bringing the wooden lances for the joust, and at the center
of the forest stood a golden castle. Before the castle gate a handsomely
dressed gentleman sat in the silken ferns weaving a garland of roses for
the infant prince. This elaborate scene appeared to be drawn by two
great beasts, a lion of damask gold and an antelope of silver, with golden
horns and tusks, chained to the pageant car with huge gilded chains.
Troops of green-clad wild woodsmen walked before the structure, leading the lion and antelope, and two beautiful women rode on the backs of
the beasts.

When it reached the queen and her ladies the forest halted, the
foresters blew their horns, and from four openings in the artificial hills
four "Knights of the Savage Forest" rode out of the pageant and down
onto the tilting ground. Each of the four was in full armor, with a
plumed helmet and a lance in his hand. Though their visors obscured
their faces the crowd knew well enough by his height that one of the disguised knights was the handsome nineteen-year-old king. On the trappings that blanketed their horses were the chivalric names of the four
defenders: Sir Loyal Heart, Sir Valiant Desire, Sir Good Valour, Sir Joyous Thought. At the sight of the defenders the crowd roared its welcome
and to the sound of trumpets and drums the noble challengers, their
horses trapped in crimson satin embroidered with golden pomegranates,
rode onto the field from the opposite side and the jousting began.

Sir Loyal Heart—as the king called himself that day—was easily the
most skillful jouster at the tourney, shattering more lances than any of
the other combatants and, assuming his performance that day was true to
form, wearing out four or five mounts. From all accounts Henry did not,
as one would expect, triumph over his opponents merely because he was
the king; he genuinely surpassed them in size, strength and skill. He was
by sixteenth-century standards a very tall man. His standing armor,
preserved in the Tower of London, accommodates a man of about six
feet two, and the size of his jousting armor suggests that he may have
been even taller.[1] Like Richard Lionheart and his maternal grandfather
Edward IV, Henry towered over his courtiers and guardsmen, and when
he walked in a crowd he was easy to distinguish. He was not only tall but
powerfully built, with broad shoulders and muscular arms and legs, and

with no trace of the repulsive girth he acquired at the very end of his life. "He is well made, tall and stout," an observer wrote of the king at twenty-one, "and when he moves the ground shakes under him."[2]

Henry seems in fact to have combined the force of his massive size with good coordination and unusual dexterity. Proficiency in the joust, for which he regularly trained and toughened himself two days a week, required both accuracy of aim and the stamina to withstand repeated blows to the chest and head. For to win a tournament required not only breaking the most lances but breaking them on the helmets, rather than the saddles or body armor, of the opponents. And striking the tilt, or wooden barrier, more than twice, or striking a horse instead of his rider, or losing your helmet twice, or, unthinkable dishonor, striking a disarmed knight or one with his back turned, all meant immediate disqualification.

The jousting lasted until dark, when the challengers, including the earl of Essex and Lord Thomas Howard, were defeated by the four Knights of the Savage Forest. The king was applauded and cheered one final time as he rode off the field, still in the guise of Sir Loyal Heart. His triumph once again bound the spectators to him by an emotion stronger than loyalty to a sovereign and not far short of gratitude to a savior. He had entered the lists not as their king but as their champion, a half-enchanted knight emerging from a mysterious forest. And by the true valor of his arms he had won the day.

On the following day the combats were introduced by a chivalric procession climaxed by Henry's solemn entry in his own person, as sovereign, under the canopy of royalty. Again, the queen and her ladies in place, the trumpeters summoned the jousters, and a parade of gentlemen rode in single file up and down the length of the lists, testing their horses and displaying their arms and devices. A group of lords in russet and cloth of gold followed, and a party of knights in the same colors. Then came a great party of gentlemen and yeomen on foot, the former in silk, the latter in matching damask, with scarlet hose and yellow caps. They surrounded the king, and held the supports of the miniature pavilion of cloth of gold and purple velvet under which he rode. The canopy, richly embroidered, had a fringe made from thin gold wire, and was surmounted by an imperial crown. Sewn all over it were replicas of Queen Katherine's monogram, the letter K, cast in fine gold. Henry, in gleaming armor, rode a prancing horse in golden trappings and with a horn attached to its forehead like the horn of a unicorn. The golden letters, hearts and pomegranates covered his armor and horse cloths, and as he made his horse curvet and bow the gilt spangles that hung from the plume of his helmet shook and glittered in the sunlight.

Next the three disguised knights from the previous day rode onto the field, each with his own pavilion of crimson and purple topped by a large gold K, and with fifty attendants on foot. And finally, to remind the company of the absent prince whose birth had occasioned the jousts, twelve "children of honor" were led in on great war horses, no two dressed alike. With this the king's party was complete.

Then, as the crowd looked to the opposite end of the tiltyard to see the entry of the opponents, led by Henry's closest friend Charles Brandon, duke of Suffolk, they fell silent. Instead of a fanfare and a procession of panoplied knights they saw a solitary figure ride toward the pavilion where Katherine sat, not a knightly figure but a man in the brown hooded cloak of a monk or recluse. Stopping his horse in front of the queen, he petitioned her to give him leave to joust in her presence, adding that if it pleased her he would begin at once, if not, he would leave as he had come. When she smiled and nodded he threw off his cape and signaled his attendants to bring his armor. The religious was none other than the strapping Brandon himself, and the spectators watched with delight as his armor was tied in place and his helmet and lance supplied. When his horse had been similarly barbed and arrayed, he rode to his assigned place. After Brandon came a small pageant car carrying a castle tower or turret, out of which rode Henry Guilford, principal defender for that day, in brown and silver. He and his liveried attendants also asked Katherine's permission to joust, as did the marquis of Dorset and Thomas Boleyn, who made their appearance dressed as pilgrims returning from the Spanish shrine of St. James of Compostela, their pilgrim staves and the golden shells that symbolized the shrine their only ornaments. The earl of Wiltshire, entered in another pageant, called "The House of Refuge," at the center of which was a huge golden pomegranate tree; the spreading branches of the tree covered the house and the knight, who was all in silver.

When the defenders for the day were in place, the jousting began, and by the time it was over the king and his three companions had again prevailed. Whether because he broke the most spears or because—as we know he did at a joust in 1515—he accomplished the rare feat of forcing to the ground both a man and his horse, Henry "achieved valiantly," and attained the prize.

The prize of arms won at the prince's tournament was only the capstone to the greater triumph of the prince's birth. No kingdom was secure, no people's loyalty guaranteed, until the ruler had provided a male heir to succeed him, and now that Henry had done that he could relax and congratulate himself for a while. He could even allow himself to look ahead to the future. The prince would in time be king as Henry IX, third Henry of the house of Tudor and ninth in a line of Henrys stretching back five hundred years: Henry I, son of William the

Conqueror; Henry II Plantagenet, friend and slayer of Becket and ruler of half of France; Henry III, saintly patron of learning and builder of cathedrals; Henry IV, adventurer and founder of the ill-fated Lancastrian line; Henry V, the beloved Prince Hal and legendary victor of Agincourt; Henry VI, whose long reign ended in madness and the chaos of the Wars of the Roses; the Tudor Henry VII, who ended those wars by his victory at Bosworth Field; and, finally, the exuberant Henry VIII, whose fame as a soldier or diplomat or ruler—indeed as anything but an expert jouster—was yet to be achieved.

In the craft of kingship Henry was very much a novice. His fellow rulers on the continent were well over twice his age, and treated him with avuncular disdain. He had as yet taken no part in European politics, though his father-in-law, Ferdinand of Aragon, was urging him to throw the weight of English arms and money against the dominant French. The pope too, the bellicose Julius II, was a suitor for Henry's support in his fight against the French in Italy. Nine months earlier he had sent Henry the traditional golden rose, anointed with the sacred coronation oil and sprinkled with pungent musk, that symbolized the long-standing sentimental alliance between the papacy and the English kings.

With the dimwitted, bankrupt Emperor Maximilian, ridiculed throughout Europe as the "man of few pence," Henry had had little to do, while the aging French king Louis XII saw in his inexperienced young English counterpart no threat to his ambitious designs. At the opening of the year 1511 the battleground of Europe was Italy, where for a generation the armies of France and Spain had fought over the spoils of the Renaissance city-states. For the moment, France had triumphed, but the peninsula's other great territorial lord, the pope, was determined to drive the French out. Even now, in midwinter, Julius was leading his soldiers through the snow in a futile campaign against the French in the north of Italy.

If he lacked a military or diplomatic reputation, Henry did possess one enviable political asset: a full treasury. The costs of his extravagant costumes, tourneys and court revels had not even begun to deplete the wealth his father had left him. And the continental powers were not slow to capitalize on that wealth. Already he had become a sort of royal pawnbroker, making loans secured by diamonds and other jewels and, in one instance, by the armor of the great fifteenth-century duke Charles the Bold. Four months earlier the Venetian ambassador wrote his home government that the English king had agreed to loan the Signory 150,000 ducats on jewels.

Of course, the infant prince gave Henry a further bargaining counter. As soon as possible, English diplomats would begin negotiations at all the European courts for his betrothal. The diplomatic credit to be gained

from a marriage alliance with France, Portugal or the Austrian Hapsburgs was wonderful to contemplate, and by no means out of reach. The
prince was certain to be a handsome and promising child, heir to a stable
throne; these benefits, plus Henry's flowing coffers, would surely lead to
a splendid match. Already the diplomats were spreading news of the elaborate christening ceremony of the young Henry, and of the organization
of his personal household and his Council of State. They would describe
the tournament, too, expanding on its grandiose pageantry and the king's
well-known prowess.

Henry's pleasurable speculations about his son were understandable,
for since his marriage he had had ample reason to doubt whether his wife
could give him a son at all. Katherine's childless first marriage, the frailty
of her health and a miscarriage the previous year had all pointed to the
possibility of barrenness.

Katherine of Aragon had come to England ten years earlier, when
Henry was a boy, to marry his older brother Arthur. The joining
of the Tudor heir to a younger daughter of Ferdinand and Isabella of
Spain raised England's prestige abroad, but only temporarily. Katherine
did not become pregnant—indeed she was to swear later that the marriage had not been consummated—and the death of the consumptive
prince left her widowed at sixteen. Kept in England as a hostage until
her father paid the final installment of her dowry, something he showed
no inclination to do, Katherine spent the next eight years uncertain of
her status and her prospects. Apart from the title Princess Dowager she
had nothing to show for her time in England. She had no money, no
friends outside her small retinue of Spanish servants, and she was an
obvious nuisance both to her father-in-law Henry VII and her father
Ferdinand. Her beloved mother, the valiant Isabella, was dead; her
favorite sister, Joanna, wrote at first infrequently and then not at all.

In her anxious isolation Katherine turned to God. By the time she was
twenty she had apparently decided to renounce worldly things and subject herself to the harsh demands of an ascetic life. Someone at the court
became concerned enough about the harm this relentless praying and
fasting might do to write to the pope. Julius wrote back ordering that
her regimen be relaxed, and stating specifically that it threatened to ham-
per her ability to conceive and bear children in the future. It must certainly have made worse the ailments that had afflicted her since reaching
adolescence: tertian fever and a troublesome irregularity in the menstrual
cycle which, after her marriage to Henry, led Katherine into repeated
misjudgments about whether or not she was pregnant.
the house and the knight, who was all in silver.

When Henry became king on his father's death in 1509, the same
diplomatic advantages that had compelled Arthur's marriage to Katherine
now led Henry to marry her, after receiving the papal dispensation

required to legitimize in the eyes of the church the joining of a man with his brother's widow. To Henry's relief, Katherine's bedchamber women pronounced her pregnant soon after the wedding in June, but late in the following January the child was born prematurely, a stillborn daughter. No one but the king, two Spanish women and Katherine's physician and chancellor knew of her misfortune; Henry kept up the pretense of her continued pregnancy by ordering sumptuous fittings for the royal nursery for the confinement expected in March. The queen was willing to go to any length to hide the truth, and went through the public ceremony of withdrawing for her confinement knowing she could not prolong the deceit much longer. In a transparent attempt to save face it was given out by Katherine's confessor that she had been pregnant with twins, only one of which had been stillborn, and that she was confined to await the birth of the second child. But through his spies the Spanish ambassador had learned that she had begun to menstruate again, at least for a time, and from February through the end of May reports of abdominal swelling and deflating, ceasing and returning of the menses succeeded one another to everyone's confusion. Henry was annoyed and his privy councilors angry, though they had the tact to blame not Katherine but her bedchamber women for the "error." The ambassador's own conclusion was that "some irregularity in her eating and the food she takes cause her some trouble, the consequence of which is that she does not menstruate as she should."

Adding to the queen's anxieties was Henry's first recorded infidelity. The woman was a sister of the duke of Buckingham, who lived in the palace with her husband. Another of the duke's sisters found out about the affair, and told both her brother and her sister's husband all she knew. A scene between Buckingham and the king followed, and the upshot was that the duke, mortally offended, left the palace and the king's mistress was shut away in a convent where no one was allowed to see her. Henry took out his anger on the talebearing sister, banishing her permanently from the court. This in turn angered Katherine—the girl was among her intimates—and led to a fiery exchange between the king and queen. Courtiers wrote that the atmosphere was thick with tension between them, and harmony was not fully restored for some time.

Through all these domestic upheavals what Katherine feared most was her father's displeasure. Late in May she finally found the courage to write him about the stillbirth. She had not written before, she explained, because a stillbirth "is considered here an ill omen." She begged Ferdinand not to be angry with her, but to look on her ill luck "as an act of God." And she hurried to add the good news that she believed herself pregnant once again.

This time there was no error. The child came to full term without incident, and the birth was normal. The doubts about the queen's capacity for motherhood were laid to rest. On New Year's Day, when by custom valuable gifts were exchanged at court, Katherine presented Henry with the finest gift of all: a son.

When the jousts were over and the prizes bestowed, the knights retired to disarm and, after evensong, went in to supper. A banquet had been prepared, and all the foreign ambassadors joined the nobles and officials of the court and their ladies in dining with the king and queen. When the tables had been removed, the entire company reassembled in a great hall to see the entertainments. Benches and a scaffolding of wooden railings held a sizable crowd from outside the palace. The gentlemen of Henry's chapel, whose singing observers called angelic, sang an interlude, and several new songs written for the occasion. After the singing Henry called for O'Donnell, an Irish lord, whom he knighted in the presence of the ambassadors. And then, at his signaling the minstrels to play, the dancing began.

At first the king joined in the dancing (the queen was not yet able to), partnering in turn several of Katherine's waiting maids while she looked on, smiling at his nimbleness and enthusiasm. In dancing as in jousting, Henry customarily did better than anyone else, especially in the quick hops, turns and double steps of the *saltarello*. At the height of the dancing, the king contrived to slip away; only Katherine and a few others knew that he had gone. It was a favorite amusement of his to leave a group without being noticed, then to return incognito at the head of a troupe of players or musicians, or as the chief performer in a pageant. He loved to confront the courtiers in disguise, then to watch their perplexity —for they never knew which mask hid the king's face. Catching people off balance was a childlike way of reminding them that behind his affable appearance Henry was always in control of the situation. He meant to be playful, but the habit had more than a hint of menace about it. It was manipulative, and Henry's actual power to manipulate his subjects gave it the double character of a jest and a threat.

Katherine was a favorite target of this game. Late in her first pregnancy the king and a handful of courtiers strode into her bedchamber very early one morning, dressed as Robin Hood's outlaws, their faces hidden under hoods of rough cloth. The queen was startled and embarrassed. No one was allowed to enter her private rooms unannounced. The ladies who were attending to her dress and arranging her hair took fright at first—the outlaws were armed with long swords and bows and arrows—but relaxed as the queen regained her composure and went along with the artifice. The outlaws demanded to dance with the ladies;

the queen agreed. Finally after a half hour or so of this Henry pulled off his hood and the dancers laughed with relief.

A few minutes after Henry disappeared from the great hall, the dance music ended and trumpets sounded to announce the entry of yet another pageant on wheels. It was rolled part way into the hall, the rest remaining behind a large tapestry, and a richly dressed gentleman came out of its garden setting to explain the theme of the spectacle. He was standing in a bower of pleasure, he said, and in a golden arbor within the bower were lords and ladies who desired to entertain the queen and her ladies, with her permission. Katherine answered that she and all the assembled company were very anxious to see the performers in the arbor. Immediately the tapestry was removed and the pageant rolled into full view.

For a dazzling instant, in the light of the torches, it was as if the fairy-tale world of chivalric romance had come to life in the great hall. Growing in the garden of pleasure were hawthorn, wild roses and flowering vines, and beneath them a thick growth of flowers. All were made of green damask, silk and satin, enclosed by pillars covered in cloth of gold. In the gilded arbor stood six ladies in green and silver gowns, their skirts overlaid with a network of golden letters H and K laced together. The dresses and high headdresses of the women and the rich coats of their six companions were covered with glittering spangles, and the caps, hose and purple satin garments of the men bore both the golden monograms and letters spelling out their names: Loyal Heart (the king), Good Valour, Good Hope, Valiant Desire, Good Faith and Loyal Love.

When the crowd had had time to admire them the twelve performers came down out of the pageant, which was rolled into a corner to make room for them to dance. Minstrels in matching costumes began to play, and the six couples paced out the intricate pattern of steps they had been learning for weeks. They had not finished their dance, though, when from the crowd seated on the scaffolding dozens of people suddenly rushed to the pageant and began tearing off the gold and silver ornaments. (On the previous day the forest pageant had been brought into the great hall after the joust, where the king's own guardsmen and gentlemen of the court had torn it to shreds, carrying off every scrap of valuable cloth and every carefully made tree and shrub. Two of the men set to guard it had had their heads broken, and the others were driven off by force. Nothing but the bare timber, the revels master wrote, was left for the king's use.) The Lord Steward and head officers of the hall now ran into the crowd and called loudly for the guard, but fearing a brawl if they tried to use force, they stood back as the pleasure garden was stripped to the boards.

Henry, who had gone on dancing during the interruption, finished his measure and then, overlooking the turmoil at the far end of the room, invited the noblewomen and ambassadors among the onlookers to take the golden letters off his costume and keep them as gifts. But "the common people perceiving," a chronicler wrote, "ran to the king and stripped him into his hose and doublet, and all his companions in like wise." One of the dancers, Thomas Knevet, tried to escape the plunderers by climbing up onto a stage, but they climbed after him and he too "lost his apparel." Not until the crowd began despoiling the ladies did Henry call in his guard. Their abrupt appearance startled the crowd, which was pushed back far enough to let Henry and Katherine and her ladies get away through a side door.

Upstairs, in Henry's chamber, a midnight supper was ordered for all the survivors of the rout. Henry, more amused than angry at what had happened, "turned all these hurts to laughing and game," and told his companions to consider all they had lost as largesse, bestowed on the spectators as a mark of honor. Apparently he was convincing, for the supper was an unusually merry one, and the two days of celebration ended in "mirth and gladness."

There was gladness too among the "rude people" who managed to bring away the golden spangles and other ornaments. With a few exceptions, they were found to be of fine gold, made from the bullion in the royal treasury; Henry had ordered the gold bars to be melted down for the use of the revels master. Many of the adornments were of great value. A sailor who managed to take several of the golden letters from the dancers' coats sold them afterward to a goldsmith for nearly four pounds —an enormous sum at a time when master mariners earned three pounds a year.

The sailor, the guardsmen and grooms, the Londoners and the courtiers would long remember the tourney for Prince Henry, and the king who had been champion, dancer, playactor and, in the end, helpless victim of the greedy crowd who adored him. But the object of the celebrations, the infant prince, they would soon forget. Despite the care of his nurses and rockers at Richmond Palace, he grew sickly. Eight days after the tourney ended he died.

Katherine, who had been away from her baby for weeks, was inconsolable. Her child was dead, and with him her renewed hope of motherhood. Henry, bewildered and grief-stricken, wept and swore and bellowed at his servants. His grandiose plans for the boy's future and his own were thwarted. He consoled his wife and then stalked off to ride out his frustrations on the tilting ground.

II

 Whoso that wyll hymselff applye
To passe the tyme of youth joly,
Avaunce hym to the companye
Of lusty bloddys and chevalry.

Two years after the death of the New Year's boy Henry VIII crossed the Channel and, at the head of a large army, rode to war against the French. He had long since ceased to mourn the tragedy of his son's death. At twenty-one he was still under the tutelage of the councilors who had guided his government since the beginning of his reign, but more and more his own style was asserting itself. The expedition to France was clear evidence of this. No English army had invaded the continent within living memory, and it had been the considered policy of Henry's father to gain his diplomatic ends without the expense and risk of war. Henry's advisers urged the young king not to endanger England by subjecting himself to the hazards of battle, but their arguments were merely logical. Other persuasions touched Henry nearer his heart.

At the start of the sixteenth century the business of war was still central to the chivalric imagination. It was the nature of a great king to be a knight first and a statesman afterward; all of Henry's most famous predecessors had proved that, from Edward I campaigning in Wales to Edward III and his sons in the Hundred Years' War. The feudal society that produced the warrior aristocracy had disintegrated generations earlier, but the personal values of the knightly class—fearlessness and hardiness in combat, indomitability, generosity, courtesy to enemies and allies alike, fidelity to a strict code of honor—were all the more fiercely prized as the knights' purely military usefulness waned. And models of individual valor were more plentiful now than at any time since the days of Richard Lionheart and Saladin. Chief among them was Henry's older contemporary the Chevalier de Bayard, whose exploits in the Italian wars were well known at Henry's court. On one occasion, it was said, he defended a bridge against an assault of two hundred Spanish soldiers, and another time he magnanimously refused a reward of twenty-five hundred ducats offered by a grateful nobleman whose wife and daughters Bayard had saved from dishonor. Until he had proved himself worthy of a similar reputation, Henry would not attain full stature as a monarch. And so, in the spring of 1513, he laid his plans for war.

By June the thousands of bowstaves, arrows, and barrels of flour and beer were assembled and loaded. Suits of armor had been ordered from the armaments factories of northern Italy, and hundreds of tents were sewn and folded for shipment. The larger tents had names: White Hart, Greyhound, Feather, Cup of Gold, Mountain, Gold Hynd, World, Flower de Lyce. The artillery pieces too—the minions, lizards and demi-culverins—had been christened Crown, Garter, Rose and Virago. One of the great curtows was called The Sun Arising. The serpentines bore the heraldic titles of Mermaid, Griffon, Olyvant and Antelope; the largest cannons of all, whose twenty-pound iron shot took so long to load they could only be fired thirty times in a day, were dubbed The Twelve Apostles.

The term was apt, for Henry's campaign had the official status of a crusade. Julius II's anger at the French king led him to issue a papal brief taking the kingdom away from Louis and giving it to Henry, to take effect as soon as Henry had made himself master of France by conquest. Late in July Henry's men filed out of the English-held town of Calais, where they had landed three weeks earlier, and made their way southeast-ward in alternating rain and suffocating heat toward the town of Thérouanne. The ordnance was carried in the van, setting the pace for the entire force. Then came the king's household guard, under the banner of the Trinity, the duke of Buckingham with his four hundred soldiers, and three ecclesiastical corps under the bishops of Durham and Win-chester and Wolsey, the king's almoner. Under Henry's own banner was a picked guard of six hundred men, followed by the priests and singers of his chapel—a small army in themselves, 115 strong—his secretaries, kitchen staff, bedchamber attendants and his lutanist. In the rear marched another large force under the Lord Chamberlain and the earl of North-umberland.

Except for the misfortune of the elderly and sour-tempered bishop of Winchester, who was kicked by a mule en route, the army arrived with-out incident before the walls of Thérouanne. They set siege to the town, and were soon joined by a band of Burgundians under the Emperor Max-imilian, which he offered to put at Henry's disposal provided the English king paid them. With the arrival of his Hapsburg ally Henry's siege force took on the character of a respectable international host which the French could not afford to ignore. It was at least worlds apart from the ill-fated expedition to Spain a year earlier, which had gained no military advantage whatever and threatened permanently to damage the prestige of English arms.

The design of this venture called for a force under the marquis of Dorset to sail to Spain, then move northward with the support of Ferdinand's Spanish soldiers to retake the former English lands in Guienne. From the outset the undertaking was frustrated by incompetent planning and the notorious unreliability of Ferdinand. There were no tents, no beer, and few other provisions. The tropical weather enervated the English, and the high prices of local goods quickly drained their pockets. Ferdinand capriciously announced that he preferred to fight in Navarre rather than Guienne, and left the English to attack alone. Dorset was not the man to organize a campaign on his own, and like many of his soldiers he soon fell ill. A rebellion among the troops seeking higher pay was put down, but all semblance of military training ceased and a fair number of men deserted. By September quarrels among the commanders allowed the English fighting men to arrange their own affairs. They ordered ships, baked enough biscuit to get home on, and left. Henry was furious, but by the time the disobedient army reached England he had decided to pretend that the entire disgraceful episode never happened.

Now, however, he was in personal command of a loyal, well-provisioned and self-sufficient army, whose successes would atone for Dorset's fiasco. In the third week of the siege of Thérouanne his first opportunity came. A body of French knights attempted to relieve the town by means of an assault on the besiegers. Driven back by Henry's cannons, they retreated past a village called Guinegate, with the English knights close behind them. In their panic, the English boasted, the French lost their spurs, and the brief engagement was given the memorable name "Battle of the Spurs." In fact the French lost several of their standards and a number of French knights were taken prisoner. Among them was the matchless Bayard himself, who graciously yielded his sword to an astonished English knight in acknowledgment of the English triumph. Henry, determined to outdo the gallant Bayard in magnanimity, released him after a brief imprisonment.

Other triumphs quickly followed. Thérouanne fell in a few days, and after taking possession of the town in a splendid ceremonial entry Henry handed it over to Maximilian, who ordered every building but the old church destroyed. The city of Tournai held out only eight days before the English siege, and this prize Henry kept for himself. With two towns taken and a shipload of valuable French prisoners whose ransoms, once paid by their anxious relatives, should repay much of the cost of the campaign, Henry took his army home. It had been a profitable and even a pleasant crusade—between sieges Henry had stopped for several weeks of feasting and entertainment at the court of the regent of Flanders, and did so again on his way back to Calais. More important, it had given Henry the military reputation he badly needed. The standards and spurs of the French were worthy spoils from a first campaign. His next venture might indeed imperil the French crown.

Paradoxically, the most decisive English military victory of 1513 came about in Henry's absence, under the nominal command of Katherine. When he went abroad in June he had left her as head of his government and remaining military forces, knowing that his departure would be the signal for at least minor incursions by the Scots. As early as February Lord Dacre, guardian of the northern border, warned Henry that the Scots king James IV was mustering his men in preparation for an invasion. He had provided himself with up-to-date siege artillery, and narrowly missed harm when one of the newly cast guns he was trying out in Edinburgh Castle exploded on firing.[1]

James' defiance, carried by Ross Herald, reached Henry in the midst of the siege of Thérouanne. He sent the bishop of Durham to London to oversee the organization of defense in the northern counties, but left the major responsibility with Katherine and the Lord Treasurer Surrey, Lieutenant General of the North. Katherine personally handled many of the administrative details, and set her women to sewing banners for the knightly contingents forming under Surrey's command. A highly intelligent and capable woman, she enjoyed coordinating the enterprise. "My heart is very good to it," she wrote to Henry. On September 9 the invading Scots met Surrey's forces in the hills at Flodden just inside English territory, and within three hours they were beaten. The slaughter was terrible. The commanders—the earls, the great churchmen, the king himself—chose to fight to the death though conscious that they were giving ground hopelessly to the English. When the battle was over Flodden Field was strewn with noble corpses; among them was the disfigured body of King James, fallen near his banner. The bishop of Durham praised Surrey and his men, but attributed the victory to the protection of St. Cuthbert, under whose banner the men of Durham had fought. Katherine was overjoyed at the outcome, and sent the Scots king's bloody shirt to her husband as a trophy.

A week after the carnage of Flodden Katherine gave birth to a stillborn son. A little over a year later she bore a living son who died within a few days. Her father, whose patience with her failures in childbirth had long since run out, sent a doctor and a Spanish midwife to England to ensure that future sons would survive. What their techniques were we don't know, but common medical remedies for infertility included drinking the urine of pregnant goats and sheep and treating the cervix with steam, produced by a brass lamp and funneled into the vagina through a pessary. Folk remedies called for the woman to wear herbs and charms—dock seeds bound to the arm, magical or religious names written in amulets—and to suspend from a girdle worn under her clothing the fingers and anus of a deadborn child. To whatever cures her physicians advised Katherine undoubtedly added assiduous prayers for a son. And Henry, whose piety was less fervent than Katherine's but no less sincere, prayed too for his long-desired heir.

The blame in all cases of childlessness fell by custom on the wife, but Henry could not overlook the evidence that there was weakness on his side of the family as well. He had been one of seven children, three boys and four girls. Three of the children had died in infancy, and a fourth, Prince Arthur, lived only into adolescence. Of course, many women lost half their children in infancy, but Katherine had so far lost them all. And she was nearing thirty.

Katherine's pregnancy in 1515 was to all appearances normal. The child was expected in February of the following year, and news of the impending birth made the rounds of the diplomatic network. The new king of France, Francis I (Louis XII had just died), felt snubbed because Henry did not personally invite him to send a representative to stand as godfather to the child at the christening; instead he asked his brother-in-law Suffolk to give Francis the message. Francis announced he would send no one; Henry was bound to be very angry. The Venetian ambassador Giustinian, always anxious to preserve good relations between Henry and other monarchs, went to see Henry's chief advisor Wolsey in an attempt to cushion the insult.

Katherine's baby was born before dawn on Monday, February 18.[2] It was a girl, but this disappointment was temporarily outweighed by the fact that it did not immediately die. Three days after her birth the child was christened in the friars' church near the palace at Greenwich. The silver font reserved for royal christenings was brought to the church for the ceremony, but apart from the exalted status of the sponsors and godparents the event was unexceptional. The muddy ground was covered first with a thick layer of gravel and then with rushes, and scaffolding was set up along both sides of the path the christening procession was to take from the court gate to the porch of the church. The princess was carried by her godmother, and she was wrapped so tightly against the cold that not even her face was visible to the spectators. A low wooden archway had been built just in front of the church door and covered with tapestries. Under it the godparents stopped, and a priest blessed the child and gave her her name. She was called Mary, after Henry's favorite sister, the beautiful Tudor Rose.

This part of the ceremony over, the company moved into the church itself for further rites. A group of gentlemen and lords filed past the needlework hangings studded with gems and pearls that lined the walls and walked to the high altar, where the accouterments of the christening—the basin, tapers, salt and chrism—were assembled. Four knights carried the gold canopy of estate above the princess, now held by the countess of Surrey. Her sponsors and godparents were of the blood royal or of ducal rank: Katherine Plantagenet, only surviving child of Edward IV, and Henry VIII's aunt; Margaret Plantagenet, countess of Salisbury, Edward IV's niece; Charles Brandon, duke of Suffolk, the baby's uncle and husband of the Tudor Rose; and the duke and duchess of Norfolk. Immediately after the christening came the ceremony of "bishoping," or confirmation. At its conclusion the heralds came together at the front of the church and loudly proclaimed Mary's title and style:

> God give good life and long unto the right high, right noble, and right excellent princess Mary, princess of England and daughter of our sovereign lord the king.

Giustinian took his time about congratulating the new father on behalf of the doge of Venice. "Had it been a son," he wrote in a letter to the doge, "it would not have been fit to delay the compliment."[3] A daughter was another matter. Nearly a week after Mary's birth the ambassador sought an audience with Henry and complimented him on the good health of his wife and daughter. At the same time he made it plain that the doge would have been happier with a prince, adding a carefully prepared series of sentiments to the effect that Henry himself would have been more contented with a son but that he ought to resign himself to the inscrutable will of God. Henry cut through this rhetorical lacework to remark that, since both he and his queen were young (an arguable point in Katherine's case), there was no reason for resignation. "If it was a daughter this time, by the grace of God the sons will follow," he concluded, and plunged without interruption into the more serious matter of stirring up Venetian worries about the maneuverings of France and the empire.[4]

Mary Tudor came into the world in a season of mourning. King Ferdinand, who had been in ill health for some time, died late in January, and the news reached England just before Katherine was delivered. Katherine was not told of her father's death until after Mary was born, but she must have grieved then to think that he did not live to know of the princess' birth. Katherine did not love her father: she had not seen

him for twenty years, he had treated her more as a piece of merchandise
than as a daughter, and in any case he was not a lovable man. But she felt
a strong sense of duty toward him, and considerable fear. Besides, his
death broke another of her ties to Spain, and to the cherished memory of
her mother. Ferdinand's last illness was too much a tragicomic affair to
evoke deep grief, however. Several years earlier he had determined to obtain a son by his second wife, Germaine de Foix. As he was over sixty the
task promised to be strenuous, and to give him extra strength his wife had
a powerful aphrodisiac baked into his food. The potion gave him convul-
sions, and attacked his reason. After two years Germaine had had no children but Ferdinand was more or less continuously ill and insane. He
still enjoyed his favorite sport of hunting, though, weakening what
resistance he had left. Finally in January of 1516 "he expired," the
humanist Peter Martyr wrote, "of hunting and matrimony, either of
which are fatal to most men at the age of sixty-three."[5]

Ferdinand's death marked the passing of the generation of Mary's
grandparents: she would not know any of them, though she bore their
imprint strongly. Her Spanish grandparents were the more romantic and
illustrious. Ferdinand, heir to the Mediterranean kingdom of Aragon,
spent his youth fighting alongside his father in the civil war against the
rebellious Catalans; after he married the heiress Isabella at eighteen he
joined in her campaign to secure her right to the throne of Castile. Competent rather than brilliant as both a soldier and governor, Ferdinand was
destined to be overshadowed by his admirable wife. Warrior, conqueror
of the Moors, indefatigable administrator and self-taught patron of culture and exploration, Isabella of Castile had the mentality of a feudal
knight. She embodied the most hallowed of Spanish ideals: the tradition
of the crusade. When her brother, Henry IV, died leaving no legitimate
children Isabella refused to recognize the claims of his niece, and fought
doggedly for her own rights until she had driven her rival from the
country. Her marriage to Ferdinand gave him no control over her kingdom, and she ruled there as an independent sovereign, contending with
revolts, the restlessness of the proud Castilian nobility, and the everyday
tedium of government. When she was not campaigning she received ambassadors, conferred with her councilors, and attended to matters of law
and war from morning till evening, then spent most of the night dictating
to her secretaries. She had not been educated to handle affairs of state,
and her Latin was poor; in her spare time she studied until she mastered
it. By no means a learned woman, Isabella respected knowledge—always
provided it remained congruent with piety—and bought many manuscript books and endowed a convent library at Toledo.

Important as they were to Isabella these benefactions went unnoticed
by the majority of her subjects, who knew her best as the armor-clad

conqueror of the Moors. Since the middle ages the Christian kingdoms of
Spain had defined themselves in opposition to the Moorish domination of
the peninsula. One by one the territories of the Moors had been
conquered, until in Isabella's time only Granada remained. A decade of
sieges and assaults under the queen's banner, interrupted only when Isabella paused to give birth to her fourth child Katherine, culminated in
the fall of Granada in 1492. By their marriage the "Catholic kings," as
Ferdinand and Isabella were called, had created a unified Spain. Now
they had made it an entirely Catholic kingdom as well. Two more events
rounded out their efforts at purification. They introduced the Inquisition
to crush heresy and they expelled the Jews.

From a triumphant heroine Isabella sank in later life to a melancholic
recluse. She became inactive and moody, and her tears of religious sentiment were indistinguishable from those she wept over Ferdinand's
infidelities. Over the coarse robes of a lay sister of the Franciscan Third
Order she now wore only black gowns. Of her four daughters the eldest
was dead, the youngest far away in England, the third at the distant court
of Portugal. The fourth daughter, Joanna, the most beautiful and spirited
of them all, would soon go mad.

Mary's paternal grandfather Henry VII never spoke of Ferdinand and
Isabella without touching his hat as a sign of respect.[6] After Katherine
and Arthur were married he liked to say that he and his wife were now
"brother and sister" to Ferdinand and Isabella, and in the presence of the
Spanish ambassador he solemnly swore, his hand on his heart, that if he
heard any of his subjects speak against the Catholic kings "by the faith of
his heart he would esteem him no longer."[7] Henry did not expect to be
taken completely seriously in his extravagant admiration of Ferdinand
and Isabella, but as the parvenu king of a minor country he did feel
keenly the difference in their status.

When he seized the English throne in 1485 he was in fact an outlaw
under the stigma of attainder—forfeiture of titles and lands. Through his
mother he had a claim to the crown, but he was without money or supporters. The attainder drove him to the continent, where at twenty-eight
he mustered an invasion force and fought and defeated the king, Richard
III, at Bosworth Field. Henry's coronation nullified the attainder, and
Parliament declared all those who had opposed him at Bosworth to be
traitors, yet his title remained precarious. Preserving it meant overcoming
the major threat of Perkin Warbeck, who persuaded most of the rulers of
Europe that he was the younger of the two murdered sons of Edward
IV, and crushing a minor threat from the Irish pretender Lambert Sim-
nel, who called himself Edward VI. It meant surviving occult intrigues
like that of the conspirators who obtained from a Roman astrologer an
ointment which, spread on the walls of a passageway in the palace, was

supposed to bring about the king's murder "by those who loved him best."8 Above all it meant building a new image of the monarchy in England.

This Henry was well equipped to do. He was a handsome man of moderate height whose expression and bearing inspired confidence. He had the irreplaceable gift of winning the hearts of his soldiers, his councilors, and the ordinary people who crowded the roadways and gathered on rooftops to see him wherever he went. The chronicler Hall imagined him on the day of the battle of Bosworth, "his aspect cheerful and couragious, his hair yellow like the burnished gold, his eyes grey shining and quick." And when he rode through York shortly after his coronation, "a great crowd of citizens" threw gifts of comfits and wheat in his path and shouted their delight at his accession: "King Henry! King Henry! Our Lord preserve that sweet and well favored face!"9 The way to a new image, Henry saw, was to surround himself with magnificence and with the symbols of royal power. Over fifteen hundred pounds was spent on the finery worn at his coronation, and twenty-one tailors and fifteen furriers were kept at their workbenches for three weeks fashioning the liveries for his knights and henchmen. As king Henry kept a personal bodyguard of archers in attendance at all times, and introduced at his court something of the elaborate ceremonial he had observed in France. By the end of his reign he had created an appearance of order and strong personal rule, and bequeathed these, along with a full treasury, to his son. For his audacity, popularity and skillful rule he was to be known in time as "a wonder for wise men."

Henry VII's wife, Elizabeth of York, lived the restricted life of a medieval queen, bearing children at regular intervals and adding the prestige of her Yorkist ancestry (she was the daughter of Edward IV) to her husband's authority. At her splendid coronation she rode in a litter of cloth of gold, in rich robes and with a jeweled circlet crowning her "fair yellow hair hanging down full behind her back." But afterward, taking as her motto the phrase "humble and reverent," she retreated into a twilight of confinements and royal nurseries, and saw two of her children die in infancy. In giving birth to her last child, a weak little princess who lived less than a year, the queen herself died.

Of the children of Henry VII and Elizabeth of York the sturdiest and most boisterous was the second boy, the one known throughout his childhood as Prince Hal. A round-faced child with a ruddy complexion, he was given an array of titles before he was a year old—Warden of the Cinque Ports, Constable of Dover Castle—and at three he was created a Knight of the Bath and elected to the Order of the Garter. By the time he was four he could sit a horse well enough to ride in state to Westminster Abbey to be created duke of York, as Perkin Warbeck, who claimed the same title, was preparing his invasion on the continent. Erasmus, who met the young prince when he was eight, declared him to possess the qualities of dignity and courtesy in kingly proportion, and thought highly of his prospects. As a younger son Henry was free from the obligations and pressures placed on the heir to the throne, but at age ten and a half his brother's death suddenly exalted him to the status of prince of Wales. From then on he began to acquire the chivalric skills and popular reputation of a future king. At sixteen Prince Hal was taller than his father, with "limbs of gigantic size." The Spanish ambassador declared that there was "no finer youth in all the world than the Prince of Wales," and another observer went even further. "If the names of all the princes who have been called handsome were to be collected," he wrote, "that of Henry would stand first."[10] The people who had loved Henry VII worshiped his son. Popular ballads about Prince Hal told how he liked to put on rough clothing and seek out the company of common folk; invariably he would be discovered, recognized, and brought in honor to the palace again surrounded by his devoted subjects. The sturdy little boy became a vigorous and beloved youth, and gave every hope of becoming an able king.

Henry's sisters, Mary's aunts, could not have been more unlike one another. Margaret, two years older than Henry, was a robust and sharp-witted young girl of fourteen when her father married her to James IV of Scotland. James was twenty-eight, and a man of vast and unscrupulous experience with women. (While his marriage to Margaret Tudor was being negotiated, his beautiful mistress Lady Margaret Drummond died in unexplained circumstances.) Margaret endured her marriage, but not without complaint; homesick and humiliated by her husband, she wrote piteous letters to her father in England. James IV's death at Flodden freed her from her unhappy marriage, but a second marriage to the earl of Angus led to further conflict and eventually to civil war. Margaret had by now become a heavy and somewhat mutton-faced matron, and a considerable woman of the world in her own right. While still married to Angus she took several lovers, including the man who became her third husband, her Lord Chancellor Henry Stewart.

If Margaret was ill-favored and unfortunate in her domestic life, Henry's younger sister Mary was probably the most envied woman of her generation. Her portraits confirm the unanimous opinion of contemporaries that she was an extraordinary beauty. Her lovely high forehead and even, delicate features were set off by a complexion fair almost to the point of pallor. Unlike Henry she had dark hair and eyes, and a docile sweetness of expression. She was strong-willed, though, and the knowledge that she was among the most desirable princesses in Europe gave her confidence. She agreed to marry the elderly French king Louis XII (after an earlier betrothal to Charles of Castile, the future Charles V, was broken off) but made the stipulation that her next husband would be of her own choosing. It was well known that her choice would fall on Charles Brandon, Henry's intimate companion, and when soon after the wedding Louis died, it was Brandon who was sent to France to console the widow. While he was there he and Mary were secretly married. Henry was furious, but was too fond of both Mary and Brandon not to let them return to court. His revenge was to seize Mary's plate and jewels, and to force her to repay the cost of her expensive French wedding; she was still paying off the debt at the enormous rate of a thousand pounds a year when she died.

Princess Mary's English and Spanish ancestry was rich in enterprising, combative, courageous and independent men and women. She too would carry those traits, and though raised as an Englishwoman she was also taught to honor her Spanish blood and acknowledge it proudly. She was after all cared for by a mother whose English was never really fluent, and who continued to pray in Spanish all her life. In personality and spirit Mary would most resemble her grandmother Isabella. She would show Isabella's tenacity, her bravery, her taste for long working hours, her tendency to melancholy. Mary shared something of Isabella's desire to purify religious belief as well, but in circumstances so different from those of fifteenth-century Spain as to defy comparison. Had she lived amid the archaic honor, piety and religious idealism of medieval Spain Mary might have been a heroine as splendid as her grandmother; amid the crisis-ridden climate of treachery, doubt and religious revolution of Tudor England she was to find obstacles even Isabella could not have conquered.

III

 I pray daily ther paynys to asswage
And sone to sende where they faynest wolde be,
Withoute disease or adversyte.

In the winter of 1517 a great frost struck London in the middle of January. The streets were slick with ice, and the Thames froze solid. Men with business at the courts had to travel from London to Westminster on foot instead of by boat, and when the river showed no signs of a thaw the townspeople cleared a "common way," or high road, in the ice. The weather was no better in February. Giustinian, who had to go to Greenwich to see the king, complained that going by boat was still impossible and that the "frozen and dangerous roads" made travel of any kind hazardous. The frost came in the midst of a great drought. No rain fell in southeastern England from September to the following May. The lush green pastures turned brown, small streams dried up and farmers had to drive their cattle three or four miles to water.[1] And soon after the first long-awaited rains fell, the sweating sickness broke out all over London.

The sweat, now thought to have been influenza with pulmonary complications, struck its victims "with a great sweating and stinking, with redness of the face and of all the body, and a continual thirst, with a great heat and headache." A pimply rash appeared on the head or body, sometimes accompanied by pricks of blood, and almost before treatment could be applied the sufferer was dead. It was the pitiless suddenness of death from the sweat that horrified survivors. People fell ill on the street, at their work, at mass; they rushed home to collapse and die. A doctor who studied the disease closely wrote that it killed "some in opening their windows, some in playing with children in their street doors; some in one hour, many in two, it destroyed; . . . some in sleep, some in wake, some in mirth, some in care, some fasting and some full, some busy and some idle; and in one house sometime three, sometime five, sometime more, sometime all."[2] Often there was no time to make a will, or to send for the priest, and those who died either intestate or without the last rites were denied burial in consecrated ground.

All who could fled the city at once, but most had to stay—to bury their dead, to guard their goods, to earn their livings. And before long there was nowhere to go, for the countryside was as full of infection as the city. By midsummer Londoners had become acclimatized to the fear of death—to the barred windows and doors, the self-professed healers selling cures and preventives in the streets, and the panic that went through a crowd when a passer-by, moaning and holding his head, stumbled past on his way to die. The French ambassador in London wrote home describing how he saw men and women "as thick as flies rushing from the streets or shops" when they felt ill; the sight of an infected person was enough to clear the street. Tens of thousands died in the summer of 1517; for the survivors it was a return to the nightmare mortality of the medieval plague. Many accounted this affliction worse than the plague, which at least gave warning to its victims and allowed them to linger for days or even weeks before they died. They christened the sweat "Know thy Master" and "The Lord's Visitation," and they made black jokes about friends who had been "merry at dinner and dead at supper." They drank the preventive medicines sent by other friends whose households had escaped infection, and murmured prayers at each sounding of the death bell.

The epidemic of 1517 was not the first of its kind. In the summer of 1485 and again in 1508 the same mysterious disease had swept through southern England, brought on, it was said, by divine displeasure at the severity of Henry VII's government. Its reappearance in his son's reign called forth an array of cures, preventives and restoratives; clearly this contagion that had come in with the Tudor line was here to stay. One remedy was compounded of endive, sowthistle, marygold, mercury and nightshade; another called for "three large spoonfuls of water of dragons, and half a nutshellful of unicorn's horn." (Swordfish blades were reverently preserved in English treasuries as unicorns' horns.) The latter potion was said to have brought Lord Darcy and thirty members of his household safely through one pestilent summer without illness, though they were all exposed to the sweat. A third preventive was called the "philosopher's egg," and was made from a crushed egg, its white blown out, mixed shell and all with saffron, mustard seed and herbs, and more unicorn's horn. This electuary could be kept in glass boxes for twenty or thirty years, and improved with age.

The most thoroughgoing treatment for the sweat was the series of medicinal recipes ascribed to the king himself. Probably because of his phobic dread of illness and in particular of epidemic diseases he became an amateur apothecary, and liked to send remedies for all sorts of ailments to friends and relatives. The first stage in the king's cure was a preventive made from "sawge of virtue," herb of grace, elder and briar leaves and ginger; mixed with white wine and drunk in small quantities every day for nine days, this kept one "whole for the whole year, by the grace of God." If the sweat should strike before the ninth day of the treatment, the second element—water of scabiosa, betony water and a quart of treacle—should be drunk. And if the disease should after all reach the critical stage marked by the appearance of the rash, the ingredients of the first medicine, made into a plaster and applied directly to the skin, would be certain to "draw out all the venom," and restore health.

Henry's medicines did not succeed in keeping his household free of infection. His Latin secretary Ammonius died the day before he was to leave for a sweat-free country house. Wolsey barely escaped death shortly afterward, and a number of his servants died. The bishop of Winchester, the ambassador Giustinian and his son were all stricken, and when the pages who slept in Henry's bedchamber began to die off one by one the king panicked and sent the entire court away. With Katherine and the infant Mary, three of his trusted gentlemen and his favorite organist Dionysius Memo, he traveled to "a remote and unusual habitation" to wait out the epidemic. But even there the infection haunted him, and rumors of deaths from the sweat drove him from one country place to another, keeping just ahead of its ravages. Meanwhile his courtiers too moved from one palace to another in hopes of escaping danger, but in the spring of 1518, when the sweat reappeared more strongly than ever and the measles and smallpox that now accompanied the disease increased its morbidity, the king's pages again began to die. Now every man or woman who had lost a relative or servant to the disease was ordered not to leave the house without carrying the white rod that symbolized infection, and had to hang wisps of straw from the doorway to warn visitors and others to stay away.

These rudimentary efforts at quarantine were intended to contain infection, but the more grave agencies of contamination—germ-infected food, water and living conditions—were left alone. London in the early sixteenth century was a medium-sized city rapidly growing into an overcrowded, slum-ridden metropolis. Every decade saw thousands of peasants and villagers from the economically troubled countryside move to the capital, settling into the ramshackle suburbs and putting added demands on the inadequate water supply. Since medieval times water had been available to Londoners in stone cisterns, inspected yearly by the Lord Mayor with much ceremony, but as the city grew those who lived at the outskirts had to buy their water from the growing group of professional water carriers who sold it by the three-gallon tankard. There was barely enough of it for drinking, cooking and perhaps rinsing out the chamber pots; cleaning and bathing were a luxury even in the great houses of the rich. There were fleas and lice everywhere—in the woodwork, the floors, the beds and wardrobes. Bugs of many kinds lived in the food stores and in woolen clothing; spiders invaded the city every spring, and flies every summer. There were public bathhouses (which were also brothels), and fastidious people bathed now and then in wooden tubs in front of the fire. But clothing was really clean only when it was new, for when they came to London country people continued to do their laundry as they always had, with cow dung, hemlock, nettles, and remnants of soap, and clothes may well have smelled worse clean than dirty. Clothing was always in short supply among the poor, and beggars were said to welcome the sweating sickness if only because they inherited the coats and shoes of the dead.

If the houses of Tudor London were unhygienic its streets were corridors of filth. Unpaved, rutted, alternately muddy and dusty, they were repositories of every kind of leavings, waste and ordure. Household garbage and the outscourings of cooking pots and dye tubs mingled with the droppings of horses, dogs and fowl. Chamber pots from every house facing the street were emptied out of front doors or upper windows into that street every morning. As the mounds of refuse grew they were raked into heaps at street corners and infrequently dumped into the river or along the highways leading out of the city, but not before they had become unimaginably foul-smelling. The heady and lingering perfumes of the age were in part designed to counteract the stench of the streets, putting a sweet-smelling barrier between the wearer and his or her surroundings. The fastidious Wolsey never left the palace without holding a scented pomander to his nose.

To be sure, there were critics of these conditions who argued that dirt must augment disease. The king was among them, but though he tried to command clean surroundings for himself and especially for his daughter, he did nothing to improve the plight of his subjects. The best-known opponent of unhygienic English customs was the Dutchman and famed humanist Erasmus. In letters to friends he gave careful descriptions of how English houses were built to maximize drafts yet minimize exposure to fresh air and sunlight. The streets, he declared, should be cleaned of mud and urine, and, above all, the dirty habit of spreading rushes over the clay floors of houses to catch food scraps, spilled ale and bones should be abandoned. The rushes were changed when their smell became intolerably sour, but a bottom layer, stuck fast to the floor by years of accumulated spit, vomit and "the leakage of dogs," remained,

according to Erasmus, for decades. He objected to other practices on the
grounds that they spread disease: overcrowding in badly ventilated inns,
infrequently changed bed linen, communal drinking cups and the pro-
pensity of the English to kiss one another when they met. Erasmus' views
met with some sympathy, but some ridicule as well. He went too far,
some thought, in claiming that even the hallowed religious customs of
confession, the communal baptismal font and pilgrimages to distant
shrines spread infection! And besides, his hypochondria was proverbial;
he corresponded with numerous doctors on the subject of his own health
problems, and sent one of them daily reports on the condition of his
urine.[3]

Most people connected disease not with unsanitary living conditions
but with supernatural forces. For every doctor who treated his patients
afflicted with the sweat by bleeding their veins or sealing them (usually
with fatal results) in a hot room wrapped in blankets, there were a
dozen practitioners of superstitious and occult healing. An act of Parliament complained of a "great multitude of ignorant persons," including
"smiths, weavers and women," who were undertaking to perform amazing cures involving sorceries and witchcraft and medicines of questionable value, "to the high displeasure of God." These self-educated healers
used the prayers and holy formulas of the church as incantations,
invoking the cross of Christ, his "title of triumph" Jesus of Nazareth
King of the Jews, the Christian mystical sign of the Greek letter *Tau*,
and even estimates of the exact "measures," or heights, of Mary and
Jesus. One spiritual preventive called for the Pater Noster and Ave Maria
to be recited by the practitioner under the patient's right ear, then his
left, then under both armpits, at the back of both thighs, and finally over
the heart. Biblical or cabalistic words spelled backward were believed to
bring about cures by magic, especially when written in certain ways.
"Write these words on a laurel leaf," a charm to break fever begins.
"Ysmael, Ysmael, Ysmael, I adjure you by the Angels that you cure this
man." The sufferer's name was added and the leaf placed under his
head. When accompanied by a diet of lettuce and seeds ground in ale,
any fever, even the sudden and fiery fever of The Lord's Visitation,
would cool.

Behind these occult treatments lay a fundamentally providential view
not only of disease but of all human affairs. The men and women of the
Tudor age accepted the ravages of the sweating sickness as they did the
destruction of floods or the mass deaths of cattle and sheep—as part of a
vast hidden design. The author of this design was God, but it was only in
the broadest sense religious: it was more a matter of faith in the power of
order over chaos. No one welcomed the sweating sickness, yet everyone

took a morbid comfort in the belief that it had been sent by a higher power for a distinct purpose.

This belief was strained, though, by the fact that the sweat struck hardest those who should have been least vulnerable to it. The "youngest and likeliest" men and women were carried off, and the "men of middle age and sanguine complexion." The poorest and weakest in the population were, paradoxically, those most likely to survive. Children, women of childbearing age, exceedingly thin men and laborers of all kinds were either spared or, if they caught the disease, survived its crisis phase and eventually recovered. Men of substance in their middle years died in great numbers.

That the best fed, wealthiest and most privileged members of society should be most victimized by the epidemic offended the prevailing faith in the order of things. It raised the unnerving possibility that order had only a tenuous advantage over anarchy, and that the future might hold the unexpected along with the predictable. It touched the most deep-seated phobia of the age—the fear that the entire social order might collapse. This fear gnawed at the English throughout the second season of the sweating sickness, until in the winter of 1518 the sweat receded with the cold weather and, to their unbounded relief, did not return in the spring.

It was in this time of panic and sudden changes of residence that the Princess Mary spent the early months of her life. She was at first put into the care of a wet-nurse—Katherine Pole, daughter-in-law of the countess of Salisbury. Later Lady Margaret Bryan replaced Katherine Pole with the title "lady mistress." Lady Bryan was responsible for the small group of servants that made up Mary's immediate household: her four rockers, Margery Parker, Anne Bright, Ellen Hutton and Margery Cousine, her launderer Avys Woode, and her chaplain and clerk of the closet, Sir Henry Rowte.[4] The princess had a state household as well, headed by the countess of Salisbury and including a chamberlain, treasurer and gentlewoman of the bedchamber. The attendants in this state household all wore liveries in Mary's colors of blue and green. When the sickness threatened the palace, however, the formalities of the official household were forgotten and the king simply packed up his family and a few intimates and moved as far from the infection as he could get. His London residences—the apartments in the Tower, the spacious Baynard's Castle in Thames Street—were out of the question. His favorite residence, the red brick palace by the Thames at Greenwich with its sprawling lawns and flowering gardens, was too near the heart of the city for safety during the epidemic. The turreted royal apartments at Richmond in Surrey offered refuge for a time, but before long word would reach Henry that a nearby village had been wiped out by the sweat and in a matter of hours he would be on his way again. The magnificent medieval castle at Windsor he disliked intensely, finding it claustrophobic and austere. What Henry liked were parks and gardens, the open country and, if possible, the river at his doorstep. At Greenwich he could walk down to the dock and inspect his ships and talk with the gunners and sailors. At Windsor he was surrounded by paved courtyards and, in the chapel of the Garter, the tombs and monuments of the Garter knights and military relics of the Plantagenet kings. Farther into the countryside the royal residences were small and in some cases dilapidated. Eltham in Kent could accommodate a severely reduced household, but the manor of Woodstock in Oxfordshire, built to house the king while he hunted in the summer and dating back to Norman times, was both cramped and shabby, and was not fit to be occupied for long.

By the fall of 1518, when Mary was two and a half years old, the court had begun to settle back to its accustomed routine. There were still periodic "removals" from one palace to another, of course. Royalty lived semi-nomadic lives, and rarely spent more than a few weeks in any one palace. But in normal times changes of residence were planned, and followed an established order, and it was to this order that Henry's court now returned.

For Mary the readjustment marked her first opportunity to play an important role in affairs of state. Rivalry between France and England was as strong as ever, and Henry now saw a way to put his daughter to use as a diplomatic tool. The new French king, Francis I, was anxious to prove his strength and that of France, and only a war or a flattering gesture of brotherliness from Henry would satisfy him. Francis had a son, Henry a daughter. A marriage alliance between them was the obvious alternative to war.

In September of 1518 the negotiations were concluded. A treaty of universal peace was to bind England and France, sealed by the proxy marriage of the dauphin and the English princess which would be consummated when the dauphin turned fourteen. Among the provisions relating to her dowry rights was the highly significant stipulation that if Henry died without a male heir, Mary would succeed him—the earliest statement of her right to the throne.[5] To the negotiators of the treaty the point was a minor one. There was still a good deal of hope that Henry would have a son—Katherine was pregnant again, and near her term— and in any case no woman had ever been crowned queen of England in her own right. But as evidence of a real if remote possibility the statement was revealing, and prophetic.

In mid-September ambassadors from the French court arrived in England to sign the treaty and solemnize the marriage. The French made an impressive showing as they rode through London in their silk doublets, surrounded by the Scotsmen of the French king's guard and a welcoming escort of English nobles and guardsmen, fourteen hundred horsemen in all. At each of the ceremonies and banquets in the following days the French appeared in fresh robes of slashed silk, to the astonishment of the English courtiers. The seemingly inexhaustible wardrobes of the ambassadors were matched by their purses. They gambled heavily, and no state banquet was complete without the card games and dicing the king loved. At a lavish feast given by Wolsey—now a cardinal of the church and papal legate, and rapidly becoming the most powerful man in England next to the king himself—to celebrate the treaty of universal peace, golden bowls of ducats and dice were set out after dinner for the guests to play at mumchance. After midnight, when all the others had left, Henry "remained to play high with some Frenchmen."

The treaty arrangements were sworn to by both parties before the high altar of St. Paul's, and then came the wedding ceremony. At eight o'clock in the morning of October 5 the betrothal parties and their retinues assembled in a hall at Greenwich. Henry stood in front of his throne, with Katherine, his sister Mary, Wolsey and another papal legate, Cardinal Campeggio, at his side. During the bishop of Durham's long oration in praise of the marriage—at least the third such declamation to which the French visitors had been subjected since their arrival—Mary's nurse stood at Katherine's side holding the princess in her arms. Mary was dressed in cloth of gold, wearing over her golden curls a black velvet cap that was studded with jewels. She was small for her age, and delicate, with her father's fair skin and light eyes. Her coloring and even features made her a very pretty child, and she remained smiling and poised throughout the long ceremony, true to Henry's proud boast that "his daughter never cried." When the bishop had finished the ambassadors asked for Henry and Katherine to consent to the marriage, the French admiral Bonnivet consenting on behalf of the dauphin, and Wolsey slid a tiny ring onto Mary's fourth finger. In it was a very large diamond—his wedding gift to the princess. The admiral, acting for the absent bridegroom, passed it over her second joint in a final solemnity, and then the entire company adjourned to the gorgeously decorated chapel for a celebratory mass. Yet another banquet closed out the festivities, and the dancing that followed it lasted until three in the morning, long after the bride had been put to bed.[6]

The visit of the French ambassadors to England was only half of the process of peacemaking and matchmaking; to complete it English ambassadors had to travel to Paris to sign the treaty and stand in place of the princess at a repeat of the proxy wedding. Early in December the English party arrived in Paris, and a few days later the king gave them a public

audience. He received them in a large hall whose high ceiling was decorated with the lilies of France. Tapestries covered the walls. Half the room
was taken up by an elevated stage several feet higher than the floor. A
second platform rising from this stage, at the extreme end of the room,
held the throne—a chair covered with cloth of gold under a trailing canopy of gold brocade. King Francis was seated on his throne, wearing a
sumptuous silver robe embroidered in flowers and lined entirely in
Spanish heron feathers. His feet rested on a cushion of cloth of gold;
the dais was carpeted in violet-colored velvet ornamented in lilies. On the
stage below the king stood several ranks of great nobles and churchmen,
the papal nuncio, and the foreign ambassadors resident at the French
court. Far to the king's left on a lower platform, hidden from the company in the hall by screens, were Queen Claude and the king's mother,
Louise of Savoy, and other gentlewomen.

The English ambassadors, who had put on their richest doublets, gold
chains and jeweled girdles for this reception, were preceded into the audience hall by a guard of two hundred gentlemen carrying battle axes,
who brought them up the steps of the raised stage to stand below the
king. Francis, who up to this point had maintained his kingly pose un-
moving, responded to their deep bows with the warmest courtesy, getting up from his throne and descending to greet them each by name.
Their credentials were presented and accepted, speeches of welcome and
cordiality were exchanged, and finally Francis came down from his
throne once more to embrace each of the English representatives in turn,
exactly as Henry had embraced the French ambassadors at their audience
two months earlier.

A few days after this formal reception the two parties swore to
uphold the treaty at a high mass in Notre Dame, and afterward Francis
and Claude on behalf of their son espoused the Princess Mary, represented by the earl of Worcester. Throughout these proceedings Francis
did his utmost to appear magnificent yet approachable—to fulfill the exalted image of sovereignty while being affable and companionable to his
English guests. He took them bear hunting and stag hunting; he jousted
with them and for them, and he provided food and entertainment on a
scale to match and, he hoped, to surpass the ostentatious banquets at
Henry's court. In the open courtyard within the Bastille a wooden floor
was built, with a huge space for dining tables and three galleries for spectators around the sides. The entire area was covered with a ceiling of blue
canvas to form a pavilion, and hangings in the king's colors of white and
tawny formed the walls. Here Francis gave a splendid feast, sitting under
his golden canopy and surrounded by his relatives and courtiers in order
of pre-eminence. The English sent detailed accounts of the evening to
Henry, describing the wonderful effect of the huge chandeliers, each

blazing with sixteen torches, throwing their light across the starry blue ceiling painted in gold with the signs of the zodiac and the planets. The food was served on plates of solid gold and silver, and some of the courses "emitted fire and flames," to the wonder of the diners. Each dish was presented with a degree of pomp usually reserved for visiting dignitaries. A flourish of trumpets announced its approach, with guardsmen and six attendants following the trumpeters. Five heralds then proclaimed the arrival of the eight seneschals of the king's household, who ushered in the Lord Steward; his staff of twenty-four pages of honor and two hundred guardsmen carried in the meat or fish or game.

Six companies of masquers danced in turn after the dining tables were cleared away: boys in white satin, men in long black satin mantles and white wigs and beards, and a group in "long gowns with tall stockings and short bolstered breeches." In the midst of the masquers Francis appeared, in a costume which perfectly evoked his magical and sacramental character as king. He wore a long, close-fitting white satin gown made in the shape of a cross like the white robe of Jesus in a religious painting. His youth and dark hair and beard heightened his resemblance to the familiar image of the savior, and his handsome face and solemn bearing created a profound and disturbing effect. Fastened to the white gown were "compasses and dials"—occult symbols—whose meaning eluded the onlookers and added to his air of mystery. The appearance of a group of girls dressed in low-cut bodices in "the Italian fashion" handing around wine and sugared confections broke the spell, and the evening ended with dancing and drinking. Fortunately, the ambassadors wrote, the canvas ceiling had been well waxed so that only a few drops of the heavy rain falling on the pavilion dropped on the heads of the guests. Francis' immense investment in the banquet, which they estimated at 450,000 crowns, was protected.

Midway in these ambassadorial exchanges occurred the last of Katherine's great disappointments. Her child had been much hoped for. "God grant she may give birth to a son," Giustinian wrote home to Venice in the last month of her pregnancy, "so that having an heir male, the king if necessary may not be hindered embarking on any great undertaking soever." A son would make certain that the crown would not pass to Mary and, through her, to her future husband the dauphin. A son would anchor the dynasty, reassure the king and satisfy his subjects.

In her eighth month Katherine gave birth to a stillborn daughter. Giustinian pronounced the misfortune "vexatious." "Never had this entire kingdom ever so anxiously desired anything as it did a prince," he declared, "it appearing to everyone that the state would be safe should his Majesty leave an heir male, whereas, without a prince, they are of a contrary opinion.''[7] Katherine was heartbroken, Henry temporarily glum. The betrothal of the princess was a calculated risk. Henry was gambling that long before the dauphin reached marriageable age his claim on the English throne in right of his wife would be invalidated by Henry's son or sons. For the time being, he had lost his wager. Giustinian expressed his private belief that if the outcome of Katherine's pregnancy had been known before the treaty was signed and the marriage promises exchanged, the entire diplomatic venture would have been abandoned. It is "the sole fear of this kingdom," he observed, "that it may pass through this marriage into the power of the French."

IV

 And I war a maydyn,
As many one ys,
For all the golde in England
I wold not do amysse.

Katherine's stillbirth meant that Mary would not, as her father hoped, fade into the background, eclipsed by a brother. Instead she remained an important focus of political attention—so important that her health was the subject of the most assiduous attention at the French court. Through her betrothal to the dauphin Mary had become the living embodiment of peace between England and France; as such it was important that she stay healthy. Queen Claude took to asking the English ambassador Thomas Boleyn how the princess was every time they met, and diplomats and courtiers began to exchange oblique inquiries about "whether the princess had been sick lately" as a matter of course.[1] A few months after her espousals a rumor circulated in Paris that she was dead, causing a few days of confused alarm, but before long Boleyn was able to quiet the disconcerted courtiers with the assurance that Mary was in perfect health.

The size and expense of her household now reflected her diplomatic importance. Before she was three years old the cost of maintaining her establishment had risen to fourteen hundred pounds, and an inventory of her household goods included enough hangings, bedding and other furnishings for a sizable apartment in the palace. Listed in the inventory along with the tapestries, rugs, featherbeds, linen, brassware and pewter basins were the necessary fixtures of a household constantly on the move: five thousand hooks and two thousand crochets for hanging and rehanging the tapestries, hammers for driving the hooks into the walls and nailing shut the lids of chests and coffers, dozens of yards of canvas for covering loaded carts and rope for securing bundles and tying the canvas in place.² Included too was a miniature throne—a little chair upholstered in cloth of gold and velvet—with a golden cloth of estate to be suspended over it and small gold cushions to go under the princess' feet.

By age three Mary had made herself the darling of her relatives and Henry's courtiers. At New Year's in 1519 she was showered with gifts—a gold spoon from Katherine's close friend Lady Devonshire, a gold pomander from her aunt Mary, two smocks from Lady Mountjoy, wife of Katherine's chamberlain, and from Wolsey a handsome gold cup. She was beginning to take part in the life of the court now, and was dressed up and shown around the room at banquets and other state occasions. She joined in family ceremonies of all kinds, and when her cousin Frances Brandon was born in the summer, Mary was called upon to be her god-mother.³

That the king kept a close watch on his daughter at this time is evi-dent from a letter his secretary Richard Pace wrote to Wolsey in July of 1518. Henry and Katherine were staying at Wolsey's estate of the More, and spending the long summer days hunting. Sometimes they rode to-gether, sometimes the queen rode alone the four miles to the little hunt-ing park on Sir John Pechy's estate that was her favorite. Neither of them returned until late in the evening, and it was after dark on the night of July 17 that Henry heard the news that one of Mary's servants was sick with "a hot ague." Mary had not come to the More with her parents, but was only two days' ride away, and Henry and Katherine received frequent messages from her household. Reports of small-scale outbreaks of both plague and the sweating sickness had been reaching the court all summer, and Henry was doubtless worried that the "hot ague" might be the sweat. He quickly told his secretary to write to Mary's servant Richard Sydnour ordering him to bring her to the More by way of Bisham Abbey, skirting the known infected areas. At the same time he told Pace to write Wolsey, who was in charge of all household affairs, asking him to work out safe itineraries for both Henry and Mary for the rest of the summer, and giving suggested routes.

Though he saw his daughter from time to time Henry's concern for Mary was usually expressed at a distance. Intimacy between the princess and her royal parents was not built up through daily contact as in less ex-alted families, but through occasional visits, exchanges of gifts and of money, letters and messages carried back and forth by household ser-vants. In her earliest years Mary spent the greater part of her time sur-rounded by her gentlewomen and by Margaret Pole, countess of Salis-bury, a long-faced, plain featured woman who in time became as dear to Mary as a grandmother.

Her parents moved through her life with the impermanence of

pleasant dreams, Katherine in her ash-colored court dress or her hunting skirts, her face always bright with laughter, Henry looming tall and strong in his velvets and jeweled caps. Mary was with them longest at holidays and in the seasons of panic during her second and third summers, but even then she saw them when they sent for her and not when she needed them. And she saw them often from the far end of the banquet hall, or looking out a window at the tiltyard. She may have been allowed to watch the pageant celebrating the French peace treaty in October of 1518, at which knights dressed as Turks and Christians fought an apocalyptic mock combat in front of a mountainous artificial "rock of peace" representing harmony among the European states. But there is no record that she was there. More likely on that evening Henry sent word ordering the princess dressed in her most splendid clothes and jewels, hugged her and carried her once around the room in his arms, and then gave her to an attendant gentlewoman to be put to bed.

Henry certainly admired and cherished his daughter—when he thought about her—and he was capable of a sentimental affection for her that reappeared at intervals throughout his life. But his idea of fatherly behavior was to be boisterous and demonstrative with his daughter for a few moments and then leave her in other hands. He saw to it that they were capable hands, but that was all. He made certain she was well cared for, but made no effort to get to know her or to involve himself in her life as she grew older. There would be no confidential intimacy between Henry and Mary. For that he needed not a daughter but a son.

Elizabeth Blount first came to Henry's court as a young girl sometime after the birth of the New Year's boy. A niece of Lord Mountjoy, she was blonde and very beautiful, and became one of the queen's maids of honor during the period when Katherine was vainly trying each year to produce a son. Elizabeth soon became "Bessie" to the king and his gentlemen, and was an especial favorite of Charles Brandon. Her beauty was put to use to adorn the pageants and revels, and at a court where graceful dancers and clear singing voices were at a premium Bessie Blount danced and sang extraordinarily well.

Bessie was still in her teens when she became Henry's mistress. She was not the first, of course. Beyond the king's indiscretion with the duke of Buckingham's sister there had been rumors of a Flemish mistress during the 1513 campaign, and dozens of the brief or lasting courtly flirtations which were a little more than an extension of good manners. But Bessie was different. She was certainly the most beautiful girl, if not the most intelligent or fascinating, at Henry's court. His association with her lasted for several years, not merely a few days or weeks. And most important, she bore him a son.

The boy was born sometime in 1519, when Mary was three years old.

Bessie left Katherine's service when the signs of her pregnancy became an outrage to the queen—for like everyone else she knew very well who the child's father was—and went to a monastery in the country for her delivery. Her child was christened Henry, with the honorific surname Fitzroy. Bessie herself was henceforth known at court by the unofficial title "mother of the king's son," and out of gratitude Henry arranged for her to marry a substantial gentleman, Sir Gilbert Talboys. The king's liaison with Bessie did not continue after the young Henry's birth, but Henry and Bessie remained linked through their son, and to Katherine's immense displeasure both Lady Talboys and her child were revered almost as if they had become part of the royal line. Certainly many observers assumed that, if Katherine had no son of her own, the king's bastard would rule in place of his legitimate daughter. And to keep this possibility open, Henry gave his infant son a princely household and a succession of titles that gave him every appearance of being heir to the throne.

In Mary's young childhood Henry VIII was at the apex of his popularity. He had taken the ideal of chivalric monarchy to heights undreamed of by his medieval predecessors. He had led an army to victory in France; he ruled a turbulent but adoring people; he had proven himself to be among the wealthiest and most generous of European rulers. Whether they glimpsed him in his red-plumed helmet and golden armor covered with little golden bells, laughing and throwing the bells to Maximilian's soldiers at the siege of Thérouanne, or riding to the hunt with the entire court at his heels, Henry captured and held the admiring attention of his contemporaries as no earlier king had done. His reign was unfolding as a vast drama in which he played the starring role. His love of costumes and of surprise changes of character, his taste for theatrical spectacles, his constant effort to be unpredictable, to do the unexpected both in his court and in affairs of state, fascinated all who came near him. Henry forced himself on the consciousness of his age and held his central place there until the very end of his life. In a remarkable feat of sustained image-building, he was re-creating the English monarchy in his own likeness.

Mary's childhood was spent in Henry's giant shadow. There was a total identification, in the popular mind, between father and daughter, but Mary was seen as the king's adored plaything, another ornament like his huge jewel-studded admiral's whistle or his collar of enormous diamonds. His nickname for her denoted a precious adornment to his court: he called her his pearl, "the greatest pearl in the kingdom." The name aptly conveyed her worth in Henry's eyes. She was a treasure to be protected, hoarded, and, when the time came, spent to procure a lasting

diplomatic advantage. That she might some day succeed her father was
no more than an alarming improbability. And so throughout her childhood she was groomed, conditioned and taught not how to rule England,
but how to make a successful transition from daughter to wife—to move
from ornamenting her father's court to adorning that of her future husband. Central to this conditioning was Mary's formal education, which
taught her to see herself as a weak and inferior being who could
redeem her inherent sinfulness only by an attitude of subservience
and vigilant self-denial. The contrast between her gloriously successful
father and her admired yet repressed self pervaded Mary's childhood, especially during her formative years.

This contrast was heightened by the fact that she saw her father, as a
rule, only on favored occasions. From about the age of three Mary saw
her parents only at Easter and Christmas; during the long months in between she rode in her litter from Windsor to Hanworth to Richmond to
Greenwich—to wherever, at Wolsey's order, fresh rushes had been laid
and the rooms "sweetened" for the princess.[4] Christmas became the high
point of her year, for then she not only visited her father and mother but
celebrated the holiday with twelve days of feasting, dancing and masques
climaxed by the arrival of New Year's gifts. At her fourth Christmas a
company of children performed a play for Mary, under the direction of
the royal dramatist John Heywood. In the following year she was allowed her own Lord of Misrule—one of her household valets, John
Thurgood—who planned and presented entertainments with morris
dancers, carillons and hobbyhorses. For Mary's sixth Christmas Thurgood
outdid himself. Mary's Christmas this year at Ditton was a miniature version of Henry's great festivities at nearby Windsor. Her Christmas feast,
like his, featured a gilded and painted boar's head; her mummers appeared
in visors and armor, rabbit skins and tails. Her nine morris dancers
wore ten dozen tinkling bells, and one of her "disguisings" required
"straw to cover twelve men." Another entertainment was a gory mock
battle whose props included twelve crossbows, gunpowder, four gunners,
two dozen morris pikes and "a man to kill a calf behind a cloth." Her
New Year's gifts were becoming more costly each year: a gold cross
from the countess of Devonshire, twelve pairs of shoes from Richard
Weston, a tall gold salt cellar set with pearls from Wolsey, and from
Henry a standing cup of silver gilt overflowing with coins.[5] And from "a
poor woman of Greenwich" a rosemary bush (one of the Tudor symbols) hung with gold spangles.

We know very little about the dim world of Tudor childhood. For
Mary it meant the loud noises and crowded halls of the great palaces, the
long silences and green vistas of the smaller manors, candlelight, torchlight, black darkness. It meant journeys through the countryside at all

seasons, barge rides from Richmond to Greenwich and back again, animals, sudden rain showers and the sweet scent of cherries and strawberries from the gardens of Hanworth and Windsor. It was prayers, priests, music, her jewels, her little throne. It was not a world of indulgent parents or nurses. Visitors to England in the late fifteenth century were struck by the terror children showed in the presence of their parents. Even as adults English men and women stood in nervous silence when their parents entered a room, and did not speak until they were spoken to. Children were governed through fear as a matter of course, and if they failed to obey they were slapped and beaten until they did. Thomas More, who wrote proudly that if he flogged his children at all it was with the tail of a peacock, was famous for his gentleness, but the attitude of his friend Richard Whytford was more typical of his time. Whytford composed a little prayer for children to repeat to their mothers every morning:

> If I lie, backbite or steal
> If I will curse, scorn, mock or swear,
> If I chide, fight, strive or threat,
> Then am I worthy to be beat.
> Good mother or mistress mine,
> If any of these nine
> I trespass to your Knowyng;
> With a new rod and a fine
> Early naked before I dine
> Amend me with a scourging.[6]

If children were taught to fear the consequences of disobedience, they were kept in terror of the uncontrollable world of the occult. They were told to "double the thumb"—to enclose their thumb under their clenched fingers—in the presence of danger, for this shape of the hand resembled the Hebrew name of God. Their imaginations were opened to the invisible troupe of menacing beings which wandered the night or waited in the forest. The list of these unseen tormentors was enormous: spirits, witches, hags, satyrs, pans, sylens, tritons, centaurs, dwarfs, giants, imps, calcars, nymphs, incubi, hobgoblins, Robin Goodfellow, the spoorn, the mare, the man in the oak, the hell-wain, the firedrake, the puckle, and the terrifying "Boneless." Ruling them all was the ultimate horror, compounded of all the animals children fear most: the Devil, "having horns on his head, fire in his mouth, and a tail in his breech, eyes like a Bason, fangs like a Dog, claws like a Boar, a skin like a Niger, and a voice roaring like a Lion, whereby we start and are afraid when we hear one cry Bough!"[7]

These dark imaginings were offset by the sunlit pleasures of riding and hawking. At six Mary rode well, and Lord Abergavenny sent her a horse of her own. Henry sent her a goshawk, and she seems to have spent many hours in the summer of 1522 learning to hunt with her. One entire August day Mary and her attendants rode in the forest near Windsor Castle, picnicking on bread and ale.[8] The princess' household establishment was quite large by the early 1520s. At age six she had seven gentlemen, ten valets and sixteen pages, plus stableboys, kitchen urchins, her laundress and woodbearer. The lists of goods supplied to her bakehouse, butlery, kitchen, and accatry grew longer each year, until her table was costing the king nearly twelve hundred pounds annually.[9] Among the members of Mary's growing household were two who would be in her service for decades, Beatrice ap Rice, her "lavender" or laundress and David ap Rice, who was at first a page but soon became yeoman of the chamber. More ephemeral are the names of minstrels who were in her pay for only a few months at a time, English and French names in most cases but occasionally a Welshman like Elandon, who joined her establishment when she was nine.

Music was the most intimate of the links between Henry and Mary. Among Henry's prodigious talents was the ability to play, with the bravado of a gifted amateur, on a good many musical instruments—among them the gittaron, lute, cornet, and virginal. He liked nothing better than to follow up an afternoon of strenuous jousting with an impromptu evening concert, where he performed in alternation with the professional musicians of his court and often played nearly as well as they did. He collected instruments, and was always looking for advancements in design and sonority; in his collection was a mechanical virginal, described as operating "with a wheel without playing upon."[10] His serious compositions —motets and masses—were no less praised than his lighter songs, and among the popular tunes of Mary's childhood—"Hay the Eye," "Maugh Murre," "Bonny Wench"—was the king's own "O My Heart."

Henry collected musicians as he did instruments. In 1519 he had at least three very distinguished soloists at his court, a French clavichordist, a German keyboard player who so impressed the king that he took him along on his summer progress to entertain him at Woodstock, and the famed Venetian organist Dionysius Memo.[11] Memo, who was organist of St. Mark's, arrived at Henry's court with his own organ, "brought hither with much pain and cost," and a group of virtuosi; the king promptly made him chief of his musicians and chaplain. He almost certainly became Mary's teacher as well, for his stay at court coincides with her early childhood and by the time she was three or four she was playing the virginal for visitors. Mary shared both Henry's love of music and his natural aptitude. As a child in arms she learned to recognize Memo across a room full of dignitaries and would call out loudly to him to play for her.[12] She became a skilled player in her own right, with a facility for rapid and intricate passagework, and when she grew older she taught the women and girls in her household to play.

Mary resembled her father in many ways besides her musical gift and fair coloring, but her formal education took no account of this resemblance. Instead she was taught to deny in herself all traces of Henry's spontaneous flamboyance and self-assertion, and to perceive the overriding truth that for her, as for all women, life must be a grim battle against temptation and weakness, a battle she was destined to lose.

We know a good deal about what and how Mary was taught in her childhood. At Katherine's request the Spanish humanist Vives designed a plan of study for her, set out in several educational treatises. One of these prescribed a curriculum in the classics, describing how the princess was to acquire the rudiments of pronunciation and grammar and then read simple Greek and Latin stories before going on to Plato, Plutarch, Cicero and Seneca. The Christian Latin poets and the writings of the church Fathers were to be emphasized, and, of course, Mary was to read passages from the scriptures every morning and evening. For recreation she was to read stories about self-sacrificing women. Vives recommended in particular Livy's account of the virtuous Roman matron Lucretia, who after being raped by the son of Tarquin the Proud, stabbed herself to death, and the story of the patient Griselda, whose husband put her through endless trials to assure himself of her devotion. These were to be her models, in addition to the suffering holy women whose lives she knew intimately from the legends of the saints.

More important to Vives than Mary's mastery of Greek and Latin was her education in virtue. Every young girl, he wrote in his work *On the Instruction of a Christian Woman*, ought to keep constantly in mind that she is inherently "the devil's instrument, and not Christ's."[13] To Vives as to most humanists the central dilemma of female education was the inherent sinfulness of women. This negative premise was the foundation of Mary's training, and everything she learned was to be chosen in the light of whether it was likely to palliate or entrench the inescapable perversity of her nature. When Katherine asked Vives to draw up a plan of education for Mary, she envisioned it primarily as a form of protection for the young girl, to guard her "more securely and safely than any spearman or bowman whatever."[14]

The protection she referred to was, first and most obviously, protection of Mary's virginity. Erasmus, who at first saw no point in education for women, was persuaded in England that "nothing so completely preserves the modesty" of young girls as learning, for without it "many from simplicity and inexperience have lost their chastity before they knew that such an inestimable treasure was in danger."[15] At courts where the learning of girls is ignored, he wrote, they spend their mornings dressing their hair and painting their faces, showing themselves off at mass, and gossiping. In the afternoon they lie about on the grass in fair weather, joking and flirting, "with men leaning over on to their laps." Their days are spent among "sated and indolent servants, very squalid, and of impure morals." In this atmosphere modesty cannot thrive, and virtue has little meaning. Vives hoped to keep Mary from these influences, and in consequence he devoted as much attention to the environment in which the princess was to be educated as he did to the content of what she learned.

From earliest infancy, he insisted, she should be kept away from the company of men, lest she become attached to the male sex. Since "a woman that thinketh alone, thinketh evil," she was to be surrounded at all times with "sad, pale and untrimmed" servants and taught to weave and spin when her lessons were over. Weaving Vives recommended as inducing a "love of sober sadness," an approved frame of consciousness likely to discourage the sensual musings native to all females. Of the "foul ribaldry" of popular songs and books the young girl should know nothing, and should beware of romances "as of serpents or snakes." Lest she trust herself too much, he advised, she should be encouraged to fear being alone; she should be trained to require the company of others and rely on them for everything. Vives' recommendations amounted to a deliberate programming for helplessness, with the feelings of inferiority and depression that accompany it.[16]

But his warnings against sensuality were even more harmful. The child's movements should be watched, he noted, to prevent "uncomely gestures or moving of the body." Only the blandest food should be served, which would not "inflame the body." He recommended that as an adolescent Mary should fast to "bridle the body and press it down, and quench the heat of youth." Fasting, always a mark of the ascetic life, became in the early sixteenth century the special hallmark of young female saints. Popular pamphlets told of the prodigious fast of one young girl in the Netherlands, Eve Fliegen, who gave up all food and drink and subsisted for years entirely on the scent of roses.[17] Weak wine was permissible, Vives thought, but water was best, since "it is better that the stomach ache than the mind."[18] All adornment of the body was of course hazardous. Like the sight of men, perfumes and ointments "fire the maid with jeapardous heat" and were to be avoided, and Mary's guardians were to impress on her that an alluring woman is "a poisoner and sword" to all who see her.

Mary's education was intended to provide her with an intellectual chastity belt—a view of herself and of the spiritual dangers facing all women that would frighten her into an attitude of withdrawn virtue. For it was a vital corollary to this concept of self that it was only compatible with a life of domesticity. Public life in any form was impossible for women, for it meant loss of chastity and good repute. Vives' model of female behavior envisioned a woman at home and silent, with "few to see her and none at all to hear her." Leaving the house was full of perils; it demanded that she "prepare her mind and stomach none otherwise than if she went to fight." In streets and public places "the darts of the Devil are flying on every side," Vives insisted, and her only defenses were the good examples she had been taught, her determination to remain chaste and "a mind ever bent toward Christ."[19] To forestall prying eyes she should cover her neck and veil her face, leaving "scarcely an eye open to see the way."

Vives' educational doctrines called for claustration, cultivated prudery and an exaggerated horror of sensuality in every form. They were more the product of Spanish than English attitudes toward women, but Vives took many of his teachings directly from the works of St. Jerome, whose views on female education had been a respected part of Christian culture since antiquity. That women were morally inferior to men was a commonplace of theology, and the fathers and scholastics of the middle ages had elaborated dozens of antifeminist formulas. The traditional starting point of these arguments was the Christian story of creation itself, in which Adam was made directly by God but Eve was made only indirectly, by means of Adam's flesh. Eve was thus not made in God's image but in Adam's, and was inferior to him. It was Eve, too, who tempted Adam to disobey God and was responsible for mankind's fall. To these sins scholastic theologians added the Aristotelian teaching that all female creatures are "misbegotten males"—biological accidents and imperfections. Man was seen as the norm of humankind, woman as the abnormal exception, and some Christian writers wondered whether, at the last judgment, women would rise from the dead in female form or whether they would be resurrected in the perfect form of men.

What gave these teachings their enduring authority was that they were biblical in origin and thoroughly integrated with the other doctrines of the church. St. Paul had written that "the husband is the head of the wife, even as Christ is the head of the church," and had forbidden women to speak in the Christian congregation; women, he taught, should reverence men and remain in proper subjection to them. Several New Testament passages implied that men were to serve as mediators between their wives and Christ, just as Christ served as mediator between man and God. Male superiority was in an important sense essential to salvation—a part of the revealed truth of Christianity. To doubt the inferiority of women, then, was to doubt salvation itself.

Social doctrines also supported this view of women. English men and women of the Tudor age believed that society was held together by a complex network of relationships between superiors and inferiors. Each individual had a preordained place in this network, and only by staying in that place could the social order be maintained. Women were ranked in the social hierachy according to the status of their fathers, first, and later according to that of their husbands; if they presumed to throw off their subservient role they risked upsetting the entire social structure.

Of course, Mary had only to read and to look around her to see contradictions to the principle of female weakness and inferiority. Medieval women had worn armor and led feudal armies; they had conducted sieges and organized the defense of towns and castles. Fist fighting was known in fifteenth-century England as "fighting like women," and the chronicles of the age were full of accounts of embattled women. In her grandfather Henry VII's reign, during fighting in Flanders a small group of English soldiers were left to guard Nieuport against the French. Many of the soldiers were wounded, and the others proved too sick or exhausted to defend the town when the French attacked. Just as they entered the gates, however, a shipload of English archers from Calais landed, and the women of the town joined them in pushing back the attackers. Crying "Help, Englishmen!" they rushed on the French with knives and cut their throats as fast as the archers could shoot them.[20]

Examples of learned women were equally numerous. Mary's great-grandmother Margaret Beaufort translated French works into English and was praised as a "right studious" woman with an "upholding memory"; she kept an apartment at Cambridge and founded Christ's College there. On the continent, the Italian courts were noted for their learned women, and the daughters of the German humanist Pirckheimer were famous throughout Europe for their scholarship. Closer to home, Thomas More's daughter Margaret was a brilliant scholar whose treatise on the *Four Last Things* More pronounced superior to his own.

The most obvious exemplar at Henry's court of female strength, courage and intellect was the queen. Born in a military camp as her mother's forces were besieging Granada, Katherine had survived a bitter adolescence in a strange country, suffered the deaths of a young husband and all but one of her children, and now lived with the ignominy of her husband's infidelities. Yet she did not give way to frustration or resignation. She took pride in her ancestry, her capabilities as a ruler in Henry's absence, her imperturbable dignity and her ever gracious smile. She took pride also in her learning, for which Erasmus called her "a miracle of her sex." Vives concurred in this judgment, but here the compliment to Katherine the woman ended and the insistence on woman's weakness began again. For Vives' highest praise of the queen was that it was only an "error of nature" that she was not a man. "There was in her feminine body a man's heart," he insisted.[21] "But for her sex," Thomas Cromwell would say of Katherine later, "she would have surpassed all the heroes of history."[22]

Both Mary's education and her observation taught her in childhood that as a woman she must fear her nature for its weakness and her character for its tendency to sin. Her wit might be considerable, but it would never be trustworthy or profound. She must fear to think or judge or act on her own, and must limit her aspirations to a retired life of quiet obedience to a husband chosen for her by others. If she surpassed herself, she might someday, like Katherine, be compared to a man—but only in a way that pointed to lost opportunities and futile hopes.

V

 O heresy, thou walkest a-wrye,
Abrode to gadde or raunge;
Like false brethren, deceave children,
This Churche nowe for to chaunge:
Her praier by night to banish quight,
With new inventions straunge.

On April 17, 1521, a thickset young monk with the coarse features of a peasant stood before the German Diet at Worms. The emperor, Charles V, was present, along with the leading figures in the German church and state. The young monk, Martin Luther, was confident yet overawed by the assembly. For he had been summoned to Worms in hopes that he might take back the heresies he taught—that the pope was only a fallible man, and that salvation did not come through the seven sacraments of the church.

The pope, who saw Luther as just another heretic, had excommunicated him, but in the empire he was already a popular hero. His writings were eagerly received by Germans of all classes who resented the political and economic stranglehold of Rome and saw in his teachings a rallying point for rebellion. North of the Alps, Luther was a dangerous man. Rather than force him into open revolt by publishing the papal bull of excommunication the emperor summoned him to Worms. Here he was shown a pile of his books. Would he stand by everything he had written, he was asked, even where it went against the age-old teachings of the church? How could he be certain that he was right and all those who had gone before him were wrong?

Luther appeared to falter under the pressure of his examiners and the solemn weight of the occasion. He asked for time to prepare his reply. He went back to the freezing attic that was the only lodging he had been able to find in the city and pondered whether he might have overstated his views. The next day he returned to face the Diet, convinced that he could alter none of what he had written. If he did not yield, the officials warned him, the only possible outcome would be bitter division and civil war throughout the German lands. But Luther was adamant. He had to follow scripture and his conscience, and no one else. Charles V left the room, unconvinced. Luther was outlawed, and left Worms in fear of his life. In the following year the first in a wave of bloody revolts that would devastate German society in the 1520s was under way.

On the day the Diet of Worms ended Henry VIII's secretary Richard Pace found the king in his chamber reading one of Luther's works. It was his new treatise *On the Babylonian Captivity of the Church*, in which he argued that there ought to be only two sacraments, the Lord's Supper and baptism, and not the seven defined by Rome. The treatise provided Henry with just the focus he needed for a project he had long had in mind. Since 1515 he had been at work on and off on a theological treatise of his own. Now he would turn it into an assault on Luther. The grateful pope would, he hoped, reward him by giving him another clause to add to his official title. A medieval pope had conferred on the line of French kings the title "Most Christian." Henry wanted a similar designation for himself and his heirs.

As a preliminary to his personal assault against Lutheran doctrines Henry and Wolsey planned a formal denunciation. The king was not able to preside in person—a tertian fever confined him to his bed—but the cardinal conducted the proceedings with impressive solemnity. He sat under a golden canopy on a platform in the churchyard of St. Paul's, and his magnificence was awesome—worthy of the pope himself, in the view of one eyewitness. The proceedings were opened by John Fisher, bishop of Rochester, who spoke for some two hours to the assembled clergy, lay lords and commoners, praising Wolsey and announcing that Henry was at work on a theological refutation of Luther's heresies. Wolsey then rose to promulgate the papal bull excommunicating Luther and cursed him and all his followers. To dramatize the condemnation he ordered quantities of Lutheran writings heaped up in the churchyard and set on fire, and the smoke from the burning books and pamphlets rose over the platform as he spoke.[1]

The elaborate denunciation of Luther was prompted, at least in part, by the embarrassing accuracy of his criticisms. The English church, like the German, was a highly imperfect vehicle of belief. Some clerics were pious and self-sacrificing, but many others disgraced their offices. They wore bright-colored clothing and silver girdles like laymen; they curled their hair like courtiers; wealthy bishops trapped their horses with costly furs and wore gold buttons and lacings on their caps. To meet a priest was, in the words of one church critic, "to behold a peacock that spreadeth his tail when he danceth before the hen." And while many parish priests were so poor they could barely feed themselves, some among the higher clergy were extravagantly wealthy. Ruthal, bishop of Durham and Wolsey's chief factotum, carried about with him an inventory of his extensive lands and treasure, and Wolsey, easily the richest ecclesiastic in England, had a personal income larger than the king's.

Wolsey's wealth came from another clerical vice condemned by Luther: pluralism. By church law every cleric could hold only one parish, deanery, diocese or archdiocese. In 1521, Wolsey held at least two such benefices—the archbishopric of York and the bishopric of Bath and Wells—and in addition he enjoyed the income from the bishopric of Worcester whose bishop, an Italian, was out of the country. Beyond his own numerous offices Wolsey gained most of the profits from the church livings bestowed on his bastard son Thomas Wynter. While he was still a schoolboy Wynter became dean of Wells; later he was made provost of Beverly, archdeacon of both York and Richmond, and chancellor of Salisbury, holding in all a group of livings earning some twenty-seven hundred pounds a year.[2]

Cardinal Wolsey was fast becoming a symbol of the worldly power and wealth concentrated in the English church. In the king's name he claimed authority over every other noble or cleric in the land, and did not hesitate to bully and rough up foreign dignitaries if they threatened England's interests. He caused a scandal in 1516 by seizing the papal nuncio Chieregato, taking him into a private chamber and "laying hands on him," demanding to know whether Chieregato was conspiring with the French and Venetians. In "fierce and rude language," Wolsey made it clear that unless the nuncio confessed freely, he would be put to the rack, and in fact he was not allowed to leave the kingdom until his house had been ransacked and all his papers and ciphers seized and read.[8] On another occasion Wolsey summoned Giustinian and threatened him in the strongest possible language against sending dispatches abroad without his personal consent, "under pain of the indignation of the king." As he spoke Wolsey became more and more beside himself, until in his frustration he began to gnaw at the cane he was holding in his hand and scrape it roughly against his teeth.[4]

If Wolsey did no more than threaten, other clerics were not above criminal intrigues. In 1514 Cardinal Bainbridge, archbishop of York, was poisoned at Rome by a self-proclaimed agent of the bishop of Worcester. Conclusive proof of the bishop's guilt was lacking, but it was thought the matter was hushed up because Wolsey succeeded to Bainbridge's see and later Worcester helped Wolsey to become cardinal.[5]

Clearly the English church was marred by abuses, vice and worldliness, but the idea of a fundamental change of religious sentiment was as foreign to the English as it was welcome to Luther's eager supporters in Germany. If the Lutherans were ridiculing the veneration of relics, the English were still taking to the roads in spring and summer on pilgrimages to the shrines of St. Cuthbert at Durham, the two Hughs at Lincoln, the Saxon St. Etheldreda at Ely, St. Joseph of Arimathea at the holy shrine of Glastonbury and, most beloved of all, the jewel-encrusted tomb of St. Thomas Becket at Canterbury. If Lutheran doctrine condemned the sale of indulgences—papal pardons which claimed to shorten the sinner's time in purgatory—the English were still moved to buy them for themselves and their dead relatives. Thomas More conjured a piteous image of the torment of souls in purgatory, condemned by God's inexorable judgment to writhe in fire hotter than any earthly flame, "sleepless, restless, burning and broiling in the dark fire one long night of many days," and torn by "cruel, doomed sprites, odious, envious and hateful." To ease this unthinkable anguish English men and women were glad to pay for indulgences that promised them a year, or five hundred years, or, as in one formula from Salisbury, 32,755 years of pardon. The love of saints, the fear of punishment for sin, the place of the church feasts in the timeless cycle of the agricultural year—these and not theological disputes were for the majority of the English the unchallenged substance of belief in the 1520s.

The general indifference of his subjects to the new doctrines from Germany put no damper on King Henry's enthusiasm for his new project. He rushed ahead with his treatise during May and June of 1521, calling it the *Assertion of the Seven Sacraments* and adding to the copy being prepared for the pope a verse of dedication in his own handwriting. By August the *Assertion* was completed, and twenty-eight copies were sent to the English ambassador in Rome, John Clerk, who took them to Pope Leo. The pope was immediately taken with his own copy, which was bound in cloth of gold, and urged Clerk to stay while he read the first five pages or so, nodding his head in approval as he read. Looking up from his reading he remarked on Henry's "wit and clerkly conveyance," and paid him the high compliment of comparing his work favorably to that of men who devoted their entire lives to learning. Leo's eyesight was almost too dim to make out Henry's dedicatory verse, but once it was pointed out to him he read it again and again, and praised it and the king in the most grateful terms.[6]

Leo presented the *Assertion* later at a private consistory, and on the following day he announced his intention to give Henry his coveted title Defender of the Faith. The pope requested copies of the royal book for his cardinals as if he expected it to be used against Luther, but in fact the twenty-eight presentation copies were allowed to gather dust in his library, and a year later Clerk noticed them there, still unread.[7] Other clerics welcomed Henry's efforts with extravagant praise, however, calling the *Assertion* a "golden book" and its author an "angelic rather than a human spirit." Outside Rome Henry's treatise was read, and translated from Latin into German and English. Certainly it did not hurt the papal cause to have such a celebrity as the king of England declare himself in opposition to Luther at a time when most humanists were reluctant to denounce him and the German knights were rebelling in his name. One of Luther's opponents exclaimed that Henry's work was "multiplied into many thousands," and "filled the whole Christian world with joy and admiration"; another was ready to turn over to him the whole field of learning. "If kings are of this strength," he wrote, "farewell to us philosophers."

Of course there were those who claimed that Henry could not have written his book without help; some said More or Erasmus or, as Luther believed, Erasmus' enemy Edward Lee was the true author. Modern scholars are equally reluctant to give the king credit for the *Assertion*, although at least one cites the mediocrity of the treatise as proof of its royal authorship. By his own admission Henry disliked putting pen to paper, but he may have dictated the treatise to a secretary. And if he had help in choosing and organizing his arguments, still the impetus to write it and the persistence to complete it were his. Henry disliked allowing others to take recognition he could earn for himself, and he rarely took credit for other men's feats. In all probability the *Assertion of the Seven Sacraments* was largely the king's own book.

Certainly the abuse heaped on the reformer in the treatise was worthy of Henry. He called Luther a "venomous serpent, a pernicious plague, an infernal wolf . . . an infectious soul, a detestable trumpeter of pride, calumnies and schism, having an execrable mind, a filthy tongue, and a detestable touch."[8] To Luther, "Squire Harry" was nothing but "a damnable rottenness and worm," and he showed no deference to royalty in his rude response to the *Assertion*. Henry and Luther proved themselves masters of invective, if not of theological argument, but after their first exchange the king left it to others to defend his side of the controversy. Under a pseudonym Thomas More took up the battle against "Lousy Luther," and Henry shifted his assault on the reformer from the religious to the diplomatic realm.

It was no coincidence that Luther's chief enemy, after the pope, was the man Henry and Wolsey were courting most assiduously, the Emperor Charles V. When Henry wrote to Charles execrating Luther as "this weed, this dilapidated, sick and evilminded sheep," his abuse was intended to echo Charles' own view and to convey England's readiness to support the emperor in his fight against the Lutheran rebels. Charles was

Katherine's nephew, the son of her mad sister Joanna. He was Henry's nephew by marriage, and in recent years Henry had been taking full advantage of his avuncular role to court an imperial alliance, inviting Charles to England and entertaining him lavishly. In features and temperament Charles fell far short of the handsome, chivalric image of monarchy dear to Henry's heart, but his wealth and power more than made up for these shortcomings.

Charles was an ill-favored man whose narrow blue eyes, lusterless white skin and enormous, disfiguring jaw and chin lent him a vaguely imbecilic air. He had bad teeth and a fragile digestion, and his lifelong habit of gross overeating gave him an expression indicative of perpetual indigestion. He looked best on horseback, where the severe plainness of his dress passed for understated magnificence and his face took on a heroic stubbornness. In the saddle he was convincing as the ruler of European lands significantly larger than those of France and nearly five times those of England. The extent of his subjects and wealth in the New World was only beginning to be estimated, but even leaving them out of account he controlled the financial center of Europe and his fleets and armies made him master of the continent. It was already apparent that Charles lacked brilliance and flair, but he was conscientious and shrewd. His bursts of activity were interrupted by long periods of listless depression during which no state business was conducted and courtiers and ambassadors wondered whether the emperor might slip into a permanent melacholy of the kind that imprisoned the wits of his mother. But then energy would return to his limbs and voice, and to the "greedy eyes" the Venetian envoy saw in his disconcerting face, and the emperor would again confront the task of administering his far-flung empire.

In the fall of 1521 Charles' energies were directed toward war with France, and Henry was supporting the imperial side of the conflict. Francis had returned to his preoccupation with surpassing Henry—now he was building a ship larger than Henry's thousand-ton warship the *Great Harry*—and Wolsey was engaged in drawn-out negotiations of a betrothal between the young emperor and Mary. (The French betrothal had been set aside.) There was no doubt in Henry's mind that the emperor's forces would defeat the French, but the war news was not encouraging. Letters from France informed the king that the French were sweeping into the territories of the emperor, burning everything in their path and cutting off the fingers of little children as a warning of worse cruelties to come.[9]

In the midst of the fighting Charles visited England a second time, in June of 1522. London was prepared for his arrival as if for a royal coronation, with buildings along his route of entry newly painted and decorated with hangings, and pageants staged in several quarters of the city. Charles was greeted by the Lord Mayor and aldermen, and by a Latin oration from Thomas More. All the clergy of Middlesex were assembled to cense him as he rode past, and the members of every occupation and company stood together in their liveries. Two giants welcomed Charles and Henry to London, addressing them as "Henry defender of the faith, Charles defender of the church," but most of the pageants made no allusion to religion and instead elaborated the themes of the English Order of the Garter and the imperial Order of the Golden Fleece, and the genealogical links between the two rulers. One representation was made in the shape of the island of England, surrounded with rocks and silver waves, and with its mountains and woods full of beasts and fish, trees and flowers. When the emperor passed this pageant the animals began to move, the fish to jump and the mechanical birds to sing, and two armed figures made to resemble Charles and Henry threw away their swords and embraced. At that moment "an image of the father of heaven all in burned gold" appeared above the island, under a banner proclaiming, "Blessed are the peacemakers for they shall be called the children of God."[10]

During Charles' visit the two kings played tennis and rode together, and the English knights jousted against the emperor's attendants, the prince of Orange and the marquis of Brandenburg. Henry and Charles took the lists themselves in a gorgeous tournament, wearing horse bards of russet velvet depicting "knights on horseback riding upon mountains of gold." A play was presented in the great hall at Windsor, mocking Francis and celebrating the English and imperial enterprise against him. An untamed horse representing France ran wild across the stage until the king and emperor, in the person of Amity, sent their messengers Prudence and Policy to tame the horse and their envoy Force to bridle him once and for all.[11]

There were banquets as well during the emperor's visit, and exchanges of compliments and effusive camaraderie, but this royal meeting was of the utmost seriousness. Despite his youth Charles was a mature ruler on a diplomatic mission of the gravest import. He knew exactly what he hoped to gain in England and what he was willing to give in return. Preliminary meetings had raised and settled most of the major points of dispute months before, and there was agreement on the central issues of the betrothal and the English declaration against France that would follow it. The betrothal contract had been hammered out with some difficulty. Charles' negotiators first insisted that Mary be delivered to them as soon as she reached the age of seven, so that she could be trained as a lady of the imperial court for some years before her marriage. Wolsey refused, fearing that the princess might in some way be "repudiated, violated or disparaged" once she arrived in Brussels. Next Wolsey's request for dower lands in Flanders and Spain to the value of 20,000 marks was refused as excessively large, and he in turn refused an imperial request that England declare against France at once, without waiting for the betrothal to be sworn. Finally compromises were worked out on all these points: Mary would not go to Brussels until she was twelve, her dower lands would total ten thousand pounds in value, and the English declaration would be deferred until the time of Charles' personal visit. Mary's dowry of eighty thousand pounds was reluctantly accepted, though the imperial negotiators pointed out that it was less than the king of Portugal was offering to give with his daughter.[12]

Some months after these negotiations the Spanish ambassador came to Richmond, and while he was there Katherine insisted that he see the emperor's future bride. Mary was dressed beautifully and brought before him to dance. She danced a slow dance first, "and twirled so prettily that no woman could do better," and then began the leaping steps of the galliard, "acquitting herself marvellously well." She played the virginal for the ambassador too, and showed such poise and skill that he marveled at her ability and wrote that she might be envied by a woman of twenty. He pronounced her pretty and, surprisingly, tall for her age—probably implying that she was taller than Spanish girls of six.[13]

After several weeks of visits and entertainments Charles, Henry and Wolsey closeted themselves to finalize the alliance. Plans were made for the invasion of France and the division of French lands between the two sovereigns afterward. On June 16 war was declared against France. At Windsor the matrimonial treaty was signed, and when Mary kissed Charles goodbye as he left to make his way to the Channel for the return crossing to Brussels it was no longer as his cousin but as his affianced bride. In six years they would marry, and the princess would become Empress Mary, co-ruler of half the known world.

Over the next four years this awesome prospect dominated Mary's life. She was to be transformed, as rapidly as possible, into a young Spanish lady. To begin with, she was to be dressed "according to the fashion and manner of those parts." Cloth was sent to the imperial court to be cut into gowns under the supervision of Margaret, regent of Flanders. Margaret was "to devise for the making thereof after such manner as best shall please her," then return the garments to England.[14] Mary spoke her mother's Spanish; now she was to be trained in Spanish customs and politeness as well. It was strongly urged that Mary be sent to Spain, at least for a time, but Henry would not part with her. Katherine could teach her all that she needed to know, he insisted, and after the marriage Charles could educate her as he wished.

The letters Charles sent to the English court during these years rarely mentioned Mary; from the emperor's point of view the betrothal was only a minor detail of a diplomatic alliance. He did ask for news of "my best sweetheart the princess, the future empress" in a letter to Wolsey in 1523, but doubtless she remained very much in the background of his thoughts.[15] As for Mary, she seems to have had a strong romantic feeling for Charles—or at any rate for the idea of a husband—and it seems clear that the women around her encouraged her to imitate the behavior and to express the emotions of a lover. When she was nine Mary sent Charles an emerald ring, together with the solemn message "that her grace hath devised this token for a better knowledge to be had (when God shall send them grace to be together) whether his majesty doth keep constant and continent to her, as with God's grace she will to him." The ambassadors who were to deliver the emerald were instructed to add that Mary's love for Charles was so passionate that it was showing itself in jealousy, "one of the greatest signs and tokens of love." Sending the emerald may or may not have been Mary's own idea, but it was certainly the kind of thing that Katherine and her ladies encouraged. It was a gesture of playful courtesy, the act of a medieval princess testing the fidelity of her knight. Regardless of its origin, there is every reason to believe that Mary, who in later life took matters of the heart very seriously indeed, meant the gesture sincerely and cared very much about her future husband's fidelity.

Charles, who was anything but continent and was by this time considering marrying someone else, made the chivalrous reply the situation called for. He inquired politely about Mary's health, education and looks, and then, smiling, stuck the emerald ring on his little finger and ordered the ambassadors to say that "he would wear it for the sake of the princess."

VI

My soverayne lorde for my poure sake
Six coursys at the ryng dyd make,
Of which four tymes he dyd it take;
Wherfor my hart I hym beqwest,
And of all other for to love best
My soverayne lorde

It may have been during Mary's betrothal to Charles V that Henry decided to look seriously into the question of whether her future husband would have a strong legal claim to the throne. He called together the chief justices, along with Stephen Gardiner, bishop of Winchester and the Garter King of Arms and asked them to determine, first, "whether men were by law or courtesy entitled to hold baronies, and other honours, in right of their wives?"

This point, at least, was beyond dispute. Under English law not only women's property (saving only their dowries) but their titles and incomes passed to their husbands when they married, along with governance of their persons. This premise of feudal law, supported by the canon law of the church, had been in force since the twelfth century and still governed the customary process of inheritance in England in default of the male line. It had never been tested, however, in the case of the monarchy itself, and for that reason the experts had to decide Henry's next question without benefit of precedent. "If the crown should descend to Mary," he asked them, "should her husband use the style and title of king of England?" Here at least one of the chief justices gave a conclusive opinion. Mary's husband could not call himself king by right, because the crown lay outside the bounds of feudal law. She could grant him the title and style of king, though, if she chose.[1]

That Henry raised these issues in a formal way implied two things.

First, it meant that, assuming Mary did eventually succeed, it would be as a married woman whose husband would be the real ruler. Her role would be solely that of a dynastic link between Henry and his grandson, a carrier of the bloodline without any presumption to govern in her own person. No provision was ever made to prepare Mary to handle affairs of state; her education, though broad in its scope, was intensely personal. She was trained to govern herself in the most vigilant way, but not to govern others.

Second, Henry's inquiry showed that, each year, he was resigning himself more and more to the probability that Mary would be his only legitimate heir. By 1525 it was obvious that Katherine would have no more children. At forty, she was still Henry's loving companion, for whom he sometimes showed tender affection, but she was no more than that; it is very doubtful whether they slept together. Bessie Blount's place as royal mistress was now held by Mary Carey, the eldest daughter of Henry's gentleman Thomas Boleyn. Boleyn had served the king in a variety of capacities, from holding the canopy at Mary's christening to serving as diplomatic envoy to the French court, and he was honored that Henry should choose his daughter—married though she was—as his mistress. Mary Carey was an obliging if colorless girl who drifted from one unsavory situation to another at the Tudor court without leaving a distinctive impression on her contemporaries. She was not a beauty like Bessie; she was neither accomplished nor witty; she cannot even be given credit for carrying on a successful intrigue behind her husband's back, for he knew all about the affair from the beginning and was as willing as Mary to comply in order to gratify the king.

If there were to be more royal children, they would be the children of Henry's mistresses, it appeared, and not his wife. This realization brought into added prominence Henry's only son, Henry Fitzroy. Fitzroy was a handsome and promising boy, blond like his parents, and though Henry did not say so publicly it was evident that he was being prepared to succeed his father if, when the time came, that suited Henry's plans. When he was six years old he was made a knight of the Garter, and in a lengthy ceremony that taxed his memory he was created earl of Nottingham and duke of Richmond and Somerset. These were the titles of a prince, and were traditionally reserved for the heir to the throne. Richmond had been Henry VII's title before he became king, and was afterward conferred on Henry VIII before his accession; Somerset designated the legitimized heirs of John of Gaunt.[2] The earldom of Nottingham had belonged to Richard, duke of York, younger son of Edward IV. More significant was the fact that these titles gave Fitzroy precedence over every other noble at court, even Princess Mary.[3] Here Katherine, who rarely attempted to override Henry's judgment, objected. No bastard, she

said, ought to be exalted above the daughter of the queen. Henry was so
angry at her protest that he sent away from court the three Spanish
gentlewomen Katherine turned to most often for advice, and though she
was hurt and offended, she said no more.[4]

Fitzroy's surroundings, household and education were in every respect those of a prince. Like Mary he had a little throne and canopy of
estate, made in cloth of gold fringed with red silk.[5] He learned to ride a
spirited pony and to handle a bow, and in his sixth summer he killed his
first buck in one of the royal hunting parks. Fitzroy's tutor, Richard
Croke, taught him Greek and Latin and helped him with the brief letters
he wrote to his father in a very large hand. Croke was proud of the boy's
intelligence, and by the time he was eight he was translating Caesar
unaided. His progress was in part the result of Henry's promise that
Fitzroy could have a suit of armor like his father's when he had mastered
part of the *Commentaries,* and from the age of eight or nine he was
clearly distracted from his learning by the allurements of hunting and
knightly sports. Croke wrote exasperated letters to Henry complaining
that Fitzroy's gentlemen were taking him away from his books and
ridiculing his tutor, while wasting the king's money on expensive food
and wine for their riotous companions.[6] Fitzroy's household seems to
have had the same climate of disorder as Henry's before it was reformed,
and eventually he was brought to live closer to court.

Assuming the king lived to enjoy a normal life span, of course, the
issue of the succession would remain purely hypothetical for a long time
to come. But two incidents that occurred when Henry was in his early
thirties reminded him and his frightened courtiers that he was not immor-
tal, and that an unforeseen accident might suddenly make the succession
the most urgent problem in the country.

In the spring of 1524, Henry appointed a joust to be held so that he
could try out a new invention of his—a suit of armor "made of his own
devise and fashion," and unlike any jousting armor ever seen in England.
Just what the innovations were is not recorded, but they were almost certainly confined to the body armor proper, and not the headpiece, because
Henry's attention was anywhere but on his head as he took up his position at the end of the tiltyard when the joust began. His opponent was
Charles Brandon, and Brandon was heard to remark that he could not see
the king as he took his spear and moved his horse into position at the opposite end of the lists. Brandon's vision was obscured because his headpiece, properly in place and with the visor fastened down, blocked out
everything but what was immediately in front of him. Henry, though, by
his own carelessness and that of his attendants, had not lowered his visor,
and the two combatants spurred their horses toward one another at an
earthshaking gallop before anyone noticed the king's mistake.

The crowd soon saw the danger, though, and cried to Henry and

Brandon to stop, but both men rode on, Henry with his face "clean naked" against Brandon's oncoming spear. It struck his headpiece at its weakest point—the cassenetpiece on the forehead, never made strong enough to resist a blow because it was meant to be covered by the lowered visor. As soon as it hit the spear shattered, sending a hundred sharp wood fragments flying into the king's unprotected face. Had the spear or even a small splinter entered his eye he would probably have been killed instantly; as it was he narrowly avoided a concussion. His mangled headpiece was full of splinters when he took it off, but he assured the panic-stricken crowd, his horrified attendants and the white-faced Brandon that he was uninjured and that "none was to blame but himself." To reassure them further he walked about briskly and, calling his armorers to "put all his pieces together," remounted and ran six more courses without incident, "by which all men might perceive that he had no hurt."

A second accident was less spectacular but equally dangerous. Henry was hawking, and in the course of following his hawk he had to cross a ditch full of water. He tried to swing himself across on a pole, but it broke under his weight and he fell head first into the muddy stream. Luckily one of his footmen, Edmund Moody, saw what had happened. He leaped into the water and pried the king's head loose. Without Moody's aid, the chronicler wrote, Henry would surely have drowned.

These two brushes with death, coming within months of one another, may have convinced Henry of how precarious a thing his power was. Certainly they had some influence on the status to which he now elevated his daughter. In the same year that Henry Fitzroy received his titles Mary was officially designated princess of Wales—the first girl to be known by that title.[7] In Henry's early childhood, when his brother Arthur had been prince of Wales, his father Henry VII had sent Arthur to Ludlow in the Welsh Marches, repairing and enlarging Ludlow Castle to be his residence. Now Mary would be sent there, with an "honorable, sad, discreet and expert council," to preside over a viceregal court that would help to bring the fiercely independent Welsh more closely within the power of English law.

Wales in the 1520s was to the English a remote and hostile place, populated by a treacherous and foreign people unlike themselves in every respect. Their language was unintelligible, their customs barbarous; what order their chieftain rulers maintained was indistinguishable from violent chaos. English justices saw life in the Welsh Marches as a panorama of criminality. In the words of one official pronouncement, the Marches were the scene of "manifold robberies, murders, thefts, trespasses, riots, routs, embraceries, maintenances, oppressions, ruptures of the peace, and many other malefacts," and the local population steadfastly refused to accept rule from London as a panacea for these ills.[8]

Wales was not yet a part of England, only a dependent territory, and the Welsh hated the English as unwelcome conquerors interfering in a way of life they made no effort to understand. It was a tense and potentially dangerous situation, and in fact both Mary's household and her Council would remain very close to the English border throughout their stay. The Council would hold court for the Marches; the justices carried with them into Wales a great triple-locked chest containing the books of landholding records and other documents, and their commission instructed them to verify the Marcher lordships against these records and to bind all the lords in person, clerics and laymen alike, to uphold the conditions of tenure originally imposed by Henry VII.

Because Wales was full of sanctuaries and liberties—pockets of territory immune from royal jurisdiction—the justices were to scrutinize each of these claimed enclaves and disallow those whose status could not be proven by royal writ or charter.[9] Sanctuaries were havens for robbers, murderers and others who had been outlawed; without the protection of these refuges, the offenders could be brought before the court and either pardoned or sentenced. "A chest with irons for keeping the prisoners" was among the Council's effects. The commissioners were expected to bring some degree of order and respect for English authority into an untamed region whose mountainous hinterland had resisted that authority for centuries. For defense they had only the household guard, two gunners, and an unspecified amount of ordnance and artillery.[10] There were arms stored at Cardiff far to the south, but they afforded little security to Ludlow. In all, the undertaking was full of uncertainties and hazards. Writing to the Council members just as their work was beginning, a Shropshire archdeacon noted that he was glad to hear of their commission, since few justices had been sent to Wales for many years. "Our lord send you good assistance," he wrote, "for there is jeopardy."[11]

In the late summer of 1525 the princess set out for Ludlow. Dozens of carts had to be borrowed from Bewdley, Thornbury and neighboring establishments to carry the furnishings for her greatly enlarged entourage. Mary's own hangings, furniture, featherbeds and wardrobe, and the wardrobes and belongings of her gentlewomen and Council members were only a small part of the load. Some sixteen hundred yards of damask and less costly cloth, all in the princess' colors of blue and green, had been purchased for liveries. Dozens of yards of Brussels cloth for tablecloths, towels and napkins were piled into chests and loaded onto carts, plus black velvet for the gentlewomen's gowns and other cloth for vestments for the chaplains. The chapel furnishings—standing candelabras, heavy mass books with their golden covers and carved stands, kneeling cushions and prayer stools—took up a good deal of space, for there would be three altars in the chapel itself and a fourth in Mary's bedroom.

Even before Mary and her retinue started on their journey repairs

were begun at Ludlow. Richard Sydnour, surveyor general to the new
court, had hired a crew of Welsh workmen to restore the chamber to be
used by the countess of Salisbury and renovate the wardrobe and great
chamber, and a locksmith to make a key for the wicket of the great gate.
A team of woodsmen were set to work felling trees and sawing timbers
in a forest near the castle, and carpenters restored the paneled walls and
mended the broken stairs and loose floor boards.

Mary's journey north was a leisurely one. She stopped at Coventry
and made a formal entry into the city, where a pageant was mounted in
her honor. When she left she was presented with a kerchief and a gift of
a hundred marks.[12] On the way to Ludlow a temporary household was
set up at Thornbury, the exquisite manor house that had been the chief
residence of the duke of Buckingham until his execution four years
earlier, when it was forfeited to the crown. With its gothic windows and
turreted walls Thornbury was well suited to house a royal establishment
indefinitely, but before long the carts were repacked for the final transfer
to Ludlow.

Ludlow Castle, "a fair manor place, standing in a goodly park," was
just west of the town of Bewdley, "on the very knob of the hill." It was
to be Mary's home for the next year and a half. Here, from the time she
was nine until just after her eleventh birthday, the princess was the center of her own imposing court. For the first time she was more than an in-
cidental adornment of her father's establishment. Here she was the essential representative of Tudor monarchy, and though she was in fact no
more than a figurehead she must have felt very important indeed. Walking through the great galleries or presiding over banquets at Ludlow it
was easy for Mary to dismiss the fact that Henry Fitzroy now held the
princely titles of duke of Richmond and Somerset, and that there were
those who questioned the right of a female to the throne. Mary was now
old enough to understand that her dynastic position was unusual, and that
though her father treasured her he wished she had been born a boy. But
she understood too that in making her princess of Wales he was breaking
convention and recognizing her as his heir. That he also appeared to be
recognizing Fitzroy troubled her less now that she sat in the presence
chamber at Ludlow, surrounded by guardsmen and ushers wearing her
livery, and now that she possessed some small degree of authority to issue
writs in the king's name.

Mary's court in Wales was in fact nothing less than a miniaturized
version of the royal court in England. The major household officers (the
steward, Lord Ferrers, the chamberlain, Lord Dudley, who was later to
forget his loyalty to Mary and attempt to keep her from the throne, the
vice-chamberlain Philip Calthrop, whose wife was one of Mary's gentlewomen, the treasurer, Ralph Egerton, the controller, Giles Grevile,

whose relative Thomas Grevile was marshal of the hall, and the almoner, Peter Burnell), all of whom were members of the Council, directed a full complement of lesser officers and a swarm of servants. Three gentleman ushers, six gentleman waiters, two sewers of the chamber and one of the hall, a herald, a pursuivant and two sergeants-at-arms, a dozen clerks and an array of stable, cellar and kitchen personnel complemented one another in following a carefully designed list of household regulations.

The countess of Salisbury, Lady Governess, was in charge of some fourteen gentlewomen, including Katherine Montague, Elizabeth and Constance Pole, nieces of the Lady Governess by blood or marriage, and Katharine Grey. All the gentlewomen were married, and were ordered to dress in sedate black gowns; there were no waiting maids to distract the gentlemen and undermine the princess' modesty. Also attached to the household were Dr. Butts, Henry's physician loaned to Mary while she was in Wales, and his assistant and apothecary, the princess' schoolmaster Richard Featherstone, a water carrier, a grounds keeper, a minstrel named Claudyon and Thomas, "keeper of the princess' nag." They totaled some three hundred and four in all, and it seems clear that the chief impact of the royal establishment on the Marches was not in suppressing disorder but in providing employment and a ready market to the local population. Lists of the chamber, stable and kitchen servants show many Welsh names, and for every man or woman who actually worked in the household there were others who profited from selling their cattle, lambs and eggs to its purveyors.

The business of the court was to dispense justice, but it also had a ceremonial function. The throne in the presence chamber, attended at all times by at least twenty ushers, waiters and grooms, bore the charisma of majesty, and suitors to court, local officials and aristocratic visitors were brought in to see and do honor to Mary as a matter of course.[18] Keeping court at Ludlow brought about a minor transformation in the way the nine-year-old princess saw herself. As never before, her life became geared to her office. She was often called away from her studies with Featherstone or from an afternoon of riding to sit in state and receive reverential attention from local landowners who had never before entered the presence of majesty. She now grew accustomed to being a public figure—to being gracious to strangers, to representing her father with dignity and to acting the part of the queen she might some day become. Mary came to Wales a sheltered girl of nine; she left it a seasoned royal personality of eleven. Though she had learned nothing of the art of governing she had learned to recognize the difference between her private and public lives, her familiar self and that self she presented when on view in the presence chamber. She saw herself as special, set apart from all others by the particular calling of her lineage. She would never again be only an admired child; from now on she would expect to be treated as the revered heir to the throne of England.

The surviving records of Mary's life at Ludlow offer only fleeting glimpses of this transformation. We see her sending thanks to Wolsey for his discharging of her affairs—unspecified—while she is in Wales, through the president of her Council, the bishop of Exeter.[14] With the Lady Governess, she spoke with the Council at least once a month, and gave account of the progress of her education. She was certainly caught up in the toils of courtier rivalries. Wales had its share of castles to hold, forests to govern, and parks to be administered. The offices of castellan, forester and parker were in the king's gift, and whoever had influence with the king when the offices fell vacant stood to enrich himself if he could acquire them. Mary was constantly being asked to use her influence on some courtier's behalf, and came face to face with the intricacies and dissimulations of the ambitious men surrounding her.

In at least one area Mary was able to issue writs on her own. She had, by Henry's command, "authority to kill or give deer at her pleasure in any forest or park" within the territory under the jurisdiction of her Council. In at least one instance, though, this authority was questioned. Mary issued a warrant to her secretary, John Russell, to kill a buck in Shotwick Park. The parker for Shotwick was Henry's gentleman William Brereton, a groom of the privy chamber, whose kinsman Randolph Brereton looked after his affairs from Chester. It was Randolph who received the warrant, and hesitated before allowing Russell his buck, asking William whether or not he should honor the princess' authorization. Personally he thought Russell ought to have it, because of his status as secretrary, and added that if Mary's warrants were not served, "displeasure will ensue." Apparently Russell enjoyed his day of sport in Shotwick Park.[15]

As the months went by the Council for the Marches fell into difficulty in carrying out its legal mandate. The original procedure to be followed—with cases coming before the Council only on appeal, after being tried by local "stewards and officers"—was being undercut by contrary orders from the royal justices in England. Lord Ferrers wrote to the bishop of Exeter that subpoenas were being issued directly to Caermarthen and Cardigan for suitors to appear at Westminster, as part of an unprecedented effort to extend the power of the royal courts into the farthest of the Welsh territories. The legal powers of the Council were being ignored.

Worse than that, the Welsh shires were responding to this threat of tighter control from Westminster by refusing to pay their taxes. "The shires say plainly," Ferrers wrote, "that they will not pay one groat at this present Candlemas next coming, nor never after, . . . but they had rather run into the woods." Clearly English rule in Wales was at a crisis point. Ferrers declared the situation to be "the most serious thing that has occurred since I first knew Wales," and the danger of large-scale rebellion eventually cut short the mandate of the Council and put an end to Mary's first taste of public authority.[16] Crime continued to flourish, even in the Council's back yard. Only a few miles from Ludlow in the town of Bewdley a murderer had taken sanctuary and the townspeople refused to hand him over for trial. The man was a notorious felon who had killed his wife's father and mother, but rather than acknowledge the jurisdiction of the justice for North Wales the people of Bewdley claimed that their town was able to grant sanctuary to all offenders, and a dispute arose over the authentication of this privilege.[17]

All these considerations led to the breaking up of the Ludlow court early in 1527. The traveling carts were borrowed again, loaded, and sent southeastward toward London. Probably Mary did not greatly regret leaving behind the beautiful but inhospitable hills, the anxious courtiers and fuming councilors, the complaining gentlewomen homesick for the gaiety of Henry's court. Besides, she had the best possible reason for leaving Wales: negotiations for a new betrothal had just been concluded.

Henry's cordiality toward Charles V had cooled, and Mary's hand was now to be part of a complicated alliance with France which when finalized would see her promised either to Francis I, who was now a widower, or to one of his sons. The alliance would be celebrated with weeks of revelry at Greenwich, and Mary was now old enough to participate in the masques and other entertainments. There would be new gowns and slippers and new jewels, masquing costumes to be fitted and dances to learn. Mary had learned to be a figure of royalty in a castle on a hill; now she would try her hand at becoming a court lady.

VII

Ravished I was, that well was me,
O Lord! to me so fain,
To see that sight that I did see
I long full sore again.

I saw a king and a princess
Dancing before my face,
Most like a god and a goddess,
I pray Christ save their grace!

When Mary returned to her father's court early in 1527 she found it dominated as never before by the masterful, ebullient king. Henry was now thirty-six, but he seemed ten years younger. After seeing him a foreign visitor wrote home that "never in his days did he see any man handsomer, more elegant, and better proportioned than this king, who is pink and white, fair, tall, agile, well formed and graceful in all his movements and gestures." He had ruled England for nearly twenty years, yet he preserved a boyish freshness of manner and appearance that made him seem eternally youthful. Barring accidents, his would be an unusually long reign, and the two chief advantages of a long reign—stability and momentum—were already beginning to be apparent in England.

More and more the diffused powers of government were gathering around the person of the king and his omnipotent chief minister Wolsey, and Henry's personal magnificence kept pace with the growth of royal authority. Supplicants, diplomats and other dignitaries vied with one another in finding phrases to describe his grandeur, calling him "most famous lantern of grace" and comparing him to the sun and stars.[1] One royal servant, Clement Urmeston, employed to design the torchlit chandeliers and "dancing lights" for Henry's banquets, became convinced that the king possessed occult powers by virtue of his exalted office and believed that these powers were concentrated in his seal. The visual impact of the seal, properly directed, could influence the course of public affairs, Urmeston believed, but no one at court took his speculations seriously.[2] Soon after Mary's return Henry himself acknowledged his increased celebrity by assuming the style of "majesty" instead of the traditional referent "your grace."[3]

Every European court knew of his uncommon abilities; cordial wishes and gifts arrived from many of these courts in a steady stream. The marquis of Mantua sent splendid horses for Henry's stables; Francis I sent a shipload of wild swine to be bred for his table. The chancellor of Poland, Christopher Schidlowijecz, sent him a rare great gerfalcon and four falcon chicks from Danzig, and from another ruler came a tame leopard.[4] Christian II, king of Denmark, sent his councilor George Menckevitz, an adventurer and man of arms who hoped to enter Henry's service when he went to war again.[5]

In fact Henry could no longer afford to go to war, and his last efforts to raise money by asking his nobles and clergy for an exorbitant "Amicable Grant" had led to rioting and resentment. He continued to stage the elaborate mock wars performed on his tilting ground, however, and he was still the chief performer, fighting both on foot and on horseback. He continued to order armor made according to designs of his own, and one afternoon he and his company tilted in new armor, "of a strange fashion that has not been seen," against the men of the marquis of Exeter until nearly three hundred spears had been broken.[6]

No matter what he did, Henry was the star attraction of the court. Whether he was exercising or riding or just walking in his gardens, invariably the palace would be deserted and a crowd of courtiers and sightseers would collect to dog his feet and applaud his every move.[7] During the day he shone at sports and outdoor pastimes; at night it was dancing. Henry was not only a graceful but a virtually indefatigable dancer, and he loved to lead his courtiers in the intricate steps of the galliard late into the night. Mary was now old enough to join in the dancing, and now and then, to the delight of the entire court, Henry would take Mary as his partner. Her steps were as nimble, if not as long, as her father's, and with their similarity of coloring and pleasing features they made a handsome pair. Vives' treatises had warned Mary against the madness of dancing, which both the sober ancients and the church Fathers had condemned. "What meaneth that shaking unto midnight, and never weary?" he asked disapprovingly.[8] But the princess evidently thought little of the warning, and Katherine, now very much a background figure at most entertainments, forgot to worry about her own worsening hold on the king's affections and was happy when she saw Henry and Mary together.

There would be dancing enough when the French ambassadors arrived for the final stage of the marriage negotiations. Mary's betrothal to Charles V had been broken off shortly before she left for Wales, and for nearly two years Wolsey had been attempting to arrange a French match once again. Francis I needed a wife, but had promised to marry Charles V's favorite sister Eleanor, the thirty-year-old widow of the king of Portugal. Francis had expressed a preference for Mary, acknowledging her beauty and virtue and admitting to Wolsey's representative that "he had as great a mind to her as ever he had to any woman."[9] Compared to Eleanor, Mary "weighed down the balance by a great number of ounces," but she was still a child; though he was pleased with the portrait of the princess Henry sent him (together with a portrait of Henry himself), Francis was in no hurry to commit himself irrevocably to either Mary or Eleanor.[10] He wrote Mary a gracious letter, calling her "high and powerful princess" and assuring her of his loyalty as her "good brother, cousin and ally," but in truth he was far from being an enthusiastic suitor.[11] He had been thoroughly humiliated by the emperor, and for the time being his fate was not his own. He was, he said, willing to marry anything, even Charles V's mule, if it meant regaining his dignity.

Francis' dismay was the result of another shuffling of interests and alliances among the European powers that occurred while Mary was in Wales. The realignment was triggered by events in Italy, where an invading French army was routed at Pavia in 1525 by the forces of Charles V and Francis himself was taken prisoner. Charles lost no time in exploiting Francis' awkward position. The French king was imprisoned in Madrid and forced to buy his freedom; he agreed to give Charles the duchy of Burgundy and sovereignty over the French territories of Flanders and Artois. Charles' other demand was harsh indeed. Francis' two sons, the dauphin and the duke of Orléans, became the emperor's hostages, guaranteeing their father's good faith.

Once he was back in France, Francis immediately renounced his oath to Charles, claiming that because it was taken under duress it was not binding. But though the pope santioned the breach of faith he could not force Charles to return the two hostages, and Francis was badly in need of help from any quarter. He turned to England, where the betrothal of Mary and Charles had just been officially ended. The imperial emissaries had been instructed to tell Henry that "he could have with much thank the lady princess [back] in his hand, which is a pearl worth the keeping."[12] Immediately Henry and Wolsey approached the French king, and though it seemed more and more certain that Francis himself would be forced to marry Eleanora in order to placate the emperor and free his sons, he was open to the betrothal of the duke of Orléans and the princess.

It was in this diplomatic atmosphere of coercion and fear that four French envoys arrived at Dover six days after Mary's eleventh birthday. They were the bishop of Tarbes, president of the *parlement* of Toulouse, the vicomte of Turenne, and La Viste, president of the *parlement* of Paris. Two months of hard bargaining followed. The English had the advantage: Francis reportedly feared more for his sons' safety than for his own, and badly needed English men and money to make war on Charles. He faced a tortuous dilemma. If he married Eleanor, he would be bound to the emperor by ties of kinship; their children would have a claim to both France and Hapsburg lands. As yet, Charles had no successor, and his pregnant wife was sickly. If on the other hand Francis did not marry Eleanor, he had reason to fear for the lives of his hostage sons. As Wolsey continually reminded the French negotiators, "there is no malice like the malice of a woman," and the jilted widow might take a cruel revenge. Francis sent his envoys several sets of instructions. In one set he told them to oppose all the anticipated English demands and objections and to insist that Mary be delivered to him in France as quickly as possible. In secret dispatches, however, he authorized them to agree to anything that would hasten the progress of the talks and lead to a quick agreement.

Wolsey and Henry worked as a smooth team. Wolsey, who held talks with the ambassadors nearly every day, alternated between openness and warmth and icy displeasure. He claimed to favor France, and made it clear that he had worked to restrain Henry from invading the country when Francis had been a helpless captive. Yet at the slightest opposition from the French negotiators he became hostile and adamant. At this point they would apply for an audience with Henry, who would proceed to disconcert them by his affability. Taking Turenne by the shoulders, the king would dismiss the difficulties with a wave of his hand and expand on his affection for Francis. If only they were ordinary gentlemen and not kings, he mused, he would be constantly in Francis' company. On other occasions Henry would turn cold, sending the French scurrying back to Wolsey's palace at Hampton Court in hopes of finding a compromise with the cardinal.

A primary issue was the English insistence on an annual pension of 50,000 French crowns. At first the French refused this outright, but later made a counteroffer of 15,000 crowns. Wolsey took no more account of this counteroffer "than if they had given him a pair of gloves," and Henry dismissed it with the remark that he had lost more than that in a single night of cards. When a stalemate arose Wolsey for the first time suggested that instead of taking Mary for himself Francis might marry her to his second son, adding that as a further inducement the duke of Richmond could be betrothed to Francis' daughter. As it became apparent that Mary would not be allowed to go to France for several years, this alternative seemed more and more desirable, and eventually, when the interlocking treaties of perpetual peace, the military alliance and the marriage contract had all been drafted and redrafted several times, Henry signed them on May 5.

There had never been any real doubt in the king's mind that the negotiators would eventually agree. Six weeks before the French arrived he had ordered work begun on a banqueting hall and disguising theater on one side of the tiltyard at Greenwich. These would be the scene of a magnificent feast and entertainments to celebrate the signing of the treaties. Two teams of artisans and laborers were employed to complete the structures before the diplomats completed their negotiations. The basic carpentry went quickly, but the ornamentation of the interiors was another matter. Four Italian painters and gilders, with their assistants, were brought in to work around the clock decorating the moldings of the high windows in the banqueting hall with carved crests and "savage work." The antique candlesticks, "polished like amber," that fitted into the moldings had to be painted and gilded, as did the five hundred "little antique leaves" that adorned the beams which held the chandeliers.

A huge triumphal arch connected the banqueting hall and the disguising house, ornamented with gargoyles, serpents, and armorial designs. Henry's motto "Dieu et Mon Droit" was carved into the arch, along with other mottoes and "antiques and devices." Six busts of Roman emperors were ranged along its sides, and in all the gilt, coloring materials, and wages to the color grinders and painters who worked on this monument came to well over three hundred pounds. On the back of the arch was a painting of the siege of Thérouanne—a reminder of Henry's victory over the French fourteen years earlier—executed by Hans Holbein. Holbein also worked on the revels house, a theater with tiers of seats around the sides for spectators. Carpets of silk embroidered with gold lilies covered the floor of the theater, and the ceiling, designed by Henry's astronomer Nicholas Kratzer, showed a map of the earth, the planets and the signs of the zodiac. Pillars painted azure blue with gold stars and fleurs-de-lis divided the rows of seats, and each pillar held a great silver basin of branching wax candles that lit up the room. The disguising house had a high ornamented arch like that in the banqueting hall, and two more paintings by Holbein were hung along its walls. Even when the talks between Wolsey and the French temporarily broke down, work on the magnificent hall and theater progressed, so that by the time Wolsey's clerks were copying out the treaties for the final time the foreign artisans were putting the finishing touches on their gilded handiwork.

For Mary the months of deliberations were a time of great excitement crowded with hours of preparation. For the first time she was to be a principal performer in the revels, and dances designed to show off her skill and grace were choreographed by Henry's dancing master and taught, step after step, to the princess and those who would dance with her. She was to be dressed in costumes of cloth of gold and red tinsel, and in jewels more brilliant than any she had ever worn; there were endless fittings of these garments, and of the headgear, hose and slippers to be worn with them. As the bride to be of a prince and the object of a hard-won diplomatic struggle, Henry wanted his daughter to be the center of attention during the celebrations. There must be no doubt that in agreeing to Mary's betrothal he was giving Francis his most valued possession, his "pearl of the world." She must be made to seem the most charming and accomplished heiress of her day.

Of her accomplishments there was certainly no doubt. Her tutor John Featherstone had taken good advantage of her intelligence and aptitude for languages, and had greatly improved her fluency in Latin, French, Italian and Spanish. At barely nine years old she was able to speak Latin "with as much assurance and facility as if she were twelve years old," and years later a humanist at her court recalled in a dedication to Mary that at eleven "your grace not only could perfectly read, write and construe Latin, but furthermore translate any hard thing of the Latin in to our English tongue."[13] The French envoys found her learning impressive: according to Turenne, she was "very handsome and admirable by reason of her great and uncommon mental endowments." Sometime during their stay in England Mary acted in a comedy of Terence staged, in Latin, at Wolsey's gorgeous palace at Hampton Court.

But no display of erudition, however rare, could compare to the long-awaited banquet and masquing held on the day following the signing of the treaties. The banqueting hall was the scene of a gorgeous array of massive gold plate and serving dishes of silver gilt. Course after course of meat and fish was carried through the gilded arch, while from a balcony above it came the music of viols and sackbuts. Mary did not sit with Henry and Katherine, but at a long table of her own, with the French envoys and "great ladies" of the court. The banquet lasted several hours, and at its conclusion the entire company was assembled in order of rank and ushered into the disguising house, where they quietly took their places in the tiers of seats. The Venetian secretary Spinelli, who was there, noted in his dispatch to the Signory that all this was done "without the least noise or confusion, and precisely as pre-arranged." The "order, regularity and silence" of public entertainments in England was a thing which amazed him, and he told in detail how the right-hand tiers of seats were reserved for the men, the ambassadors in front, the princes behind them, and the remaining guests at the back. On the left were the women, also in order of rank, "whose beauty," Spinelli wrote, "enhanced by the brilliancy of the lights, caused me to think I was contemplating the choir of angels."[14]

The performance began without delay. The children of the king's chapel sang and recited a dialogue among Mercury, Cupid, and Plutus in which Henry was asked to judge which was of greater value, love or riches. This introduced a mock combat between six men at arms in white armor, fighting at a barrier so furiously that they broke their naked swords. The combat being ended, an old man in a silver beard pronounced the conflict settled; princes, he said, had need of both love and riches—the former to gain the obedience and service of their subjects, and the latter to give as rewards to lovers and friends.

A painted curtain was now dropped at the other end of the theater and a new group of performers appeared. Eight gentlemen in gold doublets and tall plumed helmets lit with their torches a scene meant to represent a mountain, walled with gilt towers and "set full of crystal corals and rich rocks of ruby." On a rock were seated eight damsels dressed in cloth of gold, their hair gathered into nets garlanded with jewels, and the long hanging sleeves of their surcoats trailing in deep folds to their feet. Mary was among these maidens, and as she rose to her feet to the sound of trumpets "her beauty in this array produced such an effect on everybody that all the other marvellous sights previously witnessed were forgotten, and they gave themselves up solely to contemplation of so fair an angel." She shone with jewels, and as she and the others began their dance, Spinelli reported, she "dazzled the sight in such wise as to make one believe that she was decked with all the gems of the eighth sphere." The eight damsels performed an unusually complex series of steps, executing a dance unique in its variety and intricacy; then the gentlemen danced by themselves, and finally the eight couples danced a lively *coranto*. After this came another group of masqued dancers, dressed in Icelandic costumes, who "danced lustily about the place," and at the end of their performance Henry and Turenne and eight other noblemen appeared, all masked and wearing black satin gowns and hoods. For the last several days, ever since he injured his foot playing tennis, Henry had been wearing a black velvet slipper; to prevent him from being recognized, all the maskers now wore slippers like the king's. The injury, it seems, did not impair Henry's dancing, for he and the others chose partners from the audience to perform a lavish finale.

The entertainment was at an end, but Henry had one last trick to play. Mary and the other young girls came up to him as the dancing ended, and, drawing her over to where the French ambassadors were seated, he loosened the net and jeweled bands from her hair, letting her heavy gold curls fall over her shoulders, "forming a most agreeable sight." This was the image the French took back with them, of a delicate girl nearly out of childhood, dressed in golden robes, her smiling face encircled by masses of golden hair. Turenne had concluded earlier that because the princess was "thin, spare and small" she could not be married for another three years at least. Now he was convinced she would be worth waiting for.

As Henry and his court were dancing and feasting in celebration of the Anglo-French treaties an atrocity of the greatest magnitude was unfolding at the other end of Europe. The German army of Charles V, joined by Spanish troops under the duke of Bourbon, was fighting in central Italy against the combined forces of the Venetians, the French and the pope. Finding Florence and Siena too well defended to attack, the imperial forces turned southward toward Rome, their food supplies exhausted. The soldiers were mutinous; they had not been paid, there were no spoils to be had, and they were now forced to steal from the Umbrian peasants to survive. Only their loyalty to Bourbon prevented mass desertion, and it was to Bourbon that the officers now turned, urging him to march the army to Rome, besiege the city and force the pope to ransom himself for enough money to pay the troops. The imperial forces camped outside Rome on the fifth of May, and their commander sent a message to the Medici pope Clement VII explaining that he could forestall bloodshed by paying what the besiegers demanded. Bourbon's message may not have reached Clement, because there was no reply. That evening, as the condition of the hungry men became more and more desperate, they were given scaling ladders. The following morning thousands of them went over the walls, the Spaniards shouting "*Sangre, sangre, carne, carne*"—"Blood, blood, flesh, flesh"—and, in the name of Bourbon, they began to kill every Roman they could find.

The sack of Rome might have been less devastating had the duke lived to control his men, but he was killed in the first assault, and the prince of Orange, who tried to take over leadership of the armies, lacked the authority to restrain the two-week orgy of murder and desecration that followed. On the day of the assault a dark fog lay over the Eternal City, making it hard for the attackers and the few defenders to see one another's faces. What defense there was collapsed in the first two hours, leaving the way open for the imperial troops to enter the Borgo San Sepolcro by the thousands. By noon the mass slaughter had begun. At first the Germans and Spaniards spared only those they could hope to hold for ransom—the wealthiest churchmen and merchants. The terrified Romans, who had been assured until the last moment that the city would be saved by a relieving army, fled to the churches and convents or tried to take refuge in the fortified castles. The pope, who had done nothing to secure either himself or his city, now retired with thirteen of his cardinals to the Castel Sant'Angelo across the Tiber, weeping and offering to capitulate on whatever terms the imperialists asked. But the floodtide of destruction, once loosed, could not be halted. Rome, the most venerated city in Christendom, great storehouse of pagan and Christian tradition and bastion of the medieval church, was thoroughly and massively despoiled.

The readiest booty was to be found in the churches. Companies of soldiers swarmed into Rome's hundreds of holy places, stripping the altars of their ornaments and throwing to the ground relics of the saints and the bread of the mass. Catholic Spaniards and Lutheran Germans alike dressed themselves in the rich vestments of the murdered clergy and officiated at the ruined altars, bawling out tavern songs and befouling consecrated sanctuaries with excrement. The church of St. Peter and the papal palace were turned into stables, and processions of drunken soldiers and whores wound through their courtyards in imitation of holy processions. At San Silvestro the head of St. John the Baptist was ripped out of its silver reliquary and hurled to the pavement, where an old nun found it later and carried it to safety.

It was as if all the anticlerical hatred of centuries was released in a single furious burst. Friars were dragged from their convents and beheaded; nuns were beaten and raped. Abbots and cardinals were hung up by their arms or suspended head downward in wells and tortured until they revealed where their wealth was hidden. Others were branded like animals or horribly mutilated, or their mouths were forced open and filled with molten lead. The cardinal of Ara Coeli was seized and carried through the streets on a funeral bier while his captors sang the office for the dead. Fearing for his life, he was made to serve his best wine to his tormentors in the golden chalices reserved for the mass. Clergy and lay men and women alike huddled in Rome's medieval castles hoping to escape the slaughter. Five hundred nuns were found in one large room of the palace of Pompey Colonna when it was plundered, and hundreds of women were carried off whenever a great house fell to the invaders. Even the palace of the Portuguese ambassador, said to be the best fortified stronghold in the city, could not hold out. All the merchants, nobles and moneylenders who had taken refuge there were brought out and imprisoned, and their goods, which totaled some half a million ducats in value, were divided among the imperial troops.

As the days passed the soldiers, leaderless and crazed by their crimes, alternated between dazed stupor and unreasoning frenzy. They picked up fortunes in the burning remains of palaces only to lose them in a single throw of the dice. Loyalties to countrymen or coreligionists meant nothing; the houses of Spaniards and Germans in Rome were looted as mercilessly as those of the Italians. And after they had plundered the wealthy, the imperial soldiers plundered the poor, stripping even the hovels of the street sweepers and water carriers. Hearing that the pope had finally paid the wages of the Germans, the enraged Spaniards attacked their allies and demanded their share. The longer the sack continued the more the city's food supply dwindled, and as the surviving Romans and their invaders sank deeper into disorder the final nemesis of plague and panic set in. In their thoroughness the soldiers had looted the shops of the apothecaries, and there were now no medicines left to fight disease. Famine and pestilence overtook the entire population, and what began as a human tragedy was ended by broader forces of destruction no human agency could control.

"Everyone considers it has taken place by the just judgment of God," one imperial official in Rome wrote to the emperor, "because the court of Rome was so ill-ruled."[15] This view of the meaning of the Roman nightmare was not widely shared. As news of events in Rome traveled northward it was received with profound shock and horror. The sack of the papal city was seen as more than the barbarous act of a brutalized army. It was an assault on faith itself. With the desecration of the Eternal City Christian spirituality lost its anchor. The immense power and authority of Rome had been breached as surely as its walls. Christendom had been deeply wounded, not by any external enemy but from within, and would not be the same again.

PART TWO

The King's Troubled Daughter

VIII

 And wylt thow leve me thus?
That hathe louyd the so long,
In welthe and woo among?
And ys thy hart so strong
As for to leve me thus?
Say nay, say nay!

News of the sack of Rome reached the court of Henry VIII on June 1. Letters sent to the king and Wolsey told in bloody detail how the soldiers of Charles V had defiled the venerable city and threatened the pope, who was still a captive of the imperial forces. Wolsey, who saw in Clement VII's misfortune an opportunity to take over leadership of the church himself, made plans to convene the cardinals at Avignon in France and to preside over a papal court in exile. Henry cursed his nephew Charles as an enemy of the faith, and lamented that "our most holy lord, the true and only vicar of Christ on earth," had been taken from his flock. Without him the church would surely collapse, the king insisted, and he sped Wolsey on his way.

Henry's concern about the condition of the papacy was sincere, but his motives were selfish and, for the time being, secret. Unknown to anyone save Wolsey and a few trusted ecclesiastics, he had made the most fateful decision of his reign. He had decided to divorce his wife.

Barely two weeks after the celebration of Mary's betrothal a church court had been called together by Wolsey to consider the validity of the royal marriage; the next step was to persuade the pope to declare it annulled. Henry was preparing to approach Clement about this when he learned of the fate of Rome. His anger at Charles V was both public and personal. The emperor had at once assaulted Christianity and thwarted Henry's urgent divorce project, and there was no telling when either of these two wrongs would be righted.

Just when and why Henry made up his mind to put Katherine aside are very unclear, but the legal issues involved were, in Henry's mind at least, quite simple. Katherine had been the widow of Henry's brother Arthur. In marrying her he had sinned twice over: once by committing incest and again by disobeying the injunction in the book of Leviticus against "uncovering the nakedness of thy brother's wife." Once he realized the enormity of his situation, Henry claimed, the burden on his conscience became intolerable. He had to free himself from the marriage as swiftly as possible—not only to ease his spiritual pain but for the sake of England's future. For if the marriage to Katherine was invalid, then Mary was a bastard, and unfit to rule. Henry's new-found scruples deprived him not only of his wife but of his sole legitimate heir, and he owed it to his subjects to remarry and beget a son to secure the succession.

In the mountains of legal opinions which soon arose to contradict the king's position several points stood out clearly. First, why had it taken eighteen years for the issues of consanguinity and the biblical prohibition to trouble Henry? Neither issue was obscure, particularly to a man of the king's vaunted theological knowledge. How could they have escaped his attention all those years? Second, whatever obstacles to the marriage of Henry and Katherine might have existed in 1509 had been removed by the granting of a papal dispensation. The pope's plenary authority gave him the power to legitimize any union, no matter how unconventional, and only the Lutheran heretics disputed the powers of the pope. Third, Henry's critics pointed out, if some passages in the Bible outlawed the marriage of a man with his brother's widow others positively encouraged it, and in any case these were matters best left to the discretion of the experts who advised the pope in Rome.

In the beginning Henry may have deluded himself in thinking that the divorce would be a simple matter, swiftly accomplished, to be arranged between himself, Wolsey and the pope. After all, European rulers had been ridding themselves of unwanted spouses for centuries by alleging the stain of consanguinity. The procedure was a time-honored one, and Henry had the best possible excuse—the lack of a male heir—to initiate it. The pope had allowed Henry IV of Castile, married to a childless queen, to divorce her and marry another woman, although he did have to agree to take back his first wife if he had no children by the second. Only a month before Henry began his formal inquiry into the validity of his own marriage he received word that his sister Margaret, whom he had severely criticized as a shameless adulteress, had been granted papal permission to marry the already-married man she had been living with for years.

Even more influential was the experience of Charles Brandon, the broad-shouldered, bluff courtier who was the king's lifelong intimate. Before he married Henry's sister Mary, Brandon had been involved in a bizarre matrimonial situation. He had given a binding pledge of marriage—betrothal "by present consent"—to a woman named Ann Brown, but obtained a papal dispensation to marry one Margaret Mortimer before he had honored his pledge to Ann. Tiring of Margaret, he applied for a second bull of dispensation, claiming that he and his wife were related within the prohibited degrees and that his conscience would not permit him to continue the marriage. That he had been married a long time, he said, only made his torment greater; like Henry, he begged for an immediate divorce. His request was granted, whereupon he married his original fiancée Ann Brown.

Many years later, at the time rumors of Henry's impending divorce were circulating, Brandon was completing a new legal action to ensure that the children of his subsequent marriage to his third wife Mary Tudor were not deprived of their inheritance. At this time Margaret Mortimer was still living, and Brandon seems to have been afraid that she might interfere in the rights of his heirs. Wolsey was largely responsible for resolving Brandon's tangled commitments to the pope's satisfaction at this time, and there is reason to believe he extricated the duke from further embarrassments in his domestic affairs that have never fully come to light. Henry conceived his plan to divorce Katherine, then, just at the time his best friend was clearing himself of all obligations to *his* first wife with the capable aid of his chief adviser. Given the king's dissatisfaction with his marriage and his recently discovered theological objections to it, he could not have had a more attractive inducement to undertake a divorce suit himself.

There were, as always, diplomatic inducements as well. When Charles V's victory at Pavia in 1525 made him master of the continent, Henry believed the moment had come for English and imperial armies to carry out his lifelong dream, his "Great Enterprise" against France. The emperor, whose wars had exhausted his treasury, was not caught up in Henry's romantic ambitions, and his lack of enthusiasm for the conquest of France, combined with his abrupt decision to marry the Portuguese princess Isabella instead of Mary, led to a breach between the two sovereigns. Katherine was a victim of that breach. Her position at Henry's court had been changing for some time, but with the dissolving of the imperial alliance it grew more awkward than ever. She had long since lost her usefulness to him, and was now little more than a relic of the early years of his reign. Henry had improved with age, and was still robust and youthful; Katherine had become stout and massive, with the fleshy jowls and sagging cheeks of an ill-favored Spanish matron. At twenty, her look of demure innocence had made her plainness appealing; at forty, the deep sadness and resignation in her bloated face made her grotesque. Sympa-

thetic courtiers and visitors who searched the queen's features saw there
an unmistakable nobility of expression; casual observers said she was ugly,
and made jokes about the young king and his old wife.

For years Katherine had been Henry's wife in name only, and with
the opening of the divorce procedures Henry's representatives became
guardedly candid about her sexual inadequacies. It is impossible to be precise about these complaints. As a young woman Katherine had been troubled by some ailment whose symptoms, including irregular menstrual periods, misled her into believing that she was pregnant when she was not.
Repeated real pregnancies may well have brought new disorders, or made
the old one worse; by the time she reached her early forties Wolsey was
hinting that there were "secret reasons" why Katherine was no longer a
fit wife. "There are certain diseases in the queen defying all remedy," he
wrote, "for which and other causes the king will never live with her."[1]
Whatever disappointment this may have caused her was sharpened by
Henry's habitual flirtations and brief seductions, and by his long-term liaison with Mary Carey. Katherine was forced to look past these indignities without complaint, keeping her inward torment from her daughter
and confiding in her few remaining Spanish gentlewomen and priests.
Her only close relative was her nephew Charles V, and as she grew older
and more unhappy she maintained the affectionate bond that had grown
up between them on his successive visits to England.

It was precisely this bond that now made her an irritant. For if
Katherine was indecorous and superfluous, she was also, in Wolsey's eyes
at least, potentially traitorous as well. She had never said or done anything to arouse suspicion, but her sympathies were all on the imperial
side, and as Wolsey maneuvered toward a reopening of the alliance with
France he became more and more fearful about the queen's loyalties. He
kept himself informed about whom she saw and wrote to, and saw to it
that she did not communicate with the emperor's ambassador in England.
He paid spies to live in her household and report all that they saw and
heard, and even bribed her trusted servants. One serving woman, torn between Wolsey's pressure and her love for Katherine, left the court entirely rather than betray her mistress.[2]

Beyond all the talk of biblical law, diplomatic necessity and the need
for a male heir lay a more disruptive motive for the divorce: Henry's celebrated passion for Anne Boleyn. Cynics then and since have claimed that
if he had never met Anne Henry would have remained complacently
married, content with his pattern of routine infidelities and untroubled
by scruples of conscience. Or, they have speculated, if the king had
wanted Anne a little less and she had yielded a little more, his ardor
would have burned itself out in time and Anne would have gone the way
of Bessie Blount and Anne's sister Mary Carey. But as it happened,

Henry's attraction to Anne was unaccountably strong, and her sense of her power over him unusually acute. For seven years she kept herself in the center of his attention, yet just out of reach, until in the end he discarded and persecuted his wife and daughter, cast off England's immemorial allegiance to the pope and raised himself to new heights of power verging on tyranny, all in the attempt to make Anne queen.

Anne Boleyn was a black-eyed brunette of about fifteen when she came to Henry's court in 1522. She was then a thin and somewhat gawky adolescent with a neck too long for her heart-shaped face, but over the next four years she blossomed under the attentions of her cousin, the poet Thomas Wyatt, and Henry Percy, son of the earl of Northumberland, who pined after her and wanted to marry her. Four years at the French court had made her more sophisticated than most English girls, and four more spent observing the king's relationship with her sister gave her a jaundiced view of the way powerful men treated the women they used for pleasure. Mary Carey was a willing, uncomplaining plaything who submitted to a one-sided bargain in which she gave Henry everything he wanted and got nothing in return. By the time she was nineteen, Anne was determined to make a better bargain than her sister, and it may have been that rivalry with her predecessor which helped her to keep her resolution in the face of Henry's years of wheedling, coy reproaches and clumsy wooing.

She was helped, too, by the relatives and friends who promoted her romance with the king in order to further their own fortunes and political interests. In 1527 nearly all of Henry's close companions were linked to Anne. Charles Brandon and William Compton were her close friends, Francis Bryan was her cousin, Henry Norris her near relative and admirer. Her brother George was prominent at court, and her father, Thomas Boleyn, had recently been made Viscount Rochford. Beyond these immediate advantages she had aristocratic connections and royal ancestry. Her grandfather was the second duke of Norfolk, the powerful third duke of Norfolk was her uncle, and both her parents could claim Plantagenet descent.[3] Henry, who was too shrewd not to take all these things into consideration, pushed them to the back of his mind and indulged his lovesick preoccupation to the hilt. From the summer of 1527 he shut Katherine out of his consciousness, gave little thought to Mary, and put Wolsey in charge of arranging his divorce. He composed inarticulate love letters to his sweetheart and showered her with gifts, and in the evenings he put on his diamonds and brocades, drank as much wine as he could hold, and danced until daybreak.

Katherine found out about her husband's plan to divorce her several weeks before he had the courage to tell her himself. She heard about

Wolsey's secret court of inquiry, and informed the imperial ambassador Mendoza. Before long the entire matter was an open secret.

Toward the end of June Henry came to the queen's apartments and said simply that he now found they had never been legally married, and that he was taking steps to have the situation rectified by the pope. Katherine wept, and Henry, unnerved, left the room. Even though she had known it was coming, hearing of the divorce from his own lips shattered Katherine's composure, and left her agonized. The sheer heartlessness of the blow was what alarmed her most; in her eighteen years as Henry's wife she had not known him to be so openly, deliberately cruel. He had exposed her to a thousand humiliations, and had lashed out at her in anger, but this blunt, pitiless malevolence was new.

As soon as her panic passed she sent for help. Her courier reached the court of Charles V late in July, carrying a letter which confirmed the startling news of Henry's plans. The emperor's response was unambiguous yet cautious. He sat down and wrote a letter to Henry in his own hand, urging him to abandon the divorce as injurious to England's security and likely to lead to "everlasting feuds and partialities" over the question of the succession. At the same time he sent a message to Katherine emphasizing the enormity of the king's action, "calculated to astonish the whole world," and assuring her that he would "do everything in his power on her behalf." Privately he wrote to Mendoza that the entire issue must be treated as a family matter for the time being; if possible, he must prevent it from becoming an affair of state. Above all, Charles feared that through Henry's ill-advised whim both Katherine and Mary would be irrevocably dishonored, "a thing in itself so unreasonable that there is no example of it in ancient or modern history."[4]

As the months passed Henry's sudden, scandalous decision was transformed into an interminable, highly technical legal debate. Embassy after embassy was sent to Rome—first Henry's chosen negotiator William Knight, then Wolsey's representatives, bishops Gardiner and Fox, and still later Francis Bryan and the diplomat Peter Vannes. None of these legations moved Pope Clement, who was still attempting to recover from the destruction of his city and the indignities of captivity. Charles released him seven months after his troops seized Rome, and the pope was trying to rebuild his court in exile at Orvieto, but he was no longer capable of acting independently even if he had been a man of strong character, which he was not. He would not offend the emperor by granting the divorce; he feared to alienate Henry by an outright refusal to grant it. In short, he did nothing, and he did it with every semblance of purposeful activity the papal bureaucracy could devise.

After a year the papal legate Cardinal Campeggio came to England, bringing with him authorization to convene a court to examine the case, but Clement had told him to delay a conclusive decision for as long as possible, meanwhile urging Henry to take Katherine back. Soon after Campeggio arrived Katherine threw all Henry's previous efforts into confusion by producing a second papal bull pronouncing her marriage to Henry valid. The need to discredit this second bull led to further diplomatic convolutions, and ultimately, by the spring of 1529, to a complete stalemate in the negotiations with the pope.

As if to complement the murky frustrations of these proceedings the sweating sickness broke out again in London. Once again without warning the cycle of chills, "fervent heat," delirium and death broke in upon ordinary lives. Forty thousand were affected in the first outbreak alone, and Londoners fleeing the infection carried it into the countryside where it struck thousands more. Commerce and government slowed, and then stopped altogether; courts were adjourned and countinghouses locked up. Wolsey, who had come safely through the sweat once, made certain to avoid infection by locking himself away until the visitation was over. Anyone who wished to speak with the cardinal, the French ambassador wrote, had to shout through a trumpet. Householders of all degrees, from the king on down, brought out the vials and boxes of medicines they had kept from the last assault of the sweat ten years earlier, but the disease was as fatal as ever. In the words of one who lived through it, the sweat "brought more business to the priests than the doctors," and was so "pestiferous and ragious" that the only safety lay in moving from place to place, staying one step ahead of infection.

When Henry's gentleman William Compton caught it and died, and Anne Boleyn and others of the court were very ill, the king moved suddenly to a manor in Hertfordshire, leaving his courtiers and his sweetheart to struggle along as best they might. He wrote Anne an encouraging note reminding her that the disease spared women more often than men, but by the time she was able to read it she was probably out of danger, and was certainly angry at his desertion. The king took particular care for Henry Fitzroy, ordering him moved from Pontefract Castle when six people in the neighboring parish died of the sweat. He worried that there was no doctor within reach, and personally compounded preventives for the boy and his household. "Thanks be to God and to your said highness," Fitzroy wrote to his father when the epidemic had died down, "I have passed this last summer without any peril or danger of the ragious sweat that hath reigned in these parts and other, with the help of such preservatives as your highness did send to me, whereof most humble and lowly I thank the same."[5]

Whether Henry dosed his wife and daughter with his medicines is unknown, but they were with him in his Hertfordshire retreat, and for a time the bitter issue of the divorce took second place to the more pressing question of survival. Mary had been ill with smallpox slightly before the sweat appeared and was in fragile health, while Katherine's constitution was beginning to weaken under the strain of the drawn-out delays and difficulties in the king's proceedings. In her dealings with Henry she chose to behave as if nothing had changed, but her cheerful and loving manner toward him was kept up at great cost, and her confessor and Spanish gentlewomen knew well what anguish she kept hidden.

Katherine's anguish was made worse by the constant efforts of Wolsey, Campeggio and others to separate her from Henry, if possible, by some means short of divorce. One obvious alternative was to persuade her to enter a convent—an action which, under church law, would have released Henry from the marriage as irrevocably as her death. At first this solution was proposed to her under the mildest of conditions; she would lose nothing but "the use of the king's person," and would be allowed to keep her dowry, her income from rents, and her jewels. Most important, her entry into religion would in no way diminish Mary's succession rights. But Katherine was not tempted, even for a moment, to agree to any proposal under which she would cease to be Henry's wife, and she did not even take time to think it over before refusing. Other proposals angered her. Campeggio and Wolsey both favored a scheme which would satisfy Henry's desire to be rid of Katherine while preserving Mary as his heir. This plan called for the princess to marry Fitzroy after a papal dispensation overcame the obstacle of their blood relationship, but though it was suggested more than once no one took steps to implement it. Still another ingenious if unconventional solution, which seems to have originated with Clement VII himself, was that Henry marry Anne without divorcing Katherine, becoming the first bigamous monarch in Western history.

The longer a definitive resolution was delayed the more impatient Henry grew, and his impatience put unbearable pressure on those who served him. He pressed Wolsey hardest, and the cardinal used every tactic at his command to obtain the divorce. He badgered the pope, he hounded the papal legate, and when Campeggio tried to persuade him to withdraw his support for the king's cause he found Wolsey "no more moved than if I had spoken to a rock."[6] Wolsey was in fact being torn in two by the growing rift between Henry and Clement. As a cardinal of the Roman church he was a servant of the pope, and of papal interests, while as chancellor and principal churchman of the realm he owed primary allegiance to the king. As long as English and papal policies coincided, as they did throughout the earlier years of Henry's reign, Wolsey's two roles were complementary, but now they had become irreconcilably opposed.

He blamed Anne for his dilemma. If Henry had to take a second wife, he said to him in private, let her be a princess from the French royal house, not a coquettish woman of the court. It galled him that neither Anne nor her relatives respected his high status; he was accustomed to having his wants attended by dukes and earls, and even those who admired him most admitted in after years that he was "the haughtiest man that then lived." That Anne had usurped his powers of persuasion over the king he found unforgivable, and he slandered her openly. "I know there is a night crow that possesses the royal ear against me," he said, "and misrepresents all my actions." Henry, of course, sided with Anne, and so brought further tensions into a court already divided in its loyalties.

Henry's sister Mary, Katherine's gentlewomen and countless others who admired the queen were outraged that the king should try to put another woman in her place. They found the divorce and everything connected with it morally offensive, and only their fear of Henry and of the growing power of his sweetheart kept them from making spirited complaints. As it was, Anne was the object of open contempt and sarcasm; as Katherine's position at court declined, Anne became hated.

Henry's impatience with Katherine's resolute determination to remain his wife now led to threats and disgrace. He sent the queen a written message, delivered by two bishops, ordering her to comply with his desire to put her aside or Mary would be taken from her. In a parody of her real conduct, he accused Katherine of tormenting him, and of trying to turn his subjects against him by acknowledging their cheers of support and affection. He warned her that, should "certain ill-disposed persons"—meaning agents of the emperor—try to assassinate Henry or Campeggio, she would bear the full weight of punishment. As before, Katherine was not intimidated, and held her ground. But she saw now the full depth and menace of the king's own resoluteness. He meant to have his way, and he meant to harm whoever opposed him. If Katherine would not yield, she must be made to comply by force. She was moved away from Greenwich, and Anne Boleyn was installed in her apartments there. The transition from Queen Katherine to Queen Anne was well under way.

Another step came with the summoning of the long-delayed legatine court in the summer of 1529. Here Katherine made two dramatic gestures. She flung herself at Henry's feet and begged him to take her back, and when this had no effect she defied him, announcing that she refused to accept the biased judgment of a court assembled in England under Henry's control. She appealed to the pope, she said, and walked out of the room.

Katherine had in fact considered contesting the divorce in the legate's court. She sent to Flanders for two imperialist lawyers to argue in her favor, but they never arrived. The emperor had stated that no English court could arrive at a just judgment in the matter, and to send lawyers to act in such a court would be contradictory. The imperial ambassador Mendoza disapproved of this decision. Katherine's chief supporters were the English people, he wrote, "who love her and generally take her part in this affair." If they saw that she was abandoned by her relatives and friends on the continent, he feared they would lose courage and think her cause hopeless.[7] His fears were disproved, though, by the reception that greeted the queen as she left the court. A large crowd was waiting for her, and shouted approval and encouragement as she passed. Those who described the scene noted the large numbers of women who called out to Katherine and cheered her on. If it were left to the women to decide, the French ambassador wrote in a dispatch, Henry would be certain to lose his case.

But the affair of the royal divorce had long since ceased to be a quarrel of the English court in which the people of London took sides. It had quickly become an international scandal. Henry commissioned legal experts at the leading European universities to pass sentence on the merits of his cause, and Charles V paid others to refute them. In the process of collecting favorable legal judgments large sums changed hands, and the case was clouded by new ramifications of procedure and precedent. Wolsey was still urging a papal settlement, but the legatine court had been adjourned before a decision was reached, and Clement VII's future as arbiter was in peril. Wolsey had been warning Campeggio that, if the pope did not act soon, England might slip out of his grasp just as Germany had when Luther received no satisfaction from the pope. Like Luther's demands for reform in Germany, Henry's demand for a divorce had become the most urgent matter in England. If the pope continued to delay a settlement, or if he pronounced against Henry, Wolsey assured the Italian legate, "the authority of the See Apostolic in the kingdom will be annihilated."[8]

IX

 That was my joy is now my woo and payne;
That was my bliss is now my displesaunce;
That was my trust is now my wanhope playne;
That was my wele is now my most grevaunce.
What causeth this but only yowre plesaunce
Onryghtfully shewyng me unkyndness,
That hath byn your fayre lady and mastress.

For Mary the tortuous years of the royal divorce were a time of shocks, disillusionment and anguish. One month the court had been taken up with the joyous celebration of her betrothal; the next month she was all but forgotten as news of the king's decision to divorce Katherine became the dominating preoccupation of the entire court. One moment she was the adored child of loving parents; the next she was caught up in the emotional turmoil that wrenched the little family apart and destroyed all her expectations. From the time she was eleven and a half until she turned sixteen Mary lived in a constant state of uncertainty and suspended hopes, always looking for the imminent vindication of her mother's cause yet living under constant strain as that vindication was further and further delayed.

In the meantime everything old and familiar was falling away. Her father, though he still took occasional pleasure in Mary, was now capricious and cruel. Her mother was a beleaguered woman struggling to maintain her dignity as her husband abused her and another woman gradually took her place. The court became a wasp's nest of enmities, petty jealousies and backbiting, and at its center, instead of the gracious and smiling queen, Mary saw a shameless, petulant woman who by her scheming ambition had destroyed the old order of things.

Worst of all, Mary herself, once the radiant pearl of her father's court and his presumed heir, was now only the daughter of his castoff queen. As long as Katherine remained queen Mary would still be princess, but her father and the powerful men who served him were attempting to dethrone Katherine with every means at their command, and if they succeeded, Mary would be no more than the king's bastard. Like Henry Fitzroy she would be of royal blood, but baseborn, and a baseborn female would be of little use or standing in the royal court. As the dispute over the divorce dragged on, Mary's adolescence became a stormy and anxious interim between an idyllic childhood and a dubious future.

Much of what she endured during these years must be presumed, for she largely drops from sight in the official records, dispatches and letters of the divorce era. One thing is very clear, however: from the start Mary watched and wept over her mother's trials, and took her part. Katherine's heroism was the one fixed point in the shifting circumstances of Mary's life, and what she learned from her mother about wifely obedience, steadfast fidelity to conscience and resignation in the face of suffering was a lesson she would never forget.

"My tribulations are so great, my life so disturbed by the plans daily invented to further the king's wicked intention, the surprises which the king gives me, with certain persons of his council, are so mortal, and my treatment is what God knows, that it is enough to shorten ten lives, much more mine," Katherine wrote to Charles V.[1] By the time she wrote this letter in November of 1531 she had lived through nearly five years of what she called "the pains of Purgatory on earth."[2] Time and again she had been confronted, without warning, by deputations of royal councilors sent to browbeat her into submitting and relinquishing her stand on the divorce. They accused her of disobedience, stubbornness, ill temper, shrewishness. They insulted her and tried to trick her with words. They taunted her with the old pain of her stillborn children, saying that God had shown his abomination of her marriage "by the curse of sterility."[3]

The queen stood up bravely to each assault, trying to ignore the insults while using the arguments of her accusers to support her own position. As she grew more heated she told them all to go to Rome, with as much contempt as if she were telling them to go to hell. She answered them not only convincingly but with a sharpness of intellect and logic that at first startled them and later, or so the imperial ambassador Chapuys believed, won their sympathies and made them "secretly nudge one another when any point [she made] touched the quick."[4] Those who claimed that Henry's lawyers and churchmen were "confounded by a single woman, and all their designs turned topsy-turvy," were not far wrong. Henry, who knew well the queen's articulateness and skill in debate, waited anxiously to hear the outcome of these encounters, and each time he found that Katherine had come off the victor he shook his head, saying he feared as much and "remaining very pensive."

In the early years of the conflict he had taken Katherine on in person. One night toward the end of 1529 they dined together and disputed the issues of the divorce throughout the meal. Henry lost ground at every turn, and finally tried to take refuge behind the most recent of the expert legal judgments he had bought. Katherine, who had an impressive list of experts on her side, dismissed his point with a laugh and boasted that she could collect a thousand opinions favorable to her for every one of Henry's. At this he left the room suddenly and appeared "very disconcerted and downcast" for the rest of the day. At supper Anne realized what had happened, and was angry.

"Did I not tell you that whenever you disputed with the queen she was sure to have the upper hand?" she asked him reproachfully. "I see that some fine morning you will succumb to her reasoning and that you will cast me off. I have been waiting long, and might in the meanwhile have contracted some advantageous marriage, out of which I might have had issue, which is the greatest consolation in this world."

Anne played on his depression, his shame at losing the argument, his ever present concern about the succession. Then came her ultimate barb.

"Alas! Farewell to my time and youth spent to no purpose at all."[5] Anne had every advantage in the tug of war with Katherine, but still Henry continued to argue with the queen. Even after he stopped seeing Katherine they continued to quarrel by letter, with Henry's letters composed by teams of secretaries and officials and revised over and over before they were sent. Henry had allowed himself to become caught between two very shrewd women, and would need more than strong logic to extricate himself from his uncomfortable position.

Other forms of pressure were, of course, being applied to sway Katherine. One was Henry's maddeningly capricious behavior toward her. In person and through messengers he conveyed the most alarming threats and warnings, yet until the summer of 1531 he made a point of dining with the queen at all the great festivals of the year. He was sometimes surly and vicious, sometimes good tempered and even affectionate. He kept Katherine off balance, never allowing her to accurately guess his intentions or his true feelings. He was angry when she showed concern about Mary, yet more angry when she did not. She risked increasing his displeasure with everything she did, and there was no discerning when or how his next blow would fall.

His cruelest tactic was to keep Katherine and Mary in separate yet neighboring establishments, letting them see one another just often enough to make their loneliness unendurable when they were apart. Or he would force Katherine to choose between his company and Mary's, telling her in no uncertain terms that if she visited the princess she might be forced to stay with her permanently and lose what little claim she still had on Henry's companionship.[6] The queen tried to remain undisturbed by heart-rending choices of this kind, saying only "that she would not leave him for her daughter nor anyone else in this world," but she was inwardly distraught. "If you had experienced part of the bitter days and nights which I have endured since the commencement of this sad affair," she told one of her tormentors, the dean of Henry's chapel, "you would not have considered it precipitation to desire a sentence and determination of this affair, nor would you have accused me so carelessly and inadvertently of pertinacity."[7]

But if Henry's treatment afflicted and grieved the queen, even crueler attacks came from Anne. She saw to it that the few men who had been in the habit of visiting Katherine and bringing her news from court were kept away, and sent her own spies to augment those Wolsey had placed in the queen's household some years earlier. She spoke of disgracing and harming Mary, and was overheard to remark that she "wished all Spaniards were at the bottom of the sea." She persuaded Henry to give her Katherine's jewels, and though at first Katherine refused, arguing that "it was against her conscience to give her jewels to adorn a person who is the scandal of Christendom," in the end she obeyed Henry even in this.[8] Anne was reported to be involving herself in the diplomatic issues raised by the divorce. She tried to persuade Henry that Charles V, who was himself guilty of breaking church law in marrying his cousin Isabella of Portugal, could not in good faith complain of Henry's attitude to Katherine, and would certainly not go to war on her behalf. And if he did, Anne added, her relatives would pay for ten thousand soldiers for the king's army for a whole year, forming the core of an invincible army of defense.[9]

Katherine's purgatory was a solitary one. She was by no means friendless, but there was little her friends could do. The emperor's verbal protests lost their effect after it became clear he would not back them up with force. His ambassador Chapuys was some comfort, but his visits were infrequent and he brought more bad news than good. Allies at court occasionally got news to Katherine by surreptitious means—the duchess of Norfolk sent her some poultry dressed with oranges, and in one of the oranges, a letter from a papal official in Rome—but there were too few of these gestures to alleviate the queen's growing certainty that she would have to endure her agony alone.

This view of her situation was confirmed by the priests in her household and by the only other Spaniard to whom she opened her heart, Mary's onetime tutor Vives. Katherine turned to Vives, he wrote in a letter to a friend, as both a countryman "who spoke the same language" and as one well read "in matters of morals and consolation." She confided to him her anguish that "the man whom she loved more than herself should be so alienated from her, that he should think of marrying another, which was the greater grief the more she loved him." His reply subordinated the human conflict to the higher design of Christian martyrdom. Katherine's torment proved that she was dear to God, he told her, for God only tests those he cherishes, in order to strengthen their virtues.[10]

As time went by Katherine slipped easily into the role of a martyr, willingly submitting to injustice in this world and trusting that her self-sacrifice would be rewarded in the next. She ceased to expect vindication during her lifetime, and instead transferred her hopes to the broader arena of eternal justification. "In this world I will confess myself to be the king's true wife," she wrote, "and in the next they will know how unreasonably I am afflicted."[11] She adopted the vocabulary of self-immolation, declaring that "wherever the king commanded her, were it even to the fire, she would go."[12] Her admirers had cast her in this role for a long time. One imperial diplomat wrote to the empress urging her to preserve all the letters she received from Katherine, for in the years to come they would surely be valued as relics.[13]

It was while these traumas were unfolding that Mary's adult personality was beginning to take shape. She came to maturity in an atmosphere of extraordinary stress, and her character emerged as a response to crises. She was jolted painfully out of childhood and forced to come to terms with a confusing and deeply tragic situation. Understandably, she looked to Katherine as her model during these disturbing years, but in patterning herself after her mother she was taking on the behavior of a desperately troubled woman. The marks of this unique rite of passage would be with Mary all her life.

Katherine had come to an agonizing crossroads in her own character. She was being pulled three ways. She was attempting to fulfill her duty as a wife, to honor her conscience, and to retain her dignity as queen. In her present circumstances, these three compulsions demanded different, contradictory reactions, and no small part of her distress came in struggling to reconcile them. As a wife her first duty was to be ruled by her husband, yet her conscience also had its imperatives; as a queen, strictly speaking, she ought not to be ruled at all but should rule others. As a wife she was bound to submit to punishment, even torture, by her husband yet her conscience forbade her to comply with unmerited punishment, and her royal dignity was incompatible with mistreatment of any kind. Wives suffered ignominy and humiliation in silence; a woman of conscience stood up and fought against these to protect her good repute, while a monarch took swift and terrible vengeance against the slightest insult. Katherine was called upon to be an obedient inferior, a heroine and an exalted ruler all at the same time, though any one of these roles demanded all the strength she had. Had she taken her obligations as a wife less seriously, had she been more flexible in matters of conscience, had she not been the proud daughter of Queen Isabella of Castile, Katherine would have found her ordeal far easier to bear. As it was the warring selves kept up their battle within her almost to the end of her life, and without understanding clearly what she was seeing Mary saw and imitated them all.

That conscience ought to take precedence over all other considerations was a premise supported by Mary's careful, exhaustive religious instruction. But no instruction had prepared her for the more complex conflict between Katherine's roles as wife and queen. Mary must have heard, for example, how when Katherine made her dramatic exit from the legatine court she acknowledged and deplored her disobedience to Henry at the very moment she defied him. "I never before disputed the will of my husband," she declared, "and I shall take the first opportunity to ask pardon for my disobedience." The same duality marked Katherine's behavior toward Henry in less climactic circumstances. She endured every assault on her worth and peace of mind and said only loving words in return. She continued to adore and honor Henry no matter what he did, and she urged Mary to continue to love him too. But she would not allow him to rob her of her status and regal poise. She took refuge in magnanimous self-mutilation, and found in willing masochism a perfect compromise between her self-respect and her obligation to Henry. Because it was voluntary, it allowed her to preserve the illusion that she and not Henry controlled her life; because it meant abasement and abuse, it satisfied the demands of wifely subservience.

Up to the age of eleven Mary had been a romantic little girl, encouraged to dream of marriage to a prince or emperor and to think of the way men and women treated one another as an affair of love tokens, gallantry and blushing excitement. She mistook the pleasureful pastime of flirtation for the deep bonds of love; certainly she perceived nothing of the emotional intricacies of a marriage of state, made and, if need be, broken to satisfy the arbitrary logic of power. Now, without abandoning her romantic images, Mary added another, far darker dimension to her understanding of how men and women treated one another. She watched her beloved father turn against her adored mother and injure her in a hundred ways. She watched her mother respond by treading a tortuous emotional path that ultimately resolved itself into voluntary self-destruction. She observed her mother's wretchedness in the face of her father's flagrant infidelity and the other woman's cruelty. Mary came away convinced that when she married she must expect torment, obey and honor her tormentor, maintain a serene exterior in all crises, and turn inward all her feelings of hatred and lust for revenge.

There was reason to believe that Mary's married life might not be far off. Her imminent debasement in status did not discourage all offers for her hand, and Henry, whose plans for his daughter seem to have fluctuated widely, sometimes saw marrying her off as a way of eliminating her from the miasmic tangle of the divorce. The Scots king was among her suitors, and it was rumored Henry was negotiating a betrothal to a potentate somewhere in southeastern Europe. The son of the duke of Cleves was another possibility, though his value as a potential son-in-law was offset by the fact that the duke was reputed to be insane and the son on his way to the same infirmity. When the princess was fourteen it was suggested that she might marry Francesco Sforza, duke of Milan, though he was "without feet or hands, or had lost the use of them, which comes to the same thing."[14] A marriage of this kind would dishonor Mary and break Katherine's heart, putting it squarely in line with the king's general policy toward his wife and daughter, but Henry continued to defer settlement of any marriage contract until long after Mary had reached marriageable age. This left room for some hope that he might in the end arrange an honorable marriage for her, or in some way involve her in the succession. Some of his advisers continued to urge him to choose his preferred successor, then marry him to the princess. This would certainly please the people, who from the time the divorce question first arose had insisted "they would acknowledge no successor to the crown but the husband of the Lady Mary." When the princess was sixteen Norfolk was assuring Chapuys that Mary was "still heiress of the kingdom," and that if Henry died without a male heir she would take precedence over any other daughters he might leave.[15] But these reassurances were little more than matters of form, and the ambassador was well aware that Mary's status would not be secure as long as Anne was doing her best to turn the king against her.

If Anne detested Katherine, she hated Mary even more. Henry's affection for Katherine lessened year by year, but in his ambivalent way he continued to be fond of Mary. One summer when she wrote to him asking to be allowed to come and see him before he left for four months of hunting, he not only agreed but traveled to where she was staying, spending an entire day in her company and "showing her all possible affection."[16] The following summer he again "visited her and made great cheer with her," and spoke of her in his old way as the greatest pearl in the kingdom.[17] When he praised Mary in Anne's presence, though, Anne swore at her and called her names, and Chapuys believed Anne was constantly scheming to have Mary moved as far from the court as possible in order to prevent Henry from seeing her.[18]

At fifteen Mary was still being dressed as a princess. In 1531 Henry ordered his master of the Great Wardrobe to provide her with new gowns of cloth of silver tissue, purple and black velvet, and crimson satin, and kirtles of gold and silver. One of the gowns and a "night bonnet" were to be trimmed with ermines, and to go with these new clothes he ordered sixteen pairs of velvet shoes, two dozen pairs of Spanish gloves, French hoods and a cloak of Bruges satin. There was fine Holland cloth and linen for smocks and underclothing, and yards of ribbon for trim.[19] Beyond what he paid for her wardrobe and household expenses Henry sent Mary sums of money, ten or twenty pounds at a time, to celebrate Christmas, or to distribute in alms in Eastertide, or simply "to disport her with." But these amounts were no more than he paid out in a single day to people who entertained him or did him small services—the woman who returned his dog Cutte, the man who brought home Ball, another dog that was lost in Waltham Forest, the poor woman who gave him pears and nuts while he was hunting, the dumb man who brought him oranges, the blind woman who played the harp, "the fellow with the dancing dog," or the visiting acrobat Peter Tremezin, "who rode two horses at once."[20] And what he spent on Mary in a year could not compare to the sums he lavished on Anne in a week.

Henry showered Anne with clothes, costly trinkets, lands and revenues, and jewels. His jewelers made rings, gem-studded collars and girdles, diamond buttons and sleeve ornaments for her, and he designed extravagant keepsakes for her himself. Such were the "twenty-one diamonds and twenty-one rubies set upon roses and hearts, for Mistress Anne" he bought in 1531, and the "nineteen diamonds set in trueloves of crown gold" he gave her shortly afterward. There were huge diamonds set into hearts to be worn in her hair, and smaller stones meant to adorn its luxuriant thickness when she wore it unbound.[21] For himself Henry bought a somewhat sobering gift. He had just turned forty, and was troubled by a painful ulcer in his leg. To ease his pain he needed a walking stick, and had one made in coarse gold, with room inside it for a foot measure, a compass and tongs. The beauty of its workmanship could not distract Henry from the uneasy realization that the walking stick was a first sign of age; to make it appear more a matter of fashion than of necessity he had several others like it made for his younger gentlemen to use.

Time was pressing the king harder than usual, and so was Anne. Impatient to be queen, she was already setting up a royal household in miniature, complete with almoner and other officers. She surrounded herself with "almost as many ladies as if she were queen," and took Katherine's place at the king's side when he rode to the hunt. She and her servants made themselves at home in the sumptuous quarters in every palace that used to belong to Katherine. In her black satin nightgown, lined with taffeta and velvet, she tried her best to make these rooms her own, and to make the king feel young again when he visited them. By 1532 she had clearly succeeded. In January Katherine sent Henry a gold cup as a New Year's gift, "with honorable and humble words" attached. He returned it without explanation. At the same time he presented Anne with her New Year's gift—an entire bedroom newly decorated with beautiful tapestries and a magnificent bed, furnished in cloth of gold and silver, crimson satin and rich embroideries.[22]

Month by month Anne was taking on not only the quarters and entourage of a queen but a queen's power as well. Henry's treasurer Henry Guildford, once one of the king's "minions" and always an irreverent wit, had no use for Anne and let her know it. As for the divorce, Guildford found all the theological sophistries on both sides absurd, and once suggested jokingly that "it would be the best deed in the world to tie all the doctors who had invented and supported this affair in a cart, and send them to Rome to maintain their opinion, or meet with the confusion they deserve."[23] Anne found him infuriating, and told him archly that once she was crowned she would see to it that he was sent away from court. He retorted icily that he would leave of his own accord long before that happened, and complained to Henry about the insult. The king frowned and told Guildford he "shouldn't trouble himself with what women said," but the bad feeling remained. There was no love lost between Henry's sister Mary and Anne; Anne accused Mary's husband Charles Brandon of incest with his own daughter.[24] Anne's aunt, the duchess of Norfolk, who sided with Katherine, was sent away at Anne's insistence because she spoke her mind too publicly, while her uncle the duke lived under the pressure of Anne's constant suspicion. She feared he had a plan to marry his son to Princess Mary and one day to make him king; finally to put an end to her oppressive imaginings he made a hastily arranged, disadvantageous match for the boy.

Anne's net was spreading ever wider, and soon no one would be immune from her attacks. As Mary waited in fear for the trials to come she knelt often at the altar in her bedchamber and repeated the little prayer of Aquinas she had been given to translate when she was eleven. In keeping with all her education, it was an entreaty for moderation and decorum. "My God, make me humble without feigning, merry without lightness, sad without mistrust," she begged, "fearing without despair, obedient without arguing, patient without grudging, and pure without corruption." But it was also a prayer for serenity amid crises, "that in prosperous things I may give thee thanks, and in adversity be patient, so that I be not lift[ed] up with the one, nor oppressed with the other. . . ."[25] Mary would need all the comfort her faith could provide to face the critical years that lay just ahead.

X

 Who shall have my fayre lady?
Who but I, who but I, who but I,
Undir the levys grene?

On the last Thursday in May 1533 a flotilla of royal barges, boats and ships of all sizes assembled at Tower Wharf for the short trip down the Thames to Greenwich. Leading the procession was a swift foist full of ordnance, and mounted in its bow was a great red dragon belching flames into the water. Monsters and wild men disported themselves around the dragon, and behind it, in another foist, was a pageant of the queen's device, a mount with a crowned white falcon standing on it surrounded by red and white roses. The barge of the Lord Mayor, Stephen Peacock, came next, followed by forty-eight barges supplied by his colleagues in the haberdashers' company. Each was hung with tapestries and banners and pennons of the arms of the crafts in fine gold. Every barge was equipped with guns, "the one to hail the other triumphantly as the time did require," and with musicians playing trumpets, shawms, flutes and drums in such harmony that they sounded like "a thing of another world." They were going to Greenwich to greet Anne Boleyn, and to escort her to apartments at the Tower where she would be prepared for her coronation.

Anne was waiting at the palace in a bark painted with her colors and rigged with many banners. Another hundred vessels joined the parade for the trip back upriver, each fitted out with masts and rigging ornamented with taffeta flags and gold foil that shone brightly in the sun. All the little boats along the route joined in until the whole river was covered, and as the queen's barge passed by all the great warships moored at Greenwich, Radcliff, and before St. Katharine's shot their guns. The cannons at Limehouse and in the Tower itself gave out such a thunderous pounding that in the nearby foreigners' quarter every pane of glass was broken and the houses shook so violently it seemed as if they would come crashing down. The blaring of trumpets that cut through the booming guns as Anne stepped ashore at Tower Wharf gave the spectacle an apocalyptic air, and a Spaniard who described it all afterward wrote that "verily it seemed as if the world was coming to an end."

Two days later Anne rode in procession through the city, preceded by the great nobles, judges, abbots and ambassadors. The newly created Knights of the Bath rode together in their hooded blue gowns, and the French merchants, their horses trapped in violet taffeta with white crosses, wore doublets of violet velvet with one sleeve in Anne's colors. Anne rode in a litter covered inside and out with white satin and drawn by two palfreys in white damask. Her surcoat and mantle were of white cloth of tissue, the mantle furred with ermines. Her hair hung loose down her back, and on her head she wore a coif with a jeweled circlet. Constables in velvet and silk marched with the procession, using their great staves to keep the crowds from snatching at the finery, while from every window along the route of march people leaned down to wave and shout to the celebrities as they passed. Following Anne were the principal women of the court: the chief married noblewomen in cloth of gold on horseback, the dowager marchioness of Dorset and Anne's grandmother, the dowager duchess of Norfolk, in litters, twelve unmarried ladies on horseback in gowns of crimson velvet, and several dozen lesser gentle-women in black velvet. At the rear came the royal guard, in new embroidered coats of goldsmith's work.

Tapestries, carpets and rich cloths of scarlet and cloth of gold were hung from every house and shop, and at each of the stages on the traditional procession route the queen was saluted by pageantry and music. Choirs of children sang ballads in her honor, and at the conduit in Fleet Street was a group of "such several solemn instruments that it seemed to be an heavenly noise, and was much regarded and praised." At Gracechurch, Apollo and his Nine Muses sat on the mount of Parnassus and recited verses to Anne, playing their instruments in accompaniment, and at Leadenhall another group of performers presented an elaborate pageant written by Nicholas Udall, in which a white falcon, representing Anne, lighted on the Tudor rosebush and was crowned by an angel, while St. Anne looked on. At Cornhill she was saluted as worthier than the Three Graces, here called Hearty Gladness, Stable Honour and Continual Success; at the lesser conduit in Cheap a play with music depicted the Judgment of Paris, with the golden apple for the fairest of goddesses and mortals awarded to Anne. Here her nobility, virtue and beauty were praised in verse:

> Queen Anne so gent,
> Of high descent.

> Anne excellent
> In nobleness!
> Of ladies all,
> You principal
> Should win this ball
> Of worthiness!
>
> Passing beauty
> And chastity,
> With high degree,
> And great riches;
> So coupled be
> In unity,
> That chief are ye
> In worthiness.[1]

The mocking reference to Anne's chastity—she was six months pregnant at the time of her coronation—was not lost on the people who lined the streets to watch Henry's new wife pass. They called her "a strong harlot" and "a goggle-eyed whore," and one man was heard to declare that he was neither fool nor sinner enough to ever take "that whore Nan Bullen to be queen." She was already pregnant when Henry finally married her, earlier in the year, and Katherine at least believed they had been living as husband and wife for much longer.

There had been no official papal annulment of the marriage to Katherine. Instead, spurred toward a conclusive settlement by Anne's pregnancy, Parliament declared that all ecclesiastical cases were hereafter to be settled in England, without appeal to Rome or anywhere else. This enabled the convocation of the clergy of southern England, early in April, to declare Henry and Katherine's marriage invalid, and to make his marriage to Anne, already celebrated in January, a legal and binding union.

But the Londoners who had greeted Katherine on her coronation progress through the city nearly twenty-five years earlier and still loved her could not find it in their hearts to wish Anne well. Not ten people in the crowd called out "God save the queen!" an eyewitness wrote; instead they pointed to the royal initials H and A painted and stitched into the decorations along the parade route and read them as "Ha ha!" Katherine's partisans seized on every imperfection in Anne's appearance as if it were a monstrosity. She wore her dress high up around her throat as if to hide a goiter; the crownlike wreath she wore emphasized the scrofulous scars on her neck; seen from the right angle, the ears of the mule behind her appeared to project from her head "like two sharp horns, making many people laugh."

The solemnity of Anne's coronation on June 1 did nothing to discour-

age these jibes, and both before and after their marriage Anne was a
source of considerable embarrassment and inconvenience to the king.
During the summer of 1532 he took her with him on what was to be an
extensive hunting trip to the north, and as his custom was he passed
through village after village to show himself to the people and to receive
their acclaim. This time, though, for the first three or four days of his
journey he met with only shouts of derision and criticism. Anne was
roundly hooted and hissed, and the villagers shouted to the king to take
back his true wife Katherine. These insults spoiled Henry's anticipation
for the hunt, and he and Anne abruptly returned to London.[2]

Justices and magistrates were ordered to take severe action against
anyone speaking against the king or Anne. In a country town a sixty-
nine-year-old Derbyshire soldier, "sore bruised" in Henry's early wars,
said in a conversation with a vicar and two others that he could not believe the king would forsake "so noble a lady, so high born, and so gracious" as Katherine to marry another woman; a few months later he
found himself a prisoner in the Marshalsea.[3] All the crafts and guilds assembled in their halls in London were enjoined to say nothing injurious
to the king's dignity, and to prevent their journeymen and servants and,
"a more difficult task, their own wives," from insulting Anne. As the day
of the coronation approached, cash rewards were offered to anyone
bringing "talkers and slanderers" to the notice of the royal officials, and
proclamations ordered the suppression of "fond books, ballads, rhymes
and other lewd treatises" disparaging Henry's second marriage.[4] But it
was impossible, as the Lord Mayor remarked on the day of Anne's progress, "to restrain the people's hearts, and even the king didn't know how
to do it," and when at a public sermon shortly after the marriage the congregation was asked to pray for Anne's health and welfare, nearly all
who were present left the church "in high displeasure and with sad coun-
tenances" without waiting for the rest of the sermon.[5]

Within the court the factions supporting Katherine and Anne had
recently come to blows. Henry's sister Mary had affronted Anne by her
"opprobrious language." To avenge the insult, Anne's uncle Norfolk ordered twenty of his men to assassinate Brandon's chief followers in the
sanctuary of Westminster. Brandon and many of the courtiers were so
outraged that they were preparing to invade the sanctuary and drag out
the murderers by force. Henry restrained them, but it was only fear of
his anger that kept even larger brawls from occurring.

Meanwhile Anne's enemies had found a subtler way to assault both
her peace of mind and her influence with the king. Anne had gained her
power because of the king's weakness for women; she could lose it in the
same way. Young girls, noblemen's daughters, arrived at court every
month to take up residence as waiting maids. The king flirted with them

all, and from time to time singled out one for special favor. In 1532 he was said to be "courting" one of these ladies, and was "very much in love" with her. The anti-Boleyn faction gave him every encouragement and help in this new affair, much to Anne's displeasure, but the new love could not compete with Henry's abiding infatuation for his "sweetheart."[6] The disgruntled courtiers had to admit Anne's strength, and consoled themselves by making mean references to her disfigured hand. Growing out of the nail of one of her fingers was another, superfluous nail—possibly the stub of an extra finger. It was so slight a blemish that she could easily keep it covered with the tip of the next finger, but all those who hated Anne made much of it, as they did of her every defect and failing.[7]

After seven years of Anne's perilous coquetry Henry was no more blind to her faults than he was entirely faithful to her, but when she told him she was pregnant he forgot everything else in his delight at the prospect of a son. For Henry, this was the climactic event, the ultimate conclusion to the long wranglings of the divorce. All the plans, expectations and celebrations which had greeted the arrival of the New Year's boy so long ago were now to be revived. Those who for decades had predicted only disaster for England in the absence of a legitimate male heir would be confounded at last. To provide a suitable setting for the birth of his son Henry ordered that the most beautiful bed he owned, "the most magnificent and gorgeous that could be thought of," be brought from his treasure room to the room where the queen was to be delivered. As Anne's time drew near, physicians and astrologers were called in to confirm Henry's hopes about the child's sex, and armed with their assurances that it would be male Henry proclaimed a splendid tournament to be held soon after the birth. Expecting that the arrival of Anne's son would silence her detractors once and for all, her relatives and friends prepared to make a triumphant showing at the tournament, and sent to Flanders for the best horses they could find.

Two events, one merely bizarre, the other slightly ominous, marred the final weeks of Anne's pregnancy. The first was the remarriage, for the fourth time, of Charles Brandon. His wife had died toward the end of June, and barely six weeks after her interment the following month he had taken a new bride, a girl of fourteen. Like the Princess Mary she had a Spanish mother—she was the daughter of one of Katherine's former waiting women—and was very pretty, but apart from the scandalous difference in the ages of the bride and groom what made the match virtually unprecedented was that the girl was betrothed to Brandon's ten-year-old son.

At about the same time Henry indulged his passion for one of the court ladies—her name is not recorded—and took her as his mistress.

Anne's coronation was barely over when their amours began, and in her extreme jealousy Anne "made use of certain words which he very much disliked." Pregnant though she was, the king did not spare her in his angry reply. She had no right to complain, he snapped. She must simply "shut her eyes and endure as those who were better than herself had done"—a pointed reference to long-suffering Katherine—and would do well to bear in mind who it was that had exalted her to the status of queen. He threatened her with the painful truth that "he could at any time lower her as much as he had raised her," and resumed his amorous pastimes with a vengeance. Much "coldness and grumbling" between the spouses followed these remarks. Both Henry and Anne were headstrong and inclined to be moody, and now that they were married Anne had surrendered some of her leverage in an argument. Henry reportedly did not speak to Anne at all for two or three days, and she seems to have entered her month-long confinement without the comfort of a reconciliation.[8]

Her child was born at midafternoon on September 7. To her intense regret it was a girl. Henry swore and sulked, but did not despair. The child was healthy enough, and when the first disappointment had passed he realized there was every reason to think the next one would be a son.

It was at first proposed that the girl be named Mary. She would be taking the former princess' place as heir to the throne; why not let her take Mary's name as well? No more unambiguous symbol for the supplanting of one daughter by the other could have been devised, but for some reason the idea was discarded. Mary's downgrading in rank, though, was made almost brutally clear within moments after her half-sister's birth. As soon as the midwives were certain the child was liveborn and breathing, a herald proclaimed to the courtiers in the adjoining chamber that the old princess of Wales was no longer to be considered such, and as if to finalize her degradation the badges bearing her device worn on the coats of her servingmen were ripped from their sleeves and replaced by the king's arms. At the christening of the new baby, who was called Elizabeth, a herald again proclaimed her to be princess and rightful heiress of England, and Chapuys, who reported these events to Charles V, added the current rumor that Mary's household and allowance were soon to be greatly reduced. "May God in his infinite mercy," he added, "prevent a still worse treatment!"

Chapuys, Mary and Katherine had all seen the blow coming. There had never been any real question that, in the ambassador's phrase, "as soon as Anne sets her foot firmly in the stirrup" she would take from both women the last vestiges of their dignity. Anne had been threatening Katherine for years, swearing she would rather see Katherine hanged than acknowledge her rank as queen.[9] As soon as she took Katherine's place as Henry's wife Anne lost no time in using her new-found authority to take her revenge. As queen, Anne needed her own barge. She took the one that had been Katherine's, and ordered Katherine's arms removed from it and "rather ignominiously torn off and cut to pieces."[10] Anne already possessed nearly everything else of value that had once belonged to her rival; all that remained was to remove her person from the vicinity of the court, reduce her establishment, and change her title.

In July of 1533 Katherine was moved to Buckden in Huntingdonshire, to an old brick palace from Henry VII's time that loomed forlornly over the great fens. The palace was strong and easily defended, and in a location so remote and thinly inhabited that it made an effective prison. Katherine was allowed to take with her her Spanish ladies in waiting and her faithful Spanish officers—Felipez, head of the household, the physician De la Sà and his apothecary, the chaplain Jorge de Ateca, bishop of Llandaff. But she was under strict guard, and more cut off than ever before from news of Mary and of those who were still trying to help her.

Ever since the second marriage was made public, Chapuys had been urging Katherine to save herself by escaping, with the emperor's help. Within England, he told her, there were many "people of quality" who were ready to come to her defense with money and the rudiments of an army. All they needed was encouragement from Charles V or possibly from the Scots, since the people were so angry at the king's treatment of her that they would aid any army organized to restore her to the throne by force. No king, not even Richard III, was ever hated so thoroughly as Henry now was, these potential rebels insisted. Now was the time to put an end to his wicked treatment of his rightful wife and daughter.[11] But though she realized the danger she was in, Katherine was determined to stay in England. Otherwise, as she told Chapuys, she would be "sinning against law and against the king." What was more, she would be running away from what, in her mind at least, was the most significant question of conscience yet to arise.

With the judgment of the clerical convocation that Henry's first marriage was invalid, Katherine lost her claim to the title of queen under English law. She received word that from now on she would be known as "the old dowager princess," the title she merited as Prince Arthur's widow.[12] She ignored the change, continuing to sign herself as "Katherine the queen" and crossing out the title "princess dowager" wherever she saw it written. After three months of resistance Henry sent orders to those he had placed in charge of Katherine to accuse her of "arrogance, selfishness, and inordinate vainglory" in refusing to abandon a title that was no longer hers, and telling her that stubbornness over this issue would assuredly lead to civil war and disputes over the succession. "Much blood would be spilt," they were to say, and "the kingdom totally destroyed," and the king's conscience would be "greatly troubled." If Katherine acquiesced, she would be honorably treated; if she did not, she would feel his displeasure, not only against her but against her friends and companions, and her daughter.

Without hesitation Katherine answered that, despite all pretended judgments to the contrary, she was Henry's true wife, and would never be known by any other title than queen. There was no arrogance or vainglory in her attitude, she said, "for she would certainly take greater glory in being called the daughter of Ferdinand and Isabella than the greatest queen in the world against her own conscience."[13] The evocation of Isabella was pointed and appropriate. Henry was overheard to admit more than once that he feared Katherine would imitate her famous mother and take the field against him. The image of the heroic crusader queen, riding armed into battle, still lived to trouble the musings of the powerful king of England nearly thirty years after her death.

Mary too was immediately affected by Anne's official designation as queen. On one terrible day she was informed, first, that her parents' marriage had been, once and for all, pronounced invalid and second, that Henry and Anne were now man and wife. At the same time she was told that she could no longer communicate with the princess dowager either through intermediaries or in writing. Despite the panic she must have felt at these announcements, Mary remained outwardly thoughtful and composed, and seemed "even to rejoice" at the news of Henry's marriage. She sat down right away and wrote the king a letter which, when he read it later, made him "marvellously content and pleased, praising above all things the wisdom and prudence of the princess."[14]

Henry's pleasure in Mary was always a source of extreme annoyance to Anne, as was the obvious affection the people had for her. When Mary traveled from one residence to another shortly after Anne's coronation the villagers came to see her and to cheer her as they did Katherine. "As much rejoicing went on as if God Almighty had come down from heaven," Anne complained, and she planned to punish both the princess and the people who stood behind her.[15] Anne boasted that she intended to make Mary wait on her as a maid of honor in her royal household, and that, once she was installed in this position, Anne might perhaps "give her too much dinner on some occasion"—that is, poison her—or "marry her to some varlet."[16]

No threat was as dangerous, though, as the tacit threat of her unborn child. Shortly before Elizabeth's birth Katherine wrote Mary a letter which shows clearly how fateful she saw Mary's situation to be and how she advised her to face it. "Daughter," she wrote, "I heard such tidings this day that I do perceive (if it be true) the time is very near when Almighty God will provide for you." The "tidings" concerned Anne's menacing remarks, coupled with the nearness of her expected delivery. Anne's child would make Mary superfluous, and therefore expendable; to protect the succession rights of his new heir Henry might yield to Anne's pressure and order the princess killed.

Knowing this might be the last letter Mary received from her, Katherine poured into it all the love and encouragement she could put into words. Her overriding message was that of the Christian martyrs she had come to resemble: the message of cheerfulness and rejoicing in the face of danger. "I would God, good daughter, that you did know with how good a heart I write this letter unto you. I never did write one with a better." She told Mary what Vives had said to her long before, that tragedy and persecution are signs of divine favor and that "we never come to the kingdom of heaven but by troubles." Whatever happens is God's will, no matter how men and women deceive themselves that it is their own, she wrote, and this too should be cause for rejoicing, even if his will means suffering and death. "Agree to his pleasure with a merry heart," Katherine told Mary, secure in the "sure armor" of his commandments and with faith that "he will not suffer you to perish if you beware to offend him." What she meant was not that God would preserve Mary's life but that he would spare her the eternal death of hell; she might be killed, but she would know everlasting life beyond the grave. The final words of the letter were a resigned yet scornful acknowledgment that, for both mother and daughter, the end seemed near. "And now you shall begin, and by likelihood I shall follow. I set not a rush by it, for when they have done the utmost they can, then I am sure of amendment."[17]

Katherine's morbid cheerfulness was echoed in the little book she sent to Mary along with her letter. It was an edition of the letters of St. Jerome to Paula and Eustochium, a classic of Christian asceticism for women. In many ways these letters rounded out the education Mary had been receiving since she was a young girl. The treatises Vives wrote for her in childhood were drawn largely from these and other letters of St. Jerome outlining an ideal of female behavior that was not unlike the rule of a professed nun. Now, as Katherine tried to prepare Mary for the greatest danger she ever had to face, she could think of no better examples for her to follow than those of the sheltered, prudish women Jerome described, who shunned all men, feared every sensual impulse they felt, and prayed that they might be rid of their youth and beauty so that they could devote themselves fully to God. Jerome's letters were exhortations to imitate the stolid asceticism of young Roman women who shrouded themselves in garments that "reminded them of the tomb" and wore out their lives in ascetic disciplines.

One story must have made a strong impression on seventeen-year-old Mary. It described the holy life of Blesilla, a Roman girl of about Mary's age who when her husband died so starved and exhausted herself with fasting and prayers that within a few months she had followed him to the grave. Jerome's theme was the never ending battle of spirit against flesh, Christian self-discipline against the overripe sensuality of the Roman world. Mary's battle was to be, like Katherine's, a conflict of mental endurance, pitting the strength of her individual conscience against the shame of disobedience and the fear of death. But Jerome's rousing persuasion to fight the good fight was filled with biblical exhortations well suited to inspire Mary nonetheless. "Thou shalt not be afraid for the terror by night nor for the arrow that flieth by day; nor for the trouble which haunteth thee in darkness; nor for the demon and his attacks at noonday. A thousand shall fall at thy side and ten thousand at thy right hand; but it shall not come nigh thee."[18] And in her isolation Mary must have found comfort in Elisha's words: "Fear not, for they that be with us are more than they that be with them."[19]

The popular view of Mary's circumstances was far different from Katherine's. To the country people who knew of her chiefly through songs and the stories of travelers, Mary's life was that of a fairytale heroine, full of romance and peril yet veiled in unreality. Thus the villagers of Yorkshire and Lincolnshire were quite prepared to believe the story of an eighteen-year-old girl who impersonated the princess in the northern counties toward the end of 1533. The girl, Mary Baynton, called herself Lady Mary and told how she had been "put forth into the broad world to shift for her living" by her father, and went from house to house asking alms. To those who took pity on her and welcomed her as if she really were the princess she told a curious story. As a little girl, she said, she had been with her aunt Mary while the latter was in her bath, reading. Looking up from her book her aunt had said to her, "Niece Mary, I am right sorry for you, for I see here that your fortune is very hard; you must go a-begging once in your life, either in your youth or in your age." "And therefore," Mary Baynton told her fascinated listeners, "I take it upon me now, in my youth." And telling them she intended to take ship to join the emperor over the sea, she took the coins they offered and went on to the next town.

As the real Mary Tudor read and reread her mother's letter and the exhortations of Jerome in her room at Beaulieu, many a Lincolnshire housewife took comfort in the misguided thought that she had helped to speed the princess to safety in Flanders.

Patience, though I have not
The thing that I require,
I must of force, god wot,
Forbere my moost desire;
For no ways can I finde
To saile against the wynde.

In April of 1534 a celebrated visionary was hanged at Tyburn. She was Elizabeth Barton, called "the holy maid of Kent," and she had been convicted of a peculiar sort of treason. She had dared to announce to the world that God found King Henry's divorce abhorrent, and she had told the king so to his face. Her prophecies threatened Henry's future and the succession at a time when both were in peril. So along with those who encouraged and, in the end, probably coached her in her revelations, the holy maid of Kent was arrested, tried and eventually hanged.

The career of Elizabeth Barton is a fascinating enigma. A woman of undoubted spiritual gifts, she came to be surrounded by opportunists who made her a charlatan. Yet she inspired belief and fear in many highly educated, ordinarily skeptical people. And in some occult way she spoke for the thousands of Henry's subjects who hated what he was doing but had no persuasive means of telling him so. She was both a throwback to an older time and a harbinger of a new era when matters of revelation and faith would once again be central to English life.

The fame of the holy maid began when, at age sixteen or seventeen, she was struck by a severe illness. As she lay in a semi-conscious state she fell into a trance and saw visions of heaven, hell and purgatory, and was able to recognize the departed souls she glimpsed there. In one of these visions she was told to visit a certain shrine of the virgin, and when she was taken there and laid before the virgin's statue, "her face was wonderfully disfigured, her tongue hanging out, and her eyes being in a manner plucked out, and laid upon her cheeks, and so greatly disordered." Witnesses told later how a strange voice was heard coming from her belly, sounding as if it came from within a barrel, speaking "sweetly of heaven and terribly of hell" for some three hours. These events attracted a large crowd, and when after a still longer time the girl awoke with no trace of her former illness the onlookers declared they had witnessed a miracle. The clergy too pronounced Elizabeth Barton's seizure and recovery miraculous, and the story made the rounds of the Kentish countryside both by word of mouth and in the form of a printed book. Further revelations told the holy maid to enter a convent, and shortly after her cure she became a nun at St. Sepulchre's, Canterbury.

Retirement to convent life only increased her fame, and before long she was being petitioned by letter and in person to advise and help all sorts of people. Monks asked her for guidance in their spiritual lives, and for her prayers. Katherine and Mary's supporter Gertrude Blount, marchioness of Exeter, had the "nun of Kent" brought to her to speak of the fate of her unborn child. Her other children had not survived, the marchioness told the nun; she hoped desperately that the one she now carried would live, and asked the holy girl's intercession. Clerics of all ranks came to St. Sepulchre's for advice, impressed by the illiterate nun's ability to speak "divine words" she could only have received through revelations.

For eight years Elizabeth Barton enjoyed growing repute as a revered local oracle. She acquired a "spiritual father," a monk of Christ Church, Canterbury named Edward Bocking, who transcribed the visions she received and in time compiled them into a large book. St. Sepulchre's became renowned through her fame, and she was called upon to give opinions and advice about everything from the spread of the Lutheran heresy to the likelihood of war.

From 1527 on, however, the nun of Kent was consulted most often about the king's divorce. The unambiguous clarity of the nun's pronouncements about this issue was a welcome contrast to the disagreements among lawyers and theologians about the validity of the royal marriage and the indecisiveness of the pope. According to Elizabeth Barton Henry imperiled his soul when he put away his wife, and if he married Anne Boleyn he would not live six months. He was already "so abominable in the sight of God that he was not worthy to tread on hallowed ground," she said. If he took the ultimate step of a second marriage God would destroy him and many others in a plague more devastating than any yet seen in England.

The nun was now receiving messages from an angel, she explained, and the angel instructed her to tell the king in what danger he stood. Whether because he believed in her powers or merely out of deference to her popular reputation Henry ordered Elizabeth Barton brought before him several times. Each time she warned him of the consequences of his sin, and though he didn't find her prophecies alarming enough to make him change his mind about Anne she must have made a strong impression nonetheless, for Henry seems to have offered to make her an abbess. He was angry when she refused his offer, and still angrier when he heard that she claimed to be using her psychic powers to prevent his marriage. In fact the nun's claims to power and supernatural influence escalated as the royal divorce dragged on. She boasted that through clairvoyance she could overhear the king's private conversations, and that she had observed how devils conversed with Anne and put detestable ideas into her mind. Other occult abilities enabled her to prevent ships from leaving the harbor and to free souls from purgatory. Her angelic messages frightened the archbishop of Canterbury so badly that he refused to perform the marriage ceremony for Henry and Anne; thus in a sense she had, as she claimed, prevented their union singlehandedly.

By this time Elizabeth Barton had become the tool of political forces. She was being used by opponents of the divorce, and at least some of her revelations and messages were coming from Father Bocking's pen. Bocking and others, among them pro-Katherine monks of the Observant and Carthusian orders, carried accounts of the nun's prophecies to every courtier and high official who would listen. Mary's former governess Margaret Pole, her chamberlain John Hussey and his wife Anne, Gertrude Blount and other partisans of Katherine and Mary were heartened by the revelations. Thomas More "greatly rejoiced" to hear that in time the injustice done to Katherine would be avenged, but to protect himself he refused to hear anything the holy maid said about the king. Bishop Fisher, who had defended Katherine valiantly in the legatine court in 1529 and continued to be an outspoken opponent of the divorce, wept for joy when the nun's messages were read to him, and pronounced her to be entirely credible.

Until 1533 the holy campaign of the nun of Kent was tolerated. But in that year, when Anne became not only Henry's legal wife but England's crowned queen, the nun's fulminations began to sound dangerously like treason. She was now saying that in marrying Anne Henry had forfeited his right to rule. In God's eyes he was no longer king, and the people were sure to rise up and depose him. He would soon be forced to leave England forever and seek an obscure death among pitiless foreigners. She was certain of these predictions, the nun added, because while in a trance she had been shown both Henry's destiny and the exact place prepared for him in hell. Should anyone doubt the origin of her in-spiration, he had only to hear of a letter she had recently received from Mary Magdalene in heaven, a priceless relic written in characters of gold.

The political menace in these prognostications was unmistakable. With unrest high and Anne's child about to be born, Henry could not afford to spare the famous nun. In July Elizabeth Barton, Father Bocking and a number of others associated with them were arrested and ques-tioned, and all printed accounts of the life and predictions of the holy maid were collected and destroyed. She confessed that some, if not all, of her revelations were fraudulent and nine months later she and her com-panions were hanged.[1]

Far more disturbing to Henry than Elizabeth Barton's visions and prophecies was the broad force of popular mysticism she represented. She belonged to that underworld of folk belief that showed itself at times of public crisis and that followed no causal logic. When she first became a popular oracle the nun of Kent had no intention of feeding discontent or promoting rebellion; to the end of her life she saw herself primarily as God's mouthpiece, fulfilling his will. Though she was eventually ex-ploited by others she came forward initially on her own. There was something uncanny, something of the everpresent supernatural world in her appearance and message, and Henry, knowing that world to be be-yond even his sovereignty, shuddered when he saw the holy maid and tried to put her out of his thoughts.

But though she was the most famous, she was not the only visionary to articulate the workings of the popular imagination. The wife of the former master of Henry's jewel house, Robert Amadas, began in 1533 to spread "ungracious" statements about the king's occult destiny through-out the court. Prophecies known to her for some twenty years were now unfolding, she said. These prophecies foretold how Henry, called the Mouldwarp, was to be "cursed with God's own mouth" and banished, while his kingdom would be conquered by the Scots and divided into four parts. Mistress Amadas kept a painted roll of her predictions, which told of the coming of "the dead man in the island," the deaths of many of Henry's favorites and a great "battle of priests" in which the king would be destroyed.[2] Prophets and oracles were multiplying outside court circles. A clairvoyant living in the household of Sir Henry Wyatt was receiving urgent messages from the supernatural world for Queen Anne throughout 1533, which he delivered to various clerics in her serv-ice.[3] Former supporters of the divorce were dreaming visionary dreams in which they were shown their errors in graphic and terrifying forms.[4] It was as if the vast forces of the invisible world were gathering against the king and speaking their opposition through the ancient seers, loretel-lers and revelatory dreams of folk belief.

What Henry may have sensed was that the nun of Kent and the others represented only the beginning of a ground swell of popular opposition to his rule. He sensed an ever-increasing upsurge of feeling against everything new, everything that challenged tradition and the old ways. And far from conciliating that feeling, Henry was moving faster than ever toward a radical break with the past. For at the very time that Elizabeth Barton and her colleagues were suffering at Tyburn Parliament was preparing legislation so sweeping it would permanently change the church, the faith, and the monarchy.

In 1527 Henry had made the momentous decision to divorce his wife. Now in 1534 he made an even more fateful decision: he would make himself head of the English church. In a series of acts the authority of the pope in England was destroyed and the autonomy of the clergy dissolved. The "bishop of Rome," the lawmakers asserted, had long ago seized powers that rightfully belonged to the king of England as supreme and plenary ruler of all his subjects, lay and clerical alike. Now these powers were restored. The clergy were forbidden to make laws or render judicial decisions without royal permission, and from now on the king himself would choose bishops and abbots, oversee the spiritual health of the monasteries and reform errors in belief. The pope's "false pretended power" was ended once and for all; hereafter Henry would take his place in everything, short of consecrating clergymen and celebrating mass. With his usual habit of confusing self-interest with righteous idealism, Henry convinced himself that these changes were needed in order to free English men and women from the stranglehold of papal rule. Henry was Moses delivering his people from bondage, a selfless ruler carrying out his "sacred duty" to defend the "liberties of his realm and crown."

As he took on the mantle of papal authority in England Henry took on the aura of sacred majesty as well. Since the middle ages English rulers had enjoyed an exalted status somewhere between laymen and priests. Their persons were sanctified by holy oil at their coronations, and they inherited the power to heal persons afflicted with the "king's evil," scrofula, by touching them with their hands. But the lofty eminence Henry now attained was something new. His advisers spoke of him as "excelling among all other human creatures," and ascribed to him the combined virtues of Solomon and Samson. His glory was dazzling. "I dare not cast my eyes but sidewise upon the flaming beams of the king's bright sun," one man wrote to Henry. His will was indistinguishable from the divine will, since he ruled at God's pleasure. Thus he was to be obeyed without "one syllable of exception," no matter what he ordered. "The king is, in this world, without law," a theorist of royal authority declared, "and may at his lust do right or wrong, and shall give accounts but to God only."[5] From here it was only a short step to comparing the king on earth to the king of heaven, and Henry was in fact called the "Son of Man" who carried the divine imprint in his person. The king, Bishop Gardiner wrote, "represents as it were the image of God upon earth," and deserves the reverence and obedience not unlike that which God commands.

No one could have foreseen that, as a result of Henry's conflict with Pope Clement over the status of his marriage, he would one day be pope in his own kingdom, aspiring to godlike eminence. In the beauty, strength and towering height of his physical presence he had fitted the role for a quarter of a century; his new powers were in one sense only a capstone to a symbolic stature established long before. But he now added to the appearance of semi-divine monarchy all that he had learned from a quarter century of rule. And for the last four years it had been personal rule. The giant figure of Wolsey, once pre-eminent in government and statecraft, had fallen victim to Henry's impatience in 1530. Caught between the king's demands and the pope's indecisive delays, Wolsey was forced to resign his offices, handing over to Henry his great seal, his wealth and his gorgeous residence at Hampton Court.

Henry was not yet conscious of the full extent of his might—that consciousness would require years to mature—but his new glory added another dimension to an ego already monumental in its scope. Against his clerical enemies at least he felt himself to be invincible; when other opponents appeared, he would deal with them in their turn. Certainly he need no longer tolerate resistance from the two friendless women who galled him most: his ex-wife and bastard daughter.

The Act of Succession passed in the first parliamentary session of 1534 transferred to Anne's heirs the right to succeed to the throne. Mary, already a bastard, was now excluded by every legal mechanism from the succession. If Anne had no son Elizabeth would be the next ruler. More distressing to contemplate was that, under the provisions of the act, if Henry died while his heir was still a minor Anne would become sole regent of the kingdom; there could be little doubt that as regent her first act would be to order the executions of Mary and her mother.

In anticipation of the parliamentary act Mary's living conditions had undergone a rapid and dramatic change. Late in September of 1533, only a few weeks after Elizabeth's birth, Mary's chamberlain John Hussey was ordered to tell her that the time had come for her to abandon her pretensions and to recognize that she was no longer a princess. No one must call her princess in future, not even her personal servants, and to make the distinction between Mary and her half-sister Princess Elizabeth as clear as possible Mary would live in Elizabeth's household from now on.

Mary immediately protested the informality of this announcement, with no notification in writing from either Henry or his Council, and wrote to the Council that "her conscience would in no wise suffer her to take any other than herself for princess." She would obey the king, she said, in moving to any residence he liked, but to confess to her loss of title would dishonor her parents and "the deed of our mother, the holy church, and the pope, who is the judge in this matter, and none other." The pope had in fact bestirred himself at last. In a decree issued to coincide with the birth of Anne's child he proclaimed Henry's marriage to Anne invalid. The vindication Katherine had been seeking for so many years was finally at hand, though it came far too late to bring any change in her status or treatment. It was a moral victory, but as Clement knew perfectly well, it carried no political weight now that Henry had forced through his own solution. It did not prevent Katherine from remarking afterward that she did not know who was guiltier, Henry for initiating the wickedness of the divorce or Clement for hesitating so long in denying it.

Mary's protest produced an official written order for her to leave her establishment at Beaulieu, referring to her as "the lady Mary, the king's daughter." When she saw it she wrote to her father, signing herself "your most humble daughter, Mary, *Princess*," and pretending to believe the omission was an oversight. "I could not a little marvel" at the letter, she wrote, "trusting verily that your grace was not privy to the same." "For I doubt not that your grace does take me for your lawful daughter, born in true matrimony."

It was a brave response, if a futile one. Without replying to his daughter Henry gave orders that she was to move at once from Beaulieu to a far meaner and smaller residence, in bad repair and open to the fog and rain of autumn. Beaulieu was given to Anne's brother George Boleyn, who lost no time in taking possession of it as if he meant never to leave.

At about this time Mary was visited by a team of commissioners like those who had been sent again and again to Katherine. Mary must have heard from several sources, including Katherine herself, how the former queen had met these persecutors head on and how she had learned to maximize her defense against them. Mary knew to summon her entire household—still some hundred and sixty strong—to hear her exchange with the royal representatives, certain that before so many witnesses they would be forced to weigh their words and to treat her with minimal courtesy. She knew to answer their arguments calmly, point by point, leaving them exhausted with frustration when their "prayers, threats and persuasions innumerable" failed. And thanks to Chapuys, who followed everything that happened to Mary with close attention and wrote it all down for the benefit of the imperial court, Mary was learning that to keep her title she had to watch carefully everything she did and said. The slightest careless word, uttered in the presence of witnesses, might be used later to damage her claim to be called princess; even to acquiesce without protest when others called her by a lesser title could prejudice her rights.

Chapuys drew up for Mary a formal statement of protest, declaring that she had never said, done, or condoned anything detrimental to her status as princess. She was told to keep this document with her at all times, in case she was taken without warning to a place of imprisonment or torture, or compelled to enter a convent or to marry against her will. The ambassador believed that Henry might condemn his daughter to any one of these fates at any time, and besides her written protest he wrote out for her several brief verbal protests which she was to memorize and repeat to anyone who came for her. In essence these statements were elaborations of a single formula which Chapuys hoped would placate Henry yet preserve Mary's birthright—a formula combining submission and defiance. "If the king wished it to be so," she was to say, "she submitted, but she protested in due form against whatever might be done to her prejudice." From now on the repetition of these statements became a part of her daily ritual, like her daily attendance at mass. Surrounded by her most intimate servants, she repeated again and again the words that might make the difference between treasonable disobedience and tolerated self-defense.[6]

Henry was neither so vindictive nor so foolish as Chapuys feared. For the time being at least he would do with Mary what he had originally decided to do in September. She would live in Elizabeth's household at Hatfield, deprived of all marks of her former rank, as a maid of honor in Elizabeth's service. In these surroundings, compelled to show deference to the infant princess and with none of her supporters to turn to, her rebellious spirit would in time be broken.

On December 10 the duke of Norfolk came to carry out the king's orders. He told Mary she must prepare herself to be taken to the residence of Elizabeth, whom he called "princess of Wales." "That is a title which belongs to me by right, and to no one else," Mary replied, pretending to find everything the duke said strange and inappropriate. Norfolk, who saw that the conversation was headed for an impasse, said curtly that "he had not gone thither to dispute, but to see the king's wishes accomplished," and Mary, realizing the moment for her written protest had come, asked for a half hour to herself.

Alone in her bedchamber she took out Chapuys' draft and copied it in her own hand. Returning to Norfolk she handed him the document, and then proceeded to ask what arrangements would be made for her servants when she was transferred to her new quarters. Would her household officers be given a year's wages if they had to be dismissed? How many of her household would accompany her when she moved? What of her maids, her chaplain and confessor? The duke told her that she would find plenty of servants in the new household, and would need very few of her own. A number of Mary's servants had been sent away some weeks earlier, ostensibly for "encouraging her in her disobedience."[7]

The one person who, after her mother, meant most to her, would not be allowed to make the journey to Hatfield. Margaret Pole, countess of Salisbury, who had looked after Mary all her life, was told she would not be needed. She offered to continue to serve Mary at her own expense, and to pay the wages of an entire household if necessary, but Norfolk was adamant. Two maids of honor would be a sufficient retinue for the king's bastard daughter, he said, who had better try to forget her old governess and the hundreds of other familiar faces that had formed a reassuring background to her daily existence for nearly eighteen years.[8]

Just before Christmas Charles Brandon came to take Mary to her new residence. When they arrived at Hatfield there was a repeat of her exchange with the duke of Norfolk earlier in the month. Mary told Brandon that she, and not Elizabeth, was the true princess, and that though she would call Elizabeth "sister," just as she had always called Henry Fitzroy "brother," she would never use the style of princess to refer to anyone but herself. Before he left her, Brandon gave her one final chance to give up her struggle and satisfy her father. He asked whether she had any message for the king. "None," she replied, "except that the princess of Wales, his daughter, asked for his blessing." Brandon blustered and frowned, and said he wouldn't dare deliver that message. "Then," said Mary, "go away and leave me alone."

As soon as Brandon left, Chapuys later reported, Mary went into the room she was to live in for the next several years and wept. It was "the worst lodging of the house," he wrote, and unfit even for a maid of honor.[9] He speculated on the "bad designs" of her new caretakers. What they wanted, he said, was "to cause her to die of grief or in some other way, or else to compel her to renounce her rights, marry some low fellow, or let her fall prey to lust, so that they have a pretext and excuse for disinheriting her." The last suggestion was an odd one, given Mary's upbringing and complete innocence. She was, to be sure, an uncommonly pretty girl about to turn eighteen, and with another girl of eighteen it might have been reasonable to suppose that a lover might succeed in compromising her where threats failed. But Mary was not just any girl. She was the sharp-witted, resolute daughter of a fearsome father and a courageous mother, and she would not be cajoled into surrendering her title any more easily than she would be persuaded to it by force.

The first eight months of Mary's life in Elizabeth's household were the worst. The constant struggle over privilege and precedent was an exhausting irritant. Every time she heard Elizabeth called "princess" she had to object; every time she was called "the lady Mary" she was obliged to remind the speaker that she did not acknowledge that title. Because the infant Elizabeth was given the chair of honor in the dining hall and Mary was assigned an inferior place she refused to eat there and took her meals in her chamber. Later, when Anne heard of this and forbade it, Mary repeated her verbal protest every time she sat down to eat. When Elizabeth was carried along the roads in her velvet litter Mary was forced, complaining loudly, to walk beside her in the mud, or on longer journeys, to ride in the leather-covered litter appropriate to a woman of lower rank.

Whenever Mary protested she was punished, first by the confiscation of all her jewels and fine clothes, then of virtually everything she owned. When she found herself "nearly destitute of clothes and other necessaries," she sent word to Henry of her condition, instructing her messenger to accept either money or clothing if he offered them, "but not to accept any writing in which she was not entitled princess."[10] When all else failed force was used. Late in March the entire household left Hatfield for another house, and when Mary, as usual, refused to travel under any conditions which gave Elizabeth the appearance of higher status "certain gentlemen" seized her bodily and pushed her into the litter of her governess Lady Shelton. Mary, who was not accustomed to being manhandled, gasped out her formula of objection and rode the rest of the way in troubled silence.

Lady Shelton, Anne's aunt, now had complete authority over Mary. If she did not actually come to hate Mary—it is impossible to tell anything of her character from Chapuys' descriptions—she nonetheless felt a strong enough loyalty to the interests of the Boleyn family to play the role of persecutor with thoroughness and vigor. To her credit she resisted this role at the beginning. When George Boleyn and Norfolk first saw her with Mary they were angry at her for treating the girl "with too much respect and kindness," when she deserved only a bastard's abuse. Lady Shelton retorted that even if Mary was only the bastard of a poor gentleman, and not the king, "she deserved honor and good treatment for her goodness and virtues." That Mary could win such praise from Anne's aunt is convincing proof that she was less the stubborn and obstinate ingrate Henry complained of than a young woman of impressive piety and purity of life. But under pressure from Anne and her supporters Lady Shelton became their willing tool. Anne urged her to slap and hit Mary whenever she claimed to be the true princess, and to swear at her "as the cursed bastard she is."[11] Often when visitors came to Hatfield, ostensibly to pay their respects to Elizabeth but hoping to see

Mary as well, her governess locked her in her room and nailed the windows shut.

Beyond this ceaseless mistreatment of her own person Mary's captors added to her anxieties by harassing those around her. Anyone in Elizabeth's household who showed her the slightest humanity was sent away. Anne Hussey, the wife of Mary's former chamberlain John Hussey and a woman who continued to worry over Mary's health and spirits long after she left her service, was arrested and imprisoned in the Tower. Informants reported that on a rare visit she made to Mary at Hatfield she fell back into her old habit of calling her "princess." On one occasion she asked for "drink for the princess," and a day later she said the "princess had gone walking." Under grueling interrogation Mistress Hussey admitted that she had from time to time sent Mary secret notes and received "tokens" from her in return, and she named several others who were sympathetic to her cause. After signing a confession and begging Henry's forgiveness she was released, but the incident caused Mary nearly as much anguish as it did Anne Hussey herself, and the revelations about clandestine messages led Lady Shelton to keep a stricter watch on her charge.[12]

Henry had suspected for some time that Mary was being encouraged in her continued resistance by letters smuggled in and out through a go-between. The logical suspect was Mary's only servant, a young chambermaid whose name has not been preserved but whom Chapuys acknowledged as his channel of news and messages. Through her he sent Mary letters from Katherine and news from his own sources, and received in turn the brief notes Mary wrote him in the moments when she was not being watched. The maid had refused to swear an oath of fidelity to the Act of Succession, and only after she was locked in her room and told she would be sent to the Tower unless she swore to it did she relent.[13] Less than a month later Henry questioned Lady Shelton about the maid, and this time she was sent away. Mary was "much grieved at this," Chapuys wrote, since the girl had nowhere to go and no money, and because "she was the only one in whom she [Mary] had confidence."[14]

One day in the third month of her time at Hatfield Mary had a most alarming visitor: Anne Boleyn, now Queen Anne. The two women had not seen one another since Anne became queen, and the meeting was traumatic for them both. For Anne, it meant facing the young woman whose mother she had hurt and dishonored, and whose own life and prospects she had all but destroyed. For Mary, it meant confronting the woman who was the "scandal of Christendom," the woman who had broken up her family and alienated her father's affection, and whose baby daughter now held the honors that by right were Mary's own.

Anne was at first civil, asking Mary to come to court and pay her respects, and saying that if Mary would honor her as queen she would at-

tempt to reconcile her to Henry. Anne promised to intercede for Mary
and to see that she was "as well or better treated than ever." Mary's reply
was equally polite, though her face betrayed unspoken rage. "She knew
of no queen in England but her mother," she said, but if Anne was
willing to speak to Henry in her behalf she would appreciate it. Anne
repeated her offer, emphasizing the benefits of the king's favors and the
dangers of his anger, but Mary was unmoved. In the end Anne became
angry, and left swearing that "she would bring down the pride of this
unbridled Spanish blood" if it was the last thing she ever did.[15]

Chapuys' informers at Henry's court made it clear that she fully intended to carry out her threat. Not long after the tense interview between Anne and Mary a "person of good faith" told the ambassador that
he had heard Anne say more than once that as soon as Henry was out of
the country, leaving her as regent, she meant to use her authority to have
Mary killed, "either by hunger or otherwise." When her brother warned
her that Henry's wrath would be monumental, Anne answered defiantly
that she would do it anyway, even if it meant the worst conceivable punishment, "even if she were burned alive for it after."[16]

Henry's behavior toward his daughter was on the whole as implacably
hostile as Anne's. He too referred to Mary's "obstinate Spanish blood,"
and gave at least one diplomatic envoy the impression that he hated her
thoroughly.[17] He tortured her by coming to Hatfield often to see his
other daughter and ordering Mary to be shut in her room throughout his
stay. From Lady Shelton Mary heard a frightening report that the king
had said he would have her beheaded for violating the law in refusing to
acknowledge the Act of Succession, and according to Chapuys, she was
convinced by this news that she must indeed prepare to die.[18]

But Henry was capricious, if not exactly ambivalent, in his attitude
toward his daughter. When he complained of her stubbornness to the
French ambassador, who remarked that she was nonetheless a girl of
good breeding and virtue, his eyes filled with tears and he had to agree.
Like Anne, he tried at least once to bribe Mary, offering to give her "a
royal title and dignity" and to restore her to favor if only she would lay
aside her claims. She refused, but the offer was tantalizing. Though her
loyalty to Katherine was primary, some part of her must have longed to
give in to the father she feared, despised and loved. His changeability tortured her, however, just as his well-known insincerity left her bewildered.

One incident haunted her memory for the rest of her months at
Hatfield. On one of Henry's visits Mary, who had been ordered not to go
near the room where her father was, sent word to him begging to be allowed to kiss his hand. Her entreaty was denied, but just as he was
mounting his horse to leave she slipped away from her guards and went

up to a terrace on the roof to watch him go. Someone may have told him she was there, or he may have caught sight of her by mere chance, but when he looked up to the terrace he saw Mary, on her knees, her hands clasped together in supplication. If he was moved at the sight he did not show it, but he did not ignore Mary either. With a gesture that lay somewhere between simple courtesy and fatherly affection he nodded his head and touched his hat to her before he rode off toward London.[19]

XII

 My thought oppressed, my mynd in trouble,
My body languishing, my hart in payn;
My joyes, dystres; my sorows dowble;
My lyffe as one that dye would fayne;
Myn eyes for sorow salt ters doth rayne:
Thus do I lyve in gret hevenes
Withowte hope or comfort off redresse.

Two weeks before her nineteenth birthday Mary Tudor fell desperately ill. Henry waited six days before doing anything to help her, but
he finally summoned Chapuys and informed him of her danger. He
wanted the ambassador to send doctors of his own choosing to visit Mary
along with the royal physicians. If Mary died the king wanted the blame
to fall as heavily on the imperial doctors as on his own. He told Chapuys
that his physicians had pronounced Mary's disease incurable, adding that
because of this Katherine's physician had refused to leave his patient in
order to diagnose Mary's condition.

The imperial ambassador was alarmed. He knew of Mary's illness
from his own sources, but the story he pieced together was very
different from the account Henry gave. According to Chapuys' informants, Henry's chief physician Dr. Butts told the king Mary's illness was indeed grave, but not incurable. Without good care she
might not survive, Dr. Butts said, but all she really needed was to
be released from the climate of anxiety and persecution in which Henry
kept her. Chapuys had learned too that all the physicians were convinced
Henry meant his daughter to die, and that the king was using their fears
to forestall a cure. His own doctors refused to treat Mary unless
Katherine's Spanish physician was present and involved in the treatment;
the Spaniard in turn refused even to attempt a cure unless Mary was
brought to live near her mother, believing that their separation was what

harmed Mary most. Chapuys himself hesitated to send doctors, fearing that their failure might prejudice the imperial cause. Paradoxically, the sicker Mary became the less likely she was to be treated, for no doctor was eager to risk having to take responsibility for her death.

As the days passed Mary's condition grew worse as a result of neglect and "continued vexation," and the ambassador feared it might very well "carry her off." He did what he could from a distance. He was not allowed to see Mary, who was at Greenwich under Lady Shelton's untender care, but he sent his servants every day to find out how she was, and kept himself far better informed than the king about the stages of her illness. He pestered Henry's chief secretary Cromwell with such persistence that in the end Cromwell arranged for Dr. Butts to attend Mary. At court he tried to counteract Henry's tale of incurable disease with truthful rumors of his own. But the king chose to be pessimistic, and his courtiers and councilors followed his lead. Several Council members approached Chapuys to remark that since no human agency had been able to reconcile Charles and Henry, God would "open a door" by taking Mary to himself.

Behind Chapuys' anxiety, the doctors' hesitancy and the resignation of the councilors was the unspoken fear of poison. Everyone remembered Anne's threats against Mary all too clearly; no one was willing to be implicated in a poison plot. The suddenness and gravity of Mary's sickness pointed to a toxic dose of some sort in her food or drink, and the fact that she had no food taster had long been a source of worry to Katherine and Chapuys. Henry's seeming unconcern about his daughter's condition—Chapuys believed he was actually pleased at it—certainly meant that, if there was a plot to poison her, he did not oppose it.

Only one person had nothing to lose by nursing Mary in what might be her last illness: her mother. She wrote to Chapuys, asking him to beg Henry to let her care for their daughter at the house where she was staying. Katherine was at Kimbolton, once a duke's residence but now a decaying ruin with buckling walls and weed-choked grounds.[1] She was none too well herself; Kimbolton was a notoriously unhealthy place, and in addition to her real infirmities Henry was spreading rumors that his former wife was both dropsical and demented. But she offered to treat Mary "with her own hands" nonetheless, putting her in her own bed and watching her night and day. Like many at court she "had great suspicion as to the cause" of Mary's illness, and knew she might not recover. If God took Mary while she was in Katherine's care, she wrote, "her heart would rest satisfied; otherwise in great pain."[2]

Henry's response was a tantalizing compromise. Mary would be moved nearer Kimbolton, but she and Katherine could not meet. By the time Mary was moved she was already beginning to improve slightly. The doctors bled her at least twice, and when it looked as though she might recover Katherine's Spanish apothecary, who had been prescribing Mary's medicines for four years, came forward with pills and draughts.

When she was able to write Mary sent word to Chapuys, urging him to ask the emperor to intercede with her father on her behalf. Surely after what she had been through he would allow Mary and Katherine the comfort of each other's company, especially if Charles requested it. What Mary did not say was that, coupled with the strain of her illness, the hostility of her jailers was becoming unbearable. Chapuys heard from his informants how, as Mary lay helpless and in pain, Lady Shelton and others in the household said in her hearing that they hoped she would die. Her death would promote peace, they told one another, while incidentally ridding them of the inconvenience of looking after her.[3]

It may have been a death threat of a more formal kind that brought on Mary's malady in the first place. The Succession Act was being enforced with greater rigor than ever, and those who refused to swear to uphold it faced execution. Late in 1534 Mary was told that she must take the oath, and that if she called herself princess or her mother queen even once she would be sent to the Tower.[4] Clearly Henry meant to do what he said. Several prominent opponents of the divorce, including John Fisher, bishop of Rochester and the former chancellor Thomas More, were already imprisoned, and their numbers were growing. Throughout January the danger to Mary had increased. Katherine's physician warned her that Henry was determined to make Mary swear to the statutes passed against Katherine and herself, and that her refusal would mean either death or life imprisonment.[5] The warning was passed along to Mary; a few days afterward she fell ill.

Though it was by far the most serious it was by no means Mary's first serious illness. She had been troubled on and off since 1531 with pains in her head and stomach, and had sometimes been unable to keep her food down for eight or ten days at a time.[6] Katherine's physician and apothecary had always been called in to treat her, except on one occasion when treatment by an unfamiliar doctor led to unfortunate results. In September of 1534 Mary had complained of headaches and indigestion, and an apothecary Lady Shelton brought in gave her pills, "after which she was very sick and he so much troubled that he said he would never minister anything to her alone."[7] Henry's physician Dr. Butts heard what happened when he came to examine Mary afterward, and wrote to Cromwell explaining the entire matter. Mary, who lived in dread at the best of times, probably thought she had been given poison, and Chapuys was at first certain of it. The apothecary was probably innocent, and Mary's aggravated condition could have been anything from a simple allergic reaction to the drug in the pills to a psychosomatic response to an imagined menace. But however innocuous the circumstances actually were, the incident left its mark, and made Mary afraid to get sick again. And because every added fear put added strain on her health, it undoubtedly helped to bring on her grave illness the following February.

Mary did not recover completely from this onslaught. Late in March she was still convalescent, and having to keep a special diet in order to avoid repeated relapses. She needed meat first thing in the morning, and was allowed to take a large breakfast instead of waiting until the middle of the day to eat a meat dish as was customary in Elizabeth's household.[8] But although she was permitted this special favor Mary was by no means out of political danger. Cromwell was dropping dark hints to Chapuys, asking the ambassador what real harm Mary's death might do, even if it did offend the people and temporarily annoy the emperor. After all, Cromwell pointed out, Mary was the cause of all her father's problems; any sensible observer would understand why he wanted to be rid of her. Cromwell stopped just short of wishing Mary dead, but his meaning was clear.

Henry expressed the same sentiments with a vengeance. When Mary had a serious relapse in mid-March, Henry proclaimed himself anxious to see her "as a father should," but once he arrived at Greenwich he spoke only with Lady Shelton and the waiting women, not with Mary herself, nor did he consult her doctors. When Dr. Butts took it upon himself to come before the king unbidden Henry accused him of disloyalty; he was exaggerating Mary's illness, Henry said, in order to promote her political interests and have her moved to Kimbolton. From there the two women would raise a revolt against him. Again the specter of Isabella troubled Henry's mind. Katherine was so "haughty in spirit," he blustered, that she might "raise a number of men and make war, as boldly as did queen Isabella her mother." The idea was not at all farfetched, since both Katherine and Mary had more than enough fortitude to lead an army along with the heroism to inspire it. But even if Katherine had been in good health, which she was not, her announced determination to obey Henry in all things saving her conscience would have prevented her from even the most trivial breach of faith. And without Katherine's acquiescence it was hard to imagine Mary acting alone.

With his imagination dominated by fantasies of rebellion Henry was in no mood to console his daughter, or to allow her the comfort of his presence. Instead he sent word to her through Lady Shelton that she was his "worst enemy," and that he knew her behavior was part of a calculated plot to turn his subjects against him. She had already succeeded in turning most of the Christian princes of Europe against him, he raged; what could she expect from him but anger and vengeance?[9]

To the extent that Henry sensed rebellion in the air he was not far wrong. For a year and more Chapuys had been receiving visits, messages and encouraging indications of other kinds from dozens of nobles eager to take up arms against Henry and in defense of Katherine and Mary. Their grievances ranged from personal injuries and resentments to broad political and religious issues. Thomas Dacre, former warden of the Western Marches, was incensed at his recent trial for treason; his acquittal showed the solidarity of the peers in the face of unpopular royal policies. Lord Dacre was only one of a large group of northern nobles—one lord told Chapuys there were some sixteen hundred of them—pledged to support any armed attempt to force Henry to give up Anne, reverse his blasphemous religious legislation and restore Katherine and Mary to their rightful status.

All those who hoped for an armed rising in the countryside welcomed the news of dissension and dissatisfaction at court. Henry and Anne now quarreled frequently and bitterly, and even those who hated Anne most for what she had done to Katherine and Mary had to admit that she had now entered a purgatory of her own. To say that Henry tired of Anne after Elizabeth's birth fails to do justice to her enduring attraction for him, an attraction which never really faded and which he eventually attributed to witchcraft. But soon after their marriage Henry had taken up again the round of flirtations, seductions and romantic intrigues that had characterized his life with Katherine. Anne became one love among many, and when she protested Henry simply refused to be moved by her agonized pleas for fidelity and told her to stay in her place.

Anne's strongest hold on her husband was the possibility that she might give him a son, and in the spring of 1534 she told him she was pregnant again. For a few months their life together resumed its old course, but when in early summer Anne had to admit that she had been mistaken about the child Henry's vengeance was swift. He took as his mistress an old love, a "very beautiful damsal" of the court whose identity is unclear but whose loyalty to Katherine and Mary suggests that she was allied with the growing anti-Boleyn faction.[10] Anne's sister-in-law tried to break up the affair but the king banished her from court, and Chapuys noted that Anne grew more subdued and unsettled the longer the infatuation lasted.

There can be little doubt that Henry wanted revenge. He felt cheated by Anne's false pregnancy, and he attacked her both by putting another woman ahead of her in his affections and by insulting her child's primacy in the succession. For the first time since she joined Elizabeth's household Mary became the object of an official visit by the principal courtiers. At Henry's request, "nearly all the gentlemen and ladies of the court" paid their respects to her at the country house where she and Elizabeth were staying, and when she left for Richmond she was riding in a velvet litter just like Elizabeth's.[11] The significance of the courtiers' visit and the velvet litter was not lost on Anne, who was "greatly annoyed" at Mary's temporary promotion in rank and even more put out to learn that Henry's new favorite had sent the king's daughter an encouraging message. She was Mary's true friend and devoted servant, she said, and she urged Mary to look for a favorable change in her circumstances in the near future.[12] Anne's renewed protests at these incidents were received coldly. Henry told his wife that she would do well to feel thankful for her present rank and luxury, adding frankly that if he had it to do over again he would not marry her.[18] The implied threat was clear enough. He had divorced one wife; he could divorce another.

Chapuys' dispatches during this period show Anne as a calculating murderess with limitless opportunities to strike out at her enemies. He reported her conflicts with Henry, but he always added that she knew so well how to handle the king that in the end she invariably came out ahead. Other observers, who were not so severely biased by loyalty to Henry's ex-queen, saw Anne differently. Behind her scheming they saw desperation and fear; behind her mistreatment of Mary they perceived a struggle to preserve the rights of her own child. Anne was queen and Elizabeth princess, but only at Henry's sufferance. No European sovereign acknowledged Anne's title, and at every court where Katherine was pitied Anne was called "the Concubine" or "the Great Whore." If Henry decided to put her aside, no church, no government, no lawyer would come to her defense. Her relatives would disown her, and her few remaining friends at court would denounce her more loudly than her enemies. A French envoy who visited Henry's court in the month of Mary's severe illness, February of 1535, wrote that Anne was severely restricted in her movements and in some fear for her safety. Her looks betrayed anxiety and nervous exhaustion, he said. He described how she had sought him out and confided to him that her position had become even more tenuous than it had been before her marriage. She was being watched so closely she could neither speak freely nor write to anyone, she whispered, and then left him so abruptly that he felt certain she was not exaggerating her predicament.[14]

Anne's relations had begun to treat her as shabbily as the king did. In their determination to preserve their own interests they brought to court Margaret Shelton, daughter of Lady Shelton and Anne's cousin, hoping that she would become Henry's next mistress. Margaret did supplant the unknown girl who had encouraged Mary, but not for long. New flirtations followed, including Henry's revived fascination with the daughter of a Wiltshire gentleman, Jane Seymour. Henry did not abandon Anne entirely, of course, but though she still gave him pleasure at times he was coming to feel trapped by his marriage, and disappointed that his wife had produced only a daughter. Anne knew where her salvation lay. More than anything in the world, she told a lady of the French court, she wanted a son.

Heartened by every sign of discord and especially by Henry's disfavor toward Anne, dissatisfied nobles pressed Chapuys harder than ever. Lord Bray asked the ambassador to obtain for him the exact wording of a prognostication circulating in Flanders to the effect that Henry would face a widespread revolt in 1535. He meant to send the prophecy to all the conspirators, and with it a code they might use to correspond secretly with one another. All they needed was a show of military support from the emperor. The appearance of a few imperial ships at the mouth of the Thames, filled with seasoned troops, would send the government into a panic. Meanwhile a tough company of German mercenaries, led by trusted officers and backed up by arms and ammunition, could be landed in the north to signal the start of the rising.

Chapuys forwarded the urgent pleas of the rebel lords to his master, knowing that for the time being, Charles' own military situation did not permit him to intervene in English affairs. He was currently engaged in a dramatic attempt to reconquer lands seized by the Ottoman Turks in central Europe and North Africa, and he had continually to be on the alert against the French. Neither his sympathies nor his political interests were directed toward England, and the family ties Katherine and Mary counted on so heavily were for Charles only one small piece in an intricate political puzzle. It is hard to avoid the conclusion that, where Katherine was concerned, the emperor saw little reason to take any action whatever, particularly now that Henry had married Anne and started a new family with her. As for Mary, there were remedies short of war which could solve her difficulties. Marriage to a respectable prince—preferably one with strong ties to imperial interests—would accomplish several objectives without leading to conflict. It would remove her from her semi-captivity, it would help to initiate a rapprochement between Henry and Charles, and it would shut the mouths of those who continued to criticize Henry for dishonoring his daughter.

Chapuys did not pass on Charles' true strategy to the English rebels. Instead he gave them every encouragement short of what they wanted most to hear: that imperial ships and arms were on the way. In actuality there was no need for help from any continental power. There were more than enough disaffected nobles and commoners within England to make a strong showing against Henry's forces. But they lacked leadership. Katherine, their natural leader, refused to abandon her oath of obedience to Henry, and no other figure appeared with the determination or quickening energy to trigger the revolt. The moment came and, through inaction, was lost.

As the lords of the Marches were struggling to bring the revolt into being the pivotal figure in their plans fell ill. Like the emperor's potential involvement in the rising, Mary's health was among the imponderables of the insurrection. She had not been entirely well since about the age of fourteen, when with the onset of puberty she began to experience symptoms of a disorder known to Renaissance doctors as "strangulation of the womb" or "suffocation of the mother." These violent terms described several distinct complaints grouped together in a paramedical theory about female sexuality. The separate symptoms were, first, the irregularity or cessation of menstrual periods, or amenorrhea. A depressed mental state characterized by "heaviness, fear and sorrowfulness" was another indication of the general disorder, as were difficulty in breathing and swelling and pain in the abdominal region.

In young unmarried women like Mary any one of a wide range of symptoms could point to strangulation of the womb: "headache, nauseousness, vomiting, want of appetite, longing, an ill habit of body, difficulty of breathing, trembling of the heart, swooning, melancholy, fearful dreams" and "watching, with sadness and heaviness."[15] Sixteenth-century doctors, like their predecessors in antiquity, believed that these afflictions were brought on by sexual abstinence. Every woman, whatever her age, rank or degree of virtue, was at the mercy of her voracious uterus—what for centuries had been called the "raging womb." Widows, or wives suddenly deprived of the "company of a man," fell into an aggrieved state of melancholy and were troubled with amenorrhea. Even young girls who were kept strictly away from men suffered pain, mental anguish and irregular menstruation, and the only satisfactory cure was marriage.

Widows suffering from strangulation of the womb were urged to marry again; wives were advised to engage in "wanton copulation" with their husbands. Physicians told the parents of young girls to arrange matches for them without delay, and in the meantime to send them out riding for several hours a day. More bizarre remedies were also recommended. A woman in a near-catatonic state was laid on her back, her clothes loosened and her hair hanging free around her shoulders. Calling her name in a loud voice, the doctor seized her by the hair and yanked it until she regained consciousness. At the same time he pulled at her pubic hair, both to increase the pain and to "draw downwards" the "sharp and malign vapor" that was ascending from the womb and threatening to damage the other organs. Another common treatment was uterine fumigation. A medicated pessary, a curved cylindrical tube, rounded at one end, made of gold or silver and perforated at the closed end with a number of small holes, was inserted into the patient's vagina, closed end first. Fastened in place by means of cords tied around the waist, it allowed steam from a vessel of boiling liquid to reach the mouth of the uterus and, so the doctors thought, alleviate its unnatural state. Along with horseback riding, fumigation was the method of treatment most often prescribed for "bashful and shamefaced" young maidens; matrons underwent the horrifying treatment of having horse-leeches inserted into the neck of the womb.[16]

As Mary lived through her adolescence, along with the racking anxieties of her own and her mother's situation she had to come to terms with the dangers and indignities of recurrent strangulation of the womb as well. No record of the specific treatments she was given survives, but it is certain that she followed the recommended therapy of daily horseback rides, and that when she joined Elizabeth's household these rides stopped. Her horses were taken away along with her fine clothes and jewels, and this change in the pattern of her daily exercise cannot have improved her general health.

The fact that Katherine knew at first hand what her daughter's illness meant made their separation especially painful. In a letter to Cromwell Katherine said she had been "ill of the same sickness" as Mary, and a curious document unearthed during the legal battle over the divorce confirms her claim. It was a memorandum headed "Questions to be asked of those persons who know the circumstances of the marriage of queen Katherine of England," and it listed specific points to be raised with legal witnesses who had reason to know whether or not Katherine came to Henry as a virgin. Among the queries was one asking whether, after Arthur's death, Katherine was "weak and crippled, and discharged humors from her mouth." Weakness in the limbs and some sort of oral discharge were among the symptoms of strangulation of the womb, and the physicians who examined Katherine after her marriage to Arthur agreed on the common diagnosis of the "raging womb," its passion unassuaged because the girl was still a virgin. Their recommendation, according to the document, was that Katherine marry a "competent person," namely Henry; the disappearance of her symptoms after her marriage to Henry showed that their prognosis was correct.[17]

Remembering her own discomfort, and the obstetrical complications linked with it that plagued her during the first fifteen years or so of her marriage, Katherine knew what Mary was going through and what reassurance she could offer her. If Mary came to Kimbolton, she wrote to Cromwell, "the comfort and cheerfulness she would have with me would be half her cure." "I have found this by experience," she added, hoping to add a slightly clinical tone to her request.

But Henry was firm. Mary was not allowed to go to her mother, or even to come within thirty miles of her forsaken residence during the critical weeks of her illness in February of 1535. Katherine was half prepared to hear that her daughter had died when the news finally reached her that Mary had passed the crisis point and was recovering at Greenwich.

XIII

 They did robe and spoule al the Kynges frendes
They called them heretikes with spight and disdayne
They toffled a space lyke tirantes and F[e]indes
They put some in preson and sume to greate payne.

It was during Mary's convalescence that the most outrageous executions of the English Reformation were carried out. The priors of three Carthusian monasteries and a Brigittine monk of Sion were tried and convicted of treason, taken to Tyburn and hanged. They were hanged in their religious dress, an unheard-of affront to the entire religious community and an unprecedented departure from judicial custom. The brutality of their treatment was also unusual, even in an age of brutal executions. They were cut down from the gallows still living; their torsos were slit open and their vital organs torn out. Afterward their beheaded corpses were paraded through the streets, the severed heads and feet displayed at the city gates and the remains burned.

The execution of the traitorous monks was given highly visible endorsement by the court. The duke of Norfolk, Thomas Boleyn (now earl of Wiltshire), and Henry Fitzroy were prominent among the spectators, along with other courtiers, and the notables were careful to stand near the scaffold where they could be seen to greatest advantage by the crowd. The king's chamberlain Henry Norris clattered into the throng with an escort of forty mounted men. Five strangers disguised as Scots Borderers, their visors lowered to hide their faces, watched the bloody proceedings from a distance. When one of them temporarily lost his visor and was recognized as the duke of Norfolk's brother speculation began about the identity of the others. It was noticed that all the courtiers showed unusual reverence to the disguised men, and this, plus the persistent rumor that the king wanted to witness the event in person, led to the widespread belief that one of the Borderers was Henry himself.[1]

The four monks were only the first in a series of victims of judicial murder. Within weeks three other Carthusians were apprehended and imprisoned, and awaited their trial fastened in a standing position against the dungeon wall. Iron collars pinned them at the neck and iron fetters bound their feet. For seventeen days they could neither sit nor lie prone, and their chains were never "loosed for any natural necessity." Finally they too were tried, condemned and hanged.

Three days later the crowd witnessed an even stranger spectacle. The spare, ascetic bishop of Rochester, John Fisher, was brought to Tower Hill to face the executioner's sword. Thousands came to see him die, few of them believing him capable of the treason for which he had been condemned. Fisher was in fact guilty of the treasonable act of writing letters to Charles V inviting him to invade England, but in his own view he was acting in response to a higher logic than that of the law. Summoning an imperial invasion was a means of saving the lives of Katherine and Mary and, even more important, saving the Catholic church in England. As Fisher told those who crowded around the scaffold, "Christian people, I come hither to die for the faith of Christ's holy Catholic church."[2]

In executing the bishop of Rochester Henry was committing the greater sacrilege of killing a cardinal of the Roman church; Fisher had been raised to the cardinalate during his imprisonment. Londoners who looked up at the bishop's bony head, impaled on a pike on London Bridge, believed their king had killed a saint as well. The head did not decay. Day after day the sober features continued to look down "sadly and constantly" on passers-by with the same expression the bishop had worn in life. Another grisly execution came and went, this time the killing of the revered humanist Thomas More, and still Fisher's skull-like head kept its reproving vigil. Finally, when the inevitable talk of a miracle began, the head was taken down and dropped in the river.

From a procedural point of view the nine victims were unarguably guilty of treason. They had refused to take the required oath to uphold the succession, thereby making their loyalty to the king and his designated heir, the Princess Elizabeth, open to serious question. It made no difference that what the nine men objected to was not Parliament's right to change the succession but the phraseology of the oath. Its wording contained an explicit denial of papal authority, and this, they pointed out, was a matter unrelated to the succession and offensive to their consciences.

Yet their protest came at a time when the oath was being enforced with greater rigor than ever. In November of 1534 a parliamentary edict

specified its wording in greater detail and spelled out the procedures surrounding its enforcement. To refuse to swear, this new law stated, was
tantamount to being convicted of treason, since a certificate of refusal
signed by two of the commissioners administering the oath had the same
weight as a treason indictment arrived at by twelve jurors. Fisher and
More, who were already in prison, had been unmoved by this new threat,
and when the Carthusian priors met at the London Charterhouse near
Smithfield and announced their opposition to the oath Cromwell had
them arrested and taken to the Tower. They were accused, along with
the learned Bridgettine Richard Reynolds, of denying that Henry VIII
was head of the English church. They argued at their trial that to affirm
the king's headship of the church was to challenge the pope's authority.
Yet papal primacy was essential to the salvation of every believer. No
manmade law could cancel out this overriding truth of the church, they
claimed, and they were prepared to die rather than sin by forswearing it.
At the monks' trial the lines were clearly drawn on both sides. The king
and the royal Council, who until now had stopped short of carrying
through their threats to punish with death those who refused to swear,
decided not to hesitate any longer. From early in May to the middle of
July the news out of England was filled with accounts of trials, executions and martyrs to the faith.

On the continent, churchmen and devout laymen were horrified. In
Italy, the bishop of Faenza, papal nuncio, recorded the account that
reached him, describing how the English king had caused "certain
religious men" to be "ripped up in each other's presence, their arms torn
off, their hearts cut out and rubbed upon their mouths and faces."[3] This
outrageous king who had badly mistreated his wife and daughter and
made his brazen mistress queen now made it plain that he was capable of
monstrous cruelty to religious men as well. Opponents of Lutheran and
other reforming doctrines condemned Henry for assaulting the true
church, while even ardent Lutherans deplored the executions of Fisher
and More. Fisher had after all agreed with Luther in upholding the validity of Henry's marriage to Katherine, while More's humanist writings
and teachings were held in the highest respect by the scholars of the
Protestant movements. And believers of every sort found the executions
of the monks repugnant in the extreme. That peaceful, withdrawn men
of prayer who wore hair shirts, denied themselves meat and drank wine
so watered it had no color presented a threat to the security of Henry's
throne was beyond credibility. The only possible explanation was that
Henry was mad.

A form of madness, it seemed, hung over all the sovereigns of Europe
in the middle 1530s. The specter of religious dissent, first conjured by
Luther at the Diet of Worms, was growing ever larger and more menac-

ing. There were now not only Lutherans to contend with but Zwinglians, Calvinists, and a swarm of nameless congregations each claiming to possess theological truth. The established governments saw in each of these pockets of unorthodox belief an incitement to political rebellion, and as they proliferated government servants, clerics of the old faith and the rulers themselves grew more and more severe in their response. Only a few days after the martyrdom of the English Carthusians three Lutherans were burned at the stake in Paris, and one of them, a Fleming who insisted to the end that he was right and his persecutors wrong, was slowly roasted alive. The French king Francis reportedly joined a religious procession marching to the site of a mass execution of Protestants and, with his sons, had stayed on to watch the torturing and burning. His presence was taken to be a sign of complete royal approval of the policy of burning heretics, and his example was followed in other capitals.[4]

In Catholic countries the Inquisition was called upon to step up its age-old process of weeding out the tares in the spiritual vineyards, and the numbers of those holding erroneous opinions who were "relaxed" to secular governments for burning leaped upward in the third and fourth decades of the century. But even in regions where the Protestants made themselves a majority—as in Calvinist Geneva, the Zwinglian cantons of Switzerland and the Lutheran territories under Charles V's rule—men and women of differing views were subjected to savage repression. Of all these dissidents the most feared were those their opponents called Anabaptists, congregations whose belief in the necessity of adult baptism radically alienated them both from the faith of Rome and the doctrines of other Protestants. In Catholic and Protestant lands alike Anabaptists were mutilated, drowned, garroted, burned and suffocated without mercy. Their lands were seized, their houses torn down, their children driven off to beg their bread.

The fear the Anabaptists attracted was increased manyfold by their remarkable reign over the town of Münster in Westphalia in 1534 and 1535. Here a group of Anabaptists led by a Haarlem baker and a tailor from Leyden took over the town council and expelled all citizens who refused rebaptism. The fleeing townspeople had to leave behind all their goods, and after the enforced exodus a minority of perhaps fourteen thousand of the regenerate, most of them laborers or craft workers, found themselves in possession of a large town and an even larger armory and treasury. The baker, Jan Mattys, immediately set about to organize the defense of the new community of saints, which was under attack by its nominal overlord the bishop of Münster. Filled with a sudden certainty that he could repeat the miracle of Gideon in the book of Judges and defeat the besieging armies with only twenty men, Mattys left the protection of the town walls and assaulted the enemy. He was killed on sight, but his death did nothing to decrease the enthusiasm of the Anabaptist flock. Instead it brought into prominence the more colorful and charismatic figure of Jan of Leyden, a fascinating opportunist who soon turned Münster into a spectacular parody of contemporary government and religion.

In a matter of days Münster became a biblical city, ruled by elders and committed to Old Testament morality. All existing laws, authorities and family relationships were swept away, and a new order brought in. Jan of Leyden proclaimed polygamy to be the natural state of mankind, sanctioned by the prophets, and set an example to his followers by taking seventeen wives. Among them was the widow of his predecessor Jan Mattys, a former nun named Divara, who was said to be the most beautiful woman in the city. Superimposed on this patriarchal society was an elaborate imitation of the regalia and ceremonial of a royal court. Jan of Leyden became King Jan, and his principal wife Queen Divara. There were chamberlains, stewards and marshals of the court, and the king's sixteen lesser wives served as matrons of honor to the queen. Plundered vestments and hangings from all the churches of the town provided the finery for the courtiers, and when King Jan rode through the town on one of his thirty-one splendid horses he wore a gown of cloth of silver, lined with crimson and ornamented with gold thread. Two pages, one bearing a Bible and the other a naked sword, formed his mounted escort; one of these boys was a son of the bishop of Münster, captured when the Anabaptists first seized the town. King Jan wore a rich gold crown and a jeweled orb, the insignia of royalty, with the motto "King of justice for the whole world," and both he and his attendants spoke in the most grandiose terms about the day when his rule over the remnant population of a Westphalian town would be transformed into sovereignty over the entire world.

That Henry was known to be pleased by the Anabaptist take-over in Münster made his own recent alterations in religion seem all the more radical. Henry did not sympathize with the theological views of the Münster rebels, but the fact that they were an irritant to Charles V's sister Mary, regent of the Netherlands, made them useful allies in his enduring contest with imperial interests. He came very close to making overtures to King Jan during that monarch's brief reign, and lost much of his credit with more moderate Protestant leaders in the process. In the same month that he began executing Catholics he tried to restore that credit by burning fourteen Anabaptist refugees who had recently come to England from Holland, but the gesture was forgotten in the uproar that followed the more scandalous executions.[5]

However hard he might have tried to temper or disguise it Henry was swiftly making England a Protestant country, and the deaths of the Catholic martyrs were a harsh but inescapable milestone along that path. The king's own views had certainly changed. The onetime arch-opponent of Luther now regretted his harsh stand, and fostered the view that he had written his treatise against Luther under duress. He ordered the distribution of a letter by Luther arguing that Wolsey and other clerics had been behind the entire venture, and tried to clear himself of involvement in the affair.[6]

To be sure, Henry's altered attitude toward Lutheranism was rooted in political expediency. He was seeking allies among the enemies of the empire; many of those enemies were Lutheran. In the summer of 1534 he welcomed embassies from the Lutheran free cities of Hamburg and Lübeck with great pomp, and as they rode upriver in the royal barge Londoners remarked on the bright red liveries of the Lübeckers, with their motto of indomitability, "If God be for us, who can be against us?" In breaking with the pope and casting his lot with the continental Protestants Henry was putting English trade and commerce in jeopardy, and even risking the possibility of food shortages among his subjects. The commercial repercussions of English diplomacy were widespread. English merchants in Flanders, Spain and France found their markets so hostile they had no choice but to sell their wares and come home. Those who stayed were abused, boycotted or robbed, and their rights under the law of nations governing international trade were ignored. Even the English fleets that fished off Iceland and Newfoundland were liable to be attacked or sent home by agents of the Danish king.

There were those who argued that until the conflict between England and the pope was ended the English people forfeited their place in Christendom. This highly abstract view had little direct impact on the practical lives of the English, but it did lend support to continental debtors who withheld payments from their English creditors, and to foreign merchants, who engaged in reprisals—legalized piracy—against English ships. Most damaging of all was the policy of the Hanseatic merchants, who now refused to supply England with grain. In a year of poor harvests, this put the country at the severe disadvantage of having to turn to grain suppliers in the unfriendly territories of France and the Low Countries.

The harvest of 1535 was among the worst within living memory. The rain began falling, so the people said, on the day the Carthusians were hanged, and it showed no sign of stopping. God was taking vengeance on his faithful for the wickedness of their ruler. The king ordered the preachers to say that God was merely testing his chosen people, but they knew better. It was Henry, they said, who was testing the Lord, and he had finally gone too far. When the fields were harvested the barns were less than half full. There would not be enough corn to last the winter.

Everywhere the king was blamed and reviled, and bitter songs about his impiety, his tyranny and his despised wife were sung at every bride-ale and wake.

The constant rain irked Henry as much as it did his unloving subjects. It spoiled the summer's hunting, and kept him cooped up with his reproachful, neurotic wife. It spoiled his temper as well. When his favorite fool, Will Somers, chose the wrong moment to joke about the king's "ribald and bastard"—meaning Anne and Elizabeth—Henry struck him so hard he nearly killed him, and the terrified Somers had to take refuge in a nobleman's house until the incident blew over.[7]

Henry had a great deal on his mind that summer. His legs were bothering him, he was starting to put on weight, and he had recently ordered nine men of conscience to their deaths. One of them, Thomas More, had been among his few genuine friends in earlier years, a man whose wit had amused him and whose unfailing good sense he had relied on completely. And there was Anne, now grown querulous and vengeful, and still barren of sons. He was thinking of ridding himself of her, except that he might then have to take back Katherine and face the ridicule of every petty priest and royal servant in the Christian world. Meanwhile the new pope, Paul III, was showing himself to be a much more vigorous enemy than Clement had been. The execution of Cardinal Fisher had spurred him to launch a fresh assault on Henry's power. The pope wrote to the European rulers announcing his intention to deprive Henry of his kingdom and asking their aid. His only weapon was the loyalty of the Catholic sovereigns, but that loyalty could be counted on to injure England in a hundred ways short of war. And as the rainy summer dragged on Henry felt more and more disinclined to bestir himself to retaliate.

It was while these troublesome thoughts were plaguing him that Henry slipped away one night on a whim. He heard that a play mocking the clergy was to be presented in a village far from the censorious eye of the London clergy, and taking nothing but a swift horse and a two-handed sword he set out for the place on his own. He rode the first twenty miles but had to walk the last ten, trying to forget the ulcers on his legs and the weight of the sword against his thigh. He walked most of the night, until he finally came to the house where the play was in progress. He was in disguise, of course, but once he saw himself represented on the stage he could hardly keep silent. He was so delighted when the actor who represented him "cut off the heads of the clergy" that "in order to laugh at his ease, and encourage the people," he made his identity known.[8] To most of Europe he might be a monster, but to the handful of Protestant sympathizers who had gathered on that summer night to revile the church, he was their hero once again.

XIV

By me al women may beware,
That se my wofull smart:
To seke true love let them not spare,
Before they set their hart,
Or els they may become as I,
Which for my truth am like to dye.

The executions of 1535 made Mary desperate to escape. In the week the Carthusians suffered, Lady Shelton was "continually telling her to take warning by their fate," and reminding her for the hundredth time that she was a superfluous nuisance who had long ago been marked for death herself. A servant of the imperial ambassador Chapuys who visited Mary during that week reported to his master that escape was on her mind day and night, and "she thinks of nothing else than how it may be done, her desire for it increasing every day."[1]

The idea of escape was not new. Chapuys had brought it up from time to time, and every plan for political revolt brought to him over the last year had included the kidnapping of Mary and Katherine, who were to be taken to a safe hiding place to await the outcome of the rising. When Mary fell sick in February the ambassador was in the process of designing another escape plan, and each time the tension mounted around her he recalculated the distances, the obstacles and the means necessary to carry Mary to freedom in Flanders. So far each crisis had eased before the escape plans matured, but that was no guarantee she would not have to escape in the future. In the spring of 1535 Mary felt her danger to be greater than ever. She sent word to Chapuys "begging him most urgently to think over the matter [of her escape], otherwise she considered herself lost, knowing that they wanted only to kill her."[2] She was at Eltham when she sent the ambassador this message, and was still troubled by illness. She suffered another relapse in mid-April, but remained so intent on escape that she talked long and urgently to Chapuys' man about it from her sickbed, and what she said was very affecting. "If I were to tell you the messages she sent me," the ambassador wrote to Charles V's chief minister Granvelle, "you could not refrain from tears, begging me to have pity on her, and advise her as I thought best, and she would obey."

On first consideration the ambassador thought Eltham might be the ideal site for Mary's escape. In the Kentish countryside about five miles south of the Thames at the nearest point, it was far enough from London to be inaccessible by the king's guard yet near enough to the river to provide swift access to the Channel ports. Mary felt certain it would be impossible for her to get out beyond the walls at night, but flight might be possible during the daytime. It seems she was now permitted, probably for health reasons, to walk in the grounds and perhaps even to go hawking, for Chapuys suggested that she could be carried off while "going out to sport" at some little distance from Eltham. There she could be seized, put on horseback, and escorted to the river somewhere below Gravesend, where a rowboat would be waiting to take her to a Spanish or Flemish ship. A gunboat would provide what protection would be needed, and within hours Mary would be within sight of the Flemish coast. They would need a favorable wind, of course. But if the wind drove them back against the coast the armed escort vessel could hold off any pursuing English ships, while any wind that might favor the pursuers would also drive Mary's ship all the faster toward Flanders.[3] And once ashore there she would be taken to Brussels, to become a celebrated guest at the court of her imperial cousin, honored in her exile as Princess Mary, sole heir to the throne of England.

The easiest part of the plan, Chapuys thought, was the Channel crossing. There were Spanish and Flemish merchant ships in the Thames at all times, and imperial warships hovered just off the coast. Even as he wrote a great galleon lay only a short distance downriver, and he knew of "several Spanish ships" which were in a position to take Mary aboard at a moment's notice.[4] He did not worry about those who might try to follow Mary and her abductors. Once she was past the household guard she would encounter only friendly faces between Eltham and the coast. The country people were all on her side, and even those sent in pursuit would, he felt certain, "shut their eyes and bless her saviors," and would "make no hurry" to catch up with her.[5] Apart from her recurrent illnesses Mary herself presented no problem; her passionate desire to escape, combined with her proven "great prudence and courage" convinced Chapuys she would play her part well. "It is very hazardous," he concluded about the escape plan, "but it would be a great triumph and very meritorious."[6]

The most significant thing about Mary's desire for flight was that in making up her mind to leave she was for the first time departing from Katherine's model. Katherine had sworn never to tarnish her honor as queen, never to disobey her husband, and never to leave England. Until this year of 1535 Mary had repeatedly stated her intention to follow Katherine's example in every way, and the few letters she received from her mother urged her to continue in that resolve. But now, without telling Katherine, she decided to save herself by running away. (That Katherine knew nothing of the plan seems beyond doubt. In a letter to Henry written just at this time Katherine offered to pledge her own life as a guarantee against Mary's flight if the king would allow their daughter to come to Kimbolton.)

It would be easy to say that Mary's decision was nothing more than a simple survival reflex—an overwhelming urge to get away once and for all from an intolerable situation. She was, after all, a semi-prisoner in the hands of pitiless and hostile strangers; her health was breaking under the continual strain and she was in dread of a relapse; she had good reason to believe Anne was trying to poison her; and her father, the murderer of innocent monks, had recently announced that she was his worst enemy. Under such pressures as these anyone might break and run.

But Mary's new-found determination did not come from blind panic. It was a well-considered, deliberate choice. And it was a choice which marked a break with many of the strongest influences in her upbringing. It went against her education, which taught her to be helpless, to distrust her judgment, to fear to leave home and above all to obey her father. It went against the object lessons of prayer, patience and martyrdom offered by the saints of the church. It departed from her mother's life-long example of heroic masochism. And it was of course a decision which, if carried out, would have represented an act of political defiance of the greatest consequence.

Mary would never abandon the premises impressed on her in childhood and continually reinforced by her environment. But from now on there would be another force at work, a force impelling her to act decisively and with courage in the face of crises, to arrive at her own opinions, and to be true to a sense of her own destiny that was slowly taking shape in her mind.

As it turned out, there was to be no escape for the time being. Much as Mary tried to bring it about, the indispensable elements in the scheme —the ships, sailors and armed men on horseback—were beyond her control. And Chapuys, who probably had the means to engineer the adventure, was really not the best man for the job. He was far more at home in the private recesses of the king's Council chamber than galloping along the highroads of Kent, and in any case the emperor had not yet ordered him to act.

Meanwhile the climate of tension increased. Cromwell was openly lamenting the fact that by their very existence Katherine and Mary were preventing good relations between England and the empire. He reminded the emperor's ambassador that, after all, the two women were only mortal. Katherine was ill and aging, and would probably not live long; if Mary were to die her death would do far less harm than good, since the most immediate result would be a treaty of mutual good will between Henry and Charles.[7] It was not hard for Chapuys to see what Cromwell was hinting at, and he tried his best to impress on the chief minister that if Mary were harmed the emperor would be less rather than more disposed to come to an accommodation with her father. But by summer Cromwell's hints had turned to curses. He now blamed Katherine and Mary for all the king's troubles in recent years. If only God had "taken them to himself" no one would have questioned Henry's marriage to Anne or the right of their daughter to succeed him. The entire dispute would have long since been forgotten, and the possibility of internal revolt and war with the emperor would never have arisen.[8]

Chapuys hoped that Cromwell's casuistry was a substitute for more violent assaults on Katherine and Mary, though he could not be sure. He was fairly confident that Cromwell felt no personal malice toward them; they were merely added complications in the difficult diplomatic balance sheet he was trying to maintain. To have them permanently out of the way would have made his job easier, and in his professional capacity Cromwell could not afford to let pity interfere with statesmanship. But if Cromwell would have found the deaths of Katherine and Mary a diplomatic convenience, Anne saw it as a dynastic necessity. When Henry ordered Fisher and More to the scaffold she talked loudly of the injustice of allowing the two royal women to live, calling them worse rebels and traitors than the others. She accused Mary in particular of "waging war" against the king and, in an odd reversal of the truth, of conspiring Anne's death. "She will be the cause of my death unless I get rid of her first," Anne insisted. "But I will so manage that if I die before her, she shall not laugh at me."[9] In her mind Anne magnified the conflict over the succession to a final apocalyptic struggle from which only one of them would emerge alive. It was said that to quiet Anne down Henry had promised her that as long as he lived he would not allow Mary to take a husband. Without a husband to help raise a revolt she was less dangerous to Elizabeth and to the son Anne was longing for.

Anne's most ingenious stratagem against Katherine and Mary turned on this most sensitive of all issues: the need for a male heir. Ever since the affair of the nun of Kent the air had been full of revelations and occult messages, and the nun's accusation that Henry's second marriage was cursed still rang in Henry's ears. Now Anne claimed to have discovered a visionary whose messages supported her interests. She paid a man to swear that he had received a revelation about the royal succession. He was clearly shown in a dream, the man said, that Anne would be unable to conceive again as long as Katherine and Mary were still alive. The suborned prophet was sent to Cromwell first and then to the king, and though there is no evidence that Henry took the prophecy to heart it was the sort of thing that bothered him and added to his irritation.[10]

He was uneasy throughout 1535 about Mary's security. He knew perfectly well that an attempt might be made to kidnap her, whether with her consent or against her will. He seems to have believed that her kidnappers would most likely be French and not Spanish or Flemish, however. He was counting on Charles' studied policy of belligerent noninterference to continue for the time being, but the French might see in Mary a tempting hostage. Everywhere but in England Mary was considered heir to the English throne, and possession of her person might well provide the diplomatic leverage France needed to restore her tarnished influence in Italy and elsewhere. Mary was no longer a minor, and could be married to a prince of the royal house; equipped with an invading army, her husband could then undertake the conquest of England in his wife's name, confident of the support of the rebellious lords and disaffected courtiers who had been hoping for just such an eventuality for several years.

In an effort to prevent this alarming possibility Henry saw to it that an armed watch was kept around every house where Mary stayed, and ordered that no one but trusted household servants and known visitors like Chapuys' men were to be allowed anywhere near her. Every seaport within a day's ride of her residence had its armed guardsmen, alerted to look out for a girl taking ship with an escort of foreigners. When Chapuys told Cromwell he might have to go to Flanders on personal business the secretary turned pale, thinking the ambassador's business might concern the abduction of the king's bastard.[11]

There must have been some reason for optimism now, for despite Henry's precautions Mary was writing to her cousin Mary, regent of the Netherlands, that she had recently heard "an efficient remedy would be found for these troubles." The reference was very vague, but the letter had an unmistakably hopeful tone in spite of its ominous close. Above her name Mary signed "written in haste and fear, the 12th of August."[12] The regent must have sent some good news in her own earlier letter, and

Mary knew from the ambassador that continuous prayers were being said in all the churches of Spain for the safety and health of herself and her mother.[13]

In the fall, though, Mary's hopes fell as her cycle of illness began again. The doctors were called in September to treat a "rheum" in her head, and recommended that she be moved at once to "some place where she may get recreation and pleasure." Because of her fear of poison she now "detested all sorts of medicine," and became a difficult patient,[14] and when she fell sick again the following month Lady Shelton kept it a secret even from the physicians for twelve awful days,[15] probably hoping that this time Mary would not have the resiliency to survive.

When Mary was well enough to write again her letter to Chapuys had none of the optimism she had shown during the summer. She wanted now to write to the emperor directly, but didn't dare to, "fearing," as she told Chapuys, "lest those who are constantly watching me should get hold of the letter." Instead she wrote to the ambassador, urging him this time to send a personal envoy to Brussels to lay her case before Charles. Perhaps Chapuys' dispatches were too dispassionate; what she and her mother needed was an eloquent advocate whose description of their plight would soften the emperor's heart. Surely, she wrote, he could be made to see that saving his wretched kinswomen would be a work "highly acceptable in the eyes of God," and no less glorious than his current conquest of Tunis. Even the conquest of all of Africa could bring him no greater honor, she added grandiloquently.[16]

Mary could not have known as she wrote this that within weeks her plea for imperial aid would be taken seriously. What in fact roused the emperor to action at last was not his cousin's pitiful message but distressing news from London about the king's altered state of mind. The news came via an interesting source. Gertrude Blount, marchioness of Exeter and longtime ally of Katherine and her daughter, heard through highly-placed courtiers that early in November Henry had gathered his most valued advisers together and told them bluntly that Katherine and Mary had to be dispatched. He would no longer endure the "trouble, fear and suspense" they caused him, he said, and he wanted them judged once and for all at the next session of Parliament. He was not only firm but angry, the marchioness wrote to Chapuys, and he "swore most obstinately that he would wait no longer." From his tone and manner the councilors he spoke to understood the seriousness of his purpose, and they linked his meaning to a remark he had made earlier in the month about Mary. Then, in response to some reference to her lack of company, the king snapped that soon he would see to it "that she would not want any company, and that she would be an example to show that no one ought to disobey the laws." The time had come, he raged, for him to fulfill what had been foretold of him—"that at the beginning of his reign he would be gentle as a lamb, and at the end worse than a lion."

When these dark fulminations continued for three weeks the marchioness went to Chapuys in person to underscore the urgency of her earlier messages. She came in disguise, he told the emperor, and would without question have been in danger of her life had she been discovered at his residence. She brought fresh evidence of Henry's determination to carry out his purpose. Talking openly about how he meant to be rid of his stubborn ex-wife and daughter, the king noticed that some of those who heard him were so upset they started to cry. This made him even angrier. "Tears and wry faces would not move him," he had said loudly, "because even if he lost his crown he would not change his intention."[17]

These were things "too monstrous to be believed," Chapuys told the emperor after seeing the marchioness, yet he was certain his informant was trustworthy and that this time the king was in earnest. Henry had clearly become so exasperated by the stumbling block Katherine and Mary represented that he was prepared to go to war over the issue of their execution. He had shown the same impatient severity before the killings in the spring and summer, and those who cared most about Katherine and Mary's safety had been saying for months that as a result of those executions the king had become too calloused and "inured to cruelty" to shrink from ordering his former wife and daughter to their deaths. Besides, another matter nagged at him. Anne was pregnant, and if her child proved to be a boy his way would be made much smoother by the elimination of his potential rival and her obstinate mother. And it is just possible that, in the back of his mind, Henry recalled the dire prophecy of Anne's visionary and vowed he would take no chances with the survival of this child.

Whatever his motives, Henry succeeded in convincing his advisers, Chapuys, and finally the emperor himself that if Katherine and Mary were to be rescued it would have to be done immediately. In December the emperor took the first step toward giving the rebel English lords the support they had been seeking, and then, believing that the success of the venture would hinge on Mary's role, he laid plans for her abduction. Charles seems to have had a far different plan in mind than simply freeing Mary from captivity and probable attainder. As he saw it, the coming revolt would be carried out in her name. She would be more than an aggrieved victim of Henry's reckless policies; she would be a pretender to his throne. Once the rebels had seized power Mary would rule, her mother at her side, along with a carefully chosen husband and under the constant supervision and advice of her imperial cousin. England would be brought securely within the orbit of Hapsburg influence, and Henry's recent break with the pope and alterations in religion would be reversed.

With this bold plan in mind the emperor told the count de Roeulx, his captain general in the Netherlands, to send the best man he could find to England to make arrangements for bringing Mary to a temporary refuge in Flanders. She would wait there, in constant contact with Charles, while the northern lords were armed and prepared. As soon as the fighting began she would make ready to return to claim the throne. If she expressed any doubts about the justice of the undertaking she would be reassured by the recent publication of a papal sentence of excommunication against Henry, depriving him of his kingdom and declaring him to be outside the community of Christian souls. To take an excommunicant's throne was a worthy act in the eyes of the church, and if Mary did not seize it some foreign prince undoubtedly would.

In the first days of the new year 1536, the imperial agent arrived in England. He learned all he could from Chapuys, and then drew up his plans. Mary would be taken to Flanders in February; the rebellion would take place in March or April. By the first of May England would be in new hands.

Though she knew nothing of the impending revolt Katherine too felt the urgency of the political climate in late 1535. She wrote to the pope, entreating him to remember Henry and Mary, and describing England as a land of "ruined souls and martyred saints." If only the pope would intervene and protect the wayward people, who were straying "like sheep without a shepherd," she wrote, then the godless tyranny might be brought to an end. "We await a remedy from God and from Your Holiness," Katherine concluded. "It must come speedily or the time will be past!"

Part of her continued to struggle against the enduring injustice of which she was a victim, but she was gradually giving in to the mental burdens that oppressed her. Living in a single small room with a dreary view of the ruined moat and unkempt hunting park of Kimbolton, Katherine saw only her three maids of honor, her half dozen chamber women and the faithful Spaniards who looked after her material and spiritual well being: her physician, apothecary, confessor and chamberlain. The other members of the household she viewed, quite correctly, as her jailers, and by staying in her tiny apartment she avoided seeing or encountering them. The men Henry put in charge at Kimbolton, Sir Edmund Bedingfield and Sir Edward Chamberlain, were kept at a distance by Katherine's self-imposed isolation, and most of the guardsmen who watched the gates and grounds never saw their royal prisoner.

These highly restrictive living conditions helped Katherine to preserve a measure of dignity, but they were hardly conducive to either mental or physical health, and as the year 1535 drew to a close she entered what would be her final illness. What oppressed her most was the terrible thought that in some way she was responsible for all that had befallen England over the last eight years. In maintaining her cause, in refusing to acknowledge that she was now or ever had been anything but queen, Katherine had been true to her conscience and her faith. But what if, fallible as she was, she had misperceived the greater truth that by persisting in her claims she had forced Henry to cut England off from the Roman church and court the Protestant heresy? What if, in doing right, she had done a great wrong? The issue became more poignant still when she recalled the deaths of her beloved supporters Fisher and More, and of the blameless monks who had shared her scruples about the succession. Perhaps by giving in to the king's demand that she abandon her queenly pretensions and enter a convent she would have done a greater good, both for herself and for the others who had suffered and would suffer in future.

Other griefs crowded in on Katherine's mind during the long months of her isolation. One she had carried on her conscience for more than thirty years. When her marriage to Prince Arthur was being negotiated, her father had objected to the fact that Arthur's inheritance seemed insecure. The Tudor dynasty was not yet two decades old, and there was a Plantagenet claimant (Edward, earl of Warwick, son of Edward IV's brother George) whose pedigree was strong enough to make him a threat to Henry VII's successor. Ferdinand of Aragon's objection to the earl's continued existence prompted Henry to have him executed, and the marriage negotiations proceeded to a successful conclusion. Probably the English king would have had the unfortunate Warwick killed eventually even without Ferdinand's prompting, but Katherine believed to the end of her life that, through her father, the earl's blood was on her hands, and she told the other surviving representatives of the Plantagenet line—chiefly the countess of Salisbury and her son Reginald Pole—that her troubles were God's punishment for her father's sin.[18] Along with the old wound of the divorce and the ever fresh pain of her five-year separation from Mary, Katherine wrestled with these guilts until she became convinced that from the start her life had been fated for tragedy. Her state of mind was shown in the way she occasionally signed her letters: "KATARINA SIN VENTURA REGINA"—"Katherine, the unhappy queen."

On December 30 Chapuys left the court to go to Kimbolton. Katherine had been ill for nearly a month, and Henry had given permission for her to move to a less pestilential house. The ambassador carried this good news, and was in the best of spirits himself. The coming months were to be filled with intrigue and excitement, and he was to be at the center of it all. He could not tell Katherine any of the details, but the encouragement he gave her during his stay was fed by his own un-feigned enthusiasm. Of course, some of what they said to one another had been arranged beforehand, and was said solely for the benefit of the officials who were present. Bedingfield and Chamberlain, whom Kath-erine had not seen for more than a year, were allowed to be in the room during Chapuys' first meeting with Katherine, and a "friend of Crom-well's"—a spy, sent to record all the ambassador did and said during his visit—was also present.

But when the obligatory statements about Katherine's high status, powerful relatives and vital significance for "the union and peace of Christendom" had been made, their talk became more personal. Chapuys stayed at Kimbolton for four days, and each day he sat for several hours by her bedside, answering all her questions about Henry's health, his standing with other rulers, Mary's health and situation and the new house Katherine would live in as soon as she was well enough to be moved. They spoke too of how no one had yet come forward to defend her cause, and of the heresies that had taken root in England because of Henry's break with Rome over the divorce. On both these troublesome issues Chapuys felt he was able to console Katherine. He pointed out that even as they spoke the pope was preparing to enforce his sentence of deprivation, and was pressuring the French to abandon their lukewarm alliance with England. As for the spread of Protestant doctrines, the am-bassador reminded Katherine that God always uses such weapons to prove the faithful and confuse the wicked, and that she was in no way re-sponsible for the delusions of the few who were taken in by them.

Chapuys' presence and the sound of his voice were as much comfort to the bedridden woman as his words. It was the Christmas season, and there was a little gaiety and a few gifts. One of the ambassador's men loved to tell jokes, and on the night before Chapuys and his party left Kimbolton he made Katherine laugh again and again. She seemed to be much improved, and her physician told Chapuys there was no reason for him to stay. If her condition worsened, he said, he would send word im-mediately. But as it happened there was no time to summon him back. On January 7, the day after the Feast of the Three Kings, Katherine knew she was dying. She heard mass and spent the morning in prayer, pausing only to dictate a brief will and to write to Henry. She left the small sum of money she had to her servants, begging the king to supplement her small legacy to each with a year's wages. She asked that someone make a pilgrimage to Walsingham on her behalf, giving money to the poor along the way. She wanted masses said for her soul, beyond the daily prayers being offered in every parish church in Spain, and she left to her daughter her furs and a gold collar that had been part of her trousseau when she came as a bride from Granada.

Her last message to Henry was full of love. There was no longer any need to remind him of her true title, or of the long conflict that had estranged them. She forgave him everything; she hoped he would look to the good of his soul; she urged him to be a good father to Mary. "Lastly," the letter ended, "I make this vow, that my eyes desire you above all things." She prayed for him, and for Mary, until in midafternoon she died.[19]

Even before Katherine's death there had been strong suspicion of poison. The doctor ruled out the possibility that she had been given "simple and pure poison," whose sudden and dramatic effect would have made it unmistakable. But he thought a "slow and subtle poison" might have been put into some Welsh beer she drank just before her final relapse, and an elaborate rumor of a poison plot quickly took shape. The poison came from Italy, it was said, and was smuggled into England by a brother of the papal protonotary. It was an inescapably lethal toxin, and its effects were evident in what the chandler of Kimbolton found when he opened Katherine's corpse. The heart, he reported, was completely black and hideous; it would not come clean in any of the three "waters" he washed it in. Inside it was a cancerous growth, also black in color, which seemed to the doctor who heard the chandler's account clear evidence of slow poison. None of Katherine's partisans were willing to be cheated of their revenge by admitting that the old woman they had loved for so long had simply died of grief.

XV

 Adew, adew, my hartis lust!
Adew, my joy and my solace!
Wyth dowbyl sorow complayn I must
Untyl I dye, alas, alas!

Four days after Katherine died Lady Shelton went to Mary and, "most unceremoniously without the least preparation," told her her mother was dead. It had been said at court that Henry might take this excuse to visit his daughter in person at last and bring her the sad news, or that he would at least send one of his principal courtiers, but he did neither. Chapuys was afraid that hearing of Katherine's death might be too great a blow for Mary to bear, knowing how she "loved and cherished [her] as much, perhaps more than any daughter ever did."

No one but Lady Shelton knew how Mary actually took the news, but by the evening of the day she heard it she was composed enough to request that Katherine's physician and apothecary be allowed to visit her. The king refused at first, saying that if she was sick it was only the "natural affliction" of grief and nothing more serious, but at Chapuys' urging he relented. What Mary wanted from the two men was not treatment but an account of Katherine's last hours and of the manner of her death. Like everyone else she wanted to know for certain whether poison was involved, and since the doctor strongly suspected it he must have passed on these suspicions to Mary.[1]

Closeted in her room, wearing her black mourning robe and veil, Mary spent the next weeks writing endless letters. Chapuys had given a consoling note to one of the waiting maids, telling her to pass it on to Mary once she had been officially informed of Katherine's death, and Mary now answered it, eloquently and without bitterness. The ambassador had encouraged her to be brave and persistent, as Katherine had always been; Mary wrote back that she would try, at the same time preparing herself for whatever change in her own situation might come. As she looked out over the bleak winter landscape it was hard for Mary to imagine any but the darkest future as long as she stayed in England, and she felt again a strong desire to escape. Letters from the emperor and his sister made her long to be among her understanding relatives across the Channel, even though she hardly knew them. The letters were intended for Katherine, but arrived too late to be shown to her. Mary treasured them now, as she did the little gold cross with the relic that her mother had willed to her just before she died.

This legacy at least had been respected, but few of Katherine's other wishes were carried out. She had wanted to be buried in a convent of the Observant friars, but as the order had been suppressed several years earlier this wish could not be fulfilled. As for her bequests, Henry weighed them carefully. He wanted to see for himself what her robes and furs were like before allowing Mary and the church to have them, and he later ordered Mary to give up even the gold cross that meant so much to her. At the same time he ordered one of the gentlemen of his chamber to take inventory of Katherine's furnishings as queen, all of which had been stored away in the London palace of Baynard's Castle ever since her imprisonment began. Her old beds, hangings, and cushions were still there, embroidered with the arms of England and Spain, along with the painted tables and brazier that bore her picture and Henry's and their joint monogram. Everything had been preserved, even the smocks that she wore in childbed, the hangings for the nursery and the little cradle trimmed in yellow cloth of gold and crimson velvet. Few of these reminders of Katherine's past interested Henry, but he did take her ivory chessmen and black velvet writing desk, while Anne helped herself to a money chest, an ivory stool and a beautiful horn drinking cup decorated with antique figures.[2]

It was certainly no comfort to Mary to hear that, on learning of her mother's death, Henry organized a display of rejoicing calculated to impress on the representatives of foreign courts how great an obstacle to peace she had been. When he first heard the news Henry shouted "God be praised, now we are free from all suspicion of war!" and ordered entertainments and jousts to be prepared to celebrate England's deliverance. The next day he dressed himself as gaily as possible, all in yellow from doublet to stockings, with a white feather in his yellow cap. He went to mass to a loud fanfare of trumpets, carrying Elizabeth in his arms, and then after dinner danced with the ladies of the court "like one transported with joy." When the dancing ended he went off to the tiltyard and broke a dozen lances with a vigor he had not shown for years. Anne too was happy to hear that her old rival was dead, and generously rewarded the messenger who told her so, but she seemed troubled by the news as well, and did not take a central part in the rejoicings at Greenwich.

At the imperial court Chapuys' dispatches describing Katherine's last days were received with some dismay. The emperor put on black and wept, saying that he still could not understand how Henry could have left "so sage, virtuous and sainted a wife" for a whore.[3] With his eight-year-old heir Philip at his side he heard a mass in Katherine's honor, and announced to the ambassadors at his court that he believed she died like a saint. But if he blamed Henry for her death Charles did not hold a grudge. Within a few months he was welcoming the approaches of English diplomats eager to restore good relations, and was agreeing with them that, since Katherine no longer presented a problem, there was no reason why the old friendship between the Hapsburgs and the Tudors should not be restored. If this rapprochement confirmed Katherine's former diplomatic significance it also showed just how little Mary counted in the game of continental politics. She might be useful to have at hand in marriage negotiations, or as a pretender installed by a rebel army, but Charles was not prepared to remain estranged from England over the issue of her disinheritance or ill treatment. It was Katherine, not Mary, whose rights had caused an upheaval in European diplomacy.

Katherine may have died like a saint but she was buried like a princess —to be precise, a princess dowager. An account of her burial arrangements referred to her as "the right excellent and noble Princess the Lady Katherine, Daughter to the right high and mighty Prince Ferdinand, late King of Castile, and late Wife to the noble and excellent prince Arthur, Brother to our Sovereign Lord King Henry the 8th."[4] When the body had been "seared, trammeled, leaded and chested with spices" it lay for some days under a canopy of state before being enclosed in a leaden coffin, and placed before the altar within a "burning chapel," a display of dozens of wax candles kept alight in a blazing circle. Around the coffin were four crimson banners with the arms of England and Spain, and four great golden standards painted with the images of the Trinity, the virgin, St. Katherine and St. George. Wherever the arms of England appeared they were left ungilded, and the crown that surmounted them was the unclosed circlet of a princess, not the closed crown of a queen.

After more than two weeks the new mourning clothes were ready, and the mourning procession formed. Katherine's niece Eleanor, daughter of Mary Tudor and Charles Brandon, was chief mourner; she and sixteen other ladies and fifty of Katherine's serving women followed the hearse in slow stages to the abbey of Saltry, where another burning chapel was lit and the party rested overnight. Then, accompanied by forty-eight poor men in black hoods and robes carrying long torches, the company made the final journey to the Benedictine abbey of Peterborough where Katherine was to be interred. Here, surrounded by a thousand candles, by banners of all the great ruling houses to which she was related—those of Spain, Aragon, Sicily, Portugal, and the Holy Roman Empire—and by the aristocratic arms of the house of Lancaster and the white scutcheon of Prince Arthur, Katherine received her final homage. Her symbol, the pomegranate, was represented in several pennons, and her device, "Humble et loyale," was spelled out in huge golden letters around the walls.

Her humility and loyalty Henry could afford to celebrate, but not the principles she had maintained in life. Her funeral sermon was an assault on the pope and on her marriage, and the bishop who delivered it was persuaded to say, in exact contradiction of the truth, that on her deathbed Katherine had at last admitted that she had never been England's rightful queen. The sermon satisfied the king's conscience, but convinced no one else. All those who truly mourned Katherine knew better, and the six hundred poor women who were given black robes in which to mourn her more conspicuously prayed for her not as princess but as Queen Katherine as the coffin was placed at the lowest step of the high altar, a site unworthy of her place in their memory.[5]

Mary found the funeral arrangements such a dishonor that she advised Chapuys not to attend the ceremonial interment. Except for the controller Guildford, Anne's great enemy, the courtiers judiciously stayed away. Henry found little to say about the affair except to complain about the cost of a memorial to be displayed in Katherine's honor at St. Paul's.[6] Beyond bewailing the expense, he could hardly be bothered with the trivia of his first wife's funeral when all he could think of was how to rid himself of her successor. Anne had disappointed him again. On the day of Katherine's burial she miscarried her child, and the midwives who pored over the tiny fetus declared it to be male. Henry showed "great distress" when he was told, and was quite uncivil to his anguished wife. The miscarriage gave substance to the long-standing rumor that since Elizabeth's birth Anne had been incapable of bearing another child.

Anne tried to excuse her misfortune by saying that she lost the child through worry over the king. A few days earlier Henry had fallen heavily during a joust. He was mounted on a great warhorse, charging at an opponent in the tiltyard at Greenwich, when suddenly both horse and rider came crashing to the ground. For a terrible moment it looked as though the king was dead, but then his grooms saw that, though unconscious, he was breathing. He was senseless for more than two hours, and when he finally opened his eyes he found himself surrounded by churchmen and distraught courtiers. It was only after he was himself again that Anne was told what had happened, but she blamed the miscarriage on her shock at the news, and took the opportunity to blame Norfolk as well for telling her too abruptly. With her waiting maids, though, she took quite a different tone. Seeing them in tears over the loss of her child Anne consoled them by saying that all was for the best, since she could now conceive her next child all the sooner. What was more, she added, the new one would be free from any possible taint of bastardy now that the king's first wife was dead.[7]

Whatever Anne may have thought, Henry believed—or so he said—that her miscarriage was the result of malignant forces. Gertrude Blount got word to Chapuys that the king had told one of his intimates "in great confidence, and as it were in confession," that he now understood that he had been seduced into marrying Anne against his will, by witchcraft.[8] Such a marriage was accursed, he said, and could not produce sons. Furthermore it ought to be considered invalid, and he confided that in his own mind he already believed himself free to take another wife.

Everyone, including Anne, knew the woman he had in mind. She was pale, shy Jane Seymour, a monumental contrast to Anne in every respect, and Henry had been showing her every attention and giving her "very large presents" for months. Anne made a final pitiful effort to win back her husband's affection, telling him that "her heart broke when she saw he loved others," but it was too late. The king hardly spoke to her any more, and spent all his time in the palace apartments of Edward Seymour, where he could meet Jane in her brother's presence and avoid scandal.[9]

No one was more distressed over Anne's miscarriage and disgrace than Lady Shelton. She saw at once that, if Mary realized Anne's true situation, she would become ungovernable, and she sent her daughter and niece to try to find out from a woman whom Mary trusted, possibly Gertrude Blount, just how much Mary knew. If she had heard about the loss of the child, so much the worse, but "they would not for the world that she knew the rest."[10] In fact Mary's relationship to Lady Shelton was already changing. Thanks in part to a steady stream of bribes from Chapuys, Anne's aunt was allowing the ambassador's servants to see Mary whenever they liked, even without the requisite order countersigned by the king, and there were other signs that her icy harshness was thawing.[11] Until now Lady Shelton had owed her place at court to Anne's status, but if Anne fell she would need a new protector. There was talk that Mary might be restored to something like her former state, and the king might even decide to punish those he had told in the past to mistreat her. To guard against this possibility Lady Shelton was now hedging her bets.

Through Chapuys Mary too had heard the talk of "increasing her train and exalting her position," and her father's attitude seemed for the moment to be benevolent. He sent her a hundred crowns to distribute in alms, and he returned to her Katherine's gold cross, having satisfied himself that it had no value beyond the relic of the true cross it was said to contain.[12] But Mary had no wish to wait for the rumored mending of her fortunes. Like Chapuys she had come to fear "the scorpion lurking under the honey," and her desire to escape had only been heightened by Katherine's death. The emperor's agent had not been idle, and had made plans to get Mary safely to the coast. Transport from there was still to be arranged, however, when she was moved suddenly to Hunsdon in Hertfordshire and the entire project had to be redesigned.

Hunsdon was badly situated for even the most ingenious escape scheme. It was forty miles by horseback from Gravesend, where Mary would embark for Flanders—a distance requiring several changes of mount and many extra horses and men. Beyond this, the escape party would have to ride through several large villages, where only a sizable armed bodyguard could prevent a hue and cry. The risk of discovery and capture was overwhelmingly great even if, as Mary thought, she was being guarded more lightly than ever. If they made it safely to the river their ship would be subject to repeated searches and the uncertain tides might delay them still further. Mary thought that, if she had a sleeping draught to give her women, she could let herself out of the house without interference, provided she could get past Lady Shelton's window; once she reached the bottom of the garden it would be easy enough to open the gate—or break it if need be—and join the waiting horsemen on the other side.

Chapuys found the project far too hazardous and recommended waiting until after Easter, when Mary expected to be moved again. In April or May, with better weather and calmer seas, the chance of success would be far greater, and the king's probable absence from the vicinity of London would only increase the odds.[13] In the meantime he told Mary to continue in the semi-seclusion of mourning, and if approached by the king's officers to beg them to leave her in peace with her grief. If pressed, he suggested she tell them she was thinking of entering a convent as soon as she reached full age, a startling and unprecedented move calculated to stun them into indecision and to give her time to prepare for flight in the spring.[14]

Before new escape plans could be made, however, Queen Anne's tortured reign reached its dramatic conclusion. Throughout April Henry was actively looking for a way out of his marriage, hoping that one of his lawyers or theologians would discover a hidden impediment or a flaw in the original proceedings that would prove his union with Anne unlawful. Sensing the impending shift in influence from the Boleyns to the Seymours, the courtiers formed new alliances and began to tell tales on the Boleyns that they had up to now kept to themselves. That Henry passed over George Boleyn for membership in the Order of the Garter late in April was very significant. The Garter was an honor held by very few men, and only when a member died could a new Garter knight be chosen. The death of the redoubtable old Lord Abergavenny created an empty place, and Anne coveted it for her brother. Henry gave it to his Grand Esquire Nicholas Carew, who had recently become openly and stridently critical of the Boleyns and was advising Jane Seymour on how to advance her progress toward the throne.[15]

Carew and others of the king's chamber sent word to Mary at about this time telling her to take heart, and boasting that all the Boleyns would soon be forced to "put water in their wine" and learn humility. Geoffrey Pole, a younger son of the countess of Salisbury and hotheaded opponent of Anne and her relatives, spread the word that Henry had asked the bishop of London whether some grounds could be found which would allow him to abandon his wife, and it appeared to be only a matter of time before Anne was, in the crude phrase of the courtiers, "dismounted" and another mare put in her place.

Anne's spirits had been sinking since January. She was tormented by the gossip about Henry and Jane, and Henry did not spare his wife the sight of his demonstrative affection for his new love. She had to bear the sneers and contempt of all those she had sneered at and abused for so long, and their laughter as well. She was haunted too by an old prophecy that in her days a queen of England would be burned alive. In the early years of her involvement with Henry Anne had assumed that the queen of the prophecy would be Katherine, but now she dreaded that it might well refer to herself. She was badly frightened when a fire broke out in her bedchamber early in 1536, and her satisfaction at Katherine's death was clouded by fears for her own life. Toward the end Anne seems to have conceived a mystical link between Katherine's death and her own, and when she heard that the old queen was gone at last she grew increasingly morbid about her future.

When no flaw could be found in the legalities of the marriage Henry determined to rid himself of Anne on political grounds. Alleging that the misconduct of a queen, if it threatened her husband's security, was treasonous, he ordered Cromwell, Norfolk and a commission of others to investigate her morals. What they found convinced the commissioners, and the twenty-six peers who ruled unanimously against her at her trial on May 15, that the queen was a flagrant adulteress who had conspired with at least one of her lovers against the king's life. The specific charges against Anne were that she had been unfaithful to Henry with three of his courtiers (Henry Norris, Francis Weston and William Brereton) and with a musician named Mark Smeaton, that she was guilty of incest with her brother George, and that she and Norris had exchanged a vow to marry after Henry's death—taken by her accusers as proof of a conspiracy to assassinate the king. There were lesser charges as well: that Anne and Norris exchanged medals implicating her in Katherine's death by poison; that she gave money to Weston (which she admitted); that she laughed at Henry's clothes and person, and, with her brother, made fun of the ballads he wrote; and that "she showed in various ways she did not love the king but was tired of him."[16]

The most sensational of the indictments brought against Anne and her alleged accomplices revealed the sordid undercurrent of recrimination and bizarre conjecture in sexual matters that had spread through the court during Anne's reign. George Boleyn was charged with "having spread reports which called in question whether his sister's daughter was the king's child." In other words, it was being said that Anne's brother had accused his sister of conceiving Elizabeth by someone other than Henry. The accusation was odd in that according to some accounts George Boleyn was himself held to be Elizabeth's father, but other evidence brought out during the trial made it more plausible. Among the statements George was asked to confirm or deny was that Anne had told her sister-in-law that Henry "was impotent, having neither vigor nor strength [for intercourse]."[17] This accusation, which despite stern admonitions the accused read aloud, much to the embarrassment of the court, may have been true, at least when Anne said it, or it may have been her way of attacking the king where he was most vulnerable in a moment of spite. But the suggestion alone was enough to cause a great deal of talk, and every ambassadorial dispatch that left London that week noted it in full.

A final charge accused Anne of a unique form of theological promiscuity. Chapuys recorded that the most Protestant of the bishops taught Anne that "according to their sect, it was allowable for a woman to ask for aid in other quarters, even among her own relatives," whenever her husband was incapable of satisfying her. This outrageous accusation brought even the church into complicity with the adulterous queen, and showed just how eager Henry was to discredit her.

He was not disappointed. Though both Anne and her brother defended themselves ably—the latter made such a good impression that at one point spectators wagered ten to one he would be acquitted—both were condemned, along with Anne's four other alleged lovers, who had been tried separately. Anne was sentenced to be beheaded, the first English queen to die on the block for treason. She asked, as a final courtesy, that her head be neatly severed, as in French executions, with a sword.

The evidence at Anne's trial consisted of little more than the bawdy whisperings of courtiers, yet what made it significant was the inescapable importance of the succession, and the aging king's reluctant admission that he might die without leaving a legitimate son. His preoccupation with this problem led the men and women of his court to dwell on his sexual exploits, his married life and his potency with an exclusive fascination which at another court they would have reserved for their own. Anne Boleyn was in a sense a casualty of their collective preoccupation, and perhaps for this reason even her worst enemies found themselves in the end strangely disturbed by her fate and angry at the king for making such a spectacle of his relief at it.

During the two and a half weeks that Anne lay in the Tower Henry gave himself up to the carefree enjoyments of springtime. He banqueted every night in the company of beautiful women, danced lustily, drank until he could not stand, and then made his way back to the palace to the raucous accompaniment of shawms, drums and many choruses of tavern songs. Long after midnight the royal barge could be heard coming back to its mooring at Greenwich, with the king and his chamber singers bawling out songs from the stern, his voice booming loudest of all. The "skinny old hoyden" was out of the way at last, he told his companions with delight, and repeated again and again that Anne had been unfaithful to him with a hundred men, and had only kept his love through her spells and enchantments.[18]

On Friday, May 19, at eight in the morning, Anne was beheaded on Tower Green, before the great White Tower, by a swordsman from St. Omer. During her imprisonment she had joked about her coming execution, saying she would be known to posterity as Queen Lackhead, but in her hours of serious preparation for death she spoke often of Mary. Chapuys reported that she was genuinely remorseful about mistreating Mary and plotting her death. Charles V's sister Mary, though, was cynical about the entire affair, and looked forward to the time when Henry, having tired of still a third wife, might order her to execution. "I think wives will hardly be well contented if such customs become general," she wrote. As a vigorous and capable widow with no intention of remarrying, Mary of Hungary was in no danger from the precedent of Anne's death, but she joined all women in hoping for deliverance. "Being of the feminine gender," she wrote, "I will pray with the others that God may keep us from it."[19]

Before the high altar at Peterborough the monks were reporting a miracle. The candles near the grave of Katherine of Aragon were lighting and extinguishing themselves of their own accord. The king was notified, and thirty men from his court arrived to witness the remarkable event. When they reported the sign to Henry he chose to interpret it as an occult confirmation, from the one she had wronged most grievously, of the justice of Anne's execution. In some macabre way the king believed he was receiving permission from his first wife to carry out the ultimate punishment of his second.

XVI

My wofull hart in paynfull weryness,
Which hath byn long plongung with thought unseyne,
Full lyk to drowne in wavis of dystres,
Saffe helpe and grace of my lord and soverayne,
Is nowe be hym so comfortide agayne
That I am bownde above all erthly thyng
To love and dred hym as my lord and kyng.

Anne Boleyn's death put an end to nine years of uncertainty, danger, constant tension and sorrow. Anne had moved into Mary's life at its happiest point, when as princess of Wales she was the admired center of her father's banquets and entertainments and about to become the bride of a French prince. All that was swept away when the cataclysm of the divorce burst over the court, and the king's outrageous fascination with his new sweetheart pushed Mary and her mother further and further into the background. What began as an indulgent flirtation became an international scandal, then a notorious legal issue and finally a serious influence in European politics. Through it all the princess of Wales was at first ignored, then dislodged from her household and ultimately disinherited. At eighteen she had become a friendless bastard, separated from her mother and living in humiliating subjection to the infant half-sister who was now princess in her stead. For most of the three years that Anne Boleyn was queen Mary lived in fear of death, menaced by her guardians, her terrifying stepmother and her heartless father. The older she grew the more the shocks, tensions and persecutions increased, and the pattern of her life was one of deepening and unrelieved misfortune. Then, as abruptly as it had begun, Anne's power came to an end. The harm she had done remained, but the shadow of future harm was lifted.

Mary grew to adulthood surrounded by personalities, circumstances

and extremes of emotion exaggerated to the point of caricature. Her father was an outsize man of incalculable, semi-divine authority. Her
mother was a heroine of remarkable personal courage whose life became
a celebrated martyrdom. The woman who destroyed the calm of her
family life was the Great Whore, probably the most reviled woman of
her time. The discord in which they were involved became conflated into
conflict between nations, creeds and spiritual powers. The contours of
English religious life were being vastly changed as a result, and a new
sort of Christianity without the pope was being attempted. Living in an
ever worsening climate of hostility, mistrust and mortal danger Mary
watched events unfold around these figures knowing that her life was at
risk to their outcome.

All this amounted to a magnification of experience that predisposed
her to see life in monumental proportions. She came to think in terms of
absolutes, of overriding forces intervening to shatter, rescue or sustain
her. If her life was to be significant, it too would have to be defined with
reference to a purpose beyond the ordinary. In the months that followed
Anne Boleyn's death Mary was helped to define that purpose in a way
that linked her personal fate to the political future of the English people.

In the first days after Anne died an atmosphere of lightness and gaiety
spread over the court and capital, reflecting the general mood of popular
rejoicing. "I cannot well describe the great joy the inhabitants of this city
have lately experienced and manifested" at the "fall and ruin" of the
queen, Chapuys wrote at the time of her execution. The king appeared
dressed entirely in white, as if to belie even the faintest inclination of
mourning. Plans for his wedding to Jane Seymour were being finalized,
and he set up a temporary residence for her a mile from the palace where
she was waited on by officers from the royal household and feasted by
the king's cooks. The king's silkwomen and embroiderers had been at
work dressing her sumptuously for some time, and her wedding clothes
were already being prepared when Francis Bryan arrived to tell Jane the
good news that Anne was dead.

A large measure of the people's delight in the spring of 1536, the ambassador explained, came from their hope that Mary would be reinstated
in her rights.[1] The years of Anne's ascendancy had not lessened Mary's
popularity. Few in the country had seen her since she was a child, but she
had grown in the folk imagination from the beloved princess of Wales to
a forlorn, motherless bastard—a figure deserving not only love but pity
and warm loyalty besides. Katherine's great legacy to Mary was the firm
allegiance of the majority of the English people.

Wherever Mary was kept during her years of semi-captivity small
crowds of country people always formed to watch her pass in her litter,
or to catch a glimpse of her at a window or walking across an open ter-

race on her way to mass. They looked for her now, waiting outside the palace and repeating the rumor that she would soon become princess of Wales again. When the countess of Salisbury returned to court it was assumed that Mary would be with her old governess, and a huge throng gathered at the palace gate to watch for her. Henry himself came out to speak to the crowd, explaining that Mary was not yet reinstalled in the palace but that she soon would be. The presence of so great a crowd so close to the palace reminded Henry how potent a political symbol his daughter had become, and made him irritable when his privy councilors brought up the delicate subject of what should now be done with her.

Three days after Anne went to the Tower Mary was moved to a more honorable residence, escorted with marked respect by Elizabeth's household officers. In the new house dozens of well-wishers came to congratulate her on the reversal of her fortunes, and several members of her own and Katherine's former households offered to enter her service. Mary was overjoyed to have these old servants near her again. Many of them had been dear to her when she was a child, and others had helped her to bear the hard years of her disgrace. But following Chapuys' advice she did not take any of them into her service for the present; she would wait until Henry approved them. She must do nothing now to anger the king, who was being pressed from all sides to bring her to court, to give her a large establishment, to restore her to a place in the succession.

Chapuys was systematically visiting the privy councilors one by one and pointing out to each the diplomatic and political advantages of bringing Mary back to court, and was trying, through his contacts outside London, to put pressure on the gentlemen who would be coming to the Parliament summoned for the first week in June. Within the king's Council the marquis of Exeter and the treasurer Fitzwilliam were urging a complete restoration of Mary's rights, while even closer to the king's ear his intended bride was now Mary's most constant advocate.

Jane Seymour had been pressing for a reconciliation between Henry and Mary for months. Her entreaties were rooted as much in sentiment as in political expediency. She spoke for many who held the naïve conviction that a restoration of harmony between the king and his daughter would sweep away all the disruptive changes in government and religion that had arisen out of the rift in the royal family. Henry, however, was looking forward, not back, and told Jane "that she must be out of her senses to think of such a thing," and that she ought to think instead of her own future children. But Jane insisted that the people could not be content until Mary was returned to her place at her father's side, and that without their reunion the country would face "ruin and desolation."

The sincerity and imploring ardor of his new beloved touched the king, who had in any event already determined to recall Mary. In view of her popularity he had no choice but to give her back some degree of honor, though the issue of her place, if any, in the succession would have to wait until Parliament met and redrafted the Act of Succession. She was recalled to court briefly late in May, and publicly received. There were feasts in her honor, and as an additional mark of favor many of Anne's jewels were given to Mary. Some of these jewels had almost certainly been Katherine's, for Anne had taken nearly every gem and chain her predecessor owned. There was an ironic justice in the fact that the jewels now came to Mary, but to judge from what she told Chapuys she was not eager for revenge in any form.[2] Throughout Anne's trial Mary had been hoping grounds for a divorce would be found, but less because of the injuries Anne had done to her mother and herself than for the sake of "the king's honor and the relief of his conscience."[3] In a message to the ambassador she declared she had "willingly forgiven and forgotten" the past, and hated no one. Using a favorite expression of Katherine's, she wrote that she "didn't care a straw" whether Henry and Jane had sons whose succession rights were stronger than her own. Clearly what mattered most to her was the king's affection—that he accept her, without qualification, as his beloved daughter.

Mary's appearance at court shortly before the king's marriage was only a first step toward that acceptance. She now appealed to Cromwell, whom she addressed as "one of her chief friends," to help her gain the full measure of Henry's benevolence. "Nobody dared to speak for me as long as that woman lived," she admitted, but now that Anne was gone she hoped Cromwell would act as her go-between, interceding with the king on her behalf and assuring him of her desire to obey him as far as her conscience allowed. It soon became obvious that nothing less than the most abject submission would satisfy him. By her unshakable resistance to all the overt and subtle pressures to which Henry had subjected her Mary had cost him a good deal of frustration. She and Katherine both had reminded him that there were limits to his power at a time when he was pushing back those limits to an extent undreamed of even a decade earlier. In Henry's view, his daughter had much to atone for. The price of his restored affection would be Mary's complete and painful humbling to his will.

Her suit was in any case a peripheral matter, for the king was once again a bridegroom. Eleven days after Anne's execution he married Jane Seymour at York Place in London, and following a brief country honeymoon brought her back to be proclaimed queen. She was not formally crowned, but in lieu of a coronation procession there was a parade of boats to escort her from Greenwich to Westminster, the king and queen riding in the royal barge and the guardsmen of the king's bodyguard in a single great barge behind them. The warships and shore guns roared out as they passed, and at Radcliff they slowed to admire the display and entertainment arranged by the imperial ambassador. A large tent bearing the arms of the empire had been erected on the bank, ornamented with banners that fluttered in the wind and flanked by an impressive display of ordnance. Under the tent stood Chapuys, resplendent in purple satin and surrounded by gentlemen in velvet coats. On his signal two small boats, one full of trumpeters, the other carrying musicians playing shawms and sackbuts, headed out into the river and followed the royal barge as the procession made its way toward the Tower, and the forty cannons he had assembled were shot off to salute the king and his new queen.[4]

The rise of the Seymours was associated with imperial interests and the cause of the old faith, and Chapuys was eager to maintain close ties with Jane in her new role. Two days after her return to Westminster he went with Henry to her chamber after mass and spoke to her awhile. After congratulating her on her marriage he alluded to Jane's fidelity to Mary, remarking that of all the recent changes at court the one that pleased the people most was Mary's return. He elaborated this opinion with the awkward sentiment that, without the pain and anxiety of labor, Jane had gained in Mary a treasured daughter who would please her more than her own children by the king.

Jane assured Chapuys she would do all she could to make peace between her husband and stepdaughter, though it was plain the king was bent on little but amusement. With a zest that recalled the early days of his reign he was passing the time with Jane and her ladies, dicing with his courtiers or honoring favored nobles with his presence at banquets. With a boatload of disguised companions he went one afternoon to a sumptuous entertainment that followed a triple wedding. He was dressed as a Turk, in long garments richly embroidered with gold thread and a black velvet hat with white feathers. After he had danced awhile he took off his mask and received the homage of the wedding guests, and then ordered his cooks to bring in the forty dishes of meat and decorative "subtleties" he had brought with him from the palace.[5]

Henry could no longer joust; the injuries from his heavy fall and his ulcerated legs now prevented it. But he could enjoy the "jousting and triumph" organized for his amusement in the early weeks of his marriage. Four boats loaded with combatants in full armor met on the river before York Place and exchanged fire from their guns for two hours. When one of the boats was disabled fighting men from the others boarded her, and in the confusion some of them fell in the river. Nearly all of them were fished out again, as it was low tide, but one, a servant of Sir Henry Knevet named Gates, was drowned. After this misfortune the king insisted that all the combatants exchange their metal swords for harmless wooden ones, and put wool and leather tips on the ends of their darts and pikes. Even so one of the ships sank when a gun exploded on firing, and the experiment was quickly ended. The soggy mariners trotted off somewhat disgruntled to change their armor and prepare for a second joust on land, with Henry and Jane watching from the gatehouse.[6]

While the king enjoyed these pastimes his servants in and out of Parliament had been formulating a new succession act. All of Henry's children—Mary, Elizabeth and Henry Fitzroy—were now bastards. Fitzroy had been born one, Mary declared one by the 1534 act, and Elizabeth became one when the archbishop of Canterbury, Thomas Cranmer, pronounced Henry's marriage to Anne invalid in May. The new act took account of the absence of a legitimate heir, but instead of conferring the succession on the as yet unborn children of Henry and Jane it took the unprecedented step of giving the king the right to name any heir he chose. For the first time since Henry became king the succession issue was divorced from his domestic life. The continuation of the Tudor dynasty no longer depended on the precarious happenstance of the king's true wife giving birth to a male heir of undisputed parentage.

This altered situation put Henry's marriage and his children's status in a new perspective. He might now without hesitation name the seventeen-year-old Fitzroy as his heir instead of waiting for Jane to produce a son. Some of his privy councilors had always favored this course. Robert Ratcliffe, earl of Sussex, remarked at a Council meeting in Henry's presence that, as both Fitzroy and Mary were now on the same footing, "it was advisable to prefer the male to the female for the succession to the crown."[7] What Henry himself thought is unclear, but Fitzroy was given a prominent place in the formal opening of Parliament in June. He walked just ahead of the king in the ceremonial procession, bearing his cap of maintenance, and was given greater honor than Sussex, who bore the royal sword, or Oxford, who carried the king's train.[8]

Fitzroy had been kept away from court throughout his childhood. He was given the titles, the household and the education of a future king but little else. While Henry made certain that the boy was prepared to step in should an emergency create the sudden need for an heir, he had little to do with Fitzroy personally, and it is hard to avoid the conclusion that they did not get on well. The endearments, the companionship, the close personal affinity Henry displayed (however fleetingly) toward Mary in her childhood were missing in the king's relationship with his son. Fitzroy's marriage to Norfolk's only daughter, Mary Howard, completed his preparation for power, though his alliance with the Howards was troubled by the hostility of Anne Boleyn. Fitzroy was prominent among the spectators at Anne's execution, and it was being said that Henry "certainly intended to make him successor," but by early summer he was in poor health and showing no sign of improvement. Toward the end of

July he died. The king ordered Norfolk to arrange an obscure burial for him, with no public mourning and no funeral procession. The sealed coffin was put in a wagon, covered with straw, and taken off to a provincial town to be buried. Henry was determined to keep Fitzroy behind the scenes even in death.

For Mary the passage of the revised Act of Succession brought on the definitive crisis of her youth. She had asked Cromwell to mediate her reconciliation with her father, and he now undertook to do so in the light of the altered arrangement enacted by Parliament. He drew up a letter for her to copy out in her own hand and sign, full of the most self-abasing phraseology. "In as humble and lowly a manner as is possible for a child to use to her father and sovereign lord," the letter began, Mary acknowledged all her offenses against her father, "since I first had discretion unto this hour." She begged him to forgive them all, and professed herself to be "as sorry as any creature living" for what she had done that was contrary to his will. She asked his "fatherly pity" on her frail condition—"I am but a woman, and your child," was how Cromwell phrased it for her —and added that though her soul belonged to God her body was Henry's to order according to his pleasure.

When this letter brought no immediate response from the king Mary wrote again, repeating Cromwell's formulas of self-abnegation and begging her father to envision her "most humbly prostrate before your noble feet, your most obedient subject and humble child." This time she signed herself "Your majesty's most humble and obedient servant, daughter, and handmaid." When she sent this letter via Cromwell Mary added in a separate letter to the secretary that she hoped she would not have to do more than make a general admission of guilt to unspecified "offenses." In sending the humiliating letters she had already done as much as her conscience would allow, she told him; she could not bring herself to acknowledge all that the new Act of Succession implied in more explicit terms. She could never recognize the illegality of her mother's marriage, or her own illegitimacy, or the nullity of papal power in England. She would rather die than displease her father, she told Cromwell, yet "if I be put to any more (I am plain with you as my great friend) my conscience will in no ways suffer me to consent thereto."[9]

But in making a vague and sweeping plea for forgiveness Mary was giving the king free reign to interpret her submission in any way he chose. Taking advantage of her claim "to be ordered according to his pleasure," he sent several of his privy councilors to obtain her assent to precisely those points to which she could not in conscience subscribe. Norfolk, Sussex and the bishop of Chester, Roland Lee, were deputed to carry out this task. That the king knew his commissioners were likely to encounter resistance from Mary is evident from the written instructions he prepared for Norfolk before the duke and the others left for Hunsdon.

This document began by condemning Mary's earlier refusal to obey her father as a "monster in nature"—a freakish departure from the natural obedience of a daughter toward her father. Any other man would have sent such a daughter as Mary away long before, but because of his clemency, his pity, and his "gracious and divine nature" Henry was willing to withhold his displeasure if she swore to submit to him, to his laws and to the all-important official positions on his first marriage and headship of the church. Norfolk's instructions left no room for compromise. Mary was to be forced to consent to every demand the councilors made. And because Henry recognized the "imbecillity of her sex"—a formula from Roman law describing the intellectual incapacity of women—he wanted his commissioners to find out from Mary who it was that instructed her to be defiant for so long. It was unthinkable that her resistance arose out of inner conviction or loyalty to her mother; someone must have "emboldened and animated" her to defy him.[10]

Armed with these directives, the commissioners went to Hunsdon. Mary had been returned there, it seems, in anticipation of the final confrontation with the king's representatives, and was back under the governance of Lady Shelton. They put the king's terms to Mary; she repeated her old familiar arguments in reply. She would obey her father in all matters save those that injured her mother, her personal honor or her faith. The commissioners were furious. If they failed this time they, along with Mary, would suffer the king's violent displeasure. They had no pity for her. She was no longer a fragile girl but a resolute woman of twenty, a woman who now more than ever recalled her mother in her rigorous logic and steadfast defiance. Norfolk and Sussex shouted at her and called her names, and one of them swore he could not believe she was in fact the king's daughter, for no child of his, not even a bastard, would be as willful and obdurate as she was. In a rage he stormed that if she were his own daughter he would beat her to death. He would pick her up and dash her head against the wall again and again until he cracked it open and "made it soft as a boiled apple." And he would be more than justified. Any father would do the same.

There is no doubt that Norfolk—if it was he who made these threats—was fully capable of carrying them out. Shortly afterward he brutally punished his own wife, whose only offense seems to have been that she resented her husband's mistress. Elizabeth, duchess of Norfolk, wrote to Cromwell explaining her circumstances. Norfolk "chose her for love," she wrote, and not for her dowry; they had been married for twenty-five years and had five children. But though she had been a good and virtuous wife, serving beside her husband at court for many years and making many sacrifices for him, he repaid her by gambling away her jointure and seducing younger women. He fell in love with one of these women, Bess Holland, and when he heard his wife had spoken out against her he "came riding all night" from the court and locked her in a small room, taking away all her clothes and jewels and leaving her only a small allowance to support herself and twenty others "in a hard country." When she objected he ordered some of the serving women to bind her arms and legs and keep her thus bound and imprisoned until she accepted her situation. And, the duchess wrote to Cromwell, the women bound her until the blood came out at her finger ends, and sat on her breast until she spat blood, and though her husband knew it he did nothing to stop them. Since then she had been plagued by "much sickness and cost in physic," and could no longer live on the pittance the duke allowed her.[11] It was a sordid story, though by no means a unique one, but if nothing else it showed how real Mary's danger was.

The three commissioners kept up their barrage of threats for some time, with Lady Shelton adding dire verbal bludgeonings of her own, until it became obvious that Mary would not yield. They left her then, giving Lady Shelton strict orders not to allow her to speak to anyone. She was to be watched day and night, and kept in a state of fearful expectation of further persecution.

When they returned to court and reported that Mary was as adamant as ever the king was beside himself with anger. He was now convinced that a group of conspirators was using Mary to thwart him and wreck the new design for the succession. He lashed out at everyone he suspected, dismissing Exeter and Fitzwilliam from the Council, interrogating a number of aristocratic women and sending Lady Hussey to the Tower, grilling Mary's principal servant and subjecting the unfortunate Cromwell to an agonizing week of fear for his life. For most of that week, he confided to Chapuys, "he considered himself a dead man" for having represented Mary to her father as penitent and obedient.[12]

When he could uncover no conspiracy Henry apparently decided to order Mary to be tried for treason. Jane's "prayers and exertions" to the contrary were "rudely repulsed." The judges were commanded to proceed with the legal inquiry into her guilt and to sentence her, in her absence, as contumacious. At the same time the king was heard to say, Chapuys wrote, "that not only Mary but Exeter, Cromwell and many others would suffer" once the judgment was rendered.

The only thing that saved Mary, it appears, was the squeamishness of the royal justices. They too were threatened with harsh punishments if they failed to indict Mary, but they did not want her blood on their hands. To gain time they proposed that she be given a paper to sign, declaring all that the king wanted her to affirm, and that if she refused to sign it legal proceedings could then be begun. A document, called "Lady Mary's Submission," was accordingly drawn up and sent to Hunsdon. It acknowledged that Katherine and Henry had never been legally married, that their daughter was illegitimate, and that the "pretended authority" of the bishop of Rome had no legal ground in England. The Submission reiterated Mary's request to be forgiven for her obstinacy and disobedience, and declared that she now swore to these truths "with all her heart" and "inward sentence, belief, and judgment."

Mary was warned from trusted sources that the Submission represented her last chance to save her life. Cromwell, in a long, self-righteously indignant letter, made it plain that he had lost all sympathy for Mary and would not lift a finger to help her in future unless she signed the document. He echoed the commissioner's abuse, and said it was a pity Mary had not been given exemplary punishment long before. Cromwell was genuinely shocked by her disobedience, and bewildered by what seemed to him a contradiction: she had signed the groveling letters he wrote for her yet she refused to yield to the king in specific points. The only satisfactory explanation was either that someone else was manipulating her or that, like all women, she suffered from perverse stubbornness. "I think you the most obstinate woman that ever was," Cromwell wrote, adding that she was an unnatural ingrate and unfit to live in the community of Christians.[13]

Cromwell's letter revealed the depth of his insensitivity to Mary's character. Like the privy councilors and the king himself, Cromwell could not give Mary credit for holding strong convictions on abstract issues of conscience. He could not perceive that, as she wrote him, she was in "great discomfort" because she was torn between two strong desires. She sincerely loved her father and wanted to obey him, yet she believed deeply in the rightness of her dead mother's cause and in the old religious order. This belief had sustained her when nothing and no one else had; to abandon it would have meant giving up a vital part of her identity. That a girl of twenty might be capable of such complex loyalties was inconceivable to Cromwell, who would have had little sympathy for them even if he had perceived them. Women were meant to do as they were told, not to ponder the merits of the command. For them to behave otherwise upset the natural order and caused pointless inconvenience. It is odd that Cromwell, who had been such a staunch admirer of Katherine, should fail to see and admire the similarities in Mary's character, but he did not. And of course he had never come even close to putting his head on the block for Katherine's sake.

But if Cromwell threw up his hands in disgust at Mary's behavior, Chapuys did not. He alone understood where her problem lay, and why she felt as she did. He had in fact foreseen the crisis, and had already sent

Mary a protest to sign along with the Submission, explaining that the former invalidated the latter in the eyes of God and preserved her conscience. The ambassador was aware, though, that this time no such stratagem would be sufficient in itself to convince Mary to submit. He would have to appeal to a higher, more all-encompassing logic. And it was here that, summoning all his diplomatic expertise, his persuasiveness in argument and his concern for Mary, Chapuys hit on the key argument that at last induced her to give in.

He appealed to her sense of her own destiny, to that future Mary had been protecting when she determined to escape instead of following her mother's example of passive martyrdom. If she yielded now, he told her, she would be doing much more than saving her own life. She would be preserving the instrument of England's tranquillity to come. She was the country's hope. Only if she survived could all the disorders of recent years be reversed and true government and the true faith restored. To dissemble in the small matter of the document of submission was to serve the great matter of her own and her country's future.[14]

The idealistic hope Chapuys appealed to in Mary had little or no political substance. Few now believed she would ever come to the throne. Her sex, her clouded status in law, and Jane's unborn children all stood between Mary and the crown. But though Mary saw these things as clearly as anyone else she persisted in the belief that she had up to now been spared in order to perform an important work, and Chapuys made her see that she must not thwart this destiny by refusing to use any means possible to save herself.

Swayed by the ambassador's urging, and impelled by an inexplicable faith in a hidden future, Mary made up her mind to act. She did not read the Submission—a final protection allowing her to say later that she did not know the contents of what she was endorsing—but she signed it, writing out the protest at the same time and leaving the rest to God.

PART THREE

"The Unhappiest Lady in Christendom"

XVII

Weep, weep O Walsingham!
Whose days are nights;
Blessings turn'd to blasphemies—
Holy deeds to despites.
Sin is where Our Lady sat,
Heaven is turned to hell;
Satan sits where Our Lord did sway:
Walsingham, Oh, farewell!

Shortly after Mary's twentieth birthday the destruction of the monasteries began. The monks and nuns were turned out, the convent buildings were plundered of their treasures, and when everything of value had been taken, the walls were thrown down. Old abbeys whose walls were too strong to be breached were mined and then blown up with gunpowder.[1]

Royal officers took possession of each of the houses in turn. All that had belonged to the monks was now the property of the king, to be administered through his new "court of the augmentations of the revenues of the king's crown," and nothing of value was overlooked. The treasure in the crypt, the golden vessels, altarpieces and candlabras were packed in chests and carted off to the royal treasure house. The jewels the faithful had given to adorn the tombs and reliquaries of the saints were ripped from their settings and confiscated, and every ornament, bowl, pitcher and wooden trencher was seized, boxed and sent to London. The furnishings and hangings were sold, along with the cows, sheep and pigs and the grain and other foodstuffs in the barns. The crops were harvested and marketed by the royal commissioners, and the outbuildings were emptied of their tools, presses, plows and hayrakes. Even the lead from the roofs was stripped off and melted down for resale. The bells, many of them cast three or four centuries earlier and each lovingly named and christened by the monks, were taken down from their towers and hauled away.

By July of 1536 the effects of the campaign of destruction were highly visible. Monastic ruins scarred the countryside, and the human detritus too was very much in evidence. "It is a lamentable thing to see a legion of monks and nuns who have been chased from their monasteries wandering miserably hither and thither seeking means to live," one observer wrote. Many of these men and women had known no other home but the cloister since childhood; without their religious vocation they "knew not how to live."[2] More ominous were the social changes brought by the dismantling of the monasteries. They had been important economic as well as religious institutions, renting thousands of acres of land to rural tenants, employing villagers as laborers and servants, and buying locally produced crafts. Their disappearance would radically change rural life, and even those who hated the church admitted with alarm that the passing of the monks would mean hardship for the country people they had lived among for so long.

At first only the smaller houses were suppressed, those with twelve or fewer religious and worth less than two hundred pounds a year in revenues. Some effort was made to find refuge in other houses for the displaced monks and nuns, and a few of the monks became secular clerics. But though the destruction of monastic life would not be complete for several years its course was already clear. It could not be long before the crown seized the larger houses, putting an end to a monastic tradition stretching back to the days of the Venerable Bede in the early middle ages. In 1537 the first of these great old foundations, the Cistercian abbey of Furness, was surrendered to the king by its abbot, and in succeeding months other Cistercian and Benedictine establishments followed the same pattern.

It is thought that fewer than ten thousand religious were affected by the first wave of closings, but numbers alone tell little about what the final interruption of monastic spirituality meant to the population as a whole. The pulling down of the abbeys was evidence of the most startling and immediate kind that England was being swept into a new religious order. To be sure, the king's breach with the pope had been as radical an alteration in the faith as the destruction of the monasteries, if not more so. But the pope's influence had been invisible, whereas the monasteries were an immemorial part of the landscape. There were something less than six hundred religious houses in England, one for every ten parishes at least, and few in the population lived far from the sound of monastery bells or the sight of monastery fields. The generation born in the 1530s would grow to maturity amid monastic ruins.

Of course, since medieval times the very ubiquity of the monks and nuns had led to bitter criticism from laymen. The monks were accused of corruption, immorality and spiritual apathy; the nuns were denounced as luxury-loving and immoral. These time-honored criticisms the agents of Henry VIII now proposed to document, in order to provide a moral justification for the suppression. Teams of inspectors, or visitors, traveling in Yorkshire in 1536 found more than enough evidence of spiritual decline. The most obvious abuses were sexual sins. Dozens of monks admitted they had broken their vows of chastity; one monk confessed to incest with his own sister, another, who was prior of his house, told the visitors he had had seven mistresses. Pregnant nuns were not rare, and one religious at Cartemell had six children. Homosexuality was by far the most common sin against the monastic rule. Nearly every monastery had its "sodomites," and some mature monks were accused by their colleagues of seducing the young boys brought in as novices at the age of thirteen or younger. There was criminality too—theft, assault and, at Pontefract, a conspiracy among three monks to murder the prior.

The official visitors took careful note not only of abuses of this kind but of superstitious practices the religious encouraged among the country people. Every monastery had its relics, its shrines and its saintly images, all of which were severely discredited by the Protestant teachings now sweeping England. The nuns of Wallingwells treasured the comb of St. Edward, the monks of Shelford preserved the candle Mary carried at her purification. At Arden the countrywomen prayed to the image of St. Bride to help them find their lost cows or cure their sick ones. Pregnant women in every parish sent to the local monastery for the girdle of St. Francis—or St. Thomas, St. Peter, St. Bernard or the virgin Mary— to place over their bellies to ease delivery, and touched the wimple of St. Ethelrede when they had sore throats. Simon de Montfort's foot was also efficacious, as was Thomas of Lancaster's hat. At Repton, St. Guthlac's bell was said to relieve headaches, while at Bury St. Edmunds the faithful put the skull of St. Petronilla on their heads, hoping to be delivered from fever. As significant as the corrupt morals and superstitions the visitors reported was the overwhelming evidence that many, in some cases most, of those living the religious life were persisting in it against their will. Everywhere they found men and women who "sought to put off the habit"; at Langley, they noted, "almost all seek release."[3]

That so many monks and nuns should long to be delivered from what to them had become a burdensome life was perhaps the most eloquent testimony that monasticism was collapsing under its own weight. The ascetic ideal had not been entirely lost, but it was thriving best among the poor theologians at the universities, who rose before dawn, studied fifteen hours a day, and were content to share a "penny piece of beef" and its broth among four. These "living saints" had no fires in their rooms, and were forced to run up and down the halls for half an hour before going to bed to make sure they didn't freeze during the night. By comparison a religious like John Melford, abbot of Bury St. Edmunds, lived the life of a dissolute courtier. He "delights in the company of women," the York visitors wrote, "and in sumptuous banquets; he delights in cards and dice, lives much in his granges, and does not preach."[4]

However fixed their place in English society, the monasteries had clearly fallen on evil days. But if the monasteries were indeed in need of reform, the remedy provided by the royal government was equally harmful to spiritual life. Once the monks and nuns had been expelled, the lands of the church, which may have totaled as much as one-third of all the land in England, were sold off to peers, courtiers, crown officials, industrialists and country gentlemen for just under £800,000. A small percentage of the properties were given away to royal servants like Cromwell, who along with his nephew Richard received twelve abbeys, but most were sold outright to finance the growing cost of government. Cromwell, who as vicar general was the chief strategist of the dissolution, was acutely aware of the depleted royal treasury and of England's precarious diplomatic situation. If there should be war, bankruptcy would come sooner than victory, and no strong Protestant alliance had yet been forged to replace the old ties to France and the empire. Monastic wealth was sacrificed to the fiscal needs of the state, and from the king's point of view only good could result.

The ultimate outcome of the transfer of monastic properties to secular hands, though, was a harvest of cynicism. Where the cloisters and chapels were not simply left to rot their new owners put them to bizarre or blasphemous uses. One gentleman built a mansion on the site of a former Carthusian house, using the cloister itself for a parlor. A cloth manufacturer, Jack of Newbury, bought up as many abbeys as he could to use as factories. And most enterprising of all, the former prior of the Gilbertine house of Watton, Robert Holgate, took advantage of the dissolution to strike an unholy bargain with the king. He traded his monastery to Henry in return for the right to keep its revenues for himself as long as he lived. Holgate made himself useful to the king as archbishop of York, bringing some sixty-seven manors into Henry's hands, all the while amassing greater and greater personal wealth from the profits of the dissolution. In less than ten years he was reputed to be the wealthiest prelate in England.

Holgate's example was far from unique. In the end Catholics bought more church land and profited more from the spiritual traffic with the crown than Protestants. Overall the destruction of the monasteries unleashed a degree of greed far greater than any the corrupt monks had ever displayed. It embittered many among the devout without consolidating the loyalty of any segment of the population, while in the north, where rebellion had been in the air for years, it was soon to trigger a massive appeal to religious sentiment and tradition in the rising known as the Pilgrimage of Grace.

As the monastic households disintegrated Mary's was being reorganized. In the aftermath of her capitulation Henry gave orders that new officers and servants should be chosen for her, and considered, with his Council, the many requests he received from persons hoping to enter her service. There were, first of all, several men and women who had been in Katherine's tiny suite. One of Katherine's women, Elizabeth Harvey, asked to be allowed to join Mary's household but was refused; another, Elizabeth Darrell, had already asked to be taken into Jane's service some months earlier, as she saw no hope that Mary would ever yield to her father and so despaired of her future. Katherine's apothecary Juan de Soto, who was to have a long future in Mary's household, now joined its rolls, as did Anthony Roke, sometime courier for Katherine and, in Mary's words, "an honest man" whom she "loved well" and wished to repay for his fidelity. Three other women she asked for in particular. These were Mary Brown, her former maid, "whom for her virtue I love and could be glad to have in my company," and Margaret Baynton and Susan Clarencieux, two women who according to Mary regretted her former disobedience and were glad when she "inclined to duty."

Susan Clarencieux deserves particular emphasis. She had served Mary since the latter's childhood, and along with one or two others was the most long-established member of Mary's suite. Her name was Susan (or Susanna) Teong, but because her father had been Clarencieux Herald she was always referred to as Mistress Clarencieux. Perhaps because she was someone Mary had loved as a child, she became the unofficial favorite among the ladies and gentlewomen now appointed to attend her. She remained with Mary, "ever in principal place about her," for the rest of Mary's life. Familiar faces from Mary's former household as princess of Wales now reappeared: her cook, restored to her with the help of Henry's councilor Thomas Wriothesley, and Randal Dodd, an avuncular figure named often in her letters who had been among the last to leave Mary in 1533 and was now among the first to return, with the office of gentleman usher. The rest of those who made up her establishment—the yeomen, grooms, footmen and menials of the kitchen and laundry—are anonymous in the records, though at least one of them, a clerk of the kitchen, came from Henry Fitzroy's household, disbanded after his death.

Long before the household list was complete the climactic event of Mary's summer took place. She was brought from Hunsdon, riding at night with a few attendants, to a country house near the court. Henry and Jane met her there, and in this informal setting Mary and her father met and spoke, not as king and subject but as father and daughter, for the first time in five years. He had last seen her as a girl of fifteen, when to judge from a portrait of Mary painted at about that time she was a wide-eyed, thin-faced waif with a slightly hunted look. He now saw a woman of medium height and trim build who looked arrestingly like himself. She had his fresh coloring, his firm, small mouth, his pale eyebrows and intense gray eyes. Mary's face was heart-shaped, and dominated by a very wide, high forehead which was made to appear even more prominent by her smoothed hairstyle and domed headdresses. Her face was alert and highly intelligent, and her habitual expression was one of faint amusement that sharpened readily to sarcasm or disdain. Like her father Mary was nearsighted, and what many took to be a look of penetrating scrutiny in both father and daughter was in fact the frown of myopia.

What Henry must have found most startling in his grown-up daughter was her voice. For though she looked very much a woman Mary Tudor sounded like a man, with a low-pitched, resonant voice that carried well in a large room. According to the French ambassador Marillac Mary had "a voice more manlike, for a woman, than [Henry] had for a man," and combined with her customary outspokenness the effect must have been a powerful one.[5]

If Henry was at all taken aback by the self-determined woman he now recognized as his daughter he did not show it. From midafternoon until after vespers, when the king and Jane left to return to court, "there was nothing but conversing with Mary in private and with such love and affection, and such brilliant promises for the future, that no father could have behaved better towards his daughter."[6] Much was left unspoken, of course. Henry said nothing about Katherine, who had been in her tomb at Peterborough only five months, or about Anne, whose memory Jane seems quickly to have erased. He expressed deep regret at having kept Mary apart from him for so long, but gave every evidence that he would make up the loss in time, putting a draft for a thousand crowns in her hand for "small pleasures" and telling her there would be more whenever she needed it. Jane gave her a valuable diamond ring, and she was told that in a few days preparations would be made for her permanent return to court.[7]

Mary's return was delayed for several months, until after Henry came back from the long end-of-summer hunting tour he took every year. She stayed on at Hunsdon, surrounded by her growing household and receiving frequent gifts, messages and visitors from Cromwell and other royal servants. Edward Seymour, now Lord Beauchamp and Henry's chamberlain, asked her to send a list of whatever clothing she needed; Cromwell himself, who returned to his old role as Mary's chief friend in the Council, sent her a "well favored horse" and a beautiful saddle.[8]

Mary spent the long summer days walking in the fields, riding her horse and writing frequent letters to Henry. She took a warm interest in little Elizabeth, who at nearly three years old was as precocious as Mary herself had been. Mary wrote about her to the king, remarking on her unusual gifts and future promise, though remembering to add her customary reference to Henry's hope for a son. While at Hunsdon Mary received the clothes and jewels that had been taken from her two and a half years earlier. The clothes would have to be recut, the gowns made into kirtles and the trimmings removed to be used again. The jewels Mary put in her jewel chest along with those she had received just after Anne's death and those Henry and Jane often sent her. The news that the messengers and couriers brought from court along with their letters and packages marked the passing of an era. Henry Fitzroy was dead of tuberculosis; Anne's father Thomas Boleyn, who had been overheard to say at the time of Katherine's death that it was a pity her daughter was not keeping her company, was deprived of his lands and title. And Thomas Abel, Katherine's former chaplain and defender, was in prison for preaching against the royal Council, and no one believed he would ever be released.[9]

Ostensibly Mary and Henry were reunited, yet in Chapuys' phrase there were "a few drachmas of gall and bitterness mixed with the sweet food of paternal kindness."[10] Mary had been made to come to heel in signing the Submission, but her look and demeanor were anything but submissive. She was overtly deferential, and genuinely loving, but disturbingly intelligent. And she was, after all, very like himself, and Henry was guile incarnate. To ease his mind the king met with her again, and this time, believing he had won her confidence through his display of affection, his gifts and the disarming pomp of her new household, Henry asked Mary to tell him privately whether she had signed the Submission voluntarily or merely as a ruse, maintaining the opposite opinions in her heart. He hated nothing more than dishonesty, he said. Sometimes he was advised to conceal the truth from ambassadors, or even to lie to them, but he never did as his councilors told him, preferring to speak the truth at all costs. Mary should now show herself his true daughter, he concluded, by telling him in all confidentiality whether she had dissembled when she agreed to sign the document.

Mary assured him her submission had been sincere. She had no other choice than to say this, unless she wanted to abandon the course she had decided to follow and return to a sure sentence of death. For weeks she had been writing to Henry in the most self-deprecating terms imaginable, begging him "prostrate at your most noble feet, humbly, and with the very bottom of my stomach," to believe the sincerity of her repentance.[11] She declared herself his "bounden slave," his "most humble faithful and obedient child," and announced that she would rather be a servant in his chamber, favored with his presence, than an empress away from him.[12] He could hardly ask anything more of Mary, except that she repeat, in letters to Charles V, the pope and the regent of Flanders, her change of heart about her mother's marriage and her illegitimacy, telling them that she arrived at her new opinions freely and without coercion. Mary wrote these letters, following drafts the king provided, and declared herself willing to take any other steps he asked to prove her complete loyalty. Finally Henry professed to be satisfied, for the moment at least, but in fact he had gained nothing. Mary was becoming more than a match for her father in the game of deceit. The two dissemblers—the expert and the novice—had squared off in a fresh display of artificial candor, but neither had come away the wiser.

Of course, Mary protected herself at every step in this latest round of hypocrisy. She had asked for papal absolution from all vows or oaths forced from her against her conscience.[13] With every letter she wrote she signed a protest invalidating it. She asked Chapuys to write to the emperor, forewarning him of the false declaration Henry would be forwarding to him on her behalf, and advising him of the reply she felt would serve her interests best. In these maneuverings Mary was firmly at the helm, steering her own course among the obstacles and dangers to her soul, her honor and her political future. Chapuys was involved at every turn, but he was no longer in charge. Mary knew well her danger. She told the imperial ambassador in Rome, Cifuentes, that if the king found out what she was doing it would be as if a knife were placed at her throat. But she persisted, spurred on by the sense of destiny she had discovered earlier in the year and undeterred by the atmosphere of capricious menace that hung over the king's personal rule.

Mary's relations with her father were on a new and dangerous footing. She loved him as a father, but reached a new accommodation with him as her king. She was outwardly obedient, but inwardly defiant. Like all successful diplomats caught between irreconcilable interests she stumbled at last on the one workable policy: say one thing but believe another, relying on a higher morality, a transcendent purpose, to justify the deceit.

It was among the many ironies of Mary's situation in the summer of 1536 that she was given a tangible symbol of her new-found posture of submission to wear in token of her change of heart. Cromwell had a gold ring made for Mary, with portraits of Henry, Jane and herself on the top and verses inscribed around the sides. He wanted to give the ring to her himself, but Henry usurped the honor, perhaps wishing he had thought of the idea first. The Latin verses celebrated obedience and humility, in words which echoed the language of the Magnificat, the song the virgin sang after submitting to the divine purpose in the miraculous conception of Jesus. Christ's life too, the poem said, was a model of obedience and humility. With these holy patterns to follow Mary could not fall into willfulness and arrogance again. Obedience leads to unity, the verses read, unity to constancy and a quiet mind, and these are treasures of inestimable worth. For God so valued humility that he gave us in his son a perfect exemplar of humility, who in his obedience to his divine father taught us to obey our parents in turn.[14]

Through the ring she now wore in commemoration of her reunion with Henry, Mary was being told in yet another way that obedience was her divinely ordained function. But unknown to her father, she had glimpsed another role, sanctioned by the same divinity but leading to a destiny nearer her own choosing.

XVIII

 God save King Henry with all his power,
And Prince Edward, that goodly flower,
With all his lords of great honour—
Sing in, troll away, sing, troll on away,
Heave and how, rumbelow, troll on away—

In October of 1537 Jane Seymour gave birth to a son. He was born at Hampton Court, and because his birthday fell on the eve of St. Edward he was given the saint's name. Within hours of his birth Te Deums were being sung in every parish church in London for Prince Edward, and all the bells were ringing. There were bonfires in every street, and at St. Paul's all the priests, canons and regular clergy of the city were assembling in their richest robes, with their best crosses and candlesticks carried before them. When the bishops of London and Chichester, the dean of St. Paul's, the judges and the Lord Mayor and aldermen arrived a public feast was spread and distributed at the choir door of the church, and later a great Te Deum and anthems were sung. The king's musicians played, and at the Tower, "a great peal of guns" was shot.

The celebrating lasted well into the night. New fires were lit in every street and lane, and the people in each neighborhood sat around them "banquetting with fruits and wine." Hogsheads of wine were set out in various places at the king's order, and at the Steelyard the merchants lit a hundred torches and provided wine and beer to all comers. The mayor and aldermen rode up and down the streets thanking the citizens for their good fortune, and urging them to "praise God for our prince." It was ten o'clock before the bells stopped ringing, and even later before the Tower guns shot their two thousandth round and fell silent.

The bishop of Worcester, Hugh Latimer, sat down at the end of this eventful day to record the immense delight of the English people at Edward's birth. "Here is no less joying and rejoicing in these parts for the birth of our prince," he wrote, "whom we hungered for so long, than there was, I trow, by the neighbors at the birth of John the Baptist." Latimer's rhetoric was unbounded. The prince was, in his view, the gift of "an English god" who was no longer angry with his people. Edward's birth discouraged traitors and stopped the mouths of those who spoke against the king. The prince was "the stop of vain trusts, the stay of vain expectations." He defied all the prophets who had pronounced the king cursed with childlessness; he ended the rumors of impotence once and for all. If he proved to be a sturdy child he would become Henry's most treasured possession, his true heir, the new hope of an aging king.

The public anticipation of Edward's birth had begun months earlier. Late in May Queen Jane appeared in the open-laced gown and stomacher of a pregnant woman, and on May 27, Trinity Sunday, a Te Deum was sung "for joy of the queen's quickening with child." Then too there had been bonfires and wine for the Londoners, and throughout the summer wagers were made on the sex of the child and on the exact day when he (for it had to be a prince this time) would be born.[1] Henry took no chances with this baby. There was no court gossip about new mistresses, no indiscretion of any kind. Though it was prime hunting season Henry stayed close to the queen at Hampton Court, knowing that the birth was expected in October and realizing that his absence might upset his wife and harm his son. The king explained in a letter to Norfolk that though Jane's "reverend conformity" made her content with anything he asked of her, still, "being but a woman, upon some sudden and displeasant rumors and bruits that might by foolish or light persons be blown abroad in our absence, being specially so far from her she might take to her stomach such impressions as might engender no little danger or displeasure to the infant." The Council urged Henry not to travel more than sixty miles from the capital, and he concurred.[2]

The plague kept Henry away from Hampton Court on the night Edward was born, but he joined his pale, exhausted wife soon afterward. Jane's labor had lasted more than fifty hours, and she was weaker than anyone realized. Her condition, though, went all but unnoticed amid the attention given to the newborn prince. Overnight Hampton Court became a nursery, and every person and object in the household came under stringent regulations ordered by the king to ensure the health of the prince. Henry's painful memories of the death of his first son in 1511 still haunted him; there must be no repetition of that tragedy now. The recent outbreak of plague made the need for scrupulous cleanliness and isolation all the greater, and the king gave orders that neither Londoners, country people nor beggars were to be allowed within the palace gates. Every hallway and courtyard was to be washed down and swept daily;

every blanket, dish and cushion brought near the baby was to be spot-lessly clean. Even the christening had to be planned in accordance with these instructions, though it was to be a splendid celebration nonetheless.

There had been no christening of a prince in England for more than a quarter century, and every care was taken to make the event as elaborate and impressive as possible. Mary was to be Edward's godmother, and she ordered a new kirtle of cloth of silver for the ceremony, paying the London cloth merchant an enormous sum for the fabric.[3] Every no-table of the court and government was present as the christening proces-sion formed in the queen's apartments. Jane received the courtiers from her bed, and she and Henry watched as the churchmen and officials took their places and walked two by two toward the chapel. The ceremony lasted for hours. Finally the tapers carried by the gentlemen of the court were lighted to indicate that the naming was complete, and the Garter King of Arms proclaimed the child "Edward, son and heir to the king of England, duke of Cornwall and earl of Chester." Mary stood behind the marchioness of Exeter, who carried the baby in her arms under a canopy. Mary's christening gift was a golden cup, and to the nurse, midwife and cradle rockers she gave a generous thirty pounds. As the group left the chapel Mary took Elizabeth by the hand and led her out, with Lady Kingston and Lady Herbert bearing their trains. It was after midnight when Edward was brought back to the queen's apartments to be blessed once more, by his parents and in the name of God, the virgin Mary and St. George, and then food was provided for the entire company, hypocras and wafers for the nobles and bread and sweet wine for the "gentles and all other estates."[4]

Latimer's hope that the birth of an heir would put an end to rebellion was not mere rhetoric. The spectacle of so many nobles and clerics solemnly assembled to confirm the king's heir in his rights was meant to give an appearance of popular stability and content, but in fact the king had only recently faced the most dangerous revolt of his reign. It had broken out just twelve months earlier in the north, revealing the true extent of the people's disloyalty and the precariousness of the royal authority.

The unrest had been building for years. Economic hardship hit the northern counties very hard in the 1530s, striking at the clothiers of the West Riding, the farmers impoverished by high rents, and all those affected by the suppression of the monasteries. Sentiment against the religious innovations was very high in the north, where distrust and hatred of the king had been widespread since the early days of his di-vorce from Katherine. When Anne became queen the people cursed her; when Henry declared himself head of the church they refused to accept his supremacy. They swore to uphold the Act of Succession, but it only

The young Henry VIII, by Joos van Cleve. (*The Royal Collection* © *Her Majesty The Queen*)

Henry Fitzroy, duke of Richmond, natural son of Henry VIII and Elizabeth Blount. *(The Hulton Deutsch Collection)*

Henry, his jester Will Somers, and Mary, by Holbein. *(The Hulton Deutsch Collection)*

Margaret Pole, countess of Salisbury. Artist unknown. *(The National Portrait Gallery, London)*

Katherine of Aragon in middle age. Artist unknown. *(The National Portrait Gallery, London)*

Henry, circa 1536. Portrait after Holbein. *(The National Portrait Gallery, London)*

Anne Boleyn. Artist unknown. *(The National Portrait Gallery, London)*

Catherine Parr, by William Scrots. *(The National Portrait Gallery, London)*

ANNO DNI · · · 1544

LADI MARI · · · DOVGHTER
THE · MOST · · · VERTVOVS · PF
KING · HENRI · · · THE · EIGHT

THE · AGE · OF · · · XXVIII · YE

The Princess Mary at twenty-eight, in 1544, by Master John (Johannes Corvus).
(The National Portrait Gallery, London)

Elizabeth Tudor, circa 1560. Artist unknown. *(The National Portrait Gallery, London)*

Fantasy portrait, circa 1545, of Henry VIII with his family: the king with Edward Tudor and Jane Seymour in the centre, Mary at left and Elizabeth at right. Will Somers is pictured in the background far right, and the woman at far left is probably Jane Bold, Mary's fool. School of Holbein. *(The Royal Collection © Her Majesty The Queen)*

Edward Tudor at age ten. Artist unknown. *(The Royal Collection © Her Majesty The Queen)*

Edward Seymour, duke of Somerset, the Protector. Artist unknown. *(The National Portrait Gallery, London)*

Thomas Cranmer in 1546, by G Flicke *(The National Portrait Gallery, London)*

Lady Jane Grey, circa 1545, attributed to Master John. *(The National Portrait Gallery, London)*

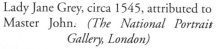

Sir Thomas Wyatt, leader of the 1554 rebellion. Artist unknown. *(The National Portrait Gallery, London)*

Philip and Mary in 1558, now attributed to Hans Eworth. (*By kind permission of the Marquess of Tavistock and Trustees of the Bedford Estate*)

Mary Tudor in 1555, by G Flicke. *(The Dean and Chapter of Durham)*

made them more angry, more eager, when the time came, to join forces against the king. "Even the rude people," Chapuys reported, "said it was evident the statute was of no value, since they were compelled to swear, which had never been seen before."[5] Like Mary they told one another that an oath exacted by force was not morally binding, and besides this they demonstrated their opposition to the new political and religious order in direct and emphatic ways.

When preachers were sent among them to denounce the pope and the old practices of relic worship and the granting of indulgences they called them seditious. One preacher who presented a play about the pope and his "councilors" Error and Incredulity found the doors of all the parish churches closed to him. At Kendal in Westmorland the parishioners, some three hundred strong, "threatened to cast the curate into the water unless he would proclaim the pope to be head of the church." Local priests continued to uphold the pope, to maintain the efficacy of the saints and their remains, and to dispense indulgences. They denounced the relaxed Lenten observances instituted by the king as head of the church, and they heard with horror of the Ten Articles, Henry's redefinition of belief which made no mention of confirmation, matrimony, holy orders or extreme unction. There was no telling how far the destruction of the traditional faith might go. If the king could annihilate four of the seven sacraments, why not the other three? Already he was ordering his clergy to say that masses had no power to deliver souls from purgatory, and there were rumors that in the near future many churches would be closed and all religious ceremonies taxed.

The final provocation to rebellion, though, came with the destruction of the monasteries. The rebel leader Robert Aske, when questioned about the grievances of the Yorkshiremen who followed him, spoke eloquently about the different meaning the religious houses had in the northern counties. The abbeys "gave great alms to poor men," he said, and taught God's law to unlettered people living in the "mountains and desert places." The monks had kept up the sea walls and dikes, and had built bridges and highways—something no one else did in the remote regions of the kingdom—and provided weary travelers with food and rest in country where villages were sparse. Moreover the monasteries were the guardians of tradition, both literally and metaphorically. For the nobility they were ancestral graveyards, for the common folk they embodied the past in a way that defied explanation. They were landmarks in both a historical and geographical sense. In Aske's phrase, the abbeys were "one of the beauties of this realm to all men."

As the pulling down of the abbeys accelerated the climate of opposition in the north grew more heated. Priests denounced Cromwell and his assistants as agents of the devil in their thorough and efficient work of demolition, and assured their congregations that all who took part in the suppression would be damned. Some clergy urged the monks to resist by force, and when this failed, encouraged their own parishioners to take up arms.

The first risings were in Lincolnshire, where the shoemaker Nicholas Melton and his sworn companions dedicated themselves to revolt on behalf of "God, the king and the commons for the wealth of holy church." In a nearby village the country people took as their symbol the Five Wounds of Christ, and within days there were said to be some forty thousand men following the banner of the Five Wounds, including hundreds of priests and monks. The rebel army seized Lincoln, but failed to hold the town after a royal herald arrived with a threatening message from the king. The commons of Yorkshire, however, now defied their sovereign and supported the lawyer and country gentleman Robert Aske, who with his "Pilgrims" took the city of York and became the effective ruler of the county. Henry, who had dismissed both the rebels and their petitions for reform as beneath his notice, now grew uneasy and sent Norfolk and Suffolk to put down the revolt. Already the success of the Yorkshiremen was encouraging unrest in East Anglia and Norfolk, and there was always the danger of intervention from the Scots or from continental powers. In fact the pope gave legatine powers to Reginald Pole, the son of the countess of Salisbury and scion of the Plantagenet line, and sent him to Flanders to wait for an opportune moment to cross to England and lead the rising.

While Pole waited the rebels sent the king a new list of demands. Headship of the English church was to be returned to the pope in matters that concerned the "cure of souls"—that is, spiritual and ecclesiastical affairs. Parliament was to be reformed, the recent Act of Succession repealed, and the monasteries restored. Full pardon for all rebels would have to be guaranteed before York would be surrendered to the royal forces. The demands were stringent, but the king appeared now to take them seriously. Through his deputy Norfolk he granted the Pilgrims the pardon they asked for—or so it seemed—and Aske convinced them to disband.

Before the Pilgrims realized that the king had deceived them his agents were at work rounding up all who believed they had been pardoned and bringing them to trial. Hundreds were summarily executed, many of them sentenced by juries coerced into rendering guilty verdicts. The rebel leaders, including Lords Hussey and Darcy, were beheaded, and Robert Aske was "hanged in the city of York in chains till he died."[6] Many country people were hanged in their own gardens as examples to their fellow villagers, and monks of Sawley Abbey, a suppressed monastery which the Pilgrims had re-established, were hanged from the steeple of their church.

It was this rebellion that Latimer meant to conjure in his fervent welcome to the new prince as the sure remedy against conspiracies. Now that the king had a male heir he would be much less vulnerable to attack from those who might try to use the uncertain succession as an excuse to overthrow him.

In particular, it weakened those who supported Mary and wanted to see her rights restored. For if the Pilgrimage of Grace had been primarily a conservative protest against religious innovations it also prominently raised the question of Mary's status. In the north Mary was still looked on as the king's legitimate daughter, who on her mother's side "came of the greatest blood in Christendom" and whom the Roman church had never proclaimed to be baseborn. "She is marvellously beloved by the whole people," Aske said, and it is certain that not only the commoners but the aristocrats and gentry among the rebels, many of whom had been prepared to take the field against the king since 1534, supported Mary's claim to the throne.[7]

Yet so complete was her restoration to favor that the rebellion did nothing to dislodge her. Henry assumed, correctly, that his daughter was not connected with the rebels in any way, despite their advocacy of her cause. Throughout the fall and winter of 1536 she associated herself more and more closely with her father and stepmother, riding beside them in the royal barge or, when the river was frozen, through the streets of London.[8] At court she held the place of honor just below the queen, sitting opposite her, "a little lower down," at table and enjoying the privilege of serving both the king and queen with the napkin when they washed their hands before the dishes were brought in.[9] She stood with Jane at the font at the christenings of noblemen's children, and rejoiced with the queen as her pregnancy advanced. Mary sent her stepmother quails in June—Jane ate them by the dozens as the summer went on, and could not seem to get enough—and attended to her obligations as mistress of a growing establishment of officers and servants.[10]

Some members of the new household proved to be troublesome. One of Mary's yeoman cooks, Spencer by name, was implicated in a robbery in Oxfordshire, and had to answer to the bailiffs of Reading.[11] Shortly afterward it came to light that a tailor's servant who had been given access to a manor house where Mary stayed from time to time abused his master's trust and spent the day in the empty residence. Two of his friends were with him, and while they did no harm—one played the virginals and lute, another read a book, and all three explored the "gentlewomen's chamber" with inordinate interest—their unsupervised stay

worried the porter when he found out about it and indicated some carelessness on the part of Mary's household steward, John Shelton.[12]

In the fall Mary was back at Hampton Court waiting out Jane's
confinement with the rest of the nobility. In her capacity as godmother
to the prince she was an important figure in the celebrations that attended
his birth, but a more somber honor fell to her when Jane, weakened by
her ordeal and humored in her craving for "unwholesome" foods, became
fatally ill and died. The rejoicing over Edward's birth was barely over
when Jane's obsequies began, and Mary was now called upon to be chief
mourner. Her responsibilities were especially grave in that Henry, who
was deeply grieved by Jane's death, rode off almost immediately to get
away from the morbid atmosphere of the court and left the funeral arrangements in the hands of the Council and chief mourner.

The king was both affronted and alarmed by reminders of death. His
preoccupation with medicines and hygiene, the terror of plague and dread
of all other disease all point to a phobia that clung to him throughout his
reign. Years later a member of Edward's royal Council recalled that
Henry "ofttimes would not only dispense with all mourning, but would
be ready to pluck the black apparel from such men's backs as presumed
to wear it in his presence." Henry's sorrow at the loss of his wife sharpened his horror of death in general and made him more anxious than
ever to take refuge away from court.

In his absence the cumbersome sequence of vigils, masses and processions that made up a royal funeral was set in motion. Jane was first laid
out in her coffin in the palace, surrounded by candles and mourned by
the household servants who had now to find other work. Mary distributed the funeral dole among them—a sovereign each to the chamber
women, forty shillings to the page, and three shillings to the queen's personal gardener at Hampton Court.[13] After a few days the corpse was
placed in the palace chapel, and Lancaster Herald ordered all present to
kneel. "Of your charity pray for the soul of the queen!" he called out,
then made way for the priests and chapel boys to sing the dirge.

Weeks of vigils followed. Watchers surrounded the hearse at all hours
of the day and night, with the clergy, gentleman ushers and officers of
arms presiding at night and the chief mourner and her ladies taking over
during the daylight hours. There were several masses each day, among
them the offering mass at which every mourner gave a piece of gold for
the soul of the deceased. Finally on November 12, eighteen days after she
died, Jane was escorted to her burial place in the Garter chapel at Windsor. Two hundred poor men walked ahead of the procession wearing her
badge and carrying lighted torches. Mary, her horse trapped in black velvet, rode just behind the coffin, followed by twenty-nine ladies and
gentlewomen. At every town and village through which the procession

passed the poor men formed a corridor of honor with their torches, and the villagers lined the road, their caps in their hands, to watch the queen pass.

At Windsor the dean and college met the funeral party at the outer gate, and the pallbearers carried the coffin into the chapel where the archbishop of Canterbury awaited it in his pontifical robes, flanked by six bishops and as many abbots. Mary followed, attended by seven ladies and with Lady Rochford carrying her train. After another day and night of lessons, dirges and masses, the women mourners offered their velvet palls —as chief mourner Mary presented seven of these—and then Jane was buried between the stalls and altar of the chapel.

Her epitaph compared her to a phoenix who in dying gave the realm another like herself.

> Here lies Jane, a phoenix
> Who died in giving another phoenix birth.
> Let her be mourned, for birds like these
> Are rare indeed.

Jane would be honored for the rest of Henry's reign as the mother of his heir, though the king's enemies would in time embroider the circumstances of her death with a dark legend. It would be said that, to save his son, Henry ordered the baby torn out of the womb at the cost of Jane's life. Henry had become so despised by many of his subjects that even his bitterest personal tragedy was charged to his own cruelty.

For Mary the period of mourning had a painful postscript. Her days and nights of watching and attendance at mass after mass gave her a bad toothache, and as soon as Jane was in her grave Mary had to have the tooth pulled. Henry sent his own man, Nicholas Sampson, to do the extraction, and either the procedure was very time-consuming or Sampson was very skilled, for beyond giving him the forty-five-shilling fee Mary sent him back to court with six gold angels in his purse.[14]

XIX

 Shee may be calde Marigold well,
Of Marie (chiefe), Christes mother deere,
That as in heaven shee doth excell,
And Golde in earth, to have no peere:
So (certainly) shee shineth cleere,
In Grace and honour double folde,
The like was never earst seene heere,
Such is this floure, the Marigolde.

Mary Tudor was now in her early twenties. She had already lived through more in her short lifetime than courtiers three times her age, but though the inner strains would become apparent soon enough her outward appearance was still that of a young girl. "With a fresh complexion she looks not past eighteen or twenty," the French ambassador Marillac wrote in 1541, when she was twenty-five.[1] And he added "she is one of the belles of this court." He went on to describe her person and habits, relying on one of her chamberers, a woman who had served Mary on and off from infancy, for his information. He reported that she was of middle stature, with her father's features and her mother's neck. Once she was married, the woman told Marillac, Mary was "of a disposition to have children soon," implying both that she was capable of bearing children and that she looked forward to having them.

In manner Marillac found Mary sweet and benign, but with the prudence and reserve appropriate in a woman of her rank. The ambassador's description of her daily life portrayed a reasonably healthy, vigorous and gifted woman. She is active, he wrote, and seemingly robust. She liked to exercise in the mornings and often walked two or three miles after breakfast. Her French and Latin were very good, and she read the Latin classics for pleasure. She had become an impressive performer on the virginals, and played (and taught her women to play) with unusual dexterity. In all, Marillac found Mary to be a very suitable candidate for marriage to a younger son of the French king, or to a duke of the royal blood. Her illegitimacy, plus the doubts surrounding her recurrent illness —which the chamber woman tried to dispel—were her only handicaps in the marriage market. Marillac would have liked to send his master a portrait of Mary, but her father refused. There would be no portraits of his daughter to send to prospective bridegrooms or fathers-in-law unless he approved the proposed match, and he did not approve.

Mary's regular features, clear complexion and fresh coloring attracted admiration, and the clothes she chose helped to make her a center of attention. She loved to wear bright colors—reds and rich purples and the shimmering cloth of gold that sold for more than ten pounds the yard. Like her father she was inclined to be gaudy, and to decorate herself, some said to excess, with finery and jewels. When the secretary of a Spanish grandee met her at court he found her wearing a kirtle of cloth of gold and a violet gown of heavy three-piled velvet. Her headdress sparkled with "many rich stones."[2]

Among her favorite jewels was a single ruby set in the shape of a Gothic letter "H," Henry's monogram, with a pendant pearl. She also owned a jeweled letter "M", set with three rubies, two diamonds and a huge pearl.[3] She supervised the inventory of her jewels closely, checking each page and signing it when she found it correct. Biblical jewelry filled the pages of this jewel book, with brooches of Old Testament scenes such as Moses "striking water out of the rock" and "Jacob being asleep" in mother of pearl complemented by stories from the life of Jesus. There was a brooch of Noah's flood with little diamonds and rubies, a pendant "tablet" depicting the Trinity, and a brooch of Jesus healing the palsied man, adorned with a great table diamond.[4] Among her dearest treasures was a miniature golden book that had somehow survived the attempted obliteration of all references to the king's first marriage. It too was ornamental, and it showed "the king's face and her grace mother's"—that is, it bore facing portraits of Henry and Katherine.[5]

Now that she had money to spend Mary indulged her taste for finery. To one of the king's envoys who was traveling to Spain she gave forty shillings to buy her small luxuries; to another bound for Paris she entrusted twelve pounds to buy more costly goods. But if her personal tastes now flourished her father's preferences were never far from her mind, even in matters of dress. At Easter, 1538, when the court was putting off mourning for Queen Jane, Mary was anxious to wear what pleased Henry most. She sent Lady Kingston to the privy councilor Wriothesley, to ask him to inquire through Cromwell what the king wanted his daughter to wear. Mary thought he might like to see her in an old dress of white taffeta edged with velvet, "which used to be to his own liking whensoever he saw her grace, and suiteth for this joyful feast of our Lord's rising."[6] Lady Kingston carried the message to Wriothesley, who relayed it to Cromwell, who finally asked Henry about it. He answered brusquely that Mary could wear whatever she liked.

Henry was preoccupied with continental affairs during 1538 and 1539, and paid scant attention to his children. Mary saw him infrequently, and spent her time at Richmond, Hampton Court, and the country houses of Kent and Surrey. Life in these country establishments was especially pleasant in summer and fall, when the farmers and villagers brought their fruits and vegetables to the gate of the great house to sell, and there were fresh peaches, apples, pears and strawberries in abundance. Gentlewomen sent quince pies and orange pies to Mary's cook, and there was always deer from the neighboring hunting parks. There were bucks sent up from Eltham, does from Lady Sussex and other game brought by servants of Nicholas Carew's; the king sent partridges when he happened to think of it, and the local people supplied as many chickens as the household could consume. Villagers whose children Mary had sponsored at their christenings brought her pheasants, baskets of vegetables and other things from their gardens out of gratitude, and country women came every week with dishes of butter, or confections, or flowers for the king's daughter.[7]

It was characteristic of Mary to form close ties with the members of her household. She attracted their devotion, and they her care and compassion. The affection between them took many forms: the stability of the household staff from one year to the next, the competition for a place among Mary's attendant ladies and gentlewomen, the frequent celebrations and exchanges of gifts among those who did enter her service. There were always gifts at New Year's, but birthdays and holy days were also observed with small presents. On St. Valentine's day the men drew the women's names as their Valentines, and gifts of spaniels, caged birds, artificial flowers, smocks or lace or embroidered sleeves for gowns were exchanged. Sometimes the gifts were very valuable. When the widower Anthony Browne drew Mary as his Valentine she gave him a gold brooch set with an agate and four small rubies, enameled with the story of Abraham.[8] Mary gave christening gifts to all the children she held at the font, and many of them were sons and daughters of household officials or servants. At the christening of Dr. De la Sà's child his godmother Mary presented a large ornamental saltcellar in silver and gilt, and an entry in her expense book shows that it cost sixty-six shillings. To the children of her longtime servants Beatrice and David ap Rice Mary became a patron. She paid the girl's board in London and the boy's at Windsor, where he served in some capacity at the court, and she continued this support until both children were able to make their own way in the world.

Mary's establishment was always a source of charity. She relieved hundreds of poor men and women each year, giving something to all who came to her. On her daily walks she carried a purse full of pennies to give to needy folk she happened to meet, and many times she met women whose husbands were in jail, or men whose crops had been trampled or lost through drought or frost, and in every case she gave the petitioner something to help him or her make a fresh start. In 1537 she gave seven shillings to a "poor man whose house was burned" to build it again. Whenever she received a lump sum of money from the court she gave much of it away in alms, usually on the same day that she received it. Like other compassionate Christians in the 1530s and 1540s, Mary found the sight of impoverished monks, nuns and priests heartbreaking, and she helped them whenever she could. When she found that one Father Beauchamp, an old priest attached to Windsor Castle, had been deprived of his income and had nothing to live on, she took over responsibility for his support herself.[9]

The Spanish envoy who reported on Mary's looks and disposition at this period wrote in his account that, beyond her "very great goodness and discretion, among other praises I heard of her is this, that she knows how to conceal her acquirements."[10] The acquirements Mary had to work hardest to conceal were her musical skills and her learning. She was as proficient on the regals and lute as she was on the virginals, and several of her instruments were moved with the itinerant household from one residence to another. Repairmen came regularly from London to replace strings, make needed adjustments and tune the virginals, and Mary's keyboard teacher "Mr. Paston" and lute teacher Philip Van Wilder were salaried members of her establishment.[11]

As for her proficiency in languages, she had no regular tutor but continued to read on her own. The works of the Greek and Roman historians, philosophers and poets had occupied a special place in her life for many years. Mary confided to the chamberwoman who was Marillac's informant that throughout the trying period of her mother's divorce and even in the darkest months of Anne's reign she had turned to the classics for comfort. The "humane letters" dear to the Renaissance humanists were Mary's solace during her sleepless nights at Hunsdon, and they meant a good deal to her on that account.[12] Mary was at no time part of a scholarly or artistic circle, but she did maintain close ties with Lord Morley, who presented her with either a translation or an original work of his own every year. At least some of his works were undertaken at

Mary's suggestion, and the range of his interests—his translations included patristic, scholastic and humanist treatises—must have coincided
with hers at many points. In the doctrinal and scholarly controversies of
the 1530s Morley's tastes placed him among the followers of Erasmus,
who though he re-edited and purified the Christian texts did not share the
Protestants' radical reinterpretations of them. Morley translated Erasmus'
treatise in praise of the virgin Mary, and the new edition by the
humanist Poliziano of a work by the Greek doctor Athanasius. He also
made a new translation of Aquinas' treatise on the Hail Mary, a biblical
passage that was always significant for Mary Tudor.[13]

In her talents and cultural preferences Mary was clearly among the
most accomplished women of her time, but her temperament was in no
sense that of a withdrawn intellectual. She loved the outdoors, and spent
hours walking in the gardens and tending plants of her own. Jasper, head
gardener at Beaulieu, sent Mary roots and herbs to grow in the gardens
of Richmond and Hampton Court, and her household records show her
preoccupation with growing things. Riding was another of her delights.
She had always ridden for health reasons but in her twenties, with a sizable stable and several very good riding horses, she resumed her old pastime of riding to the hunt. Her mother had taught her to love hunting,
and in the last years before they were separated Mary and Katherine had
hunted together in the royal parks, forgetting for a few hours the tragedy that was closing in around them. Mary now kept a kennel of hunting
hounds, and liked to be painted with Italian greyhounds at her feet.

In the winter months there were indoor amusements. Mary shared her
father's taste for gambling, and when she played cards with Lady Hart-
ford or Lady Margaret Grey she often lost twenty shillings at a single sitting.[14] Most of the entertainment, though, was provided by a jester
whose name appears more often in Mary's household books than any
other: Jane the Fool. Jane was one of Henry's jesters, the only woman
fool on a par with his favorite Will Somers. (Anne Boleyn had a woman
fool, but what became of her on her mistress' death is unclear.) Henry
provided Jane's board and paid her wages, and occasionally supplied her
with cloth for her gowns and other necessities, but from 1537 on she
lived with Mary, and it was Mary who looked after her everyday expenses. She paid for Jane's hose and shoes (she wore them out every few
months), and for the cloth for her smocks, gowns and bed linen; she paid
the bills submitted by one "Hogman" who kept Jane's horse, and found
someone to care for her during a long illness she suffered in 1543.

Jane the Fool must have been a startling parody of a court gentlewoman. She wore damask gowns and silk kirtles, but her hose and shoes
were those of a clown. She kept her head shaved as bald as an egg, and a
barber came to shave it once a month at a cost of fourpence. Jane had a

companion who was known as Lucretia the Tumbler, and between them they kept Mary amused for hours with their jokes and songs and tricks.[15]

But if Mary's time was spent agreeably enough in these years it was nonetheless time spent in expectation. The natural next step in her life was marriage, and rumors about who Mary's husband would be were more or less constant at court and in the council chamber. In November of 1536, five months after her submission, Henry told Mary at dinner one night that he was seriously searching for a husband for her, and that he had a very suitable one in mind. He said much the same thing a few days later, now adding that the man he had in mind was Dom Luiz of Portugal, Charles V's brother-in-law and preferred choice as Mary's husband. In the fall of 1536 Henry was discouraged about the prospect of Jane's having a son, and confided to Mary that since his queen would not provide him with a male heir he hoped his daughter would give him one. A legitimate grandson, he said, would be better than a bastard son.

Reports that the king intended to marry off his elder daughter were commonplace throughout the 1530s. Charles V had seen marriage to a foreign prince as by far the best solution to Mary's dilemma during Anne's reign, and recommended King James of Scotland, the French dauphin, and Dom Luiz as honorable matches for her. Henry let it be known that he was considering the voyvode of Poland as a potential son-in-law from 1532 on, and later, when he began to seek new political alliances with the Lutherans, he considered bestowing his daughter on a German prince. There was always the possibility that to punish Mary and remove any threat to his security she represented Henry might marry her to an Englishman of low birth, or to one of his trusted officials. Shortly after Katherine's death Chapuys heard a rumor, taken seriously by most of Mary's friends and supporters, that the king meant to marry her to Cromwell. Chapuys could not bring himself to believe it, but he traced the story to "one lord and one gentleman" who sincerely thought Henry was considering giving Mary to his principal secretary.[16]

By the fall of 1536, though, the field of candidates had narrowed. As the privy councilors noted shortly afterward, both Mary and Elizabeth were diplomatic assets which ought to be used to make allies. The two great powers on the continent, France and the empire, were currently alienated by England's Protestant leanings (though both were actively soliciting Mary's hand). Why not ease the diplomatic strains by means of a marriage alliance? Henry appeared to favor such a policy, and welcomed envoys from both the Hapsburg and Valois courts when they arrived in England empowered to negotiate the terms of a marriage contract. The French negotiator Gilles de la Pommeraye bustled about the court, telling every courtier in sight how advantageous a marriage between Mary and Charles, duke of Orléans and second in line to the

French throne, was bound to be. To the king's councilors he repeated again and again Francis' offer of a dower of eighty thousand ducats in revenues, plus a force of mercenaries to help put down the rebellion then troubling the north of England. Henry pretended not to hear these offers and took little notice of La Pommeraye, but he and his associates persisted, making themselves odious to Mary with their constant attentions and hints that they hoped she would soon be the bride of a Frenchman.[17]

In the end the French match fell through, chiefly because La Pommeraye had been instructed to insist that before the marriage contract was drawn up Mary's legitimacy had to be restored. The issue of her legitimacy and succession rights were to prove an obstacle to any marriage settlement, for several reasons. First, any prospective suitor would obviously prefer a bride with a claim to her father's throne. But beyond this Mary's status had a special importance. She was the living symbol of the scandal of Henry's divorce and repudiation of the pope. To acknowledge her illegitimacy in the terms of a marriage contract would be to approve all that Henry had done to affront Katherine, the pope and the community of Christians. Much as he liked the idea of marrying his son to Henry's daughter, Francis could not bring himself to accept her without a full restoration of her rights.

The emperor was less scrupulous, and gave his envoys much more flexibility in coming to terms with Henry. In offering the hand of Dom Luiz, the Portuguese infante, they were simply to make the best bargain they could. If Henry agreed to naming Mary as his successor in default of a male heir, so much the better. But if he would not agree to this, the imperial representatives were to draw up a settlement omitting all mention of the succession, and to be content with a large dowry of lands in England.

Henry gave the impression that he favored the imperial match. The infante was reported to be a "person of mature age, sensible, virtuous, and well-conditioned," and would on his marriage to Mary be "entirely in the king's power."[18] He was agreeable to living in England—Henry flatly refused to let Mary leave the country until Jane had a son, which at that time seemed unlikely—and he appeared to have no inconvenient political views or loyalties beyond his allegiance to his relative Charles V. Dom Luiz was a man of princely appearance, whose portraits showed a handsome, resolute, yet benevolent face. He was muscular in build, with a broad chest and strong arms, and he had proven himself fighting alongside Charles V at Tunis. He seemed in many ways the ideal son-in-law for Henry, despite the drawbacks of his staunch Catholicism and fidelity to the pope. But the imperial envoys got no further with Henry than the French. When he demanded that both Charles and the king of Portugal declare his marriage to Katherine null as a preliminary to finalizing the betrothal, they balked, and though Dom Luiz remained a potential suitor the negotiators returned to Brussels.[19]

From Henry's point of view the diplomatic rivalries generated by Mary's availability were far more important than any betrothal that might be concluded. What he feared most was that France and the empire might end their current war and join forces against him, and his principal reason for favoring the candidacy of the infante was the prospect of an Anglo-imperial alliance against the French. His talk was less of dowries and grandchildren than of war and the threat of war. He was both frightened and angered by the recent behavior of the French king, who was becoming more and more belligerent and breaking the agreements he had made with the English long before. "Since Francis is trying to strengthen himself with alliances against me," Henry was overheard to say, "I will take the initiative. I fear him not!" He paced up and down the Council chamber denouncing the French, gesticulating with his hands and swearing he did not give a fig for Francis.[20]

But if Henry showed no eagerness to conclude a marriage for his daughter those who opposed him had long known whom she ought to marry. The courtiers who had supported Katherine—the marquis and marchioness of Exeter, the Carews, the Poles and the northern lords who rose in the Pilgrimage of Grace—all favored a marriage between Mary and Reginald Pole. Next to the Emperor Charles, Pole had been Katherine's choice for Mary, and she and Margaret Pole often spoke of uniting the two families both for dynastic reasons and as a way to atone for the judicial murder of the countess' brother Edward, earl of Warwick, in 1499. Mary was predisposed to like Reginald by her strong affection for his mother, and though he was sixteen years her senior it was said she had been in love with him as a young girl.

In the mid-1530s Pole was the most important English exile on the continent. Educated in England and Italy at the king's expense, he had nonetheless refused to allow Henry to use his prodigious learning to promote the divorce. He did collect the opinions of other scholars for the king—for which he received a handsome remuneration—but would not commit himself against Katherine. As Henry moved closer and closer to a breach with Rome Pole decided to leave England for good, taking up residence in various Italian cities and finally at the Vatican, where Pope Paul III made him a member of a committee organized to reform the church. He had by this time become a celebrated international figure, as well known for his opposition to the divorce as for his learning. Charles V urged him to take a leading role in an English rebellion to overthrow Henry in 1535 and again during the northern rising in the following year, and the pope now made him a cardinal and gave him authority to act as papal legate in England. Before he could get there the Pilgrimage was crushed, but Pole had shown himself willing to oppose Henry, whose tyranny and heresy he now denounced in the bitterest terms, on the battlefield if necessary. Henry saw him as a dangerous man, and dispatched assassins to kill him. Pole became a fugitive, traveling in disguise and with few attendants in order to escape notice, aware that other English exiles in Italy were being encouraged to regain Henry's favor by murdering him.

Despite the highly adventurous life forced on him by circumstances Reginald Pole was the gentlest of men, preferring the quiet of his study to the turbulence of international politics. He was tenderhearted to a fault, and he wept easily; the uprooting of trees in a Roman garden once moved him to floods of tears. He was hardly a dashing figure, but he had courage and carried the blood of the House of York in his veins. He spoke with a moving eloquence that stood out in an age of rhetorical bombast, and he had the wisdom of a reflective thinker. All these qualities, combined with Pole's stout adherence to her mother's cause, could not but appeal to Mary. In the minds of a large number of her supporters, the match was already made.

Apparently Pole himself took the possibility of the marriage seriously, for in the spring of 1537 he confided to the emperor's agents that he thought the unrest in England might lead to "his marrying the Princess himself."[21] With this eventuality in mind he was careful to take only deacon's orders, not the full orders of a priest, so that although he was a cardinal of the Roman church he remained free to marry. Chapuys thought that Pole was the only Englishman Mary would accept as a husband, and Pole's relatives, who were becoming more and more outspoken in their hostility to Henry's authoritarian rule, began to speak of the union of Mary and the cardinal as a foregone conclusion. Margaret Pole's two other sons, Henry, Lord Montague, and Geoffrey, put their hopes for a change of government in their famous brother, and believed Mary's natural place was by his side. A servant of Lord Montague's reported that he heard his master say "it were a meet marriage for Reginald Pole to have the Lady Mary, the king's daughter," and Montague's principal household officials echoed this judgment. Geoffrey Pole had an even more idealistic vision. He saw the marriage of his brother and the true Tudor heiress as part of a grander scheme for change, with Henry's perverse innovations swept away and the old order restored. With all the determination he could muster Geoffrey was heard to swear that "the lady Mary would have a title to the crown one day."

XX

 Twene hope and drede
My lyfe I lede.

The search for Henry VIII's fourth wife had begun within hours of his third wife's death. The diplomats who conducted it found no shortage of eligible girls. There was the Danish Princess Christina, a captivating sixteen-year-old widow and niece of the emperor; there were other Hapsburg relatives, and the two lovely daughters of the duke of Cleves. There were so many French girls—among them Francis' daughter Margaret, Anne of Lorraine, and the three daughters of the duc de Guise, Marie, Louise and Renée—that Henry decided they should all be brought in a group to Calais where he could inspect them, dine and dance with them, and then make his choice. That anyone else could choose for him was unthinkable. "By God," he told the French negotiators, "the thing touches me too near. I wish to see them and know them some time before deciding."

There was a romantic simplicity in Henry's attitude toward marriage. His union with Katherine had been a matter of state, but they got on well together during their good years and he was undeniably fond of her. His next two marriages had been love matches, with no diplomatic significance whatever. At forty-six, Henry had no stomach for a cold marriage of state. He wanted someone he could be comfortable with; he wanted to fall in love again. Hence his proposal to disport himself amid the French ladies at Calais. The French found the suggestion insulting and far from chivalrous. "Is this the way the knights of the Round Table treated their women?" they asked sarcastically. Henry would have to make his selection through an intermediary first: then that girl and no others would be brought to Calais for him to see.

Henry may have been overbearing in his matrimonial dealings, but then he was generally in a mood to make unreasonable demands. He had just ordered hundreds of workmen to level an entire Surrey village to make room for the grandest palace yet built in England. Henry had never before been able to commission a palace to be constructed from the ground up; he had always lived in renovated royal dwellings built by his predecessors. But the palace he planned to raise in the fields of Surrey would live up to its name—Nonsuch—and would rival even the splendid palace of the French king at Chambord. Craftsmen were brought in great numbers to cut the timbers and build the walls of the huge structure, and Italian carvers, plasterers and sculptors were imported to ornament it. Tents erected for the artisans and laborers to live in for the years they worked at Nonsuch soon formed a new village to replace the one they had demolished, and it was not until 1541 that the king was able to move into the completed wings of the palace. Long before then, however, he came down to the site to watch his sculptors and stonemasons shape mythological and historical carvings around the walls and gates. At the center of the inner courtyard was the most imposing representation of all: a huge statue of Henry himself, many times larger than life, on his throne in a pose of majesty.

Nonsuch was an architectural metaphor of power. It was built with the spoils from another proof of royal power, the revenues from the sale of monastic lands. The dissolution of the greater monasteries was accomplished in these final years of the 1530s, and the undercurrent of outrage it produced reached its height with the spoliation of the country's most venerated shrine. The tomb of Thomas Becket at Canterbury, an opulent, gorgeous monument to medieval piety, was as famous for its treasure as for the healing virtues of the martyr himself. The casket which held Becket's body was encased in sheets of solid gold, and over the centuries pilgrims had brought sapphires, diamonds, emeralds, pearls, small rubies and the great rubies called baleases, coins and semi-precious stones to be fastened into the goldwork as a memorial to the saint. Some of these gems were said to be as large as goose eggs, but the most precious of them was a ruby, "not larger than a man's thumb-nail," which had ornamented the shrine for more than three centuries. It was called the "regal of France," and it had such fire and brillance that even when the church was dark and the weather cloudy it could be seen clearly, glowing in its niche to the right of the altar.[1]

The shrine at Canterbury had long been the object of the king's greed. Now in a unique if one-sided test of strength with the long-dead saint Henry managed to take Becket's treasure for his own. First he proclaimed that "Thomas Becket, sometime bishop of Canterbury, and made a saint by the bishop of Rome's authority, should from hence forth not be esteemed, named, reputed, nor called a saint," and ordered all

Becket's images removed from the churches. His festival was no longer to be observed, nor were services or offices to be read in his honor, "because it is found that he died like a traitor and rebel to his prince." Becket had in fact been murdered by agents of his prince, Henry II, but he was now summoned to court as if he were a living traitor and brought to judgment. When he did not appear in answer to the summons he was convicted in his absence of rebellion and treason, and sentenced to be burned. (His bones were thrown into the flames.) As a traitor his goods were forfeit to the king, and royal agents methodically stripped the tomb and altar at Canterbury of their incalculable wealth in jewels.[2] The spoils filled two huge chests, each of which could barely be moved by eight strong men. In the twelfth century the martyred Becket had triumphed over his king; in the sixteenth the king reversed the order of power again. No force from within the church was to be allowed to stand in his way, not even the beloved St. Thomas. Now when Henry sat on his throne, he wore in his thumb ring Becket's flashing jewel, the regal of France.[3]

Henry's extravagant matrimonial conditions, his grandiose building plans and his arrogant humbling of Becket were all part of a cultivated pose of might intended to disguise a growing feeling of vulnerability. The most urgent purpose of his marriage negotiations was to forestall a feared declaration of war from the combined forces of France and the empire. Henry was prepared to go to any lengths to buy off either partner in this dreaded alliance. When the French candidates proved unsatisfactory, or took other husbands, Henry proposed quadruple, even quintuple weddings with Hapsburg partners. One plan would have paired Henry and his three children with four eligible relatives of the emperor; another saw him offer himself, Mary and Elizabeth plus Mary Howard and his niece Margaret Douglas in a similar bid. Meanwhile he tried to use the long-delayed negotiations with Charles over the proposed marriage of Mary and Dom Luiz of Portugal to alienate Mary from the emperor and draw her more securely to him.

In the spring of 1538 Henry began to speak very disparagingly of Charles' intentions whenever he saw Mary, telling her the emperor was only pretending to favor the marriage to Dom Luiz while offering such dishonorable terms that Henry could not possibly accept them. On into the summer months he continued to try to turn her against her imperial cousin, until finally at the end of August he urged her to complain about the delays to Chapuys. Cromwell wrote a letter setting out her supposed grievances, and told her to communicate these to the ambassador, "coupled with such gentle terms as her own wisdom and natural discretion might suggest."

When Mary saw Chapuys she did as she was told. Following Cromwell's letter point by point she complained about the emperor's dissimulation, his failure to show her the cousinly kindness and friendship she expected of him, and his miserly dower. Even merchants give one fourth of their yearly income to their daughters on their wedding day, she said, echoing Cromwell; surely an emperor could offer more than the twenty thousand ducats Charles proposed. Why, after so many fine words had been exchanged, had nothing been settled? She was only a woman, Mary concluded, and could not help saying these things. It was not that she was anxious to have the matter settled for reasons of her own, but that she wanted to obey her father "in whom, after God, she placed all her trust."[4]

Having rehearsed all of Cromwell's points and arguments Mary told Chapuys her real feelings. She understood that the inconclusiveness of the negotiations was not the result of bad faith on the imperial side. She did not believe what her father said against Charles, and she stood ready to do whatever he asked of her in the issue of her marriage. She had complete trust in Charles, she assured Chapuys, "in whom next to God she placed all her hopes." Her assurances of loyalty were expressed in language so strong it seemed almost forced. She held the emperor in the place of "father and mother," and was so affectionately attached to him that "it seemed to her almost impossible to have such an affection and love for a kinsman."[5]

Mary's effusiveness was almost certainly the product of new uncertainties about her safety. With the possibility of war looming, Henry was restricting her movements and doing his best to direct her thinking as well. If he thought that merely by denouncing his enemy's bad faith he could destroy Mary's loyalty to the man who had been the symbol of her hopes for ten years and more, he was deluded. In fact he constantly underestimated Mary's shrewdness and overestimated both her gullibility and his own charm. But however deep his misreading of her Mary was still in an awkward political position, and Chapuys was uneasy enough about her safety to raise again the old subject of a possible escape. She replied that for the time being she preferred to wait and hope that her situation would improve, and that her father would "show more consideration for her, or cause her to be more respected and better treated than she had been until now."[6]

In the summer of 1538 Mary was uneasy, if not yet fearful, about where she stood in her father's estimation. She still wrote to him, and to Cromwell (her "sheet anchor next the king") in the most subservient language imaginable, aware that even the slightest rumor or hint of suspicious behavior might anger them both. A letter she wrote to Cromwell at about this time reveals her state of mind. She had taken some strangers into her house for a brief time—who they were is not recorded—and the incident had been reported to the Privy Council in a way that put Mary's trustworthiness in doubt. Cromwell wrote her a strong letter of warning, ordering her not to do anything in future which "might seem to give any other occasion than should be expedient" for her. Mary wrote back thanking Cromwell for his "gentle and friendly" letter and assuring him she would never lodge anyone in her household again. She begged him to continue to advise her and to be her advocate with her father, adding that she would rather endure physical harm than lose even the smallest part of the king's favor.[7]

Her reference to physical harm was in keeping with the atmosphere of menace that hung over the court and country in these years. Henry was becoming more and more capricious, and he seemed to take inordinate pleasure in his powers of life and death. Executions, threatened and real, multiplied in the late 1530s and early 1540s, keeping pace with the mounting popular opposition to the king. Ballad makers who put political verses to traditional tunes were arrested and condemned; at least one of them dared to set new words against Henry to one of Henry's own tunes. In the English-held territory of Calais two priests were hanged and quartered for treason, and the story of how they lived on during their torture was carried back across the Channel to be told and retold all over London. After they were hanged, it was said, they were cut down alive and helped the hangman to take off their clothes. Then, strapped to a board beside the scaffold, their bellies were cut open and their intestines pulled out and burned, and still the priests did not die but "spake always till their hearts were pulled out of their bodies."[8]

Random violence in the London streets seemed to follow the pattern of judicial executions. Citizens on their way to mass or to business were shot or stabbed by anonymous attackers; thieves became bolder than ever. And there was a rash of suicides. One Mrs. Allen, a clerk's wife, cut her throat with a knife "by the instigation of the devil," and when the curate and the neighbors burst in to try to save her she could not speak. Because she knocked on her breast and held her hands up as a sign of contrition the priest gave her the last rites, and did not insist that she be given the burial of a suicide in unconsecrated ground. The grisly climax to these events was the execution of the hangman of London himself, a man who had become a macabre celebrity in his own right and who was known as "a cunning butcher in quartering of men." With two accomplices he had robbed a booth at Bartholomew Fair, and was caught and hanged in his turn.[9]

At court too crime seemed to be increasing. Two archers of the guard named Davenport and Chapman were hanged when it was found they had waylaid and robbed a merchant near the palace.[10] A serving boy in the pay of one of the privy chamber gentlemen was found guilty of stealing a purse with eleven pounds in coin and one of the king's jewels. A gallows was built at the end of the tiltyard at Westminster, the noose was placed around the boy's neck, and the hangman was just taking the ladder from the gallows when the king sent his pardon and the boy was freed.[11] In some dark way it gave Henry particular satisfaction to order a dreadful punishment, let the victim suffer all the agonies of hopeless anticipation of it, and then set him free at the last moment. When Sir Edmund Knevet struck another courtier the king sentenced him to lose his hand. A chopping block was immediately brought and the hand bound to it. The master cook, always ready to stand in for the executioner in minor mutilations, sharpened his hatchet. The sergeant of the scullery stood by with his mallet, and the irons were placed in the fire to sear the wound before the surgeon bound it with his searing cloth. When all was in readiness the king suddenly postponed the procedure until after dinner and then, when the unfortunate Knevet had sweated away another several hours, just as suddenly pardoned him.[12]

In the intervals between episodes of bloodshed there were rumors of impending harm. For the first time since the demise of Anne Boleyn a poison scare swept the court. One of the gentlewomen told a servant of Lord Montague that when the king's envoy Sir Thomas Wyatt returned from Spain he brought news of a potent poison. Applied to an arrowhead, it caused instant death with the merest pricking of the skin, and the only known antidote was the juice of a quince or peach. When Wyatt asked Henry whether he should bring any back with him the king said no, but the knowledge that such a powerful drug existed in itself gave rise to lurid fantasies of royal assassinations, and greatly increased the discomfort of any courtier who angered the king.

There can be little doubt that a principal animator of the climate of fear was Cromwell. To be sure, he was not completely heartless, and managed to acquire a particular reputation for helping women. When the much-injured duchess of Norfolk appealed to him for help she said she did so principally because she "heard how good he was to lady Mary in her troubles"; ultimately his aid to the duchess increased his repute.[13] But if Mary never tired of assuring Cromwell of her profound gratitude for all he had done for her, her fear of him was as obvious as her reluctant dependence on him, and most courtiers felt the same mixture of fear and inescapable reliance on the Lord Privy Seal as Mary did. Few of them trusted him completely, and many agreed with Chapuys' assessment when he wrote of Cromwell that "his words are fair, but his deeds are bad, and his intentions much worse."

Cromwell came to power at a time of grave crisis, and maintained his influence during England's most troubled decade since the wars of the last century. But he contributed to the tensions around him by creating a network of spies and informants and then using it to entrap both genuine rebels and harmless malcontents. Believing that kings rule best when their subjects fear them most, he set out to surround the royal power with an aura of magisterial caprice, and he was given to composing memoranda under the rubric "For the putting the king's subjects and other in more terror and fear." Certainly he succeeded in making himself both feared and despised, especially by the great aristocrats who considered themselves Henry's natural advisers and the ambitious officials who coveted his power. He maneuvered Suffolk and Norfolk out of power, and kept lesser men away from the king by sending them on diplomatic embassies or commissions which took them far from court. His enemies found themselves suddenly out of favor, banished from the king's presence, or worse. Just before New Year's of 1539 Nicholas Carew, the Grand Esquire who had close ties to the marquis of Exeter and the Poles, was seized without warning and taken to the Tower. Cromwell's agents entered his houses and took everything of value, including the beautiful diamonds and pearls of Jane Seymour's which Henry had given Carew's wife after Jane's death.[14]

Cromwell felt a particular enmity toward Reginald Pole, whom he called "Brainsick Pole," that extended to everyone associated with the cardinal. (Pole returned the insult by calling Cromwell the "vicar of Satan.") When the rumors about the Spanish poison were being spread, there was no doubt in anyone's mind that Pole was the victim Wyatt and his masters were thinking of. In the summer of 1538, with war in the air and the cardinal's denunciations of Henry growing more and more shrill, the king and his chief minister decided to make an end of the troublesome family once and for all.

The weakest of the Poles was used to entrap the others. Geoffrey, brother of Reginald and of Henry Pole, Lord Montague, and youngest son of Margaret Pole, countess of Salisbury, was taken to the Tower. He was a rash, ill-considered young man, sensitive and easily terrified. Under Cromwell's grilling and the abuse and torture of his agents Geoffrey broke down and told what he knew about his brothers and their friends. What he said was not in itself proof of treason, though his description of Lord Montague's opinions and behavior told much about the rough hatreds that rankled below the surface gentility of court life.

Like Henry Courtenay, marquis of Exeter, Henry Pole had grown up with the king from childhood. They had not liked one another as boys—according to Pole, even Henry VII didn't like his son, "having no affection or fancy unto him." When Pole became Lord Montague and his royal cousin became Henry VIII, they liked one another no better, and when the king began to pull down the abbeys, choose anti-papal bishops and fill his privy chamber with "knaves," Montague began to say openly that his character was changing for the worse. Once when Henry remarked to those about him that "he would go from them one day, and where be you then?" Montague replied without hesitation "If he will serve us so, we shall be happily rid." Behind the king's back he was overheard to say that "he had seen more gentleness and benignity in times past at the king's hands than he did nowadays," and that "the king never made [a] man but he destroyed him again either with displeasure or with the sword."

Remarks of this sort, along with unkind references to Henry's corpulence and ulcerous leg ("the king is full of flesh and unwieldy," Montague said, "and he cannot long continue with his sore leg"), may have been irritating but they were hardly treasonous. Nor were the hints of Reginald Pole's great future and hoped-for marriage with Mary that Geoffrey Pole repeated under threat of death. But Cromwell and his master were satisfied that what evidence they had was proof of Henry Pole's treason. As for Pole's ally the marquis of Exeter, the king had been convinced for years that it was the marquis and his wife who had, in Cromwell's words, "suborned" Mary during Anne's reign and encouraged her to defy her father. This plus copies of letters exchanged by Exeter and Reginald Pole, and other letters from Katherine and Mary found in the marchioness' possession, proved to the king's satisfaction that Exeter planned to take over the kingdom by marrying his son to Mary and destroying Prince Edward; that Lord Montague was in on the conspiracy was substantiated by the messages carried back and forth between them by "a big fellow in a tawny coat."[15]

Montague, Exeter and another alleged conspirator, Sir Edward Neville, were imprisoned, brought to trial, and executed in December of 1538. The marchioness, her son, and Montague's young heir were also taken prisoner, and though the marchioness was eventually released the two children stayed on in the Tower. Exeter's son, young Edward Courtenay, would eventually be freed in Mary's reign; the fate of Lord Montague's son remains a mystery.

From a political point of view the elimination of the Poles and Courtenays was a sound dynastic expedient. All those executed or imprisoned, including Edward Neville, had a claim to the throne, however distant, and the Poles were relatives of an undoubted traitor. In dangerous times such subjects represented a risk too great to be tolerated. In human terms, though, the wreckage of the Pole family left two tragic figures: the cardinal, whose personal grief now lent added urgency to his crusade against Henry, and the wretched brother who in his fear and weakness had betrayed those he loved. Geoffrey Pole was spared execution with the others because of the testimony he gave against them. Armed with a royal pardon, he was free to live out his days without fear of royal punishment. But his inner peace had been permanently shattered. He tried to kill himself and failed. Utterly miserable in England, he joined his brother Reginald as a continental exile, restlessly wandering from city to city while slowly going mad with grief. Through his brother he was able to gain a papal pardon for what he had done, but he could never forgive himself.

For Mary the executions were a harsh reminder of her father's vengeance and seeming omnipotence. His capacity for destruction, already formidable, was increasing, and his hand was not stayed by affection or ties of blood. Even as she mourned the passing of those who had supported her mother and herself so faithfully she grew frightened about her own future. Her father was seeking to eliminate all those who threatened Prince Edward's right to the throne. In the opinion of many, Mary's own claim was stronger than Edward's, despite her degradation by Parliament. What was to prevent the king from suddenly deciding to eliminate her as well?

Adding to these fears was the king's rumored instability of temper. He was certainly intoxicated with power; some said he was losing his mind. Among Lord Montague's remarks about the king was that "he would be out of his wits one day, for when he came to his chamber he would look angerly [sic], and after fall to fighting."[16] The image of King Henry as a snarling, quarrelsome private man who felt himself to be increasingly hated and hateful is in keeping with other details of his life at this time. Mary knew both the charming public figure and the vicious tyrant, and she felt menace from both.

In a sad epilogue to the events of 1538 Mary's "second mother," Margaret Pole, now fell under suspicion along with her relatives. She was questioned remorselessly, her possessions and residence searched and finally, despite her age and illness, she was brought to the Tower. Among her things the royal agents found an armorial design symbolizing the union of Mary and Reginald Pole. The painter had joined pansies, the emblem of the Poles, with marigolds for Mary, and from the center of the intertwined flowers grew a tree in token of Christ's passion. To the king's deputy the design was treasonous in its intent. The countess had dared to anticipate Mary's marriage to a Yorkist and a traitor, and hoped for the restoration of "the old Doctrine of Christ."[17]

The countess was attainted in June of 1539 but she was not executed until nearly two years later. Then in the spring of 1541, on the pretext that she might somehow have encouraged a minor rising in Yorkshire, Margaret Pole was brought to the block on Tower Green. More than a hundred people came to hear the sixty-nine-year-old woman say her last words. She asked them to pray for the king, the prince, and for her beloved "Princess" Mary. Then she knelt and put her head on the block. In the absence of the usual Tower executioner the ax was given to a clumsy-fisted boy. Before Margaret Pole was finally dispatched her head and shoulders were hacked nearly to pieces.

XXI

All you that be at libertie,
and would be void of strife:
I speake it on experience,
ne're venture on a wife.

By January of 1540 the prolonged marriage negotiations of the past two years had borne fruit—at least for the king. After considering dozens of princesses and heiresses Henry decided to trust his ambassadors' recommendation that he marry Anne, daughter of the recently deceased duke of Cleves and sister of the reigning duke.

Anne of Cleves was represented to Henry as a girl of matchless beauty, and the portrait Holbein painted for him from life pleased him well enough. A copy of that portrait shows a girl with a lovely, doll-like face whose delicate eyes, mouth and chin are only slightly marred by a rather large nose. Besides, the match had more to recommend it than Anne's good looks. Cleves was among those regions which, like England, was neither Catholic nor Lutheran but something in between. In marrying Anne Henry avoided having to cast his lot with either of the warring religious factions on the continent, while lending support to a known opponent of the emperor. Anne's brother was at odds with Charles V, and the English connection strengthened his hand; for Henry it meant a plentiful supply of sturdy German mercenaries and an ally on the emperor's doorstep.

Unfortunately, the king's first sight of his intended bride drove all thought of these advantages from his mind. He rode to Rochester to see her shortly after she landed in England, but instead of falling in love at first sight, as he had hoped, he found Anne disappointingly unlike the woman he had imagined from her portrait. Diplomatic misunderstandings arose too between the German negotiators and the Privy Council, and

Henry, who was wildly casting about for a way out of the marriage, declared that he was "not well handled" and cursed the day he let another man choose his wife for him. No way out was found, so rather than waste the elaborate preparations that had already been made, and to avoid "making a ruffle in the world," the king decided to make the best of the situation. He "put his neck in the yoke," as he said, took Anne to the altar, and in due course took her to bed. There he found, as he told Cromwell, that "his nature abhorred her." Her breasts and belly were not those of a virgin, he declared. This discovery "struck him to the heart," leaving him "neither will nor courage to prove the rest."[1]

Anne took her place at court despite the utter failure of the marriage, settling into her large household and enjoying the king's generosity. He was not vindictive—the revulsion he felt did not extend to Anne's personality—and after several months of chaste cohabitation he was still hoping to master his disinclination long enough to beget a child. But though he "did as much to move the consent of his heart and mind as man ever did," he failed. By spring he was seeking a pretext for divorce. Anne was meanwhile showing herself "willful," and she and Henry quarreled, at least briefly, over Mary. All things considered the Cleves union was a fiasco. "Before God," Henry swore, "she is not my lawful wife."

Henry's displeasure with Anne was common gossip in foreign courts. The French queen told Cardinal Farnese, who told the pope, that besides being "old and ugly" Anne was not pleasing to her husband in her German dress, and was forced to change her wardrobe to the French fashion.[2] It was said in Flanders that besides being old (she was thirty-four at the time of her marriage) Anne was overly fond of wine and indulged in "other excesses."[3] But whatever her faults she was remarkably accommodating. She agreed to divorce Henry in return for an annuity and a comfortable private life in England, and she did not mind that her husband's eagerness to end the marriage was heightened by his infatuation with her nineteen-year-old maid of honor Catherine Howard. In fact, some months after Henry had made Catherine his fifth wife Anne paid a call on the newlyweds at court. She presented herself at the gate of Hampton Court with a New Year's gift of two large horses trapped in violet velvet for the king and asked to see the royal couple. Catherine received her warmly, embarrassed by Anne's insistence on kneeling in her presence, and when Henry came in he bowed to Anne and kissed her familiarly. Anne and Catherine stayed up after supper long after the king had gone to bed, dancing together and doubtless comparing notes on his merits as a husband. The next day the three dined together, and when Henry presented Catherine with a gift of a ring and two lapdogs she handed them over to Anne.[4]

In the end Catherine Howard proved to be far more unsatisfactory than Anne of Cleves. For if Henry found Anne distasteful, Catherine broke his heart. In contrast to Anne, Catherine was an earthy girl with a sensual face and expression that invited passion. Like Anne Boleyn before her, she was a niece of the duke of Norfolk, and it was no accident that the king's fancy should light on her instead of some other girl. The duke arranged for Henry to see Catherine often at his London house, and Lady Rochford, George Boleyn's widow, advised her on how to behave toward her royal suitor. Norfolk was using Catherine to regain his standing in the king's favor, knowing that if Henry divorced Anne of Cleves Cromwell's power would be destroyed. The king's infatuation took its course; Anne was set aside; and on the day Henry married Catherine Howard Cromwell was beheaded.

It is baffling that Norfolk and his relatives should have urged on the king a girl whose hearty sexual appetites had already disgraced her more than once. Before she came to court she had been the lover of Francis Dereham, who had "lain in bed with her, in his doublet and hose, between the sheets an hundred nights." Catherine's liaison with Dereham was so disgraceful—it lasted for three years, and there was "no question nor talk of a marriage between them"—that the maid who also slept in her bed declared she would sleep there no longer "because she knew not what matrimony was." When she was even younger Catherine had allowed a servant in her aunt's household to "feel the secret parts of her body," and he boasted about his knowledge of a "privy mark" there.[5] These indiscretions were hardly obscure; all of the serving women in the duchess' household knew the stories, and the duchess herself cannot have been ignorant of what was being said about her niece. Norfolk may not have realized what danger there was in promoting the marriage, or he may have thought that once she was queen Catherine's nature would change.

Whatever he may have believed, he was deluded about Catherine's trustworthiness. Henry was delighted with his young bride, but she found him old and unappealing. She contrived to bring Dereham to court, and made him her letter writer and messenger with plenty of excuses to be alone with her in her bedchamber. And by the time Henry began a great progress to the north in 1541 she had taken a new lover, Thomas Culpepper, a gentleman of the king's chamber who "slept at the bottom of his bed." With Cromwell and his informers gone for good and the king blinded with love, the queen indulged herself extravagantly with Culpepper while Lady Rochford served as go-between and set her servants to keep watch outside the queen's chambers. Later Culpepper confessed how he and Catherine met behind the king's back at Lincoln, Pontefract, York and other places along the progress route. When the royal party halted for the night at a strange castle the queen would "in every house seek for the back doors and back stairs herself," and then send for Culpepper.

Catherine seems to have had a naïve expectation that she and her lovers could go on as they were forever, though she did warn Culpepper not to reveal their secret to the priest at confession since "surely, the king being supreme head of the church, [he] should have knowledge of it."[6] Finally, though, a servant in the Norfolk establishment told what she knew of Catherine's conduct before her marriage, and a series of interrogations eventually brought out the rest.

Henry was wounded to the quick by these revelations. His "heart was pierced with pensiveness," and his sorrow was so deep he could hardly speak. In the end, when all the evidence had been gathered in great secrecy, "with plenty of tears," he gave orders that the queen was to be seized and questioned. Catherine was terrified. She wrote out a confession, but finding that to be only the beginning of a grueling inquiry she began to go to pieces. She would not eat or drink, and she paced up and down in her room "weeping and crying like a madwoman." All the heavy and sharp objects in the room had to be taken away for fear she would "hasten her death" by suicide.

Fearing for their own lives, Catherine's relatives denounced her more loudly than anyone else. Norfolk bewailed the king's tragic loss and the dishonor to his family, and declared that his niece deserved to be burned alive.[7] As Henry got over his grief he too talked wildly, calling for a sword to kill the girl he had loved so much and vowing never to marry again. Doubtless he felt keenly the irony of his situation. At fifty, his young wife was inflicting on him the same humiliation and pain he had brought on Katherine of Aragon many years before. His fury mounted, then gradually subsided into ill temper and then into melancholy as one by one the queen, Lady Rochford, and the guilty lovers were executed. After five wives Henry was a bachelor again.

Mary stood on the sidelines as her third and fourth stepmothers played out their brief reigns. With Anne of Cleves Mary had little to do, though she was among the ladies deputed to welcome Anne on her arrival in England. When Catherine Howard became queen an awkward situation arose. Mary was some five years older than Catherine, and Catherine's close ties of blood to Anne Boleyn put a barrier between her and her stepdaughter. Evidently Mary made her distaste for Catherine's parentage obvious in small ways, for after Catherine had been queen for a few months she complained to Henry that his daughter was not treating her with the same respect she had given Jane Seymour and Anne of Cleves. Catherine persuaded Henry to dismiss two of Mary's maidservants, much to Mary's concern, but Chapuys found out what the minor furor was about and warned Mary. She attempted to smooth things over by sending Catherine a handsome New Year's gift, but the insult was not so easily healed.[8] The girls were not allowed to return to Mary's service, and one of them, it seems, actually died of grief at being separated from her mistress. Mary was "exceedingly distressed and sad" at this, but later in the year Catherine had apparently forgotten the injury she felt Mary had done her and was giving her valuable presents. By the time the court was following the king on his great progress the two women must have been on civil terms, for at Pontefract Catherine gave Mary a gold pomander set with an enameled clock ornamented with rubies and turquoises.[9]

Mary was hustled off to the country, along with Edward and Elizabeth, when the scandal surrounding Catherine Howard and her lovers became public knowledge, and once there she resumed her now familiar routine of brisk morning walks, riding, reading and improving her skill on the virginals and lute. Occasionally the king would spend an hour or two with her on his way from one palace to another, but her place in his thoughts was small. Chapuys never ceased to look out for her, though he had to acknowledge that her "wisdom and discretion" in handling her own affairs were remarkable.[10]

Still the tacit fulfillment of her life, marriage to a foreign prince or a great English nobleman, was continually postponed. In keeping with the expected attitude of a gentlewoman, she affected disinterest in marriage, as Vives' treatises and her mother had taught her to do throughout her childhood. She was "a young maid and willing to continue so," she said in one letter, and in another professed to "prefer never to enter that kind of religion, but continue a maid for life."[11] But if these conventional sentiments do not reveal Mary's true feelings about marriage little evidence of those feelings exists. What she observed of her father's marital adventures cannot have made her sanguine about taking a husband, though she still cherished the romantic idea of marriage she had conceived as a child. Much later both the anticipation and reality of marriage gave her enormous pleasure, and released a flood of sentimental associations which had almost certainly been nourished over many years. Mary wanted a husband and children; that no marriage was arranged for her disheartened and depressed her.

It was not that there were no suitable candidates for her hand. When Henry was first contemplating an alliance with Cleves he considered proposing Mary as a wife for the young duke, and later, when the emperor became a widower, Henry approached him about reviving his suit.[12] Just before Henry married Anne he was thinking of giving Mary to Duke Philip of Bavaria, who came to England to help prepare for Anne's reception and marriage. A draft agreement was drawn up, and Mary was told to receive Philip when he arrived. He sent her a diamond cross as a sign of his love, and if Mary was not delighted with him she did say she would marry him if her father decided she should. The negotiations seem to have ceased abruptly—probably they were a casualty of the dismal Cleves marriage—and the diamond cross went to Cromwell.

Several years later the possibility of a French marriage was again being discussed, but only as a diplomatic ploy. The French ambassador Marillac went through the motions of discussing terms, interviewing the prospective bride and composing long dispatches about the mutual advantages to be gained on both sides, but he was convinced that nothing would come of the matter. "The king will not marry [his daughter] out of England," he wrote, "lest the crown of England should be claimed for her as legitimate by the church and not for those born since the withdrawal of obedience to the Holy See, like the prince."[13] Henry was even more blunt. "I love my daughter well," he told Marillac, "but myself and honor more."

No one understood the apparently irresolvable dilemma of her unmarried state better than Mary herself. She saw clearly that in marrying her off, Henry would be undermining the strength of his throne. If he married her to a foreigner he increased the risk, already high, of invasion from the continent; if he gave her to an English nobleman he risked civil war. These two dangers were not new: Henry had faced them when he first betrothed Mary at the age of two and a half. What made them so urgent now was Mary's disputed dynastic status coupled with Henry's weak position among the European sovereigns. And as neither of these difficulties seemed likely to be removed, it was becoming more and more evident that, at least during Henry's lifetime, Mary would remain unmarried, and unhappy.

Mary expressed her predicament neatly to one of her chamberwomen, a reliable informant who, because she had a French husband, was willing to talk freely to Marillac. "It was folly to think that they would marry her out of England, or even in England, as long as her father lived." She knew all the arguments on her father's side, as well as the point of view of the emperor and of the French. She considered the French offers the most sincere, for economic reasons; her dowry would help to cancel their enormous debts. But money alone was not a sufficient reason for Francis to marry his son to an illegitimate Tudor, she said bitterly, and in the end "nothing would be got from them but fine words, for she would be, while her father lived, only lady Mary, the unhappiest lady in Christendom."[14]

The high destiny Mary had envisioned for herself was to be thwarted by obstacles beyond her control. She could not marry, and now that Edward was proving himself a sturdy child there was no chance that she would rule. Her life was comfortable, her relations with her father intermittently strained, but bearable. Yet the thought that she was to live out her days in the genteel backwater of the court, moving from one country house to another, coming to Greenwich or Richmond occasionally but never being useful or important, weighed on her more and more heavily. By the early 1540s it was helping to make her ill again.

The sharpest irony of Mary's predicament was that the illness brought on by her feeling of uselessness was itself hindering negotiations for her marriage. Every envoy sent to Henry's court to make an offer on behalf of a continental prince was told to make inquiries about Mary's rumored weakness and uncertain health. In particular, of course, prospective husbands wanted to be absolutely sure that Mary's disorder was nothing that might hinder her ability to bear children. Katherine's repeated miscarriages, stillbirths and fatally weak infants were not forgotten—diplomats at foreign courts kept track of such things—and it was feared that Mary might have inherited her mother's handicap.

What clouded the issue was that Mary's illness did not follow a consistent pattern or conform to a known disease. It was linked to recurrent episodes of amenorrhoea, depression and eventual restoration of the menstrual cycle, but this sequence was not invariably mentioned (though it may have been present) in the brief accounts and references to her bouts of illness. It was roughly seasonal, coming on most severely in the fall and early spring, yet it did not appear every year, or at least not in a severe enough form to be recorded. And it sometimes struck in the winter and summer months as well. The symptoms varied widely from one attack to the next, and the only name given to the disorder, melancholy or melancholia, referred primarily to Mary's emotional state and did not take into account the wide range of other complaints that accompanied it.

Mary had been seriously ill twice since she entered her twenties. In December of 1537 and January of 1538 she was sick for at least several weeks, falling ill at Christmas and growing steadily worse until by New Year's Day "she could neither sit nor stand but was fain to go to her bed, for faintness."[15] As usual Dr. De la Sà was cautious in his treatment, asking for "more counsel" before prescribing any medicines and turning to Henry's physician Dr. Butts for his experienced opinion as "he had been with her in such cases in times past." She was sick again in March and April of 1542, of a "strange fever" that weakened her and brought on heart palpitations, and so debilitated her that at times "she remained as though dead."[16] According to Chapuys she was in "extreme danger," and Henry was sending frequently for news of her condition.[17] By the first week of May she was out of danger, though by no means completely recovered.[18]

By the time she was twenty-six, when Marillac was instructed to make inquiries about Mary's suitability as a wife for Francis' son Charles, duke of Orléans, her reputation for weakness and possible incapacity for child-bearing was well established. He was told to find out whether she was able to bear children and to ask her physician, if possible, "if this melancholy which she has so long worn has not brought on some malady which might prevent her having issue, as is said."[19] Marillac went to his usual source, the chamberwoman who had served Mary for years. What she told him added to the confusion about the nature, gravity and frequency of Mary's disorder. When Katherine was first set aside, the woman said, Mary was "sick with melancholy," but after being "visited and comforted by the king," she soon recovered and had shown no symptoms of the affliction since. It is understandable that the chamberwoman would want to minimize Mary's condition in hopes of enhancing her chances for marriage, but what the apothecary Juan de Soto told Marillac is less easy to reconcile with the other evidence about Mary's complaints. He never gave Mary anything but the lightest medicines, he told the ambassador, "which she took more often because it was her father's command than because she needed them."[20] These accounts, plus Mary's active way of life and personal energy, made Marillac wonder whether the gossip about her debility was exaggerated.

Yet as Mary entered her late twenties the doubts about her health grew greater, and she became more and more convinced that she was destined to live and die a superfluous, unmarriageable spinster. These dark speculations undermined her composure and embittered her view of the future. In time they too would take their physical and emotional toll.

XXII

God save his noble grace,
And grant him a place
Endless to dwell
With the devil of hell!

It took some time for the king and his court to return to normal after the disgrace and execution of Catherine Howard. For months the dejected king remained isolated and withdrawn, nursing his bad leg, listening to his harper and talking to his fool Will Somers. By the summer of 1542, though, he was coming out of his depression and seeking female company. His taste for "carousels and pageants," and for "paying court to ladies" returned, and Mary was among the first to enjoy his attentions. In September he was "entertaining and feasting her beyond measure," showering her with jewels, and asking her to come to court to take the place of a queen in entertaining the ladies he meant to invite for the holidays.[1] Hampton Court was renovated for the Christmas festivities, and workmen labored day and night to prepare apartments for Mary and the many women who would attend her. On December 21 Mary rode through the city "in triumphal manner," and was received at Hampton Court gate by nearly all the courtiers and by the king himself, who "spoke to her in the most gracious and amiable words that a father could address to his daughter."[2]

The king's high spirits and enthusiastic cultivation of Mary continued throughout Christmas and New Year's, and on into the early months of 1543. Amid the feasting and dancing he sought Mary out and "addressed her in the most endearing terms," while giving her costly rings, chains and silver plate; among his gifts of jewelry were two large rubies "of inestimable value." Mary was the gracious center of the lively court, overseeing the receiving and lodging of the courtiers and visiting guests and leaving her father free to "rejoice himself."

Both the king and his daughter suddenly found themselves in unaccustomed roles: he a widower in need of a daughter to be his hostess, and she a twenty-seven-year-old spinster eager to be needed by an effusively affectionate father. Their relationship was cordial rather than intimate, and the old wounds he had given her would never heal, but in this interval between wives Henry was genuinely glad of Mary's company, and he let her know it. If he behaved more like a suitor than a father, substituting gallantry, charming speeches and gifts for friendship and sincere affection, it was only that he had never learned to be a father to any of his children, and it was far too late for Mary to teach him.

It was being said that the primary object of the round of entertainments at court was to give the king a chance to choose a new wife. To Anne of Cleves, however, it seemed as if her hour had come again. Ever since Catherine Howard's fall Anne had been hoping that Henry might take her back, and had recently come to live near Hampton Court in that expectation. The ambassador of Cleves, an obscure figure who lived in one room over a tavern with a single servant and was rarely seen at court, was rumored to be working for Anne's restoration as queen, probably to offset stories of her ill treatment then circulating in the German courts. It was rumored that after her divorce Anne was kept in England against her will, cruelly bound in a dungeon. A woman claiming to be Anne, newly escaped from captivity, appeared at the court of the prince of Coburg, and it was some time before her imposture was discovered. In March of 1543 Anne herself was allowed to visit the court, perhaps to plead her own case. Henry saw her only once during her stay, though, and she spent her time with Mary instead.[8] In fact Henry was paying more and more attention to Catherine Parr, a young widow of "lively and pleasing appearance" who not only liked to dance and provide convivial company but shared his taste for learning and Erasmian theology as well.

When he was not in her company, or visiting Mary in her chamber—something he now did two or three times a day—Henry was inspecting the coastal fortifications and choosing the sites or new ports for his warships. France and the empire had gone to war the previous summer, and in February Henry and the emperor became allied against the French. By June Henry was sending thousands of foot soldiers to the continent and putting more ships in the Channel, and war with the French was imminent.

The rapprochement between Charles and Henry had a good deal to do with Mary's current high standing at court. As usual she kept herself well informed about continental affairs, and passed on to Chapuys anything she overheard that might be of use to the imperial side. Since the outbreak of war she had been sending to the ambassador for news of

Charles and Mary, regent of Flanders, and she told Chapuys often "how displeased and sorry she was at the troubles and annoyances by which both were surrounded." Her concern for the regent was especially great. "There is nothing in this world," Chapuys wrote, "that the princess herself would not sacrifice and throw away for the sake of relieving the perilous situation of the queen's affairs."[4] Beyond praying incessant prayers for their health and prosperity Mary did all she could to help in more practical ways. She kept herself informed about the activities of the French ambassador at court and in the Privy Council, and regularly reported to Chapuys what the king was saying about the French.[5]

Henry was enjoying himself thoroughly in these months, gearing himself and his forces for war, keeping his enemies and allies alike guessing what his real intentions were and uncertain about how well he guessed theirs. He amused himself with banqueting and entertainments, and surrounded himself with beautiful women, one of whom he had begun to woo in earnest. At fifty-two he was bald and paunchy, and the quantities of game, fowl, breads and sweets which he devoured at every meal had long since begun to make him mountainously fat. Armor made for him two years earlier measured fifty-four inches around the waist, and he was growing stouter every year. He was still vigorous, riding for hours, putting in long days of travel and walking across the fields when the condition of his legs allowed. He "crept to the cross" on Good Friday on his knees—a practice which, with typical inconsistency, he condemned at the very end of his life as romish and superstitious—and sometimes served at mass. He rode up and down the coast and through the countryside of Kent and Surrey, checking the fortresses and the warning beacons to be lit on the hillsides in case of invasion. He still kept as large a stable as ever, with eighty-eight coursers, stallions and geldings besides seventeen carriage and sumpter horses for his personal use.[6] But though he continued to be a formidable hunter the game now had to be brought to him; on his progress in 1541 beasts of the northern forests were driven by the hundreds into vast enclosures where the king and his companions were waiting to slaughter them. Hawking replaced the chase as his principal sport, and he kept more fewterers and hawks than ever in his last years. He still loved to go "with his noblemen to the park to shoot the popinjay" and, when in a merry mood, he still "used himself more like a good fellow than a king." But as he aged his dark moods were fearful, and they were made worse by his phobias and physical complaints.

Henry's horror of the sweating sickness was now obsessive. When the sweat broke out in the summer of 1543 he gave strict orders that no one who had passed through the infected area of London could come within seven miles of his person. He tried to forestall sickness, and mischance in general, by consulting astrologers and hiring alchemists, and on at least one

occasion hazarded the deep waters of the occult when a "stranger of Per-
pignan" was paid to show the king "quintessences." But the older he got
the more his ailments multipled. The bills from his apothecary lay bare
his afflictions. He was dosed with eyebright, stomach and liver plasters,
rhubarb pills and "a fomentation for the piles." He had a stomach bag of
red sarcenet to ease indigestion, and took endless varieties of medicinal
powders, oils and waters.[7] As always Henry acted as his own apothecary
as well, dosing himself and those around him, making up plasters to heal
swelling in the ankles, ointments "to take away itch," and an intriguing
potion for Anne of Cleves "to mollify and resolve, comfort and cease
pain of cold and windy causes."[8] Even his hawks and hounds were
treated with horehound water, licorice and sugar candy.

What hampered and tormented the king most were his swollen legs,
now so corrupted and sore that they kept him bedridden at times. One
leg had to be kept elevated on a stool. The medical evidence indicates
that the king's condition started either as a varicose ulcer or a chronic
septic infection of the thighbone. Treated with barbarous inefficacy and
abused by constant overactivity for many years, the infection spread to
both legs and led to severe complications.[9] In 1538 a clot worked loose
from one of the fistulas and became lodged in his lungs. He nearly
suffocated; he couldn't speak, went "black in the face," and was obviously in great danger. The clot dissolved, but the infection continued to
flare up time after time, and the compounds he mixed most frequently
for himself were those intended to heal ulcers and "excoriations in the
legs." One plaster "to heal ulcers without pain" was made in part from
powdered pearls.[10]

In July of 1543 this hulk of decaying manhood, limping on his throb-
bing leg, announced that he was about to marry his sixth wife. Catherine
Parr was perhaps his best choice since Katherine of Aragon. She was
thirty-one and had been twice widowed, and the king felt certain that she
was free of the flaws that had destroyed his last two marriages. Unlike
Anne of Cleves, Catherine would hold no sour mysteries in store for him
in the bedchamber, and she was unlikely to indulge in the girlish indiscretions of Catherine Howard. In appearance Catherine Parr was quite
ordinary, and if her portraits show perspicacity they reveal almost no
charm. She was an intellectual, a woman of considerable common sense
and earnest piety, a good companion and a sympathetic nurse. She was
not ambitious, and—much to her credit—she was not afraid to marry a
man who had doomed four of her predecessors either to the divorce
court or to the block.

The wedding was arranged with impulsive haste. There was no time
for the publishing of the banns, and Cranmer was called in to license the
ceremony to take place without them. Then on July 12 the king, his

bride and the witnesses gathered in the queen's privy closet at Hampton
Court. Mary and Elizabeth were there, and many of the privy councilors.
Anne of Cleves, understandably, was not invited though she made her
views about the marriage clear to all who would talk to her. She was humiliated and hurt that Henry should marry Catherine, who in her opinion
"was by no means so handsome as she herself is," and whose barrenness
during her two previous marriages seemed to confirm the general opinion
that she would have no children by the king. But Anne's views were little
heeded. Henry was satisfied with the son he had, and the Seymours,
Prince Edward's uncles, were much in evidence at court. Jane Seymour's
brother Edward, now earl of Hertford and fast becoming the dominant
figure in the Council, attended the wedding with his wife, though his
brother Thomas was absent. Thomas Seymour, an extremely handsome
man who had won Catherine Parr's love and would have married her if
the king's preference had not supervened, saw to it that he was away on
official business when the king married his sweetheart.

When all the witnesses were present Stephen Gardiner, bishop of
Winchester, began the ceremony. He first asked whether anyone present
knew of any impediment to the marriage—an ironic question in Henry's
case—and then turned to the king and asked him to recite his vows. Taking Catherine's hand, Henry repeated them, "with a joyous look," and
then Catherine spoke hers. After the giving of the ring, the traditional
offering of gold and silver, and the benediction, the witnesses signed the
notarial document registering the proceedings and then gave hearty congratulations to the royal couple.[11] This marriage, as it turned out, would
survive the king's worsening temper, the factional struggles within his
Council, the rumors of new favorites, and even an attempt to accuse the
queen of heresy. Catherine Parr was to be Henry's last wife.

Mary was so solidly in her father's favor at this time that he insisted
she go along on his honeymoon. Henry, Catherine, Mary and their suite
started out to spend the summer visiting the king's favorite hunting parks
but before they had gone far Mary became sick and had to turn back. She
spent the next months recuperating in the company of Elizabeth and Edward, and looking after her own servants, many of whom were more ill
than she was. Her chamber woman Bess Cressy had to be boarded and
cared for in a private house, as did Jane the Fool. Mary paid for their
care, and looked after her gentleman usher Randal Dodd when he too
was bedridden. By February of 1544, though, Mary had rejoined the
court, and with a new standing.

Recognizing that he might not live much longer, and that even if he
did the chances of his having more children were slim, Henry decided to
restore to Mary and Elizabeth their succession rights. If Edward died

without heirs, Mary was to become queen, and Elizabeth was to be next in line if Mary had no children. Mary's readmission to the succession, a change of momentous importance to her future, was accomplished with little fanfare. It was made to seem a natural result of Henry's newfound rapport with his older daughter, and of the closer family feeling Catherine was working to create among the king and all his children. They had never before been brought together to live with him on a more or less permanent basis; now the new queen not only made a home for them at court but set about to make the royal nursery a training ground for the humane rulers the king's children might someday be. She set them a personal example of serious, studious interest in the life of the mind, and brought in the humanist John Cheke to train them in the classics and in the felicitous if overly elaborate style of speaking and writing at which they all excelled.

As learned women Mary and her new stepmother shared a special bond. They belonged to that growing company of noblewomen that the scholar Nicholas Udall described as "given to the study of devout science and of strange tongues." Catherine's treatise *The Prayers stirring the Mind unto Heavenly Meditations* appeared two years after she became queen, and among her other projects was a translation of Erasmus' *Paraphrases on the Four Gospels*. Udall served as editor of the book, and Mary was one of the translators; the queen financed its publication.

A Spanish visitor to Henry's court in 1544, just before Mary's twenty-eighth birthday, left a description of his meeting with the queen and princess in the queen's apartments. He was the duke de Najera, a soldier in the service of the Emperor Charles, who on his way back to Spain came to pay his respects to the English king. The duke wanted to see at first hand this amazing prince, who, he noted, had ordered more executions of those who opposed his opinions than any other ruler "Christian or infidel."

Arriving at Greenwich the Spaniard was escorted through three large halls hung with tapestry. The first was empty, the second held two long rows of halberdiers of the king's bodyguard in red livery, and the third, the presence chamber, was full of sumptuously dressed nobles, gentlemen and knights. All of these courtiers paid reverence to an empty chair of estate whose customary occupant was nowhere to be seen. The king never did come into the presence chamber—because he feared assassination, the duke conjectured—but in time the Spaniard and two of his companions were summoned into Henry's inner chamber. After an audience of half an hour the visitor was taken to the queen's apartments, where he found Catherine, Mary and Henry's niece Margaret Douglas flanked by dozens of gentlewomen and other attendants. Although Catherine was "a little indisposed" she wanted to dance "for the honor of the company," and, taking as her partner her brother William Parr, she led a measure "very gracefully." Then Mary, Margaret Douglas and the others danced, and a Venetian of the royal household danced some galliards with the spectacular agility the king had displayed twenty years earlier. After several hours of this pastime the duke took his leave. He kissed the queen's hand and turned to kiss Mary's, but she offered her lips instead—a gracious familiarity usually reserved for relatives or those of equal rank. In all he found both the queen and princess to be agreeable in their looks, dress and manners, and the impression left by his account is of an orderly court, centered on an increasingly inactive king yet enlivened and ornamented by two distinguished and accomplished women. Catherine was only four years older than Mary, and if as Chapuys noted she "did her all the favor she could," it was more as a friend than as a stepmother.[12]

The calm, harmonious atmosphere the duke de Nájera observed at court filled Mary's life as a whole during her father's final years. Apart from occasional periods of illness, including an episode of what Chapuys called "colic," she lived the uneventful life of a royal favorite, haunted as ever by the seeming impossibility of marriage but outwardly content within the intimate circle of her women and household staff. She was an advocate for present and former servants in their lawsuits and property settlements. She saw her officials Charles Morley and John Conway well set up with rents and lands, and when her gentleman usher of the chamber, Robert Chichester, married Agnes Philip she arranged for the couple to receive lands and a manor in Suffolk by a royal patent. For her favored gentlewoman Susan Clarencieux she obtained first an annuity of thirteen pounds a year and later the manor of Chevenhall.

Mary's contacts outside the court widened during these years. A Spanish nobleman wrote to ask her about an impostor who was traveling through England on the strength of a forged letter of recommendation in the nobleman's name. An Aragonese noblewoman who heard of Mary's fondness for Spanish gloves sent her ten pairs, with a letter. And Princess Mary, daughter of King Emanuel of Portugal, wrote to say she had heard so much about Mary's "virtue and learning" that she hoped they might exchange letters and literary works from time to time. Whenever a messenger was available, she assured Mary, she would try to write again.[13]

Mary's answers to these correspondents were brief and formal. Often she dictated them to be written by others, when the headaches or illness or exhaustion of which she complained made it impossible for her to write herself. Despite the opportunities that now presented themselves for contacts of a more expansive kind Mary preferred to turn her energies inward, above all toward her father. She stood beside him at christenings; she was in his sickroom when he took to his bed. Like Catherine she thought a good deal about his comfort and about how to please him.

In the fall of 1543 she ordered work to begin on the most unusual New Year's gift he would ever receive. She had a joiner build him an enormous chair, big enough to accommodate his girth, and had it upholstered in fine cloth. She hired a French embroiderer, Guillaume Brellont, to decorate it, and paid eighteen pounds for his elaborate designs and skilled craftsmanship.[14] Next to his chair of state, Henry must have valued Mary's gift as much as he did his golden walking stick or the stool on which he set his tortured leg.

In the spring of 1544 Henry rose above the limitations of his age, bulk and afflictions to lead his army to war against the French. It was agreed that he and his ally Charles would each equip more than forty thousand men and bring them to Calais and the Champagne frontier, respectively. Then Charles' men would advance through Champagne along the Marne to Paris, while Henry's forces would make their way south through Artois to meet them there. When he heard that Charles was to lead his army himself Henry made up his mind to do the same. He was still the envious, fiercely competitive monarch he had been a quarter of a century earlier. He considered it "a part of honor to do what the emperor does," Chapuys wrote, and he begrudged Charles his slight advantage in age and his long experience in campaigning.

Henry's advisers were dismayed at his decision. Even in the comfort of his palace his "chronic disease and great obesity" required "particular care." How could he survive in a military camp, living in an unheated tent, eating and drinking rough food, vulnerable to extremes of weather and to all the hazards of warfare besides? Even if he survived these rigors, and the fatigue they brought, how could he ride into battle when he was reported to be "so weak on his legs that he could hardly stand?"[15] Everyone around Henry tried to dissuade him from going, both for the sake of his health and because he promised to present the worst kind of liability to the armies in the field. His commanders, Norfolk and Suffolk, threw up their hands; the emperor sent two envoys to urge him to change his plans, but without success. The only way out seemed to be for Charles to hand over command to one of his generals and retire from the campaign himself, allowing Henry to back out without dishonor. But this solution would impugn the emperor's vigor and ability, and was unthinkable.

In confident disregard of the fears of everyone connected with the venture Henry continued his preparations for war. Some years earlier he had ordered cast the largest guns ever made in England; now he hired two foreign gunsmiths, Peter Bawd and Peter van Colin, to make mortars and shells. Ten warships, with the flagship the *Great Harry*, were loaded with the cast-iron pieces and other guns, hackbuts, pikes, baggage wagons and horse harness. Each ship carried hundreds of men, their horses, and much of their food. The beer brewers were told to keep a certain number of vessels loaded with filled casks, ready to sail with the fleet when the call came. To assure a plentiful supply of bread, the other staple of the army on the march, Henry ordered mills for grinding grain to be mounted on wagons, and constructed in such a way that they ground as the wheels of the wagon turned. There were portable ovens too, to be carried on wagons behind the mills.

Finally in June the "king's great army on the sea" moved out into the Channel, augmented by long oared vessels of Henry's own design whose deadly guns were placed for maximum advantage against the French galleys. The main force under Norfolk and Suffolk crossed first; Henry followed. He had decided to split his forces into three contingents, leaving the most burdensome objectives to his two commanders. Norfolk, with a singularly ill-equipped army, would besiege Montreuil; Suffolk, with an army that included two hundred seasoned Spanish troops under Beltrán de la Cueva, was sent to take Boulogne. Henry would skirmish with the French in the vicinity of his headquarters at Calais.

He rode out of the city, "armed at all pieces" and mounted on a great courser, on July 25. Mounted drummers, fifers and trumpeters preceded him, and behind him a knight carried his headpiece and spear. The violent thunderstorm that drenched the camp that night left him undaunted. He rode and marched like a young man during the following days, and made the thirty-mile journey from Calais to Boulogne in a single hard day of riding. He spent long hours in the fields, looking over the lay of the ground and planning where to put his troops and guns. He even found time and energy to keep a journal. To the amazement of his men, his captains and the diplomats who watched his every move this arduous life seemed to rejuvenate Henry. After weeks of campaigning he appeared to be in better health than when he started out, and more determined than ever to remain in personal command. All his life, he told the imperial agent De Courrieres, he had been "a prince of honor and virtue, who never contravened his word." He was "too old to begin now, as the white hairs in his beard testified." His weeks of effort were rewarded when with the help of de Cueva Suffolk took Boulogne in mid-September. The king entered the city in triumph, reliving his victorious conquest of Thérouanne thirty years before, and stayed on for a week to celebrate his success.

Then, forgetting everything but that he had spent a season marching and maneuvering on French soil, that he had besieged a city and proven wrong those who said he was too feeble to fight again, Henry returned home. The emperor, for reasons of his own, had already made peace with the French. The campaign ended badly, with Norfolk struggling to keep command of his mutinous soldiers and Suffolk abandoning Boulogne when he heard that a French army was about to attack. In the end there was little to show for the staggering cost of the expedition, but Henry, at least, had kept his honor and proved his remarkable stamina.

Two years later he was dying. In the fall of 1546 his ulcerated leg gave rise to a fever which, though he tried to shake it off by exercising, hunting and meeting with ambassadors as usual, persisted. By December he thought it prudent to make his will.

His last months had been filled with intrigue, as the men around him prepared for the transfer of power they knew could not be delayed for long. Along with John Dudley, Viscount Lisle, who had become Lord Great Master of the household, Edward Seymour was the controlling presence in the Privy Council. Both the bishop of Winchester and the powerful duke of Norfolk had been ousted from their positions of influence, and as the king slowly lost ground to his fever Norfolk lay in the Tower under sentence of death.

Mary was untouched by these shifts of power. Henry continued to show her every sign of favor, showering her with so many jewels that the French were saying she might rule when Henry died and not the nine-year-old Edward. One of the last entries in the king's household accounts is the purchase of a horse for Mary, a "white grey gelding." Catherine Parr was less fortunate. An attempt was made to remove her on the grounds that she held heretical opinions, and the king signed the bill of articles drawn up against her. Catherine fainted from fear when she found out what was being planned, but when she asked Henry to pardon her religious fervor and forgive any erroneous views she innocently held he pardoned her, and protected her when the chancellor Wriothesley came to make the arrest.

The legend of Henry's amorous disposition remained with him to the end, and it was rumored that Catherine might be put aside not for her supposed heresy but for another woman. Charles Brandon's beautiful fourth wife, Katherine, was the object of these speculations. Brandon's death in 1545 left her a widow, and it was said that the king was showing her "great favor" in her bereavement. The rumors were persistent enough to annoy Catherine considerably, and as far away as Antwerp merchants were wagering "that the king's majesty would have another wife."[16] Henry and his matrimonial changes had become a fixture of European political life, and it seemed as if both would go on forever.

The king grew dramatically worse in January of 1547. Very early in the morning of January 28 he died. News of his death was kept from everyone but the Council members for three days. In the banquet hall his meals were brought in to the sound of trumpets as usual, and envoys who requested audiences with him were told that he was overwhelmed with business or indisposed. Finally the announcement came that he was dead, and his will was read out in Parliament. Henry lay in state in the chapel of Whitehall for twelve days, surrounded by candles and mourners, and at the Leadenhall and St. Michael's churchyard in Cornhill a dole of one groat apiece was given to some twenty thousand paupers of the city.[17] Next to the coffin was a lifelike waxwork figure of the king, dressed in costly robes covered with jewels. An Italian traveler who left a description of the scene counted nearly five hundred gems on the effigy.

The funeral procession that followed the corpse to Windsor was four miles long. The wax figure too rode in its own chariot, drawn by eight horses trapped in black velvet and attended by pages in black livery.[18] According to the terms of Henry's will he was to be buried with Jane under a monument in the chapel at Windsor. His design for the monument called for a large base with statues of himself and Jane, the latter in repose, "sweetly sleeping." At the corners of the tomb he wanted the sculptor to carve children, seated, throwing down jasper, cornelian and agate roses from baskets they held in their hands. The monument was begun but never finished. Henry's long coffin was buried in Jane's tomb, under the floor of the chapel, in the center of the choir. After it was lowered into place his household officials took their staves of office, broke them over their heads, and threw them into the grave.

At the news of Henry's death the French king panicked. He had long since come to believe that his life and Henry's were mystically linked; if Henry died he would soon follow him. Francis tried to throw off his apprehension by exhausting himself in his hunting park, but he caught a fever and died two months after his lifelong rival of England.[19]

The ambassadors who had reviled, feared, mistrusted and yet admired Henry now outdid one another in formulating expansive tributes to his greatness. They called him "a mirror of wisdom for all the world," and lamented his passing with the sincerity of men seasoned in professional deceit. "He is a wonderful man and has wonderful people about him," a French envoy had written several years earlier, yet the same man conceded that Henry was "the most dangerous and cruel man in the world."

Henry VIII ended his reign as a dark enigma, and it was as such that he entered popular folklore. In the 1540s the English swore "by the king's life" as if it were sacred, but after Henry's death they gave his name to the devil. Along with "Old Nick" and "Old Scratch," "Old Harry" became synonymous with the Evil One in the north of England, among the men and women of York and Lincoln who cursed his memory.

XXIII

 Sing up, heart, sing up, heart,
and sing no more down,
For joy of King Edward, that
weareth the crown!

The death of Henry VIII put England's future into the pale hands of a rather undersized boy of nine. King Edward VI was an intelligent, lively child whose white skin, reddish hair and delicate, elegantly proportioned body gave him the look of an expensive china doll with a slight flaw—one shoulder was higher than the other. He had always been an exceptionally beautiful child. A noblewoman who saw him when he was thirteen months old wrote that he was "the goodliest babe that ever I set mine eye upon," adding, "I pray God make him an old man, for I should never be weary of looking on him."[1]

Apart from occasional illnesses in early childhood Edward gave his father no worries. Under the tutelage of John Cheke he mastered Latin and had made a good beginning at Greek; he knew French well by the time he came to rule, and could keep up with the other boys in his household at fencing and riding to the hunt. In his religious instruction he was entirely a child of the Reformation. The religion he learned was the hybrid orthodoxy of Henry's court; the services he heard were conducted in English, and he grew up unencumbered by the nostalgia for the old church and the Latin mass that haunted the generation of his parents. His mother, had she lived, might have been allowed to teach him to revere the least offensive of the old ways and could have told him something of the nature of country faith before the abbeys were pulled down. But she was not there to teach him, and the only other adherent of the old belief he knew well was Mary. Despite the twenty-one-year difference in their ages Edward and Mary were very close, but they did not discuss religion.

"Imitate your father, the greatest man in the world," ran verses inscribed on Holbein's portrait of Edward. "Surpass him, and none will surpass you." To follow a king such as Henry had been would have overburdened any child, but Edward did not fall short of the challenge merely because of his youth. As a boy Henry had already become a king in miniature. Erasmus, who saw him briefly then, remarked that he had something regal about him. Henry had been a commanding presence at nine; Edward was not. Both his good and bad points were on too modest a scale. He was cheeky but not defiant; alert but not shrewd; gracious but not charming. Worst of all, he had none of his father's robust vitality or breakneck zest for athletic contests and tournaments. Try as he might, Edward would never imitate, let alone surpass, his fearsome, bellowing father; he could not create the illusion that, in his sacrosanct person, he was the locus of power.

Of course, Edward was not expected to rule alone. In his will Henry had designated sixteen of his "entirely beloved councillors," including the chief men in his government, to form an advisory body to guide the young king during his minority. Two of the sixteen, Edward Seymour (who became duke of Somerset soon after Henry's death) and William Paget, took over at once. They made the decision to withhold news of the old king's death for three days, and added to it the much more audacious decision to alter the mechanism of rule. At the first full meeting of the Council Paget persuaded his fellow councilors to name Somerset as head of the Council and Lord Protector of the king. Outwardly the change appeared to be both slight and natural; Somerset was Edward's nearest male relative and natural guardian, and Edward himself approved of the arrangement, signing the commission giving the Protector his powers. But in reality the alteration was fatal. It substituted for the deliberations of a committee of equals bitter squabbling between the supporters and opponents of the increasingly offensive Protector, and it opened the way to an orgy of opportunism, corruption and ineptitude in government.

None of this was yet apparent, however, when Edward made his ceremonial progress through London on the day before his coronation. He was dressed in cloth of silver embroidered in gold, and his belt and cap sparkled with rubies, diamonds and pearls. His horse was trapped in crimson satin, and as he rode through the freshly swept streets he was greeted as a "young king Solomon" who would continue his father's noble work of restoring "ancient Truth" and suppressing "heathen rites and detestable idolatry." These pointed references to Edward's Protestantism were set in elaborate pageants in which children representing Faith, Justice, Grace, Nature, Fortune and Charity spoke to the king and Edward the Confessor and an armored St. George on horseback reminded him of his lineage and patriotic duty. One scene recalled his parentage: a phoenix, representing Jane Seymour, came out of an artificial heaven of "Sun, Stars and Cloudes" to where a crowned golden lion—King Henry—greeted her lovingly. A young lion, their offspring, then appeared, and after two angels crowned him the phoenix and the old lion vanished, leaving him to rule on his own.

The solemnity of these representations was relieved by a death-defying spectacle played out in the air above St. Paul's churchyard. A rope was stretched taut from the steeple of the church to a "great anchor" in the yard below. As Edward rode up before the church an Aragonese acrobat, who had been waiting on the roof, lay down on the rope at its highest point and, spreading out his arms and legs, "ran on his breast on the said rope from the said battlements to the ground," like an arrow out of a bow. Edward paused, delighted, while the Aragonese saluted him and kissed his foot before climbing back up the rope to begin more tricks. When he got halfway up he began to "play certain mysteries" on it, tumbling and hopping from one leg to another, and finally hanging by a second rope tied around his ankle. Edward and his attendants "laughed right heartily" at this entertainment and stayed a long time watching it before going on to Westminster to complete the progress. On the following day, February 20, the young king was crowned, and on successive days the coronation was celebrated by tournaments at which the dashing Thomas Seymour, the Protector's brother and now Lord Admiral, won the prizes.

Edward began his reign in a climate of unclouded approbation. His councilors, officials and subjects welcomed him as David, Samuel, and "the Young Josias." His beauty, wit and amiability were exalted; he was praised as the "gentlest thing of all the world." His gravity far exceeded his age. "It should seem he were already a father," said a court observer, "yet passeth not the age of ten years." Few in the crowd of admirers perceived that Edward would prove to be little more than a symbol of the continuity of Tudor rule, vulnerable to the manipulative ambitions of the men around him and "opportune to treacheries."

Mary had always stood next to Henry in Edward's affections. In his early childhood she never failed to send him gifts—an embroidered coat of crimson satin, a gold brooch with an image of St. John the Baptist set with a ruby—and he sent her in return baskets of vegetables and, when he learned to write, brief, precise letters in elegantly turned Latin. The letters were more schoolroom exercises than outpourings of brotherly feeling, but Edward's sincere love for Mary was not entirely stifled by the rhetoric. In one letter he worked out the sentiment that, although he did not write to her often, still he loved her most; he wore his best clothes less often than the others yet he loved them more.[2] He wrote solicitous notes to Mary when she was sick, and sent greetings to her women. And once, when he was only eight, he felt the need to remind her that "the only real love is the love of God," and that her inordinate enjoyment of dancing and entertainments imperiled her respectability. He urged her from then on to avoid "foreign dances and merriments which do not become a most Christian princess."[8] According to Mary's gentlewoman Jane Dormer, who spent a good deal of time in Edward's company as a child and whose autobiographical memoir contains valuable accounts of his reign and Mary's, the young king "took special content" in Mary's company. He treated her with the respect and reverence of a mother, asking her advice and promising to keep secret anything she confided to him.

Edward's accession put a barrier of ritual deference between the boy king and his sisters. When they ate with him they had to sit on low benches, not chairs, and etiquette required that they be placed far down the table, so that the cloth of estate which hung above the king did not cover them. Even when talking to him in private in his apartments they did not dare to sit in armchairs but on benches or cushions, and when entering his presence they were required to kneel several times. The barriers of precedence, though, were slight compared to those erected by the Protector and Council. To these politicians Mary represented a diplomatic and confessional liability, and a potential focus of discontent and even of rebellion. As such she had not only to be kept away from the king but from the court as well.

The authors of this policy toward Mary were committed to a political and religious program far removed from Mary's beliefs and remote too from the ideals of that large group in the population which was devoted to her. Encouraged by the Protector, Parliament was sweeping away many of the characteristic laws and policies of the last reign. Many of the changes were beneficial. The treason laws, the foundations of Henry's authoritarian power, were being struck down, making it much more difficult for the sovereign to obtain a treason conviction from the courts. New social legislation aimed at tapping the wealth of the booming cloth industry and restoring the old patterns of farming disrupted by the enclosure of lands for sheep raising was being formulated, and old legislation enforced, with the full approval of the Protector and Council. But where religious legislation was concerned, the changes were alarming to Mary and others like her. The Henrician religious settlement was being swiftly and radically overturned, to prepare the way for thoroughgoing Protestantism.

For a decade and more English religious life had been prey to royal and governmental assault. The pope had been vilified and his power in England destroyed; the monastic establishment had been uprooted and plundered. The sacraments were reduced to three, and the adoration and invocation of saints condemned. Theology, the exact definition and redefinition of what was to be believed about the mass, the clergy and the process of salvation, was left in confusion. And since many of those who tried to clarify that confusion were burned as heretics, little clarification was attempted.

The result was a harvest of anticlericalism. Time-honored hatreds of clerical wealth and privilege were unleashed with a vengeance. Everything once held sacred was profaned. The clergy were ridiculed. The "nodding, becking, and mowing" of priests performing mass was compared to the posturing of apes. The saints were insulted, the virgin Mary reviled. The pope was condemned as "the misty angel of Satan" or worse; the Protector claimed that, among ordinary folk, "the name of the pope is as odious as the name of the devil himself." Penance and Lenten fasting were dismissed as unnecessary practices; purgatory was denounced as a fantastic invention of priests. Christening, it was said, was a superfluous gesture which could be performed just as well by immersing the child in a tub of water at home or in a ditch by the roadside. As for holy water, it made a good sauce for mutton if a little onion was added to it; failing that it was good medicine "for a horse with a galled back." Praying to the saints for help was like "hurling a stone against the wind," for saints can do no more to help a man than wives to help their husbands. And priests, the authors and perpetuators of all these delusions, were little better than agents of the devil; their tonsures were "the whore's marks of Babylon."[4]

In Edward's reign violent insults soon gave way to violence itself. Churches and ruined monasteries were plundered until every holy image they contained was destroyed. Altars were smashed, tombs laid in ruins, stained-glass windows shattered into heaps of colored glass. The hostility spilled over into the streets and public houses. Men were shot at as they went to church, and clerics were assaulted. Innkeepers changed the names of their establishments to avoid attracting the consequences of religious prejudice: the sign of the Salutation of the Angel became the Soldier and Citizen; the St. Katherine's Wheel became the Cat and Wheel. Even King Edward, eager to purge his institutions of all taint of popery, objected to the association of St. George with the Order of the Garter.

In a purely negative sense the explosion of anticlericalism laid the foundation for doctrinal change. The condemnation of good works as useless to salvation prepared the way for the Protestant teaching of justification by faith alone. Ridiculing the mass wafer as a "round Robin" or a "jack in the box" and deriding the "roaring, howling, whistling, murmuring, tomring and juggling" of the mass and offices set the stage for the introduction of the simpler English communion service. The

sweeping condemnation of the externals of the old faith—"hallowed candles, hallowed water, hallowed bread, hallowed ashes"—made way for
the Protestant emphasis on internal conversion and the devotion of the
heart. And by adding to the general bewilderment about belief this furor
of invective made at least some in the population doubly eager for the
new orthodoxy when it came at last.

It was the intention of the Protector and Archbishop Cranmer to ride
the crest of this tide of dissatisfaction and to harness its discontent
through the formulation of a new creed. The first steps were taken soon
after Edward's accession, when all the legislation regulating the Henrician church was repealed. Restrictions on the printing and reading of the
Bible were lifted, and Cranmer began work on an English communion
service to replace the mass, which would come into use early in 1548. It
was essential that there be no organized Catholic opposition to this program, and it was here that Mary presented an embarrassment. As the
official faith of England moved further away from Rome, Mary could be
counted on to remain loyal to the old faith. While Henry lived her Catholicism had been tolerated, once she renounced allegiance to the pope.
But when the new teachings and services came into existence her adherence to the mass, the festivals and the doctrines of Rome would seem an
insult to the religious establishment, and would encourage the vast numbers of Catholics who had never been reconciled to any change in the
faith to resist.

And as always, the issue of religion had its diplomatic dimension. Any
move toward Lutheranism in England was bound to bring on the disapproval of the emperor, who in the spring of 1547 was stronger than ever
after achieving a significant victory over the German Protestants at
Mühlberg. The French, always intent on driving a wedge between imperial and English interests, were already at work raising fears of invasion.
Within six weeks of Henry's death the French king was telling the English ambassador in Paris that the emperor planned to make war on the
English, on the pretext that Mary and not Edward was the true heir.[5]
Even if he did not invade England Charles was certain to support Mary's
continued fidelity to her Catholic confession, and to back any rebellion
against the Protestant government that might take shape as the religious
alterations advanced.

What made matters worst for the Council was that Mary was now heir
apparent. It was common knowledge that, should Edward die without an
heir, Mary was designated his successor under the terms of the late king's
will. Certain knowledge that a Catholic would succeed should harm come
to the king was bound to give rise to assassination plots and political
conspiracies both in England and on the continent, where for years the
pope had been urging Reginald Pole and others to find the means to de-

stroy Protestantism and restore the true faith. In the light of these dangers the most influential of Edward's councilors took varying attitudes toward Mary. The Protector, fearing above all the international complications she might trigger, thought that if she could be kept in the background, away from court and out of the view of the public and the diplomats, the twin problems of her divergent faith and her popular influence would be minimized. Obsessed as he was with waging war against the Scots, he tended to treat Mary as a minor irritant to be dealt with as the need arose. There had never been any personal enmity between Mary and Somerset up to now, and Mary was known to be on good terms with his wife Anne, whom she called her gossip and "her good Nan." Anne Seymour had been a maid of honor in Katherine of Aragon's household; apparently this endeared her to Mary, who now wrote her on behalf of several elderly former servants of Katherine. They were infirm and without employment, Mary explained, and she wondered whether Nan would ask her husband to secure them pensions.

The three Council members who stood next to the Protector in influence—Paget, Dudley and Thomas Seymour—had somewhat different views. Paget, a supple man of impermanent commitments, echoed Somerset's recommendation at the Council table but privately worried that Mary posed a greater threat than the Protector realized. Paget favored conciliatory talk up to the last possible moment: then expedient action. Mary should be allowed to live and worship as she liked until it gave rise to problems; then she would have to be given an ultimatum and, if necessary, dealt with by force. Dudley, an able, unprincipled soldier who was now the third man in the Council, saw Mary as only one of many components in a rapidly shifting political game. He was prepared to force her to renounce her faith if that became necessary, but his primary concern was taking over leadership of the Council himself, and supplanting Somerset. The last of the leading figures, Thomas Seymour, had the most original suggestion for bringing Mary under the control of the Council: he offered to marry her.

Thomas Seymour, whose unsavory charm and ambition were as obvious as his transparently gauche tactics, had like Dudley made up his mind to rise to the top position in the Council. He saw two ways to do this—by winning the heart of his nephew the king and by making a royal marriage. In the admiral's pay was one Thomas Fowler, a gentleman of Edward's privy chamber who brought the king presents from his uncle and spoke on his behalf whenever he and Edward were alone. On one occasion Fowler brought up the issue of Seymour's marriage, and asked the king whom he would recommend as a suitable wife. Edward's first suggestion, Anne of Cleves, would doubtless have chilled the admiral's blood, but on second thought Edward told Fowler "I would he married my sister Mary, to change her opinions."

Greatly heartened, Seymour next went to gain the approval of his brother the Protector. But far from giving his brother permission to marry the heir to the throne Somerset "reproved him, saying that neither of them was born to be king, nor to marry a king's daughter." They must "thank God and be satisfied" with their present honors, and not presume higher. Besides, the Protector added, Mary would never consent. (In fact it was rumored that before approaching either his brother or the king the admiral had proposed to both Mary and Elizabeth, who flatly turned him down.) The admiral, offended, answered that all he sought was approval for the match, and that he would overcome the obstacle of gaining Mary's consent in his own fashion. But this led to another sharp burst of outrage from Somerset, and the conversation ended with bad feeling on both sides that never fully healed. In a few months Thomas Seymour secretly married his old love Catherine Parr, while she was still in mourning for Henry.

In keeping with the Protector's policy Mary was kept away from Edward and the court from the start of Edward's reign. She moved back and forth from Havering, Edward's old residence in Essex, to Wanstead House, New Hall and Framlingham Castle in Norfolk, near the estates which now provided her modest income. She saw little of Catherine Parr either before or after her marriage to Thomas Seymour, and was so far from court that the imperial ambassador, François Van der Delft (Chapuys had left England in 1545), could not see her easily. He learned indirectly that she was being held in "very little account," and was upset over some vague slight from the Council; she was also put out, he heard, that the Protector did not write or visit her with the news of Henry's death for several days after it occurred.[6]

When Van der Delft was finally able to speak to Mary at some length in July of 1547, he found her to be in semi-seclusion out of respect to her father. Henry was still "very rife in her remembrance," she wrote at about this time, and to Van der Delft she explained that in deference to his memory she had not dined in public since his death. She made an exception for the ambassador, and insisted that he dine with her. Mary did not hesitate to put her trust in Chapuys' successor. "She seemed to have entire confidence in me," he wrote afterward, and though their conversation was relatively casual he felt and appreciated Mary's customary openness and lack of formality. They spoke of her income, which Van der Delft thought was far too low considering her standing in the succession; of her father's will, whose authenticity she doubted, but could not prove one way or the other; of the amount of her dowry, about which she knew nothing; and finally of the marriage of Catherine Parr and

Thomas Seymour. Mary asked Van der Delft what he thought of it, and after indicating his general approval he alluded to the rumor that the admiral had proposed to Mary first. She laughed, saying that "she had never spoken to him in her life, and had only seen him once," and made light of the suggestion.[7]

The admiral was in fact fast overreaching himself. He had offended the Protector and Council by marrying Catherine without their approval. He was putting pressure on Edward to advance him beyond his brother, and he was known to be searching the lawbooks for a precedent in which, with the king a minor, one uncle governed the kingdom and the other the person of the king. After a year or so his attempts to win Edward over were at least partially successful, but his swaggering efforts to become the first man in the Council made him universally despised. He tried to ride on his wife's former rank as queen dowager, but fierce confrontations between Catherine and the tenacious duchess of Somerset were the only result. He intrigued to marry Edward to his cousin Jane Grey, a daughter of Edward Grey who had been brought up in the admiral's household, contrary to the Protector's cherished plan to marry the young king to Mary of Scotland. And he abused his office with a thorough and imaginative criminality remarkable even in an age of accomplished corruption.

Among his earliest commissions as admiral was the task of capturing one "Thomessin," a pirate operating out of the Scilly Isles and preying on the ships of all nations. Seymour returned from his mission without Thomessin, but having discovered a profitable new avenue of self-enrichment. He agreed with the pirate and his confederates that he would not interfere with their trade provided they gave him a share of everything they seized. He made similar agreements with the privateers of the southern coast, and in effect became a pirate himself. Taking advantage of the Protector's absence in Scotland he tried to organize a force of sworn adherents and boasted that he could call ten thousand men to his aid if need be, and could arm them from a large private cache of weapons and ammunition. Through a confederate he arranged to embezzle funds from the Bristol mint to finance his illegal private army, and by the fall of 1548 he had become the most dangerous man in the kingdom.

It was then that his schemes began to backfire. Early in September Catherine Parr died giving birth to a daughter, and Seymour's immediate renewal of his proposal to Elizabeth—with whom he had enjoyed a long and scandalous flirtation—made his unashamed ambition more obvious than ever. Determined somehow to use the king for his own ends he obtained first a stamp of Edward's signature and then keys to many of the royal apartments, and late one night he broke into the king's bedchamber, his retinue at his heels, and shot Edward's little lapdog when it tried to bite him. The sheer folly of this adventure seemed to prove that in his desperation the admiral had lost his judgment. He was arrested and, as his misdemeanors came to light, charged with high treason. In March of 1549 he was executed on Tower Hill, the first victim of the self-devouring coterie of councilors that was daily drawing more and more power to itself.

XXIV

 The poor at enclosing do grudge,
because of abuses that fall,
Lest some men should have but too much,
and some again nothing at all.

In the spring and summer of 1549 the commons of England rose in massive protest against the government. There was violence in Hertfordshire, Essex, Norfolk, Gloucestershire and a half dozen other places; in Oxfordshire an incipient revolt broke out. In Cornwall pent-up grievances exploded early in June when by government order the new English communion service was read on Whitsunday in place of the Latin mass. The following day the parishioners of one Cornish village forced their priest to promise to bring back the mass, and before long the new service was thrown out in many Cornish towns and the mass restored. Meanwhile parts of Devon had risen and a large crowd was massing for an assault on Exeter, the largest town in the West Country.

The rebels besieged the town while the force sent by the Council to subdue them stood by and did nothing. The commander Lord Russell, a seasoned veteran of Henry's campaigns, saw that his fighting men were too few, and waited for reinforcements. As he waited the rebel army grew stronger, and the siege of Exeter gave added urgency to the insurgents' demands. They complained of food shortages and high prices, but their principal demands concerned the religious changes. They wanted to keep the mass and to have the old statues and pictures of Jesus, the virgin Mary and the saints restored. The litanies, offices and familiar sacraments should be brought back, they insisted, along with the blessed bread and holy water, and at Eastertime, the palms and ashes. Two of their demands show how eager they were to return to the days before reform doctrines had been mooted in England: they wanted two abbeys re-built in every country, and they wanted Cardinal Pole to be brought back from his exile and placed in King Edward's Council.

In August the West Country rebels were finally defeated, but not be-fore the commons of Norfolk had risen in a widespread and potentially dangerous protest that had something of the millennial character of medi-eval popular revolts. Led by the wealthy tanner Robert Ket, the Norfolk rebels tore through the grazing lands around Norwich, pulling up fences, breaking hedges and obliterating every boundary marker that symbolized the private seizure of what had been common land. After a time they gathered in a huge camp at Mousehold Heath, two miles from Norwich, and as their numbers grew they set up a loosely organized community whose leaders called themselves "commissioners" of the "King's Great Camp at Mousehold." There were at least ten thousand of them—some said nearer twenty—and it took an alarmingly large royal force to subdue them. Dudley was at the head of that force. He took Norwich on August 24, and three days later faced Ket and his men at Dussindale. Leaving much of the fighting to his German mercenaries, Dudley's men carried out a merciless slaughter. When the battle ended, more than three thou-sand rebels lay dead on the field. The survivors straggled home, their leaders seized as prisoners and executed. Ket was hanged on Norwich Castle, and nine others on the "Oak of Reformation" on Mousehold Heath.

The revolts of 1549 seemed to confirm the worst fears of the Coun-cil—that beneath the uneasy acquiescence of the people lay deep dissat-isfactions with religion and government which an inflammatory incident or a popular leader could trigger into violence. In mid-July, when the revolts in the west and north were in full cry, spontaneous uprisings in the counties around London made Council members frightened for their own safety. Mobs of angry tenants moved in disorderly fashion toward the capital, coming so dangerously close that at one point they broke the fences of one of the king's parks at Elton near Greenwich. It was said they planned to besiege London until all rebel prisoners were returned to them alive, and rumors of every sort—including revived fears of reprisals against foreigners—spread throughout southern England in the anxious weeks before the rebellions ended.[1]

Behind the rebels' immediate grievances lay the pent-up frustrations of decades of severe hard times in the countryside. The process known as enclosure, in which large areas of farmland and the meadows and pastures that for centuries had been held in common were fenced in by landlords to make grazing land for sheep, swept away many small farms and caused entire villages to shrink or to disappear altogether. Social critics of the time bemoaned the hundreds of deserted villages to be found throughout

England, their ruined churches and houses a poignant witness to the once flourishing rural life that had gone forever. Sometimes the very ruins themselves were obliterated. "I know towns," wrote one observer, "so wholly decayed, that there is neither stick nor stone standing."

The displaced farmers wandered the roads searching for another few acres to make a fresh start. Some made it to the capital, and survived there; many did not, and became a marginal vagabond population, distrusted by all who saw them and treated with brutality or indifference by the government that feared them. Those who hung on to their farms amid the upheaval in rural life found themselves faced with enormous increases in rents and other fees; landlords were accused of inhuman exploitation and every sort of rapacity. Edward VI's Primer contained a "Prayer for Landlords" asking God that "they, remembering themselves to be thy tenants, may not rack, and stretch out the rents of their houses and lands." Between the enclosing of the fields and the raising of rents fewer acres were being farmed, so that as the numbers of the landless and the unemployed grew, there was less and less food to go around. A contemporary believed that for every plow idled six men lost their livings, and seven more their sustenance. And this at a time when the population as a whole was increasing faster than at any time in the last two hundred years.

In the face of this turmoil the frightened members of the ruling Council took refuge in shrill reiterations of the importance of obedience and maintenance of the social order. To be discontented with one's lot was a sin against the divine order, they insisted. For God has ordained that "some are in high degree, some in low, some kings and princes, some inferiors and subjects, some rich and some poor," and to chafe against these preordained categories was to loose the evils of "abuse, carnal liberty, enormity, sin and babylonical confusion."[2] Take away the agents of the divinely appointed social hierarchy—rulers, magistrates, judges and the natural leaders, the aristocracy—and the result would be that "no man shall ride or go by the highway unrobbed, no man shall sleep in his own house or bed unkilled, no man shall keep his wife, children and possessions in quietness."

Beyond making pronouncements such as these the government did little to alleviate the crisis. The one positive policy was the ill-advised expedient of debasing the coinage. Henry VIII had periodically ordered more base metal mixed with the gold and silver of his coins, and in other ways manipulated the currency for profit. He made perhaps half a million pounds in this way to add to his treasury, but by the 1540s his debts were so huge that the profit from the mint could not begin to cancel them. The 1544 campaign in France and the border warfare with the Scots in the final years of his reign cost him more than two million pounds, and he had to borrow heavily from the merchant bankers of Antwerp to keep barely ahead of his creditors at home. When Henry died he left his debts to his son, and in Edward's name the Protector ordered still further debasement. By 1549 most coins had dropped to slightly more than half of what they had been worth when the decade began, with the result that food costs doubled or tripled.

It had been difficult enough for Henry to hold the country together in the face of these forces of disunity. He had done it by retaining an image of serene mastery, by finding temporary ways around each successive wave of the continuing crisis, and when all else failed, by prompt and terrifying displays of force. Through it all he had remained awesome. No rebellion succeeded in robbing him of his power. But it was evident from 1547 on that neither Edward nor his uncle had the prestige to remain aloof from the unrest that was closing in around them. Popular loyalty was eroding under intolerable economic and social pressures. "What weapons can pacify or keep quiet the hungry multitude?" the author of an anonymous treatise asked the Protector. "What faith and allegiance will those men observe towards their prince and governor which have their children famished at home for want of meat?"[3]

In this atmosphere of fear and insecurity suspicion fell heavily on Mary. Writing to William Cecil about the risings Sir Thomas Smith, secretary of state, referred to "the Marian faction" in the population as if it posed an even greater threat than the rebels of the west and north. "As for the Marians, the matter torments me greatly, or rather, it nearly terrifies me to death," he wrote. "Pray God of his mercy averts this evil from us."[4] He had good reason to be afraid, for though she remained aloof from the political struggles in the Council Mary was taking on an increasingly important public role.

To English Catholics Mary was becoming a popular symbol of resistance to religious innovation. As the religious policies of the Council were transforming the official faith she made her adherence to the old faith as obvious as possible. Where before she had heard the customary one daily mass she now heard two or even three or four, and had prayers in her chapel every night.[5] When she went north to see the estates that had been assigned to her in Norfolk in the summer of 1548 the predominantly Catholic population gave her an enthusiastic welcome, and she made a display of her devout practices everywhere she went. "Whenever she had power to do it she had mass celebrated and the services of the church performed according to the ancient institution," Van der Delft reported to the emperor.[6]

It was almost certainly this public defiance of the religion of the king and Council that led members of the government to meet with Mary on her return. What they said to one another we don't know, but Mary's popularity in the north was very much on the minds of the Council members when the men and women of Norfolk rose in revolt the following summer. The rebellion was in no sense a religious protest; Ket's camp on Mousehold Heath followed the new English communion service and the rebels' grievances were focused on their economic survival. Mary was back in the north when the revolt broke out, and she saw clearly that it had no confessional flavor. "All the rising about the parts where she was," she said, "was touching no part of religion."[7] If proof were needed that Mary had nothing to do with promoting the rebellion, it could easily have been supplied. The rebels did protest on her behalf that she was "kept too poor for one of her rank," but they treated her fences as roughly as those of any other landlord, pulling down the enclosure of her park and tramping through her lands.[8]

What no one in the government could have seen clearly as yet was that Mary was undergoing profound inner changes to accommodate the public role she felt herself called upon to play. She had always been predisposed to see life in monumental terms; now Catholicism and Protestantism became the huge polarities that overshadowed and drew to themselves every act and event in her experience. Her Catholic faith became much more to Mary than the dear belief of her childhood, the faith of the emperor and the regent, the church that had sustained her mother and for which so many of those she cherished had died. It was becoming the cause to which she devoted her being—as absolute and unyielding a commitment as that she had felt toward her mother's cause long before.

Mary had always been a faithful Catholic. But what took shape within her now was so fundamental a merging of her self with her faith that it transcended religious devotion. It was a virtually complete identification of her personality and her destiny with the cause of Catholicism. Many years before Chapuys had urged Mary to save her life by giving in to her father and signing the Submission. He argued that in doing so she would be preserving herself to fulfill a higher destiny. Now that destiny was beginning to become clear. It would somehow be linked to her unswerving allegiance to the old faith, and to her emerging role as representative of all English Catholics.

The process was a slow one. It began when the remaining vestiges of Catholicism in England came under attack in 1547; it would not be complete until Mary herself took power. But signs of the transition were apparent from the first months of Edward's reign, and by the spring of 1549 she saw clearly that she would soon come under pressure to abandon her faith and conform to the usages in Cranmer's Book of Common Prayer—the form of service whose introduction in June of that year led to the western rebellion. When Van der Delft saw Mary on March 30 she confided to him how apprehensive she was about the consequences of her defiance. Her public manner was dignified, confident and determined; in private she felt vulnerable, anxious, increasingly concerned about the welfare of the country. To the ambassador she "complained bitterly of the changes brought about in the kingdom, and of her private distress, saying she would rather give up her life than her religion."

Open conflict with the Council could not be avoided for long. When it came, she said, the emperor would be her only defender. This was true enough, though it is hard to believe Mary was entirely sincere when she told Van der Delft that "her life and her salvation" were in Charles' keeping. She knew well enough that an attitude of helpless entreaty was what her imperial cousin expected of her, just as her father had, and exaggerated her desperation accordingly. But though Mary was no longer the terrified girl who had looked to the emperor almost as a savior in the 1530s, she still clung to the memory of what he and his sister had meant to her in those traumatic years. She showed the ambassador faded letters they had written to her at the time of her submission more than twelve years earlier. The letters were among her most cherished possessions, she said, and she took constant pleasure in them.[9]

Charles was unmoved by Mary's sentimental gesture in keeping his letters, but he was concerned about her situation all the same. Her status as heir apparent gave her more political importance than ever, and the possibility that, through Mary, he might bring England within the Hapsburg fold was never far from the emperor's mind. He had been hearing conflicting rumors about her safety. It was said in Flanders that Thomas Seymour's rash invasion of the king's bedchamber had been meant as only the first step in a much vaster plot to kill Edward and Mary both.[10] In France it was being said that Mary herself uncovered the plot.[11] And in England, Paget was alleging that "it was plain in every respect" that the admiral intended to assassinate Edward and his sisters, and that he had long since recommended putting Mary in the Tower.

That such a conspiracy could be divised and attempted from within the government Charles found distressing, especially as he had other grounds for complaint against the regime as well. Corruption in the policing of the seas, in the collection of customs duties and in the treatment of foreign merchants had been straining relations between England and the empire for some time. When Thomas Seymour's goods were searched after his arrest it was found he had amassed a huge treasure in the purloined property of Flemish merchants—his share in the plunder of the pirates who were his confederates. Seymour's successor as admiral, Lord Clinton, continued to ally himself with the privateers and to heap up riches from Flemish ships; when accused by the aggrieved foreigners he pretended ignorance. No justice was available to Flemish seamen in the Admiralty Court, and the fees charged by customs officials were twice what the law prescribed.

Orderly government in England appeared to be breaking down at an appalling rate, and imperial interests there were being damaged. Charles was therefore all the more predisposed to do what he could for Mary when she wrote to him in April, shortly after Van der Delft's visit to her. She wrote of the plight of all English Catholics in "these miserable times" and stressed that "after God, your Majesty is our only refuge." "We have never been in so great a necessity," she went on, and alluded to the recent enactments making the English service the only tolerated form of worship. Mary urged Charles to do his utmost to ensure that she could "continue to live in the ancient faith, and in peace with her conscience." "In life and death I will not forsake the Catholic religion of the church our mother," she swore, even if compelled by "threats or violence."[12]

Late in May, just before the violence of the summer months broke out, Charles began to put pressure on the Protector and Council to exempt Mary from obedience to the recent laws governing religion. Van der Delft asked Edward Seymour to give Mary "letters of assurance" guaranteeing that she would not be compelled to give up her faith and embrace the new orthodoxy. Seymour refused, saying he had no authority to act against parliamentary law, and that even if he did he could not bring himself to grant something so dangerous to the kingdom. Given the character of the nation, he said, "if the king and his sister, to whom the whole kingdom was attached as heiress to the crown in the event of the king's death, were to differ in matters of religion, dissension would certainly spring up." Mary could continue to worship as she liked, at least for the time being, but the Protector could offer no assurances for the future. The emperor was indignant, and told the ambassador to persist in his efforts, always "making use of all his cleverness so that the Protector may not interpret our words as threats of any kind, or imagine that we might resort to violence." Van der Delft was to walk a tightrope between perseverance and intimidation; he was a far less skillful diplomat than Chapuys had been, and he found it hard going.

On the day that the new service was to become official, two commissioners from the Council, Secretary Petre and Chancellor Rich, came to Mary's residence and informed her that she and all in her household were subject to the Act of Uniformity in religion. She stood firm and gave them a curt refusal, but they had not been sent to enforce the law, merely to state it unequivocally, and the confrontation was relatively mild. Not long afterward, however, Mary received a second message insisting on her compliance and peremptorily ordering two of her household officers, her controller Sir Robert Rochester and her chaplain Dr. Hopton, to appear before the Council.

Both the order and the summons angered Mary. She replied in a letter that her controller could not be spared and her chaplain was sick. As for her mass, she had broken no law in maintaining her manner of worship, she told the councilors, "unless it be a late law of your own making," which could not be held as binding on her conscience. And she went on to lecture them about how they had broken the oath they took "upon a book" to keep King Henry's religious settlement intact. The evil results of their changes were apparent "to every indifferent person," she wrote —and even as she composed her letter revolts were spreading in Devon and Norfolk. They had brought displeasure to God and disquiet to the realm, and she would not lend support to their innovations lest Edward should later hold her accountable for them when he grew to manhood.

Mary's protest was disregarded entirely. Rochester, Hopton and a third man in her household, Sir Francis Englefield, were summoned again and this time Mary let them go. The Protector's tactic was two-edged. He hoped to frighten Mary, and to make her anxious about her servants; at the same time he seems to have believed that, if told by her own trusted men to alter her religion, she might obey. Rochester refused utterly to try to command his mistress, or even to convey a message to her from the Council. Hopton, slightly more flexible, agreed after being closely questioned by the Protector about his theological views to carry back "instructions" about the changes Mary was expected to make.

By this time the rebels were in control of large sections of the country, and no effective counterforce had yet been mustered. Exeter was in the hands of the insurrectionists, and Norwich soon would be. Van der Delft was worried because rebel ground lay between London and the country house where Mary was staying; he could not be sure of sending or receiving messages from her. Though he was preoccupied with meeting the growing threat to his government Somerset agreed to see the ambassador in mid-July. He was remarkably cool and reasonable, under the circumstances. Mary could continue as she was, he said, provided she no longer made a spectacle of her worship. "We have not forbidden the Lady Mary to hear mass privately in her own apartment," he reiterated. "But whereas she used to have two masses said before, she has three said now since the prohibitions, and with greater show." He added the frightening insinuation that through one of her chaplains Mary was implicated in the risings in the west. The Protector had heard that "the head of the Cornish rebels was her chaplain once," he said, but made no further reference to the matter. (At the same time the Council wrote to Mary complaining that her receiver, one Pooley, was "a leader of the worst sort of the rebels in Suffolk." According to Mary both accusations were ground-less.)[13]

As the summer wore on the bloody course of the rebellions held the attention of the Protector and Council. Van der Delft and Somerset met once again in mid-August, but it was not until September, after the con-clusive battles were won, that Paget and another councilor, Paulet, were deputed to state the Council's position to the ambassador. They spoke of Mary with a surprising degree of deference and respect. They were sorry, they said, that such a "wise and prudent lady, the second person in the kingdom," was so fixed in her views that she could not conform to the new service without doing violence to her conscience. They could not give Van der Delft the written letters of assurance the emperor asked for, but they were prepared to make a verbal promise "that she should freely and without hindrance or interference continue divine service as she had been accustomed to have it celebrated in her house, and that her priests and the members of her household should incur no risk."[14]

Van der Delft was not satisfied with this solution, but Mary was. Written guarantees were in reality no more binding than verbal ones, and in any case Chapuys had trained her long ago to be wary of anything put in writing. Letters of assurance, she told the ambassador, might imply an acknowledgment of the laws against the mass which she had no wish to give. "These innovations were not laws," she insisted, "for they were not duly given, but contrary to God, to her father's will and the welfare of the realm."[15]

Mary had come safely through the dangerous summer of 1549, but there were already signs of political upheavals to come. Somerset would soon come under attack, and Mary was under pressure to become part of the coup. She knew that her only safety lay in remaining aloof from po-litical involvements until Edward came of age, yet her mounting concern for the state of the country tempted her to take action. There were some in the Council, notably Dudley, who would like nothing better than to accuse her of treason, and if the Protector were ousted Dudley would be-come the most powerful man in the Council.

In her dilemma Mary read and reread her old letters from the em-peror and regent, prayed daily that God would have mercy on the coun-cilors and "that matters might be restored as they were when the king her father left them," and composed meditations to lift her thoughts above the vexed conditions of politics and the faith. She tried to remind herself that for the true Christian this world is only a temporary resting place on the soul's journey to its home country. Beyond the pains of mundane life stretch the joys of eternity, when all that was once obscure shall be made clear in the light of God's wisdom.

"This natural life of ours is but a pilgrimage from this wandering world, and exile from our own country," she wrote in a "Meditation Touching Adversity" in 1549.

And lest the pleasantness and commodity of this life should withdraw us from the going to the right and speedy way to thee, thou dost stir and provoke us forward, and as yet ward prick us with thorns, to the intent we should covet a quiet rest, and end of our journey. Therefore sickness, weepings, sorrow, mourning, and in conclusion all adversities be unto us as spurs; with the which we being dull horses, or rather very asses, are forced not to remain long in this transitory way. Wherefore Lord, give us grace to forget this wayfaring journey, and to remember our proper and true country. And if thou do add a weight of adversity, add thereunto strength, that we shall not be overcome with that burden: but having our minds continually erected and lift up to thee, we may be able strongly to bear it. Lord! all things be thine; therefore do with all things without any exception as shall seem convenient to thine unsearchable wisdom. And give us grace never to will but as thou wilt. So be it.

XXV

 But Styll as one all desperate,
To lead my life in misery,
Sith feare from hope hath lockt the gate
Where pity should graunt remedy;
Despair this lot assigns me ever
To live in pain, joy shall I never.

The rebellions of 1549 put an end to the Protector's authority. His ability to maintain order had been discredited. His reputation, largely undeserved, as "the good duke" who had tried to correct the evils of enclosure had helped to incite the rebels. His popularity in the countryside was more than offset by the hatred of his colleagues at court, who saw him as incompetent, arrogant and dangerously near to forgetting that he was only the overseer of Edward's government and taking the royal powers into his own hands. By the time the risings had run their course Somerset had made himself so odious that under Dudley's leadership the Council moved as one to depose him.

During his time as Protector Somerset had one overriding preoccupation: to bring the Scots to heel and to establish a lasting peace between the two lands. He defeated the Scots at Pinkie Cleugh in September of 1547 in a battle more fearful in its carnage than that of Flodden three decades earlier, but his hoped-for goal of marrying Edward to the five-year-old Mary Queen of Scots was thwarted. The engagement was broken off and the heiress sent to safety in France, and Somerset now combined revenge and apocalyptic militarism in hoping for a war "to make an end to all wars." His drawn-out enterprise against the Scots so obsessed him that he neglected more urgent threats from the empire and France. Charles V, irritated by the licensed piracy against Flemish merchants in English waters, was antagonized by Somerset's Protestant innovations; beyond his concern that Mary be allowed to keep her Latin mass, he opposed the spread of Protestantism anywhere in Europe and considered it his duty to support its overthrow.

By 1549 England and the empire were at odds, leaving the English without a continental ally against the French. The new French king, Francis I's successor Henri II, lost no time in profiting from Somerset's preoccupation with the Scots. France and Scotland were traditional allies, and any war on the northern border had in fact to be waged on two fronts. But the Protector did little or nothing to fend off war with France. By ignoring the defenses of the English holdings at Calais and Boulogne he invited Henri to attack them, and in August of 1549, when Somerset had his hands full suppressing revolts at home, Henri took the outer fortresses of Boulogne. England and France were once again at war.

Somerset's presumption, greed and hotheaded disposition made even more enemies than his myopic foreign policy. He was no more eager to enrich himself than many others in the Council, but his prominence made his peculation more obvious. He flaunted his wealth in ostentatious building projects, ordering two churches razed to the ground to make room for the palatial magnificence of his residence, Somerset House. He was given to inordinate fits of rage, lashing out at everyone around him and indulging what even his friend Paget criticized as his "great choleric fashions." On one occasion Somerset roared out his anger at Richard Lee, a courtier who had the misfortune to displease him. When the cascade of abuse ended Lee was reduced to tears. He went weeping to Paget's apartments, where after more tears he grew angry and complained that he had been treated far more harshly than necessary. And, Paget added, he "seemed almost out of his wits, and out of heart."[1]

As the months and years of Somerset's rule passed his habitual look of melancholy deepened. He had not won his war to end all wars; his government was careening toward bankruptcy; he was surrounded by corruption and discontent. He was surrounded, too, by relatives and in-laws impatient to share the advantages of his power. His wife, "a woman of a haughty stomach," coveted his wealth for their nine children and forced him to disinherit those he had by a previous marriage. His household was a turmoil of squabbling; at court he was hemmed in by petty skirmishes over precedence. Thomas Seymour refused to take off his hat in the presence of the duchess of Somerset; she in turn refused to hold his wife's train. That Catherine Parr Seymour had once been queen was a circumstance her envious sister-in-law could not forgive, and the Protector was constantly besieged by his wife's demands that he put Catherine in her place once and for all. These sordid quarrels came to an abrupt end when Catherine died in childbed and Thomas Seymour on the block. It was a sobering solution to the problem and, for the Protector, a prophetic one. Seven months after he signed the warrant for his brother's execution Somerset was himself arrested and imprisoned in the Tower.

An initial benefit of Somerset's fall was that relations between Mary and the Council temporarily improved. Van der Delft heard a rumor that she might be made regent for Edward, but it was only wishful thinking on the part of her supporters.[2] Her support was sought when the Protector was ousted, but in keeping with her practice since Edward became king she took care not to ally herself with any faction or political policy. She had in fact been considering the possibility of escape. Earlier in the year she sent the emperor a ring, which he took to be a sign that she wanted to be rescued and brought to Flanders. He sent instructions to Van der Delft that she was not to be encouraged in this, both because of the logistical problems involved in getting her out of England and—here he was blunt—because he had no wish to pay the cost of maintaining her and the household she would require.

Mary took no comfort from her brief rapprochement with the Council. She was treated with greater deference than before, and there were small signs that the Protector's restrictive policy toward her had been replaced by a more relaxed attitude. Sir Thomas Arundell, a gentleman "of the old faith" whom Somerset had kept from entering Mary's service in the past, now made his request again, this time with the approval of the Council. Because Arundell had been an important figure in the plot to depose the Protector Mary did not at first accept him into her household, but she noted the significant reversal of Somerset's position.[3]

Still, to Mary the brief months of closer accord with the Council in the fall of 1549 were only an interlude between tyrannies. Somerset was out of the way, but Dudley was pushing himself to the fore; it was only a matter of time before he would impose his own style of control over the Council and the king. Both within the government and outside it she saw only mounting chaos, criminality and unrest, along with calculated destruction of the old faith. The rebellions in the countryside had been subdued, but not entirely suppressed, and the economic conditions that had triggered them were growing worse. As long as the "disorder among nobles and peasants" continued, she told Van der Delft, no improvement in the religious situation could be expected. She had come through the recent upheavals personally unscathed, and her confrontation with the Protector over her use of the Latin mass had not put her in real danger. But she saw herself in the eye of a storm which might at any moment break with fury over her head. "She thinks she is the only person here exempt from scandal and trouble," the ambassador wrote after a conversation with Mary. She was waiting to see what the Council would do next, he said, "not without apprehensions."[4]

Mary was apprehensive on several levels. On the political level, she feared the subtle Dudley more than the overbearing Somerset; he was shrewder and even more unprincipled, and lacked Somerset's pretense of courtesy toward her. Where religion was concerned she had even more to fear. Beyond the issue of her private worship there was the threat of the vague "Marian faction" that some in the Council saw forming around her, and the everpresent reality that she, a Catholic, was heir to the throne. As one member of the Council put it, Mary was "the conduit by which the rats of Rome might creep into their stronghold."

But Mary was looking beyond the human dimension. In trying to understand events in England she was turning more and more to theological explanations, and to analogies from the Bible. She saw the rebellions in the west and north as signs of divine displeasure, and believed that the worst was still to come. If the men in power continued to destroy the church and persecute the true believers, then God's punishment was to be feared in the form of a revolt so widespread and so devastating it could not be suppressed. England was like Egypt in Moses' time, she said. The English Catholics, like the Israelites of that day, were pleading for their freedom, but in vain. "He hath hardened the hearts of the councilors as he did pharaoh's," Mary said to Van der Delft in an oracular tone. And she feared he meant to loose plagues on England more harmful than any the Egyptians had endured.[5]

In December relations between Mary and the Council took a new turn. Elizabeth was brought to court, "received with great pomp and triumph," and conspicuously entertained in Edward's presence. Because Elizabeth did not hesitate to conform to the religious decrees—she had never known any faith but that of Henry VIII's church—she was being favored over Mary, who remained at a house thirty miles from London. There Mary received a letter in the king's hand inviting her to join her brother and sister at court for Christmas. Mary suspected a trap. There could be only one reason for the invitation, she told the ambassador: to force her to celebrate the holiday according to the Protestant observances. "They wished me to be at court so that I could not get the mass celebrated for me," she explained, "and that the king might take me with him to hear their sermons and masses. I would not find myself in such a place for anything in the world," she added. She excused herself on grounds of ill health, and made plans to visit the palace after the holidays, when she would be free to stay in her own London house and hear her chaplains say mass without hindrance. But she would stay only four or five days even then, to avoid becoming entangled in a theological debate with the king. She had heard that Edward was being encouraged to pose as an authority on religious questions and to be very vocal in his opposition to the Roman faith.[6]

There was no doubt in Mary's mind about who was encouraging him. Dudley was clearly using Edward to carry out his own designs, remaining behind the scenes yet carefully manipulating the course of events. He was a master of the art of court politics, having risen to eminence at the court of Henry VIII despite major disadvantages. He began life with a grave handicap. His father, Edmund Dudley, was beheaded at the very start of Henry's reign, leaving the eight-year-old John Dudley friendless and deprived of his inheritance. Another courtier, Edmund Guilford, later took over the boy's education, and he made the best use of his cleverness in attaching himself successively to the service of Charles Brandon, Wolsey and Cromwell. He managed to profit by the patronage of the cardinal and the Lord Privy Seal, while avoiding the consequences of their fall from favor, and by the end of Henry's reign Dudley had become a Knight of the Garter, Lord High Admiral, and the most respected soldier in England.

In the shift of power that took place after Henry's death Dudley took the safest possible course, acquiescing in Somerset's assumption of the office of Protector while quietly amassing influence of his own within the Council. The victory over the Scots at Pinkie was, militarily, Dudley's victory, and his crushing of the northern rebels at Dussindale made him a hero once again. He was energetic, bold and restless, and possessed a remarkable capacity for intimidation. At the same time, however, he was a man of considerable cunning. His cleverness was such "that he seldom went about anything but he conceived first three or four purposes beforehand," one diplomat remarked. Dudley seems to have combined the bluff, athletic physical endowments of Suffolk with the mental adroitness of Cromwell. By 1549 he had come to represent decisiveness and authority, while the Protector was seen as muddled and ineffective. With Somerset in the Tower Dudley was moving to the forefront of the Council, and its policies were becoming his.

Van der Delft thought at first that Dudley's leadership might prove to be a change for the better. He had been opposed to the ultra-Protestant Somerset, and had allied himself with the Catholics in the Council in plotting his fall. It was Mary who deflated the ambassador's hopes, pointing out that Dudley was "the most unstable man in England" and that only envy and ambition, not religious motives, had prompted the coup. "You will see that no good will come of this move," she warned Van der Delft, "but that it is a punishment from heaven, and may be only the beginning of our misfortunes."[7]

Mary's prognosis was soon borne out. Protestants were calling Dudley the "intrepid soldier of Christ," "the thunderbolt and terror of the papists," and it was apparent that he had no intention of moderating Somerset's religious policies or improving the lot of English Catholics.

According to the ambassador, Dudley saw the church as no more than an object to be despoiled. He "spends freely and possesses a small income," Van der Delft wrote, and had to find money wherever he could. He was reputedly meeting with the new bishop of London, Nicholas Ridley, and Thirlby, bishop of Norwich to claim a share in the spoils of their sees. The cargoes of foreign merchant ships were an even better source of illegal income, and here Dudley "thrust his hand in deep" as often as he could. He ordered ships seized, searched and relieved of their goods; the merchandise was sold at once, and the owners quickly found that all form of protest was futile. In March Van der Delft learned that an imperial treasure ship had been taken whose cargo of bullion from the mines of the New World was valued at four thousand crowns.

Dudley's principal associates were William Parr, marquis of Northampton and Henry Grey, marquis of Dorset. Northampton, an undistinguished courtier and mediocre military commander, was currently trying to live down a scandal; he had married a second time before the complications arising from his first marriage had been resolved. Dorset, whom Van der Delft called "a senseless creature," was a relentless if unskilled intriguer who had been heavily implicated in Thomas Seymour's escapades and was now trying to advance by attaching himself to Dudley. The earl in turn cultivated Dorset for his exalted family connections. Grey had married Frances Brandon, daughter of Charles Brandon and Mary Tudor. His three daughters were cousins to the king, and stood next to Mary and Elizabeth in the succession. Thomas Seymour had promised Dorset he would arrange a marriage between the eldest of them, Jane Grey, and the king, but failed in his plan. Now the royal heiresses were being brought within the circle of Dudley's influence—an alteration that was to prove fateful for Mary.

To make Dudley's supremacy in the Council complete Somerset was also added to his clique. The former Protector was now released from the Tower and allowed to live in his own house in London. He had signed the articles brought against him, admitting malfeasance and mismanagement of his office, and it was unlikely he would pose any political threat to Dudley, but just to make certain the earl set about to bind Somerset to him by a marriage alliance between the two families. In June, Dudley's eldest son married Somerset's daughter Anne; two months before the ceremony Somerset was restored to membership in the Council.

Dudley's primacy in the government was unobtrusive, but unmistakable. He was rarely seen in public, preferring to stay in his house and avoid the streets and crowds of the capital. Sometimes he claimed to be ill —Van der Delft thought this was only a pretense—but it was noticed that even at these times the Council members went to his house every day without fail to "learn his pleasure." "[Dudley] is absolute master here," the ambassador wrote categorically to the emperor. "Nothing is done except by his command."[8] Meanwhile the king and his courtiers were kept amused by a revival of the martial sports Dudley was known to favor. In January of 1550 a tournament was held with the grotesque theme "that love shall be hanged." At one end of the tiltyard a scaffold was erected, and a gallows. On a ladder leading to the gallows stood a richly dressed woman representing Love, whose fate was to be decided by the outcome of the fighting between the contestants at the barriers. When one of the challengers was successful she advanced one step nearer the hangman; when a defender was victorious she stood down a step. The young gentlemen of the court defended Love valiantly against the challengers, three Italians led by one "Captain Julian"; presumably Love was saved.[9]

The early months of Dudley's rule were notable for the increasing division of political influence along confessional lines. "The most dangerous crime a man can commit is to be a good Catholic and live a righteous life," Van der Delft commented. "People do not make inquiry of a man's name, but merely ask whether he belongs to the new or the old religion, and he gets treated according to his faith."[10]

Mary's household reflected this religious polarization. Service to Mary became a mark of piety among the Catholic nobility. "Her servants are all well-to-do people, and some of them men of means and noblemen too," Van der Delft explained in one dispatch. They boasted of their connection with her, and competed for places even in the lower ranks of her staff. Membership in Mary's household assured them of being able to practice their faith, and to hear her chaplains say mass. She had as many as six chaplains at any one time, among them doctors of theology and "men of irreproachable conduct." Noblemen looking for situations for their daughters urged Mary to give them places among her maids of honor. Jane Dormer, who came into Mary's household during Edward's reign, told how "in those days the house of this princess was the only harbor for honorable young gentlewomen, given any way to piety and devotion. It was the true school of virtuous demeanor, befitting the education that ought to be in noble damsels."[11]

Jane Dormer's description implies a prim and sanctimonious atmosphere that was foreign to Mary, but there can be little doubt that, with no queen at court and only the unsettled rivalries of the Council members and their wives to set the tone in the royal residence, Mary's establishment must have appeared to be an oasis of seemliness. She liked order and expected it of those who served her, and she was a diligent mistress who checked up on her officials and looked over their records herself. What impressed visitors most, though, were the religious services, performed regularly and often, and attended by the entire household. As the physical destruction of the symbols and monuments of the old faith continued Mary's vigorous displays of fidelity to the mass were keeping the hopes of English Catholics alive.

After Dudley had been in power for a few months the emperor instructed his ambassador to reopen the matter of arranging a marriage for Mary. As a preliminary he wrote to the old ambassador Chapuys, now an invalid taking the waters at a spa far from the imperial court. Charles asked his former ambassador to recall all that he could about the marriage negotiations in which he had been involved during the previous reign, and to speculate on the probable attitude of the present Council toward new proposals. In his reply Chapuys was dubious about the possibility of convincing Dudley and his colleagues to agree to any proposed marriage. The same obstacles that had hampered negotiations in Henry's reign—the need for the bridegroom to swear to the invalidity of Henry's marriage to Katherine of Aragon, the question of Katherine's dowry, the issue of whether or not Mary would be allowed to leave England—were still present, and the worrisome condition of England's relations with the continental powers created further complications.

England and France were still at war, though there had been no actual hostilities since the Protector's fall. For their part the French were sowing distrust between England and the empire by insisting that, before long, Charles would invade England and depose Edward, setting Mary on the throne and—a new element in the scenario—marrying her to his son Philip.[12] For these reasons Dudley and the others were "prey to an infinitely greater amount of fear and suspicion" than Henry had been, and would be much more reluctant to make any match for the heir to the throne. At the end of his letter Chapuys added a personal note. Nothing would please Mary more, he felt sure, than a revival of the marriage negotiations. She "has no other desire or hope than to be bestowed at the hands of your majesty," he assured the emperor, urging him to reopen the matter for her sake. That Chapuys believed Mary to be eager for marriage is of great significance. She claimed more than once during the 1540s that she preferred not to marry, but the ex-ambassador's statement to the contrary supports the view that her expressions of disinterest were only a matter of form. Chapuys knew Mary as well as anyone ever had; if he thought marriage was among her fondest hopes, his opinion must be given a great deal of weight.[13]

The subject had come up in a Council meeting as early as October, but when in response to the emperor's instructions Van der Delft formally reopened negotiations for the Portuguese match in the spring, he met with an odd response. The intended bridegroom was Dom Luiz, brother of the king of Portugal and a longtime suitor for Mary's hand. To the ambassador's amazement the Council members now professed not to know whether Dom Luiz or his nephew, Dom Juan, was to be considered. They hemmed and hawed over the problem, excusing their ignorance by saying that all the pertinent information had been given to Somerset while he was Protector, and not to any others in the government. Then, laying aside the pretense of confusion, they announced that in any case only Dom Juan would be an acceptable husband for Mary. Dom Luiz, despite his high rank, lacked sufficient lands or territories to support "so great a lady" as Mary and to provide for their children.

"We should be quite ready to pursue the matter if it were a question of the son and not the brother," they all said at once. But Dom Luiz was definitely not suitable.

Van der Delft looked pained, then affronted. "My lords," he said to the Council, "see how misguided you are; for in the whole of Christendom there is no match so suitable and well balanced as this one, and my Lord the Infante of Portugal is by no means so ill-provided with lands as you suppose."[14]

Dudley was probably not present during this exchange, though the feigned confusion over the identity of the suitor was his idea. Not long afterward Van der Delft came before the Council once again, to ask once more for letters of assurance promising Mary free exercise of her religion, and this time he encountered such vocal and undiplomatic opposition from Northampton that even his colleagues were alarmed. As usual the granting of written assurances was denied, and the issue of Mary's highly public worship was raised. The Council took the position that she had only been given permission to hear mass in her chamber, with two or three of her serving women. When the ambassador protested that Somerset had explicitly extended the permission to cover her entire household the marquis broke in irritably. "I have never heard anything said except that she alone might be privileged to do so," he snapped, "but with two or three of her women." Furthermore it was stressed that even this permission was only a temporary act of leniency, granted because of Mary's ignorance and incapacity, that might be withdrawn at any time, especially if she continued to cause scandal by allowing her entire household to be present whenever mass was said. The term the Council members used to define Mary's condition was imbecility—the same word her father had used about her long ago. "To succour her imbecility," they would continue to permit the mass until she learned more about the Protestant usages and could be persuaded to adopt them. When Van der Delft quietly observed that Mary could never be brought to "burden her conscience by forsaking the ancient religion," Northampton interrupted him again.

"You talk a great deal about the Lady Mary's conscience," he burst out. "You should consider that the king's conscience would receive a stain if he allowed her to live in error." He went on in the same vein, growing more heated and turning the discussion into a monologue on the worthlessness of Catholicism. He finally became so angry that the others had to calm him, bringing the meeting back to its starting point and reiterating their flat refusal of the letters of assurance.[15]

There could be no mistaking the import of this exchange. Parr's outbursts had been meant to convey Dudley's impatience with Mary, and Van der Delft understood very clearly the menace behind them. The tightening of restrictions around Mary's religious privilege was ominous; most likely it meant that before long she would be deprived of even her private mass. When the ambassador went to see Mary at the end of April he found her almost in despair. She had heard "through some good friends" that her household staff was in future to be excluded from all Catholic services held under her roof. Soon she would be ordered to conform to the Act of Uniformity. She would refuse, of course, and then a dread and quite probably fatal stalemate would ensue.

"When they send me orders forbidding me the mass," she told Van der Delft, "I shall expect to suffer as I suffered once during my father's lifetime. They will order me to withdraw thirty miles from any navigable river or seaport, and will deprive me of my confidential servants, and having reduced me to the utmost destitution, they will deal with me as they please."[16] Whether she realized it or not Mary was describing not only the torments of her own bitter adolescence but the isolation, semi-imprisonment and hopeless suffering her mother had endured when she too opposed the law in the matter of her divorce. Like Katherine, Mary now swore to remain faithful to the path she had chosen. Nothing could induce her to give up the mass. "I will rather suffer death than stain my conscience," she said with the simple, unwavering firmness she had heard in her mother's voice long ago. "I beg you to help me with your advice, so that I may not be taken unawares."

XXVI

And in grene waves when the salt flood
Doth rife, by rage of winde:
A thousand fansies in that mood
Assayle my restlesse mind.

In the last days of June 1550 a small fleet of Flemish ships crossed the Channel in foul weather. There were four large warships and four smaller vessels, under the command of Cornille Scepperus, admiral of the imperial fleet, and his vice admiral Van Meeckeren, and as they made their way through the heavy seas the lookouts kept a close watch for English and French ships. On Sunday the twenty-ninth they came within sight of the Kentish headlands, and turned northward past the Thames mouth and up along the Essex coast. As evening fell the fog closed in, so dense the sailors could not see from bow to stern, and the captains spent an anxious night worrying that they might run aground on a sandbank or that when the fog lifted they might find themselves to be miles away from the main body of the fleet. But in the morning all eight ships were still together, and that day they sailed farther up the coast to the vicinity of the Blackwater, where they were to wait to convey Mary back across the Channel to safety in Flanders.

It was a bad season for the venture. With the approach of summer fears of rebellion rose. Landowners in every county fortified their country houses and pledged to keep ready a contingent of armed men in case of trouble, and the local constabularies were in a near-constant state of alert. The grievances that had compelled revolt eleven months earlier had grown sharper. Prices and rents were higher, and landlords in many places were exacting rents on fields that had not been plowed the previous year because of the disturbances. None but the gentry were allowed to keep weapons, and the cottages and barns of the villagers were searched frequently for hidden arms. These measures only increased the undercurrent of resentment, and in the north and west the peasants were boasting they would rise again. Only three weeks before the arrival of the Flemish ships an incident over the capture of several highwaymen led to rioting in Kent. Ten thousand peasants assembled at Sittingbourne, setting off a wave of reaction that swept through the southeast. Officials were sent off to "scour the country" for rebels, and arrested and punished anyone making the slightest sign of opposition. One man who "began to murmur and make certain speeches" was taken and sentenced to have his ears cut off. A force of a thousand mounted men was sent into Kent to keep the peace, and another four thousand were kept in readiness on the island of Sheppey opposite the coast.

All through the spring and summer foot soldiers were being levied by the thousands. Some said they were being sent to guard Calais, others that they were to be used against the rebels at home. The new imperial ambassador Scheyfve wrote to the emperor that a force of eight thousand men was being equipped and trained to serve on twelve warships to guard the coastal waters against invasion. "All gentlemen, noblemen and merchants are said to entertain a great fear that your Majesty may declare war because of religion," he explained, "and for other causes too."[1] The roads and lanes of Essex were full of marching men that June, and a diffuse threat of war hung over the little port of Maldon, near Mary's manor of Woodham Walter, where she was to go on board the cornboat that would take her out to the Flemish fleet.

Mary had been thinking of escape for months. She knew she would come under increasing persecution from Dudley and the Council, and that when their patience ran out she would be imprisoned and possibly executed. They would not hesitate to shed her blood out of respect for her rank, fear of her cousin the emperor, or from any ethical scruple. "It is evident to all," Mary told Van der Delft, that the Council members "fear no God and respect no persons, but follow their own fancy." It was also evident that they would act soon. By late April Mary had resolved not to "delay till she was past all help," but to save herself as best she could. She made her plans to get out of her house, past the guards and the local watch, out to a small boat that would carry her to deep water where she hoped a ship of the emperor's navy would be waiting for her.

She told the ambassador her plan, and convinced him she was in earnest. Acting on the emperor's orders he tried one last time to dissuade her, reminding her that, if Edward should happen to die while she was out of the kingdom, she would have a slim chance of defending her right to the throne. But she had already thought through that possibility many times, and had come to the conclusion that she would never be allowed to succeed. "There is nobody about the king's person or in the government who is not inimical to me. They would be so afraid of me that before the people heard how it had pleased God to deal with the king, they would kill me by some means or other." Van der Delft came away believing Mary meant to do as she said. "She is quite determined not to wait here till the blow falls, for any consideration whatever," he wrote to the emperor, adding that she had already taken the first step by moving to Woodham Walter, a house only two miles from the port of Maldon and best situated of all her residences for reaching the coast without detection.[2]

It was at first arranged that Mary's escape would be coordinated with a change of ambassadors. Van der Delft had been in England nearly six years, and had long since begun to suffer from the time-honored complaints of the ambassadorial service: gout and bankruptcy. His recall would not cause suspicion, and once he had formally taken his leave he could divert his ship to the waters off Maldon for long enough to meet the boat bringing Mary out of the harbor. His replacement, the Dutch merchant Jehan Scheyfve, was to be kept in ignorance of the plan, both for his own protection and to ensure that no hint of it would leak out.

By mid-May the change of ambassadors had been arranged. Scheyfve arrived; on May 30 Van der Delft officially took his leave. But from here on problems arose. The man Mary had counted on to take her in his boat from Maldon harbor out to sea—a "trusted friend" of her controller Robert Rochester—changed his mind at the last minute, and when Van der Delft came to see Mary to finalize the arrangements no one had been found to take his place. At the same time, all the towns and villages near the coast were put in an increased state of alert. Householders were told to watch the back roads and lanes by night, and not to allow anyone to pass without an urgent errand. "There were no roads or crossroads, no harbors or creeks, nor any passage or outlet that was not most carefully watched during the whole night," Van der Delft wrote.[3] It was obvious Mary could not get away unless she traveled on foot, heavily disguised, and with only one or at most two others with her. She was willing to do this, and begged him at their last interview to send any boat he could find, even a fishing boat, to rescue her. He left, promising to return for her himself as soon as he could. He meant to keep his promise, but once in Flanders he succumbed to gout and age, and lapsed into fatal illness. He died raving about the plans he was making to save the princess of England.

With the death of the ambassador it was left to his secretary, Jehan Dubois, and the regent of Flanders to engineer Mary's escape. The emperor had set off earlier in the month on a journey through his German lands, and could not take charge of the arrangements, but he wrote to his sister indicating approval of the scheme she and Dubois worked out. It

called for Scepperus and Van Meeckeren to sail to England and to cruise
the coastline as if looking for pirates, while Dubois would take a ship
with a light draught up the Blackwater to Maldon. He would pose as a
merchant selling grain to Mary's household; while his boat was being
unloaded Mary would be smuggled aboard. By the time her absence was
discovered she would be on one of Scepperus' ships and on her way to
Brussels.

On the morning of July 1 the eight ships disposed themselves according to plan.[4] The four warships under Van Meeckeren rode at anchor off
Harwich, while the four smaller ships went in toward the coastline, between the sandbanks and the shore, ostensibly to seek out the coves and
inlets that sheltered pirate ships. Scepperus was in one of these smaller
ships, and Dubois preceded him in a lighter oared boat of the kind used
by grain merchants. At midafternoon they were in the tidal estuary opposite Stansgate. There Scepperus remained, while Dubois went the rest
of the way to Maldon, sending his brother-in-law Peter Merchant on
ahead in a smaller boat to pass the word that the rescue ship was on its
way.

Dubois arrived in Maldon harbor before dawn on the morning of the
second, and sat down to write to Mary's controller to say that everything
was ready for her flight. Before he finished the letter, Merchant and a
servant of Mary's called Henry came on board, and it was apparent at
once that they had met with a delay. Dubois was expecting Mary herself;
now he found that she was not prepared to leave after all. He made his
note to the controller as urgent as possible. "I am obliged to write now to
point out to you that there is danger in delay," the note read. He explained that there were four ships in the coastal waters and four others
just off shore waiting to escort Mary across the Channel. To reach them
undetected would be risky unless they sailed with the next tide. As he
wrote the tide was at its highest; it would be lower each successive
night, making navigation of the Blackwater increasingly difficult. "I must
add that I see no better opportunity than the present one," he added,
"and this undertaking is passing through so many hands that it is daily
becoming more difficult, and I fear it may not remain secret."

Henry took this message to Rochester, and returned just at dawn to
say that the controller wanted to meet with Dubois. At first the secretary
was reluctant; the longer he stayed the greater the danger of discovery,
and any meeting with Rochester would be certain to arouse suspicion. He
ran a grave risk of being taken and executed as a spy, and the slightest indiscretion by the controller or one of his sailors could give him away. He
finally agreed to meet Rochester in the graveyard of St. Mary's church,
an out of the way location not far from Woodham Walter, and once
there he and the controller went on to the house of a villager Dubois

called Schurts. There in the privacy of Schurts' garden they talked, the Fleming nervously and somewhat irritably, the controller in a tone full of dark insinuations.

Rochester was evidently opposed to the escape. In the first place, he said, Mary could not possibly get past the watchmen posted every night at every passage leading to the waterside. Secondly he hinted strongly that there were spies in her household who would get word to their contacts the instant they saw her leave the house. Her household, he said, was "not so free of enemies to her religion as she imagined," and besides these specific dangers the countryside was up in arms, and the watchmen were doubly suspicious of anyone they found on the roads late at night. Besides, he said, Mary was not in imminent danger; the Council was not likely to deprive her of her mass until later in the year, and if necessary another escape plan could be devised and carried out then.

By now Dubois was confused. He had come to England in response to Mary's insistent pleas for help. He recalled how she had spoken to Van der Delft at their last meeting, where both Dubois and Rochester had been present. She had been fully aware of the dangers then—of the persecution, harassment of her servants, and probable imprisonment she faced if she stayed, and the risk of capture and possible forfeiture of her right to the throne if she left. After these points had been discussed several times over, she laid the logic of the situation aside and spoke from her heart.

"I am like a little ignorant girl, and I care neither for my goods nor for the world, but only for God's service and my conscience." Mary knew herself well; she saw that beyond her capacity for shrewdness and discernment she was impelled by simple fidelity to the religious ideal that had now become central to her personality. She regretted leaving those who served her, realizing that in her absence they might "become lost sheep, and even follow these new opinions." For their sake she would willingly stay, as long as she was left in peace by the Council. But Dudley and the others were unpredictable, arbitrary—even cruel. "If there is peril in going and peril in staying," she concluded, "I must choose the lesser of two evils." The morning after this conversation Van der Delft had sent Dubois to Mary one last time, to see whether she was still anxious to go. She assured him she was. And to put the issue beyond all doubt Mary had sent Dubois a letter a few days afterward, saying she was eagerly waiting to hear that the rescue boat was on its way.[5]

Recalling these events of only four weeks before Dubois could hardly believe that Mary would hesitate to leave now, and suspected that the controller was attempting to prevent her from going for reasons of his own. Rochester sensed his distrust.

"Sir, I beg you do not judge me thus," he said, "for I would give my hand to see my Lady out of the country and in safety, and I was the first man to suggest it. And if you understand me, what I say is not that my Lady does not wish to go, but that she wishes to go if she can."

Dubois had no time to split hairs. It was a question of yes or no, he said, and further conversation was perilous. By now Van Meeckeren's warships would have been sighted off Harwich, and within hours the Council would know of their presence. The decision had to be made at once. Rochester now took Dubois by surprise once again, telling him that Mary wanted to talk to him in person. Could he come to Woodham Walter? At first the Fleming refused, but after a day of dickering with customs officials and the town bailiff over the price of his grain, the buyer, and the amount of the duty (waived because the grain was for Mary's household) he finally consented.

The sun was low in the sky as Mary's servant Henry led Dubois "by a secret way" to Woodham Walter. Once there the secretary had another talk with Rochester while he waited for Mary to receive him, and he found the controller more mysterious than ever. Rochester told him "a mighty secret"—that Edward's death was imminent. He was "quite persuaded the king could not outlast the year," he said, "for he and others knew his horoscope to say so." Astrological prediction was rampant at Edward's court, and had already led to several arrests; apparently the controller was privy to some such reading of Edward's stars. If he passed on his occult information to Mary—and there is no reason to believe he did not—it could account for the dilemma she faced in deciding whether to stay or go. Rochester had one final card to play. He had already hinted at treachery from within Mary's establishment; now he said plainly that he knew of some threat so ominous that if either Mary or Dubois knew of it they would abandon all thought of the escape. "Neither she nor you see what I see and know," he warned. "Great danger threatens us!"

When Dubois was finally summoned into Mary's presence he found her to be calm and dignified. She inquired after the health of the emperor and regent, and thanked the secretary for all that he and Scepperus were doing to help her. She seemed strangely unmoved by the excitement of the adventure that lay ahead of her, and Dubois soon learned why. She had half decided not to go after all. "I am as yet ill prepared," she told Dubois. She had begun to pack her things for the journey, putting as much as she could into long hop sacks, but there was still more to do. "I do not know," she went on, "how the emperor would take it if it turned out to be impossible to go now, after I have so often importuned his majesty on the subject."

By this time Dubois was thoroughly bewildered. Something or someone had nearly convinced Mary not to attempt to leave—at least not for the present. Yet she had begun her preparations, and now asked Dubois if he would take her rings back with him. Without presuming too much he tried to persuade her that no better opportunity was likely to come in the future, and that if she was bold enough to send her rings "she might as well go with as after them." Here she turned to Rochester and to Susan Clarencieux, who had been keeping watch at the door throughout the interview, and the three spoke together for a few minutes. It was during this hurried conference that Mary made up her mind. When she turned back to Dubois her look and manner were different. She was decisive, practical, precise. Whatever consideration had deterred her earlier had been pushed aside.

She spoke rapidly now, asking detailed questions, making certain every contingency was reviewed. She could be ready on Friday. She and her ladies would go to the beach at four in the morning "to amuse herself and purge her stomach by the sea," as she often did. At four the watch retired and the roads would be clear. She asked Dubois whether the tide would be high enough, whether he could get word to Scepperus, what Van Meeckeren might be expected to do. As they made their final arrangements she grew more voluble, telling Dubois things Rochester had kept to himself. The very day Van der Delft left London two royal galleys, the *Sun* and the *Moon*, came up the Blackwater to anchor off Stansgate. No warships had ever come so far up the river before, she said, and what was more, one of the galleys was captained by the vice admiral, "the greatest heretic on earth." "It is more than time I was hence," she added, growing more and more vehement, "for things are going worse than ever. A short time ago they took down the altars in the very house my brother lives in."

Just then there was a knock at the door of Mary's chamber, and Rochester went out. When he returned his face was white. "Our affair is going very ill," he said in an undertone, speaking chiefly to Dubois. "There is nothing to be done this time, for here is my friend Mr. Schurts, who has ridden hard from Maldon to warn me that the bailiff and other folk of the village wish to arrest your boat, and suspect you of having some understanding with the warship at Stansgate"—Scepperus' ship. They meant to arrest Dubois and his crew, board his boat and find out exactly what its purpose was. The secretary was dismayed. The delays had been fatal, just as he predicted. If the officials did board his ship the secret would be out for certain. His sailors had not been told that they were coming for Mary, but he had overheard them guessing at the truth, and remembering the abortive escape planned many years earlier.

Rochester's announcement had a profound effect on Mary. She lost her command of the situation and grew fearful. "What shall we do?" she asked Dubois. "What is to become of me?"

The controller elaborated on the danger. "My friend here says there is something mysterious in the air, and that you had better depart at once, for these men of the town are not well disposed." Schurts would try to take Dubois back to Maldon by a back road, hoping he could bluff his way through if he were questioned by saying that Dubois had gone to Woodham Walter to get payment for his grain. There was no longer any chance that Mary could reach the harbor, even if she could find the courage to make a desperate run for freedom. "They are going to double the watch tonite," Rochester had learned, "and what is more post men on the church tower, whence they can see all the country round—a thing that has never been done before."

Dubois did not hesitate. There was nothing more he could do; the matter was out of his hands. Mary, temporarily paralyzed with anxiety, kept repeating over and over "What is to become of me? What is to become of me?" He was sorry for her, and unquestionably loyal—he was quite literally risking his life to bring her out of England—but he could serve her best by leaving as quickly as he could, before the suspicions of the men of Maldon could be confirmed.

The few moments that remained before dark were used to piece together the outlines of an alternative plan. Mary had recovered her composure, and it was she who suggested that the next attempt could be made from Stansgate, which had the advantage of being closer to the open sea. She would go back to Beaulieu in two or three days, and send a servant of hers to Dubois in Flanders with complete instructions for the second attempt. As the secretary left Mary told him to send her best wishes to the emperor and his sister. "You see," she said to him finally, "that it is not our fault now."

It was nearly midnight when Schurts and Dubois reached the outskirts of Maldon. There were twenty men on watch, headed by the bailiff in person, and Schurts had to bribe them to let the secretary pass by promising to give them the grain unloaded from his boat earlier in the day. The boat had been drawn up to the bank, and the tide was rising; just after two o'clock they cast off and started down toward the open sea. As he passed the church tower Dubois looked up to see the lookouts Rochester had warned him of, but there was no one in sight. He had some difficulty on the outward journey—in his haste he had left his best sailor behind on shore—but at nine the next morning he came up to Scepperus' ship and reported all that had happened in the last forty-eight hours.

For five days the Flemish ships hovered near the English coast, waiting out a violent storm that came up as Dubois left Maldon. No English ships challenged them, though the Council in London knew their location and guessed the reason for their coming long before the storm cleared.

But whether through an informer among Mary's servants or some other means they also knew that the heir to the throne had not escaped, and were taking precautions to make certain she never tried to leave England again. On July 7 Scepperus gave the orders for the return crossing. The eight vessels set sail for Flanders, with Dubois at work in the vice admiral's cabin writing a detailed account of his adventure. With them went Mary's last hope of rescue while her brother lived.

XXVII

 What remedy, what remedy?
Such is fortune! What remedy?

Word of the rescue mission to bring Mary out of England began
to leak out almost as soon as the imperial ships arrived back in Antwerp
harbor. By mid-July it was being publicly said in Flanders that Mary had
escaped, and was living at the court of her cousin the regent. Van der
Delft's deathbed ravings had let the secret out, and the Flemish merchants, always alert to any shift in the diplomatic balance between the
Low Countries and England, were telling anyone who asked how the late
ambassador had been planning the venture for months before he died, and
how others had successfully carried it through on his behalf.

Partly to counteract these rumors the English Council made public its
own version of the story. It was true the emperor had tried to carry off
the heir to the throne, they said, but he had not succeeded. They were
shocked that he should attempt anything so scandalous; they could not
imagine that so exalted a personage could be guilty of so great a wrong
against the king and his Council. All the English envoys living at foreign
courts were instructed to inform their colleagues of the emperor's
dishonorable conduct and of the Council's well justified indignation.
Unofficially it was being said that Charles had planned to give Mary to
his son Philip as a bride, giving Philip a pretext to invade and conquer
England in right of his wife.[1] Whether he married her to Philip or not,
went another speculation, the emperor wanted to remove Mary to safety
because he planned to make war on England.

Charles V was in a belligerent mood. Word reached England of his
recent ordinances against heresy—the hated placards—which threatened
savage punishments for any hint of heretical beliefs. To read or sell the

works of Luther, Calvin, or any other reformer was of course forbidden, but even to discuss points of doctrine or to speak with a heretic brought severe penalties. To sell indecent or irreverent pictures of the virgin Mary, the saints or the clergy was accounted as serious an offense as preaching heresy. In every case the offender was to lose both his or her life and property, the men to be beheaded, the women buried alive. The English were astonished at the placards, and told one another the emperor meant to revive "the real and thorough Spanish Inquisition." Twenty English merchant ships that had recently gone to Antwerp returned home abruptly when their captains read the placards, refusing to trust the promise they contained that foreign merchants would not be persecuted for their opinions "unless they gave scandal."[2]

Beyond the emperor's increasing toughness the English had a further reason to be fearful of war. With the shift of power in the Council had come a shift in diplomacy. Somerset had favored conciliation with the emperor; Dudley made no effort whatever to appease him, and was known to prefer the French. He brought the war with France to a close in the spring of 1550, selling Boulogne to Henri II—who already held its outer fortifications—and arranging for the French king to be made a Knight of the Garter in April. The rapprochement with France was bound to worsen England's relations with the empire still further, and as if to prepare for an inevitable war against the imperial forces Dudley saw to it that the country was geared for battle. He took advantage of the emergency military arrangements made during the risings of 1549 to create a standing army answerable to himself. An array of "lords lieutenant" replaced the sheriffs as heads of the military contingents in the shires, and certain of Dudley's trusted followers were put in charge of bands of men at arms paid from the royal treasury.

To channel the attention of the young king toward feats of arms Dudley ordered military entertainments to be staged for his diversion. On June 19 a water tournament was held on the Thames, organized by the Lord Admiral, Edward Clinton. A floating castle had been constructed, with three walls and a watch tower, defended by fifty soldiers in yellow and black. A galley painted bright yellow held the defenders' munitions and more men. Four pinnaces stormed the castle, driving off the yellow galley and assaulting the defenders with "clods, squibs, canes of fire, and darts," until the outer walls gave way. Then after a rally by the soldiers in the castle four more attack ships came alongside, with the admiral in command, and "won the castle by assault, and burst the top of it down, and took the captain and undercaptain."[3] The militaristic tone at court and in the countryside was unmistakable, and had its effect on the populace. "All these events combine to make the people fear that a war may follow," Scheyfve wrote early in August. "Everybody is in great perplexity."[4]

Mary's perplexity in the weeks that followed the failure of the escape attempt was heightened by the presence of hundreds of soldiers in the neighborhood of Beaulieu. Armed men were sent to every port and harbor in the vicinity, with instructions to scrutinize the ships that went up and down the bays and inlets for any sign of secret intent. The English ambassador at the French court was overheard to say that the Council meant to guard Mary much more strictly than before, and that in the light of her recent behavior her religious idiosyncrasy could no longer be tolerated. "She would have to put up with the new religion introduced by the king," he said, "or she might rue it."[5] Left with no possibility of retreat to the shelter of the imperial court, Mary had now to stand and fight the Council as best she could. She had few weapons at her disposal, beyond her own resolution. Her greatest asset was the displeasure of her imperial cousin, who had already done more on her behalf than he had for her mother and might well bring greater pressure to bear in the future. But his protection extended only so far, and had to be exerted from a distance, while his agent in England, Scheyfve, was little more than a diplomatic cipher who knew no English. With these resources to fall back on, Mary set about parrying the fresh assault on her mass that began in July of 1550.

When Mary was leaving Woodham Walter to return to Beaulieu, she sent one of her chaplains on ahead, so that he could be ready to say mass when she arrived. When she did not come he perfomed the service anyway, with many of her household in attendance. The incident gave the Council the pretext they had been waiting for. William Parr, the ill-tempered marquis of Northampton, was also earl of Essex, and the officials of the shire were under his control. He ordered the sheriff to have the chaplain, Francis Mallet, decried as an offender against "the king's edicts and statutes concerning religion." Another of Mary's chaplains, Alexander Barclay, was similarly indicted. Mallet went into hiding; Barclay stayed in Mary's house and continued to perform her mass.

The indictments gave the Council an excuse to hound Mary for months. Would she cooperate with the sheriff in bringing the two men to justice? How could she protest that she and her chaplains had been promised free use of the mass when no such promise had ever been given? Would she be so gracious as to come to court to visit the king's majesty her brother? The latter request was carefully phrased. It was an invitation, not a command, but it was delivered by the chancellor, Richard Rich, and Secretary Petre in person carrying letters of credence from the king and Council. They wanted her away from the coast and nearer the capital, preferably at court where her movements could be closely watched. Mary asked to be excused for health reasons, and was as usual quite sick with the coming of fall. Her illness was then urged as a reason for making the trip to court, since the change of air might be beneficial. But the contagion was not in the air of Essex, as she pointed out in a letter written toward the end of November. "The truth is, that neither the house nor air is herein to be suspected, but the time of the year being the fall of the leaf, at which time I have seldom escaped the same disease these many years."[6]

Rich tried in every way short of force to persuade Mary to leave Beaulieu. He attempted to talk Rochester into using his influence on Mary, but he gravely misread their relationship. Like others in the Council he was incapable of seeing Mary as a figure of authority in her own house; the controller, he presumed, must stand in lieu of a father to her, or a guardian. Surely Mary did not make her own decisions, and Rochester was the obvious man to make them for her. When Rich approached him the controller made it plain that he had no particular influence over Mary, and that she was not at all likely to change her mind about joining her brother in any case. The chancellor did not believe him, and became very angry, but it did no good. When this approach failed Rich tried a more oblique tactic. He returned to Beaulieu with his wife in tow, and the two of them took Mary hunting. After the hunt he urged her not to let their pastime end, but to come to visit him at his house where he would arrange special entertainments for her. Mary saw through this and declined.[7] She did agree to borrow his house while Beaulieu was being cleaned, but that was all.

In November the attack on her chaplains was renewed. Mallet and Barclay were summoned to appear before the Council, a step which underscored the gravity of their crime. Their guilt or innocence turned on the much-disputed issue of the verbal assurances given to Van der Delft that Mary could practice her religion in peace, and in December Mary and the Council reopened their debate on this point. Mary's letters were direct, factual and concise. It was her policy, she told Scheyfve, to "write roughly" to the Council in order to convince them she would not waver in her resolution. In keeping with this policy she wrote the plain truth as she knew it, sparing no embarrassment to those in the Council who had once acquiesced in her free use of the mass and were now attempting to take it from her. Those who claimed to have no recollection of the verbal promises were lying, and she knew it; "you in your own consciences," she wrote to them, "know it also."

In the weeks before Christmas Mary visited the court to back up her case. She defended her position as best she could, but found herself arguing in a vacuum. No one listened to her objectively, least of all the king, who opened the discussion with the peculiar statement that "he had heard a rumor that Mary habitually heard mass." As Mary's staunch Catholicism had always been public knowledge, it was evident someone had been coaching Edward in what to say to his sister. Instead of the child who had loved her like a son Mary now saw in Edward the unfeeling puppet of his councilors. "But when I perceive how the king, whom I love and honor above all other beings, as by nature and duty bound, had been counselled against me, I could not contain myself and exhibited my interior grief," she wrote describing this interview. At the sight of her tears Edward's façade fell away and he too cried, telling Mary to dry her eyes and reassuring her that "he thought no harm of her." Edward's councilors intervened before the tender feelings between brother and sister could go any further, and no more was said about religion.

In the letter she wrote to the Council after this meeting Mary tried to distinguish between her feelings of loyalty and duty to her brother and her wary mistrust of the Council members, to whom she owed no obligation. "To the king's majesty my brother," she wrote, "I confess myself to be his humble sister and subject, and he my sovereign lord; but to you, my lords, I owe nothing beyond amity and goodwill, which you will find in me if I meet with the same in you."[8] The distinction was important to her. However Dudley and the others wronged her, as long as Edward kept his old feeling for Mary she had something to hope for. Jane Dormer recorded how strong that feeling was. Whenever Mary came to visit Edward, Jane heard from one who was present, he would "burst forth in tears, grieving matters could not be according to her will and desire." Edward urged Mary to "have patience until he had more years, and then he would remedy all." He was always very sorry to see her go, kissing her and asking for something to give her. The jewels he was allowed to present to her were never fine enough to please him, and this plus his regret at her leavetaking made him sadder than before. Realizing that Mary might try to use her influence with the king to the Council's disadvantage, the men around Edward saw to it that Mary's visits became more and more rare. Her presence "made the king sad and melancholy," they said, and affected him too deeply for his good.[9] Mary in turn took comfort from her brother's assurances that, once he was old enough to rule on his own, he would stand up to her persecutors and take revenge.

In the meantime, Dudley was doing all he could to head off this eventuality by shaping Edward's opinions and character to serve his own ends, and the young king's chilling reception of his sister in December was proof of the earl's partial success. Edward had grown into a slight, delicate youth of thirteen who carried one shoulder higher than the other and had to squint to see at any distance. To his doll-like beauty was now added an incongruous pose of rough majesty—a wholly unconvincing imitation of his hearty, burly father. He put his hands on his hips and strutted about on his thin legs, frowning with dissatisfaction and piping out "thundering oaths." He cultivated a bad temper that contrasted oddly with the religious doctrine that streamed so readily from his lips. He was very much an unformed boy, but he had the makings of an intellectually fastidious, pedantic king, impressive yet unappealing. And his frailty had become alarming. "He will be the wonder and terror of the world," Bishop Hooper wrote of Edward in the fall of 1550, "if he lives."

Each year Edward took on more of the work of government, though he was far from exercising any real control over affairs of state. In August of 1551 he began to sit in regularly at meetings of the Council, and was giving thought, in a very abstract way, to how the Council and government were organized. He ordered the *Great Harry* rechristened the *Great Edward*, and looked into enlarging her and improving her design. Even the warlike sports the young king practiced at Dudley's insistence had their political significance; when envoys from foreign courts came to England it was important that they take away an impression of Edward as a vigorous and accomplished athlete. Here he proved to be a marked disappointment. He could hunt, shoot and ride moderately well, but when it came to the skills of the tiltyard he foundered badly. When he tried tilting at the ring—riding at a target instead of a moving opponent— he invariably missed his aim, and after humiliating himself at several small-scale tournaments held against opponents his own age, the king seems to have given up tilting altogether.

Mary's adolescence had been an agony of persecution, uncertainty and neglect; Edward knew only adulation, security and constant attention. But both extremes were harmful, and the hypocrisy and servility that surrounded the young king gravely handicapped his development. Pressured by his advisers in a dozen different directions, besieged by intrigues and petty politics, Edward's own personality—and with it his peace of mind —was all but lost. The outspoken preacher Hugh Latimer warned the king against the influence of the "velvet coats and upskips" that swarmed about him, but he lacked the strength to hold his own. Van der Delft wrote to his master in 1550 that Edward, who was "naturally gifted with a gentle nature," was being "corrupted" by radical Protestant doctrines, by the behavior of his scandal-ridden Council, and by his own inability to escape the push and pull of factional politics.[10] He was learning to "say only what he is told to say," and to take on the ruthlessness of the men around him. He could not help himself, yet he realized what was happening, and resented bitterly those who were exploiting him.

According to Cardinal Pole, who heard the story from "people whose testimony should place it beyond doubt," Edward conveyed his resentment in a particularly cruel and graphic way. In the presence of some of his attendants he took the falcon he kept in his bedchamber and plucked its feathers one by one. Then, when it was naked, he tore it into four pieces, "saying as he did so to his governors that he likened himself to the falcon, whom everyone plucked, but that he would pluck them too, thereafter, and tear them in four parts."[11]

It was to this anguished boy that Mary now looked to preserve her right to keep her faith.

On March 17, 1551, Mary rode toward London in the midst of a great procession of horsemen, gentlefolk and supporters. Fifty knights and gentlemen in velvet coats rode before her, and eighty gentlemen and ladies behind her, and as she neared the city hundreds of Londoners ran out through the fields to meet her and to join her retinue. "The people ran five or six miles out of town and were marvellously overjoyed to see her," Scheyfve wrote, "showing clearly how much they love her." By the time she reached the city gates there were four hundred people in her train, but even more striking than their numbers was the badge of religion Mary and all her household and attendants wore. Each of them had hung a large rosary conspicuously around his or her neck, and there was no mistaking the symbolic meaning of the procession. Their loyalty to Mary was inseparable from their loyalty to her faith, and her faith was now on trial.

It is highly probable that the wearing of the rosaries was Mary's idea, for she saw the coming meeting with Edward as a climactic event in a great struggle. In her mind her conflict with the king and Council was more than a matter of politics, more than a tactical device to demonstrate the supremacy of the men in power: it was a supernatural conflict as well. The rosaries dramatized this dimension of the coming confrontation, surrounding it with an atmosphere of solemnity and portent. Onlookers caught up in this otherworldly atmosphere believed they saw in the sky visions like those the medieval crusaders saw as they marched against the Saracens in the Holy Land. Armored horsemen were glimpsed amid the clouds, and extra suns, so bright they outshone the true sun and filled the crowds with wonder. The earth seemed to shake underfoot, and the sky to glow with its three suns in an unearthly way, until the procession took on the character of a holy pilgrimage.[12]

What brought Mary to London in a state of such determined piety was the deterioration of what remained of her relations with the king and Council. Not long after the inconclusive meeting between brother and sister in December Mary received a letter, composed by the Council but including a paragraph in the king's own hand, demanding once and for all that she conform to the Anglican liturgy. Whatever leniency might have been shown her in the past was now withdrawn; only her "wayward misunderstanding" kept her from recognizing that no promise of exemption from the king's laws concerning religion had ever been allowed her. "It is a scandalous thing that so high a personage should deny our sovereignty," the letter read, and the point was a reasonable one. "That our sister should be less to us than any of our other subjects is an unnatural example."[13] No further disobedience would be tolerated in future, on pain of the customary penalties for heretics. A passage in Edward's personal postscript left no doubt of the firmness of his intent. "Truly, sister, I will not say more and worse things," he wrote, "because my duty would compel me to use harsher and angrier words. But this I will say with certain intention, that I will see my laws strictly obeyed, and those who break them shall be watched and denounced."[14]

Edward's letter had referred to Mary as "our nearest sister," the one who should be to him "our greatest comfort in our tender years," but more and more Mary was taking second place to the sister who obeyed the religious laws, the seventeen-year-old Elizabeth. As Edward's letter to Mary was being composed, Elizabeth rode into the capital "with a great suite of ladies and gentlemen," and enjoying the privilege of a royal escort of a hundred horsemen. The councilors went out of their way to receive her with honor, "in order to show the people how much glory belongs to her who has embraced the new religion and is become a very great lady."[15] Mary was not ignorant of the preferential treatment given her sister, and her pain was reflected in her reply to Edward's letter. His accusations "caused her more suffering than any illness even unto death," she said. She affirmed that she had done him no harm, and had no intention of bringing any injury to the king or his kingdom in future. But she could not do otherwise than to follow God and her conscience. "Rather than offend him and my conscience, I would lose all I have left in the world," her letter read, "and my life too."[16] Scheyfve protested to the Council in February, but in vain, and it was then, with full realization of the danger she faced, that Mary determined to go to court again and defend her mass in a last battle.

The streets were so crowded as Mary and her supporters made their way to Westminster that the horsemen who accompanied her could hardly move through the throng. It was the greatest demonstration of loyalty in recent memory, and its meaning was not lost on Dudley and his colleagues. They took care to make Mary's official reception as perfunctory as possible. No one from the court met her; instead the controller of the royal household escorted her to a gallery where Edward and the full Council were waiting. After a minimum of ceremony Edward took Mary into a still smaller room to face the Council alone.

Two hours of argument and counterargument followed. The Council harangued Mary on the outlawing of the mass, the king's insistence that she obey his laws, and a new accusation: that in defying the Council she was disobeying her father's will. She answered in language as blunt as that of her letters. She would not back down from her claim to the promises made to Van der Delft. No one was more humble than she, or more obedient, though she did hope that Edward would "show her enough respect" to realize how hard it would be for her at her age to change the faith in which she had been bred. Time and again she tripped up her accusers, turning their arguments against them, cutting through their assertions and, in the end, goading them to anger by her relentlessness in debate. When Edward claimed to be ignorant of any agreement made with Van der Delft, because "he had only taken a share in affairs during the last year," Mary retorted that "in that case, he had not drawn up the ordinances on the new religion," and therefore she was not bound to obey them. As to the councilors' insistence that Henry's will obliged Mary to "submit to the Council's instructions," she answered that she had read the will, and found that it obligated her to the Council only where her marriage was concerned, and on this point she had given no offense. If anyone had betrayed Henry's will, she added, it was the executors—most of whom were in the room—in neglecting the late king's orders that two masses be said for him daily, and four obsequies annually, according to the rite he left in force at his death.

Whenever her father's name entered the discussion Mary invariably grew heated, as if in recalling him she took on more of his character. Remembering Henry's fearsome yet dedicated rule she could not help insulting the self-seeking, unprincipled men who stood before her now. Her father, she said, had "cared more for the good of the kingdom than all the members of the Council put together." Here Dudley interrupted her. He had as usual been staying in the background of the argument, hoping to make it appear as though Edward were in command. He was pushing Edward more and more into the forefront of policymaking, both to disguise his own actual control of the government and to give the king the illusion of leadership. But Mary was clearly getting the best of the situation, and now she had gone too far.

"How now, my lady?" he broke in. "It seems that your grace is trying to show us in a hateful light to the king our master, without any cause whatever."

Mary replied that this was not her intention in coming, but that since they pressed her so hard about the will she had no choice but to tell the whole truth as she saw it. At the end of two hours of fruitless debate the parties stood where they had been at the outset. It was left to Mary to make a final statement. She addressed Edward, hoping she could touch him by phrasing her earnest plea for leniency in terms he was accustomed to hearing from other sources. "In the last resort," she told him, "there were only two things: soul and body. Her soul she offered to God, and her body to his majesty's service, and might it please him to take away her life rather than the old religion, in which she desired to live and die."

It was a moving appeal. Edward quickly assured her he had no wish to ask for any such sacrifice, and gave her permission to return home. She was not well—"My health is more unstable than that of any creature" she had written in January—and the strain of this meeting was bound to affect her. Asking her brother "to give no credit to any person who might desire to make him believe evil of her," and repeating again that she "would remain his majesty's humble, obedient and unworthy sister," she took her leave.[17]

The next day Scheyfve delivered a formal message from the emperor. If Mary were to be denied the mass, he would declare war on England.

XXVIII

 When Wyt with Will and Diligent
Applie themselves, and match as mates,
There can no want of resident
From force defend the castell gates.

Scheyfve felt certain that it was only Charles V's threatened declaration of war that saved Mary. He knew "from a good source" that without the emperor's timely intervention "they intended to use her very
roughly, keeping her here in this town if she refused to conform with the
new religion, and taking away her servants, especially those whom she
trusted, in whose place they would have set others of their way of thinking."[1] Mary agreed completely. She was not deluded about her pow-
erlessness. She fought the Council not because she believed she could
win but for the sake of her honor. Mary knew perfectly well that, "had
the Council only had to deal with her, they would long ago have
deprived her of the mass and the old religion, and attempted to force her
into the new."[2] Doubtless Mary saw her cousin's threat as providential,
for it led to an immediate mellowing of the councilors' tone and attitude.
She was allowed to leave the court without hindrance, and to resume her
customary way of life, carrying with her assurances of "the most cordial
affection" from the king and Council, delivered by Secretary Petre the
day after the emperor's message arrived. Though Petre found Mary sick
in bed at her London residence of St. John's, he did not hesitate to reiter-
ate the arguments impelling her to abandon the old faith. Lifting herself
up out of the pillows, she asked him to excuse the brevity of her reply
and said simply that her soul was God's, her body Edward's to command.
With the king's permission she left a few days later for Beaulieu.

Despite Petre's reference to the mass the Council had in fact drawn
back from the issue, ostensibly to allow time for a new English envoy,

Nicholas Wotton, to go to the imperial court and confer with the emperor. Edward's own notes of the discussion among the Council members describe something closer to capitulation than to a mere postponement of the religious issue. The king was dismayed to find his three principal bishops—Cranmer, Ridley and Ponet—now persuading him to tolerate Mary's mass at least for a time, arguing that while it would be wrong to actually give her permission to use the Catholic liturgy it was not sinful to simply look the other way.

Behind this blatant rationalization were grave fears that any further irritation of the emperor might touch off a whole chain of explosions, not merely an Anglo-imperial war. The ruinous debasement of the coinage, which at first had increased the demands of the Flemish wool merchants for English cloth, had finally led to a glut of English wool in Flanders; the cloth industry was a shambles, and in the north thousands of workers were starving. Londoners rioted against the presence of foreign workers and merchants in the city, exaggerating their numbers and blaming them for the high prices. "Ruffians and servingmen" and other "evilly disposed persons" gathered in large numbers to advocate the slaughter of all foreign residents, until in May the Council issued an order warning "the lower sort of people" against becoming "like those sick madmen" who "have presumptuously taken upon them the office of his majesty," and were "attempting redress of things after their own fantasies."[3]

War between England and the empire would certainly worsen the crisis in the cloth industry, and there were other risks as well. In the spring of 1551 the English government was amassing armaments and military equipment in Flanders. If war broke out the entire valuable stockpile —including seventy-five tons of gunpowder, quantities of armor and other goods—would fall into enemy hands.[4] A recent diplomatic embarrassment had also to be considered. The English ambassador in Brussels, Richard Morison, had dared to lecture Charles on theology with such vehemence that the emperor lost his temper and ordered him out of the room. The incident was smoothed over, with Charles apologizing for his sour temper and blaming it on his gout and advancing age, but it contributed to the smoldering enmity between the two antagonists, and made it all the more necessary that the Council adopt a conciliatory attitude toward the emperor (and Mary) in the coming months.

Mary was left in relative peace until late summer. The discovery and imprisonment of her chaplain Francis Mallet in April led to a sharp exchange of letters between Mary and the Council, but the chaplain remained in the Tower nonetheless. By this time, though, the business of government was taking second place to the more urgent business of survival. The sweating sickness returned in the late spring and summer of 1551 with a virulence unknown since the early years of the century. As always it carried off the most robust men in their prime; the weakest in the population were spared. Before the infection died down fifty thousand victims had been carried off, though official accounts minimized the mortality of the disease. With a threat of imminent war it was unwise to let the other side know how badly the fighting men had been devastated; beyond this there were always troublemakers eager to seize on any destructive plague as a sign of divine wrath at the religious policies of the king and his ministers.[5]

But there was no disguising the seriousness of the disease to Londoners, who spent the summer either trying to outrun infection by traveling from one village or manor to another or by staying in the city and applying the exotic remedies sold on every street. Persons of every trade—"carpenters, pewterers, brasiers, painters"—became dispensing apothecaries overnight, posing as healers from Constantinople or India or Egypt and "promising help of all diseases, yea incurable." Their medicines, which a contemporary doctor found to be "so filthy, that I am ashamed to name them," were of various kinds, but all priced as high "as though they were made of the sun, moon or stars." There were draughts of many kinds, and other cures ranging from the spiritual to the practical —"blessings, Blowings, Hypocritical prayings, and foolish smoking of shifts, smocks, and kerchieves."[6]

The sweat attacked several men in Mary's household, driving her from Beaulieu to a smaller house. It was there, in mid-August, that she received a letter summoning her controller, Rochester, and two of her gentlemen, Edward Walgrave and Francis Englefield, to appear before the Council. When all three finally appeared at court—Rochester could not at first be spared—they found they were to be the agents of the Council's will. If Mary would not obey the king's laws, and if any attempt to coerce her would mean scandal, then the enforcement would have to come from within the household, from men who could be threatened with imprisonment, as Mary could not. Rochester, Walgrave and Englefield were surprised to hear themselves described as "the chief instruments and cause that kept the princess in the old religion." Without their instigation, she would have accepted the Protestant orthodoxy long before. The three household officers, startled by the sweeping error of this accusation, assured the councilors that "as for her religion and conscience" Mary "asked nobody's advice and, what was more, not one of her ministers dared broach the matter in her presence."[7] But it was no use. The three were to return to where Mary was staying, at Copt Hall in Essex, and forbid the chaplains to say mass any longer.

They failed, of course. As they knew she would, Mary responded angrily to the Council's strategy, saying "she found it very strange and unreasonable that her ministers and servants should wield such authority in her house." She flatly forbade the three officials to carry out their orders, and sent them back to Hampton Court to face the fury of Dudley and his colleagues. They were ordered again to stop the celebration of mass at Copt Hall; they pointed first to the futility of the effort, and then refused. On August 23 all three were committed to the Tower.

The attempt to coerce Mary through intimidating her servants had failed. The Council would have to enforce its own laws, or else tolerate Mary's persistent breaking of them. But whether they sensed it or not, there had been another change. The emperor's once uncompromising stand on his cousin's mass had grown more flexible. His public utterances were as stern and angry as ever, of course. In June he burst out to Wotton "I will not suffer her to be evil handled by them," meaning the Council, and appeared to stand firmly behind his earlier threat of war. But later he added the morbid sentiment that "if death were to overtake her for this cause, she would be the first martyr of royal blood to die for our holy faith, and would for this earn glory in the better life."[8] And in dispatches to Scheyfve he was urging Mary not to provoke the Council too far, and assuring her that even if her chaplains were forbidden to say mass, as long as she did not adopt the Protestant liturgy she would be guilty of no sin. The regent agreed that as a "victim of force" Mary would be "blameless in God's sight."[9]

So matters stood when at the end of August Rich, Petre and Wingfield came to Copt Hall determined to root out all vestiges of Catholicism. The chancellor handed Mary a letter from Edward, which she knew contained another demand for full conformity in religion. She received it on her knees, "saying that she would kiss the letter because the king had signed it, and not for the matter contained therein, which was merely the doings of the Council."[10] She then read it over to herself, exclaiming under her breath—but loud enough for the councilors to hear— "Ah! good Mr. Cecil took much pains here." Cecil was Dudley's secretary, and there was no mistaking the meaning of her remark. When she had finished reading the letter she urged the visitors to be brief, speaking in an irritable, almost offhand tone. When they offered to point out to her all the names of those opposed to her use of the mass she cut them short.

"I care not," she said, "for the rehearsal of their names, for I know they are all of one mind therein. And rather than use any other service than that ordained during the life of my father, I will lay my head on the block," she added. Whatever happened she knew Edward was not to be held responsible for what the three councilors were about to do, for "though his majesty, good sweet king, have more knowledge than any other of his years, yet it is not possible for him, at present, to be a judge of all things." As for the silencing of her priests, she implied that she would endure it with resignation, though she would under no circumstances tolerate the introduction of the Anglican liturgy into her house.

"Howbeit, if my chaplains do say no mass, I can hear none, no more than my poor servants. As to my priests, they know what they have to do, if they refuse to say mass for fear of imprisonment; they may set therein as they will, but none of your new service shall be said in any house of mine, and if any be said in it I will not tarry in it an hour."

Rich and the others now told Mary of the obstinate refusal of her three officials Rochester, Walgrave and Englefield to attempt to enforce the Council's orders a second time, and how all three had been imprisoned. This news gave her great satisfaction. She thought them "honester men" than she had supposed, and could not help pointing out to the chancellor and his companions that it had been foolish to send her own servants to control her, "for, of all persons, she was least likely to obey those who had been always used to obey her implicitly."

When the old question of the promises made to Van der Delft and Charles V arose Mary began to lose patience. She had a letter from her cousin substantiating her position, and gave it more credence than any words of the Council. But even if they thought so little of the emperor, she said, "yet should you show me more favor than you do, even for my father's sake, who made the most of you what you are now, almost out of nothing."

Now that she had brought her father into the discussion Mary lost her temper. When the councilors told her that another controller had been appointed to take Rochester's place her reply was both blunt and imperious.

"I shall appoint my own officers," she said, "for my years are sufficient for the purpose; and if you leave your new controller within my gates, out of them I go forthwith, for we two will not abide in the same house." Her last words to Rich were a threat. "I am sickly, yet will I not die willingly; but if I chance to die," she warned him, "I will protest openly that you of the Council be the cause of my death." As a final gesture she went down on her knees again and, taking off one of her rings, asked that it be given to Edward as a token "that she would die his true subject and sister, and obey him in all things except matters of religion." "But this," she added cynically, "will never be told his majesty," and she left the room.

Relieved that they had only had to deal with Mary's anger and not the tears and hysteria they had doubtless been expecting, the chancellor and his colleagues called all of Mary's servants together and informed them that from now on no mass was to be said in the house, on pain of the full punishment of the law. They directed their words to three of Mary's chaplains in particular, warning them that if they read any but the service in the Book of Common Prayer they would be guilty of treason, and wringing from them a promise to obey. (To free them, both from this promise and from the anguish of conscience they now faced, Mary officially dismissed them all the following day.)

A fourth chaplain could not be found, and Rich, Petre and Wingfield delayed their departure while one last search for him was made. While they waited Mary appeared at an open window and called out to them insolently.

"I pray you," she said, "ask the lords of the Council that my controller may shortly return; for since his departing I take the accounts myself, and lo! I have learned how many loaves of bread be made of a bushel of wheat! I know my father and mother never brought me up to brewing and baking," she went on, "and, to be plain with you, I am weary of my office. If my lords will send my officer home again, they shall do me a pleasure; otherwise, if they send him to prison, beshrew me if he go not to it merrily, and with a good will." In a final burst of impudence she wished them on their way with a wry insult. "And I pray God to send you well in your souls, and in your bodies too, for some of you have but weak ones."

On this saucy note the long conflict over the mass ended. The prohibition was in force, and there would be no more public masses said in Mary's house, with the gentry from neighboring houses and farmers from the villages streaming in to join in the worship. But in another sense Mary had come out ahead. She had succeeded in protecting her servants from punishment, and by hiding away one of the chaplains she provided herself with a way of continuing her worship in secret. If discovered the fugitive priest could correctly say he had not personally been forbidden to perform the sacrifice in Mary's house; technically he was exempt from the order. And so, "unknown to more than three of the most confidential persons at the utmost," Mary continued to hear mass for the next two years, conscious of the grave danger she would be in if she were found out.[11]

Her fear of discovery and punishment was not lessened by the fact that under Dudley's leadership the country was gradually coming to pieces. With his favorites Northampton and Dorset he spent his days dominating the Council, supervising the shaping of the king's mind and opinions and browbeating peasants accused of disobeying the religious laws. Voices could be heard up and down the galleries outside the Council chamber, shouting loudly and violently at the unfortunates and "handling them roughly."[12] Inflation was a far more serious problem than heresy in Edward's reign, but all Dudley could think to do for it was to repeat Somerset's disastrous policy of debasing the coinage. Coming on the heels of uncontrolled inflation in the early years of the reign, the new debasements created appalling hardships. In 1551 coined money was worth a little over half its value in the closing years of Henry's reign, while prices had tripled. Ignorant of the fact that when coins are worth less, goods cost more Dudley blamed the inflation on "diverse insatiable and greedy persons" who raised prices simply to enrich themselves, and the cycle of devaluation and higher and higher prices continued.

Widespread unrest continued with it, and rumors of rebellions being plotted at country manors far from London. It was said the earls of Derby and Shrewsbury, who absented themselves from court because of political differences with Dudley, were prepared to raise a rebel army of sixty thousand men on a few days' notice, and as the months passed more and more of those who had once looked to Dudley as a deliverer secretly hoped he would be overthrown. One of these disillusioned men, Lord Warden of the Cinque Ports Sir Thomas Cheyne, confided to Scheyfve that "he would spend all he had to help in restoring matters to a better condition than we see them in now."[13]

A conspicuous sign of the decay of the political order was the ceaseless preoccupation with security. The government was as hard hit by the inflation as the king's angry subjects, and new and inexpensive ways had to be found to maintain an armed force to keep order at home and discourage invasion from abroad. Beyond the five hundred foreign troops now brought in to form an expanded royal bodyguard, Dudley was experimenting with a semi-feudal arrangement under which gentlemen and lords were to provide several armed horsemen each to a national fighting force in return for a nominal sum from the king. In this way it was thought that four thousand horsemen might be kept at the ready at a cost to the royal treasury of only ten thousand pounds.[14]

In October of 1551 the need for security was emphasized when Somerset, who had continued to sit on the Council ever since his release from the Tower nearly two years earlier, was arrested again and charged with high treason. According to the Council, Somerset had plotted to seize the Tower, use the arms stored there to take over the city, and then stir up the commons to revolt. Accomplices in other parts of the country would seize the strong places and subdue the local population. Then in a bloodthirsty epilogue the duke had planned to invite the Council members to a banquet at which they would all be assassinated.[15] The sinister plan was discovered and forestalled just in time, and the duke, who could hope for no leniency this time, was executed the following January.

In the same month that Somerset was charged, Dudley and the principal men about him advanced themselves in rank, taking new titles and greatly enlarging their estates. Dudley, already earl of Warwick, became duke of Northumberland; Grey, marquis of Dorset, was given the recently extinct title duke of Suffolk. (With the death of Charles Brandon in 1545 the title duke of Suffolk had gone to his brothers, both of whom died of the sweat in 1551; Grey was married to Brandon's daughter Frances, and so had a claim to the dukedom through his wife.) The treasurer, Paulet, became earl of Wiltshire, while Herbert became marquis of Winchester and earl of Pembroke.

With the frantic efforts to support fighting men, the alarms of the conspiracy, and the flourishing of new titles and styles within the government, Mary and her mass were virtually forgotten. At the end of the year she heard a rumor that an attempt might be made to force her to adopt the Anglican liturgy, but nothing came of it. In the spring of 1552 Rochester, Walgrave and Englefield were quietly released from captivity and allowed to return to her service. From then on Mary came to the attention of the Council only in passing, in connection with routine matters. On one occasion she exchanged four of her manors—St. Osyth, Little Clafton, Great Clafton and Willeigh—for others, a transfer not without significance, as St. Osyth was at the mouth of the Blackwater in Essex, even closer to the sea than Woodham Walter. At other times money was sent to her to repair her houses, or her flooded lands "decayed by the rage of the water."[16]

The emperor and regent watched the course of English politics with astonishment. They saw a disorganized tyranny presiding over a disintegrating society. A king who might not live to manhood was at the mercy of a coterie of insecure opportunists that was gradually turning in on itself and devouring its own. The regent wrote to her chief minister about the volatile situation, describing a dark scenario of what might happen in the near future. The men at the head of affairs saw their own shortcomings all too clearly, she wrote. Knowing they could never give a good account of their stewardship to the king at his maturity, they might well kill both Edward and Mary and avoid the day of reckoning. "Stranger things have been seen in England," she remarked, "and done with less motive."[17] In view of this possibility, "many people are of opinion that the kingdom of England would not be impossible to conquer, especially now that it is prey to discord and poverty." She suggested three men who might be counted on to lead an expedition to England to "take the king out of the hands of his pernicious governors": Archduke Ferdinand, Mary's longtime suitor Dom Luiz of Portugal, and the duke of Holstein. The latter might count on his brother, the king of Denmark, for help, "for the Danes claim England, have often invaded it, and have actually held it for a number of years."[18]

The regent had read her history thoroughly, but there was no precedent for the sudden change in fortunes that now overtook England. Edward's health began to decline. He lost his vitality, his weight dropped, and he fell prey to a series of diseases. He was "thin and weak" in the summer of 1551, and the following spring he took to his bed with measles and smallpox. His convalescence was very slow, and though he was able to make a summer progress the following July and August "it was observed on all sides how sickly he looked, and general pity was felt for him by the people." When the Milanese physician and psychic Girolamo Cardano saw Edward in the fall of 1552 he was impressed with his abilities but pessimistic about his future; he bore, Cardano wrote, "an appearance on his face denoting early death." And he added, "His vital powers will always be weak."

By the early months of 1553 Edward was showing the symptoms of an advanced case of tuberculosis. He was racked by a "tough, strong, straining cough," which seemed to get worse every day. At the same time he showed a "weakness and faintness of spirit" which betrayed the decline of his vital parts. When Mary came to court in February she heard rumors that her brother's sickness was growing "by a slow-working poison." He was too ill to see her, but after three days of waiting she was finally allowed into his bedchamber. A week later, with the cough and other symptoms growing more severe despite every sort of medical treatment, the doctors all but gave him up. To protect themselves they warned the Council that Edward was in peril of his life, and that if any other "serious malady" supervened he would not be able to survive it.

It now appeared that, unless Edward made a miraculous recovery, Mary would soon be queen of England. Whether Mary herself believed this possible is unclear. At one time she speculated that, if Edward died, she would be killed very quickly, before there was time for a popular rising on her behalf. She may have felt the same fear for her life now, or she may not have been aware that Edward's illness had reached a critical point. She was away from court during Edward's last months; she knew he was seriously ill, but she may not have realized until shortly before news of his death reached her that he had been fatally ill.

The thought that Mary might come to the throne had haunted the minds of Dudley and the Council ever since Edward's increasing debilitation began in the spring of 1552. The prospect was a grim one indeed, for as queen Mary would certainly overturn the Protestant religious settlement, bring England back within the jurisdiction of the pope, and take vengeance on those in the Council who had mistreated her, exploited her brother and illegally enriched themselves. With Mary in line to succeed, Edward's death would bring in a prolonged day of reckoning that would shake the kingdom to its political foundations, putting most of those who had ruled for the past six years in the Tower.

But even as they contemplated these horrors the councilors did nothing to forestall them until the late spring of 1553, when two distinct forces—Edward's firm opposition to Catholicism and Northumberland's desperate ambition—came together to exclude Mary from the succession.

In mid-May, as the king lay wasting away at Greenwich coughing blood, his body covered in ulcers and his mind disturbed by the fever that never left him, he wrote out in his own hand a document altering the succession established by his father's will. This "Device for the Succession" passed over Mary and Elizabeth and named the heirs to the throne in the following order: first the male heirs of Edward's cousin Frances Brandon, then the male heirs, in turn, of her three daughters, Jane, Catherine and Mary Grey, and finally the male heirs of Margaret Clifford, like the Greys a granddaughter of Charles Brandon and Mary Tudor.

That Edward should redraw the plans for the succession was not as unorthodox as it might seem. His father had changed the succession several times, until it seemed more a matter of the royal will than the royal blood. And there was the urgent issue of religion. Under Dudley's tutelage Edward had become so staunchly opposed to the old faith that he could not tolerate the thought of a Catholic on the throne. This explained his exclusion of Mary, despite his fondness for her, but the exclusion of Elizabeth can only have been on grounds of her sex. By a dynastic quirk all of Henry VIII's heirs but Edward had been female. Since he had no son of his own Edward was bound to pass his crown to one of these women, yet in his "Device" he specifically named their male offspring as his heirs. Assuming that Edward was determined to assure himself a male successor, it was obvious he could not look to his unmarried Protestant sister Elizabeth to produce his heir, so he named the sons of his remaining female relatives. There was only one difficulty: none of the five women had any sons.

Here Dudley's determination to hold onto his power fell into line with Edward's rearranged succession scheme—and of course, the entire plan may well have been Northumberland's creation. Before the Device was drawn up the duke had announced that his son, Guilford Dudley, would marry Jane Grey, eldest daughter of Henry Grey, duke of Suffolk, at the end of May. Jane Grey stood second in Edward's Device, but the woman who stood first, Jane's mother Frances, was not likely to have more children. Thus if all went well, the son of Jane and Guilford Dudley would be the next ruler of England, and his grandfather Northumberland would be allied to the royal house by marriage. Three other matches were arranged at the same time, all of them intended to strengthen Northumberland's faction. Herbert's eldest son was to marry Jane Grey's sister Catherine, while the third Grey daughter was betrothed to a man not previously aligned with the duke (and not related to the bride's family), Lord Grey. Finally, Dudley's daughter Catherine was to marry the son of the earl of Huntingdon—another influential man who had not until now been of the duke's faction.[19]

Jane Grey married Guilford Dudley on May 21, with no public announcement of the altered succession. To allay Mary's suspicions about his scheme Dudley went out of his way to put himself on good terms with her. He kept her informed of Edward's condition, though he was careful not to go into detail. He even sent her "her full arms as Princess of England, as she used to bear them in her father's lifetime"—contradicting his earlier insistence to Scheyfve that the title "Princess of England" was not hers to use or claim.[20] But there was no mistaking the purpose behind the match he made for his son, his amassing of money and provisions, and his sending of his most trusted followers to many of the chief castles and strongholds to secure them in case of rebellion. The king was slowly dying; once he was dead there would be a struggle for the throne, and Dudley meant to be the victor.

At the end of May the duke learned that the struggle would be upon him even sooner than he had expected. Edward's doctors informed him that it was now their opinion that the king could not live through the autumn. There would be no time for Jane to bear a son; if things remained as they were Edward would die without an heir, leaving the way open to confusion and civil war. It was probably at this time that Dudley made a slight alteration in Edward's Device. Inserting two extra words he changed the order of succession to read "the Lady Jane and her heirs male." Now the document identified a successor, Jane Grey. She was to take precedence over the nonexistent male heirs Edward had hoped for.

In this revised version the Device was put into legal form in June and signed by the members of the Council and others. Some objected to it, but most were too busy preparing for the immense wave of popular protest they knew would come once Mary's exclusion was announced. "All the councilors down to the very secretaries are buying up armor and weapons," Scheyfve reported in June, and in the midst of their hurried preparations the dying king himself was neglected.

During June Edward withered into agonized immobility. He was kept drugged with opiates, and when he did struggle into consciousness it was only to bring up a livid black sputum that gave off an unbearable stench. His digestive system no longer functioned; his hair and nails had dropped out and "all his person was scabby." When in his final days the doctors gave up on the king a woman offered to try to cure him, "if she could have a free hand." She dosed him with something vile which made his shrunken body swell like a balloon. His legs puffed out painfully, and all "his vital parts were mortally stuffed." His pulse began to fail, his skin changed color, and he could hardly breathe or speak. After several days of this new agony, on the sixth of July Edward died, leaving it to God and Dudley to work out the succession to the throne.

PART FOUR

Queen Alone

XXIX

When they forth went, lyke men they were, most fearefull to beholde;
Of force and eke of pusaunt power they semed very stronge;
In theyr attemptes, also, they were both fearse and wonders bolde.
If god wolde have ben helper to such as stryveth in the wronge—
But at the last he helpèd us, though we thought it ryght longe.
The Nobles here proclaymed her queene, in voydyng of all blame;
Wherfore prayse we the lorde above, and magnyfie his name.

On July 4, two days before Edward's death, both Mary and Elizabeth received messages summoning them to the bedside of their dying brother. Elizabeth did nothing; Mary, who had been staying twenty miles from court at Hunsdon, moved cautiously toward the capital, to give at least the impression that she meant to go to Greenwich as ordered. It is doubtful that she would have gone very much nearer, for she had been warned by a friend the previous day to go farther into the country for her own safety, and had already made plans to travel to Framlingham in Suffolk, where "she had confidence in her friends."[1] Scheyfve had no doubt that if she went to Greenwich she would be playing into Dudley's hands. "It is to be feared that as soon as the king is dead they will attempt to seize the princess," he wrote to his master in Brussels. On July 4 Scheyfve had just heard about the official designation of Jane as heir apparent; whether Mary knew of it we don't know.

Mary reached Hoddesdon on the evening of July 6, the day Edward died, intending to spend the night there. But before the household was asleep a messenger arrived to say that the king was dead, and the summons was a trap.[2] Without waiting for dawn, she left Hoddesdon at once, stopping only to send word the imperial envoys in London that she was on her way to Kenninghall. As Edward lay dying, the emperor had sent three special representatives to England, officially to inquire about his condition but actually to oversee the transfer of power that he knew could not be long in coming. Two of the envoys, Jacques de Marnix and Jean de Montmorency, were to have a marginal role in Mary's future, but the third, Simon Renard, was to influence the early years of her reign in a decisive way. Mary was relying on them to help her now, as she fled in the night with only two women and six gentlemen to protect her. The anonymous messenger may have told Mary that one of Dudley's sons, Robert Dudley, was making ready to ride to Hunsdon with an escort of three hundred guardsmen to take her prisoner; perhaps to avoid meeting him on the highway she and her little retinue made their way along the Newmarket road, the route that led directly toward Yarmouth and the sea.

Dudley let it be known right away that instead of coming to see her brother as decency demanded Mary had "gone towards the provinces of Norfolk and Suffolk, being the coast opposite Flanders, with intent to involve the kingdom in troubles and wars, and bring in foreigners to defend her pretensions to the crown."[3] It was rumored that she had escaped to Flanders, and the duke, fearing that this was the obvious preliminary to an invasion by the armies of Charles V, put his navy in readiness. He sent seven heavy warships to lie off the Norfolk coast, to watch for any sign of ships from Flanders and, if the rumor proved to be untrue, to prevent Mary from escaping before she could be captured.

It was an awkward situation, for though Edward had been dead for nearly forty-eight hours no official announcement of his death or of Jane's accession had yet been made. When the imperial envoys asked to see the king on July 8 they were told he was too ill to receive them, but it was obvious from the heightened pace of military activity in London that Mary's dash for the seacoast was not the only climactic event of recent days. The emperor's representatives knew in fact that Edward was already dead—Renard had found out the news the day before—and they watched with great interest as Northumberland and his confederates made their final preparations for war. The Tower was secured, and with it the largest cache of arms and other military supplies in the kingdom. The admiral, Lord Clinton, was put in charge of the Tower and its garrison, and he ordered all the great ordnance there hauled to the top of the White Tower and mounted for immediate use. In the prison itself the three most eminent prisoners—the old duke of Norfolk, Gardiner, former bishop of Winchester and Edward Courtenay, son of the ill-fated marquis of Exeter who had grown to manhood confined in the fortress—were ordered to prepare themselves for death.

On the tenth of July, late in the afternoon, Queen Jane was brought to the Tower and installed there, in accordance with custom, to await her coronation. It was a hollow ritual, with none of the excitement or pageantry of a state entry. Only a small crowd was present, and the few spectators watched in silence. A little later in the day two heralds and a trumpeter went through the city proclaiming Jane to be queen, and declaring that Mary, "unlawfully begotten," and a papist, was not fit to rule.[4] The announcement met with a melancholy response. "No one present showed any sign of rejoicing," the emperor's envoys noted, "and no one cried 'Long live the queen!' except the herald who made the proclamation and a few archers who followed him." There were murmurs of dissatisfaction, and a few shouts of defiance. A young barman, Gilbert Pot, was arrested "for speaking of certain words of Queen Mary, that she had the right title." The next morning Pot was solemnly set on the pillory and both his ears were cut off.

The girl who was now exalted to the throne was a thin, pale bride of sixteen whose complete surprise at finding herself queen was exceeded only by her dismay in discovering that she was expected to make her husband Guilford Dudley king. "I sent for the earls of Arundel and Pembroke," she wrote to Mary later, "and said to them, that if the crown belonged to me I should be content to make my husband a duke, but would never consent to make him king." Jane had an instinct for ruling, but she was treated as a powerless cipher by those around her. When she refused to give her husband a crown of his own his mother was furious, and "persuaded her son not to sleep with me any longer as he was wont to do." Jane might have made a capable ruler in time, but for the immediate future it was up to Dudley to control the dissatisfied populace, dominate the disgruntled Council and give an illusion of majesty to the makeshift royal household in the Tower. He had expected this, and was gambling on his ability to deal with any emergency as it might arise. But there were two eventualities he had not reckoned on: that Mary might elude capture and gather an army of her own, and that he might have to leave London in order to deal with it.

On the same night that Jane was proclaimed a letter was brought to the councilors from Kenninghall. It was from Mary, and it was a forthright statement of her right to the throne. The letter proved that she had evaded Robert Dudley and his guard, and that she was committed to resist Jane's usurpation. The councilors were "astonished and troubled" by Mary's letter, but the next day brought even more disquieting news. Reports reached them from Norfolk that a number of nobles and gentlemen —the earl of Bath, the earl of Sussex, Sir Thomas Wharton, Sir John Mordant, Sir Henry Bedingfield—were either with her at Kenninghall or on their way to her there, and that in addition she had gathered to her banner "innumerable companies of the common people." A force had to be sent to disperse this rebel host—for since Jane's accession was hedged about with legal sanctions, Mary's opposition was nothing less than rebellion—but who could be spared to command it? Henry Grey, duke of Suffolk, Jane's father, was an obvious choice, but the queen grew frightened at this suggestion and burst into tears; Suffolk would have to stay beside her in the Tower. The most feared commander in the kingdom was Dudley, and the councilors reminded him that only four years earlier he had won his greatest victory in the very region where Mary was now drawing her support. The battle of Kenninghall could be as glorious a triumph as the bloody field of Dussindale, they told him, and, seeing no alternative, he reluctantly agreed to go.

On the night of July 12 carts loaded with big and small guns, bows, spears, morris pikes, arrows, gunstones and gunpowder rumbled through the streets to the Tower, where Dudley's army was gathering. There had been a muster that day in Tothill fields, to take in men "for a great army toward Cambridge," where, it was said, the duke was going to "fetch in the lady Mary . . . to destroy her grace."[5] Now all those who had agreed to join the muster for tenpence a day were formed into companies in the courtyard, and prepared to move northward. Two days later the duke marched out of London, having left to Suffolk the difficult task of representing him in the Council and keeping order in the city.

Dudley had with him some three thousand mounted men and footsoldiers, thirty cannon from the Tower, and as many cartloads of ammunition. He controlled the capital, the government, the treasury, and the queen. No commander was superior to him in experience or skill; he seemed to have every advantage. The imperial envoys gave Mary little chance to win against such odds. How could one woman prevail over such a concentration of power, they wrote to Charles V, even if she was the rightful queen?

But what Renard and the others did not take into account was the power of popular feeling. Dudley was hated; Mary was adored. As earl of Warwick, the dark presence behind Edward, and now as duke of Northumberland, father-in-law of the spurious queen they did not accept, John Dudley was "the tyrant," the "bear of Warwick," the man many suspected of poisoning the king in order to bring the crown into his own family. "The duke's difficulty is that he dares trust no one, for he has never given any one reason to love him," the imperial ambassadors admitted in a dispatch written while Dudley's army was camped in Cambridge.[6] Mary, on the other hand, was now reaping the full measure of popular loyalty. There were some who fought for her because they hated "the ragged bear most rank," Dudley, but most joined her because, in their minds, she had always been princess of England, and this was the first opportunity they had been given to fight in defense of her rights.

At about the time Dudley left London Mary rallied her forces at Framlingham in Suffolk, a large, strong castle that had belonged to the old duke of Norfolk but had recently come into Mary's possession. Its forty-foot walls were eight feet thick, and crowned with thirteen square towers; the highest watchtower provided a good view of the sea. Here dozens of gentlemen brought their horsemen and their retainers and mounted knights, in numbers that grew astonishingly from day to day. With the thousands of peasants from Norfolk and Suffolk that swelled the ranks Mary had an army of nearly twenty thousand by July 19, plus an abundance of ordnance and provisions. Those who could not fight for her sent her money, or mercenaries, or carts full of bread, beer and freshly slaughtered meat. And one by one the towns of the southeast proclaimed Mary to be queen, and not Jane; the biggest of them, Norwich, declared for Mary as early as July 12.

In some places, to be sure, loyalty gave way temporarily to expediency. Armed bands from Framlingham would ride into a town, proclaim Mary to a delighted crowd, and then ride on; "as soon as they were departed the inhabitants, for fear of the Council, proclaimed Jane anew, and all were in arms in the greatest confusion in the world."[7] But there was no wavering at Framlingham itself, where, "to encourage her people," Mary rode into the camp to give orders for the expected battle with Dudley's forces. Her appearance was greeted by "shouts and acclamations," and her troops threw their helmets into the air and shot off their guns wildly, crying out "Long live our good Queen Mary!" "Death to traitors!" The noise and excitement made Mary's horse unmanageable; she dismounted, and walked the entire length of the mile-long camp on foot, followed by her nobles and ladies, "thanking the soldiers for their good will."[8]

If Mary spread confidence and encouragement among her troops she felt little herself. She was in communication with the emperor's envoys, and looked to them to provide support for her cause by whatever means they could manage. "Destruction was hanging over her head," she told them, unless they or the emperor helped her. If she had known of the disarray in Dudley's camp, though, Mary would surely have taken heart. The duke had stopped at Cambridge, unable to go on because of the threat of a rising in London if he moved farther north. He mistrusted his troops, his captains, and the people who every day "muttered against him" and prepared to declare for Mary as soon as he had moved on. There were quarrels between prominent men over which candidate was the true queen, and the duke himself got into a violent argument with Lord Grey that came to blows. Grey left Dudley's camp and joined Mary, and a good many others did the same. With his military effectiveness drastically reduced—he could only fortify Cambridge and send out small bands to levy peasants and burn the houses of those who supported Mary—the duke took the desperate step of calling in French aid. He sent

a relative, Sir Henry Dudley, to offer Henri II the precious English territories of Calais and Guines in return for a force of picked troops. There
was no sign of the reinforcements the Council had promised to send him,
but Mary's camp was said to be growing larger and stronger every day.
Three thousand French soldiers from Boulogne would tip the balance in
Dudley's favor.

While he waited for word from France the most dramatic event of
his struggle with Mary took place in Yarmouth harbor. The seven ships
he sent to guard the Norfolk coast took shelter there in stormy weather,
and while they lay at anchor one of Mary's captains, Sir Henry Jerningham, went to Yarmouth and rowed out to address the sailors. He succeeded in arousing feelings of loyalty to Mary; "from their natural love
toward her," they "rose against their captains in favor of the queen,"
shooting off their artillery and shouting "Long live our Queen Mary!"
This mass mutiny gave Mary a decisive advantage. The following day the
camp at Framlingham was augmented by two thousand sailors and the
hundred great cannon from the seven warships riding at anchor in the
harbor.

The most important result of the defection of the sailors was its effect
on the Council. Suffolk had locked all the councilors in the Tower to
await the outcome of the battle they expected any day. But when they
heard of the mutiny at Yarmouth they began to believe that Mary could
win after all. The Treasurer of the Mint escaped and went toward
Framlingham, taking with him all the money in the privy purse. Emboldened by his act, the Council members "resolved to open their bosoms to
one another" and reconsider their sworn loyalty to Dudley. Few of them
had been sympathetic to the change in the succession; they had sworn to
uphold Edward's Device (in Dudley's altered version) but "under con-
straint." Now, with their consciences goaded by the thought of what
Mary might do to them if she did win out over the duke, they decided to
turn against him. On July 18 they offered a reward for his arrest—a
thousand pounds to any noble, five hundred to any knight, and one hundred to any yeoman who would confront him and demand his surrender.
The next day a dozen of the Council members broke through Suffolk's
guard and met at Pembroke's house—the old royal residence of Baynard's
Castle—to make their plans. Arundel made a persuasive speech in Mary's
behalf, and a further inducement came in the form of a rumor that 150
London gentlemen pledged to Mary had made a pact to seize the Tower
—a venture that would almost certainly have led to the first bloodshed of
the conflict.

After informing the Lord Mayor and the imperial ambassadors of
their intentions, on the afternoon of July 19 the councilors came without

warning into the public square, preceded by their macebearers, and proclaimed Mary queen of England.

The news came as a glorious surprise. "As not a soul imagined the possibility of such a thing," an eyewitness wrote, "when the proclamation was first cried out the people started off, running in all directions and crying out: "The Lady Mary is proclaimed Queen!" Before long the news had been carried to all quarters of the city and out into the countryside, creating astonishment at first—for to speak in favor of Mary had been punishable by death—and then a mad display of joy greater than any in living memory. "For my time," one contemporary wrote, "I never saw the like, and by the report of others the like was never seen." The bells, "which it had been decided to convert into artillery," began to ring and never stopped for two whole days; their clamor was so great that "there could no one hear almost what another said." Suddenly the streets were full of people, tossing their caps in the air without caring where they came down. Men with coins in their purses threw them to the crowd, and women leaned out from their windows and flung down pennies; when the earl of Pembroke tossed up his cap it came down in a shower of angelettes. For the first time in years there was a genuine feeling of hopefulness in the air, and everyone, even the most dignified of Londoners, forgot themselves in celebrating it. Eminent citizens, "being men of authority and in years, could not refrain from casting away their garments, leaping and dancing as though beside themselves"; they joined the more ordinary folk in "singing in the street for joy."

When night fell bonfires were lit in every crowded street, and the drinking and banqueting went on throughout the night, "with great rejoicing and music." "I am unable to describe to you," a visiting Italian wrote to a friend, "nor would you believe, the exultation of all men. From a distance the earth must have looked like Mount Etna." A Spanish writer found a more devout metaphor for the eruption of joy in London that night: "it seemed as if all had escaped from this evil world, and alighted in Heaven."[9]

As the bells rang and the wine flowed freely, the duke of Suffolk came quietly out of the Tower, unarmed, and ordered his men to lay their weapons down. According to one account, he noisily proclaimed Mary himself before returning to Jane's apartment and tearing down the cloth of estate that had been hung over her chair.

In Cambridge, Dudley gave up without a struggle. With his own hands he tore down the sheets proclaiming Jane posted at the street corners, and, waving his white truncheon, shouted "Long live Queen Mary!" and threw down his weapons. That night his chief confederates Northampton and Clinton, and 140 of the knights who had led his troops, made their way to Framlingham to give themselves up to Mary, while Arundel and Paget rode to her camp from London to "ask her pardon for the offense committed in the reception of the Lady Jane." According to the imperial envoys, they craved pardon in the traditional ritual demanded by so serious a crime, on their knees and with daggers turned toward their stomachs.[10]

Arundel's first act of penance was to seize Dudley, who was by this time a doomed man. All of his associates had deserted him; even his servants were so frightened of sharing his fate that they "tore his badge from their arms in order not to be known as his men."[11] The earl of Pembroke had gathered several hundred armed horsemen to oppose the duke if he had tried to resist, but they were not needed, and precautions were now taken to secure the capital against any disturbance that might be caused by his troops as they straggled back southward. All the weapons that had been in private hands were taken back and stored in the Tower; the municipal guard had been reinforced, and roadblocks were set up to control access to the city.[12] Everything was in readiness for the triumphal entry of the true queen.

She came on August 3, having stayed at Framlingham until all the rebels had been taken and sent on under guard to the Tower. Then, disbanding her army but keeping several thousand men to guard her on her way to London, she set out toward the capital. From Cornwall Sir Peter Carew sent seven hundred horsemen to form part of the royal guard; Elizabeth rode out to join her sister with another thousand gentlemen, knights and ladies in her retinue. On the day of her entry Mary stopped at a house in Whitechapel to exchange her dusty clothing for the finery she loved so well. She put on a gown of purple velvet, cut in the French fashion, with velvet sleeves. Under it was a kirtle of purple satin, thickly set with goldsmith's work and large pearls. Her foresleeves were covered with rich stones, and over one shoulder she wore an ornamental baldric of gold, covered with pearls and gems. The stones on her headdress were even more dazzling, and her horse's trappings were of cloth of gold, embroidered in rich designs. The train of her gown was so long that it had to be carried by Sir Anthony Browne, riding behind her and "leaning on her horse, having the train of her highness' gown hanging over his shoulder."[13]

Thus arrayed Mary rode through London, preceded by more than seven hundred mounted men, with "a great number of strangers all in velvet coats." All the king's trumpeters, heralds and sergeants at arms rode with her, and behind her, splendidly dressed and with guards of their own, came Elizabeth, the duchess of Norfolk, the marchioness of Exeter, and the rest of her ladies. The spectacle loosed another wave of emotion, nearly as great as that which had greeted Mary's proclamation two weeks earlier. As she passed through the streets they were "so full of people shouting and crying Jesus save her grace, with weeping tears for joy, that the like was never seen before." At Aldgate she was met by the Lord Mayor and Recorder, who knelt to welcome her and presented her with the scepter of her office, "in token of loyalty and homage." She returned it with a gracious speech of thanks, "so gently spoken and with so smiling a countenance that the hearers wept for joy." After this Mary made her way toward the Tower, past the waits playing on the battlements of the gate, and other musicians playing and singing "which rejoiced the queen's highness greatly." As she neared the Tower the guns shot continually "like great thunder, so that it had been like to an earthquake," and at Tower Gate she greeted Norfolk, Gardiner and Courtenay, who were kneeling to ask her pardon. Then in a last gesture of good will "she came to them and kissed them, and said, these be my prisoners." She went into the royal apartments then, where she would stay awaiting her coronation.

In the weeks since the remarkable collapse of Dudley's attempt to make Jane queen the staunchest Protestants in London had begun to predict calamity in the religious life of the nation. "Several preachers, certain Scotsmen in particular, have preached scandalous things of late to rouse up the people," Charles V's ambassadors reported, "going so far as to say that men should see Antichrist come again to life, and popery in the land."[14] That Mary associated her amazing triumph with God's purposes for herself and England was certainly true. One account of the climactic events of July, 1553, told how, as soon as Mary heard the news of her proclamation, "she caused a crucifix to be placed in her chapel, being the first which had been set up publicly for several years," and sang a Te Deum with her followers.

But the overwhelming sense of pious gratitude she felt was mixed with a more complex emotion. It was a dawning confidence in the harmonious blending of divine will and popular politics—a growing certainty that her reign was to be the agency for bringing England back to a spiritual equilibrium it had not known since the early years of the century. Along the roads between Framlingham and London she had seen time and again the same inscription at every crossroad; it was repeated in the placards and banners that decorated London at the time of her royal entry. The phrase expressed perfectly the conviction she now claimed: "*Vox populi, vox Dei*"—"The voice of the people is the voice of God."

XXX

Here is my hande,
My dere lover Englande.
I am thine with both mind and hart;
For ever to endure,
Thou maiest be sure,
Untill death us two do depart.

A traveler to England in Mary's reign described the country as "a long, narrow gut of land, situated in the great sea at the extremity of the world." To visitors from the continent the island kingdom appeared a remote place, insignificant in a sense yet somehow admirable. The same traveler, the Frenchman Étienne Perlin, remarked that England was, "if compared with other small kingdoms, great"—a backhanded compliment that contradicted the more succinct judgment of the diplomat Antoine de Noailles, who always referred to England as "this nasty island."[1] Perlin admired English men, whom he found to be "large, handsome and ruddy, with flaxen hair"; English women were, quite simply, "the greatest beauties in the world, as fair as alabaster," and also "cheerful and courteous, and of a good address." Their delightful custom of kissing everyone, even strangers, when they met had sent Erasmus into raptures. "If you were once to taste them, and find how delicate and fragrant they are," he wrote, "you would certainly desire . . . till death to be a sojourner in England."

The people Mary now set herself to rule spoke a tongue foreigners found ungainly. To speak it they had to "inflect the tongue upon the palate, twist words in the mouth and maintain a sort of gnashing with the teeth," an Italian wrote, and they spoke it with a vengeance, outdoing any other nation in the range and vehemence of their swearing. Even children and young people swore astonishingly, and no one seemed to complain or punish them for it. Their parents, though, had a worse habit. They loved to belch, "without reserve or shame, even in the presence of persons of the greatest dignity" and no meal was complete without a belching contest.

This national pastime undoubtedly had something to do with the heady beer the English consumed in such quantities. Strong beer, brewed from native wheat and barley and hops imported from Flanders, replaced ale as the cheapest and most abundant drink in the reign of Henry VIII. Known as "angels' food," "dragon's milk," "stride-wide" or "lift leg," it went down well with the soft raisin-filled saffron cakes served in taverns, and no diversion was more agreeable to Mary's subjects than to resort to the Magpie and Crown, the Whale and Crow, the Bible and Swan or the Leg and Seven Stars to drink "till they be red as cocks and little wiser than their combs." The "double beer" they favored was as strong as whisky; it soon made men and women "stark staring mad like March-Hares," and left them "drinking, brawling, tossing of the pitcher, staring, pissing and beastly spewing until midnight."

The English climate was as insalubrious as the prevailing drinking habits. It was as a rule free of extremes of heat and cold, so that people wore furs all year round, but the "thickness of the air" bred diseases. There was "some little plague" every year, and at least once in a generation the "atmospheric putrescence" gave rise to the terrors of the sweating sickness.

The effects of "thick air," disease and poverty were most apparent in London, a city whose remarkable growth resulted in part from the grim want that had devastated rural England over the last twenty years. The uprooted, the unemployed and the starving all made their way to the capital, where they formed a "common abhorring" to offend respectable citizens. In the year before Mary's reign began the Hospital of St. Bartholomew, a charitable institution organized to relieve the poor and ill, reported that it had either cured or buried nearly a thousand indigents "who would otherwise have stank in the noses of the city."

But if visitors from Europe avoided London's sprawling outskirts with their festering slums, they were impressed by its landmarks, its prosperity and brisk commercial life. The towering spires of St. Paul's, London Bridge with its twenty arches and its shops with flowers in every window, the royal residences and noble houses along the river all charmed newcomers. They marveled at the numbers of ships that sailed up the river, and at the wonderful variety of goods that came from their holds. Tudor London was a merchant's town, where both foreign and native tradesmen appeared to prosper even when the government was struggling to pay its creditors. The power of the guilds was unmistakable, and those who aspired to membership provided another conspicuous characteristic of the city. "In London you will see the apprentices in their gowns," Perlin wrote, "standing against their shops and the walls of their houses bare-headed, in so much that passing through the streets you may count fifty or sixty thus stuck up like idols, holding their caps in their hands."

Below the public mainstream of London life flourished another society: the Tudor underworld. This world had its own etiquette, its guilds, its social hierarchy, with carefully observed distinctions between rufflers, rogues, vagabonds and lower orders of evildoers. Highest in rank were the rufflers, ex-soldiers or servants turned out of their jobs to "wretchedly wander" the streets of the capital, flaunting self-inflicted wounds and pretending to be maimed soldiers returning from the wars. As only the flintiest heart could resist the sight of such noble misery, rufflers made almost as much in alms as the beggars who feigned epilepsy or the "Abraham-men" who danced and sang at street corners pretending to be mad. Below the rufflers were the rogues, more ordinary thieving beggars who extorted money by such underhanded means as attaching horselocks to the outstretched arms of people who offered them money, and demanding larger sums to let them go.

Still lower in the hierarchy were the hookers or anglers, who spent their days walking from house to house, taking careful note of what in the way of clothing or linen the householder kept near the second-story window; the same night they returned, carrying a tall staff with a hook at one end, and plucked down everything of value. Hookers were said to be able to lift the bedclothes off unsuspecting citizens as they slept by their open windows, leaving them to wake cold and naked in their nightshirts and suppose that they had been the victims of goblins or elves. On good days these professionals made very good money—as much as three, four or five shillings—but on bad days they barely scraped by, or fell to robbing each other, and few escaped the hazards of their calling—the pillory, prison or the gibbet—for long. The luckiest of them got off with nothing more serious than the public humiliation of being "ridden about London" in a cart, wearing around their necks a placard listing their offenses, while householders emptied chamber pots on their heads or threw rotten eggs in their faces.[2]

With crime flourishing, rebellion frequent and public order non-existent, England had become a nation in arms. Knights and gentlemen went armed by custom, but common folk now followed their example. Churchmen too ordered their servants to carry shields, and farmers, when they plowed their lands, left their swords or bows in a corner of the field in case of need. "In this land," Perlin wrote, "every body bears arms," and he blamed the government for creating the climate of violence. Justice in England is "tyrannically administered," he observed. The kingdom appeared to be governed by "shedding human blood in such abundance as to make it run into the rivulets," and for the aristocracy, beheading had become an ancestral disease. "In this country you will scarcely find any nobleman, some of whose relations have not been beheaded."

Even more shocking to visitors, though, than the arbitrary destructiveness of the government was the physical destruction of the churches of London. "The city is much disfigured by the ruins of a multitude of churches and monasteries belonging heretofore to friars and nuns," the ambassador Soranzo reported to the Venetian Senate. The devastation marred every street. Wrecked convents, parish churches with their naves gutted and their windows broken, vestiges of demolished shrines, graveyards and statues were the striking remains of the attempted obliteration of the old faith. The ruinous condition of English churches was not entirely unknown on the continent. For years boatloads of statues and paintings salvaged from their ruins had been arriving in French harbors, to be sold at Paris, Rouen and elsewhere.[3] The French bought them eagerly, treasuring them as relics of the martyrdom of the faith in England and murmuring about sacrilege and desecration. Nothing could prepare devout Catholic visitors for the spectacle of the dismantled, dishonored churches of London, however, or for the gaunt Protestant divines, burning with conviction, who had been Edward's preachers, and who still preached in the first weeks of Mary's reign. Men like Latimer, Lever and John Knox cut sinners to ribbons with their tongues, lashing out at pride, greed and vanity in sermons that went on for two hours or more. What was less apparent to visitors from abroad, though, was that large groups within the population held only a marginal place in the community of believers. There were many English men and women whose outward observance of the ceremonies of the church covered a profound inward indifference. And there were others, in hamlets and villages and farms distant from any settlement, whose religious ideas were not far removed from the heathendom of their remote ancestors.

This heterogeneous population, archaic and conservative yet caught up in rapid change of every kind, was now to be ruled by England's first crowned queen, Mary Tudor. The advent of a female ruler was in itself a remarkable innovation. There had been a woman ruler in England in the twelfth century, Henry I's daughter Matilda, but she was not crowned during her brief reign and did not call herself queen. Matilda's title was "daughter of king Henry and lady of England"; she avoided the Anglo-Saxon term *cwen* (queen) because it meant "wife," and implied that she did not hold the throne in her own right.[4] Matilda had not been able to hold her crown securely, and her reign set an unfortunate precedent. Happily for Mary the twelfth-century queen was all but forgotten. The most recent example of a woman holding political power in the British

Isles was in Scotland, where Henry VIII's sister Margaret had been regent for her infant son. Margaret was a genuine ruler, not just a
figurehead; she controlled the appointment of officials and kept the treasury in her own hands. But her power provoked sharp criticism. Lord
Dacre, ruler of the English lands along the Scots border, complained that
the Scots "let any woman have authority, especially her," and he spoke
for nearly all the men Margaret encountered.[5] Henry VIII spent the
greater part of his reign avoiding the unthinkable eventuality of leaving a
female heir. He had not trained either of his daughters to rule; certainly
he never meant them to. All his life Henry's idea of a ruler was a
strong man leading a large army into battle, and the battlefield, he once
remarked, was "unmeet for women's imbecilities."

Yet Henry had been forced to admit the capability of some women.
Early in his reign he had left Katherine of Aragon to rule in his stead
while he was on campaign in France, and later, when he believed he had
made an enemy of her, he had no difficulty imagining Katherine at the
head of an army, leading an armed rebellion against him. The sixteenth
century was in fact an era of women rulers, and Mary had to look no farther than to Flanders to observe a highly capable one at work.

Her cousin Mary, regent of Flanders, had been ruling there for more
than twenty years, ever since Charles V appointed her to succeed her
aunt Margaret in the regency. Mary was short and delicately built, like
her cousin in England, with the distinctive Hapsburg disfigurement of a
thick lower lip, but at fifty she was as awesome as she had been in her
thirties, when she regularly outrode, outshot and outhunted her male
courtiers. Once when the humanist Roger Ascham was traveling in the
German lands he met the regent on the road. She was riding alone, miles
ahead of her retinue of thirty gentlemen, having accomplished a journey
that invariably took seventeen days in thirteen. "She is a virago," Ascham
wrote admiringly. "She is never so well as when she is flinging on horseback [sic], and hunting all the night long."[6]

The diplomats of the time unanimously conceded the regent's intelligence and her shrewdness in statecraft. She "had courage enough for
anything," they noted; in character they compared her to her progenitor
Charles the Bold.[7] Yet despite her prodigious capabilities she was denied a
place at the diplomatic table. During crucial peace negotiations with the
French in 1555 the emperor sent an urgent message to his sister, asking
her to join him and give him advice on exactly what concessions should
be made. She came, she gave excellent advice in private, yet to the Venetians at the conference she sent her regret "at being prevented by her sex
from attending . . . as she earnestly desired."[8] As a younger woman even
the ambassadors with greatest admiration for her put her biological function first in their dispatches, speculating that "by reason of her natural

volatility, and from too much exercise and motion, she will have no posterity." Her own final observation on her authority was both judicious and tragic. "A woman is never feared or respected as a man is, whatever her rank."[9]

The idea of a woman at the head of state was abhorrent on principle. For a woman to rule her husband was unnatural; for her to rule a nation was a monstrous exaggeration of that unnatural condition. Men were strong and prudent, with the force of mind and greatness of soul to govern others; women were weak and thoughtless, lacking the logic, concentration and largeness of vision to guide any political body. It was common knowledge that women, like lunatics, were governed by the moon, making them unstable and capricious. However gifted or well intentioned she might be, no woman could escape this influence. Besides, all the imagery of royalty—of all authority—was male. For a woman to mount the throne offended the very concept of majesty. Politically, a woman ruler was a symbol of national impotence. More important, no queen could fill the ruler's primary function in the larger order of the cosmos: to represent God to her people. Bishop Gardiner had defined this larger function. Kings, he wrote, were "representatives of God's image unto men." Their part in God's grand design was to reveal him more fully to their subjects. No woman could do that; given the inherent sinfulness of all women, it would be blasphemy for any female ruler to try.

Mary came to the throne at a time in English history when the idea of the monarch took on new scope. Through the sheer force of his size, his magnetism and his power to dominate others Mary's father had reshaped the office of king. Put in the simplest terms, to the average English man or woman, a ruler was someone who looked and acted like Henry VIII. It is extremely doubtful whether any man could have stepped into Henry's shoes—certainly the boy Edward had failed dismally—yet this was what Mary was called upon to do. Her task was made doubly difficult by her ambivalent feelings about her father and by the entire force of her education. During the nearly thirty-one years she had lived under his absolute authority Mary had loved and hated her father with equal force. She would never forgive him for the way he treated her mother, nor could she forget how he had treated her, yet since his death she had often invoked his presence in moments of crisis. He was her benchmark of political power; beside him all other authority faded. Mary drew strength from the fact that she was Henry's daughter as well as Katherine's, and she was aware of having inherited his authority along with his throne and title.

Yet everything she had been taught since childhood robbed her of that strength and contradicted that authority. She had been trained to mistrust her judgment, fear her weakness, and feel shame for her sinfulness. She had never been taught to confront the world; instead her gaze had been turned inward, to focus on guarding her chastity and cultivating the gestures, expressions and tones of voice that symbolized it. Her intellectual achievement was formidable, but atrophied; its only formal purpose had been to encourage fretful introspection. In short, Mary was now raised to a political status that conflicted with her sexual status at every turn. The interplay between the two was to form an inescapable backdrop to her troubled reign.

At thirty-seven, Mary was a striking woman, despite her short stature. She was almost boyishly slender, with the bright auburn hair and rosy cheeks of a much younger woman. Her eyes were of an indefinite hazel color, and very large; her nose was "rather low and wide," and gave her face character as well as a dignified beauty. In her most revealing portraits there is a defiant set to her features, and a faint sarcasm, though what impressed the Venetian Soranzo was Mary's expression of "great benignity and clemency." She set off her handsome appearance by "arraying herself elegantly and magnificently," just as her father had. Like him she changed her clothes often, alternating between the close-fitting, trailing gown and kirtle worn by English gentlewomen and the French-style gown and bodice with huge, full sleeves. She wore the latter on state occasions, but even her everyday dress was sumptuous. She loved rich embroidery and expensive velvets and brocades. She had gowns and mantles made of costly cloth of gold and cloth of silver, and wore with them great quantities of jewels—on her fingers, around her neck, and as trimming for her gowns. Mary took exceptional delight in her jewels, the Venetian ambassador wrote. "Although she has a great plenty of them left her by her predecessors, yet were she better supplied with money than she is, she would doubtless buy more."[10]

Mary's love of finery was the only sign of self-indulgence in the severely disciplined life she led as queen. She rose at daybreak, said her prayers and heard a private mass and then, without pausing to eat, worked at her desk until one or two in the afternoon, when she took a light meal. She made herself available not only to the members of her Privy Council, from whom she heard "every detail of public business," but to everyone else who asked audience of her, and went on transacting business and writing and answering letters with exhausting diligence every night until after midnight. Mary's habit of spending nearly all her waking hours at the work of government was reminiscent of her grandmother Isabella. Nothing was allowed to interfere with her regimen but religious services, which took up several hours a day at least, and at the seasons of the great church feasts, many more. For convenience the leading members of the Council had rooms in the palace; by ancient custom some of them slept there. They met early each morning under the leadership of the chancellor, Stephen Gardiner, bishop of Winchester, and conferred with Mary periodically during the day.

Visitors to Mary's court found her intelligence and competence impressive, and judged her to be "more than moderately read in Latin literature, especially with regard to Holy Writ." To ambassadors she spoke Latin, French and Spanish; she understood Italian, though she did not speak it, and displayed a quickness of mind and an eloquence of expression which left no doubt of her capacity to rule. With her servants and others she was generous—some said too generous—with gifts of money and valuable objects. She also gave them her time and her concern, which soon lent her a reputation for simple goodness that clung to her throughout her reign. But Mary was fiercely proud too, and "inclined to talk about her exalted station."[11] Renard called her "great-hearted, proud and magnanimous," and she carried with her an air of solemnity that made even ordinary events seem important. Mary's unshakable belief that she had come to the throne through divine intervention made her deeply serious about her responsibilities. According to Soranzo, her constant exclamation was "In thee, O lord, is my trust, let me never be confounded: if God be for us, who can be against us?"

Mary's natural ability, her extraordinary dedication and her confident belief that she was divinely guided helped to sustain her at the outset of her reign. But there were hindrances as well, beyond the everpresent hindrance of her sex. Mary was reported to have a weak constitution, her habitual complaint troubled her from time to time, and her long working hours gave her headaches and sometimes heart palpitations.[12] She had found a diet that suited her, but she still had to be bled quite often, and to take various medicines. The first months of her reign were emotionally as well as physically exhausting, and throughout the fall of 1553 Mary was wishing she could get away to Flanders, to visit the regent, the cousin she had never seen. The sight of Mary of Flanders would surely "cure all her natural melancholy," Mary wrote, "from which she constantly suffered." With some exaggeration she added that she had "never known what it was to be happy."[13]

Mary's extremes of confidence and melancholy only confirmed the general impression among her ministers that she was unfit to run her own government. They consistently underestimated her, confusing her deference to their views with helplessness. She was to surprise them again and again with her capacity for hard work, her courage and her leadership in crises, but each time they quickly returned to their original impression. Simon Renard, who came to know Mary as well as anyone in her government, took a very dark view of her future as queen. "I know this queen," he wrote to Charles V's chief minister Cardinal Granvelle, "so good, so easy, without experience of life or of statecraft; a novice in everything. I will tell you honestly my opinion, that unless God guards her she will always be cheated and misled either by the French or her own subjects; and at last taken off by poison or some other means."[14]

XXXI

 Haile Quene of England, of most worthy fame
For vertve, for wisdome, for mercy and grace;
Most firme in the fa[i]th, Defence of the same,
Christ save her and keepe her in every place.

A week before Mary made her ceremonial entry into London
Dudley and some ten of his captains and accomplices rode into the city
under strict and heavy guard. At the head of the armed cortege four
standard-bearers carried the royal ensign, then came a large company of
mounted men, and behind them an array of archers and men at arms.
More guardsmen lined the streets, to prevent the townspeople from
breaking through the column of horsemen and attacking the duke. During the journey south from Cambridge he had been wearing a scarlet
cloak; at the city gate he was made to take it off to make him less conspicuous among the small group of prisoners, but the crowd knew him
well enough. He held his cap in his hand, as if begging for mercy, but the
people, "greatly excited," cried out insults as he passed, and cursed him as
a traitor to the crown. "A dreadful sight it was, and a strange mutation,"
the imperial ambassadors recorded, for only a few weeks earlier the duke
had ridden through these same streets in state, magnificently dressed, es-
corting Jane Grey to the royal apartments in the Tower. Now he was
being taken there to die.[1]

Dudley's trial was brief. The court was assembled at Westminster,
where the old duke of Norfolk, as Earl Marshal, sat representing the
queen as president of the court. Mary had recently released him from his
seven years' imprisonment in the Tower, and acknowledged his primacy
among the peers. Norfolk was among those Mary might well have
wanted to punish once she came to power, for the wrongs he had done
her in the past. Given his shameless promotion of Anne Boleyn, and his

repeated cruelties to Mary and her mother during her father's reign, Mary would have been amply justified in reducing him to penniless obscurity, but she showed no hint of vindictiveness. Instead the duke was given the privilege of overseeing the condemnation of his old enemy Dudley, in a setting which did him much honor.

He was seated atop a high scaffolding many feet above the floor in a chair bearing the dossal, pall and mantle of majesty. The chief officers of Mary's government sat at his side—Paulet, Arundel, Paget and even the former chancellor Rich. Four aldermen, and an equal number of lawyers in their scarlet robes and white wigs, completed the personnel of the court. Dudley had made a full confession of his guilt in writing before the trial began; he reiterated it now, falling on his knees and begging the absent queen for mercy, saying that he had acted with the advice and consent of the Council in all he had done. When he had made his appeal Norfolk pronounced the sentence of the court: Dudley was to be hanged, "his heart to be drawn from his body and flung against his face," and his body quartered. Custom demanded that the traditional barbarous punishment for traitors be invoked; later Mary commuted it to simple beheading.

During his weeks in the Tower Dudley had undergone an amazing transformation. He was assailed by remorse for all of his sins, political and religious. To ease his conscience he wrote his confession and then, asking that Somerset's two sons be brought before him, he admitted that he had had their father wrongly condemned, and begged their forgiveness. He asked pardon of others as well, and returned all the money he had amassed from the royal treasury during his years in the government. But what was more astonishing was that, having professed the most radical Protestantism for the last four years, he suddenly recanted and returned to the old faith. He confessed his sins, heard mass with every sign of heartfelt fervor and gave himself up to prayers and devotions. He even went so far as to link his crimes to his abandonment of Catholicism, telling those who came to see him die that "since he had forsaken God and the church to follow the new religion he had done no good." His final message from the scaffold was to urge his hearers to obey the "good and virtuous" queen, who had "attained the throne miraculously" through the "hand of God." Then the executioner, a lame swordsman wearing "a white apron like a butcher," made ready to perform his office, and the duke, with a last prayer, put his head on the block.[2]

Some Protestants suspected that Dudley's change of heart was part of a government plot to discredit the established church, which Mary was eager to replace with her own, but to many Londoners his remarkable conversion was just one more sign that the circumstances surrounding Mary's accession were nothing short of miraculous. Catholics were predicting that God would soon "take pity on his people and church in England, through the instrument of a virgin called Mary, whom he has raised to the throne."[3] Protestant pamphleteers tried to refute the argument, widespread among the "common sort," that Mary's victory over Dudley confirmed that hers was the only true religion. "This is of God which our queen and old bishops have professed," they were saying. "For how has God prospered and kept them! What a notable victory has God given them!"[4] Ballads told how the duke "went forth full glad" to meet Mary, yet "came a traitor in full sad," because God subdued all her enemies. New songs welcoming her to the throne were registered at stationers' hall every few days, some of them addressing her by the old fond nickname of "Marigold."

The most eloquent statement of Mary's providential accession came from Reginald Pole, who in a letter to the new queen marveled at how, "without the aid of any other forces or resistance save that which the spirit of God roused in the hearts of men," her throne was secured. Her reign was proof that the hand of God ruled human affairs, Pole told Mary, and like the virgin Mary she should rejoice that "her soul did magnify the Lord." The queen had "more cause than any one" to sing the virgin's song of praise, "He hath regarded the low estate of his handmaiden; he hath shewed strength with his arm; he hath put down the mighty from their seats, and exalted them of low degree."[5]

It was not the first time Mary's life had been compared to that of Jesus' mother. After an earlier crisis, in 1536, after signing her formal Submission to her father, Mary had been given a ring signifying her obedience in the words of the virgin's song, the Magnificat. Now Pole was encouraging Mary again to see her life as a channel for the divine purpose, just as the virgin Mary's life had been used by God to fulfill his plan for mankind. The parallel could hardly have been more flattering, but the queen was already convinced. For seventeen years she had been living with the certainty that hers was to be a destiny beyond the ordinary. Now that destiny had been made clear. She was to bring England back to the true faith.

Mary's initial statements on religion showed considerable tolerance and flexibility. She "wished to force no one to go to mass," she told the imperial ambassador Renard at their first meeting late in July, but she "meant to see that those who wished to go should be free to do so."[6] She told her councilors it was not her intention "to compel or constrain other men's consciences," merely to provide them the opportunity to hear the truth through "godly, virtuous learned preachers."[7] She was aware that both Protestants and Catholics were waiting to see how resolute she was. In her view the funeral that had yet to be held for Edward provided the first test of her fidelity to the Catholic ritual. A Protestant funeral would make the Lutherans "more audacious," she told Renard. They would be sure to "proclaim that she had not dared to do her own will." When she ordered a Catholic funeral her Council would not object, though some members "would only consent out of dissimulation and fear." She meant to go ahead despite this, relying on her troops to prevent any serious incidents and hoping to use her councilors' dissimulation "for a great end" later.

Renard advised Mary to be cautious in making any religious demonstrations for the time being; the emperor, who imagined that she might try to alter the religious settlement overnight, had ordered his envoys to urge caution. There was no need for alarm. Mary was moving slowly though unmistakably toward her ultimate goal, at a pace designed to prevent organized opposition from her Protestant subjects. Her first official announcement on August 12 made it plain that she meant to leave her subjects free to worship as they chose until Parliament could cooperate in bringing about orderly change. "She had so far found no better expedient than to leave each one free as to the religion he would follow," the announcement read. "If some held to the old, and others to the new, they should not be interfered with or constrained to follow any other course until the coming Parliament should decide by law."[8] As if to confirm this policy Mary decided to authorize two separate funeral observances for Edward—a Protestant service in Westminster Abbey and a requiem mass in the old chapel of the White Tower. But if she saw the virtue of deferring the re-establishment of Catholicism there was no doubt she meant to complete it in time. She told Renard "she felt so strongly on this matter of religion that she was hardly to be moved," glancing as she said this toward the altar in her chamber.[9]

The court set a pious example of adherence to the traditional faith, and one that was followed in many places throughout the kingdom. Six or seven masses were being sung every day in Mary's chapel, with all the Council members in attendance. (It was noted, though, that neither Elizabeth nor Anne of Cleves had yet attended.) In the major churches of London the altars were being restored, and the crucifixes replaced. Matins and vespers had been recited in St. Paul's for weeks, and on St. Bartholomew's Day, August 24, the first Latin mass was sung there.[10] Elsewhere the Catholic ritual had been restored even earlier. At Oxford a visiting Protestant watched Catholics "dig out as it were from their graves their vestments, chalices and portasses, and begin mass with all speed" as soon as Mary was proclaimed queen. In their exuberance they "had a public festival, and threatened flames, hanging, the gallows and drowning" to all Protestants.[11] In some places, of course, secret masses had been performed throughout Edward's reign, either by daring English priests or by foreign clerics from Normandy or Brittany, many of whom could not speak English.[12]

Demonstrations against the restoration of the old faith began on the day the councilors announced Mary's accession. Shortly after she was proclaimed a man was set in the pillory "for speaking against the good Queen Mary," and before long the slander took written form. Less than a month after Mary came to the throne she published an edict against "books, ballads, rhymes and treatises" injurious to the peace of the realm which printers and stationers, "of an evil zeal for lucre," were selling.[13] Few preachers managed to get through their sermons without interruption from roving bands of troublemakers, and apprentices and servants went about from street to street insulting priests, singing anti-papal songs and disrupting religious services. Protestant preachers, including some Flemings and Frenchmen, who "interspersed seditious words" in their sermons were silenced, but not before some violence had broken out. In the week after Mary entered London in triumph an old priest said mass in St. Bartholomew's church. The sight attracted an angry mob, who "would have pulled him in pieces."[14] A few days later a "defamatory leaflet" was found scattered in the streets which exhorted Protestants to take up arms against Mary's government. In it all "nobles and gentlemen favoring the word of God" were urged to overthrow the "detestable papists" who supported "our virtuous Lady, Queen Mary," especially "the great devil," Gardiner, bishop of Winchester. Gardiner had to be "exorcised and exterminated" before he could "poison the people and wax strong in his religion," the pamphleteer claimed; otherwise the cause of the gospel would be lost.

The first really serious incident took place on Sunday, August 13, when Mary's chaplain Gilbert Bourne preached at Paul's Cross. In his sermon Bourne lashed out at the former bishop of London, Ridley, and praised the newly established Catholic bishop Bonner. The assembled crowd was so infuriated with his remarks that they broke into "great uproar and shouting, like mad people," and were on the point of rioting. A dagger was thrown at Bourne, and narrowly missed him, sticking fast in one of the sideposts of the pulpit. The preacher was hurriedly led to safety in the cathedral school nearby, and a reforming preacher in the crowd, one Master Bradford, eventually managed to quiet the crowd. Mary and the Council were outraged, ordering the people to obey the Lord Mayor and keep the peace or she would "set other rulers over them."

It was thought that the presence of the Mayor and of Edward Courtenay in the crowd had helped to prevent more harm from being done, and the following Sunday the worshipers arrived at Paul's Cross to find not only the Mayor but all the crafts in their liveries, the Council, Bishop Bonner, the captain of the guard and upwards of two hundred guardsmen flanking the preacher Mary sent to address them. The guardsmen "strode about the pulpit with their halberds," as if daring an-

other attack, while the preacher expanded on the less inflammatory subject of "rebuilding the old temple again."[15] The incident was not
repeated, but it led Mary to increase her personal guard. Beyond her ordinary mounted escort, she ordered eight cannon brought to Richmond
"for her greater safety, and to make a show of her strength and authority
for the intimidation of the seditious and those who have evil intentions."
In addition, she was said to be arming seven or eight hundred more
mounted guardsmen and two hundred footsoldiers.[16]

In these first unsettled weeks of her reign Mary was forced to come
to terms not only with unruly Protestants and would-be rebels, but with
the volatile, divisive men of her Council as well. There were more than
forty of them, drawn from among Mary's faithful household officers,
men imprisoned or out of favor during the preceding reign and, to the
surprise of many, the members of Edward's Council—the men who had
assented to removing Mary from the succession and giving her crown to
Jane Grey. From her household came Rochester, Walgrave, Englefield,
and her chaplain Bourne, supplemented by men such as Sir Henry Jerningham, now captain of her guard, who with the old earl of Sussex had
come to her defense at Framlingham, Sir John Gage, her aging Lord
Chamberlain, and Sir Thomas Cheyne. These men were utterly trustworthy, reliable, staunch in their loyalty to Mary and the Catholic
church, but lacking any experience of statecraft.

Equally loyal and far more experienced were the political outcasts,
mostly churchmen, who had suffered for their views and allegiances in
the regencies of Somerset and Dudley. The duke of Norfolk, Thomas
Thirlby, bishop of Norwich, Cuthbert Tunstal, the octogenarian bishop
of Durham and the able, outspoken and choleric bishop of Winchester
Stephen Gardiner had all managed to serve, and survive, two rulers. Gardiner had been a principal adviser to Henry VIII in the matter of his
divorce—something Mary chose to look past now—but had redeemed
himself in her eyes by becoming more and more conservative in religion
as the years passed, and by developing an inveterate hatred of Dudley.
This antipathy flattered the bishop, who was honest where the duke was
devious and deceitful, and who like Mary stood by his convictions to the
end.

More ominous for the future of Mary's government was that Gardiner was at odds with the leader of the third group in her Council. This
third group, consisting of the now-repentant councilors who had lent
their authority to Dudley's plot, were led by William Paget, a wary, cir-
cumspect man whose outstanding characteristic was his ability to adapt
himself to every political climate. Paget had advised Henry VIII in his
last years, befriended the Protector yet survived his fall, made himself

useful to Dudley and was now becoming invaluable to Mary. The men Paget spoke for—Pembroke, Petre, Arundel, Derby, Shrewsbury and the others—were in an extremely awkward position. They were all embarrassed by their association with the traitor Dudley, yet each of them tried to lay the blame for the Council's acquiescence on the others. Some, like Derby, had deserted Dudley early in the contest to bring thousands of soldiers to Mary's camp, while others had remained inconspicuous throughout the struggle for the throne. The former expected to be rewarded with offices and special favors, while the latter hoped their cowardice had not been noticed. All of them were continually on edge in the early part of Mary's reign, sometimes explosively so. Yet she would have found it hard to rule without them, for despite their disadvantages they were the only men in the government with recent experience of affairs. Besides, given the deterioration of government over the last six years there were few men in public life whose integrity was above reproach. As the imperial ambassador wrote to Charles V in August, Mary "found matters in such a condition when she came to the throne that she cannot possibly put everything straight, or punish all who have been guilty of something; otherwise she would be left without any vassals at all."[17]

Mary had gotten a foretaste of the squabbling indecisiveness of her Council in the first weeks of her reign. Between the time her camp at Framlingham was broken up and the day she made her formal entry into London Mary met with her Council several times. She was naturally curious to hear from them what had really happened in the last days of Edward's reign—whether the Device had been his own or Dudley's idea, whether or not the duke had planned to imprison or kill her, how and why she had been allowed to get away. Instead of answers her questions unleashed a barrage of mutual accusations and recriminations among the councilors, and she soon realized that she would never learn the truth about the conspiracy from these men. To her astonishment, they could not even come to a decision about whether she should hasten or delay her journey to the capital, "some saying she had better tarry a while because of the heat, bad air and danger of the plague . . . others urging her to press on as fast as possible to set her affairs in order and establish herself in the government of the country." In her first conversation with Renard Mary confessed to him that "she could not help being amazed by the divisions in the Council," whose members spent all their time trying to get the better of one another, changing their views as often as necessary to protect their reputations.[18]

What was worse, many of them were becoming enmeshed in a net of backbiting, influence peddling and petty intrigue. Some of the more obscure gentlemen who had "stood by the queen in the days of her adversity and trouble" now felt "cast off and neglected" because they had not been appointed to office or given lands or titles. Instead of approaching Mary directly, though, they took their complaints to more powerful lords who in turn spread tales of dissatisfaction to anyone who cared to listen. These lesser men let it be known that they "might easily change sides if they perceived that they received no notice," and devoted far less energy to the work of government than to the task of finding an influential patron or outmaneuvering rivals for bureaucratic posts.

Others thought they could advance their careers in the queen's service by ingratiating themselves with her women. Renard noticed in August that "the ladies about the queen's person are able to obtain from her more than she ought to grant them," and Mary was frequently approached by female friends and relatives asking favors on behalf of courtiers. In one complex negotiation the earl of Pembroke approached Courtenay to ask if he would persuade his mother to speak to the queen on the earl's behalf. Courtenay's mother was Gertrude Blount, marchioness of Exeter, one of Mary's oldest friends, and Pembroke knew that Mary would be favorably inclined to anything the marchioness proposed. To ensure Courtenay's cooperation Pembroke gave him valuable gifts— a sword and poniard, a basin and ewer, and several horses—worth in all more than three thousand pounds. The marchioness "made his peace with the queen," and Pembroke found himself named to the Council as he had hoped. At another time the duchess of Suffolk, mother of Jane Grey and wife of the conspirator Henry Grey, now a prisoner in the Tower, came to Mary's bedchamber at two o'clock in the morning to tell her that her husband had been poisoned and to beg for his release.

Even the leading figures in the Council, Gardiner and Paget, were caught up in the web of intrigue. Each resented the other's power and influence, and their enmity was becoming public knowledge and interfering with the business of government. After observing the operations for a time Renard was inclined to agree with Mary that "the Council does not seem to us . . . to be composed of experienced men endowed with the necessary qualities to conduct the administration and government of the kingdom."[19]

The shortcomings of the men around Mary were all the more crucial in that, as her reign opened, England stood lower in the estimation of the European states than at any time since the Wars of the Roses. Henry VIII had been able to create an illusion of power and majesty so convincing it made his kingdom seem powerful—or at least substantial—as well. With Edward on the throne the illusion vanished, and when Dudley became the actual ruler in 1549 England's influence in European diplomacy melted away. Paradoxically, England's very weakness gave it a new importance in the 1550s. Astute observers on the continent were convinced that, sooner or later, the country would become a client state of France or the empire, and the competition between them came to center on England as it once had on Italy earlier in the century. With Mary on the throne, Hapsburg domination seemed likely, probably in the form of a marriage between Mary and Dom Luiz or the emperor's widowed son Philip. But the French would be certain to keep their influence alive in England as well, and there was always the chance that the bold young French king might mount an invasion, as he clearly thought of doing when Dudley appealed to him for help in July.

Even if the French did not invade England proper there was no doubt that Henri II was eager to regain the English-held territories of Calais and Guines, and Mary's first concern as queen was to ensure the defense of these two possessions. The issue was urgent, for in his desperate need for military aid Northumberland had authorized his envoy to Henri II's court to discuss transferring the English strongholds to the French, and had recalled the English commander of Guines, Lord Grey. Mary quickly sent Grey back, with orders to hold the town at all costs and to inform the French that Dudley had been seized as a traitor. To emphasize her determination to hold the towns Mary ordered a muster to be held in London, specifically to enroll men to defend Calais and Guines; the muster, along with the presence of an imperial garrison in the vicinity, dissuaded the French from attacking.

The defense of the English-held territories was more than a military problem; it was also a fiscal one. At the end of July Renard wrote that Mary could "find no money for current expenses," and was struggling with the problem of paying the dissatisfied English soldiers defending Guines and Calais. The government had not been solvent for years, and beyond the huge deficits Dudley had left there were hundreds of smaller obligations of a more personal kind that had been gathering dust in the royal exchequer for decades. The government was in debt to "many an old servitor, minister, officer, merchant, banker, captain, pensioner and soldier," Mary found. She considered it a point of honor that they be paid, and announced in September that she would pay every obligation left from the two preceding reigns, no matter how long it took.[20] Even more important, she made a significant beginning in solving the long-standing crisis of the currency. New coins were issued, with higher proportions of gold and silver, set according to a fixed standard. There would be no further debasements, she announced, and although it was evident her government would have to go heavily into debt to remain solvent, the worst of the economic plagues, unprofitable foreign exchange and inflation, were already coming under control. English money began to hold its value against foreign coins once again in the money markets of Antwerp and Brussels, and in England, prices of food and other goods fell by as much as one third in 1553.

Despite the fears about her incapacity and inexperience, Mary was clearly beginning to take command. With all evidence of rebellion crushed and religious and economic problems more or less in hand, she was ready to play her role in the great political drama of her coronation.

XXXII

Blesed be, therfore, our Lorde God above,
And Marie, our Maistresse, our merciful Quene;
For unto this lande our Lorde, for her love,
Hath of his mercy most mercifull bene.

Planning for the queen's coronation began in the first weeks of the new reign. By the middle of September the major pageants for the pre-coronation procession had been written and designed, and carpenters, painters and gilders were at work building and ornamenting the arches and painted backdrops against which they would be performed. There were verses to be composed and inscribed, speeches to be memorized, music to be rehearsed. All along the procession route citizens were "hanging the streets" with tapestries and rich cloths, and the great cross in Cheap was newly washed and gilded. At St. Paul's, the weathercock that crowned the steeple was carefully taken down by the Dutch acrobat who would mount and balance on it on the day of the procession. It was made of copper, and weighed forty pounds; its underside—all that the crowd could see—was gilded, and then it was set in place again. Finally when all was ready, on the twenty-eighth of September, Mary went by barge from Whitehall to the Tower, escorted by the mayor and aldermen and guild members in their barges, to the sound of trumpets and shawms and an immense cannonade from the Tower guns.

The following day she created a number of new Knights of the Bath, giving the honor to several men who had stood by her during her conflict with Dudley. Her controller Sir Robert Rochester—now controller of the royal household—was among them, as were Sir Henry Jerningham, the earl of Surrey and Sir William Dormer, Jane Dormer's father, who with his friends and supporters had helped to uphold Mary's cause in Buckingham during the crucial days in July.[1] Mary could not perform the ceremony itself, as it called for the newly created knights to jump naked into a bath with the sovereign and kiss his shoulder; the earl of Arundel, now Great Master of the Household, carried out this part of the ritual for her.[2]

On the morning of the thirtieth the streets were strewn with rushes and flowers to cover their stench, and at three in the afternoon the first of the five hundred nobles, gentlemen and officials who rode in procession before the queen came out of the Tower courtyard and made their way at a solemn pace toward Westminster. The queen's messengers came first, followed by trumpeters, esquires of the body, pursuivants at arms and the new Knights of the Bath. Behind these were heralds, bannerets, and the members of the royal Council. Then came the Garter Knights and the rest of the nobility in order of rank. The nobles outdid themselves in splendor, wearing gold and silver on their persons and their mounts, "which caused great admiration, not more by the richness of the substance than by the novelty and elegance of the device."

Equally magnificent were the ambassadors, each of whom rode paired with a lord of the Council. Great care had been given to the choice of escort for the major ambassadors. It was decided that Paget, after the chancellor the leading member of the Council, should ride with the French ambassador while the emperor's current "resident" (no official ambassador had been appointed since Scheyfve's departure) was accompanied by Lord Clinton. Renard, whose diplomatic status was still only that of temporary envoy, rode with another councilor of lower status, Lord Cobham. The merchants, soldiers and knights who rode in the ambassadorial suites were nearly as resplendent as the great English nobles. Four Italian merchants stood out in suits of lined black velvet, "beautifully trimmed with many points of gold," and with a band of costly gold embroidery "more than a palm in width." Their mantles, horse cloths and even the liveries of the grooms who walked beside them were of the same black velvet, bordered in worked gold. Four Spanish cavaliers in mulberry-colored velvet also attracted great admiration. Their cloaks were lined in cloth of silver, "with a very fine fringe of gold all about," and their doublets and stiff Spanish ruffs "appeared to great advantage both for their richness and their elegant design."

After the ambassadors and their escorts came the members of the queen's personal suite, first the earl of Sussex, Chief Server, carrying her hat and cloak, then "two ancient knights with old-fashioned hats, powdered on their heads, disguised," who following an old custom represented the dukes of the former English territories of Normandy and Guienne. Next came the chancellor, the Lord Mayor, in crimson velvet carrying a golden scepter, sergeants at arms, and finally the earl of Arundel, bearing Mary's sword.

Behind them was the queen herself, riding in an open litter upholstered in white cloth of gold. The six horses pulling the litter were all in
white trappings reaching nearly to the ground, and Mary sat eagerly forward amid the damask cushions, sometimes holding her head in her hand
because of the weight of the golden circlet she wore. She was dressed in
white cloth of gold, her kirtle furred with miniver and her mantle with
powdered ermine. Her hair was caught up in a net of cloth of tinsel spar-
kling with precious stones, and over it she wore "a round circlet of gold,
much like a hooped garland," set with jewels of inestimable value.

Footmen in rich coats rode beside Mary's litter, and a company of
knights carried the canopy of estate that hung over her litter. Three
women also rode at her side—the marchioness of Exeter, the marchioness
of Winchester, Paulet's wife, and the countess of Arundel. Behind them
rode the fifty-two other women of the royal suite: Princess Elizabeth and
Anne of Cleves, in gowns of cloth of silver, riding in a handsome litter;
then the duchesses, marchionesses, countesses, and gentlewomen, in crimson velvet; then Mary's maids in crimson satin and her chamberers in
crimson damask. The saddles of the gentlewomen were covered with
cloth of gold, and their harnesses bore powdered ermines.

The ladies and gentlewomen were followed by nine henchmen, and
then by three hundred mounted guardsmen and archers, who rode up and
down beside the length of the procession as protection. The precautions
were greater than usual, because it was thought some attempt might be
made to disrupt the coronation festivities. A few days earlier Mary's
Master of the Horse, Sir Edward Hastings, had discovered a plot by "certain rascals or mariners" to steal all the queen's horses. The thieves were
to meet first at Blackheath, but Hastings and a number of guardsmen got
there first and prevented the robbery.[2]

The procession paused at Fenchurch Street to see a costly pageant
presented by the Genoese merchants—a triumphal arch inscribed with
verses celebrating Mary's accession, flanked by four great giants. At
Gracechurch corner the Hanseatic merchants had set up an artificial
mount and a little fountain spouting wine; by some mechanism a man
"flew down from the top of the pageant as she rode by." The most elaborate and flattering of the representations was that of the Florentines, who
saluted Mary as "liberator of her country," and pointedly compared her
to the Hebrew heroine Judith who by beheading the tyrant Holofernes
delivered her people from the threat of slavery. By Holofernes they
meant Dudley, whose beheading was still a recent memory. Mary was
also compared to Pallas Athena, and an inscription told how her fame was
so great it reached the stars. To the crowds that lined the streets the outstanding feature of the pageant was a mechanical angel, clothed in green
and carrying a trumpet. When the angel put his trumpet to his mouth a

trumpeter "who stood secretly in the pageant" blew a fanfare, so that the sound appeared to come from the angel, "to the marveling of many ignorant persons."

At the conduit in Cornhill was "a very pretty pageant made very gorgeously," in which three little girls dressed as women took the parts of Grace, Virtue and Nature. Grace wore a crown and carried a scepter, and when Mary rode by all three children "kneeled down, and every one of them sang certain verses of gratifying the queen." St. Paul's churchyard was the site of a triple spectacle. A choir of men and boys sang at the schoolhouse, with Mary giving "diligent ear" to their song. There was more singing at the dean's house, and a pageant where little children carried burning tapers "made of most sweet perfumes."

And at the top of St. Paul's the Dutch acrobat performed the amazing feat of climbing up to the weathercock by means of scaffolds he had built out from the base of the steeple, holding a little flag in one hand. When he reached the weathercock he pulled himself up until he was standing on it, and then, waving his flag, he stood on one foot and shook his other leg in the air. The difficulty of the exploit was increased by the high wind, which blew out the torches the Dutchman had fastened to his wooden structure and threatened to blow him away as well. But he went on through his series of tricks smoothly, finally kneeling on the weathercock with both knees, "to the great marvel and wondering of all the people who beheld him, because it was thought a matter impossible."[4] The Dutch acrobat was at least as popular as the Aragonese who had flung himself down from the roof on a rope at Edward's royal entry, and much more practical. His performance was unmistakably linked to the civic celebration of Mary's accession; attached to his scaffolding were huge streamers five yards long painted with the red cross and sword of the city's arms, and he was paid £16 13s by the aldermen for his pains.[5]

The pageantry of the royal entry was a festive diversion in Mary's solemn days in the Tower. As she learned the coronation ritual, rehearsed her oaths, movements and changes of clothing and regalia, she thought a great deal of the task she was to undertake. To solemnize her dedication to that task, two days before she left the Tower she called together all the members of her Council for an impromptu ceremony of her own devising. Kneeling before them, she spoke for some time about how she had come to the throne, and what she believed to be the duties of kings and queens. It was her earnest intention, she said, to carry out the task God had given her to his greater glory, and to the benefit of all her subjects. Her affairs and her person were in their keeping, she told her councilors, and she urged them to be faithful to the oaths they had sworn, to be loyal to their queen unto death. To her chancellor Mary made a special appeal. The administration of justice was in his hands, she told Gardiner, and on his conscience. Mary remained on her knees throughout, speaking reverently of the obligations that lay before them all. For a sovereign to humble herself before her office was an extraordinary thing, and the councilors were overwhelmed "by the queen's great goodness and integrity." They had never heard anything like it before, and they were "so deeply moved that not a single one refrained from tears."[6]

Sunday, October 1, was Mary's coronation day. In the morning she left the Tower to go by water to Westminster, where in a private chamber she put on the first of her sets of robes and waited with her ladies until she was summoned to the church. The cathedral had been cleansed and hung with tapestries, and the floor covered with fresh rushes. At its upper end was a wide platform, with stairs on two sides, one pair leading up from the floor of the sanctuary and the other leading down to the altar. In the center of this platform was another set of stairs, leading to a smaller platform bearing a "great royal chair"—Edward's throne—covered with damask gold and with the royal lions, turret and fleur-de-lis surmounting its back. The way from Westminster Hall to the high altar in the cathedral was carpeted with blue cloth, and the "stage royal," from the choir to the altar, was covered with cloth of gold.

At eleven o'clock Gardiner, bishop of Winchester and ten other bishops, along with the clergy of Mary's private chapel, met her in the Hall. The bishops were wearing their miters and the chaplains their copes of cloth of gold; these signs of the old ritual were augmented by the standing crosses, silver candlesticks, basins of holy water and censers their assistants carried. After they censed the queen and sprinkled her with holy water, they took her into the church, along with the same attendants who had accompanied her on her progress the day before. Mary walked behind Norfolk, Winchester and Arundel, who carried her crown, orb and scepter; she wore her Parliament robes of red velvet, and the Barons of the Cinque Ports held over her head the canopy of estate on four silver staves hung with silver bells. When she had been escorted to the throne, completing the first stage of the proceedings, she was conducted to each of the four corners of the large platform in turn, to be viewed by the people. Then the bishop of Winchester, who was standing at her side, called out in a loud voice:

"Sirs, here present is Mary, rightful and undoubted inheritrix by the laws of God and man to the crown and royal dignity of this realm of England, France, and Ireland, whereupon you shall understand that this day is appointed by all the Peers of this land for the consecration, inunction [sic], and coronation of the said most excellent Princess Mary; will you serve at this time, and give your wills and assent to the same consecration, inunction, and coronation?" In response to this elaborate formula "all the people shouted joyfully, Yea, yea," and "God save Queen Mary!"

At this point Mary made an offering at the altar, and then lay face down on a velvet cushion while prayers were said over her. After a sermon by the bishop of Chichester, "esteemed the floridest preacher" in the realm, Mary took her oaths upon the sacrament, and then lay prostrate again while the Veni Creator Spiritus was sung and more prayers recited. Then, accompanied by some of her ladies, she went behind a screen at the left of the altar to make her first change of clothing and to prepare for the holiest of the coronation procedures: the anointing with holy oil and chrism.

This most solemn of rituals marked the sovereign with the indelible stigma of majesty. Only priests and rulers were anointed with the holy oils, setting them apart from all others as designated bearers of divine authority among men. Because so much depended on her anointing Mary had taken special care to ensure the validity of the ritual. She feared that the oils to be found in England were tainted as a result of the ecclesiastical censures brought against the nation by the pope many years earlier, so she wrote to the bishop of Arras asking him to send her vials of the sacred oil and chrism from Flanders.[7] It was these Flemish unctions that Gardiner now poured over Mary's breast, shoulders, forehead and temples, after she reappeared in a purple velvet gown that left her shoulders bare.

Dressed again in her velvet robes after her anointing Mary received her spurs and sword, and was crowned successively with the crown of King Edward the Confessor, the imperial crown of the realm, and a crown made especially for her, a massive yet simply designed crown with two arches, a large fleur-de-lis and prominent crosses where the arches joined the border.[8] Of the jewels set in the crown nothing is known, but Edward's crown made only six years earlier was adorned with a very large diamond and thirteen smaller ones, ten rubies, one emerald, one sapphire and seventy pearls, and Mary's was in all likelihood more ornate. As each successive crown was set on her head, the trumpets blew a triumphant fanfare, and after the third crown was set in place the choir burst into the Te Deum. As they sang the other royal accouterments were brought for Mary to put on—the "wedding ring of England," said to have been given by the Confessor to the evangelist John disguised as an old man asking alms, the bracelets of gold and precious stones, the scepter, orb and regal of gold, and the royal sabatons, or slippers, fastened with ribbons of Venice gold.

Thus arrayed in her regalia, wearing her royal mantle and surcoat trimmed with "wombs of miniver," and a lace mantel of silk and gold, Mary was ready to receive the homage of her subjects. Gardiner swore the oath for all the bishops, kneeling and swearing fidelity, and then Norfolk made his oath. "I become your liege man of life and limb," he promised, "and of all earthly worship and faith, and all truly shall bear unto you to live and die with you against all manner of folk; so God help me, and all hallows." One by one they knelt before her, the earl of Arundel swearing for all the earls, Viscount Hereford for all those of his rank, and Lord Abergavenny for all lords, and as each man knelt he put his hands together in the old feudal gesture of homage, "in manner of lamenting," as the chronicler wrote, and then kissed the queen's cheek. As the oaths were being sworn Gardiner made the circuit of the large platform one last time, and announced the queen's "goodly large and ample pardon for all manner of offenses," clearing all prisons but the Tower of the majority of their habitual residents. Then mass was sung, and afterward Mary took off her regalia and put on a robe of purple velvet and, wearing her crown, walked back across the carpet of blue cloth into Westminster Hall to wait for the ceremonial dinner to begin.

It was nearly five o'clock when the coronation ended, and the long banqueting tables were set out in the Hall for the hundreds of celebrants who were to dine with the queen. She ate with the bishop of Durham on her left and the earl of Shrewsbury on her right, with Bishop Gardiner and Elizabeth and Anne of Cleves farther down the table. Four swords were held before her as she ate, and according to custom she "rested her feet on two of her ladies."[9] Throughout the dinner the earl of Derby, High Steward of England, and the duke of Norfolk, Earl Marshal, rode continually up and down the hall on horses trapped in cloth of gold, overseeing the banqueting and maintaining order. After the second course Mary's champion, Sir Edward Dymoke, rode into the hall flanked by pages carrying his spear and target. A herald who preceded him cried out his challenge:

"If there be any manner of man, of what estate, degree or condition soever he be, that will say and maintain that our Sovereign Lady, Queen Mary the First, this day here present, is not the rightful and undoubted inheritrix to the imperial crown of this realm of England, and that of right she ought not to be crowned Queen, I say he lieth like a false traitor, and that I am ready the same to maintain with him whilst I have breath in my body!"

With this dramatic announcement the challenger cast down his gauntlet. When no one took it up, the herald retrieved it and returned it to Dymoke, and the entire party moved on to repeat the ritual in another corner of the hall. When he had ridden to every table the champion returned to stand before the queen, who drank to him, and sent him the cup as his wage, and then he rode out again. Following another custom the officers of arms proclaimed Mary's style in Latin, French and English, calling for largesse, and after the dinner the Lord Mayor brought Mary "a goodly standing cup," from which she drank before returning it to him as a gift.

By this time the torches had been lit and the long day was ending, but

Mary found energy enough to talk with the ambassadors for a time before taking off her ceremonial robes for the trip back to the palace. And
once there, the "feasting and royal cheer" continued, with music and
dancing and the sound of royal laughter far into the night.

To the crowds that cheered Mary as she went to be crowned, tore up
the blue cloth she walked on and scrambled for the "waste-meat" set out
for them after the coronation banquet, there was only one thing lacking
to make Mary's triumph complete. She had won out over her enemies,
she had been gorgeously crowned, and she had received the homage of
every great and small lord in the kingdom, but she needed a husband.
During Jane's brief rule one of the few arguments raised in her favor was
that she was married, and a married queen was preferable to an unmarried one; on the continent it was reported that Guilford Dudley was
the new king of England. When news of Mary's accession arrived to correct this misapprehension foreign rulers and ambassadors assumed that
Mary would soon take a husband, and retreat into relative insignificance.
When the marquis of Brandenburg wrote congratulating Mary on her
coming to the throne he added as a matter of course sincere hopes "that
she would soon take to herself a worthy husband."[10]
Among her gentlewomen marriage was the primary and only subject
of conversation. It was as if Mary were a little girl again, surrounded by
women eager for her to marry and preoccupied with talk of gallantry and
romance. Then she had been a pretty child of seven, betrothed to her
cousin the emperor; now she was a handsome woman of thirty-seven, and
a queen, but the talk was very much the same. No one, it seemed, including Mary herself, seriously considered the possibility that she might
choose to remain unmarried, and reign alone.
And if there was no question that she ought to marry, in the minds of
most of her subjects there was no question who her husband ought to be.
Edward Courtenay, son of the executed marquis of Exeter and of Mary's
intimate friend Gertrude Blount, could claim the most exalted descent of
any Englishman living. (Courtenay's relatives Reginald and Geoffrey
Pole were of equally distinguished ancestry, but both were still in exile,
and Reginald was a churchman besides.) He was the great-grandson of
Edward IV, grandson of Edward's daughter Catherine. As such he had a
legitimate, if weak, claim to the throne as the only remaining Plantagenet
heir left in England—he was, in Renard's phrase, "the last sprig of the
white rose." Like Mary, Courtenay had been a victim of Henry VIII's
tyranny. At twelve he was imprisoned in the Tower with his father, and
when Exeter was killed he was not released but kept there to grow to
manhood within its confines. He had for company the grim rebels,
disgruntled aristocrats and doomed politicians who made up the curious

society of the Tower, and all that he knew of the world until his twenty-seventh year he learned from them. He was far from ignorant, however; he continued his education during his confinement and by the time Mary released him he had acquired the formal learning and gracious accomplishments of a courtier. He was well read in "letters and science," he knew the classics, and he could play several instruments well. More important, he had the refined features and elegant body of an aristocrat of the blood royal, and a "natural civility" Renard ascribed to his lineage.[11]

Unfortunately, Renard's assessment was premature. Within weeks of his release from the Tower Courtenay was proving to be an embarrassment. He had managed to acquire the intellectual attainments of a gentleman but none of the martial skills; he knew nothing of weapons, armor or riding, and it was said Mary had canceled a tournament planned to coincide with her coronation because she knew Courtenay would disgrace himself there. In fact the tournament, like the revels planned for the same festivities, had been canceled because of threats of disruption, but the preferred explanation was Courtenay's ineptitude. Noailles called him "as maladroit as can be believed, a young man who has never mounted a big horse."

His manners were as gauche as his horsemanship. "He is proud, poor, obstinate, inexperienced and vindictive in the extreme," Renard wrote when he had observed Courtenay for several months. He liked to give orders and to call attention to his own importance, and he attracted a following from among the most unprincipled of Mary's courtiers. There seemed to be no doubt in his mind that he would be the one to share Mary's throne, and it was noticed that those who were most eager to flatter him fell on one knee when they spoke to him, just as they did to Mary. He was obviously bidding for Mary's favor in every way he could think of. Here he relied heavily on his mother, who spent hours in the queen's company and slept in her bed at night. He took only Catholics into his service, and attempted to put himself on familiar terms with those closest to Mary. He insisted upon calling Susan Clarencieux "mother" and Bishop Gardiner "father," and little imagination was required to envision him calling Mary "wife."

With his airs, his callow posturing and his alarming popularity Courtenay quickly made himself a nuisance, but by mid-September he was proving to be a menace as well. When Geoffrey Pole came to the English court the would-be bridegroom swore he would avenge the deaths of his father and cousins by killing the man whose testimony had helped to convict them. Courtenay made a dramatic accusation of Pole, and to prevent him from carrying out his vow of vengeance Mary and her Council had to arrange for a special lodging for Pole, with guards inside and out to protect him.[12] Worse yet, in his indiscretion Courtenay was said to be conspiring with both Elizabeth and the French ambassador, and Renard feared that "Courtenay's friends, who include most of the nobility, were hatching some design that might later threaten the queen."[13]

Despite his obvious unsuitability as a husband for Mary and an officer in the government a large and influential group in the Council believed the queen should marry him, and defended his merits vociferously at every opportunity. Chief among Courtenay's supporters was the chancellor himself, who had spent a number of years as his fellow prisoner in the Tower. Gardiner could not imagine Mary betrothed to a foreign prince; among the English nobles only Courtenay was worthy of her in rank. Most of Mary's most loyal household officers—Rochester, Walgrave, Englefield, Derby and the Great Chamberlain John de Vere—concurred, as did the majority of Mary's subjects. Some of them began to speculate that Mary had secretly been married to "a certain prisoner in the Tower" for years; that prisoner could only be Courtenay.[14] Even the Emperor Charles appeared to favor a match between Mary and Courtenay, provided another plan closer to his heart and dynastic interests fell through.[15]

The emperor's apparent approval was the result of diplomatic intelligence circulated by Noailles, who was informed, quite wrongly as it turned out, that Mary was passionately in love with Courtenay and would not consider marrying any other man. Noailles' misjudgment seemed to be confirmed when Mary created Courtenay earl of Devonshire early in September, and gave him a diamond worth sixteen thousand crowns from among her father's heirlooms. These tokens of favor made Charles hesitate to go ahead with the alliance he had in mind for Mary. If she decided to marry Courtenay, he wrote to Renard, "nothing would stop her, if she is like other women," and to urge her to do otherwise would only win her enduring resentment.[16] Renard was cautious, but he soon found it was unnecessary. Mary told him she had no wish to marry Courtenay or any other Englishman. She had only spoken to Courtenay once—on the day she pardoned him—and in fact she considered him a serious political liability. She had already decided against allowing him to marry within England, and her suggestion that he go abroad was being ignored. She could only hope that his high birth and the further lands and titles she planned to give him would make him an attractive match for a foreign heiress, and soon.

For whatever might become of Courtenay, Mary's affections were turning in an altogether different direction—toward the man she felt sure the emperor would choose for her, the heir to the richest empire in Europe: Prince Philip of Spain.

XXXIII

Maddame dangloyse me tell you verye true
Me be verye muche Enamored wythe youe
Me love you muche bettro than I cane well saye
Me teache you parlere the fyne spaniolaye.

As the year 1553 drew to a close the Emperor Charles V looked out over the vast reaches of his land with a jaundiced eye. He was master of most of Europe and much of the New World. His dominions stretched from Spain through Italy, where he was duke of Milan and king of Naples and Sicily, up across the Franche-Comté to the Low Countries, the wealthiest region in the Christian world, and eastward through the German-speaking lands of the Holy Roman Empire. He ruled the Cape Verde Islands and the Canaries, the North African territories of Tunis, Oran and Melilla; on the other side of the world the Philippines were his. Treasure ships brought him gold and silver from the mines and ruined empires of Mexico and Peru in seemingly limitless supply, and his viceroys in the Americas ruled millions of acres of bountiful, trackless wilderness. His soldiers were the most fearsome fighters in Europe, while his Spanish and Flemish ships were more numerous and more powerful than the navies of France and England combined. He had governed these regions and marshaled these forces for nearly thirty-five years with a cautious, unspectacular decisiveness amounting to genius, and he was now a time-honored fixture in European politics. It was impossible for the kings and diplomats who had come to maturity during his long reign to imagine life without him.

Yet Charles was only too aware of how much of the world he ruled, and for how many years he had kept up the wearisome task of ruling it. In recent years his body had begun to fail him, and he would never again ride before his soldiers in golden armor on his bay Spanish jennet, javelin in hand, looking to his well-read commanders like Caesar before he crossed the Rubicon. He had not lost the inscrutability that had always amazed emissaries sent to his court, however. In 1552 the English ambassador Morison noted that neither the emperor's features nor his complexion showed the slightest emotion. "There is in him almost nothing that speaks beside his tongue," Morison wrote ruefully, adding that Charles seemed to epitomize the biblical proverb "Heaven is high; the earth is deep; a king's heart is unsearchable." But though he still played the game of diplomacy well Charles was losing ground to recurrent fevers and catarrh that affected his speech, sometimes reducing him to silence for days at a time or forcing him to speak so softly he could not be heard by others in the room. Fever blisters covered his protruding lower lip, and he had to chew herbs in order to keep enough moisture in his mouth to talk.[1] The gout that had crippled the emperor's legs for years had now spread throughout his body, so that every nerve and joint ached painfully. When even the back of his neck became affected his doctors pronounced him to be in the final stages of the disease, and did not attempt to treat him further. Hemorrhoids tormented him incessantly, swelling to such a point that he could not turn in his chair without "great pain and tears."

In the intervals between attacks of illness the emperor retired to the solitude of an inner chamber, where he passed the time designing fortresses or joking with his Polonian dwarf. He preferred the company of his grooms to that of his courtiers, and his only productive activity appeared to be the ceaseless setting and winding of his hundreds of clocks. "His single care and occupation, day and night," one of Charles' gentlemen wrote to his son Philip, "is to set his clocks and keep them going together; he had many, and they are his chief thought." The emperor invented a new kind of clock, meant to be set in a window frame, and he was as fascinated by the inner workings of his timepieces as he was by their appearance and accuracy. He was an insomniac, and in the long night hours he liked to call all his servants into a torchlit workroom and set them to helping him take his clocks apart and put them together again.[2]

What worried the emperor's advisers most, though, was that he seemed to be slipping into a fatal melancholy like that which had afflicted his mother Joanna the Mad. By 1553 his "troubles of the spirit" had become so grave they had begun to erode his "kindness of manner and usual affability." He brooded for hours, then began to "weep like a child." No one dared to approach him in these states, and the work of government piled up unattended. Ambassadors were kept waiting a month or more before they were granted an audience, and some simply lost patience and went home, muttering that the emperor must either be dead or "no longer fit to govern."[3]

It was at these times that Charles longed to pass on his enormous task to his son. He saw no reason for the inevitable transfer of power to be delayed until his death; he could teach his son all he needed to know and then, when he was sure Philip had the confidence to govern and the loyalty of his subjects, arrange an orderly abdication. The only flaw in this plan—and it was one which sent the emperor into a "notable pensiveness" —was that Philip of Spain was hated by nearly every population under imperial rule.

Prince Philip, son of Charles V and Isabella of Portugal, was a somber, stuffy and rather dull young man of twenty-six whose upbringing had left him little scope for orginality or independence. He was slight in build, and quite short, but he carried himself with dignity; it was in fact his grave, reserved Spanish dignity that was so often mistaken for hauteur by the non-Spaniards among his future subjects. His receding hairline made him appear a little taller and older than he really was, but his face had an appealing, almost childlike look of pathos about it. The large, mild eyes gazing out from his portraits reflect superiority and boredom, but also a faint wistfulness; the dark circles under them probably came from the combined effects of dissipation and dyspepsia, but they gave a noble sadness to his expression. He looked in fact as if he wished he were somewhere else, and though he performed the ceremonial courtesies of his rank with precision and exactness, he bore them like a hereditary affliction for which he would have liked to find a cure.

Philip did his best to enjoy the active pursuits of a young nobleman. He hunted a little, and held his own in the jousts. At one tournament he kept his seat tilting against the Flemish captain Count Mansfeldt, a man much older than he and with vast experience in the wars, and won the prize of the "ladies' lance," a brilliant ruby. Another time an opponent's lance struck his helm with such force that he was unconscious for some hours, but the accident did no lasting harm. The French said Philip was such a poor jouster he could barely find his antagonist, much less hit him, but their reports were too biased to be trusted. In all likelihood Philip jousted like he did everything else: correctly, but without style, feeling or commitment. By the time he reached the age of twenty-six the prince had begun to curtail his exercise for the sake of his health. His constitution was delicate, and his digestion poor; he ate little besides meat, believing that fish, fruit and other foods contained evil humors. He needed plenty of sleep, and his "domestic entertainments" were of the most subdued kind. "His nature," the Venetian ambassador Suriano wrote of Philip, "is more inclined to tranquillity than to exercise, more suited to repose than to work."[4]

When Charles V brought his son from Spain to Flanders five years earlier he soon found the young man's presence a distinct liability. He had hoped to persuade the German Electors to choose Philip as the next emperor, but they took an instant dislike to the prince. The longer he stayed in Flanders the more the Flemish grew to hate his aloof manner and uncongenial temperament. Finally, deeply disappointed, Charles ordered his son to return to Spain, knowing he was only postponing an inevitable clash between Philip and his future subjects. When Mary came to the throne in England, however, the emperor immediately saw how he might make use of his son in an unforeseen role. As Mary's husband and Charles' heir Philip would rule both England and the Low Countries, a prospect offering great commercial and trade advantages offsetting his distasteful personality. As soon as he heard of Mary's victory over Northumberland the emperor laid his plans to unite the longsuffering woman who called him "the father of her soul and of her body" with his son.[5]

At his very first interview with Mary Renard broached the subject of marriage. He conveyed Charles' feeling that the "great part of the labor of government could with difficulty be undertaken by a woman, and was not within woman's province." Mary would need "assistance, protection and comfort" in her new role; only a husband could provide this kind of support. For these reasons Mary ought to decide on a suitable bridegroom as soon as possible, relying on Charles, of course, to advise her. Nothing was said about Philip, but the suggestion was already in the air. As Edward lay dying the papal legate in Brussels wrote to his counterpart in Paris that the emperor had made up his mind to marry Philip to Mary as soon as she became queen.[6]

Mary reacted to the idea of marriage by saying that it had never crossed her mind before she became queen—not a very accurate statement, as she had been involved in marriage negotiations of one sort or another for most of her life. She readily admitted that her "public position" now required that she be married, and declared herself ready to follow the emperor's advice in choosing a husband. She was confident, she added tactfully, that he would remember that she was a mature woman of thirty-seven and not a young girl, and that he would not expect her to make up her mind before she had seen the man and heard him speak.[7]

Though Mary reiterated at this meeting that marriage was "against her private inclination," and that she would have preferred to live and die a virgin, the next time she saw Renard she showed delight at the prospect of becoming a bride. "I assure you," he wrote to Charles V's prime minister Granvelle, "that when I mentioned marriage she began to laugh, not once but several times, giving me a look that plainly said how agreeable the subject was to her." Renard now saw reason to hope that, if the emperor were to propose a match with Philip, it might prove "the most welcome news that could be given to her."

The proposal could not wait much longer, for rival suitors were already making their bids for Mary's hand. Emmanuel Philibert, duke of Savoy, had been looked on as an eligible candidate for years. A Hapsburg ally, he was an exile from his duchy and would gladly live in England. Paget supported the duke's suit, but no other councilor did, and he lacked an eloquent advocate to officially plead his cause. The Archduke Ferdinand, on the other hand, had several. The archduke was a nephew of the emperor, the second son of his brother Ferdinand, king of the Romans, and was very popular in the Low Countries. Within weeks of Mary's accession the king of the Romans sent his great chamberlain to England to propose marriage on behalf of the archduke. Anne of Cleves also came to court to speak on his behalf, but the queen was waiting for the emperor to tell her his choice and hoping, no doubt, that it would be Philip.

By the beginning of September Mary was trying harder than ever to let Charles know, without actually saying it, that she wanted to marry his son. Her professions of daughterly loyalty and gratitude to the emperor were becoming more and more extravagant. She told Renard that she saw his master as her true father, and was so devoted to him that even if Henry VIII were still alive she would obey Charles in choosing her future husband.[8] What lay behind both Mary and Charles' tactics was the complication of the Portuguese infanta. It was well known that the emperor had been trying to arrange a marriage between Philip and the king of Portugal's sister for some time, though no one at the English court knew just how deeply committed Philip was. Mary pretended to believe that the two were already married, receiving from Renard the hoped-for assurance that nothing had been concluded. Yet Charles was determined to hold both options open for as long as possible, realizing that as soon as it was known that he favored the English match the Portuguese negotiations would be broken off immediately. By September this problem had resolved itself. Philip was only slightly less unpopular in Portugal than in Flanders, and the Portuguese diplomats were doing everything they could to delay the drawing up of a final contract. Finally the news came that the infanta's dowry was to be only a little over 300,000 ducats—far less than a prince of Philip's rank could have commanded. The insult rankled, and when the emperor wrote to Philip informing him that he meant to make him the husband of the queen of England the prince found the directive opportune.

"If you wish to arrange the [English] match for me, you know that I am so obedient a son that I have no will other than yours, especially in a matter of such high import," Philip wrote dutifully. The news "arrived at just the right moment," he went on, "for I had decided to break off the Portuguese business."[9]

On October 10 Renard delivered a formal proposal from the emperor. It began with a courtly lie. The ambassador was ordered to say first that Charles would be deeply honored to marry Mary himself, if only his age and health would permit it—a sentimental reference to their betrothal in Mary's childhood. As he was an old and sick man, however, he was obliged to offer his son instead. Mary was happy and relieved to hear at last the proposal she had been waiting for, and thanked her cousin profusely through Renard, insisting that the match was "greater than she deserved." But her joy was mixed with anxiety. Despite her deep personal satisfaction at the prospect of marrying the emperor's son, two things worried her. One was the reaction of her subjects to the idea of a Spanish consort. Her first words to Renard after expressing her gratitude were "that she did not know how the people of England would take it." To satisfy them her husband would have to come and live with her, she said, and she did not see how Philip could do this when he came into his inheritance after the emperor's death. It was obviously important to her to "weigh the people's affections" before deciding to accept the proposal, and though she did not say it outright, both Mary and the ambassador had on their minds the extreme antipathy of the English to all foreigners, especially Spaniards.

Mary's other worries were much more problematic. She had never been in love, and had only an outsider's knowledge of sex. Mary was not prudish, but she was inexperienced, and almost certainly insecure about how attractive she would be to Philip. She joked to Renard about her age, saying that most of the suitors for her hand were so young she was old enough to be their mother, but behind her humor was the fear that a handsome twenty-six-year-old prince might not find her to his taste. If Philip "were disposed to be amorous," she told Renard, "such was not her desire," both because of her age and because "she had never harbored thoughts of love." Her mother had been six years older than her father, and the age difference, along with the related sorrow of Katherine's inability to bear a son, had helped to push their marriage toward its tragic end. Mary was eleven years older than Philip, and nearing the threshold of middle age; the shadow of her mother's great unhappiness surely hung over her as she considered marrying a younger man.

Deeper memories haunted her as well, memories of her mother's loving, patient instruction in piety and chastity, and of the dangers lying in wait for all young girls who give themselves up to voluptuous pleasures. She remembered Vives' warnings about how the darts of the devil are always flying on every side, and how a woman can only preserve herself by keeping her mind on Christ. Marriage was sanctioned by the Bible, but sex was something her father had indulged in; she knew that one went with the other, yet all that she had been taught and much that she had lived through forced her to experience them as distinct.

Among her recollections was a sordid memory of her father and Francis Bryan testing her purity at a court masque. Henry had been told that his daughter "knew no foul or unclean speeches"—something he found hard to believe given the good-natured ribaldry of his courtiers. He told Francis to go up to Mary and find out, probably either by paying her a vulgar compliment or, conceivably, attempting a mock-serious seduction, whether or not the rumor of her innocence was true. Her behavior convinced Bryan of her profound modesty, but the sight of her father and his notorious gentleman amusing themselves over her lack of sophistication stayed indelibly in Mary's memory. Many years later she told the story to Dormer, whose biographer recorded it in hopes of building a saintly image of Mary.

Closely linked to Mary's uncertainties about sex were doubts about how her obedience to her husband might conflict with her responsibility to her people. She would wholly love and obey the man she married, Mary told Renard, "following the divine commandment," and would not act in any way against his will, but if he tried to interfere in the government of the kingdom she would have to prevent it at all costs. Even such minor interference as appointing foreigners to office she would have to oppose, for the people would not tolerate it.

Renard gave Mary no assurances on this crucial and delicate issue, though he saw clearly enough that what lay behind it was the fact that Mary knew virtually nothing about Philip's character and personality beyond the inflated flattery of the imperial ambassadors and the alarming slanders of his numerous detractors. And the slanders were increasing daily. As the rumor of Mary's imminent betrothal to Philip spread, unsettling revelations about his precarious authority, personal repugnance and inclination to vice spread with them. It was said that because of Philip's "sinister and taciturn disposition" he would almost certainly lose Flanders once he tried to rule there, and Mary was worried by new reports that his cousin the archduke was better liked than the prince not only in the Low Countries but even in his native Spain.

Gossip about Philip's extravagant sex life—which may have prompted Mary's ladylike reference to his amorous inclinations—flourished at the English court. Paget, who after dropping Emmanuel Philibert became a staunch supporter of the Spanish marriage, was concerned by the fact that "in order to estrange the queen, people have told her that his highness is very voluptuous and has bastard sons and daughters."[10] And whatever distressing speculations these reports may have led to were hardly dispelled by the emperor's virtual admission that there was some truth in what was being said. "We admit there may be some youthfulness in our son," he wrote, "though it is far from being as grave a matter as . . . some people have sought to make out."[11]

Without meeting Philip herself Mary could not reconcile the unsettling contradictions in his public image, and shortly after Renard conveyed the official marriage proposal she asked him whether there was any chance the prince might come to England before she committed herself once and for all to becoming his wife. She had heard he was coming to Flanders before long; could he stop in England on his way? Renard hedged, saying he didn't know whether it would be possible—or proper —for so important a prince to make a detour of that kind, but to lessen her concern somewhat he told her a comforting lie. Philip, he said, had not waited for the emperor to suggest the marriage but, having heard of Mary's "great virtues," became eager to woo her on his own. Mary was flattered but not satisfied. Taking Renard by the hand she urged him to tell her whether all the praiseworthy things he had said about the prince up to now were true—"whether he was indeed of even temper, of balanced judgment and well conditioned." Renard assumed his most effective expression of candor. If his word were enough, he swore, he would back with his oath the assertion that Philip "had qualities as virtuous as any prince in this world." Again Mary begged him not to lie to her, or to speak as a servant or subject, but to tell her the full truth as he knew it. He begged her in return to take "his honor and his life" as hostages for the utter honesty of his words. Apparently he was convincing enough for, as he wrote to the emperor, Mary then "pressed his hand and said 'that is well,'" and went on to discuss other matters.[12]

While he was reassuring Mary Renard was equally busy with the task of wooing the Council. With Paget as his ally, he visited those Council members he thought he could win over most easily, carrying personal letters from Charles V. (The letters were supplied to him by the dozen from the imperial chancery in Brussels, with the salutations left blank; Renard's secretary wrote in each councilor's name as the ambassador made up his mind whom to approach.) Arundel and Petre came around to the imperial point of view fairly quickly, and Rochester, both humbled and impressed by his own personal letter from the emperor himself, was persuaded to abandon Courtenay and throw his weight on the side of Philip. All the leading councilors were given gold chains and other costly gifts. Renard distributed thousands of Spanish *escudos* as well, finding that coins were even more welcome to the English than jewelry or other valuables. In his eagerness to bring off the diplomatic coup of betrothing Mary to Philip, Renard did not scruple to make political promises he had no authority to keep. Bribing the lords with power as well as with money, he told them that, if Mary chose to marry Philip, four of them would be put in charge of the government any time she left the country—a bald inducement that he found very effective. "The English are so grasping," he wrote to the emperor, "that if one cares to try them with presents and promises one may do what one likes with them by very simple means."[13]

Winning over the Council was in the end to prove more difficult than Renard suspected, but Mary had made up her mind once and for all by the end of October, strengthened in her resolve by two of her chamberers, Jane Russell and Mistress Shirley, and by Susan Clarencieux, who was present every time the queen spoke with Renard and whose aid he valued. Mary also had the encouragement of the wives of at least three of the councilors—the duchess of Norfolk, the countess of Arundel and Lady Rochester—who favored the Spanish match over any other and who Noailles judged "more to be feared than their husbands under these circumstances." Even so Mary did not arrive at her decision easily. She spent hours deep in thought, and sometimes in tears; she stayed up until midnight writing to Renard, Paget and others about their progress with her councilors; and, of course, she prayed.

On October 27 and 28 the court was informed that the queen was ill. No one saw her but her women, and when on the evening of Sunday the twenty-ninth she called Renard into her presence he half expected her to receive him in bed. Instead he found her up and dressed, if weary, in a room filled up with an altar.[14] The altar was furnished in every detail, and this plus the affectionate greeting and shining face of Susan Clarencieux told him that he had been summoned to share in a solemn event.

Mary told Renard she had not slept for the past two days, but had spent the time in continual weeping and prayer, asking God to inspire her with the right decision about her marriage. Invoking the sacrament as her "protector, guide and counselor," she trusted it to show her the way. Then she knelt, and Renard and Clarencieux joined her in repeating the Veni Creator Spiritus. When they had finished she made her announcement. God, "who had performed so many miracles in her favor," had now performed one more. He had inspired her to make an unbreakable vow in the presence of the sacrament: she promised to marry Philip and to love him perfectly, "and her mind, once made up, would never change."

XXXIV

 Now all shaven crowns to the standard.
Make room! pull down for the Spaniard!

When word spread that the queen meant to marry the prince of Spain the news unleashed a flood of outrage. Londoners claimed to know "Jack Spaniard" well, and they did not like him. They had observed his "pomping pride," his "lusty liveries," his pretended courtesy that hid villainy and vice. All Spaniards were thieves, they said, who after they robbed a man liked to "tread his head in the dust." Every one of them, even the vilest beggar, demanded to be called a lord—*señor* in their tongue—and most of them had titles of honor besides. Their excesses with women were well known, and if Philip married Mary he would soon tire of her and seek his pleasure elsewhere, caring about as much for her as for an old pair of shoes.

Protestants in the capital swore "they would rather die than suffer Spaniards to rule this country," and Catholics liked the prospect no better. One English traveler who had visited the Spanish court sent back to England a vivid description of what Mary's palace would be like once Philip and his Spaniards were turned loose in it. The queen's orderly staff of officials and underlings would be swept away and in its place the Spaniards would bring cobblers, woodmongers, pointers, pinners and peddlers, and "all kinds of lousy loiterers," each with his open bottle tied around his neck. These drunken wretches would line the courtyards and galleries of the palace, swaying over their work, while the Spanish guardsmen—"bawdy, burly beasts"—left the halls and gates of the palace open to "beggars, slaves and all kinds of wretches." In no time at all bread and beer would be sold in the stately reception rooms, while the courtyard would be full of oxen, cows, "hoggish old swine," sheep, goats, cats, dogs, geese, ducks, cocks and hens, all "rubbing, rooting, digging, delving and donging" before Mary's chamber window.

If some found the idea of Spaniards at court ludicrous, many found it terrifying. Spanish rule was known to be harsh, Spanish governors cruel. Visions of mail-clad armies marching through the English countryside mowing down English yeomen spread panic throughout the southwest. At Plymouth, where commoners and gentry alike had hoped Mary would choose Courtenay, the mayor and aldermen sent a secret message through Noailles to the French king, asking him to take the town under his protection against the time the prince of Spain might try to land there. The men of Plymouth were resolved not to receive him or to obey his commands, they said, and the gentlemen of the region were prepared to back the townspeople in their resistance.[1]

To the French the possibility of a Hapsburg ruler in England was alarming in the extreme. When Henri II heard rumors of the impending betrothal his "countenance was sad, his words few, and his dislike of the match marvellously great."[2] He held a long conversation with the English ambassador, Nicholas Wotton, pointing out that "a husband may do much with his wife," and that it would be very hard for Mary, as for any woman, "to refuse her husband anything that he shall earnestly require of her."[3] Philip would certainly ask Mary to lend him her ships and fighting men to aid his father in his wars against the French, and before long Philip would be ruling England instead of Mary.

Wotton tried in vain to combat these fears, while in England Noailles attempted to convince Mary herself of the hidden dangers of marrying Philip. He too raised the specter of husbandly tyranny, but she assured him that God would not let her forget the promise she had made to her first husband, England, on her coronation day. Mary repeated this argument often in the last months of 1553, looking down at the ring she had worn ever since her coronation and referring to the pre-eminence of her "first husband." When other persuasions failed the French resorted to theological objections. Philip and Mary were close relatives—Philip referred to Mary as his "aunt" for want of a better term to describe his father's cousin—and as such their marriage was forbidden under church law. Marriages between persons related by blood were subject to the "impediment of public honesty," the accusation that they offended common decency, and their validity could be contested in court. While English courts did not uphold suits of this kind many foreign courts did, and even if no one questioned Mary's marriage to Philip directly, their children might later be prevented from inheriting their lands on the continent on the grounds that the union between their parents was invalid.

To the English who opposed the marriage these legal complications were part of a larger concern. They perceived the queen's marriage to be not unlike the marriage of any other gentlewoman; they assumed, without thinking clearly about it, that England would in some sense be part of Mary's dowry, and as such would become her husband's property when she married. Thus Mary's husband would obtain a vague but ineradicable sovereignty over the country whether or not he actually became king, and Mary proposed to hand over this sovereignty to the heir of the Hapsburg empire. The dilemma of a woman ruler in a society where men controlled property was becoming clear: an unmarried queen was unthinkable, yet a married queen invited fresh political dangers. That Mary might, like her grandmother Isabella, retain her autonomy within her marriage was something none of her subjects thought possible.

Yet she was clearly setting her distinctive stamp on the court and government. Not since the death of Henry VIII had the ruler's personality, taste and style so dominated court life. Mary put herself to the fore much as her father had, consciously keeping herself the center of attention by the magnificence of her dress and the dignity of her manner. Like Henry she adorned herself with innumerable jewels, setting all who saw her to speculating on their worth and rarity. She was careful to promote her symbolic image as well. One of the first things she did after becoming queen was to have a large portrait of herself painted, and the French ambassador wrote to his queen that the greatest compliment she could pay Mary would be to ask her for her portrait.[4] Shortly after her coronation Mary issued her first coins. They too bore her effigy, and on the reverse the legend "*Veritas temporis filia*"—"Truth the daughter of time." The humanist motto was a metaphor of vindication, a succinct assertion of Mary's belief that, after the long night of Protestantism and injustice her reign would restore justice and the true religion.

Mary's courtiers echoed her tastes in dress, food and entertainment. Clothing at Edward's court had been simple and subdued; Mary's ladies and gentlewomen wore rich velvets and damasks in bright colors, set off with trimmings and laces and complemented by jewels. Soon after they arrived in England the imperial ambassadors sent word to Flanders that Mary was fond of wild boar meat, and before long hunters were riding regularly through the fields along the Flemish coast, tracking wild boar to send to England. The hunting was best in the French and imperial territories, and when Mary commanded her captain at Guines, Lord Grey, to supplement the regent's gift of boar meat with some of his own, he nearly caused an international incident by leading his men over the farms of the French pale in pursuit of the queen's favorite game. The French peasants spoiled the hunt and killed the Englishmen's hounds, whereupon the English rounded up the countrymen and cut off a piece of their ringleader's ear. The incident was reported to the French commander at

Ardres, whose complaint led to an airing of pent-up grievances on both sides of the border. The quarrel was settled, though, in time for Lord Grey to send the queen a great baked boar before the end of the year.[5]

Mary celebrated her first Christmas as queen by ordering the staging of the interlude originally written for her coronation. The action of the play has not survived, but a list of the characters and costumes suggests that it portrayed the suffering of Mankind (in purple satin) at the hands of Deceit, Self-love, Scarcity, Sickness, Feebleness and Deformity (in red, green and ash-colored satin). With the involvement of good and bad angels, Reason, Verity and Plenty (in purple satin) triumphed, to the benefit of Mankind, and a black damasked Epilogue closed out the performance. A more explicitly political play was John Heywood's *Respublica*, performed in London at the same season. *Respublica* described in allegorical form the misgovernment of Somerset and Dudley and the restoration of governmental virtue under Mary. The members of Edward's Council—Oppression, Insolence, Avarice and Adulation—wronged, tormented and robbed the country mercilessly, until People, "with a wide throat," roared out against them. With the arrival of "the general Verity, Old time's daughter"—Mary—the republic was saved and the Vices overthrown, and People rejoiced that he could once again buy himself a new coat and clink a few coins in his purse.[6]

With playwrights saluting her as the savior of her people, courtiers flattering her and diplomats filling their dispatches with news of her government and her marriage plans Mary was at home with her office by the end of 1553. Her public serenity was more apparent than real, but her private joy at the forthcoming marriage grew greater with each piece of news Renard brought her. By mid-November she was declaring that Renard "had made her fall in love with his Highness," adding jokingly that "his Highness might not be obliged to him for it, though she would do her best to please him in every way."[7]

When a full-size portrait of Prince Philip arrived a few weeks later she became even more enamored of him. It was a Titian portrait, painted some three years earlier, and in it Philip wore a blue coat trimmed in white wolfskin. It was a good if flattering likeness, and Mary was no doubt relieved to see that the man represented to her as uncommonly handsome had, at least, shapely limbs and regular features. Everyone who had lived at the court of Henry VIII remembered the king's greatest mistake—Anne of Cleves—and knew the dangers of misleading portraiture. The regent, who sent Mary the portrait, told her the likeness was not exact, but made it clear that the prince was even better looking than he had been when he posed for Titian, with a more manly body and a fuller beard.[8]

At this time too Granvelle sent Antonio Moro to England to paint

Mary's portrait, but she had little time to spare for sitting idle while he sketched. Matters of diplomacy and administration, large and small, pressed in upon her with greater urgency every month. The French king asked her to mediate his dispute with the emperor. Foreign merchants asked her for licenses to avoid paying customs. Courtiers petitioned for offices, pensions and other favors. A decision had to be made about the title "Supreme Head of the church," a relic of the two preceding reigns that was part of the royal style but that Mary refused to adopt because it denied papal authority. After consulting with Renard, her councilors and, by letter, with Cardinal Pole, who told her the phrase "misbecame her sex," Mary got around the problem by putting "et cetera" in place of the actual words of the style.

Criminals of uncommon boldness and notoriety had to be sought out and brought to justice. Thieves robbed Lady Knevet of her plate in the fall of 1553, and because it was assumed they had taken it to Paris to sell, it was up to Mary and the Council to try to find them. The men's identities were known, and the English ambassador in France, Wotton, sent one of his servants to Paris to ask the French goldsmiths for help in tracking them down. The servant made the rounds of the city, looking "everywhere Englishmen commonly resort there," but without success.[9] Crimes along the Scots border took up more of the Council's time. On the pretext of fishing in the Tweed, the Scots were grouping under the walls of Norham Castle at night, to the danger of the garrison; the ancient fishing boundaries had to be enforced. The Scots complained that the English were stealing their cattle; the English retorted that the beasts were taken on the English side of the border, and their owners could only get them back on payment of a fine, and the Council concurred. A "lewd Englishman" provoked a quarrel with a Scot, and the Scots claimed it led to murder; the Council believed the report was exaggerated, but in any case the Scots were guilty of so many murders of Englishmen they could not possibly recite them all.[10]

These and similar matters—grievances of merchants, complaints of piracy and border encroachments—made up only a small part of the day to day work of the queen and her Council. It took time for the lax administrative practices of the preceding reign to be corrected. As late as January of 1554 Mary's clerks were still occasionally sending out official documents sealed with King Edward's seal instead of the queen's, leading to delays and added work for the chancery.[11] The most serious issue faced by Mary's government, however, was a severe financial crisis. The queen admitted to Renard in November that there was no money in the country, and that Dudley's rule had left the treasury £700,000 in debt. Her agent Thomas Gresham was hard at work in Antwerp, trying to raise loans, but here too the dead weight of the previous reign proved to be a handicap. Gresham had to straighten out the dishonest dealings of his predecessor Christopher Dawntesey while competing with the agents of Charles V and those of the great towns for what little money the bankers had to loan. Once he did negotiate a loan he was faced with the problem of conveying the money safely to England, and finally decided to pack the coins inside suits of armor—a method he had used before with success.

Mary was not unique in her financial difficulties, of course. Late in 1553 the French king was trying desperately to borrow all the money he could, and was taking his nobles' plate to melt down for coins. The emperor too was borrowing enormous sums from the Flemish bankers, and the regent had had to take a loan of two million florins in 1552. But in the empire finance was a vast drama in which the imperial treasury was repeatedly saved from bankruptcy by the timely arrival of ships heavy with the plundered riches of the New World. As Mary's agent Gresham was toiling to squeeze sixty thousand florins from the reluctant Antwerp banker Jaspar Schetz, Charles V's financial clerks were weighing out newly arrived treasure from the Americas worth five million ducats in gold.[12]

However serious England's financial problems might be, the men who came to Mary's first Parliament in October and November were preoccupied with the dismaying probability of the queen's marriage to a powerful foreigner. They thought in terms of the legal and political hazards of the match, and of the impossibility of binding either party to fulfill their contractual agreements. "In case the bonds should be broken between the husband and wife," one member asked, "each of them being Princes in their own country, who shall sue the bonds?"[13] There was no natural arbiter for marital quarrels when the spouses were both sovereigns in their own right, and if Philip would need no defender in such quarrels, Mary almost certainly would. On November 16 a delegation from the Commons, led by Speaker Pollard and accompanied by some dozen or more of the councilors, met with the queen in an effort to dissuade her from marrying Philip. The delegation was superfluous, as Mary had already given her solemn oath to go ahead with the marriage and most of the Council members had been won over to supporting it. But the Commons knew nothing of this, and the Speaker had taken pains preparing an eloquent discourse for the occasion.

His speech was very solemn and very long, "full of art and rhetoric and illustrated by historical examples." He told Mary how it would displease the people to have a foreigner as the queen's consort, and how the foreigners in his retinue would make themselves hateful and "lord it over the English." If Mary died childless her husband would lose no time in carrying money, artillery, and everything else of value back to his own country. He might decide to take her out of the country too, "out of husbandly tyranny," and if she left him a widower with young children he would probably try to usurp the throne for himself.

Mary listened to this outpouring for a time, but the longer it went on the more exasperated she became. Pollard had unfortunately forgotten his notes, and his extemporaneous ramblings were, she later told Renard, "so confused, so long-winded and prolific of irrelevant arguments" that she found them irritating and offensive. As he spoke Mary was formulating a point-by-point reply, for she had decided to depart from the customary practice of allowing the chancellor to answer on behalf of the sovereign. When Pollard finally finished she rose to address the assembly.

She thanked them dryly for advising her to marry, but as for the rest of the advice "she found it very strange." It was hardly traditional for Parliament to recommend to the ruler whom she should marry, nor was it "suitable or respectful." Mary tossed off her arguments with skill, her words judicious but full of anger and occasional sarcasm. History showed that even when the ruler was a minor Parliament had never interfered with the choice of a consort. All the nobles present could vouch for the fact that the behavior of the Commons was unprecedented and thoroughly inappropriate. Furthermore, if she were forced to marry a man who did not please her she would die within three months, leaving the kingdom worse off than ever and defeating the prime purpose of the marriage—namely the birth of an heir. With this direct and telling threat she closed her rebuttal, assuring the Speaker and his colleagues that she had the good of the kingdom as much in mind as they did, and that in the question of her marriage, as in all her other affairs, she would be guided by the inspiration of God.

The extraordinary sight of the queen answering the Speaker in person made almost as great an impression on her audience as the force of her logic. The nobles present backed her in this, and "said she was right," while Arundel afterward ridiculed Gardiner, saying that "he had lost his post of Chancellor that day, for the Queen had usurped it," and the other councilors laughed heartily at his expense. Mary had in fact become contemptuous of what she perceived as Gardiner's equivocation. It had not taken her long to understand his tricks, she told Renard. One day he would assure her, when it suited his purpose, that the people would obey her, while the next day, "speaking on a matter that touched him personally," he would try to frighten her with the prospect of rebellion.[14] She was beginning to understand why the Protestants called her chancellor "Doctor Doubleface," and was finding that there was more to the accusation than Gardiner's embarrassing change of views on the question of Henry VIII's marriage to Katherine.

Mary suspected Gardiner, in fact, of prompting the Speaker to address her on the subject of her marriage, and of supplying him with his arguments. Several days after her meeting with Pollard and the Commons she confronted the chancellor and accused him of intrigue with the Speaker. She wanted him to understand, once and for all, that no matter what means he used to persuade her otherwise she would never marry Courtenay. The Speaker's "disrespectful words" had nearly made her angry, she said, and she did not intend to listen to any more advice about what husband to choose.

The chancellor broke down completely. He confessed with tears that he had spoken with Pollard and coached him in his speech, and that it was true he had always been fond of Courtenay ever since their imprisonment together. Mary asked Gardiner disdainfully whether he seriously meant to suggest that she marry a man just because he had befriended him in prison, and then went on to give a cogent summary of the extreme disadvantages of Courtenay as a consort—his "small power and authority," his intrigues with the French, England's need for money, and so on. Finally the chancellor gave in entirely, saying that "it would not be right to try to force her in one direction or another," and swearing to "obey the man she had chosen."[15]

Mary emerged unscathed from her encounters with Parliament and the chancellor, and with an added measure of authority. Renard's fears for her competence were quieted, at least for the moment, and he admired her "steadfastness and courage" in dealing with Gardiner. But the marriage question, important though it was, had little to do with the deeper issues that divided the country. Parliament had begun to come to terms with some of these, revoking the "corrupt and unlawful sentence" of Henry's divorce from Katherine and, by implication, making Elizabeth a bastard again. Jane and Guilford Dudley were attainted, along with Cranmer, and a further step was taken to rid the country of the archbishop's Protestant liturgy when a law was passed making it illegal to perform any service but that in use at the time of Henry VIII's death after December 20 of the present year. All of Edward's Protestant statutes were repealed, after a week of "marvelous dispute," but the principle that the sovereign and not the pope ruled the English church remained intact. Mary had got around using the term "Supreme Head" in her title, but she had to sit by and allow Parliament to retain it on her behalf in its laws.

Any further progress toward a complete return to Catholicism would have been impossible, for throughout the parliamentary sessions there were outbreaks of violence over the clergy and the mass. In one village church an arquebus was aimed at the priest who was saying mass, but it misfired. In Norfolk and Kent parishioners rioted and prevented mass from being celebrated, and it was being said that elsewhere two priests had actually been killed. Mary herself had been living with assassination threats since September, and it was a mark of her courage and flair for rulership that she continued to appear in public ceremonies and court audiences as freely as if no danger existed. Several plots against Gardiner's life had been uncovered since the reign began, forcing him to move into Mary's palace in order to be under her protection.[16]

A week before Parliament dissolved Mary's courtiers were seriously frightened. As the queen was passing through a gallery on her way to vespers, accompanied by Elizabeth and a number of others, an unseen voice cried out loudly "Treason!" The courtiers scattered, but Mary, unperturbed by the alarm, went on into the chapel to hear the office. It was later found that the accusation was meant for Gardiner, and came from a man the bishop had imprisoned many years earlier for writing a treatise in defense of Katherine of Aragon; but at the time no one doubted that the cry was directed at the queen. Elizabeth was so frightened she turned pale and "could not compose her countenance." She was amazed, she said, that Mary had not retired to safety after receiving such a warning, given the danger of an attack on her person. Elizabeth herself could not stop trembling, and had to get Susan Clarencieux to rub her stomach until the color came back to her face and she was able to join Mary at the altar.

XXXV

 Our life is a warfare, the worlde is the fielde:
Her highnes her army hath alwayes at hande;
For Hope is her helmet, Faith is her shielde,
And Love is her brestplate, her foes to withstand.

In a "Memorial" he sent her two weeks after her coronation Renard outlined to Mary the dangers she faced as queen, as he saw them. "You have four certain and open enemies," he told her: "the heretics and schismatics, the rebels and adherents of the duke of Northumberland, the king of France and Scotland, and the Lady Elizabeth." These opponents might appear to be quiescent from time to time, but their menace could never be ignored. "They will watch for a propitious moment for carrying out their plans," Renard wrote, "and your Majesty must always bear these four adversaries in mind and guard against them."[1]

Of the four enemies, Dudley's adherents had been dealt with most directly, if inconclusively. The duke and two of his captains had been executed, and his sons and daughter-in-law Jane were condemned prisoners in the Tower. Northampton and Suffolk had been imprisoned briefly, then released, while the marquis of Winchester, Pembroke and ten others who had signed the Device disinheriting Mary now sat on her Council. Mary's decision not only to pardon Dudley's councilors but to give most of them places in her government was widely criticized; giving Suffolk his freedom soon proved to be especially dangerous.

As for the heretics and schismatics—by which Renard meant Protestants of all kinds—their opposition was growing. Mary was showing wise moderation in moving the country back toward Catholicism very slowly, but the most committed opponents of the old faith were becoming more and more vociferous in defense of their beliefs. Here Cranmer showed the way. Mary had been lenient in her treatment of the archbishop, confining him to his house but stopping short of imprisoning him as a traitor. When it was said that he might submit himself to the queen's mercy and return to the church of Rome, however, he demonstrated the strength of his faith by writing a bitter attack on the mass; in a very short space of time he joined the former bishop of London, Ridley, and the fiery Protestant preacher Latimer in the Tower. Cranmer's defiance put heart into his coreligionists, who met Mary's attempts at conciliation with vehement arguments and symbolic insults. Toward the end of October a theological discussion was arranged, at which four learned Protestants were to debate six Catholic doctors. The meeting coincided with parliamentary debate over alterations in the religious laws, but instead of enlightening the lawmakers the theologians nearly came to blows. Reasoned discussion gave way to "scandalous wrangling," leaving Parliament and the public disgusted.[2] On the day Parliament rose anonymous troublemakers took a dead dog, shaved its head in the form of a priest's tonsure, and heaved it through the windows of the royal presence chamber.

The hopes of the Protestants hinged on the last of Mary's enemies—her half-sister Elizabeth. Mary and Elizabeth inherited their hatred of one another from their mothers, and though Mary made a sincere effort to be charitable toward her younger sister there was never any neutral ground between them. Mary could never perceive Elizabeth as anything but a bastard, telling Renard sarcastically that she was "the offspring of one of whose good fame he might have heard, and who had received her punishment."[3] According to Jane Dormer, the queen clung firmly to the old slander that Elizabeth was not the daughter of Henry VIII at all but of the musician Mark Smeaton; she had Smeaton's "face and countenance," Mary liked to say, and her own morals were no more admirable than her mother's had been.[4] Elizabeth had been guilty of an indiscreet flirtation with Thomas Seymour as a young girl, and she had acquired a reputation for promiscuity. It was hardly to be expected that the daughter of Anne Boleyn would grow into a woman of outstanding virtue, and Mary liked to cite the "characteristics in which she resembled her mother" as an important reason for keeping Elizabeth from coming to the throne.[5] Renard found the princess to be like Anne in another respect. She possessed, he wrote, "a bewitching personality," a power to entrap others and make them do her will. He was certain Elizabeth was using her beguilements on Courtenay, knowing that to marry him would give her access to the queen through Courtenay's mother.

Mary and Elizabeth were far apart in age—Mary was thirty-seven, Elizabeth twenty—as well as in parentage, temperament and, most important, religion. When Protestant preachers spoke of the future they liked to say that the papists were "having their turn" but that Elizabeth would remedy all in time.[6] Nevertheless Mary insisted at the outset of her reign that Elizabeth observe the Catholic ceremonies, knowing full well that a genuine conversion was a remote possibility. When rumors persisted that Elizabeth's attendance at mass was mere hypocrisy Mary brought the issue out in the open, asking her sister "whether she firmly believed what the Catholics now believed and had always believed concerning the holy sacrament?" Elizabeth insisted that she went to mass "of her own free will and without fear, hypocrisy or dissimulation," adding that she had considered making a public declaration to that effect. Mary was relieved to see how timid her sister appeared to be, and how she trembled when she talked to her, but to Renard her behavior indicated that she was lying about the mass, and guilty of plotting against the queen besides.[7] When Elizabeth left court in October Mary embraced her and made her a gift of an expensive sable hood and two strings of beautiful pearls, but Paget and Arundel sent her off with a harsh warning against becoming involved in any conspiracy to dethrone the queen.

Any plot likely to involve Elizabeth would more than likely include Antoine de Noailles, ambassador of the "king of France and Scotland" whom Renard had identified as Mary's third enemy. Noailles was a French nobleman of high birth whose large and varied staff of informers compensated for his modest diplomatic abilities. He had spies everywhere —in the royal court, in the households of Mary's councilors, among the merchants, gentlemen and ne'er-do-wells who frequented the capital. They included a French bookseller welcome in Renard's house, a Flemish servant of Paget's, one of Courtenay's servants, and a Scottish physician said to dabble in poisons as a sideline. Among the professional informers in Noailles' pay were Étienne Quiclet, a native of Besançon who had been Renard's *maître d'hôtel* and who made his living selling imperial secrets to the French, and Jean de Fontenay, sieur de Berteville, a sometime wine merchant and soldier of fortune who marketed military secrets and had on occasion been imprisoned as a double agent.

Like all ambassadors Noailles made informers of his own servants too, and what Quiclet and Berteville could not tell him he could often find out from his cook, his well-traveled couriers or his Scots groom. For a time the Venetian ambassador Soranzo made his knowledge and his staff available to Noailles as well, in the belief that helping the French might offset the growth of Hapsburg power, but among the Frenchman's most valuable spies was a man whose only political objective was to keep England free of foreign domination: the Surrey gentleman Sir John Leigh. Leigh was on the closest terms with Rochester, Walgrave, Englefield and a fourth member of Gardiner's faction, Sir Richard Southwell. Through Leigh Noailles could trace the progress of the marriage negotiations during December and January, and was able to plan with greater accuracy how he would undermine the entire project as the new year began.[8]

The treachery of these volatile opponents of Mary's rule had not retarded the course of the marriage negotiations, which by the end of the year had resulted in a definitive treaty. The articles called for each sovereign to enjoy title to the other's lands, but no authority there. Philip was, however, to "assist his consort in the task of government"—a vague phrase meant to describe the indefinable but extensive influence he might be expected to exert on Mary's policies as queen. Philip was not to attempt to appoint Spaniards to positions at court or in the government, or to depart to any extent from the "laws, privileges and customs" of the realm. If Mary died childless Philip would have no further connection with England; in the unlikely event that he predeceased her she was to enjoy a generous dower.

Apart from the guarantee that Philip would not bring England into any present or future imperial war against the French, the most important clauses in the marriage articles discussed the rights of the children that might be born to the couple. Philip already had a son, Don Carlos, who would inherit Spain and certain other continental possessions. The oldest son of Philip and Mary would inherit both England and the Low Countries, the latter being Philip's own future inheritance from his father. If there were no son, the oldest daughter was to rule England but not the Low Countries, except on condition that she marry with Don Carlos' consent. And if the Spanish prince should die without heirs, his lands—including the Spanish empire in the New World—would pass to Mary's heir. In theory at least, the next sovereign to rule England could come into possession of nearly half the known world.

Given this possibility it was essential that the negotiators consider how the country would be governed in case Mary died leaving a minor heir. The emperor foresaw the possibility very clearly, but told his clerks to omit all mention of it in the treaty. He explained his reasoning in a letter to Renard. He wanted to avoid making the English suspicious, he said, and also to take advantage of the unwritten premise of the law that in the event of a wife's death her husband became legal administrator of their children's persons and goods.[9]

Philip could hardly have asked for more advantageous terms himself —if he had been consulted. But he was not consulted, and as soon as he signed the final draft of the treaty he signed another document invalidating it completely. In this appended clause he swore "by our Lord, by Saint Mary and by the Sign of the Cross" that the marriage articles were "invalid and without force to bind him."[10] In declaring himself free of his oath Philip was following a time-honored diplomatic precedent, but he was also letting his father know how much a matter of form he considered the English match to be. He would be obedient, but he did not intend to be foolhardy; he would keep the terms of the treaty only as long as they complemented his other commitments, and no longer.

Philip was being ordered about like a child. He was told to choose his retinue with care, bringing to England only gentlemen of "sufficient age" and judgment to behave themselves and not spend all their money right away. As for their servants, they should be honest and responsible, and not the kind of men to worsen the already bad reputation of Spaniards among Englishmen. Philip was given instructions about provisioning his ships and limiting the number of his soldiers, and even about being "friendly and cordial" to the English. The emperor thought it necessary to advise his son "to demonstrate much love and joy to the queen, and to do so both in public and in private" once he arrived, and to send her a ring or some other token once the betrothal was formalized.[11] Sending obvious recommendations of this kind had to be either superfluous or futile. At twenty-six Philip either knew already how to provision a ship and please a bride or else he would never learn.

At the end of December four marriage commissioners delegated by the emperor from Brussels landed in England. At their head was Count Egmont, who brought with him plenty of money and jewels to distribute among the English councilors, plus ten thousand ducats for gambling expenses. "With the English, more than with any other people in the world, money has power," Egmont wrote to Philip in Spain, and in fact Philip was already giving thought to how he would store the million gold ducats he planned to bring with him on his own journey some months hence. More money was sent to Renard to give out to people he hoped would "speak and act favorably" about the coming marriage, and to others who, without bribes, might "do harm and cause difficulties."[12] The imperial commissioners were prepared to face a few days of hard bargaining. The emperor had warned Renard that "the English usually consider prudence in negotiation to consist in raising as many objections as they can think of." Each of the queen's councilors would feel impelled to find at least one issue to debate—otherwise he would not be a good servant to his mistress. But before long this display of zealous disputation would give way to agreement, and the treaty would be signed with good will on both sides.

Events followed Charles V's scenario closely. After resting for a few days near the coast the four commissioners made their way to London, arriving at Tower Wharf on January 2. They sat patiently throughout the expected flurry of objections from the English, then put their names to the marriage articles, and on January 14 and 15 Gardiner presented them to assemblies of the nobility and the citizens of London. At the bargaining table all went smoothly, but in the streets of the capital the emperor's representatives were received with hostility. When their servants arrived on New Year's Day boys threw snowballs at them as they rode to their lodgings, and there were no cheering crowds to welcome Egmont and his colleagues when they disembarked.

Londoners were in no mood to tolerate meddling foreigners just then. The January weather was bitterly cold, and both wood and coals were scarce and costly. To relieve the situation the mayor ordered sea coals to be sold at Billingsgate and Queen's Hithe for fourpence the bushel, "which greatly helped till better provision might be found," but the public temper remained sour.[13] Verbal attacks on the Spaniards mounted. A gentleman was thrown into prison on January 5 for saying "that the upshot of the match would not be as the Council expected," and in the same week signs were posted at streetcorners announcing that the man the queen hoped to marry was already the husband of the Portuguese infanta.[14]

The climate of criticism was so pervasive it reached Mary herself. News of the slanders in London was brought to her by some of her courtiers; others warned her gentlewomen of the dangers of popular revolt in such graphic terms that they came running to the queen in fear. At times these reports drove Mary to despair. "Melancholy and sadness" made her ill, and she was torn with guilt at the knowledge that her vow to marry Prince Philip caused such unrest among the people who claimed her primary loyalty.[15]

But the danger that arose in the last weeks of January, 1554, came not from the people at large but from a small group of disgruntled gentlemen united—though loosely—by their opposition to the Spanish marriage and by a somewhat cloudy determination to remove Mary from the throne. The conspirators included Sir Peter Carew and Courtenay in the west, Sir James Crofts in Herefordshire, Sir Thomas Wyatt in Kent and in Leicestershire, the duke of Suffolk. Courtenay seems to have provided motivation to the group during their first meetings in November, and many believed that, from first to last, the aim of the plotters was to place Elizabeth and Courtenay jointly on the throne. But the earl was hardly one to mastermind a political coup, and in fact he did little to promote the uprising that was eventually touched off two months later. Elizabeth knew of the plot but did nothing to promote it; Noailles was brought in at the end of December, and did all he could to make it look as though the French were about to come in on the side of the conspirators in force. One bloodthirsty plotter, William Thomas, had concocted a plan to assassinate the queen, but could not persuade his colleagues to back him in this and the proposal "that the queen should have been slain as she did walk" was abandoned almost as soon as it was raised. By the time the imperial ambassadors arrived all that was definite was that there would be

four simultaneous rebellions in Herefordshire, Kent, Devon and Leicestershire, set for Palm Sunday, March 18.

Mary and the Council first learned of the serious disaffection when
news came in mid-January that Carew was attempting to frighten the
townspeople of Exeter with stories of Spanish rapine and slaughter. Mary
immediately issued a warrant for Carew's arrest, and was sending captains
and lieutenants to every county in the south to raise men at arms to prevent trouble. Carew disappeared, and his fellow conspirators, unprepared
as they were, nevertheless attempted to set off the risings that had been
planned for later in the year. Courtenay, interviewed by Gardiner on
January 21, told all he knew, and for better or worse, the rebellion was
under way.

The conspiracy might have melted away entirely at this point, but Sir
Thomas Wyatt, the Kentish gentleman who later called himself "the
third or fourth man" in the plot, went ahead with his sworn agreement
to raise the men of Kent against the queen. He gathered his forces
first at Rochester, appealing to the broadest possible segment of the
population by leaving the precise aims of the revolt unclear. His supporters rode through the villages near Wyatt's camp shouting that the
Spaniards were coming "with arquebusses, morions and matchlight," and
when the invaders failed to appear Wyatt told his men that his true purpose was to improve the advice given to the queen and change her councilors. The rebel force numbered no more than four thousand men at its
strongest—some estimates place Wyatt's total following at only two
thousand—but Londoners imagined it to be much larger, and Mary's advisers, who knew of the prearranged revolts to be staged in the West
Country and the Welsh Marches, feared the worst. A French spy had informed Renard that Henri II was hoping to open another front along the
Scots border, and had already sent agents into England carrying white
badges to be given to the English captains he expected to recruit. The
rebels had been told, Renard's informant said, that there were twenty-
four French ships and eighteen infantry companies massed on the Normandy coast, ready to sail for England on a few hours' notice.[16]

In the first days of the revolt the rebels had the initiative, though
there were already signs that Wyatt would never succeed in stirring any
but a small minority of the country population to join him. For if the
rebel lieutenants were spreading fears of invasion, councilors and local
officials loyal to Mary were riding through the same villages behind them,
offering the queen's pardon to all who would reconsider their adherence
to Wyatt and return quietly to their homes. On January 27, market day,
Sir Robert Southwell addressed the crowd at Malling in Kent in ringing
terms. "They go about to blear you with matters of Strangers," he said,

referring to the rebel persuasions, yet "he seemeth very blind, and willingly blinded, that will have his sight dimmed with such a fond mist! For if they meant to resist Strangers," Southwell pointed out, "they would then prepare to go to the seacoasts, and not to the queen's most royal person, with such a company of arms and weapon." His logic was impeccable, and his appeal to the patriotism of the citizens of Malling even more effective. When he concluded his speech with "God save Queen Mary and all her well willers!" the crowd answered with a hearty "God save Queen Mary!" and "with one voice defied Wyatt and his accomplices as arrant traitors."[17]

But if the people of Malling were willing to swear they would die in defense of the queen, few of them actually joined the bands recruited to oppose Wyatt, and when the elderly duke of Norfolk led a force of men against him five hundred of the Londoners among them actually broke ranks and joined the rebels rather than fight them.

The defection of these "Whitecoats" and the failure of the stalwart old duke marked the low point in the contest with Wyatt and his men. The sight of the remnant of Norfolk's fighting men straggling into the capital, "their coats torn, all ruined, without arrows or string in their bows," was "heart-sore and very displeasing" to the queen, and when she turned to her councilors for advice and help she found them quarrelsome and treacherous.[18] Paget and his associates blamed the chancellor for creating unrest by his intemperate religious policies; Gardiner's faction in turn blamed Paget, Arundel and the others for backing the marriage with Philip. Renard felt certain that some of the Council members were implicated in the revolt, and the curious inactivity of the body as a whole throughout the crisis lent support to his suspicions. Mary had ordered the Council to provide her with a large bodyguard shortly after the rising began; by January 31 they still had not done so even though she received word that same day that Wyatt meant to march on London. There was virtually no one in her government whom she could trust, Mary confided to Renard; she had no army, and for the first time since the middle ages, rebels would soon be at the gates of the capital.

Watch had been kept at all the gates in London since the twenty-sixth, and when the news came that Wyatt was indeed about to march on the city every possible measure was taken for its defense. Every craft provided double its normal muster of men, all wearing the white coats that identified the forces of the queen. Men in armor stood at every entrance to the city, and great guns were set in place at the drawbridge. Wyatt was proclaimed "a traitor and rebellious," and whoever took him was promised a landed estate, to be held by himself and his heirs in perpetuity.

With the city in such danger the Council finally began to consider the safety of the queen, and debated whether she should retire behind the thick walls of the Tower or retreat to Windsor. Some said she ought to disguise herself and go to live among the faithful country people until the coming battle had been decided, while a few—at least one spy among them—argued that she would be safest of all across the Channel at Calais. The four imperial commissioners set her an example by leaving London on February 1, fearing that "the fury of the populace" was about to fall on their heads.[19] They went to take leave of Mary, and found her amazingly composed and resolute in the face of such danger. She "showed a firm spirit," they wrote, asking as usual to be remembered to the emperor and regent and saying she would write them when she had time. Egmont and the others took the first ship they could find, and the ignominy of their departure was increased by the rudeness of the guardsmen who escorted them to the wharf. As soon as they embarked the guardsmen "behaved disrespectfully towards them, both by word and by firing certain arquebus shots" in their direction. They were seasick all the way home.[20]

Those who thought Mary would leave London to its fate gravely misunderstood her. On the day of the commissioners' departure she went with an escort to the Guildhall, where the citizens were assembled to try to work out a plan to resist Wyatt's invasion. She entered the great hall and went up into the place of the hustings, where a rich cloth of estate was hung. Standing beneath it, she spoke to the people in a strong, low voice that carried to the back of the hall.

"I am come unto you in mine own person," she said, "to tell you that which you already see and know; that is, how traitorously and rebelliously a number of Kentishmen have assembled themselves against us and you." She explained, in clear and direct language, that Wyatt and his followers were only pretending to oppose her forthcoming marriage, and in fact meant to attack her religion and take the government into their own hands.

"Now, loving subjects," she went on, "what I am ye right well know. I am your queen, to whom at my coronation, where I was wedded to the realm . . . you promised your allegiance and obedience unto me. And that I am the right and true inheritor of the crown of this realm of England, I take all Christendom to witness. My father, as ye all know, possessed the same regal state, which now rightly is descended unto me." As to her marriage, Mary assured her subjects that she had been moved to take a husband not out of lust or self-will, but "to leave some fruit of my body behind me, to be your governor." If she thought for one moment that her marriage would harm any one of her subjects, or any part of the realm, she said, she would remain a virgin for life.

It was a masterful speech, delivered without notes and seemingly without any preparation but the constant preoccupation of a loving sovereign with her people's welfare.

"I cannot tell how naturally the mother loveth the child," Mary told the Londoners, "for I was never the mother of any, but certainly if a prince and governor may as naturally and earnestly love her subjects, as the mother doth love the child, then assure yourselves that I, being your lady and mistress, do as earnestly and tenderly love and favor you."

At these "so sweet words," a chronicler wrote, the people took comfort, and many of them were weeping.

"And now, good subjects," the queen concluded, "pluck up your hearts, and like true men, stand fast against these rebels, both our enemies and yours, and fear them not, for I assure you I fear them nothing at all!"[21]

Cheers of "God save Queen Mary!" rang through the hall as the queen took her leave, and some were heard to add "and the prince of Spain!" Mary's councilors were dazzled, and her chancellor openmouthed in admiration. "Oh, how happy are we," he exclaimed, "to whom God hath given such a wise and learned prince!" Renard, cynical to a fault and grudging in his compliments, stated the simple truth when he wrote that "there never was a more steadfast lady than this queen."

XXXVI

 Remember well, o mortall man, to whom god geveth reason,
How he truly, most ryghtfully, doth alwayes punyshe treason.

On the morning of Saturday, February 3, Wyatt and his men entered Southwark. They met no resistance. Some of the soldiers raised to oppose them joined them instead, and the people of the suburb entertained the rebels "most willingly with their best" out of fear. Only the river now lay between the Kentishmen and the heart of London, and in the city proper all was rumor and panic. "Then should you have seen taking in wares off the stalls in a most hasty manner," wrote one Londoner. "There was running up and down in every place to weapons and harness; aged men were astonished, many women wept for fear; children and maids ran into their houses, shutting the doors for fear." All the boats in the river were withdrawn to the Westminster side, and in every quarter of the city Mary's speech was read and reread to the people to give them courage in the difficult hours that lay ahead.

Wyatt set up two cannon against London Bridge, but the citizens had placed four against him, while arquebusiers fired on his men from the White Tower and the Water Gate. The great guns of the Tower were trained on Southwark, but when one of the Tower captains came to Mary to ask whether his gunners should fire on the rebels she refused to give the order. "That were pity," she said, "for many poor men and householders are like to be undone there and killed." In the end the threat of bombardment was enough to drive Wyatt to the desperate gamble of marching his men upriver to Kingston, crossing over by night to the opposite bank, and coming into the city from the west at dawn on February 7.

The musters had been ordered for six o'clock, but it was only four when the streets were filled with the "noise and tumult" that Wyatt was only a few miles off. Mary was at Westminster, very near the rebels' path; her councilors met in her bedchamber, and begged her to save herself by taking her barge to the Tower. But putting her faith in her captains—Pembroke and Clinton—and in the gentlemen pensioners and guardsmen who surrounded the palace she announced that "she would tarry there to see the uttermost." Her courage was so great many believed she might take the field against Wyatt herself.[1]

Throughout the day the rebels and the defending bands marched back and forth through the city, with Wyatt gaining Ludgate after encountering only slight resistance from the chamberlain, Sir John Gage, and his men at Charing Cross and from Pembroke at what is now Hyde Park Corner. Sir William Howard held Ludgate against him, however, and he had to turn back, only to find that all the routes out of the city were now blocked off by troops loyal to Mary. To prevent more bloodshed Wyatt surrendered, and by five o'clock he was the queen's prisoner.

No one in the court knew until the end of the day how the battle for the city was going, and alarming rumors of defections, rebel victories and treasonous behavior from the queen's captains set the servants of the royal household to pacing the galleries anxiously and arming themselves as best they could. Mary's women expected the worst, wringing their hands and swearing "We shall all be destroyed this night. What a sight is this, to see the queen's bedchamber full of armed men!" As the day went on, one of the guardsmen wrote in his diary, there was "such a running and crying of ladies and gentlewomen, shutting of doors, and such a shrieking and noise as it was wonderful to hear."

Through it all Mary remained serene, assuring everyone around her that her captains would not deceive her, and even if they did, God would not, "in whom she placed her chief trust."[2] When one of Wyatt's lieutenants came to the court gate at Whitehall and shot arrows into the court itself, wounding one of the defenders, an attorney of Lincoln's Inn, in the nose, some of Mary's soldiers came running to her crying "All is lost! Away! Away! A barge! A barge!" But even then "her Grace never changed her cheer, nor removed one foot out of the house," and instead asked all of her courtiers to pray for victory. "Fall to prayer!" she told them, "and I warrant you, we shall hear better news anon."

By this time it was late in the afternoon, and Mary's guard, fearing an attack on the court in force, asked her to let them open the gate and defend it as long as they could. Mary agreed, after the guardsmen promised "not to go forth out of her sight," as they were "the only defense of her person this day." The soldiers marched out to take their places, and as they passed under a gallery window the queen leaned out and spoke to them again, requiring them, as "gentlemen in whom she only trusted," not to go out of her sight. But they had been at their post less than an hour when the news came that Wyatt had been captured, and the queen and her courtiers breathed easily once again.[3]

At Tower Gate a crowd of dazed spectators, bewildered first by the pre-dawn alarm of Wyatt's onslaught and again only twelve hours later by the news of his sudden surrender, watched as the traitor was led past them in his mail shirt, velvet cassock and lace-trimmed velvet hat. As he passed into the compound a knight who had fought against him seized his collar and addressed him loudly.

"Oh! thou villain and unhappy traitor!" he shouted menacingly, shaking Wyatt as he spoke, "how could you find it in your heart to work such detestable treason to the queen's majesty?" "If it were not that the law must justly pass upon you, I would strike you through with my dagger."

The knight's hand was on his dagger as he finished, but the prisoner made no stir to defend himself. He kept his arms at his side, and, "looking grievously with a grim look" at the other man, said quietly "It is no mastery now," and passed on into the fortress.[4]

Wyatt's confederates were less resigned to their fate. William Thomas, the man who had suggested assassinating the queen, tried unsuccessfully during his imprisonment to kill himself by "thrusting himself under the paps with a knife." Another of Wyatt's captains escaped to Hampshire, where he was finally captured disguised as a sailor, "his face disfigured with coals and dirt." The duke of Suffolk, Jane Grey's father, was found hiding in a hollow tree where a dog had sniffed him out.[5]

For months after the rebellion London was a city of corpses. New gallows were built at every city gate and at the principal landmarks, and in Cheapside, Fleet Street, Smithfield, Holborn, on London Bridge and at Tower Hill the bodies of those who had followed Wyatt swung and rotted and stank. The soldiers who had gone over to join the rebels were hanged at the very doors of their houses in the city, and the executions seemed to go on for weeks. "There has never been seen such hanging as has been going on here every day," Noailles wrote, and those who were pardoned had good reason to thank their luck and cheer the queen. Perhaps as many as a hundred of the rebels were hanged; the rest, bound with cords and wearing nooses around their necks, went in double file to the tiltyard at Westminster, where they knelt in the mud before Mary. There she pardoned them, and their ropes were cut and their nooses thrown off. A diarist who described the scene of the mass pardons wrote how the freed men rushed out into the streets, throwing up their caps and shouting "God save Queen Mary!" while bystanders picked up the nooses as souvenirs, sometimes collecting as many as four or five before going home.[6]

In the wave of official retribution Jane and Guilford Dudley, who had taken no part in Wyatt's revolt but who nonetheless represented a threat to the security of Mary's government, were condemned and executed on February 12. Wyatt himself was kept alive until April, when he was beheaded on Tower Hill, his "bowels burnt" and his head set on the gallows on Hay-Hill beside Hyde Park. His corpse was taken to Newgate to be parboiled, after which it was quartered and the four quarters displayed in four parts of the capital. Wyatt's lands were parceled out among the gentlemen of Kent who had helped to suppress his rebellion, but Mary took pity on his widow and five children. At first the queen allowed the woman an annuity, and later permitted her to redeem her husband's goods and a little of his property.

In the dispatches of the resident ambassadors in England the Kentish rebellion took on the proportions of a monumental uprising. All the rumors of the early days of Wyatt's threat—of large-scale unrest in Cornwall and Wales, of mass desertions from the queen's forces and of imminent, country-wide revolt—were reported in detail and sent to the imperial, Venetian and French courts with all haste. Before these exaggerated accounts could be corrected they had given rise to further distortions, until it was being said that Mary was about to be overthrown and "all England" was in turmoil. The French king circulated reports that thousands of rebels in many parts of the kingdom had seized the major fortresses, backed by the majority of the people, who preferred death to subjugation to a foreign prince. To the pope, the Venetian Signory and the rulers of the Italian states he wrote that there were hundreds of Spanish troops fighting against the rebels, and his letter was given such credence in Venice that the English ambassador there, Peter Vannes, had to send out a letter of his own explaining that the current reports went far beyond the truth.[7]

The colony of English merchants in Antwerp was thoroughly frightened, not least because local creditors would lend no more money to the English government once they got wind of the rebellion. Egmont and his colleagues, who had left London as Wyatt moved into Southwark, substantiated the worst of the rumors by claiming that the rebels were massed against the capital twenty thousand strong. When the news of the queen's victory over Wyatt finally arrived on February 14 every Englishman in the city joined in a huge celebration, lighting bonfires, providing tuns of wine to all who would drink and setting off a "great peal of guns."[8]

Though more accurate reports of the size and menace of the Kentish revolt eventually reached continental sovereigns the episode put both Mary and her government in a bad light. The revolt itself was attributed to the weakness of a woman ruler, yet its suppression was in no way credited to her strength. The royal defeat of Wyatt was in any case a

clouded triumph, for the collapse of his rebellion was to an extent his
own doing. In going ahead without the promised support of the other
conspirators Wyatt had shown determination but scant judgment. He
had not been able to recruit enough followers to guarantee success, nor
had he proved competent to lead a swift and decisive attack on London.
More worrisome to the queen and her councilors was that many of her
subjects, though indifferent to Wyatt's nebulous program to change
Mary's advisers, were equally unwilling to take up arms against the
rebels. In the long run this stubborn lack of concern might prove more
dangerous than any rebellion.

The leniency with which Mary treated three of the conspirators—
Courtenay, Elizabeth and Noailles—was particularly hard for foreign
rulers to comprehend. Courtenay had been in on the plot from the start,
but had not carried out the role assigned to him, and had actually fought
on Mary's side—where he was a distinct liability—during the final days
of the revolt. He was allowed to go abroad, though he did not leave for
some months. Elizabeth, who was strongly suspected of being in communication with Wyatt and the French about the revolt, was imprisoned
in the Tower for three months but then released under close guard. And
Noailles, though endlessly harassed and annoyed by Renard and his men,
received no official punishment.

Noailles was made thoroughly uncomfortable throughout the spring of
1554. He found his spies suborned, his agents threatened, and his
dispatches missing. He suspected, with good reason, that Mary and
Renard were reading everything he wrote, aided by a cipher key provided
by a double agent. When a new house was made available to him in
London—Mary's residence of Bridewell—he found to his chagrin that
it was Renard's old house, and that his predecessor had taken every door,
window and lock with him when he left. The only thing Renard did
leave behind, in fact, was one of his own informers, who reported everything Noailles said and did and kept all important visitors away from
his door.

There were no serious aftershocks to Wyatt's rebellion, but the
drawn-out executions and prominent gallows kept the events of February
fresh in the memories of Londoners. Foreigners living in the city became
more and more apprehensive about their safety, and some, observing
mysterious marks on their houses, believed they had been singled out for
assassination and left the country.[9] With the first days of warm weather
children playing in the open fields at the outskirts of the city carried out
a chilling re-enactment of the drama their parents had lived through. Armies of boys and girls, hundreds on each side, played "queen against
Wyatt" so roughly that some on both sides were hurt. One boy took the
part of the prince of Spain; he was taken prisoner and hanged, and the

simulation was so authentic that he was nearly strangled by the rope. Mary ordered those who had organized the mock combat to be whipped and imprisoned briefly, and no more games of "queen against Wyatt" were reported during her reign.[10]

After the collapse of the rebellion Noailles remarked wryly that "perhaps God is permitting her marriage to this prince in order to punish them both." It was the only viewpoint left for a defeated conspirator, but in seeing that the forthcoming marriage would cause Mary a good deal of anguish in the months ahead Noailles was right. She was being encouraged from all sides to reconsider her decision to marry Philip. The burghers of Flanders, while they saw clearly the commercial advantages of a closer political union with England, hated Philip with such intensity that they condemned the marriage. One of Cardinal Pole's principal servants, William Peto, wrote Mary a long letter advising her on both spiritual and practical grounds not to marry. According to Renard, Peto warned Mary repeatedly that "she would fall into the power and become the slave of her husband," and added the dark prediction that "at her advanced age she cannot hope to bear children without the peril of her life."

The latter point, Renard noted, was being made over and over again when the marriage was discussed, much to Mary's chagrin. Peto's letter arrived on her thirty-eighth birthday—an opportune moment to point out one of the principal shortcomings in the prospective marriage—and coincided too with new rumors of violent attacks on Philip once he arrived in England.[11] Renard was beginning to recommend that Philip delay his arrival until fall, and was even hinting that he wished "the whole matter" could be reconsidered. Mary, though, was unshaken in her resolution to fulfill her vow to marry Philip, and as quickly as possible. (She would not agree to marry during Lent, as it was against church law, but was prepared to have the ceremony as soon after Easter as it could be arranged.) As for Renard's fears for the prince's safety, she told him "with tears in her eyes" that she would rather never have been born than to have harm come to Philip. She would guarantee his safety personally, and he must not postpone his arrival on account of rumors of danger.

Philip had not been idle in communicating with all those involved in arranging his marriage, but his only message to his intended bride was the indirect news, conveyed through Renard, that he was pleased at the prospect of marrying her. Mary sent word back that "she would fulfill towards him all the duties which ladies were bound to discharge where their husbands were concerned," though she did not commit this involuted sentiment to writing, believing that etiquette demanded that the man be the one to begin the correspondence.[12] She did add a more down-to-earth piece of advice to Philip, recommending that he bring his own physicians and "trustworthy cooks" from Spain. Since physicians and cooks were the usual conveyers of poison this advice would ordinarily have been alarming to Philip, but he knew from other sources that the queen was preoccupied with planning every detail of his household and retinue, and he simply did as she asked.

The arrangements were complex and time-consuming. Price lists of food for men and horses had to be drawn up, so that Philip could estimate his expenses and bring an adequate sum with him when he came. Precise exchange rates for Spanish and Italian crowns and Portuguese ducats had to be determined in advance, to prevent exploitation of the Spaniards by English merchants and to discourage the growth of an illegal money market. To prevent incidents between the English and Spaniards during Philip's initial journey from the coast inland, and on ceremonial occasions, an English marshal had to be appointed. Together with Philip's Spanish marshal, this man was to prevent the exchange of insults on both sides and to make sure the English didn't "push up against foreigners as they are accustomed to do." All the officers and lesser servants of Philip's household had to be selected and approved, a gargantuan task whose completion in late March was marked by a solemn ceremony. The entire group was assembled before Mary's great master and chamberlain and made to swear an oath of loyalty, along with the hundred archers who were to join the Spanish guardsmen Philip would bring with him. The archers were chosen from Mary's personal guard, on the basis of their proven loyalty and skill in languages. It had been hoped that they could be outfitted with liveries to match their Spanish counterparts, to promote greater unity among the two contingents, but no sample of the Spanish livery could be found in time.[13]

Mary was at the center of all these preparations, just as she was, after Gardiner, at the center of political affairs. The administrative routine that had kept her busy from dawn until midnight in the early months of her reign had expanded, leaving her less time than ever to devote to the exceptional issues that seemed to arise more and more frequently. Among these exceptional matters was a fresh legal dispute about the effect of the marriage on the succession. Two lawyers came forward—prompted, Renard thought, by partisans of Elizabeth—to say that under English law, once Philip married the queen the entirety of her regal authority passed to him. Even if Mary had a son, they claimed, her throne would not pass to him but would continue to belong to her husband.[14] Fortunately for Mary, this legal position was not taken up by others in the judiciary, though her Council did debate the question of whether the queen's name or her husband's should take precedence in public documents, and this issue was decided in Philip's favor.[15]

What weighed most heavily on Mary in the spring of 1554 was the ever-worsening rift in her Council. She had hoped to improve its efficiency and reduce the time wasted in personal disputes among the Council members by creating an "inner Council" of six advisers, but the chancellor and his adherents complained so bitterly over this that they generated new conflict. The most troublesome councilor was Paget, whose animosity to Gardiner now mushroomed into an obsession. He did everything possible to disrupt the chancellor's policies, shouting him down at the Council table, organizing opposition to his proposals in Parliament and using his influence to dissuade the lords from supporting his bills. He angered Mary so thoroughly that when he came to her and asked to be excused from court for a few days she surprised him with a brusque and cutting recitation of his "acts of inconstancy," adding that since he had fallen so far short of her expectations he "might come and go as he pleased" from then on. She stopped just short of dismissing him from the government—which would hardly have been wise—but she succeeded in distressing him to the point of tears. Paget managed to mumble his excuses and left her, though after a few days in the country he was back at court again and was fast resuming his former intrigues.

Gardiner, who could not stress often enough to Mary that Paget and his supporters were "heretics" and not followers of the true faith, urged her to send him to the Tower, along with his colleague the earl of Arundel, who was said to be fortifying one of his castles near the coast and raising a force of mounted men without authorization. Paget in turn accused the chancellor of being a "man of blood," a religious fanatic whose clumsy efforts to crush the Protestants were likely to overturn the government itself. "The split in the Council is so enormous and public, and the members so hostile to one another," Renard wrote, "that they forget the queen's service in their anxiety to wreak vengeance, and no business is transacted except on definite orders from the queen." The tension was so pervasive that Renard expected fists to fly at any moment, and he dreaded what might happen once Philip came.[16] Certainly the Council did little to help Mary with the work of government, and it was the queen and not her officials who brought her second session of Parliament to a successful close early in May. Her speech to the members was interrupted five or six times with shouts of "God save the queen!" and as in February, her eloquence moved the lords and commons to renewed expressions of fidelity.[17]

Through it all Noailles, sulking over his ill treatment and extremely displeased as he watched preparations being made to receive Philip, wrote to his master in France that Mary was nothing but a "poor love-sick woman" preoccupied with her growing passion. She was becoming impatient to be married, he wrote, and while she waited for her wedding day

she could do nothing but "curse and accuse people" and condemn everything, including the weather.

Other accounts, though, showed Mary in quite a different light. She
had a great deal on her mind, but there were moments when she
could relax and allow herself to think only of her happiness to come.
One night after dinner Admiral William Howard, a bluff and gar-
rulous man whose heavy playfulness sometimes got him into trouble,
came up to Mary and, "seeing her wrapt in thought," said something to her in a low voice, then turned to Renard, who happened to be
present, and asked him if he wanted to know what he had just said. Mary
tried to stop Howard from repeating it, smiling and embarrassed, but he
went ahead anyway, pointing to the empty chair next to the queen and
saying that he wished Philip were there "to drive thought and care
away." At this Mary blushed and pretended to scold the admiral, but he
said he knew well enough she wasn't really angry, and liked his suggestion well enough. She burst out laughing then, and every courtier in the
room joined her.[18]

XXXVII

 O ladye deere,
Be ye so neare
To be knowne?
My hart you cheere
Your voyce to here;
Wellcum, myne owne!

In June of 1554 Philip the Prudent assembled his ships, his men
and his treasure for the rough sea voyage to England. Because his father
had ordered him to arrive with a "minimum of display" he was taking
with him only some nine thousand nobles and servants, a thousand horses
and mules, and three million ducats in gold, transported in a fleet of 125
ships. Twenty of the greatest nobles of Spain would travel with him,
along with their retinues and trains of servants, and—much to the discomfiture of Renard—their wives. The ambassador had warned Philip
that the presence of Spanish duchesses and countesses in his company
would lead to endless inconvenience and bad feeling; unlike their husbands, the Spanish noblewomen could not be counted on to keep their
distaste for the English in check. But the prince would not be persuaded,
although he did agree to take no unmarried women with him.

Apart from the nobles, most of those who were to accompany Philip
would not leave their ships. The majority of his retinue were soldiers
who, in accordance with the terms of the marriage treaty, could come
along to protect the prince at sea but could not come ashore. Once he set
foot on English soil Philip would have to rely on the hundred gentlemen
of his Spanish guard, conspicuous in their red and yellow liveries, and the
hundred Germans whose similar liveries had silk facings "as their custom
is to go bravely dressed," plus his bodyguard of mounted archers. Renard
had told him not to take any chances, advising him to disguise some of his

soldiers as servants and have them bring arquebuses ashore with them in their trunks, but he disdained to follow this precaution. For better or worse, he would place himself in the hands of the alien English, trusting his future wife to guarantee the preservation of his honor and his life.

Charles V had put no limitation on the size of Philip's wardrobe, and in the months before he left his capital to take ship for England the royal tailors, weavers and embroiderers of Valladolid were kept at work night and day sewing the gorgeous doublets and surcoats the prince would need when he arrived at the court of his bride to be. One of the gentlemen of his chamber wrote a flowery description of the clothes made for Philip at this time—suits of crimson velvet, gray satin, and white silk velvet, lined in satin and cloth of silver and adorned with inter-worked embroidery and precious stones and metals. One jacket was covered with twisted gold chains intertwined with silver braid, with leaves outlined in silver filigree. Gold and silver bugles adorned several of the prince's surcoats, and his doublets were embroidered so thickly in gold thread that the colors of the cloth beneath were all but hidden. With these splendid garments Philip would wear jewels at his wrists and around his neck, and he liked to wear gold chains at his shoulders and to wind them around his hats. With the addition of his gem-studded orna-mental weapons, his magnificence was complete.

Philip's wardrobe was more suited to a reigning king than a royal bridegroom, and in fact he had already begun to think of himself as a king, and to adopt the regal style. Writing to Mary's councilors in Eng-land he signed himself "Philippus Rex"—a tactless presumption that would certainly have affronted them if Renard had not intervened. The ambassador quietly destroyed the prince's letters before they reached their destinations and had his message to the councilors delivered orally.

To an extent Philip's error was pardonable. A Spaniard in Mary's serv-ice, Antonio de Guarras, had brought him news that he had already been proclaimed king, and he was merely taking advantage of this informal promotion in status. But a more experienced statesman would never have committed such a dangerous breach of diplomatic etiquette, and the inci-dent confirmed fears by many in the emperor's government that Philip might disgrace himself in some way or display before the English the same hauteur that had so far made him detested in every land he had visited. The imperial ambassador in Rome wrote Philip a cautionary let-ter advising him to yield to the English in everything, and to be as ingra-tiating as possible. "For God's sake," he warned, "appear to be pleased." Renard sent essentially the same advice, while the emperor, not content to trust Philip to be guided by his own better judgment, entrusted to the duke of Alva the delicate task of making certain the prince behaved him-self. "For the love of God," Charles wrote to Alva shortly before the wedding flotilla left for England, "see to it that my son behaves in the right manner; for otherwise I tell you I would rather never have taken the matter in hand."[1]

One of Philip's worst lapses had been neglect of his future bride. He did not write to her until the middle of May, nor did he send her any jewel to commemorate the betrothal as his father told him to do. Charles himself sent Mary a handsome large diamond after the marriage articles were signed, with the warm message that he now "considered her as his own daughter," but it was his son she wanted to hear from. Weeks passed, then months, and though Renard and the Council members received letters from the prince—some of which spoke of her in dutiful terms—the queen had none.

Just as the issue was becoming almost scandalous an envoy arrived from Spain, bringing a letter for Mary and much else besides. The letter had been written May 11, but the envoy, the marquis de Las Navas, did not come to court until June 20, shortly before the prince was expected. The gifts Philip sent with his letter, however, more than made up for the long delay. Mary and her ladies were showered with presents of all kinds, and with pearls, diamonds, emeralds and rubies of great value. Mary received three matchless jewels of incomparable loveliness. The first was a necklace of eighteen brilliant diamonds, in a dainty setting which became her delicate proportions. The second was a huge diamond with a large pearl hanging from it, to be worn over her breast on a long gold chain. Some who saw this piece called it "the most lovely pair of gems ever seen in the world," and it quickly became Mary's favorite jewel. But the third gift moved her by its sentimental value. It was a precious heirloom, a great table diamond mounted in a rose in an ornate gold setting, and it had originally been given by the emperor to Philip's mother, Isabella of Portugal. The diamond was said to be worth eighty thousand crowns, but to Mary it held a greater value; it symbolized her closer union with her mother's family, and all they meant to her. Whether Philip knew what effect this jewel would produce or whether he was guided by Alva or some other adviser the gesture achieved its effect, and made Mary long to see the man who had so honored her and who must love her as well.[2]

The English envoys who were sent to deliver the marriage contract to Philip in Spain found him very much to their liking. They met him at Santiago, where he stopped for a time on his journey from Valladolid to the coastal city of Coruña where he would embark. He was grave, dignified, and generous—he gave one of the two envoys, Lord Bedford, a piece of statuary four and a half feet high, exquisitely worked, made of solid gold. One of Philip's gentlemen who understood English overheard one of the Englishmen say to the other "Oh! God be praised for sending us so good a king as this!" after the marriage articles were signed, and he probably meant it.

At Santiago Philip was joined by his eight-year-old son Don Carlos, whom the prince could not expect to see again for several years at least. They hunted together and attended a tournament, and in the evening watched "a procession of beautiful and strange inventions" by torchlight in the plaza. There were horses disguised as elephants, and pasteboard castles full of savages from the Indies. More savages carried a green temple-like structure with a maiden inside, and following these was a miniature ship, complete in every detail, flying English and Spanish flags. A grim pageant featured a girl lying in a coffin, complaining loudly that cupid had brought her to her death, followed by an artificial cupid on horseback. As the display reached the center of the plaza the cupid was pulled upward by ropes while fireworks burst from him to the crowd's delight. The prince and his son also watched a great bullfight in the plaza which, because of one "devilish" bull which resisted death for hours, lasted all night long.[3]

After several weeks at Santiago Philip said goodbye to his son and went on to Coruña, where the fleet rode at anchor and the beach was littered with stacks of provisions, tuns of wine and casks of water, animals and their fodder, and the weapons, armor and sea chests of thousands of soldiers. When the prince arrived six hundred Guipuzcoan sea warriors lined up along the edge of the sand to receive him, lances in hand, and the guns of the fleet and the nearby castle boomed out a salute. Their firing produced such smoke that "for an hour and a half neither heaven nor earth was visible."

The English envoys wanted the prince to travel in an English ship, but he declined; he did let them choose which of his Spanish galleys would be his flagship, however, and their choice rested on a ship so elaborately decorated it resembled "a lovely flower garden" more than a seagoing vessel. It was the *Espíritu Santo,* a twenty-four-oared galley upholstered from stem to stern in fine scarlet cloth. The forecastle was hung with crimson brocade painted with golden flames, and a royal standard was suspended from the mainmast, a banner thirty yards long, painted with Philip's coat of arms. Another standard hung from the mizzenmast, while flags with the royal arms flew from the foremast and from the stays and shrouds. Alongside these stately banners were thousands of little silk pennons, attached to every inch of wood and rigging and flying gaily in the wind.

It was this vessel that Philip and his gentlemen boarded on the afternoon of July 12, as the sailors in red and yellow liveries hung from the masts and yards and performed gymnastic tricks on the ropes. The crowd of townspeople who came to watch the departure of the prince knew that he was sailing to England to be married, but there was no mistaking the larger diplomatic object of his marriage—to strengthen Hapsburg power at the expense of the king of France. As the prince boarded the *Espíritu Santo* they not only shouted out wishes for a safe voyage but "hurled defiance to the French."[4]

The fleet put out to sea in a high wind, and throughout the first night and all the next day heavy weather kept the prince and his retinue below decks. Philip was unusually susceptible to seasickness, and to make his misery as brief as possible the English envoys arranged for him to land at Plymouth instead of the officially designated port of Southampton should he need to.[5] He set sail on Friday, and by Wednesday morning the English coast came into view. The sea was calmer now, and the strong current brought the Spanish ships past the Needles and into the coastal waters between Southampton and the Isle of Wight the following day. Fortunately the prince had not been ill, and was ready to receive the first of several deputations from the shore on the very day the *Espíritu Santo* dropped anchor three miles out in Southampton Water.

The English admiral, Lord William Howard, was his first guest. Philip managed to contend with Howard's bluff playfulness, but the admiral's mocking reference to the Flemish ships as "mussel-shells" infuriated the Flemings, and he started a quarrel with the Spanish admiral as well. When Howard saw that the foreign ships had not lowered their topsails on entering English waters he shot off a gun in their direction, reminding them to do so, and his English sailors looked across the bows of their ships at the Spaniards with undisguised contempt.[6]

The next day, after receiving a boatload of young lords who begged him to accept them as gentlemen of his chamber—the eldest sons of the earls of Arundel, Derby, Shrewsbury and Pembroke, and the duke of Norfolk's grandson—Philip went on board a royal barge to be escorted the short distance to shore. While still aboard his own ship he had been invested with the Garter, and he stepped on English soil a Garter Knight. Mary was not there to meet him—she was waiting at a country house two miles away—but she had sent him a white horse, beautifully trapped in crimson velvet ornamented with gold, to carry him to church to give thanks for his safe voyage. Sir Anthony Browne met the prince as he stepped on shore, greeting him in Latin and telling him that he had been sent to serve as his master of the horse, indicating the rich mount that stood waiting. Philip replied graciously that he could just as well walk, but Browne was insistent, lifting the prince into the saddle and kissing his stirrups in the traditional gesture of deference. Browne led Philip's horse all the way to the church of the Holy Rood, stopping only at the gate of the town to allow the prince to solemnly receive the keys to the town from the Lord Mayor.

Philip stayed in Southampton three days, in apartments hung with tapestries commemorating the deeds of Henry VIII and embroidered with his offensive titles "Defender of the Faith" and "Head of the Church."[7] He slept late each morning, then dressed and met with Mary's councilors and other lords who presented themselves to kiss his hand. There was little else to occupy him in Southampton—then a small community with only three hundred houses—and it rained incessantly throughout the prince's stay. Mary had appointed her lord privy seal to report to Philip on "the whole state of this realm with all things appertaining to the same," and to give him any advice he might ask for, but as yet Philip knew too little of England and her politics even to frame a question. He did make a formal speech to the councilors, assuring them that he had not come to England to enrich himself—for, as God knew, he had enough lands and riches to content any prince living—but because he had been called by the divine goodness to be Mary's husband. He would live with her and with them, he said, as "a right good and loving prince," and hoped they would fulfill their promise to be "faithful, obedient and loyal to him" in their turns.

Philip was well aware that his every word and gesture were being noted and judged by the English, and went out of his way to create an atmosphere of casual good will in order to put them at ease about him. On his first evening ashore he joined a roomful of lords and gentlemen talking informally among themselves. He greeted them genially and then went over to talk to Lord Howard, "to whom he showed great favor." He even attempted a clumsy pleasantry, remarking to the admiral that he now realized none of the suits he had brought with him was elegant enough to wear on his wedding day, or as rich as "the greatness of the queen deserved." But he hoped to have a suit made from the trappings of the horse Mary had sent him, he added, meaning to compliment her gift and to disparage his own sartorial splendor. Just then great ewers of wine, beer and ale were brought in, and tall silver drinking pots. Philip turned to his Spanish companions and announced that from now on they must forget Spanish customs and adopt English ones, and that he would show them how. Ordering beer to be brought to him, he drank it down after the English fashion, much to the approval of the Englishmen present.

The prince gave every appearance of being a carefree young man looking forward to his wedding day, but behind his joviality he was gravely distressed. While he was still at sea word had come from his father that on June 26 the French had seized Marienbourg, a strong fortress on the border of the imperial lands, and that within days they might be in Brussels itself. Already bands of French scouts and arsonists were chasing the peasants off their lands and burning their houses and fields, while

Charles' own soldiers, taken completely by surprise, were trying to collect themselves for a counterattack. The emperor appealed to his son to come to his aid, to stay in England only long enough to get married and enjoy a brief honeymoon, then sail for Flanders.

Philip sent word from Southampton that he was willing to do as his father asked, and ordered his servants not to bring his horses ashore as he would only have to order them loaded again in a few days. The French seizure of Marienbourg troubled Mary as well as she waited to meet Philip. She feared Charles might take advantage of the new ties binding England to the Hapsburg lands to ask that English soldiers be sent to the defense of Brussels. But by the time the wedding day arrived the crisis had passed. The French were not prepared to do more than harass the countryside around the imperial capital, and the emperor's troops eventually gathered themselves to push them back across the border.

It soon became obvious that Philip would have nothing to combat but the English weather, which grew worse day by day. On his second day in Southampton Philip had to borrow a hat and cape from one of the Englishmen to protect his clothing when he rode to mass. Two days later when he left the port to ride to Winchester, where he was to meet the queen and take his wedding vows, it was raining violently, and the road became a muddy ditch. Philip covered his diamond-studded surcoat with a red felt cloak for the journey, but long before he arrived in the episcopal city he was drenched and his white satin trunks and doublet were stained and splattered. He stopped at a hospital—once a monastery—just outside the city and changed into a suit of black and white velvet covered with gold bugles, and continued on his way, flanked by the sad-looking Spanish guardsmen in their soaking liveries and his bedraggled but faithful noblemen.

The prince rode into Winchester at dusk, and went directly to the cathedral, where Gardiner and four other bishops met him and sang a Te Deum. The church was crowded with onlookers, packed so tightly "they were all in danger of stifling," and after the ceremony of thanksgiving was ended the people followed Philip as he made his way to the dean's house, where he would spend the night. The queen's guard kept the crowd at a distance from the prince, but he turned and bowed slightly, first to one side, then the other, as he passed them and they "much rejoiced to see his noble personage." Mary had come that day to the bishop of Winchester's palace, just across the cloister from the dean's house, and that night she and Philip were to meet for the first time.

If Philip felt the self-assurance of a handsome young prince matched with a woman much older and, by repute, less well favored than himself, his preparations for this first meeting did not reveal it. He changed his clothes once again, after deciding that his gold-embroidered suit and matching hat were not fine enough for the occasion, and put on a doublet and trunks of the softest white kid. Over these went a French surcoat intricately worked with silver and gold threads, and a matching cap with a long plume. Thus arrayed—"and very gallant he looked," one of his gentlemen observed—the prince and a dozen of his Spanish and Flemish courtiers crossed the narrow lane between the garden of the dean's house and that of the bishop's palace, and were admitted into a private garden, full of arbors and plashing fountains, and up a narrow winding staircase to where the queen was waiting.

Philip came into the room, a "long narrow room or corridor where they divert themselves," and stood smiling before Mary, the beloved Titian portrait come to life. A Scotsman who saw the prince at this time described how he appeared to British eyes. "Of visage he is well-favored, with a broad forehead and grey eyes, straight-nosed and [of] manly countenance. From the forehead to the point of his chin, his face groweth small; his pace is princely, and gait so straight and upright as he loseth no inch of height; with a yellow head and a yellow beard." The Scotsman found nothing whatever to complain of in the prince's appearance. "He is so well-proportioned of body, arm, leg, and every other limb to the same," he concluded, "as nature cannot work a more perfect pattern." After all the months of waiting, Philip proved himself worth waiting for.

Mary, though, was something of a disappointment to the Spaniards. It was not entirely her fault; nearly all Philip's Spanish gentlemen professed to find English women unattractive, preferring the full-bodied, olive-skinned Spanish women to the porcelain pallor and coltlike proportions of the English. But the queen, looking thinner than ever in a plain, tight-fitting black velvet gown, "cut high in the English style without any trimming," her complexion almost dead white and her small features drawn into an expression of hopeful anticipation, looked exactly what she was: Philip's maiden aunt.

Her first twelve months of rule had left her tired and careworn, and the excitement in her face on this night could not disguise the exhaustion of all she had lived through. She was naturally restless and somewhat high-strung, and the worries of the last few months had made her an insomniac. Near-constant anxiety over the safety of the country and the government, long hours of tedious work and the endless annoyance of living in the same household with an odd dozen squabbling politicians who ate, worked and slept in her immediate surroundings had all taken their toll. The circumstances of Mary's life over many years had doubtless robbed her of whatever self-absorbed sensuality she may once have possessed, and her romantic feelings for Philip had from the start been tainted by the accusation that the man who would be the best husband for her might well be the worst co-ruler for her country.

She bore the marks of these concerns now as she looked eagerly across the long corridor toward the prince and his party. Ruy Gomez, Philip's most intimate confidant, described Mary shortly afterward as "rather older than we had been told," but others in the group minced no words. "The queen is not at all beautiful," one of them wrote. "Small, and rather flabby than fat, she is of white complexion and fair, and has no eyebrows."[8]

Mary was walking up and down at the opposite end of the room when Philip came in, and as soon as she saw him she ran up to him and kissed her own hand, then took his. He greeted her in the English way, kissing her on the mouth. The only other persons in the room were four or five "aged nobles" and the same number of "old ladies." Mary had not wanted to risk showing herself to Philip in the company of her young unmarried gentlewomen. The fiancés sat down under a cloth of estate and began to talk together, searching one another's faces for signs of approval, liking, affection. Admiral Howard interrupted this most sensitive of exchanges with coarse reminders of the closeness of the wedding day, the appealingness of the bride, the prodigious capabilities of the groom, and so on, but his loud jokes did not distract Philip and Mary from one another. After a time Philip's gentlemen came up to kiss Mary's hand, and she in turn led the prince into an adjoining room where her ladies, two by two, presented themselves to be kissed.

Good manners demanded that this visit be a brief one, but when Philip was preparing to leave Mary took him by the hand and led him away for another long talk. "No wonder," the Spaniards remarked as they saw this. "She is so glad to get him and to see what a gallant swain he is." Finally, though, Mary had to let Philip go, after teaching him the English words "Good night, my lords all." He forgot it the first time, and had to be taught again, and even then the best he could do was "God ni hit," but the queen was delighted and her courtiers tolerant, and the interview ended happily.[9] Philip went off to his quarters satisfied that he had done his duty, and Mary retired to her bedchamber rejoicing that God had sent her a storybook prince.

PART FIVE

The King's Wife

XXXVIII

 But I shall do the best I can,
And marry some good honest man,
And brew good ale and tun.
Marriage by my opinion,
It is better religion
As to be friar or nun.

On the feast of St. James, patron saint of Spain, Mary and Philip were married in Winchester cathedral. The church was hung with rich tapestries and cloth of gold, and a raised wooden platform was erected at one end for the ceremony itself. On each side of the altar were two canopied seats for the bride and groom, and at the center of the wooden platform was a raised dais, upholstered in purple, where the five officiating bishops were to stand as the wedding mass was performed. Philip arrived first, wearing a white doublet and breeches and a French mantle Mary had sent him as a gift the day before. The mantle was made of cloth of gold trimmed in crimson velvet and lined in crimson satin. Thistles of curled gold were fastened to the gleaming fabric, and each of the twenty-four ornamental buttons on the sleeves was made from four large pearls. Philip also wore the jeweled collar of the Garter the queen had sent him earlier. He entered the church escorted by his principal gentlemen, and took his seat. No symbols of his titles were borne before him, but there had been an important change in his status since his arrival in England. The night before a document had come from Brussels making him king of Naples, and when it was read out, all the nobles present kissed Philip's hands in token of his royalty. Much to her pleasure Mary discovered that she would be marrying not a prince but a king.

About a half hour after Philip's coming Mary arrived at the church, the sword of royalty carried before her by the earl of Derby and the long train of her gown held by the marchioness of Winchester and the Lord Chamberlain Sir John Gage. She wore a gown of black velvet studded with precious stones, and over it a mantle of cloth of gold to match Philip's. An observer wrote that the queen "blazed with jewels to such an extent that the eye was blinded as it looked upon her," and she outshone everyone present. Mary's fifty gentlewomen, splendid in cloth of gold and silver, followed her, "looking more like celestial angels than mortal creatures."[1]

The most important part of Mary's wedding finery, though, was completely unadorned. It was her wedding ring, "a round hoop of gold, without any stone." She was a sentimental bride, and "her desire was to be married as maidens were married in the old time." The wedding ceremony, too, was in the old fashion, with bidding of the banns and offering of candles and crowns by both spouses. After a high mass the chancellor read the words of the marriage ceremony in English and Latin, assisted by his fellow bishops serving that day as deacon and subdeacon, all mitered and in their richest vestments. To calm Mary's apprehensions about the validity of a marriage performed in a country still officially under sentence of excommunication the emperor had obtained from the pope a dispensation declaring the union a lawful one by papal authority.[2] Philip had brought his own priest from Spain to perform the nuptial benediction. The solemnities lasted several hours, and all that time, it was noted, Mary never took her eyes off the sacrament. The Spaniards were uniformly impressed by her unaffected piety. "She is a saintly woman," one of them wrote admiringly.

The only tense moment came when Gardiner asked in a loud voice "if there be any man that knoweth any lawful impediment between these two parties," and invited all who objected to make themselves heard. There was no response, and he hurried on to the last part of the ritual. In place of her father the queen was given away by the marquis of Winchester, the earls of Derby, Bedford and Pembroke, "in the name of the whole realm," and then the ring was laid upon the Bible, along with the traditional three handfuls of fine gold. At this Lady Margaret Clifford, Mary's cousin and her only female relative present, opened the queen's purse and Mary, with a smile, put the gold inside. The trumpets sounded then to signal that the couple were now man and wife, and the earl of Pembroke unsheathed the second sword, to be carried before Philip now that he was Mary's wedded husband. The mass was concluded, with the spouses taking the sacrament and Philip following the old Catholic custom of kissing the celebrant, and finally the king of heralds then came forward and proclaimed the royal title and style:

"Philip and Mary, by the grace of God king and queen of England, France, Naples, Jerusalem, and Ireland, defenders of the faith, princes of

Spain and Silicy, archdukes of Austria, dukes of Milan, Burgundy, and Brabant, counts of Hapsburg, Flanders, and Tyrol."

The banquet hall in the bishop's palace was the scene of the wedding feast. Mary and Philip sat at a raised table, and four long tables at floor level were laid for the Spanish and English nobility. The guests ate standing up; only the royal pair were seated, with Mary in the favored place on the right and in a chair noticeably finer than her husband's. The Spaniards were quick to take note of this, and of the fact that while the queen ate from gold plate, the king was served on silver—a slight they hoped would be corrected once he was crowned. The quantity of valuable plate impressed them greatly. Even the least of the gentlefolk present were served on silver dishes, and tall sideboards full of platters, ewers and serving dishes stood at both ends of the hall. Behind the queen was another large display cabinet filled with more than a hundred great pieces of gold and silver plate, along with a "great gilt clock half as high as a man" and a marble fountain with a rim of solid gold.

Mary and Philip were served by the English noblemen whose hereditary privilege it was to present the basin, hold the napkin and pour the wine for the sovereign. Only one Spaniard, Don Inigo de Mendoza, was permitted to wait on Philip, and throughout the meal Lords Pembroke and Strange stood before the king and queen holding the sword and staff of state. As each dish was brought in it was saluted with low bows and a fanfare, and as this formality was repeated for each of the four courses of thirty dishes the banquet lasted several hours. Foreseeing this, Mary had ordered her surveyor of the works to arrange a place "for her highness to withdraw herself" from time to time during the afternoon. To do this he had had to break down the wall "at the back side of her table," marring the bishop's chamber for the convenience of the queen. There was only one alteration in Mary's plans for the wedding feast. The surcoat she provided for her consort—another French robe in cloth of gold with the roses of England and pomegranates of Spain intertwined in drawn gold beads and seed pearls—was left behind in the prince's apartment. With its eighteen huge buttons made from table diamonds it struck the bridegroom as ostentatious, and he chose not to wear it that day. In an inventory of his wardrobe annotated by Philip himself some years after his wedding day he wrote in the margin opposite this robe "This was given to me by the queen for me to wear on our wedding day in the afternoon, but I do not think I wore it because it seemed to me ornate."[3]

When the banquet was over and the queen had drunk a cup of wine to the health and honor of the guests the company went into the presence chamber where Philip's gentlemen attempted to make gallant conversation with Mary's ladies. As few of the Spaniards spoke English, they found this difficult. "We had great trouble to make out their meaning," one Spanish courtier wrote, "except of those who spoke Latin. So we have all resolved not to give them any presents of gloves until we can understand them." The writer added that, because of the obvious charm of his compatriots, "the gentlemen who speak the language are mostly very glad to find that the Spaniards cannot do so."[4] If conversation was awkward, dancing was virtually impossible, as neither group of courtiers knew the dances of the other. Mary and Philip found a compromise and danced together in the German fashion, though it was said that Mary, who was an excellent and enthusiastic dancer, was not adequately partnered by the unathletic Philip. The Spaniards in general were "greatly out of countenance" at the superior virtuosity of the Englishmen, especially Lord Bray, a spectacular dancer known as "a paragon in court, and of sweet entertainment."[5]

On this mortifying note the festivities ended early, and by nine o'clock the last of the guests had retired. Mary and Philip were escorted to their separate apartments, where they dined alone, then met again at the lodgings prepared for their wedding night. On the door Gardiner had ordered these rather insipid verses subscribed in Roman lettering:

> Thou art happy house, right blest and blest again,
> That shortly shalt such noble guests retain.

The bed was blessed by the chancellor, who then left husband and wife alone, still dressed in their wedding finery and in "great quantities of jewellery." "What happened that night," a hopeful Spaniard wrote shortly afterward, "only they know. If they give us a son our joy will be complete."[6]

When Philip's gentlemen presented themselves outside the royal bedchamber the next morning, Mary's shocked attendants stood resolutely between the Spaniards and the door and refused to let them in. To call on a newly married woman the morning after her wedding night was "not honest," they said; furthermore, English queens by custom did not appear in public until the second day after their weddings. What Mary's gentlewomen did not realize was that in Spain custom required that the rulers be congratulated in bed on the morning following their marriage, and if Philip had been there he might have explained the misunderstanding. But Philip was gone; he got up at seven and worked at his desk until eleven, when he went to mass and then dined alone.

Flemish affairs were very much on his mind. The French were in retreat—after taking Binche and destroying the regent's palace—and the emperor's forces were in pursuit. The raids had been costly, however, and Charles confessed to his son in England that his treasury had been badly drained and his Flemish territories exhausted by the conflict. He ordered Philip to stay with Mary for the time being, "busying himself with the government of England," and in fact the king had more than enough to do to keep him occupied, as he was readying the fleet that had brought him to England to sail immediately for Flanders. Like Mary he spent a good many hours at his desk each day, and did not see his wife until evening. Mary was left to face the intricacies of exchanging visits with her new Spanish courtiers on her own.

Courtesy demanded that the queen begin the exchange by inviting into her presence the wife of the principal nobleman, the duchess of Alva. On the third day after the wedding the duchess was escorted to the queen's apartments by all the lords and gentlemen of the court. She had just come from Southampton the day before, having missed the wedding, and this was to be her first meeting with Mary. The duchess took great care to prepare herself for the interview, dressing in an elegant black velvet gown trimmed in lace and black silk embroidery and having her hair beautifully arranged. Mary, who was doing her best to dress like a Spanish woman, wore black damask with a stomacher of black velvet embroidered with gold. Both women were doubtless apprehensive about the meeting, but the duchess was completely unprepared for the ebullience and girlish eagerness of the queen. Instead of allowing her maids of honor to bring the duchess into the presence chamber Mary waited for her in the antechamber herself. When the Spanish woman entered Mary went up to her at once, and the duchess, not knowing how to make a proper obeisance to a sovereign who was not seated on a throne, sank to her knees and reached for Mary's hand to kiss. Mary refused to give her hand, and instead stooped over and hugged the duchess as she knelt, lifting her bodily to her feet again and kissing her firmly on the mouth, "as queens of England do to great ladies of their own blood, but to none other."

Mary led her uncomfortable visitor in the direction of a high-backed chair raised off the floor, all the while telling her in an animated tone how pleased she was to see her, and asking about her journey and sea voyage. When they reached the chair Mary abruptly sat down on a cushion on the floor and graciously offered the seat of honor to the duchess. This was too much for the Spaniard, who implored the queen to take the chair herself. Mary refused, and ordered two brocaded stools to be brought. But when Mary sat on one of these the duchess would only bow very low and sit on a cushion. At this Mary returned to her cushion again, causing the duchess fresh embarrassment, and the struggle to avoid preeminence continued until the duchess, too exhausted to protest further, agreed that they both should sit on the stools.

Once the seating etiquette was settled the two women appeared to get on well, and none of the quarrels Renard feared would break out be-

tween the Spanish noblewomen and their English sisters actually occurred. As for the royal couple, they were reported to be "bound together by such deep love that the marriage may be expected to be a
perfect union." This platitudinous judgment was somewhat inexact. A
closer approximation of the truth was that Philip was doing the job assigned to him—to make himself agreeable to all the English, and especially to their queen—more capably than anyone had thought he would.
The English appeared to like him very much indeed. "His way with the
lords is so winning," Philip's closest friend and confidant Ruy Gomez
wrote, "that they themselves say they have never had a king to whom
they so quickly grew attached."[7] "The king is certainly a master hand at
it when he cares to try," Ruy Gomez added, and his mastery of the
queen's affections was in no doubt. Mary referred fondly to Philip in letters to the emperor as "my lord and husband," "him whose presence I desired more than that of any other living being."[8]

Mary favorably impressed the Spaniards fully as much as Philip did
the English. "She is so good that we may well thank God for giving us
such a bountiful princess to be our queen," one of them wrote. "God
save her!" Ruy Gomez called her "a very good creature," while another
courtier saw her as "a perfect saint." They were unanimous, though, in
concluding that her physical charms had been overrated. The problem
was partly her clothes. To the Spaniards, who disliked English clothes intensely, the queen appeared to "dress badly," but they conceded that if
dressed in the Spanish fashion "she would not look so old and flabby."[9]

The real problem, however, was not her clothes. "To speak frankly
with you," Ruy Gomez remarked obliquely in a letter sent to Spain, "it
will take a great God to drink this cup." For a prince of Philip's youth
and endowments, marriage with a painfully inexperienced, sexually un-
awakened woman of thirty-eight was bound to be something of a trial, at
least at first, but Philip had never expected a passionate match. "He treats
the queen very kindly," Ruy Gomez noticed, "and well knows how to
pass over the fact that she is no good from the point of view of fleshly
sensuality. He makes her so happy that the other day when they were
alone she almost talked love-talk to him, and he replied in the same
vein."[10] He was tactful, attentive and gallant; he missed no detail of
courtesy, and, when he was not attending to matters of state, never left
Mary's side. Their compatibility was doubtless strengthened by the fact
that they could not speak one another's language. Mary spoke only
Aragonese, though she understood Philip's Castilian Spanish; he in turn
understood no English, and relatively little of the French Mary was
forced to speak to him.

The pageantry with which Londoners greeted Philip on his first entry
into the city on August 18 seemed to confirm Ruy Gomez' feeling that

the English had taken Mary's husband to their hearts. At London Bridge two giants saluted him as "noble Prince, sole hope of Caesar's side,/By God appointed all the world to guide," and at the end of Gracechurch Street, at the Sign of the Splayed Eagle, an equestrian statue of the prince in the antique style greeted him as "worthy Philip the fortunate and most mighty Prince of Spain, most earnestly wished for." The royal consort was compared in another pageant to Philip the Bold, Philip the Good of Burgundy, the Roman Emperor Philip the Arabian and Philip of Macedonia, father of Alexander the Great, but the most flattering comparison was made in Cheap, where the prince was represented as Orpheus taming the wild beasts with his harp. The sight of the harp player, surrounded by nine "fair ladies playing and singing on diverse sweet instruments"—the nine Muses—and by men and children disguised as lions, wolves, foxes and bears, "dancing and leaping with Orpheus' harp and the Muses' melody," delighted Philip and Mary very much, as did the by now traditional appearance of the acrobat sliding down a rope stretched from St. Paul's steeple to the ground.

Though large crowds watched the royal couple make their way through the streets, and many people ran about joyfully, "calling and crying 'God save your graces,'" still by mid-August the presence of the Spaniards had begun to seem oppressive. Philip himself might be a gentleman, but the rest of the foreigners were distinctly unwelcome. Months before they arrived Mary had issued a proclamation ordering all her subjects to extend "courtesy, friendly and gentle entertainment" to the Spaniards, "without either by outward deeds, taunting words, or unseemly countenance" giving any insult to the visitors. But no proclamation could keep the distrust and hostility of the English in check. "Disagreeable incidents" between Englishmen and Spaniards began almost as soon as Philip arrived, and every inconvenience or disturbance that occurred at court was blamed on the presence of the foreigners. Their actual numbers were very small, but to the English they were everywhere. One English diarist claimed that for every Englishman he saw on the streets of London there were four Spaniards, and the taverns of the capital were full of rumors that thousands more of the strangers were about to disembark at the Channel ports.

The apparent prosperity of the visitors irritated the English almost as much as their manners and their looks. At court the elegant dress of the Spanish nobles and their satin-clad servants, and the sumptuous bed-hangings, velvet canopies and quilts embroidered in gold and seed pearls they had brought from home aroused the envy of the English courtiers. They seemed never to run out of money, no matter how high the English raised the prices of food and lodging, and when Philip's treasure was conveyed through the city for storage at the Tower Londoners marveled at its vast extent. Twenty carts rumbled through the streets, carrying ninety-seven treasure chests full of gold, and doubtless creating the impression that the supply was infinite. Money speculators were quick to set up an exchange in St. Paul's to try to profit from the superabundance of Spanish coin, while the French, hoping to deepen the suspicions of the English toward the Spaniards, put false Spanish coins into circulation.[11]

The Spanish, on the other hand, were worried lest the English realize how little money they actually had. "If the English find out how hard up we are," Ruy Gomez wrote, "I doubt whether we shall escape with our lives." Money was the key to retaining what minimal good will English officials, servants, merchants and innkeepers showed toward the foreigners; once the Spaniards ran out of money, Gomez feared, they would be abused like pickpockets.[12] Philip, whose resources were far from infinite, was alarmed to discover that he had to pay for two households instead of one. The terms of the marriage contract had been interpreted more literally by the English than by Philip and his advisers, and he now found himself having to be served by English counterparts of the men he had brought with him from Spain. Worse still, he found he was expected to pay all these English servants himself, with no part of the cost shared by the queen.[13]

These economic difficulties might be solved in time, but more intangible disparities separating the Spaniards from their English hosts grew worse and worse. The longer they stayed the more the Spaniards found to criticize. The English gossiped too much, they said, had no respect for the clergy, and lacked cultural refinement. Their dances were "strutting or trotting about," and their women immodest and unappealing. Mary's palaces were large but uncomfortable, "full to bursting" with the servants, lackeys and grooms of her enormous household. Yet the only entertainment to be found there was eating and drinking—"the only pastime they understand," the Spanish claimed. Eighteen kitchens were kept operating at full blast, one of the Spaniards wrote, "and they seem veritable hells, such is the stir and bustle in them." Dozens of cooks toiled over the carcasses of eighty to a hundred sheep every day, not to mention a dozen cows, eighteen calves, boar and deer when available, and great numbers of chickens and rabbits. As for the drinking habits of Mary's courtiers, they consumed enough beer to fill the Valladolid river, and the younger ones, inclined to be amorous on summer nights, "put sugar in their wine, with the result that there are great goings on in the palace."[14] Whether it was the copious English food or the climate—or both—by late summer most of the Spaniards had had to take to their beds with bad colds or worse illnesses. Philip caught cold right away, and some members of his Spanish household were sick enough to cause concern for their lives before the summer was over.

On top of this, the English underworld soon discovered that the Spaniards made easy marks. There were thieves in Spain, of course, but one never saw them; they worked at night, or when the victim's back was turned or his house empty. English highwaymen were an unexpected danger to the foreigners, who lost large sums to them in their first months in England. In the first week after Philip's arrival there were several major robberies, in one of which four chests of the prince's own household furnishings were taken. Bands of twenty or more highwaymen watched the roads for the red and gold liveries of Spanish servants, knowing they carried coins and valuables. "They rob us in town and on the road," an anonymous Spanish gentleman explained to his correspondent in Spain. "No one ventures to stray two miles but they rob him; and a company of Englishmen have recently robbed and beaten over fifty Spaniards." If the visitors complained of this treatment, no one listened. As far as the English were concerned, the hated Spaniards were only a temporary curse, to be endured with hostile indifference until Philip had served his purpose as the father of Mary's children. "When she has children of him, they say, he may go home to Spain," the Spanish gentleman reported, and he only regretted that Mary did not seem likely to be fruitful.

To be sure, the Spaniards found much to appreciate in the country itself. England, they believed, was the land where King Arthur had lived and died, the place whose enchanted landscape had formed the backdrop to many a tale of chivalry. "The man who wrote *Amadis* and other books of chivalry, with all the flowery meads, pleasure-houses and enchantments, must first have visited England," one of Philip's gentlemen commented, and he wrote glowingly of the forests, meadows, castles and fresh springs of the countryside. But even these delights could not compensate for the rudeness of the populace, and before long the homesick Spaniards were saying "they would rather be in the worst stubble field in the kingdom of Toledo than in the groves of Amadis," and one by one they begged Philip to let them leave. The proud duke of Medina-Celi left first, and soon some eighty lesser lords had taken ship, some to join the war in Flanders, others to go home to Spain. It was even suggested that Philip might want to follow them, provided he could be certain he would be allowed into the country again once he returned.[15]

But Philip was determined to stay in England for the time being, and a small group of Spanish noblemen and personal servants stayed with him. As the king settled into his routine as Mary's husband these servants made themselves as comfortable as they could, paying ever-rising rates for their lodging and food and attempting to insulate themselves from the mounting abuse around them. By September Renard was informing the emperor that all the Spaniards would have to be moved either to the palace where the king was staying or else far away in the country, "to protect them from the rapacity of the people." The foreigners did their best to "move among the English as if they were animals, trying not to notice them," but it seemed to be impossible to avoid violence.

By the last week of September there was fighting in the halls of the palace nearly every day, and three Englishmen and a Spaniard were hanged following a murderous brawl. In the midst of the wrangling came the first whispered hints that the queen was pregnant.

XXXIX

 Nowe singe, nowe springe, oure care is exil'd
Oure virtuous Quene is quickned with child.

When Mary's physicians told her in September that in all probability she was pregnant the news was deeply satisfying. Once again God
had intervened at a decisive moment, this time lifting her above the limitations of age and health that many said would prevent her from having
children. The event was congruent with the fortuitous course of her life,
which had been preserved amid danger and prospered in the face of
seemingly overwhelming odds. That she had outlived her father was an
amazing improbability; that she had come to the throne a near miracle.
Her triumph over Dudley, her resolute defiance of Wyatt, her determined accomplishment of the Spanish marriage were feats none of the
men around her had believed possible. To Mary these improbable triumphs were ever increasing proof that she was being guided toward the
divinely ordained destiny of restoring the true faith in England. The
culmination of that destiny would be the birth of a Catholic heir to
ensure that Mary's religious changes would not die with her.

The immediate effect of the good news was to calm the escalating
hostilities between the Spaniards and the English. The rapprochement
came none too soon, for the enmity of the English had reached such a
pitch that several mass assassinations had been plotted. According to
Noailles, one of these plots called for the conspirators to surround Hampton Court in the middle of the night, storm the palace, and slaughter all
the Spaniards inside—and the queen and her councilors with them,
Noailles felt sure. There were more than enough assaults on a smaller
scale to make this rumored conspiracy plausible. The English had begun
to carry arquebuses everywhere they went, and at the slightest alarm
they rushed through the streets, weapons in hand, falling upon the first

Spaniards they met. Renard reported seeing one of the lower court functionaries attack and beat two Spaniards as they walked in the street at three o'clock in the afternoon. He was no match for them, and soon ran off, but before he did he pulled a gun from under his cloak, pointed it at one of the foreigners, and then, "to show what a brave man he was," fired it into the air.[1] The Spaniards did not take such insults lightly. Three days after this incident occurred the injured parties found their assailant and killed him not far from the palace.

Renard had felt for some time that the one certain remedy for these disorders would be the announcement of the queen's pregnancy, and as soon as he heard of her condition he spread the word as widely as he could, "in order to keep the malcontents within bounds." A visitor to Mary's court, an ambassador sent by the duke of Savoy, spread the story further. "The queen is with child," he wrote in a dispatch. "I have personal reason to believe it, as I have noticed her feeling sick to her stomach." Like Renard the Savoyard talked to the royal doctor, who gave him "positive assurance" of the pregnancy, adding that "if it were not true all the signs described by physicians would prove to be fallacious."[2]

By October the mood of the court had changed. Courtiers who had been at each other's throats mellowed, and returned to the guarded courtesy they had shown one another on Philip's arrival in July. The Spaniards showed their good will by staging a tournament in the Iberian style—a "cane play" or joust in which canes took the place of lances. The English found the sport bland, but joined in anyway, and it was noticed that the two groups of courtiers no longer kept to themselves at banquets and dances but had begun to mingle again. At one of these dances Admiral Howard presented a masque performed by eight sailors in particolored trousers of cloth of gold and silver with jerkins and hoods to match. They danced a vigorous hornpipe, and then were joined by all those present, including the king and queen. Both were "in health, and merry," and appeared to be enjoying themselves.

Mary's pregnancy brought into sharper relief the question of her joint sovereignty with Philip. Strictly speaking he was the queen's husband and nothing more. He had not been crowned king. Whatever royal prerogative he possessed would not outlast Mary's lifetime, and those of her subjects who saw him as the future father of the queen's children and nothing more were in a sense not far wrong. But tradition was stronger than legalities, and tradition called for the wife to defer to her husband's authority in all things. How a reigning queen, a sovereign recognizing no superior on earth, might be expected to take second place to her much younger husband, a king in name but not in function and a man with few legal rights of any kind within her country, was a dilemma outside the concerns of Mary's advisers. What mattered was that, to preserve his dignity, Philip had to be given at the very least the appearance of primacy, and something of its substance as well. For to put Philip second in any way was an insult, while to put Mary second was in accord with scriptural teachings, the norms of society and the unquestioned truism that women were less capable than men.

In the months following her marriage Mary found that her delight in Philip's comforting presence had been acquired at a considerable cost. In the eyes of the men in her government she had become the king's wife, the lesser partner in the monarchy, who was expected to settle comfortably into a role heretofore denied her only because of the dynastic peculiarities of the house of Tudor. It was as if the cohesive leadership she had shown during the first year of her reign—leadership that had never failed to amaze them, and that had been forgotten by the time the next crisis arrived—was a mere aberration in the continuity of male sovereignty in England. Now that she was married this sort of authority was no longer needed.

Two things made this shift in perception both insidious and devastating. One was that it was not overt but tacit: an unspoken, all-pervasive, commonly held belief about the natural status of the king's wife. There was no malice in it either; Mary was to be subordinate to Philip less because of her personal inadequacy than because of the ponderous, impersonal weight of custom centuries old. The other was that from now on Mary had to contend with conflicting forces within herself. In childhood she had learned to expect marriage, to abhor yet emphasize her attractive powers and to esteem herself below men. In adolescence this deep conditioning had been shaken by the tormenting spectacle of her parents' divorce and her own disgrace, and since the age of twenty Mary had been sustained by an alternative vision of her future. Instead of expecting the conventional destiny of marriage she had come to believe that she would fulfill a more exalted role. This higher destiny did not preclude marriage, but it was hardly compatible with a life of passive subordination.

For the time being, however, this conflict had been resolved by the joyous compromise of Mary's pregnancy. For if in the view of those around her her condition underscored the inappropriateness of her supremacy in the government it nonetheless satisfied both her childhood expectations and her adult hopes. The child she carried fulfilled her earliest image of herself, while at the same time it reaffirmed her conviction in the divinely guided course of her life. She could afford to let Philip bear more than his share of authority while she undertook the all-important responsibility of nurturing the Catholic heir to the throne.

Even before Philip landed at Southampton Mary's courtiers were speaking of him as if they expected him to rule them as well as reign over them. The proverb *"Novus Rex, Nova Lex"*—"New King, New

Law"—was repeated at the Council table and in the letters of courtiers to one another, and English diplomats at foreign courts sent nervous inquiries about whether they should expect to be recalled once the new king arrived. There was no outward change in the procedure of government, apart from an order from the Council that a brief summary of state business should be drawn up from time to time, in Latin or Spanish, and given to whomever Philip appointed to review it on his behalf. Documents bearing the names of both sovereigns were to be signed by both, it was decided, but this too was a simple and obvious matter of administrative routine. Coins struck with Mary's image alone were replaced by new ones with the profiles of both the king and queen in mid-September, by which time Philip appeared, to foreign visitors at least, to be in command of affairs. The Savoyard ambassador reported that "the king hears and dispatches all state affairs, as it befits his dignity and authority that he should." Philip seemed to be as approachable and friendly with the English as if he were an Englishman himself, the ambassador remarked, adding significantly that "he already has the same authority as his predecessors on the throne of England."[8]

Correspondence between Philip's retainers and his councilors in Spain puts his situation in England in quite a different light. Late in August Philip was asking that a ship be sent from Spain to be "placed at his disposal so that he may return without delay." Correctly or not, the Spanish Council took this to be an urgent appeal for rescue. The Council members were anxious, and the admiral, presuming Philip to be in grave danger, drew up an escape plan. He would quickly equip a fleet, ostensibly to take soldiers to Flanders but in fact to bring Philip back to Spain. The Spanish fleet would anchor off an English port, and then, on the pretext of inspecting it, Philip would be rowed out to the flagship. Once aboard he would be safely out of English hands. He could leave without a word, or he could strike a bargain with the English under which he would agree to come ashore on condition that they "arrange matters so as to permit him to live there as befits their Sovereign Lord."[4]

Whether or not Philip was on satisfactory terms with Mary's councilors, on one point at least the queen, king and Council were agreed. Now that Mary was pregnant it was more important than ever that England be reconciled with the church of Rome.

On November 20, 1554, Cardinal Reginald Pole landed at Dover and made his way to London, where the third Parliament of the reign had been convened several weeks earlier. He had been appointed legate by the pope, Julius III, fifteen months before, but his coming to England had been repeatedly postponed. Mary had written him several times, urging him to be as patient and deliberate as she was in the work of returning

England to the Catholic fold, and though he could not agree with her policy he had no choice but to wait at Brussels until he received the formal summons from the queen. In the twenty years since he left England Pole had become a changed man. He was no longer the witty courtier whose urbanity and keen mind had won him the favor of Henry VIII. He had become "sad and grave" in appearance, and his long, somewhat drawn face with its solemn, widely-spaced eyes and feline features was that of a fastidious ascetic. It was also the face of a man deeply scarred by family tragedy and, behind the mildness and melancholy in his eyes, animated by revenge.

Pole had become a great churchman, a principal figure in the movement of reform that had been renovating the Roman church since the 1530s. Appointed to the college of cardinals by Paul III, first of a series of popes concerned with purifying the lives of the clergy and restoring to Rome the spiritual leadership of the Christian world, Pole had worked for two decades to rid the church of the worldliness and institutionalized greed that fed anticlericalism and helped Protestantism to flourish. His commitment to the cause of the church was deepened by the evident success of his efforts and by his increasingly high standing among his peers. In the papal election of 1549 a group of cardinals offered to make him pope "by adoration," but because he hesitated to accept the honor he lost the election by two votes. He made light of his lost opportunity, largely because, like Mary, he believed he was being saved for some higher purpose.

Pole's years in exile had deepened not only his faith but his bitterness. He blamed Henry VIII for the tortured course of his personal life. It was Henry's willful breach with the pope which had first sent Pole into exile, and later, when he had become the king's hated enemy, it was Henry's cruelty which brought Pole's entire family to the block. The one brother who had been spared, the pitiable Geoffrey Pole, brought the cardinal more shame than comfort, and only made the loss of his other relatives more poignant.

In the aftermath of this loss Pole seems to have conceived a sanguinary view of his experience. He envisioned the execution of his blameless old mother as a martyrdom to be compared to the deaths of Christ and the saints of the early church. He called himself the "son of a martyr," and referred to his injuries at the hands of the king as if they were physical wounds. His pain and grief he called the "stigmata of his obedience" to the church, and he clearly believed his life had to be sacrificed to God in order to avenge the wrongs done to his relatives.[5] The appropriate victim of his vengeance would have been Henry VIII, but Henry was dead. The Protestant doctrines he had helped to bring into England were still in existence, however. By helping to root them out Pole would be destroying a substantial part of the king's legacy while serving the interests of the church and ensuring the salvation of the countrymen from whom he had been estranged for so long. This, he believed, was the work God intended him for—the preordained purpose for his life.

If Mary delayed Pole's return to England for political reasons, the emperor encouraged the delay for quite different reasons of his own. A year earlier Renard had written him that Mary had more regard for Pole than for all the members of her Council put together, and the last thing Charles wanted was another influential man at Mary's court. Philip, not Pole, must remain the primary source of support and advice to the queen. Yet as much as Mary loved her husband, she was bound to the cardinal by unique ties. Both had known their happiest times in the days before England's breach with Rome. Both had had their lives shattered by the king's divorce; both had lost their mothers to the king's cruelty. Both had lived through years of isolation and suffering for the sake of the Catholic faith, living in danger of death yet believing that in the end their fidelity would result in a glorious vindication.

The remarkable similarity of their emotional experience, plus the natural affinity between them, meant that Pole's influence on Mary would be very great—and very harmful. For of all the men around the queen who minimized her authority, Pole was the most blatant. He had not been with her at Framlingham; he had not heard her speech at the Guildhall when Wyatt was at the gates of London. He had not seen her handle Gardiner or Paget, or assert her will eloquently in Parliament. He assumed that she was weak and incapable, and he had the effect of making her believe it too.

In one other respect his advice was misguided. He assumed that the religious situation in England was not unlike that in Italy, where the Protestant heresy had taken rather shallow root and had been decisively crushed by the papal Inquisition. He would never realize how profoundly the English had changed during their generation of independence from papal rule, and how hardy English Protestantism had become. Restoration of the Catholic faith in England was a far greater challenge than Pole was prepared to undertake when he sailed in the queen's barge from Gravesend to London on that November day, his silver cross shining over the prow.

On the afternoon of November 28 the cardinal came before Parliament at Whitehall and spoke to the members about the purpose of his commission. After praising Mary—"a virgin, helpless, naked, and unarmed," who "prevailed and had the victory over tyrants"—he explained that he had been given the power to formally reunite England with the church of Rome, in a spirit of forgiveness and welcome. "My commission is not of prejudice to any person," he told them. "I come to reconcile, not to condemn. I come not to compel, but to call again." Most important, he assured the members indirectly that once England was rejoined to Rome no attempt would be made to take back the lands that had once belonged to the church but had long since been in private hands. "Touching all matters that be past," he said, "they shall be as things cast into the sea of forgetfulness."[6]

Two days later Parliament made its official request for reunion with Rome. It was in the form of a petition to Philip and Mary, as "persons undefiled in the offence of this body," to intercede with the legate to grant the papal pardon. The Lords and Commons fell on their knees, and Pole pronounced the absolution. A public absolution was made the following Sunday. The legate came to St. Paul's, his cross and poleaxes carried before him. There he met Gardiner and a crowd of bishops and clergy, and a Te Deum was sung. Afterward they met Philip, who had come from Westminster with a great many of the courtiers and his four hundred guardsmen. A huge crowd of fifteen thousand people—the largest crowd ever seen in St. Paul's churchyard, it was said—heard Gardiner deliver a two-hour sermon on the text "It is time to awake out of sleep." At its end he announced that Pole had given him the authority to absolve all who were present. The entire crowd knelt for his blessing. "A sight to be seen it was," wrote a Spanish eyewitness. "And the silence was such that not a cough was heard."

The reunion with Rome was nearly complete. Now all that remained was for Parliament to enact the legal instruments that would restore the ancient faith by statute. During December this task was accomplished. In the lengthy Second Statute of Repeal all legislation hindering the authority of the pope in England was repealed, and the country declared absolved of its schismatic errors. All the clergy ordained and promoted since the schism began were declared confirmed in their orders and benefices. All the marriages performed by schismatic clerics were made legal, and the children born of them legitimate. The judgments made by the church courts were upheld, and the current possessors of church lands were confirmed in their possessions, "clear from all dangers of the censures of the church." In view of the expected birth there was legislation providing for the eventuality of Mary's death in childbirth. Philip was declared regent for the heir to the throne should the queen die while he or she was a minor. Philip expected a proposal to be made to crown him king, but there was none.

More ominous was the revival, soon after the absolution was declared, of medieval statutes prescribing how heretics tried in church courts were to be handed over to the civil officials for execution. How this bill was brought before Parliament is unclear, but it was not an unusual proposal in a session preoccupied with religious affairs. It was in any case a purely procedural change, since the death penalty for heresy was a punishment of long standing. Whatever its origin, the bill passed unanimously.

In political terms, the reunion with Rome was at best a compromise. The Lords and Commons were willing to rejoin the Catholic confession only if they were allowed to keep the spoils of the dissolution. The spiritual rights of the church could be restored as long as its temporal wealth remained in private hands. But to Mary this flaw in the proceedings was of little consequence compared to the overwhelming triumph she had gained. What her father had destroyed she and Pole had built up again. And if there were any doubt that God was directing the course of events to fulfill his will, Mary had special proof of his favor. She had received a holy sign.

In the gospel of Luke the writer described the meeting of the virgin Mary and her cousin Elizabeth. Both women were pregnant, Mary with Jesus and Elizabeth with John, the future John the Baptist. When Elizabeth saw Mary she felt her child leap within her, in recognition of Mary's son. When Mary Tudor first glimpsed Cardinal Pole, she believed she could feel her child leap in her womb.

XL

If hap may aunswere hope,
And hope may have his hire,
Then shall my hart possess in peace,
The time that I desire.

Mary's quickening was celebrated with a ceremony of thanksgiving at St. Paul's on November 28, with the preacher taking as his
theme the words of the angel to the virgin Mary: "Fear not, Mary, for
thou hast found favor with God."[1] The clergy made a solemn procession around the circuit of the church, chanting *"Salve, festa dies"* as on a
festival day, and at every mass from then on special prayers were offered
for the birth of a prince. "Give therefore unto thy servants Philip our
king and Mary our queen, a male issue," ran one of these prayers, "which
may sit in the seat of thy kingdom." Make him, the supplicant asked, "in
body comely and beautiful, in pregnant wit notable and excellent, in obedience like Abraham, in hospitality like Lot, in strength and valor like
Samson."

Every imaginable biblical parallel was employed to persuade God to
perform the miracle of a safe delivery. If the barren Elizabeth—to whom
Mary compared herself—and the ninety-year-old Sarah could bring forth
sons, then so could the thirty-nine-year-old queen; the God who "didst
safely deliver the prophet Jonas out of the whale's belly" could surely
bring Mary's child safely into the world. A prayer written by the dean of
Westminster for the children of the queen's grammar school was more a
reminder of the curse of childbearing than of the blessing of a royal heir.
"O most Righteous Lord God," the children prayed morning and evening, "which, for the offence of the first woman, has threatened unto all
women, a common, sharp, and inevitable malediction, and hath enjoined
them that they should conceive in sin, and, being conceived, should be

subject to many and grievous torments, and finally, be delivered with the danger and jeopardy of their lives, we beseech thee . . . to assuage thine anger for a while."[2] The Protestants, who took no pleasure in the prospective birth of a Catholic heir, prayed more concisely. "God turn the heart of Queen Mary from idolatry, or else shorten her days."[3]

The object of these earnest entreaties was reported to be in radiantly good health. "The queen is in excellent health and three months with child," one of the Spaniards wrote in mid-November. "She is fatter and has a better color than when she was married, a sign that she is happier, and indeed she is said to be very happy."[4] Her stomach was already visibly distended, and none of her dresses fit her. When she appeared at the opening of Parliament "her belly was laid out, that all men might see that she was with child."[5] At court the mood of reconciliation and rejoicing continued. On the day the queen's quickening was celebrated there was a masque of "six Hercules or men of war coming from the sea," who danced with mariners bearing torches. The six Hercules wore helmets made like griffons' heads decorated with figures of a three-headed Cerberus. Lions' faces adorned the breasts and backs of their costumes, which were lavishly gilded and silvered.[6]

The masque was presented at the queen's expense, but Philip, not to be outdone, arranged a round of Spanish cane play, designed as a major court spectacle. The tournament was planned on the scale of Henry VIII's athletic displays, with more than sixty knights on the field, each of them splendidly turned out in matched liveries of green and blue and yellow silk trimmed in silver and gold. Philip had given Mary's ladies and gentlewomen dozens of yards of crimson and purple velvet and cloth of gold and silver for new dresses, and Mary sat among them in her brocades and jewels, smiling and holding the prizes she would award to the winners. Philip, who rode with Don Diego de Cordova's band in purple and silver, performed creditably, though rain and the open ridicule of the English spoiled the triumph of the winning band.[7] Many months later a shady figure named Lewkner, a purveyor of cards and dice to the court, told the queen's examiners that only chance had saved Philip and his companions from assault during the cane play. According to Lewkner, some three hundred English guardsmen and others were sworn to kill Mary and all the Spaniards on a prearranged signal during the third round of cane play. Because of the rain the third round was called off, and the plan was thwarted.[8]

Philip, Pole informed the pope, now treated Mary with all the deference of a son, but his habitual affability had begun to wear thin.[9] He had gone out of his way to please everyone, including the queen; he had disproved all the rumors of Spanish domination; he had fulfilled his primary obligation of begetting an heir. Why then hadn't he been crowned king? In the feudal law of England a man who married an heiress was confirmed in his possession of his wife's lands when their first child was born. Mary was pregnant. He saw no reason to delay the coronation any longer.

Certainly the people were on his side. When he and Mary rode to the opening of Parliament, he on horseback and she in an open litter "to expose her to the public view," all the voices from the crowd were full of approbation. "Oh! how handsome the king is!" "Oh! how kind and gentle he looks!" "Oh! what a good husband he is! How honorably and lovingly he treats the queen!" The Savoyard ambassador heard these exclamations and recorded them, along with the revealing monologue of an old woman who watched the king and queen walk from the church where they heard mass to the Parliament house. "An evil death to the traitors who said our king was misshapen!" she cried out. "Look at him! He is as fair as an angel! And I hear that he is good, holy and pious. God save him and bless us!"[10]

Crowned or not, all who favored the imperial position saw Philip moving into unchallenged pre-eminence in the government. When Paget was in Brussels in November he outlined to the emperor his view of Philip's role. The Council was so out of hand that the country was "now governed by such a crowd that it was much more like a republic" than a monarchy; Philip should choose a half dozen of the best men in the Council—by which Paget meant himself and his allies, with Gardiner excluded—and let them rule while he "took his sword in hand, grew hardened to the heat and cold of campaigning," and got on with the work of "striking terror into his foes." Paget's scenario would remove the hindrance of Mary's authority while placing the Council under limited obligation to a king absent on campaign. The emperor agreed with Paget up to a point, admitting that it had been "the object of the marriage" that Philip take over the government, but he saw clearly that Mary should retain the appearance of power. Philip's goal, his father said, "should be so to act that while he in reality does everything, the initiative should always seem to proceed from the queen and her Council."[11]

No one was more pleased than Charles V at the news of the queen's pregnancy. His son was at the head of affairs in England, the papal legate was about to reunite the country with the church, and on top of this the queen would soon give birth to a Catholic heir. When the English ambassador Mason had an audience with the emperor in November he found him in remarkably good health. He was sitting at a table, looking cheerful and "as lively as I have not of long time seen the like lustiness in him," Mason wrote. His face, usually pale and puffy, was ruddy and firmer in its contours, and his limbs seemed less sluggish despite a recent bad attack of gout. He sat forward eagerly, and asked the ambassador for the latest information from the English court.

"How goeth my daughter's belly forward?"

"Sir," Mason answered, "I have from herself nothing to say therein, for she will not confess the matter till it be proved unto her face; but by others I understand, to my great joy and comfort, that her garments wax very strait."

"I never doubted of the matter," the emperor went on, "but that God for her had wrought so many miracles, would make the same perfect by assisting of nature to his good and most desired work." And since God was arranging all, he would doubtless arrange the child's sex to greatest advantage. "I warrant it shall be a man child," Charles observed.

"Be it man or be it woman," the ambassador said judiciously, "welcome shall it be, for by that shall we at the least come to some certainty to whom God shall appoint, by succession, the government of our estate." As long as she remained childless there was grave anxiety in the kingdom, Mason added. "It maketh all good men to tremble to think the queen's highness must die, with whom, dying without fruit, the realm were as good also to die."

But the emperor was so sanguine at that moment he saw no reason for alarm on this or any other grounds. "Doubt not God will provide both with fruit and otherwise," he told Mason, "so as I trust to see, yet, that realm to return to a great piece of that surety and estimation that I have in my time seen it in."[12] His optimism showed no signs of waning when, a week later, he met with Paget. The good reports out of England were "so pleasant unto him," Paget wrote to the Council, "as, if he had been half dead, yet they should have been enough to have revived him again."[18]

In December and January the first joyous reaction to Mary's expectant state gave way to greater concern for the security of her throne and government as the time for the birth approached. Philip was looking forward to taking part in the war against the French as soon as the winter weather ended, and he did not mean to wait until Mary's child was born before he left. His letters to his father were full of military plans. "I must confess that for some years past I have been desirous of leading a campaign," he told him, "and I would like it to be as soon as possible. It will be my first campaign, my first opportunity of acquiring or losing prestige; all eyes will be fixed on me."[14] Mary was alarmed, and by mid-January her fears had helped to make her ill. Almost certainly she expected a difficult childbirth, and wanted her husband to be at hand when her time came. By early February she was "very melancholy," overwhelmed by fear of rebellion in support of Elizabeth or Courtenay, and by the unceasing opposition of the Protestants. Though it was seldom expressed, the possibility that the queen might not survive her pregnancy was never far from the minds of her councilors, and as her spirits sank their disquiet increased.

The most immediate cause of their concern were the Protestants. They were a minority in the population—very likely a small minority—but they were fiercely committed to their various creeds. The recent official reunion of England with Rome appeared to make them more determined in their opposition, and their religious differences with the crown were inevitably bound up with political opposition in a way that made them by far the most dangerous group in the country. They were never a coherent body. They held widely varied doctrines and, once they left England to form colonies on the continent, they fought bitterly among themselves. But to Mary and her councilors they represented a single, organized threat to the royal and clerical powers, a conspicuous witness to the perilous security of the queen's government. They mocked the throne. They had to be silenced.

The opposition took many forms. Small congregations of like-minded believers met together in cellars, in ruined churches, in cemeteries, led in worship by a minister or spiritual guide. Individuals proclaimed themselves to be religious leaders and attracted followers or, like Anne Bokkas, who called herself "the Light of the Faith," were seized and committed to prison.[15] Still others seemed to confound worship with violent attacks on their Catholic neighbors, the clergy, and the queen herself. In a village near London a man spoke out in favor of the mass as he walked in the street; the servant of a Protestant gentleman overheard his remark, stopped him, and stabbed him twice with his dagger.[16] In Essex an empty church was burned so that no mass could be celebrated there, and in Suffolk, arsonists set fire to another church "with the entire congregation that was hearing mass inside."[17]

Since the start of Mary's reign every stage in the return to the old faith had met with ridicule and sabotage. In the spring of 1554 Easter was observed in many London parishes with the full restoration of the time-honored traditions—creeping to the cross on Good Friday, carrying the palms on Palm Sunday—and the royal arms and scriptural verses painted on the rood-lofts were washed out or covered over. The sacrament was hung or set on the altar, and at St. Paul's, in accordance with old custom, it was laid in a sepulchre at evensong on Good Friday where it was to remain until Easter morning. At high mass on Sunday it was to be taken out of the tomb with the choir bursting into song with the words of the angel at Jesus' tomb, "He is risen, he is not here." Sometime between Friday evensong and Sunday mass the host was stolen, and when the climactic moment came the joyous words of the choir's anthem were disconcertingly true. The host was not there, which led to great embarrassment and some laughter until the priest supplied another in its stead. As soon as the story came out a ballad was printed telling how the God of the papists had been stolen and lost, and a new one put in his place.[18] Rewards offered for the identities of the thief and ballad-maker produced no response, but the example was widely imitated. In May a joiner named John Street tried to take the sacrament out of a priest's hands in Smithfield. Onlookers came to the priest's defense, and Street was taken to Newgate. There, the chronicler added, "he feigned himself mad."[19]

The coming of Philip provoked fresh rumors of persecution, and a new wave of Protestant response. The pope was coming back, it was said, the monasteries would all be rebuilt and church property given back to the clergy. All those wronged by the changes of Henry VIII and Edward were to be reinstated; the priests, the rumors insisted, "were going to take their revenge." In anticipation of these horrors assaults on Catholics and the Catholic clergy increased. In Kent a priest had his nose cut off and was made to endure humiliating punishments.[20] At Paul's Cross an assailant fired a handgun at the preacher, Dr. Pendleton, and the tin pellet hit the wall of the church just behind the Lord Mayor and then fell onto the shoulder of a man in the congregation. All the neighboring houses were searched at once, but no suspect was found until six days later, and even then there was not proof enough to convict him.[21] And at a house in Aldersgate Street a servant of Sir Anthony Neville persuaded a young girl, Elizabeth Crofts, to speak and make whistling noises behind a wall, and to answer questions put to her by a clerk, an actor and a weaver who were also in the deception. The men drew a huge crowd by saying that the "voice in the wall" was an angelic spirit which could reveal the truth behind appearances and discern religious falsehoods. Prompted by the others the girl gave answers calculated to "raise a mutiny amongst the people." Asked "What is the mass?" she replied "Idolatry." Asked about confession, about the queen's marriage and the coming of the Spaniards she condemned all Catholic practices and implied divine disapproval of Mary and Philip. When the clerk cried out "God save Queen Mary!" the wall was silent, but when he cried "God save the Lady Elizabeth!" it replied "So be it." Thousands gathered to witness this imposture, and it was not until three months later that Elizabeth Crofts was made to stand on a scaffold near the preacher at Paul's Cross and confess that the "voice in the wall" was only a trick.[22]

Beyond the Protestants whose disruptions exasperated Mary and her Council in England there were others gathering in congregations on the continent, out of reach of royal punishment and free to conduct a large-scale propaganda assault against the Catholic government. In the first months of Mary's reign the Council and the chancellor had encouraged the most outspoken Protestant leaders to leave the country. Some were given warnings, then left free to make their escapes; many were given official passports. Among those who left were Bishops Ponet and Bale, the future martyrologist John Foxe, already engaged in writing a history of the victims of religious persecution in England, and the fiery Scots preacher John Knox.

Besides these luminaries hundreds of lesser men and women left England to join the congregations in exile in Switzerland and Germany—a growing exodus of farmers, blacksmiths, chandlers, masons, laborers of every kind. They found haven principally at Geneva, Frankfort and Strasbourg, and from these cities scurrilous attacks on the queen, her advisers and her Spanish husband were sent into Kent and Suffolk and were carried by agents of the exiles into London and to the royal court. The French and German printers who set the libels in type rarely knew the meaning of what they were printing, and occasionally the trail from author to printer to transport ship to reader was many hundreds of miles long. In April of 1554 the magistrates of Danzig wrote to Mary about a sheet of invective put out in their city by a printer and his son "who confessed that the work was printed by them in ignorance of the language or the purport of the libel, they only knowing the form and character of the letters required in type." The printer had been approached by an Englishman in Danzig, who had in turn been asked to have the sheet printed by an English mariner. A third Englishman provided the actual text. The mariner was to have taken the printed sheets by sea to England, where a contact would be waiting to carry them to the capital. Then they "were to be thrown in the streets and highways that people might read them."[23]

Among the exiles Ponet and Bale wrote stinging indictments of every innovation of the Marian church, focusing their sarcasm in particular on "wily Winchester" and "blow bull" Bonner, bishop of London. But the most vicious attacks came from Knox, who in the months preceding Philip's arrival in England wrote in his *Faithful Admonition to the Professors of God's Truth in England* that Mary was herself "an open traitress to the Imperial Crown of England, contrary to the just laws of the realm, to bring in a stranger and make a proud Spaniard king—to the destruction of the nobility . . . to the abasing of the yeomanry, to the enslaving of the commonalty." Her associates in treason, in particular Gardiner, "brother to Cain and fellow to Judas the traitor," ought to be assassinated in the name of justice and the true faith, Knox wrote, and his invitation to tyrannicide was published on the day Philip landed at Southampton.

The shrill criticism from abroad, the rising incidence of disturbances and assaults in the southeast counties and in the close vicinity of the court combined with Mary's approaching delivery to force a change in the official attitude toward the Protestant heretics. The recent revival of the medieval treason statutes provided the legal mechanism by which men and women could be executed by the state for theological crimes, and there were learned, decisive judges at hand to condemn them. There were prisoners in the Tower, at the Fleet and elsewhere demonstrably guilty of transgressing the queen's religious laws, and critics of the government were quick to point out that to allow these notorious offenders to go unpunished encouraged all Protestants in their eagerness to undermine the established authority.

Among the offenders was John Hooper, bishop of Worcester, an outspoken critic of both Catholics and conservative Protestants who wrote and preached on the "absurdities" of the teaching that Christ was physically present in the eucharistic wafer. Hooper had been deprived of his bishopric on the grounds that he was married and would not put his wife aside, and because of his opinions on the corporeal presence in the sacrament. He had been imprisoned in the Fleet on September 1, 1553, and kept there for a little over seventeen months. At first he was allowed the liberty of the prison, but within a week the warden, an intimate of Gardiner's named Babington, saw to it that he was committed to close prison in the Tower chamber of the Fleet, and "used very extremely." Hooper himself wrote a record of his imprisonment, telling how Babington and his wife picked quarrels with him and had him transferred from the pleasanter quarters for the privileged prisoners to the wards where common criminals were kept. Confined there with only "a wicked man and woman" for company, Hooper wrote, he was given "but a little pad of straw and a rotten covering, with a tick and a few feathers therein" for a bed. Charitable friends later sent him better bedding, but could do nothing to change the "vile and stinking" room in which he lay. The "sink and filth" of the prison itself ran along one side of the room, and the common sewer of the city along the other. The stench and foulness made him sick. He lay in his own filth, calling for help and moaning in agony, but the warden ordered the doors of his cell kept barred and chained. Within six weeks of his confinement he was so ill he prepared himself for death, and the poor men in neighboring cells begged the guards to ease Hooper in his last hours. But according to the bishop Babington forbade them to come near him, saying "Let him alone; it were a good riddance of him."

At the end of January, 1555, Hooper was brought before Gardiner and several other bishops and urged to give up his "evil and corrupt doctrine" and to confess himself conformed to the Catholic church and a faithful son of the pope. If he did, the chancellor assured him, he would have the queen's mercy. Hooper refused. The church of Rome was not the catholic church of Christ, nor was the pope head of Christ's followers. As for the queen's mercy, he would submit to it gladly, "if mercy may be had with safety of conscience, and without the displeasure of God."

Hooper was brought out to be burned on February 9, "a lowering and cold morning." He stood on a high stool and looked out over the crowd that gathered to watch him, and "in every corner there was nothing to be seen but weeping and sorrowful people." He prayed for a time, until interrupted by a man asking his forgiveness. Hooper said he knew of nothing to forgive. "O sir!" the man said, "I am appointed to make the fire."

"Therein thou dost nothing offend me," said Hooper. "God forgive thee thy sins, and do thine office, I pray thee."

Two small loads of green faggots were laid about the stool, and reeds laid on top of them reaching up to the victim's legs. Hooper took two bundles of reeds in his hands and hugged them to him, kissing them, and putting one under his arms he showed the man who was building the fire where the rest were needed to make the circle complete. The torch was then put to the faggots, but because they were green they were slow to kindle, and the reeds took even longer to catch fire. After a time the flame reached Hooper's legs, "but the wind having full strength in that place, it blew the flame from him," and the fire only teased at his feet and ankles. More faggots were brought—there were no more reeds—and a new fire kindled, but because of the wind and the heavy overcast it did no more than burn his hair and scorch his skin a little. "O Jesus, the Son of David," he prayed, "have mercy upon me, and receive my soul!" By this time Hooper's legs were being consumed, but the fire was going out, leaving his upper body unharmed. "For God's love, good people," he was heard to say, "let me have more fire!"

A third time kindling was brought and embedded in the smoking ashes, and this time the flames were strong enough to reach the two bladders of gunpowder which had been tied between the sufferer's legs. But instead of exploding upward and killing him as they were meant to do, to spare him the excruciating pain of having his torso burned away while he remained conscious, the wind blew them out away from him so that they exploded in the air, and "did him small good." He was now heard to repeat "with a somewhat loud voice," "Lord Jesus, have mercy upon me; Lord Jesus, have mercy upon me: Lord Jesus, receive my spirit!" His lips continued to move after his throat was so scorched he could make no sound, not even a scream, and onlookers noticed that even "when he was black in the mouth, and his tongue swollen, that he could not speak, yet his lips went till they were shrunk to the gums." In the end he could move nothing but his arms, yet he knocked them against his breast in the gesture of contrition until one of them fell off and the other, with "fat, water, and blood" dropping out at his fingers' ends, stuck fast to the remains of his chest. In this position he bowed his head forward and died.[24]

Hooper had been burning alive for nearly three quarters of an hour. "Even as a lamb, patiently he abode the extremity thereof," the martyrologist Foxe recorded from the accounts sent him of the victim's final moments, "neither moving forwards, backwards, nor to any side. But, having his nether parts burned, and his bowels fallen out, he died as quietly as a child in his bed. And he now reigneth as a blessed martyr, in the joys of heaven prepared for the faithful in Christ, before the foundations of the world: for whose constancy all Christians are bound to praise God."

XLI

When raging reign of tyrants stout,
Causeless, did cruelly conspire
To rend and root the Simple out,
With furious force of sword and fire;
When man and wife were put to death:
We wished for our Queen Elizabeth.

Hooper was one of several men burned for heresy in February 1555. Their sufferings are often taken to be a watershed in the story of Mary's reign, but at the time their deaths were seen not as the beginning of a bloody campaign against the Protestants but as merited punishments long overdue. Bishop Gardiner, who tried Hooper and his companions in his episcopal court late in January, had been accused of being "too mild and too gentle" toward those guilty of the "great atrocity and consummate contumely" of heresy. For heretics were uncommon criminals, not to be classed with ordinary arsonists or murderers or traitors; their crime was not merely against man, but against God as well. By maintaining lies about the nature of God and his sacraments they made themselves as loathsome to the community of true believers as lepers or victims of the sweat. They were carriers of the plague of error, a plague that brought spiritual death and denial of eternal life.

Gardiner fully shared this view of the almost inhuman evil of heresy but he realized the political danger of moving too harshly against an opposing group. "I take heresies in the church to be like boils in a man's body, which oversoon lanced wax sorer and in time putrefy their matter," he said, and though Paget and his friends in the Council repeatedly spoke of the chancellor as a "man of blood" his restraint belies the label.[1]

In fact there was no one, at Mary's court or outside it, who did not favor the burning of heretics. Mary's Council had been discussing the question since the summer of 1554, and the treasurer, Paulet, was said to be a persistent advocate of the extreme penalty for Protestants who would not recant. Pole, a man whose thoughts ran easily to martyrdoms, had for twenty years and more been closely associated with reforming cardinals determined to fight heresy with every weapon at the church's command. Among his intimates was Cardinal Caraffa, who as head of the Theatine Order showed no mercy to Protestants and as the future pope Paul IV was to oversee personally the torture and pitiless repression carried out by the papal Inquisition. Pole had been at the forefront of the militant Catholic Reformation on the continent, and he carried that militant philosophy with him into England.

According to Renard, who had unmatched respect for the Protestants' strength and threat to the throne, the bishops were eager to bring heretics to justice at the stake, and if left unrestrained would go far beyond their authority in ordering executions. Articles published by Bonner, bishop of London, in the fall of 1554 created alarm because they contained the term "inquisition," and in justifying their publication without approval from the king or queen or the Council Bonner remarked that "in religious matters it was meet to proceed firmly and without fear." Like Renard, Bonner recognized the danger of a Protestant rising out of reaction to the burnings, but he saw no reason to stop them; instead he recommended carrying them out in secret.[2]

Though he feared the rash zeal of the bishops Renard believed that Philip could control them if he chose to. That the king did not use his authority in this way was in keeping with his deep personal revulsion for even the smallest taint of heresy. To be sure, Philip ordered his chaplain to preach a sermon opposing the burnings soon after they began, in order to dissociate himself and the other Spaniards from a practice that might lead to rebellion. But he had lived most of his life in the land of the Spanish Inquisition, where the extermination of religious error had been looked on as a pious duty for centuries. His great-grandmother (and Mary's grandmother) Queen Isabella had brought the great inquisitorial machine into being and inspired its divine work. Philip's principal mentor in statecraft, his father Charles V, had by one estimate burned or beheaded or buried alive at least thirty thousand Lutherans and Anabaptists in his Flemish domains, and was in this year of 1555 ordering executions for heresy at the rate of seventy to eighty every month. Philip's chaplain in England, Alfonso y Castro, was famous as a determined persecutor of heretics whose treatise on the subject was dedicated to the Spanish prince.[3]

Philip was careful to keep his own feelings to himself, but in a revealing letter he wrote four months after he came to England he remarked that, as for the English appointed to be his personal servants in his bedchamber, "I am not satisfied that they are good enough Catholics to be constantly about my person."[4] Philip's fastidious orthodoxy showed itself not long afterward when, as king of Spain, he put new vigor into the Inquisition and presided in person over a vast *auto da fé* in the public square of Valladolid. Asked by one of the gasping victims why he had to undergo such a horrible death, the king is traditionally said to have answered, "Had I a son as obstinate as you I would eagerly carry faggots to burn him."

The records are oddly silent about Mary's attitude toward the deaths of Hooper and the others in February. In discussing the hazards of the venture Renard put the emphasis on Philip rather than Mary. He stressed Philip's pre-eminence in general, of course, but if Mary had been among the most outspoken supporters of the burnings his dispatches would surely have reflected this. Like all those around her Mary believed that heretics deserved the ultimate punishment, and that the combating of false beliefs was part of the preordained purpose of her reign. Yet the one statement she wrote "with her own hand" about the policy makes it clear that she saw it as a temporary measure only, to be carried out neither vindictively nor hesitantly but judiciously.

To prevent any one official from going about his work with a heavy hand she ordered that a Council member be present to supervise each burning in London. Throughout the statement her attention was less on the dying heretics than on the effect of their example on the living witnesses to their deaths. For if Philip found heretics physically offensive Mary found them despicable for misleading others too ignorant to understand the truth and robbing them of their salvation. "Touching the punishment of heretics," she wrote, "I believe it would be well to inflict punishment at this beginning, without much cruelty or passion, but without however omitting to do such justice on those who choose by their false doctrines to deceive simple persons, that the people may clearly comprehend that they have not been condemned without just cause, whereby others will be brought to know the truth, and will beware of letting themselves be induced to relapse into such new and false opinions. And above all, I should wish that no one be burned in London, save in the presence of some member of the Council; and that during such executions, both here and elsewhere, some good and pious sermons be preached."[5]

No groups espoused burning for the crime of religious error with greater vehemence than the congregations of Protestants. Here they differed from the Catholics only in their judgments of truth and error. John Knox was if anything more eager to see Gardiner, Tunstal and Bonner burned than any of those Catholics were to burn him. "It is not only lawful to punish to the death such as labor to subvert the true religion," he wrote, "but the magistrates and people are bound so to do." Here he echoed John Calvin, who argued that anyone who thought it unjust to execute heretics was as guilty as the heretics themselves. In Edward's reign Calvin had given Somerset advice on how to carry forward the work of religion. "Of all things, let there be no moderation," he counseled the duke. "It is the bane of genuine improvement." Nearly every Protestant leader on the continent shared this view—Melanchthon, Beza, Farel and Luther, whose followers in Germany refused to allow the Marian exiles to enter their lands because the latter denied the physical presence of Jesus in the sacrament. In England, John Philpot denounced one group of his fellow Protestants as "flaming firebrands of hell" whom the devil "shat out in these days to defile the gospel." Such wretches, he wrote, deserved to be burned without mercy.

If the burning of the first Protestants in February of 1555 caused no moral outrage it did intensify the angry opposition of their coreligionists to the queen and her government. The numbers of men and women set in the pillory for speaking "horrible lies and seditious words against the queen's majesty and her Council" rose, and the ballad-makers who had written songs in praise of the new reign now put out ballads against the queen's "misproceedings" and the brutality of the bishops. A minstrel's apprentice from Colchester went to the village of Rough Hedge to sing at a country wedding. He sang the old anti-popish songs of Henry's reign and Edward's, and a new ballad, "News out of London." The latter ridiculed the mass and the queen, and the next day the parson of Rough Hedge denounced him to the local officials, who punished him.

In Henry's reign the forces of popular mysticism had gathered against him in the utterances of visionaries and in folk prophecies. Now these occult weapons were turned against Mary.

> When boughs and branches begin to bud
> Two Marys shall go out of the Tower
> And make sacrifice with their own blood

ran one of these vague prognostications; others foretold Mary's death unequivocally, and predicted Elizabeth's accession. There were persistent rumors that Edward was not really dead, and would come to the throne again, and so great was the power of the folk imagination that this hope was sustained for many years. Mary tried to stop these tales from spreading, sending letters to her justices of the peace ordering them to "use all the best means and ways ye can, in the diligent examining and searching out, from Man to Man, the Authors and Publishers of these vain Prophesies, and untrue Bruits, the very foundation of all Rebellions," but the stories persisted.[6]

As Mary went into the final months of her pregnancy another kind of rumor was put about. It was said that the queen was conspiring to pass off another child as her own. Alice Perwick, wife of a London merchant tailor, was indicted for saying "The queen's grace is not with child, and another lady should be with child and that lady's child when she is brought in bed should be named the queen's child."[7] French agents helped to make this report better known, and rebels in Hampshire planned to use it to persuade the country people to rise against the queen and put Elizabeth and Courtenay on the throne.[8]

At court the Christmas festivities brought Spaniards and English together with predictable results. There were banquets and plays, displays of magnanimity and of short temper on both sides. There were masques of Venetian senators and galley slaves, and of "Venuses or amorous ladies" and cupids. The Venuses wore buskins "cut out of old garments" for economy's sake, but their headpieces were tall, costly helmetlike structures fitted out with hair and spangles and netting, and decorated with colored silk flowers. The cupids wore shirts of white sarcenet and carried bows strung with "twisted lace of silk," and had wings specially made by a London feathermaker.[9]

In the afternoons Philip's men took on the English nobles in tournaments, no longer the tame cane play of the Spaniards but rough tilting on foot with spears and swords. On several occasions the king and his company held the barriers against English opponents, proving they could withstand the force of the larger Englishmen's strength, but the tilting easily led to grudges and quarrels. One Spaniard was branded on the forehead and lost an ear for wounding another man in a church, and later, at the court gate at Westminster, another of Philip's household ran an Englishman through with a rapier while two Spaniards held him by the arms. The murderer was hanged at Charing Cross, but Mary pardoned his two accomplices.[10] And in the vicinity of the court a bear-baiting ended badly when the "great blind bear," maddened by the dogs that were tormenting him, broke loose from his chains and ran headlong into the crowd. He caught a servingman by the calf of the leg and bit away a huge chunk of his flesh down to the anklebone, and the man died three days later of his infected wound. The chronicler did not record the recapture of the bear.[11]

The tournaments continued throughout the winter, and by the first week of March it was evident that Philip had decided to postpone his departure for the continent until after the birth of Mary's child. By now he had acquired a taste for English-style tilting, and the tournament held on Lady Day of 1555 was the most elaborate yet seen. The challengers, one Spaniard and one Englishman, were all in white, while the king and his retinue wore blue jerkins trimmed in yellow, with great plumes of blue

and yellow feathers in their helmets. Their whifflers and footmen and armorers were turned out in satin gowns and caps, and another company,
dressed like Turks, were all in red, with falchions in their hands and carrying great targets. As the queen and court looked on the challengers and
defenders rode course after course, tiring many mounts and not stopping
until more than a hundred staves had been broken.[12]

Mary took pleasure in these displays and in her husband's performance at the tilt, but the Venetian ambassador noticed that they made her
nervous. She was relieved that Philip would be staying in England yet she
could not help but be afraid for his safety as she watched him riding vig-
orously against all comers and exchanging blows with a punctilious dispatch he had never shown in the jousts his father had organized for him.
At the Lady Day tournament "she could not conceal her fear and
disquietude" for the king, and sent him a message "to pray him not to encounter further risk" after he had run many courses. As soon as he received it he left the lists.[13]

In Easter Week the king and queen went to Hampton Court and
there, in the presence of her principal courtiers, Mary underwent the
ceremonies that signified the beginning of her confinement. In a month,
or within six weeks at the most, she would experience the "happy hour"
of her delivery. Mary would have preferred to retire to Windsor, but it
was too far from the capital. At Hampton Court she would have the protection of her full guard, troops from the city, and the arsenal of the
Tower close at hand.

Just before she retired to keep her chamber Mary witnessed the be-
ginnings of another part of her religious restoration. Since the dissolution
of the monasteries many Franciscan and Dominican monks had been living in poverty in Flanders, waiting until their lands and properties could
be restored. Now Mary summoned them back to England, returning to
them the few religious properties possessed by the crown that had not
been alienated into private hands. The friars made themselves at home in
London, and were "well received and kindly treated." The Benedictines
were beginning to revive their order in England too. Sixteen former
monks who had been living as secular men since the 1530s put on their
habits again, renounced all their goods and requested a monastery to live
in. They asked for an audience with the queen, and came before her as a
group, in their robes and tonsures. Mary had not seen so many religious
together in one place since she was a young girl, and as soon as they entered the presence chamber she wept for joy.

She carried the happy sight of the monks with her as she entered the
last days of her pregnancy. Surrounded by her waiting women she rested,
dreaming of the baby, and then woke to watch for the signs the doctors
said would indicate the approach of birth. According to Renard, the

child was expected on or before May 9, and final preparations of the delivery room and nursery were already under way.[14] The waiting women spent their time sewing the majestic counterpoint of estate and matching headpiece that went to adorn the queen's bed. Coverings and wrapping cloths had to be embroidered, and baptismal cloths for the day of the christening. For the queen there were smocks of the softest Holland cloth with delicate trimmings of silver thread and silk at the neck and wrists, and breast cloths and blankets. The physicians assembled their instruments, and oversaw the furnishing of the delivery room with tables and benches and bowls, and casting bottles to hold the perfumed water that would help to purify the odors in the room.

They were not looking forward to assisting at this delivery. Mary had turned thirty-nine in February, and though her health had appeared to improve as her pregnancy advanced she had not been entirely free of melancholy and the illness that accompanied it. They did not confide their apprehensions to the queen, of course. Instead she was given every encouragement. Shortly after her confinement began a peasant woman and her three newborn babies were brought up to Mary's apartments at Hampton Court. The woman was "of low stature and great age like the queen," yet only a few days earlier she had given birth to the triplets, all of whom were sturdy and comely. The mother was already out of bed, "strong and out of all danger," and Mary was much heartened to see them all.[15]

On Easter Sunday a Protestant surgeon, Thomas Flower, committed an act of outrageous sacrilege in the parish church of St. Margaret in Westminster. Flower, a former priest himself and a monk at Ely, clearly went to hear mass in the church intending to do mischief of some kind, for he disguised himself as a servingman and carried a woodknife. As he watched the priest in his canonicals standing before the altar, holding the chalice full of consecrated wafers, he was seized by rage. Running toward the altar he roared out accusations at the priest, shouting that he was committing idolatry and deceiving the people. As he spoke he lunged at his victim with his knife, striking him on the head and hand so that the blood from his wounds gushed out over his vestments and into the chalice. The priest sank down as if dead, and the crowd inside the church dispersed in an uproar. The shrieking of the horrified worshipers attracted a second crowd outside, and some of these men, their weapons drawn, dashed into the church to seize Flower. At first it was said that the murder of the priest of St. Margaret's was meant to be the signal for a general rising against all the foreigners in Westminster, putting the entire population of that quarter into the greatest alarm. But it was soon obvious that Flower had acted alone, and almost as soon as he was imprisoned in Newgate he was condemning what he had done as "evil and naught."[16]

Flower's crime appeared to be a response to a second series of burn-ings that took place in Essex and in the Welsh Marches as well as in the London suburbs. In the week that Mary rejoiced to see the Benedictines at court a second victim was burned at Smithfield (the first, John Rogers, had died there on February 4), and in the following week five men were sent to the stake in as many Essex towns, one a barber from Maldon. At one of these execution sites a "slight insurrection" occurred. As Lord Dacre and his men escorted their prisoners to the appointed place "so great a concourse of persons assembled at this spectacle, that it was in-credible." The condemned men spoke to the crowd, urging them to con-tinue in their faith and "to endure, as they themselves did, any persecu-tion or any torment." The onlookers were so stirred that the officials feared for their lives, for "very strong language" had been used against those who ordered the execution. The magistrates ordered the fires to be built and lighted, but as the flames rose there were loud affirmations from the crowd that the victims were "the holiest of martyrs." Their words were written down and copies of them passed from hand to hand, and after they died the ashes were combed for their remains.[17]

In response to Flower's assault and lesser incidents of the same sort the king and queen sent for more "true and faithful great men of the realm" to stay at Hampton Court with their armed retainers. More troops were raised and quartered in the immediate neighborhood of the palace, and they brought artillery with them. Similar precautions were taken in Lon-don, for fear that the "idle rogues" who infested the city might try to take advantage of any "misfortune" at the time of the queen's delivery to sack the houses of the wealthy. The number of guards at the city gates was increased, and watchmen patrolled the streets at all hours of the night.[18] The nobles were said to be gathering at the palace to be present at the birth, and every effort was made to underplay the gathering of the soldiers. Philip made a great show of attending the wedding of the earl of Arundel's son, Lord Maltravers, arriving at the earl's house with all his chief courtiers and giving the bride a beautiful jeweled necklace worth a thousand ducats. Another wedding was held at the court. The earl of Sussex's son Lord Fitzwalter married the earl of Southampton's daughter with great pomp, and afterward, to do even greater honor to the bride and groom, Philip joined the other wedding guests in a tourna-ment.[19]

On Tuesday morning, April 30, just at daybreak the news came that a little after midnight the queen had given birth to a prince. She had had little pain and was well out of danger, and the boy was fair and without blemish. Royal officials confirmed the account of the birth, and by mid-morning there were bonfires in the streets and all the bells in the city were ringing. No shops opened, and tables spread with meat and wine

were set up in the squares and in the courtyards of the merchants' companies. The clergy marched in procession round their churches singing
Te Deums "for the birth of our prince," and the sailors who left that day
from the Channel ports carried the joyful news with them to the continent.

By the evening of May 2 the imperial court was "rejoicing out of
measure" to hear of the prince's birth, and at four o'clock on the morning of the third the emperor sent for the English ambassador to hear an
official announcement from his lips. Mason said that he too had heard the
news from London, but had not yet heard anything from the court.
Charles, though, was "loath to bring the thing to any doubt," and his
sister, at Antwerp, "caused the great bell to ring to give all men to understand that the news was true." The English merchant ships in the harbor
shot off all their guns, and their captains met to plan "some worthy triumph upon the water," but before they could complete their plans fresh
reports came from Brussels that their joy was premature. The duke of
Alva sent word to the emperor from Hampton Court that the rumor in
London was false. There was no child; the queen had not yet begun her
labor. The imperial court returned to its accustomed "hope and expectation," but Londoners were disappointed and resentful.[20] "It is hardly to
be told," wrote the Venetian ambassador Michiel, "how much this
dispirited everybody."

XLII

 The baker's daughter in her russet gown,
Better than Queen Mary without her crown.

Everyone expected Mary's child to be born late in April. The chief gentlewomen of the kingdom had come to Hampton Court to witness the birth, and somehow room had been found in the palace for all of them. The sewing and embroidering had all been done, the wetnurses brought in, and the rockers engaged. The royal cradle, "very sumptuously and gorgeously trimmed," sat in the queen's bedchamber. Inlaid into the wood were verses in Latin and English, celebrating the divine benefit soon to be conferred on England:

> The child which thou to Mary, O Lord of might!
>   hast send,
> To England's joy, in health preserve—keep, and
>   defend![1]

As day after day passed and still the pains did not begin, Mary kept more and more to her room, seeing no one but her women and becoming all but invisible to the court save for an occasional appearance at a window. Outside the queen's apartments the courtiers were ordered to put on mourning for the death of the king's grandmother, and the silk kirtles and velvet doublets in gay colors were exchanged for somber black. After years of bizarre behavior and melancholic wretchedness Joanna the Mad was dead, and Philip shut himself in his rooms until a funeral could be held for her. He planned of course to put off his mourning "for the joy of the delivery," but until then he and everyone around him had to observe his official grief. His one consolation was that Joanna's income, some twenty-five thousand ducats a year, now came to him.[2]

The French ambassador dismissed the proceedings at Hampton Court as an elaborate farce. He had never had any respect for Mary, and for the past year he had been nursing a personal grudge against her as well. In the aftermath of Wyatt's rebellion she had been understandably brusque with him, yet he found her anger incomprehensible. He wrote to Henri II that she "lost all feminine sweetness" in her dealings with him, and he could not seem to understand that what infuriated her was the French support given to a group of English rebels who had escaped to France and set up a small colony at Neufchâtel. These "tall men and diverse young gentlemen," less than two hundred strong, were talking of leading an invading French army into England. They were in league with the Channel pirates, and the French king was encouraging them with everything but money and arms. Mary confronted Noailles with this information, accusing King Henri of breaking faith with her and saying "she would not have acted toward him in that way for the gain of three realms."

With that she walked out of the room, leaving the ambassador gaping disconcertedly after her. In a moment his confusion had turned to rage, and he took it out on the nearest object at hand, which happened to be the chancellor. Noailles accused Gardiner of reading instead of listening during his conversation with the queen, and reminded him of an old promise he had made but not kept to provide him with a barge. Gardiner, who had a hot temper of his own, grew angry in his turn, and the argument might have become even more serious if Noailles hadn't noticed that they were not alone. At the opposite end of the gallery was one of Renard's secretaries, pretending to be preoccupied with his own thoughts but in fact registering every word that was said to tell his master. Sputtering fresh accusations Noailles stalked out.[3]

Now as he moved among the black-robed English and Spanish courtiers at Hampton Court Noailles laughed at their solemn expectations and their prayers for the queen's child. He knew for a certainty that there would be no child, for there was no pregnancy. One of his informers, a man in the confidence of both Susan Clarencieux and a midwife who was in constant attendance on the queen, told him that both women had admitted this. Mary was "pale and peaked," but apart from the swelling of her abdomen she had none of the symptoms of pregnancy. The midwife —"one of the best midwives in the town"—believed the royal physicians to be either too ignorant or too fearful to tell the queen the truth, and she herself, "more to comfort her with words than anything," would only refer tactfully to a "miscalculation" in the time of her delivery.[4] It had been rumored for months that the swelling was "only a tumor, as often happens to women," and to make this diagnosis more plausible one of Mary's physicians had been overheard to say that she ate so little she could not possibly keep both herself and a child alive.[5] All this was more than enough evidence to convince Noailles that what he called the "seraglio" at Hampton Court was only a ridiculous pretense, and that the queen was either a blatant liar or a pathetic dupe.

The truth, though, was much more complicated than anyone realized. To begin with, in telling Noailles' informant there were no symptoms of pregnancy the midwife was inexact. To her experienced eye this may have been true, but there were signs enough to convince both the untrained observers at court and Mary herself that she was indeed expecting. Renard, a hard man to deceive, wrote with confidence that "the queen is veritably with child, for she has felt the babe, and there are other likely and customary symptoms, such as the state of the breasts."[6] The Venetian ambassador Michiel, writing several years after the events he described, assured the Signory that "besides all the other manifest signs of pregnancy there was the swelling of the paps and their emission of milk."[7] Looking back on all that he saw and heard during the months in which Mary waited to be delivered he believed "there was neither deceit nor malice in the matter, but mere error, not only on the part of the king and queen, but on that of the councilors of the whole court."[8]

According to one twentieth-century medical hypothesis Mary was afflicted with ovarian dropsy, which produced the amenorrhea that troubled her all her life and the abdominal swelling that she mistook for pregnancy. Even if she had conceived, this condition would have prevented her from carrying a child for the full nine months.[9]

An odd statement by the French ambassador Boisdaulphin referred to a freak abortion. On May 7, he said, "the queen was delivered of a mole or lump of flesh, and was in great peril of death." The report was unconfirmed and vague, and though it gave rise to a good deal of Protestant ridicule of Mary it sheds little light on her physical state.

What is clear is that Mary was so strongly persuaded of the appropriateness of her apparent pregnancy that even when it began to seem that she was mistaken she chose to believe in the illusion rather than the reality. Her fruitfulness was in keeping with the overarching design of her life; her barrenness was not. Furthermore, everyone around her, initially convinced by the same evidence as she was, continued to reassure her in her delusion even after they began to have doubts themselves. In the end the doctors, the midwives and her chamberwomen all deceived Mary, finding every reason but the true one for her prolonged confinement and searching for corroboration of the probability that her hopes were well founded. Her grandmother Isabella had given birth to her mother at age fifty-two, they told her, and such events were not rare. If she went past her expected delivery date there was simply a flaw in the calculations, not in the diagnosis.

Fresh calculations were made. The child would come, the doctors and midwives announced solemnly, either at the next change of the moon on May 23 or after the full moon, on June 4 or 5.[10] With these comforting voices all around her Mary persisted in her expectations, but the longer she waited the more she came under stress. She grew more and more reclusive, sitting in one place for hours at a time and wrestling with depression and anxiety. Such inactivity was far from natural to her, and those who saw her said she looked pale and ill. And they noted that her sitting position was one that no pregnant woman could have assumed without considerable pain. She sat on a cushion on the floor, her knees pulled up to her chin, her abdomen squeezed nearly flat.[11]

By the twenty-first of May it was reported that "her majesty's belly [has] greatly declined, which is said yet more to indicate the approaching term."[12] One of her physicians, Dr. Calagila, looked for the onset of labor "any day now," and declared that she had certainly entered her final month. Yet Ruy Gomez wrote that he had seen her walking in her garden with such a light step that he could not imagine her being brought to bed soon, and no one was willing to hazard a final deadline.[13] Meanwhile the life of the court and government all but came to a standstill, and impatient courtiers and irritated dignitaries paced the galleries exchanging rumors and worried looks as they waited for news from the queen's apartments. "Everything is in suspense," Michiel wrote, "and dependent on the result of this delivery."[14]

In London disillusionment over the false announcement of April 30 led to mounting agitation. New libels against Mary were thrown into the streets every few days, stirring up fears and encouraging rebellion. Some said the queen was dead, and printed versions of a "grace to be said at the accession of Elizabeth" appeared. Seditious talk was everywhere—in taverns, in the streets, anywhere gentlemen met to eat and gamble. Philip was so worried he wrote to his father for advice, asking what he should do about the libels, the slanderers, and the rash of impostors claiming to be King Edward. One such pretender was brought before the Council on May 10, but no sooner was he taken than another youth of eighteen was seized in Kent for proclaiming himself the rightful ruler and "raising a tumult amongst the populace." He was brought to London, whipped and mutilated by the cropping of his ears. A fool's coat was put on his back, and signs indicating his crime were fastened on his head and hung over his breast. It was announced that he was only a serving boy doing what others told him, but not before he had persuaded many of the country folk that he really was the late king.[15]

Violence at court had become so alarming that Philip enjoined secrecy on all those who knew the details of the most recent incidents. Three English thieves who robbed a Spaniard of a huge store of gold and jewels were hanged, but there was little that could be done to punish the hundreds of English assailants who appeared just outside the court gates, their swords at the ready, to take on every Spaniard in sight. What started as a brawl between a few men on both sides escalated rapidly until by one estimate there were five hundred of the English involved. Before the battle was over five or six men were dead, and nearly three dozen seriously wounded. Despite the king's stern warning the affair could not be kept secret, and the English were so elated to find that no large-scale punishment resulted that they immediately laid plans for an even bloodier assault to be attempted early in July.[16]

The continued postponements in the queen's delivery had as great an importance in international affairs as within her realm. Since the start of her reign Mary had been looked on as a natural mediator between France and the empire, and now in the spring of 1555 a peace conference was arranged under English auspices. There was a good deal at stake: the revival of England's prestige in continental politics, the improvement of relations between England and France and, of greater immediate importance, the prevention of new warfare in which Philip might try to involve England on the Hapsburg side.

There was another significant factor in the conference as well. It was planned, executed and paid for by Mary and her agents alone. Because of his obvious bias Philip had no authority or involvement in this diplomatic enterprise, and it was one of the few autonomous undertakings for which Mary could claim credit. The delegates met, under Pole's presidency, on English-held territory in the Calais pale. Five wooden buildings were constructed by the English to house the participants. The imperial, French and English delegates each had separate temporary residences, a fourth was for Pole, and a fifth provided a neutral setting for the meetings.[17]

From the start the French seemed to have the upper hand. The French delegates arrived accompanied by five hundred mounted guardsmen each, plus companies of noblemen and prelates and great crowds of servants. In their "pompous attire" they had the air of knights riding to a tournament, while the imperial negotiators, wearing mourning for Queen Joanna, were drab and funereal by contrast.[18] There was an appearance of amity as the discussions began, with the English taking the imperialists by the hand and all but forcing them to embrace the Frenchmen, but these courtesies could not take the place of meaningful concessions of territory and privileges. The French refused to return any of the lands they had seized from the empire in the recent war, and wanted still more. The emperor's negotiators insisted that all conquered territories be returned and would not offer anything of value in exchange. Bishop Gardiner did not help the situation any by urging the emperor to take compassion on "the infirmity of the French" following St. Paul's dictum that the man should pity "the infirmity of the woman." The French took umbrage at being called women, and at the massing of troops in the region of the conference.

In actuality the soldiers were being kept in readiness so that "in case the queen of England die in childbed" they could be sent immediately to England to protect Philip, but the French feared an attack on their border. This danger, coupled with Pole's ineffectual leadership and Gardiner's choleric tendencies, prevented progress toward a settlement. Finally, when Noailles' dispatches arrived with the intelligence that Mary was not pregnant, the English lost what diplomatic leverage they had possessed and on June 7 the conference came to an abrupt end.

At its start there had been much talk of how Mary, who had miraculously brought England back to reunion with Rome, should be able to bring about a similar miracle at the peace table. When the meeting ended in a stalemate it was noted that, for the first time since her good fortune began years earlier, Mary had presided over a failure.

The summer of 1555 was bleak and sunless. The air was cold even at midday, and the rain never seemed to stop. The fields were turned to mud, and the grain grew in stunted clumps, bent under the weight of the constant rain. The weather was so bad that "the like is not remembered in the memory of man for the last fifty years," Michiel wrote. "No sort of grain or corn ripens, and still less can it be reaped, a prognostic of scarcity yet greater than that of last year."[19] The peace conference had failed, the crops were failing, and at Hampton Court the queen's unyielding hope was slowly losing ground to despair.

In the first week of June the clergy began to lead daily processions for Mary's safe delivery. Her courtiers and Council members joined in, and at her request they marched around the palace court below her apartments. She sat at a small window and watched the procession every morning, bowing "with extraordinary cheerfulness and graciousness" to the dignitaries and councilors who doffed their caps to her as they passed.[20] There was more color in her cheeks now than in May, and some said she had never been in better health, though she still felt "no movement indicating parturition."[21]

The Spanish courtiers were especially anxious for any hopeful sign of the approaching birth, as they looked forward to leaving England as soon after the christening as possible. "The queen's deliverance keeps us all greatly exercised in our minds," Ruy Gomez wrote, "although our doctors always said that the nine months are not up until 6 June." When she thought she felt some pains on May 31 and again in mid-June they became excited, but when Mary did not take to her bed they grew glum.[22]

Ruy Gomez dutifully sent word of each change in the doctors' official prognostications, but he was becoming cynical, and in his private letters he made jokes about the queen's vanished girth. "All this makes me doubt whether she is with child at all," he confided to a correspondent, "greatly as I desire to see the thing happily over."[23]

The king was even more eager than his courtiers to see the conclusion of the queen's pregnancy. He had been expected in Flanders since May—on June 6 the emperor was still postponing Queen Joanna's interment in hopes that his son would arrive at any time—and he was prepared to embark as soon as he knew that the child was born and Mary was out of danger. He had already given some of the lesser members of his retinue permission to leave, and the soldiers in his personal guard were due to begin crossing to Flanders in the second week of June. With the failure of the peace conference a fresh outbreak of war seemed likely, and Philip was determined to be a part of it. He was tired of being thought of as unfit and disinclined toward war; he badly wanted a military reputation.[24] "From what I hear," Michiel wrote in a dispatch, "one single hour's delay in this delivery seems to him a thousand years."[25]

He was still living like a wealthy guest in England, dependent on the hospitality of the court yet paying all his expenses and those of his household. It was known he had not touched a penny of the revenues of the English crown. In fact he had loaned Mary a good deal of money, and it was partly as a result of this that his treasurers were at work in Antwerp early in June trying to secure a loan. Money was scarce, and it took them some weeks to complete their negotiations. In the meantime none of the Spaniards had any coins in their pockets, and when they tried to live on credit the English landlords and merchants either complained loudly or denied them lodging and food. "In truth these poor courtiers have a very bad time of it," Michiel said of Philip's retainers, "both by reason of the intolerable scarcity of everything, which has doubled in price owing to them, as also because there is no one who, either with money or credit, will succor and assist them in their need." The dreary weather and the certain prospect of a poor harvest made the English more reluctant than ever to accommodate the Spaniards, and when Philip's agents finally sent word they had negotiated a loan of 300,000 ducats they were overjoyed, even though the bankers demanded more than twenty-five per cent interest. Philip too was relieved, but apprehensive for the future, for in order to arrange the loan he had been forced to pledge all his revenues for the next two years.[26]

Crowning his worries, though, was the embarrassment of being held up to ridicule in foreign courts. English diplomats abroad could only make excuses for Mary for so long, referring to the miscalculations of the doctors and the "common error of women in reckoning their time."

Mason wrote from Brussels asking that Mary appear occasionally at mass or in some public place in order to put an end to the scurrilous rumors at the imperial court. The Council sent him back an official response telling him to counteract whatever rumors he heard, but individual Council members forewarned him later in private letters that they doubted the genuineness of the pregnancy.[27] The Venetian ambassador in Brussels had received trustworthy information that "the queen has given manifest signs of not being pregnant" before the end of May, although he confined his knowledge to secret dispatches and maintained the opposite in his public statements.[28] The French king was willing to put down the delay to "women's ways," but one of his ambassadors, who was staying at Padua for his health, busily spread the story of her freak delivery of a "mole or lump of flesh," now embroidered to include the fabrication that he had seen letters confirming the queen's death.[29]

Meanwhile Mary busied herself with ordering her secretaries to prepare letters announcing her safe delivery to be sent to the pope, the emperor, the kings of France, Hungary, and Bohemia, the doge of Venice, the queen regent of Flanders and the queen dowager of France. The date of the birth was left blank, as was the sex of the child; these important details would be filled in by clerks at the last minute. Mary signed the letters herself, and also the passports for the envoys who were deputed to carry the good news to the imperial and Portuguese and French courts.[30] She prepared a brief letter to Pole at the same time, informing him how it had "late pleased God of his infinite goodness" to add to the benefits he had conferred on her "the happy delivery of a prince."

And as if to match these premature announcements an ambassador from Poland arrived at Hampton Court to convey his sovereign's compliments to the queen. The false report of Mary's delivery that had so rejoiced Londoners on April 30 had reached Poland some weeks later. There no one contradicted it, and the king immediately sent an envoy to England in consequence. The Polish diplomat knew no English, but had prepared a "premeditated Latin oration" artfully combining condolence on the death of Queen Joanna with congratulations on the birth of Mary's son. Apparently he was unable to disentangle his sentiments, for he delivered both the sorrowful and joyful portions of his address before Philip and his courtiers, "to the laughter and amusement of many persons who were present."[31]

As the summer dragged on popular unrest was so great the earl of Pembroke and his forces had to be brought in to keep order in London. A planned rising for the last week in June was discovered by the Council in time to forestall it, and pageants scheduled for the feasts of Sts. Peter and John were canceled. Efforts were made to break up any crowd that gathered in the city, but Pembroke and his men could not be everywhere.

On Corpus Christi Day all the principal Spaniards went to worship in a certain church, intending to follow the host in procession. A huge crowd gathered at the door of the church, the English outside outnumbering the Spaniards within by two to one. The Spaniards prudently stayed inside and some of the English, "less daring and indiscreet than the rest," succeeded in dispersing the mob, but the confrontation could easily have ended in the worst bloodshed yet seen.[32] Both sovereigns did what they could to prevent the violence, issuing order after order threatening severe penalties for assaults of any kind, but Mary's distress at the mistreatment of the Spaniards only angered her subjects further. They said she was "a Spaniard at heart," and that she cared nothing for the true Englishmen who supported her. Worse still, they said that her Spanish husband was betraying her with other women. Protestant pamphleteers alleged that the king kept company with whores and commoners' daughters while Mary was confined to her rooms. "The baker's daughter in her russet gown," they rhymed, was "Better than Queen Mary without her crown."

Other ballads spread even more quickly in the summer of 1555, songs about the heroism of the Protestants burned by the queen's bishops and about the malice of the queen herself. The burnings were creating a fresh undercurrent of opposition stronger than any political rebellion. It came to the attention of the Council that two Protestants, John Barnard and John Walsh, were going about the countryside carrying the bones of William Pigot, a man burned for heresy at Braintree in March. Barnard and Walsh were showing the bones to the people as if they were relics, and exhorting them to hold firmly to the doctrines they had learned under Henry VIII and Edward as the martyr Pigot had done.[33]

In the first two weeks of June there were eight more burnings, and the "sudden severity" they indicated was odious to many. There were riots in Warwickshire in July, and fears of more disturbances in Devonshire and Cornwall, and Pembroke was again summoned to put a stop to the unrest before it reached a critical stage.[34] The English Protestants on the continent affirmed that there was a direct connection between the burnings and the queen's frustrated hope for motherhood. Gardiner had persuaded Mary that the Protestants had bewitched her, they said, and in her fear of them she had given the bishop a free hand in his cruel slaughter of the true believers. Even in London it was being said that Mary had declared her child could not be born until every heretic then in prison was burned.[35]

In July the doctors and midwives ceased their calculations altogether. By some reckonings the queen was now eleven months pregnant, and if she succeeded now in giving birth to a healthy child it would in truth be a miracle. A miracle, it seems, was just what everyone near her expected. "The universal persuasion and belief" was, according to Michiel, that a miracle would "come to pass in this, as in all her majesty's other circumstances, which the more they were despaired of according to human reasoning and discourse, the better and more auspicious did their result then show itself." Mary's child would prove to the world once and for all that her affairs "were regulated exclusively by divine providence."[36]

As the queen waited for the miracle, she wept and prayed. Her prayer book survives, its pages worn and stained. The queen's tears appear to have fallen most often on a page bearing a prayer for the safe delivery of a woman with child.[37]

XLIII

 I know wher is a gay castle
Is build of lime and stone,
Within is a gay ladie
Her lord is ryd from home.

By the first of August Hampton Court stank as badly as a London street. The kitchens and courtyards reeked of refuse, and indoors the air in the chambers and galleries was foul and stale. The constant rains had spoiled the palace gardens, and made hunting or riding impossible. The courtiers had no choice but to keep to their tiny, overcrowded rooms, going outside only to join the religious processions that still petitioned God to deliver the queen. They were bored and impatient. There were no celebrations or entertainments to occupy them and their fine clothes hung useless in their wardrobes, rotting in the dampness.

To their immense relief it was announced that the court was moving to Oatlands so that Hampton Court could be cleansed. It was a tacit acknowledgment that Mary's confinement was over, for the manor of Oatlands was a modest rural house barely large enough to accommodate a reduced royal household. Philip's attendants had been leaving for Flanders for weeks, and now even Ruy Gomez took his departure. The noblewomen who had been shut up with Mary for nearly four months ordered their servants to pack their trunks and returned to their own summer houses. There was no formal announcement that the queen and her physicians had given up hoping for a child. Instead both Mary and Philip's most intimate advisers continued to insist that she was in her sixth or seventh month, but everyone knew it was only said "for the sake of keeping the populace in hope, and consequently in check." But the people could only be fooled for so long, and they knew as clearly as the ambassadors did that "the pregnancy will end in wind rather than anything else."[1]

Perhaps they cared less than Renard and the other imperialists thought. The incipient rebellions that had been reported turned out to be far less serious than Renard's dispatches made them appear. The Warwickshire rising was in fact an angry crowd at a local market protesting the unscrupulous profiteering of some grain speculators—a serious enough matter, but no danger to the queen. The unrest in Devon and Cornwall was no more than a ripple of dissatisfaction produced by a story that the queen was dead. The only evidence that she was still alive, her daily appearance at the palace window, was said to be a fraud; it was not the queen's own face at the window but a wax replica. Another supposed rebellion was nothing more than a dispute between a landlord and his tenants.

Disturbed though the country people were by the unaccountable course of the queen's fruitless pregnancy their immediate concern was for the price of grain and beer. In the drenched fields the harvest had putrefied. There was no fresh grain to be had, either for bread or for brewing. There was no grass for the cattle, no hay or oats for the horses. In some areas the "greater part" of the sheep had sickened and died, and those that were left were being sold for the price of a small farm.[2] In normal times August was a month of abundance, but this year there was only want, and fear of famine in the months to come. As the king and queen rode eastward out of London toward Oatlands on August 3 they saw little but barren farmlands and lean cattle, and the faces of the peasants who called out to wish them godspeed were very thin indeed.

Who it was that gave the order to remove to Oatlands is unclear. Mary herself may have struggled toward a conscious accommodation with the truth, or a compassionate waiting woman may have helped her to make the difficult decision. According to one account there was at least one among the women of her suite who refused to go along with the delusion of pregnancy. Mistress Frideswide Strelley, "a good honorable woman of hers," never echoed the comforting words of Susan Clarencieux and the midwives, and when Mary could no longer endure the strain of her false hopes she sent for Mistress Strelley and thanked her for her constancy. "I see they be all flatterers," the queen told her, "and none true to me but thou."[3]

Once installed at Oatlands Mary returned to her accustomed routine. The household officials took up their posts again, and the queen resumed her governmental tasks and audiences. She had never entirely stopped seeing ambassadors and other dignitaries, even during the time court observers reported her to be most reclusive. One of these interviews concerned the abortive peace conference. The papal prothonotary Noailles, brother of the French ambassador, spoke with Mary at Hampton Court in July. He found her to be fully informed about the course the talks had taken, and thoroughly disillusioned with the obstinacy of the French. She told him "half angrily" that in view of her obligations to her husband and father-in-law she could hardly be expected to remain neutral much longer, adding that if the conference had failed it was not the fault of the English mediators. "She would not lay the blame," she said, "on anything but our own sins and demerits, and on the evil nature of the times, God's wrath not having as yet sufficiently vented itself on us."[4]

If Mary had this view of diplomatic affairs it is possible she applied the same logic to her own situation. Her confidence in God's guiding hand had been badly shaken, but she may have found some justification for her disappointment in the view that the wickedness of the age demanded punishment. If God could use her to drive out tyranny and restore the church, then he could use her barrenness to chastise his people for their sins. Armed with this dark consolation Mary took up her accustomed life once again, showing herself and conversing with her courtiers as usual and finally admitting "with her own lips" that she was not pregnant after all.[5]

Philip went to Oatlands disappointed of a son but endowed with a kingdom. Charles V had at last determined to pass on his lands to his heirs, and the choicest of these lands, the kingdom of the Netherlands, was to be Philip's inheritance. The emperor's gout and troubled mental state made it impossible for him to go on ruling any longer. He needed rest and sun and quiet, when at Brussels he found only toil and foul weather and the imminent threat of war. His ailments were so severe in the summer of 1555 that he had to treat them with waters from the baths of Liége. Mules were posted at intervals along the road between Liége and Brussels to carry skins of water in relays to the imperial court.[6] The emperor's doctors had prescribed that he bathe in the healing waters at least once every twenty-four hours, and as he could not leave his desk to go to the spa the spa had to come to him.

Charles' sister Mary was preparing to lay aside her authority at the same time he did, to make way for Philip's personal rule. To judge from her later behavior she was by no means anxious to relinquish her power, but did so in deference to her brother. She wrote Charles an official letter informing him of her decision in August, filled with self-apology and polite formulas of subservience. "Having long been burdened with a sense of her inadequacy," she began, she had decided to follow his example and give up her throne, realizing that if Charles in his wisdom felt the need to retire it was only fitting that she feel the same need "given her inferiority to him in every respect, and the fact that she is a woman." Her ability, compared to a man's, was "as black compared with white," she confessed, and no woman, however gifted, could effectively govern the Low Countries in time of war. As for her future, Mary of Flanders had modest expectations. She would rather "earn her living as best she might" than go on ruling, she claimed. She had always planned to tend her mother in her old age, but now that Joanna was dead Mary would like nothing better than to live in Spain with her widowed sister Eleanor, queen dowager of France.[7]

Philip was as reluctant to take power in the Netherlands as his aunt was to give it up. He was eager to leave England, but not in order to rule over the Flemings, who detested him. What he wanted most, he informed his father through Ruy Gomez, was to go back to Spain as soon after the abdication as possible, and he begged earnestly to be spared a repetition of his tense year in England. But with Charles himself planning to retire to Spain it was more imperative than ever that his son remain in Flanders, especially now that war with France was imminent. All that Philip had gained in England might be lost if he put himself at such a distance from London, while at Brussels he was only four or five days away from his island kingdom. What he had accomplished in England was well worth preserving. In the eyes of the foreign ambassadors he was so obviously the locus of political power there that both the Portuguese and Venetian envoys to the English court offered to follow him to Brussels in order to stay close to the heart of English affairs.[8]

Before his leavetaking Philip acted very much like a ruling king. He startled Cardinal Pole by appearing at his door, "very privately in person," to tell the cardinal he wanted him to assume charge of the government in his absence, and the following day he repeated this request to the entire Council, ordering the Council members "to defer to him [Pole] in everything." "All public and important business" was to be decided according to the "opinion and advice" of the cardinal, while "private and ordinary matters" were to be handled by the Council alone.[9] This left nothing whatever for the queen to do, and indeed Philip did not mention her in his final speech.

Mary may have had this significant oversight in mind as she prepared to accompany Philip to Greenwich, where he was to take ship for Gravesend and then travel by land to Canterbury and eventually to Dover to embark for the Flemish coast. Philip was to ride through London to Tower Wharf, where he would join Mary in her barge and travel downriver to Greenwich with her. But at the last minute Mary decided not to go by water to the wharf but to ride beside her husband in an open litter, with Pole at her side and the Lord Mayor and aldermen bearing the royal insignia before her. Her instincts were sound, for many Londoners still believed she was dead, and the sight of her created a joyful commotion. The city was full of country folk crowding in for Bartholomew Fair, and the roadway along which the royal procession passed was choked with spectators. When they heard the queen was coming, the people "all ran from one place to another, as to an unexpected sight, and one which was well-nigh new, as if they were crazy, to ascertain thoroughly if it was her, and on recognizing and seeing her in better plight than ever, they by shouts and salutations, and every other demonstration, then gave yet greater signs of their joy."[10] By her mere appearance Mary had upstaged Philip, though both were applauded heartily all along the length of their route.

On August 29 Philip embarked from Greenwich. He and Mary said their goodbyes in private, but afterward she insisted on walking with him to the head of the stairs where his gentlemen all kissed her hand. Michiel, who was present, noted that Mary "expressed very well the sorrow becoming a wife" as well as the dignity becoming a queen. She was evidently "deeply grieved internally," but she took care not to show it, "constraining herself the whole way to avoid, in sight of such a crowd, any demonstration unbecoming her gravity."

Once the king had gone, however, and she was safely back in her apartments, she sat down in front of a window which looked out on the river and began to cry. No one but her women—among them Michiel's informant—could see her there, and she was free to express her feelings. Her beloved Philip, her dear husband and helpmeet, was going with the next tide. She sat by the window for hours, watching as his trunks and chests and horses were loaded onto the barge, then watching his personal servants, his companions, and finally Philip himself step aboard and go below. She saw the sailors cast off and the ship move off downriver, and to her delight Philip came up on the deck one last time, "mounted aloft on the barge in the open air, in order to be better seen when the barge approached in sight of the window," and waved his hat in Mary's direction, "demonstrating great affection."[11] She continued to watch the river until the ship was out of sight.

Philip and his retinue stayed at Canterbury for several days, waiting for good weather and an escort fleet of Flemish ships. There were many French ships and privateers in the Channel; only a month or so earlier seventeen French vessels had burned and sunk a Flemish fleet in a bloody day-long battle. While he waited Philip read the messages Mary sent him and sent her replies of his own. Gentlemen-in-waiting were on the road between Canterbury and Greenwich nearly every hour, and messengers hung about the courtyard of the palace night and day, "booted and spurred ready for a start."

When he was not attending to this correspondence Philip talked with great interest to his traveling companion Francisco de Ribera. Ribera, an adventurer living in Peru, had come back to Europe to strike a bargain with the emperor. He and his fellow landowners wanted to buy the right to their lands in perpetuity in return for enormous sums in Peruvian silver. Ribera came to Philip first, hoping to gain his support for the plan before approaching his father. The more Philip heard of the wealth to be gained the more he was inclined to give his approval. On his journey from the New World, Ribera said, he had lost some fifty thousand ducats in bullion when his ship foundered, but the loss meant nothing since the natives would replace the silver twice over as soon as he returned. Philip needed no more convincing. By the time he and Ribera set sail for Calais they were on the best of terms, and Philip spent the brief voyage calculating his profits—"so considerable a sum that the mere mention of it is alarming."[12]

Once in Flanders Philip wrote to Mary "in his own hand" informing her that he had made the crossing safely in less than three hours. In an effort to deceive the French he had not waited for the Flemish fleet but had gone on ahead with only four vessels. It was a good thing too, he wrote to Mary, for if he had waited another day at Canterbury he would have run into a terrible storm at sea. After giving Mary this news, however, Philip turned all his attention to the situation in his newly acquired kingdom, and sent few letters to England. Mary wrote him long letters every day, in French, but his replies became fewer and fewer. When Michiel saw her on September 13 she confided in him "very passionately with the tears in her eyes" that she had not heard from her husband for seven days.[13] Mary was prepared to endure separation from Philip as a favor to her cousin Charles V, and for reasons of state, provided his stay in Flanders was brief. Not long before Philip left she had written to his father that although "there is nothing in this world that I set so much store by as the king's presence," still she had "more concern for your majesties' welfare than for my own desires," and would not oppose his journey.[14] But her devotion to him was so great that she was in some anguish without him, and the strain of maintaining a cheerful exterior while inwardly worrying about his feelings for her and about when he would return strained her nerves and threatened her health.

One of Courtenay's correspondents in England wrote to him in September to tell him that "the queen is well and merry" despite Philip's absence, but those closer to Mary saw that she was suffering. Michiel's informant told him how, when she was alone and "supposing herself invisible to any of her attendants," Mary mourned as if griefstricken, "as may be imagined with regard to a person extraordinarily in love."[15]

Now more than ever Mary found comfort and sustenance in the presence of Reginald Pole. He moved into lodgings in the palace shortly after Philip left, and took on the duty of providing solace to the queen as part of his general task of serving as regent for Philip in all but name. Pole represented everything Mary treasured. He reminded her of their joint survival of the dark days of Henry VIII. He stood for the church militant, fighting back against the advance of heresy and wickedness. And he was the symbol of England's reunion with Rome. The very sight of Pole made her spirits rise, and though he had more pity than respect for her she was grateful for his grave and consoling presence.

Something else that gave her comfort and absorbed her attention during Philip's absence was the Franciscan monastery at Greenwich. It had been her mother's special favorite, and Mary herself had been christened there. She meant to make the Greenwich convent a seedbed for the restoration of monasticism in England, and to this end she took the house into her care, spending a great deal of time among the monks and "delighting marvelously" to watch them chant the hours and celebrate mass in the chapel near the palace. Mary installed twenty-five Observant friars at Greenwich, among them Friar William Peto, "an aged man of most holy life" and like Pole a survivor of the Henrician era. Peto had recently been nominated for a cardinalate, but what endeared him to Mary was a childhood memory of being brought, probably by her mother, to say her confession to Friar Peto when she was seven years old.[16]

In his letters to Philip Pole described how Mary spent her days as she waited for his return. She "passes the forenoon in prayer," he wrote, "after the manner of Mary, and in the afternoon admirably personates Martha, by transacting business." Pole indulgently recorded how the queen "so urged her councilors as to keep them all incessantly occupied," imagining that she was moved to work with them because she "saw Philip present in their persons." Though he completely misjudged her motives, Pole found Mary's diligence in governing impressive. She worked so hard at state business "as to require energy in this matter to be checked rather than stimulated." After a long day of discussions with her councilors, audiences with petitioners and foreign dignitaries and supervision of the drafting of documents and letters, she liked nothing better than to spend "the greater part of the night" writing to Philip. Pole feared that, combined with the strain of her husband's absence, these labors might make her sick, especially as it was the time of the year when her chronic illness often appeared. His return would of course cure all, Pole told Philip, and Mary reinforced this message with every letter she sent. When Philip had been gone about five weeks she sent one of her gentlemen to him at Brussels. He brought the king a ring from his wife, and the message that she wished him "health, long life, and speedy return."[17]

Worse than Philip's absence itself was the fact that Mary had no idea when he would come back. He could not commit himself to a definite time, as he had no idea what conditions he might find in Flanders. Then too there were the abdication ceremonies, which promised to be intricate and prolonged. Philip would be called upon to take part in ceremonial transfers of power in every capital and principal town of the Netherlands, and to spend enough time in each to establish his reputation and authority. Soon after his arrival he began trying to learn to speak Walloon, the only language his Flemish subjects understood and the tongue in which he would have to make himself agreeable, if not loved. His linguistic efforts argued for a long rather than a short stay, since during his year in England Philip had never made any attempt to learn English.

What fed Mary's worries most was the slow exodus of Spanish persons and goods that went on for months after Philip's departure. At first he had left the greater part of his household behind in England—his German and Spanish soldiers, his Burgundian cavalry, his physicians and chapel clergy, most of his horses and grooms and even the pages of his chamber. But as the weeks passed the members of his household left, one after another, "with a mind," Michiel noted, "so far as they themselves are concerned, not to revisit this country for a very long while."[18] Ships carrying the king's personal effects and those of his chief companions left English ports every day, and worse yet, by mid-September Philip had made arrangements to pay off his creditors. Ten armed caravels arrived from Spain on September 16, bringing some sixty thousand ducats to be distributed among the English merchants who had supplied his household and the English servants who had helped to staff it. When the Spanish fleet left, though, it carried a far greater sum to Flanders, and it was becoming more and more clear that Philip was making himself very much at home in his new lands.

Now when Philip wrote to Mary his letters were curt and businesslike. She should revive the peace talks. She should provide ships to escort the emperor to Spain after his abdication. She should look into the prospect of having him crowned. Without being too specific Philip gave Mary "fair hope of soon seeing her," and when she suggested coming "to some place at the sea side to see him" he offered to journey from Brussels to Bruges to be nearer to her in case she decided to come.[19] But he dismissed the ship that had been kept waiting in the harbor, ready to take him to England at any time, and finally on October 19 he sent word to Mary that all his remaining noblemen, soldiers, pages, equerries and horses should be loaded onto ships and sent to him at once. This left only his confessor, two Dominican friars and his chapel clergy in England, and though he explained that he needed the others to replace the emperor's servants who were embarking for Spain Mary was angry and hurt.[20] She began fitting out a fleet to send to Flanders to bring him back, but before it could be victualed and manned word came that the emperor's formal renunciation of his lands had been postponed, and Philip could not hope to leave Brussels before November.[21]

Mary felt thwarted at every turn. She had expected to have Philip back with her for the opening of Parliament, but that looked increasingly unlikely. And just when she had need of all her allies, the most stalwart of them lay near death. Bishop Gardiner had not been well since his return from Calais and the peace conference. By October he was gravely ill, and though his physicians persisted in hoping for a recovery and Mary showed him every care, they all admitted that, "being the dead time of the year," he could not be expected to live. He died on November 12. On his deathbed Gardiner was reconciled to Paget, now severely out of favor with Mary for having disputed the validity of her pregnancy when ordered to defend it. At Mary's suggestion the chancellor made her his beneficiary, thus returning to the crown the fifty thousand ducats in property, household furniture, silver vessels and coins Mary had given him since his restoration to his bishopric. In this he acted, Michiel believed, "as became a good and grateful servant," and indeed Mary would find it hard to replace Gardiner. Michiel pronounced him unmatched as a royal servant, and though he had left a good deal to be desired as a leader he had more than made up for this deficiency by his honesty and loyalty.[22]

The Protestants in England and abroad, though, were to preserve a darker memory of the chancellor. In their view he was responsible for the hated burnings that continued to blemish Mary's reign. They envisioned him as a monstrous beast, his disfigured limbs an outward sign of the evil in his heart and conscience. He was of a "swart color," they wrote, with "frowning brows, eyes an inch within the head, a nose hooked like a buzzard, wide nostrils like a horse, ever snuffing into the wind, a sparrow mouth, great paws like the devil, talons on his feet like a gryphon two inches longer than the natural toes, and so tied to with sinews that he could not abide to be touched, nor scarce suffer them to touch the stones."[23] In the end the Protestant calumnies were to outlive both Mary's solicitude and Michiel's praise.

With Gardiner gone Mary and Pole were left to manage the unruly Parliament alone. Mary continued to hope that somehow her husband would find a way to rejoin her for at least part of the session, but she was slowly becoming reconciled to a long separation. To remind him of England she ordered her chefs to bake some of his favorite meat pies and shipped them off to him along with letters explaining that his coronation was at best a remote possibility. The pies pleased him but his wife's uncompliant response did not. For the first time since their marriage began, Philip threatened Mary. He wanted to please her by coming back to England, he said, but only if he were allowed to "share the government with her." In Spain and the Low Countries he was absolute ruler; to accept a lesser position in England would be "unbecoming his dignity, which requires him to take part in the affairs of the realm."[24] He would return, but only if Mary would make him king of England.

XLIV

 Complain my lute, complain on him
That stays so long away;
He promised to be here ere this,
But still unkind doth stay.
But now the proverb true I find,
Once out of sight then out of mind.

As the fall wore on Philip found more and more to enjoy in the lands he had dreaded ruling. He was entertained at hunts and banquets, and he was guest of honor at the weddings of prominent citizens in Brussels and Antwerp. He attended the weddings masked, and danced afterward with the aristocratic beauties of Flanders until the early hours of the morning. By December the envoys at the imperial court were noting that Philip went out masked to balls or banquets nearly every night, and when one gathering ended he went on to another, exhausting himself and his companions in drinking and merrymaking. After a year of strained reserve and forced joviality in England, the festive atmosphere of the Netherlands was a welcome relief, and Philip let himself be drawn into the carefree enjoyment without regard to his rank or reputation. His taciturn gravity fell away completely under the liberating influence of strong Flemish beer, and he took to presenting himself at the gates of noblemen's houses at all hours of the night, demanding to be entertained. One evening he danced at a wedding until two in the morning, then went to the house of the duke of Savoy, gave orders that the duke be awakened, and spent the rest of the night laughing and joking with his sleepy host.[1]

Before long Philip's nocturnal adventures became notorious. It was said at court that he "took delight in frequent masqueings, rather more than becomes the present troublous times," and his intimate servants were blamed for encouraging him in these and "similar pleasures."[2] He seemed to have forgotten that he was a married man, and it was noticed that he had developed an indiscreet attachment to one Madame d'Aler, "who is considered very handsome, and of whom he seems much enamored."[3] When Mary sent an envoy to her husband in mid-December Philip made no effort to conceal his scandalous pastimes from him, though the Englishman took it upon himself not to reveal what he had seen to Mary, "lest the queen, who is easily agitated, might take it too much to heart."[4]

Philip had not forgotten about England entirely. In the first week of December he wrote to his wife in his own hand, telling her to appoint whomever she liked as chancellor (though he recommended either Paget or Wotton) and assuring her that he would be ready to leave Flanders as soon as he completed business which compelled him to go to Antwerp. In the same week, though, he ordered his armory, his wardrobe, and all his German and Spanish halbardiers sent to him in Flanders, and well-informed courtiers in Brussels were saying he showed little inclination to return to England for the time being.

Delays and complications in the transfer of the imperial lands were prolonging Philip's stay. It took time for the emperor to divest himself of his sizable portion of the world, and each component of his sovereignty had to be passed on separately. He had formally invested Philip with the Netherlands in October, but had not yet passed on to him his Spanish inheritance; currently the emperor was occupied with drawing up the documents relating to his Sicilian and Aragonese lands. Charles' physical incapacity and the jealousies between his ministers and Philip's were creating an administrative confusion that made the task all the more difficult. There were thousands of edicts and other documents to be signed, including the acts of renunciation themselves. The emperor's gout so crippled him that he could not sign these papers, yet when Philip was approached to sign them on his father's behalf his ministers would not allow it. He must wait, they advised, until he was in possession of full sovereignty before taking over any public business. Meanwhile the clerks continued to copy out the letters notifying the emperor's principal subjects and minor officials of the transfer of sovereignty—some two thousand of them for Spain and Sicily alone—and the messengers who were to carry them to their recipients waited for news that the emperor had recovered the use of his gnarled hand.

Charles' sister Mary presented another complication. Far from showing herself eager to retire from public life, she was still attending meetings of her Council daily, and showing up the councilors by being the first to arrive every morning. There were rumors that she might resume her regency, and she still addressed the Council members and even the governor in the forceful, imperious tone of a ruler.[5] Clearly Philip would find it difficult to take power from his aunt when the time came.

He was finding it harder than he had expected to take power in England as well. If he thought that his threats would induce Mary to arrange his coronation he was mistaken. His threats wounded her, but they did not impair her political sense. She equivocated until Parliament met; then, sensing the extreme dissatisfaction in this most unruly of her Parliaments, she told Philip flatly that no proposal for his coronation had any chance of passage. He countered by hinting that she should bypass Parliament and crown him by her own authority, but his hints produced no effect. A year earlier a bill had been proposed which would have made Philip king on Mary's death—a suggestion that represented the highwater mark of his popularity in England. But in recent months anti-Spanish sentiment had been growing, fostered in part by the libels of English refugees on the continent. Pamphlets such as "The Lamentation of Naples" and "The Mourning of Milan" described in horrifying detail what suffering imperial rule had brought to those states, making the English more and more reluctant to come under the Hapsburg yoke.

But if Philip could not be crowned, he could at least make certain that his sometime rival Edward Courtenay was permanently removed from the succession. Courtenay, whose Plantagenet blood gave him a far better claim to the throne than Philip had as the queen's husband, was living out an uncomfortable exile on the continent, having recently made himself more dangerous than ever by becoming a Protestant. He had gone first to Brussels, where he and his attendants were repeatedly singled out for attack by Spaniards he had insulted when they were living in England. After the fourth assault he moved with his wounded retainers to Venice, but here too he was in danger of his life. Philip's friend Ruy Gomez tried to arrange Courtenay's assassination through a Dalmatian soldier with connections to the Uskoks, outlaws living in the Venetian countryside and eager to be of service in matters of this kind. Gomez offered the Dalmatian a thousand crowns to kill the man "who expects to be King of England," and assured him he would have Philip's favor as well, but instead of accepting the offer the soldier told the story to the Venetian Council, and Courtenay was spared. A year later he died mysteriously at Padua, perhaps of poison or perhaps, according to another account, of a fever he caught while hawking.[6]

While Philip was amusing himself in Flanders Mary faced the opposition of a hostile Parliament. The Venetian ambassador Michiel described the Commons of November 1555 as "more daring and licentious than former houses," full of gentry and nobility impatient to oppose the queen's proposals and unwilling to show her the respect former Commons had given her. Noailles had been busy organizing the opposition, and had been assured by some members that they would block any bill granting a subsidy to the government. Gardiner's experience was sorely missed. (He died some three weeks after Parliament opened.) According to Michiel, he alone knew how to control resistance of this kind, sensing "the moment and the means for humoring and caressing, threatening and punishing" the rebellious Commons.[7]

After Gardiner died Mary took on much of his workload in addition to her own, and she now took on his function as conciliator of the Commons as well. Calling together sixty of the Commons members plus a majority of the Lords, she spoke to them "with her usual gravity and dignity," explaining that the bills she hoped to see enacted were in keeping with the good of the crown and the restored church, and represented a fulfillment of her predestined role as queen.[8] Several of the disputed bills eventually went through, but the session ended in coercion and recrimination. A crown bill recalling the political exiles in France and threatening them with forfeiture of their lands met with forceful opposition. A member from Gloucestershire, Sir Anthony Kingston, locked the doors of the house and kept them locked until the bill was defeated. Kingston was imprisoned for his "contemptuous behavior and great disorder," and Parliament dissolved in a mood of bitterness on December 9.

Over the next several months a wave of popular feeling against the government swept through southern England. Rumors that Philip would soon be crowned king triggered panic in the country people who had never ceased to fear the Spaniards they had never seen, and even in the Londoners who had cheered Philip on his departure only a few months earlier. A blacksmith described how he met a man at midnight near Finsbury Fields who told him for certain that the earl of Pembroke would soon obtain the crown for Philip. Other stories imagined that the Spaniard would not hesitate to seize the crown by force. When a truce between France and the empire was finally signed early in February, it was assumed that Philip would give his idle soldiers the task of conquering England. Noailles received intelligence from a continental source that ten companies of German and Flemish soldiers were being outfitted as an invasion force. Privately he doubted the report, but he spread it as widely as he could, and even managed to see that it reached the ears of Cardinal Pole.[9]

And as if rumors of one king were not disturbing enough, Londoners suddenly found they had a second king on their hands. In January a Greenwich man was arrested for handing out leaflets informing the people that Edward VI was alive and well in France, and was only waiting for a popular rising on his behalf to return to lead his subjects against the queen. In February a man claiming to be the dead king made himself known in London. He was caught and hanged, but not before "many persons, both men and women, were troubled by him."[10] Other disorders worried Mary and her councilors during January and February. There was rebellion in Ireland, and in England, printers were issuing a stream of "false fond books, ballets, rhymes and other lewd treatises" ridiculing the queen and king. The pipers and minstrels who wandered through the countryside were often asked to sing a favorite song called "Sacke full of Newes," a lampoon against the court, and in the "north parts" a company of players calling themselves "Sir Francis Leek's Men" were drawing large crowds to see a play "containing very naughty and seditious matter touching the king and queen's majesties, and the state of the realm."[11]

The ballads that did most damage to the queen's repute were those that glorified the Protestant martyrs. Ballad-makers wove the names of the seventy-five men and women burned as heretics during 1555 into songs glorifying their heroism and blackening the clergy who burned them. The "Ballad of John Careless" was sung wherever Protestants gathered, and in many places where the Spaniards were feared and the queen's policies despised. Another song told the story of a woman condemned to the stake who gave birth to a child as she suffered in the flames; the blameless child was thrown into the fire to die with its mother.[12]

The recent double burning of Ridley and Latimer helped to shape the burgeoning popular image of martyrdom. Both men died with the resolute piety that had come to be the hallmark of those the Catholic clergy called heretics. Ridley died slowly and horribly, his agony prolonged by a badly built fire. Latimer appeared to die all but painlessly, seeming miraculously to embrace the fire and bathe his hands and face in it. Many people in the large crowd that came to witness the executions wept and shook their heads at the sight, and carried away the memory of Latimer's prophecy that the meaning of these sufferings would become clear in time. "Be of good comfort, Master Ridley," he was heard to say, "and play the man, we shall this day light such a candle, by God's grace, in England, as I trust shall never be put out."

It was in this atmosphere of turbulence and sinister excitement that the most widespread of the plots to overthrow Queen Mary took shape. Tales of plotting came to the attention of the Council regularly, but in the first months of 1556 the accounts began to sound more ominous than usual. First the English ambassador in France sent word of a conspiracy of long standing whose object was to "deprive Mary of her estate" and to use her "as she used Queen Jane." According to the ambassador's informant the chief conspirators were "strong and many," and "such as had never offended the queen before."[18] In March the outlines of a much more dangerous plot began to come to light when one of the lesser figures in the scheme went to Cardinal Pole voluntarily and told everything he knew. This man, Thomas White, had been assigned to take part in robbing the royal Exchequer of fifty thousand pounds in silver. Through the wife of the Exchequer's teller the conspirators were able to make an impression of the teller's keys, and they counted on the cooperation of the Keeper of the Star Chamber and the customs official at Gravesend who agreed to let the boat loaded with the stolen silver pass the harbor unmolested. It soon became clear that the robbery was merely a preliminary to a more far-reaching plan. The political rebels living in France, their numbers augmented by mercenaries paid with the Exchequer silver, were to cross the Channel and land on the south coast. The leader of the invasion, Sir Henry Dudley, was confident that once he and his thousand soldiers landed, "he would quickly have twenty thousand men, and the best."

White's betrayal of his fellow-conspirators meant that the invasion plan did not mature, but as more and more of the men involved were seized and interrogated it became evident that there were nearly as many would-be rebels in England as there were in France. Dozens of public officials, landholders along the southern coast, and gentry in many parts of the kingdom were deeply implicated, and there was evidence from many quarters that some members of Mary's Council gave at least tacit encouragement to the conspirators.[14] To observers at foreign courts Dudley's conspiracy exposed the grave weakness of the English government. In the absence of her spouse the queen's authority appeared to be melting away.

In fact it might have been argued that the defusing of the plot before any harm was done confirmed the strength of the government rather than its weakness, and that Dudley's menace loomed larger in the imaginations of the queen's commissioners than it would have proved in fact. But Mary took no comfort from this view of her situation. From the time the first arrests were made she did not appear in public, and Michiel noted that she was "greatly troubled" by recent events. Everywhere she looked she saw traitors. Gentlemen among her courtiers were found to be in league with the principal conspirators. Lord Bray, the nimble-footed gallant who had danced so skillfully on her wedding day, was now in close custody in the Tower. Captain William Staunton, who had steadfastly defended Mary against Wyatt's forces two years earlier, was also arrested for complicity.[15] The skilled politicians in the Council were so tainted themselves that they could not be entrusted with the task of bringing the traitors to justice; only Mary's loyal former household officials—Rochester, Englefield, and Walgrave, along with the stalwart Jerningham and Hastings—were appointed to the commission charged with uncovering the truth of the plot. According to Noailles, one of Mary's chaplains had recently tried to kill her, and she was in dread of even her personal attendants.

In the last days of 1555 Mary wrote to Philip that "she was encompassed with enemies and could not move without endangering her crown." Her apprehension grew stronger as the alarming extent of Dudley's plot became clear, and it made her reluctant to part with the few men at court whose loyalty she counted on. Chief among these was Cardinal Pole, whose continual presence in the palace helped Mary through the difficult winter months. In March she appointed Pole archbishop of Canterbury, with mixed feelings: much as it pleased her to place Pole at the head of the English church she knew he would have to leave her to go to Canterbury to take possession of his see. In preparation for his departure, she provided him with a greatly enlarged household, and episcopal robes and ornaments worth ten thousand ducats, but she dreaded his going, and in the end insisted that he delay until after Easter.[16]

Noailles, who was active in Dudley's conspiracy and took the greatest pleasure in filling his letters and dispatches with news of the queen's discomfiture, painted a very dismal picture of Mary's torment during these months. In a letter to a lady of the French court the ambassador wrote how Mary was "in that depth of melancholy, that nothing seems to remain for her but to imitate the example of Dido." "But that she will not do," he hastened to add, lest his correspondent at the French court spread the rumor that the English queen was considering suicide. To Henri II Noailles described how Mary "lets no one see her but four women of her chamber, and a fifth who sleeps with her." She fretted the hours away in crying and writing long letters to Philip, and in bewailing the faithlessness of her subjects. Her tears were futile, the ambassador remarked, as it was now plain to everyone that Philip "never meant to reside for any length of time in England," and had withdrawn all of his servants and possessions except for his confessor. Mary herself admitted that her separation from Philip was likely to be permanent. According to one of Noailles' informants, the queen "told her ladies, that as she had done all possible to induce her husband to return, and as she found he would not, she meant to withdraw utterly from men, and live quietly, as she had done the chief part of her life before she married."

Noailles' description was an exaggeration, indeed a caricature. But there is no doubt Mary found life wearying in Philip's absence and that she was under great strain. When Noailles' wife saw the queen at court in May she hardly recognized her, and told her husband that Mary looked ten years older than when she had seen her last.

Mary turned forty in February, and she was feeling her age. Philip was not yet thirty, and to all accounts he was making the most of what was left of his youth in the banquet halls of Flanders. Mary was painfully aware how little attraction she had for her husband, especially after the embarrassment of her false pregnancy. There was no conclusive proof that she could not bear children, but Philip was understandably reluctant

BLOODY MARY

to wait out another questionable pregnancy when the risk of error was great.

Perhaps in token of the approach of her fortieth birthday one of Mary's subjects gave her on New Year's Day a supply of Dr. Stevens' Imperial or Sovereign Water, a tonic guaranteed to lengthen life far beyond the normal span. The medicinal water contained a dozen or more spices ground into Gascoigne wine, and both the inventor himself and a notable prelate were able to vouch for its death-defying properties. Dr. Stevens survived to "such extreme age, that he could neither go nor ride," and he continued to live on, though bedridden, for a number of years after he had lost the strength to walk. The prelate clung to life until he was so old he could no longer drink from a cup, and had to suck his daily draught of Sovereign Water "through a hollow pipe of silver."[17] Such examples of longevity were not unheard of. Only a few weeks after Mary's birthday news of a man of truly prodigious age came out of Rome. He claimed to be 116, and the Venetian ambassador, who saw him, confirmed that his age seemed indeed to be "very great."[18] If a man born during the Hundred Years' War could survive into the reign of Queen Mary, then the queen herself had every reason to hope for a generous span of years.

Philip too had a gift for Mary. He had just completed the last of the ceremonies through which he took possession of his father's Spanish lands, and he sent one of his gentlemen to his wife "with congratulations on her being able for the future to style herself the queen of many and great crowns, and on her being no less their mistress than of her own crown of England." He had to go to Antwerp for festivities celebrating the emperor's renunciation, Philip's envoy explained, but as soon as these were over the king would return to Mary's side.[19]

The rejoicings in Antwerp proved to be lengthy. There were pageants, bonfires, free-flowing wine barrels and booming cannon. The English merchants had erected a pageant of "a goodly castle, of the antique sort, fair painted and trimmed with banners, arms, and writings," and Philip declared himself very pleased with their efforts. The celebrations were marred by a serious accident, however. The servants charged with looking after the torches in another pageant were careless, and the whole structure caught fire. A dozen people were killed instantly, and a horse and rider were felled when one of the structure's iron supports broke and came crashing down on top of them.[20]

Word now came to Mary that Philip would soon leave Antwerp for Louvain, where he would "spend as little time as he can" and then depart for a Channel port. But ten days later he was still in Antwerp, taking part in jousts and living extravagantly on borrowed money. The English ambassador Mason wrote to Petre that Philip was spending thirty-five pounds a week, and fending off the bankers from whom he borrowed it by saying he would pay them on his return to England. But the weeks went on and he showed no sign of returning, Mason added, and "in the meantime, time runneth and charges withal, and he remains tied to the stake."[21]

In March Philip was still as earnestly engaged in his familiar pastimes as ever. He was currently preoccupied with planning an elaborate joust with Ruy Gomez and others, to be held after Easter. A rival of his in the lists, Count Schwartzburg, was preparing a tournament "in honor of his sweethearts," and Philip, not to be outdone, was taking as the theme of his tournament "that the women of Brussels are handsomer than those of Mechlin."[22] To Mary he sent the soberer explanation that he was detained in Flanders because of the expected visit of the king and queen of Bohemia. She countered with the suggestion that he bring his royal visitors with him to England, but Philip did nothing about it.[23] By now he was saying openly that England was nothing to him but an expensive nuisance, and it looked as though his marriage was no more than a matter of form. At the French court the king was predicting a worse event to come.[24] "I am of opinion," he told the Venetian ambassador in private, "that ere long the king of England will endeavor to dissolve his marriage with the queen."

XLV

 But why am I so abusyd?
Syth worde and dede is take in vayne,
And my service allway refusyd,
Yet moreovyr a gretter payne,
I wote nott where I may complayn;
For where I shulde, they be mery,
When that they knowe I am sory.

On Holy Thursday of Easter week, a large hall was prepared in the palace at Greenwich for the queen to wash the feet of the poor. At one end of the hall were the bishop of Ely, dean of the chapel, and the chaplains and royal choristers. At the other end were Mary's chief ladies and gentlewomen, wearing long linen aprons reaching to the ground and with long towels around their necks. In their hands they carried silver ewers full of water, and bunches of April flowers. Ranged down both sides of the hall were forty-one poor women, one for every year of the queen's life. (Mary had now entered her forty-first year.) They sat on benches, their right feet bare and elevated on stools. In preparation for Mary's act of piety the poor women's right feet had already been washed three times—first by a servant, then by the Under Almoner, and then again by the Grand Almoner, the bishop of Chichester. When the bishop had finished Mary came into the hall, flanked by Cardinal Pole and the members of her Council. She wore a linen apron like those of her ladies, and as she knelt down before the first of the poor women she beckoned to one of these ladies to assist her. One by one the queen washed the feet of each of the paupers in turn, drying them thoroughly with the towel which hung from her neck. As she finished drying each foot she made the sign of the cross over it and kissed it, "so fervently that it seemed as if she were embracing something very precious," and then moved on down the row of benches, remaining on her knees the whole time.

When she had finished Mary went around the room six more times in all, serving the poor women with platters of salted fish and bread and bowls of hippocras, and then giving them shoes and stockings and cloth for new clothes, leather purses full of forty-one pennies, and finally the aprons and towels which she and her ladies had worn. Then, looking carefully for the poorest and oldest of the paupers, she gave her the dress she had been wearing under her apron—a gown of the finest purple cloth trimmed with martens' fur, with sleeves so long they trailed to the ground. The Venetian ambassador Michiel was present at the ceremony, and was moved by Mary's devout seriousness throughout. "In all her movements and gestures," he wrote, "she seemed to act thus not merely out of ceremony, but from great feeling and devotion."

Mary was in fact becoming as well known for her piety toward humble people and the poor as she was for her reputed cruelty to the Protestants. She liked to appear at the door of needy households, dressed as a gentlewoman and not as queen, and offer whatever help or advice was needed. When the keeper of Enfield Chase and Marylebone Forest died, Mary went to see his widow, and finding her in tears, "took her by the hand, and lifted her up—for she kneeled—and bade her be of good cheer, for her children should be well provided for." Mary sent the woman's two oldest sons to school, and paid their tuition until they were nearly grown.[1] She liked nothing more than to go with a few of her women to visit families living near her palaces, or on Pole's estate at Croydon. The carters and farmers and carpenters and their wives rarely realized who she was; she spoke with such "plainness and affability" that they took her to be one of "the queen's maids, for there seemed no difference." Jane Dormer recorded how, if Mary found children in the house, she always gave the parents money for the children's sake, "advising them to live thriftily and in the fear of God," and if the families were very large she would turn to Jane and tell her to write down their names so that afterward she could make arrangements for some to be apprenticed in London.[2]

Jane Dormer had now become Mary's most intimate companion, "particularly favored by her and affected." Jane was with Mary during most of her waking hours, and often slept with her at night. They read the offices of the church together, and the queen gave into Jane's care "her usual wearing jewels" and other valuable ornaments. When she ate it was Jane who cut her meat, and even though there were many suitors for Jane's hand Mary insisted that none of them was good enough for her, and would not let her marry.[3]

On Mary's charitable outings it was Jane who kept a record of what complaints were made about the bailiffs on the royal estates or about local officials. Mary made a particular point of asking the villagers how they lived and whether they were getting by on what they earned.

And always she pressed them to tell her "if the officers of the court did deal with them," and whether their carts had been requisitioned for the queen's use or their grain or chickens purloined for her table. If she found any evidence of mistreatment or dishonesty she dealt with it as soon as she returned to the court. Once at a collier's house she sat and spoke with the collier and his wife as they were eating supper, and the man told her that, though his cart had been taken by men from the court in London, they had never paid him. Mary asked whether he had come to ask for his money, and he assured her he had, "but they gave him neither his money nor good answer." The queen looked the collier in the eye. "Friend," she asked one last time, "is this true, that you tell me?" He swore it was, and asked Mary to intercede with the royal controller for himself and other poor men who were abused in the same way. Mary told the collier to come again and ask for what was due him the next morning, and left.

As soon as she got back to the palace the queen summoned the controller "and gave him such a reproof for not satisfying poor men, as the ladies who were with her, when they heard it, much grieved." Mary told Rochester in her loud, low voice that the men who served him were surly thieves who took advantage of the country people, and that she wanted their wrongdoing stopped. "Hereafter he should see it amended," Mary told her controller, "for if she understood it again, he should hear it to his displeasure." And every penny owed must be paid the very next morning. Rochester had had long experience of the queen's uncompromising authority, of course, but what puzzled him was how she came to hear of his officers' behavior. Then Jane and the other women explained to him about the interview with the collier, and in future he took care to see that his men paid their debts and kept their word.[4]

By 1556 word of Mary's charity had reached even the destitute Benedictine nuns of Siena. The city had been devastated by war—"Siena is wasted like a candle," one diplomatic dispatch began—and in the destruction the nuns' convent had been leveled. Since then the hundred members of the religious community had been living in a small and unhealthy house and subsisting on charity. They had no money to rebuild their convent, and in their desperation they wrote to Mary. Her generosity was well known, the letter said; would she help them build another dormitory and church?[5]

On Good Friday Mary carried out the other ceremonies traditionally performed by English sovereigns at Easter—creeping to the cross, blessing the cramp-rings and touching for the "king's evil," scrofula. She approached the cross on her knees, stopped to pray, and then kissed it, "performing this act with such devotion as greatly to edify all those who were present." Then, kneeling within a low enclosure to the right of the high altar, she began the blessing of the rings. There were two large basins of gold and silver rings, one filled with rings Mary had ordered made for this purpose, the other with rings given by their owners to be blessed by the queen, and marked with their owners' names. Reciting prayers and psalms in a low tone, Mary now began to pass her hands over the basins and to reach in and touch each of the rings in turn, shifting them from one hand to the other and intoning "Bless, O Lord, these rings." Cramp-rings were valued as healing talismans possessing the power inherent in the touch of an anointed monarch. Mary's rings were much sought after, not only in England but in foreign courts as well.

When the rings had been distributed the queen went into a private gallery to bless the scrofulous. There were four of them, one man and three women, all afflicted with the skin disorder monarchs of England and France had been healing for centuries by the touch of their hands. An altar had been raised in the room, and Mary knelt before it, reciting the confession, after which Pole blessed her and gave her absolution. Then, having cleansed herself spiritually in preparation for the act of healing she was about to perform, Mary had the first of the sufferers brought before her. As a priest repeated again and again the verse from Mark's gospel, "he laid his hands upon a few sick folk, and healed them," the queen knelt down and put her hands on the woman's sores. With her hands in the form of a cross, she pressed the raw places several times, "with such compassion and devotion as to be a marvel," and then called forward the next victim. When all four had received the healing touch they approached Mary a second time. She now touched their sores with four gold coins, and gave them the coins to wear on ribbons around their necks, making each of them promise never to part with the hallowed object except in extreme need.[6]

Throughout all these fatiguing ceremonies it was evident to observers that Mary acted out of deep piety and profound devotion. They sensed in her a quality difficult to name except by the bland and vague term "goodness." The Spaniards who came to England with Philip had seen in her that same quality, and had admired her for it. Michiel, no facile flatterer, was impressed enough to write in a dispatch to the Signory that "I dare assert that there never was a queen in Christendom of greater goodness than this one."

Beyond this, though, in the Easter ceremonies of 1556 and on similar occasions Mary displayed the same indefinable quality of majesty that had marked her father and his predecessors as beings set apart from ordinary mortals. Through her coronation Mary had become an anointed queen—the first anointed queen of England—a sacred personage with semi-divine status. Nothing in her public manner betrayed that status. Even her detractors remarked on her regal demeanor, grave yet magnanimous, and on the great dignity of her speech and bearing. As thoroughly as any king she fulfilled the image of majesty.

Yet since her marriage Mary had been working to fulfill a contrary image. When she became a wife she took on a traditional burden of subjection that conflicted with her regal status at every point. In her letters she addressed Philip "in as humble wise as it is possible," declaring herself to be "your very loyal and very obedient wife, which to be I confess myself justly obliged to be, and in my opinion more than any other woman, having such a husband as your highness is." Mary believed she owed Philip the deference any woman owed her husband, and more besides; his exalted position as king of several kingdoms and heir to much of the Hapsburg empire meant that he deserved a greater measure of subservience from his wife, even though she was herself a queen.

But the quality of Mary's subordination was broader than this. Following a commonplace of sixteenth-century teachings on marriage every wife was told to see in her husband an earthly representative of Christ. Vives, the Spanish humanist who wrote Mary's childhood schoolbooks, wrote in his treatise *On the Duty of Husbands* that "If the husband be the woman's head, the mind, the father, the Christ, he ought to execute the office to such a man belonging, and to teach the woman: for Christ is not only a saviour and a restorer of his church, but also a master." Mary was as far below Philip, then, as all sinners were below Christ. Mary had somehow to resolve the bewildering paradox that, as queen, she herself carried out healing and sanctifying functions that gave her a cast of divinity, yet at the same time she had to look to her husband as a Christlike figure, remote and awesome, appointed to teach and guide her.

Cardinal Pole put this special form of wifely piety into words. In the prayers he wrote for Mary to repeat Philip is referred to as "a man who, more than all other, in his own acts and guidance of mine reproduces Thy image, Thy image whom Thou didst send into the world in holiness and justice."[7] The identification of Philip and Christ had a powerful effect on the emotions of a woman of strong faith. Christ and his church were at the center of Mary's life; Philip was now bonded to that core of her identity and purpose.

Yet it was becoming harder and harder for Mary to see as Christlike a man who had to all appearances deserted her. By the time Philip had been gone seven months or so she felt abandoned, and wrote to her father-in-law "imploring him most humbly" to permit him to return. "I beg your Majesty to forgive my boldness," she wrote, "and to remember the unspeakable sadness I experience because of the absence of the king." She knew he was occupied with important matters, but she feared that unless he simply tore himself away he would never find an opportunity to return, for "the end of one negotiation is the beginning of another."[8]

Mary appealed to the emperor as a bereft woman, but to Philip she was showing herself more and more as an injured queen. In mid-March she sent Mason to Philip in Brussels with orders "to pray the king her consort to be pleased to say frankly in how many days he purposed returning." Mason was to tell the king that his wife was tired of the expense and inconvenience of keeping a fleet ready to escort him back to England. The ships would leave their moorings at the Thames docks, drop down to the sea, and anchor just off the coast waiting for instructions to sail to Flanders. Then, when their water became foul and their food supplies ran low, they would return upriver to take on fresh provisions and wait for the queen's order to sail out to sea again. The cycle had been repeated again and again throughout the fall and winter, and as spring approached Mary wanted to know precisely when to send her fleet in order to prevent further futile missions.

Mason did his best. He urged Philip "to comfort the queen, as also the peers of the realm, by his presence," and reminded him "that there was no reason yet to despair of his having heirs" by Mary. But all Philip would say was that he intended to come as soon as he could, though his Flemish affairs were demanding more and more of his time. Philip's advisers were more categorical. The king would have to tour all the Netherlands provinces in the coming months, they said, and they reminded Mason of the bad treatment and enormous cost Philip had endured during his earlier sojourn in England. His wife had shown him "little conjugal affection" while he was there, and the English had treated the Spaniards with shameless contempt and violence. For all these reasons Philip would be ill advised to return to England soon, Ruy Gomez told Mason, but there was another cause for delay. Philip's astrologer had predicted that a conspiracy would take shape against the king in England sometime in 1556, and he would be foolish to return while this threat persisted.[9]

When she found that Mason had failed in his mission Mary was "beyond measure exasperated." Philip was treating her with disrespect bordering on contempt, and the sovereign in her was angered. She determined to use her most effective envoy, Paget, to try to learn the truth about her husband's intentions. Paget, whose rehabilitation to royal favor had been crowned by his appointment in January as Lord Privy Seal, was the ideal mediator between Mary and Philip. Because of his new standing at court he was eager to please the queen, and he had always been the foremost advocate of imperial interests on the Council. He was "dear to the king," and "very subtle" besides; he could be counted on to discover the true reason behind Philip's long absence.[10] Paget came no closer than Mason to discovering the hidden motive behind Philip's behavior, but he did at least bring back from the imperial court a definite date for the king's return. If he did not return to Mary by June 30, Philip had said, then "she was not to consider him a trustworthy king" any longer.[11]

What Paget did not tell Mary was that, now as always, Philip was acting not out of private inclination but political expediency. Mary, and England, were two counters on Philip's vast diplomatic gameboard. He knew perfectly well that, as the regent of Milan told the Venetian ambassador during Paget's visit, it was not to his advantage "that the queen's angry remonstrances should be converted into hatred."[12] But he also knew that in the long run Mary's affection might have to be sacrificed for the sake of attaining some more important advantage in the Netherlands. Philip was in any case in close touch with the English Council throughout his absence. Minutes of the Council meetings were forwarded to him regularly, and he returned them with marginal comments in his own hand. Sometimes his comments were no more than a brief sentence of approval—"this seems to be well done"—but sometimes they were more lengthy than the minutes themselves, and there is no doubt Philip kept himself well informed about English affairs and believed he retained a measure of control over them. He asked, for example, that "nothing should be proposed in Parliament without its having been first communicated to his majesty," and continued to expect that eventually he would receive word that his coronation had been approved.[18]

But even this issue had lost some of its importance in the light of recent events. When Philip married Mary in 1554 England was in the forefront of European affairs; now in 1556 it had become a diplomatic backwater. The Hapsburgs and the French were still battling for supremacy on the continent, but England had ceased to be the focus of their rivalry. A new force had arisen to challenge the power of the Hapsburgs: the fiery Neapolitan Pope Paul IV.

Cardinal Caraffa had become Pope Paul IV in May of 1555, and was devoting his pontificate to the twin goals of annihilating heretics and fighting Philip II with every weapon at his command. He was eighty years old, but he had the vigor of a man of forty. "He is all nerve," one diplomat wrote of the pope, "and when he walks, it is with a free, elastic step, as if he hardly touched the ground." Caraffa came from hardy stock. His mother, Vittoria Camponesca, was a bold and dashing horsewoman who liked to ride at a breakneck pace over the mountain passes of southern Italy. Hagiographers recorded that, shortly before her son was born, Vittoria raced past a hermit who called out to her to stop, then urged her to travel at a gentler pace, as the child in her womb was destined to become pope.[14] His hot temper, his eccentricity, and his unpredictability made Paul IV a fearsome figure. He was sometimes eloquent and businesslike, sometimes foulmouthed and tyrannical. He shouted at his chamberlains not to dare to disturb him with church business after sunset, "even were it to announce the resurrection of his own father," and drove out cardinals who troubled him at the wrong time with a torrent of abuse and a raised fist.[15] He called himself a "great prince," and kept a princely table, washing down course after course of delicacies with black Neapolitan wine.[16]

As he dined he talked loudly to the cardinals who gathered each evening to watch him, and his conversation was invariably dominated by his hatred of Hapsburg power. The pope had been a young man when the armies of Ferdinand of Aragon swept through Naples, replacing French rule with that of the overbearing Spaniards. In middle age he had watched the forces of Charles V take Milan, and then sack Rome. Italy had become forfeit to the greedy foreigners from the north; it was time to expel these barbarians, and the pope was the natural leader of any such campaign. Furthermore, Paul IV had a deep personal grudge against Philip II. The king had had the audacity to attempt to prevent Caraffa's election as pope. His maneuverings had been secret, but after the election was over the truth came out, leaving the newly elected pope violently angry. His anger was only increased by rumors that his election had not been canonical, and he knew that Philip had asked his Spanish lawyers to look into the possibility of deposing him on these grounds. Soon after he assumed the tiara Paul IV began intriguing against Philip, hoping to assemble a coalition strong enough to drive the Spaniards out of Naples. He negotiated a short-lived treaty with the French, and in the summer of 1556 was attempting to revive the French alliance again. In Brussels Philip nervously watched the machinations of the feisty, energetic old man with alarm, and told Mary's envoys he could not leave Flanders as long as the pope's menace continued.

It had not rained in England since early in February. The fields that had been flooded in the previous summer now lay parched under the hot sun. Seeds sown in the spring lay dormant or died for lack of water, and as the summer wore on there were fears of famine and, worse still, of the sweating sickness. Drought had brought the sweat in the past, and might well bring it again. In July Mary ordered daily processions to begin, to intercede with a wrathful God, but though the clergy dutifully processed and anxious Londoners fell in behind them the skies remained cloudless and the heat seemed to grow more intense every day. To escape the oppressive weather Mary joined Pole at Canterbury, comforted, as usual, by his presence and his advice, and "intent on enduring her troubles as patiently as she can."[17]

Her frustration with Philip now showed itself in bursts of anger. A portrait of Philip that hung in the Council chamber, as if representing the king's authority in his absence, had begun to irritate Mary. She ordered it removed; her enemies said she kicked it out of the room in plain sight of her councilors.[18] She was heard to remark pointedly that "God sent oft times to good women evil husbands," and though she was speaking of Lady Bray her meaning was clear enough. Yet when Philip fell sick late in June she showed great concern for him, sending messengers to bring news of his condition every few days and insisting that his seventy-year-old physician, still in England, dispatch himself to Flanders at once despite his gout and infirmity.[19]

Neither Mary's anger nor her concern had any effect on Philip or his father. Her pleasure in Philip's company and her hope for a Catholic heir were, it seemed, to be denied her in future. Yet the diplomatic entanglements resulting from the marriage remained as firm as ever. War between Philip and the French had been temporarily forestalled by the truce signed in February, but either side could disavow that agreement given adequate provocation. And should war break out, England would almost certainly be drawn in on the Hapsburg side. All these things were on Mary's mind as she sat down to write to her cousin Charles V in July. She sent her regards to the king and queen of Bohemia (who sent her in return a jeweled fan with a crystal mirror on one side and a watch on the other, "richly wrought, highly artistic and of beautiful design"), and then stated frankly her disillusionment with the promises made to her about Philip's return. "It would be pleasanter for me to be able to thank your majesty for sending me back the king, my lord and good husband," she wrote, "than to dispatch an emissary to Flanders. . . . However, as your majesty has been pleased to break your promise in this connection, a promise you made to me regarding the return of the king, my husband, I must perforce be satisfied, although to my unspeakable regret."[20] It was as forthright a letter as Mary had ever written to her lifelong protector Charles, yet her hand trembled as she wrote it, and she knew very well it would do no good.

To those around her it was apparent that Mary's health was breaking under the strain. "For many months the queen has passed from one sorrow to another," Michiel noted, adding that "her face has lost flesh greatly since I was last with her."[21] By August she was finding it hard to sleep at night, and appearing at court with a drawn face and dark circles under her eyes. Combined with "the great heat, the like of which no one remembers," her inner anguish made her ill. She spent the latter part of August in seclusion and, significantly, "was seen no more at Council."[22]

At Yaxley in Huntingdonshire it was being said that the queen was dead. A Protestant schoolmaster and a dozen of his fellow villagers, including the parish priest, imagined that they could stir the surrounding communities to rebellion by a bold imposture. In the parish church the priest announced that Mary had died and that "the Lady Elizabeth is queen, and her beloved bed-fellow, Lord Edmund Courtenay, king." A conspirator who claimed to be Courtenay was caught and eventually executed, and twelve others were committed to the Tower.[28] But a troublemaker closely associated with the Yaxley plotters become something of a Protestant hero over the next few months.

This unnamed figure, thought to be "a captain from the other side of the Channel, an arch-heretic well acquainted with Germany," lived in the northern forests where the queen's officials were few and her laws ignored. He hid himself for a time, then appeared "with great audacity" in a town, seeking out the Protestants and "preaching to them and encouraging them to remain firm and constant, as they shall soon hear and see great and powerful personages, who will come to replace them in their religion and free them from slavery." Sometimes he was disguised as a peasant, sometimes as a wayfarer, sometimes as a merchant. After he had eluded the local officials for months a massive effort was made to catch him. Spies were sent into the forests, and the keepers and others tramped through the woods with bloodhounds "as is done to wild beasts and beasts of chase." But the mysterious woodsman remained out of sight, and finally disappeared altogether, perhaps returning to one of the emigrant colonies abroad.[24] His agitation troubled the queen and her councilors in the last weeks of summer, as the sun beat down on the withered crops and on the fires lit daily under the feet of the Protestant heretics.

XLVI

 Of sectes and of schysmes a riddaunce to make,
Of horrible errours and heresies all;
She carckes and cares and great travell dooth take,
That vertue may flourish and vice have a fall.

When Mary sent Paget to Brussels in April of 1556 it was only partly to discover the true cause of Philip's delay in Flanders. Paget also had instructions to talk to the Emperor Charles about the vexed problem of the burning of heretics.

It had been fourteen months since the first burnings began, and in that time hundreds of suspected heretics had been examined and imprisoned, and many of these had been condemned to the stake. The executions had become commonplace, but not mundane; those who watched the Protestant men, women and children die the slow death by fire found it difficult to forget what they had seen. The spectacle of a man dying in the flames, singing a psalm "until that his lips were burnt away," was a haunting image, as was the sight of a sixty-year-old widow bound to the stake, or a young blind woman, a ropemaker's daughter, sentenced to burn by a bishop she could not see.

The executioners made these grim proceedings even more memorable by their ineptness. All too often the wood for the fire was green, or the rushes were too soggy to burn quickly. The bags of gunpowder tied to the victims to shorten their agony failed to ignite, or else maimed them without killing them. No one thought to gag the sufferers, and their screams and prayers were audible often until the very moment of death. It mattered little that most of them were originally singled out for punishment by their neighbors, the jurymen of their localities, who gave their names to the justices or commissioners who passed them on to the bishops. Or that many of the victims were Anabaptists whom not only Catholics but most Protestants saw as arch-heretics to be destroyed out of hand, and whom the Protestant King Edward, had he lived, would almost certainly have burned. Or that they were brought to the stake in an age habituated to violence and frequent executions, when men and women were hanged for most petty crimes and all two hundred of the felonies recognized under English law.

What mattered was that day after day new victims, most of them ordinary villagers, were dying amid a climate of legend and martyrdom. Stories of their heroism and joyous deaths had now become as commonplace as the burnings themselves. It was told again and again how John Rogers went to his death promising to pray for his executioner and how, "as one feeling no smart," he "washed his hands in the flame, as though it had been in cold water" until the fire had consumed him. The story of Laurence Saunders was equally well known. Saunders, it was said, went "with a merry courage" toward the fire, barefoot and dressed in an old gown and shirt, and when he came to the stake he took it in his arms and kissed it, saying "Welcome the cross of Christ! welcome everlasting life!" As his body burned he seemed to "sleep sweetly" in the fire.[1]

The burning of Cranmer had done much to foster this atmosphere of dauntless piety. Already condemned by the doctors of the university, he was excommunicated by the pope in November of 1555 and deprived of his archbishopric the following month. In February he was delivered to the queen's officers as a degraded cleric sentenced to be burned for heresy, yet his execution was postponed for nearly a month. In that time the former archbishop wrote three humble recantations of his Protestant views, disavowing all that he had written and taught about the sacraments and the pope's authority during a clerical career spanning three decades. He blamed himself for much of the harm done to the faith in England, and submitted himself utterly to the queen's mercy as a contrite sinner. Mary doubted the sincerity of his penitential writings, believing "that he had feigned recantation thinking thus to save his life, and not that he had received any good inspiration." He was not worthy of pardon, she said, and ordered the execution to proceed.

Once he knew he must die Cranmer took back everything he had said and written and, to dramatize his true belief, threw his recantation into the flames. He asked the crowd to forgive him for having tried to save himself; he had only done it, he said, so that he might be of use to them all at some future time. Then, thrusting his right arm and hand into the fire, he said "This, which has sinned, having signed the writing, must be the first to suffer punishment."[2] Cranmer's recantation was published by the government, but instead of strengthening Catholicism it put Mary and her Council in a bad light. Londoners remembered only Cranmer's final gesture, not his forced surrender to royal coercion; they denounced the published recantation as a hoax, and condemned the queen and the bishop who had subscribed his name to the book as liars.[3]

The bishop, Edmund Bonner, was already thoroughly hated. Himself imprisoned in the Marshalsea during Edward's reign, and then in the Tower, Bonner had become the leading public symbol of the Marian persecution. At the start of Mary's reign her Catholic subjects had knelt to receive Bonner's blessing when he was released from prison. Now the children sang out "Bloody Bonner" as he passed, and their parents vilified him as a "beastly belly-god and damnable dunghill" whose "butcherly, bloody proceedings" made him no better than a murderer. He was so bigoted, it was said, that he would have condemned even St. Paul to the flames, and so bloodthirsty that his "great fat cheeks" were glutted with the flesh of the martyrs.[4]

Bonner was in fact a gross, corpulent man who liked vulgar jokes and carried out his grisly duty toward the condemned heretics of the London diocese with inhuman relish. But the stories told of his sadism —stories that in all probability went far beyond the truth—made him a monster. He liked to flog his prisoners, it was said, and to see them tortured. He tormented a blind man, and held the hand of another sufferer in a candle flame until the skin cracked open. Bonner represented all that was odious in the government's religious policy with none of the sincere faith that made that policy tragically plausible. He was a figure of ridicule and contempt, and in an odd way he provided the Protestants with the dark comfort of a villain they could dismiss as a savage fool.

As great a tragedy as the burnings themselves was the fact that so many innocuous villagers were condemned to the flames for holding such relatively harmless beliefs. To be sure, a sizable number of the victims in Kent and Essex were stout sectaries who preached their heretical doctrines openly and lured ignorant country people away from the church. At Colchester priests were "hemmed in at the open streets, and called knaves," and seditious talk was as common as heresy in every alehouse and tavern.[5] But in many other places the men and women singled out for destruction were only unlettered peasants or craftspeople, confused by twenty years of shifting orthodoxy and by the conflicting voices of clergymen who had changed their doctrines at least once in every reign. Young people who had grown to maturity hearing only evil of the pope were now punished for reviling him; villagers who had heard their own priests denounce the mass and the Catholic sacraments were now ordered to the stake for holding imprecise opinions on the nature of the Eucharist. Four of the women burned at Essex "could not tell what a sacrament is." One of these women, "a young maid unskilled," thought she had heard tell of one sacrament, but could not name it.

And it was almost invariably the ordinary working people, the artisans and the laboring poor, who came to the attention of the commissioners. Apart from the Protestant bishops there were few gentlemen among the victims, and only one gentlewoman. The rest were weavers, fullers, tailors, hosiers, brewers, tanners, bricklayers and their wives. There were serving men and serving women, day laborers and workers in the fields, widows and farm wives.[6] It was obvious to the officials operating the search for heretics that their procedures were entrapping those who least deserved to suffer. "I do see by experience," one of Bonner's assistants wrote, "that the sworn inquest for heresies do, most commonly, indict the simple, ignorant and wretched." The populace at large was greatly disturbed, he added, "when they see the simple wretches (not knowing what heresy is) to burn."[7]

It was as obvious to the queen as it was to her servants that the rigorous campaign to root out heresy was failing of its object. Instead of instilling devotion and a love of good doctrine the executions were creating impiety and resentment. The most notorious of the Protestants who had not fled to the continent were still at large, and error flourished in areas remote from royal control. Worse still, many good Catholics were refusing to believe that the holy work of preserving the true faith could take the unholy form of roasting human flesh. The burnings were "the evil church's persecution of the good church," some were saying. And others, who said little, simply turned from religion altogether in their disgust. One Protestant woman wrote to Bonner warning him that he had "lost the hearts of twenty thousand that were rank papists these twelve months," and she may not have been far wrong.[8]

The dawning realization that in her zeal to defend the faith she might be harming it irretrievably weighed on Mary and made her wretched. She was doing her best to rebuild the church, restoring monastic communities, renewing the clergy, giving her support to the reforming efforts of Cardinal Pole. Yet her subjects were not settling back into the familiar Catholicism of her childhood. She had believed for so long that she was destined to preside over a people happily restored to their ancestral belief. Why was that restoration so long in coming?

If Mary hoped for insight from her cousin in Flanders, her hope was vain. What Charles V told her envoy Paget in the spring of 1556 was not recorded, but the religious situation in the Netherlands was no less tense than in England. Here too the official policy of persecution was failing to discourage the spread of Protestantism. Only a short time before Paget arrived in Brussels a house full of Anabaptists was raided; three men and a woman were taken into custody, along with the woman's son, a boy of fourteen. The boy was spared, after receiving a public christening in the town square, but the four others were tortured until they revealed the names of many of their coreligionists, and then burned. Such incidents were common, yet the number of Protestants in the population was growing. The president of the Council in Brussels had begun to question the wisdom of the mass burnings, hangings and drownings of heretics. Over thirteen hundred such executions had bloodied the Netherlands provinces in the last eighteen months, he was saying, with little positive result. "For the avoidance of greater cruelty," he now suggested, "the execrable intentions of these sectarians must be tolerated as much as possible, they being in too great number."[9]

The problem of heresy had been driven into the background of the emperor's thoughts by an event of cosmic magnitude. For seven days and nights a huge comet was visible in the skies over northern Europe, arching its way across the heavens and "shooting out fire to great wonder and marvel to the people." The comet was half the size of the moon, and much brighter, with beams like bursts of flame from a torch. The "blazing star" amazed the emperor, who took it as an omen of his approaching death. "These signs speak to me of my fate," he was heard to say, and he told his servants to hurry their preparations for his departure for Spain.[10] He had given up all his powers now, but had not lost either his fascination with statecraft or his instinctive hatred of the French. He liked to mutter to ambassadors about how the French had "ever sought to dominate not a part, but the whole of the world," punctuating his remarks with graphic gestures and repeating himself for emphasis. The French king's current warlike demands, he told the Venetian ambassador, were like "stamping on his throat," and as he said it he "placed his right hand on his neck, and with great vehemence explained this conceit, and repeated it twice." But Charles was clearly near his end. The incessant pains from his gout had become so severe that at times he "gnawed his hand and longed for death,"[11] and he did not want to die in Brussels. Finally on September 16 he left for Spain, taking with him his sister Mary, his household and the accumulations of a long and turbulent reign.

Just after he left a letter arrived from his daughter-in-law in England. He never saw it—his ship had already embarked when the messenger reached the imperial court—but he could have guessed its contents. Mary was writing yet again to plead with her father-in-law to send Philip back to her. "I wish to beg your majesty's pardon for my boldness in writing to you at this time," she began, "and humbly to implore you, as you have always been pleased to act as a true father to me and my kingdom, to consider the miserable plight into which this country has now fallen." Philip's "firm hand" was needed to stop the mounting unrest and criticism of the government that seemed to reach its climax as the scanty harvest was gathered in. "Unless he comes to remedy matters," Mary wrote, "not I only but also wiser persons than I fear that great danger will ensue."[12]

The danger appeared to be coming closer and closer. Servants in her household were no longer to be trusted, and her personal guard was doubled. William Harris, one of Mary's carpenters, was overheard to slander his mistress as he sat at an alehouse. "She hath undone us," he declared, "and hath undone this realm too, for she loveth another realm better than this."[13] One of the officers of the queen's pantry, William Cox, had to be committed to the porter's lodge for receiving a seditious handbill claiming that King Edward was still alive; the matter was serious enough to come to the Council's attention and Cox was dismissed. Worst of all, while Mary was staying in the apartments Pole kept in readiness for her at Croydon someone with free access to her presence littered her rooms with copies of the ugliest and most insulting libel yet to appear. It caricatured Mary as a wrinkled hag, her shriveled bosom suckling a crowd of greedy Spaniards. Circling the drawing were the words "Maria Ruina Angliae," and the text of the bill was an exposé of how Mary, "England's Ruin," was plundering her subjects in order to send money to her faithless husband in Brussels.

Mary might have found this injury easier to bear had Philip been true to his latest promise to return. He had told the English ambassador Mason that he was "setting his stable and a part of his house in order to be sent to England," and that he would make the journey himself in August. But the summer months found him at a "house of pleasure" outside the capital, seeking refuge from the plague, and when September came and still he had not taken ship for England Mary's disappointment deepened. By now even Cardinal Pole was "beginning to be incredulous," as he told the Venetian ambassador, though he tried not to let Mary see his disillusionment.[14]

If she had known what changes Philip had undergone during his year in Flanders Mary might have been less eager for his return. For if the lighter side of his temperament had found an outlet in masquings and tournaments, his innate seriousness had also deepened. Observers now saw in him "the very image and portrait of the emperor his father," and noted the resemblance in complexion, features and even in "habits and mode of life." He was no longer the affable prince whose primary concern was to obey his imperious father; he was now a powerful ruler in his own right, consumed with affairs of state and revealing a rare taste for the tedium of administration. He sat with his councilors for four or five hours at a time, made himself available to petitioners whenever they requested it, and relished combing through every clause of the reports and dispatches of his ministers with the crawling thoroughness of the born functionary.

It was said that Philip was already becoming a very old young man, prey to infirmities and with the mentality of an invalid. His natural languor drained him of vigor and his attacks of indigestion had become more and more frequent.[15] Harassed by bowel complaints, his brow furrowed by hours of deliberations and paperwork, his dapper figure hunching prematurely into the slouch of middle age, Philip was no longer Mary's storybook prince. What was more, he had had to mortgage the income from the Netherlands provinces in order to satisfy his creditors and, like Mary, was taxing his subjects so heavily they were on the point of rebellion. And he was being pushed from all sides into war. In November Philip wrote to Mary that he saw no way of coming back to her as long as the pope continued to "injure his affairs" and the French king continued to prepare his armies and increase his arsenal. Belligerent adversaries, not indifference or amorous adventures, were keeping Philip from his wife's side.[16]

As Philip wrote to Mary his general, Alva, was leading his cavalry up to the walls of Rome. The pope had insolently imprisoned several imperial ministers in the Castel Sant'Angelo, and Alva and his troops were threatening to besiege the city. Panic-stricken Romans geared themselves to withstand the siege, tearing down churches and convents and bolstering the walls as best they could. Nearly thirty years earlier the armies of Charles V had destroyed the papal city with a vengeance; spurred by the memory of that devastation monks and nuns joined the lay citizens in digging trenches and fortifying the strongest buildings, rooting out every growing thing the hated soldiers might feed on and hoarding food and water. Pope Paul, secure in his renewed alliance with the French, was defiant. He excommunicated Philip, calling him the "son of iniquity" and accusing him of trying to "surpass even his father Charles in infamy." Philip, who had neither the money nor, below his surface bravado, the stomach for war, was forced to look to England to fill his treasury.

A rapprochement with his wife was now essential. To prepare the way Philip sent his pages, his stable, and his personal armory to England. When Mary heard that they had landed at Dover she was overjoyed, and when, shortly afterward, several Spanish shopkeepers disembarked with their goods she felt sure Philip would soon be on his way at last.[17] Two weeks later Michiel reported that the queen was "pacified" about Philip's absence, and that she was "enduring this delay better than she did."[18] In fact the threat of war was bringing out all Mary's instinctive loyalty to her husband. The fact that he was in danger made her forget his neglect, his threats and his callousness. Mary was at her best in a crisis, and she responded now by bringing every resource of her government to Philip's aid.

Messengers began to carry letters back and forth between Mary and Philip far more frequently than ever before. They kept one another informed of everything, with Philip notifying his wife of every move Alva made and Mary passing on war intelligence gathered from English agents abroad. She sent him valuable descriptions of new French war devices being deployed on the Picardy border—instruments to sap and break down walls, a specially constructed bridge made to span even the widest ditch, and a special file which could cut through the thickest chains without making a sound.[19] Philip sent "very copious letters" apologizing for his inability to return, and Mary responded with descriptions of the emergency Council meetings she called to persuade her ministers to support Philip in his time of need. Through forced loans she amassed 150,000 ducats, and sent them to Philip, along with a promise of naval support against the French. Within a few weeks so much freshly coined money was put into circulation that the merchants, remembering the drastic fiscal measures of Henry VIII and Edward, feared a massive depreciation of the coinage. By December there were signs of financial panic in London, with wildly fluctuating exchange rates and debtors scrambling to pay their alarmed creditors before they found that the coins in their pockets were worthless.[20]

By January of 1557 England was being drawn closer and closer to war. The sheriffs in the counties nearest the capital were summoned to court to report on the numbers of fighting men they could supply, and the royal guard was newly outfitted. Ships were repaired and manned, and the garrison at Calais received fresh troops and was put in a state of alert. After holding off as long as possible the Council agreed to send Philip the six thousand foot and six hundred horse soldiers which England was obligated to provide in the event of a French attack on the Netherlands, and on January 20 a muster of the royal pensioners was held at Greenwich Park before the queen.

The men at arms rode past her three abreast, mounted on great war horses and carrying spears painted in white and green. Every pensioner had three hired soldiers with him, wearing the Tudor colors of green and silver-white, and as Mary stood on a high platform they rode up and down in front of her at the park gate, their trumpeters blowing and their standards waving in the wind. The standards bore a new design, one which combined Philip and Mary's arms and symbolized the union of the two powers against their common foe. On one side the Castilian colors of red and yellow surrounded the white hart of England; on the other was the black eagle of the Hapsburgs with gilded legs. The pensioners hired a tumbler to perform before Mary, and as they rode by he "played many pretty feats" before her, "so that her grace did laugh heartily." When the muster ended Mary "thanked them all for their pains" and went back into the palace much heartened.[21] She and her loyal guardsmen had no need to fear the French. The combined forces of England and Spain would be more than a match for the pope and his allies.

The new French ambassador in England, François de Noailles, took a far different view of Mary's preparations for war. Like his brother Antoine, whom he officially replaced as ambassador in November of 1556, he saw the coming war as the ultimate tragedy of Mary's unwise marriage. Mary's authority was already strained to the limit; war with France would surely lead to her overthrow. "I do not know," he wrote, "whether, if she tries to bend the bow still further, the wood and the string may not fly into fragments." Noailles saw more clearly than Mary herself the mental anguish the war would cause her. "She is on the eve of bankrupting either her own mind or her kingdom," he insisted. "It is impossible that the crown will not fall from her head and roll so far that someone else may pick it up before she has wept for her sins."

Ageynst the Frenchmen in the feld to fyght
In the quarell of the church and in the ryght,
With spers and sheldys on goodly horsys lyght,
Bowys and arows to put them all to flyght:
Englond, be glad! Pluk up thy lusty hart!
Help now thi king, thi king, and take his part!

On March 8 Philip left Brussels for Calais, where he would take ship for England. He took with him only two gentlemen of his chamber, six nobles, and half of his household officers, leaving the bulk of his household behind. He traveled by slow stages, stopping at Ghent, Bruges, Oudenbourg, Nieuport, Dunkirk and Gravelines, and did not embark from Calais until March 18. He was in no hurry to return to his island kingdom, and the small size of his retinue argued for a short stay once he arrived. But having weighed all considerations of diplomacy, military strategy and finance that faced him in this spring of 1557, Philip had decided that he needed England as an active ally in his quarrel with the pope and the French king. Mary had been able to give him some money and to promise him a limited number of troops, but he needed much more of both. More important, he needed what the English Council most dreaded to consent to: a formal declaration of war.

A forty days' truce concluded in November between the captain of Philip's armies in Italy, Alva, and the pope had spared Rome the indignity of a siege, but when the truce expired at the beginning of the new year mutual hostilities began again. Paul IV ordered all Spaniards to leave the papal city on pain of death, and set up a commission to try both Charles V and his son as rebels against the authority of the Holy See. Meanwhile Henri II, who swore he would come to the pope's aid even if it cost him his crown, sent an army into Italy under the duke de Guise, and as Philip made his way toward the Channel the French and papal strategists were meeting in Rome to draw up a joint plan of attack.

That the attack would come in Italy was obvious, and Philip's most effective counterattack would therefore have to be made in the north. If Philip's Spanish troops could be massed in force against the Franco-Flemish border—France's weakest perimeter—then the French army in Italy would have to be reduced in order to strengthen the border defenses and the initiative would pass to the imperial side. What he needed, then, was a large army and a full treasury from which to pay it. But this meant trying to take new loans at a time when he lacked the funds even to pay the installments on his old ones. He was in fact technically bankrupt. In January he had sent orders to the treasury in Seville not to honor any of the payment orders he signed, thus defaulting on every fiscal guarantee he and his ministers had made in recent months.[1] His only hope, short of the miraculous appearance of a treasure ship from the New World, was to try to exploit the good repute he had left behind him in England, counting always on the obedience of his wife.

Early in February he sent Ruy Gomez to England to prepare for his arrival. He had instructions to tell Mary the long-awaited news that her husband was returning to her at last, but he was to make it very clear that the price of Philip's return was a guarantee of an English declaration of war against France. Mary understood only too well, but she eagerly agreed to do all in her power to move the Council. Before he left Gomez had persuaded Mary to part with another £100,000, and to give her promise to bring England into the war.[2] On February 21 she wrote to Philip, begging him "not to be afraid to come" and telling him confidently that his presence would be sufficient to sway the councilors to agree to his demands.

On the evening of March 18 Philip landed at Dover, and the next day he joined Mary at Greenwich. His homecoming was celebrated with a great ringing of bells and the shooting of all the Tower guns, and on March 23 the king and queen rode through London flanked by the great nobles and saluted by the London crafts and the Lord Mayor and aldermen. Outwardly Philip appeared to be resuming his old role as Mary's deferential husband, but in truth both spouses had changed. Mary was quick to note the transformation her husband had undergone in Flanders, while Philip in turn found her hemmed in by doubts and deep worries, her face deeply lined and drawn.

Michiel described the queen and her sorrows in his report to the doge and Senate written only two months after Philip came to England. In appearance Mary was "very grave," he noted, and very "seemly," "never to be loathed for ugliness, even at her present age." Whenever she spoke she commanded attention, her rough voice carrying so that "she is always heard a long way off," but her eyes were her most arresting feature. "Her eyes are so piercing that they inspire, not only respect, but fear, in those on whom she fixes them," Michiel wrote, adding that she had become so nearsighted that she had to hold whatever she needed to read very close to her face. Mary's "well-formed" features were marred by wrinkles, "caused more by anxieties than by age," but whatever shortcomings there were in her physical appearance her mental endowments were vast. The facility and quickness of her understanding were so remarkable that nothing seemed too complex for her to grasp. Her gift for languages was much esteemed, while "the replies she gives in Latin, and her very intelligent remarks made in that tongue," Suriano remarked, "surprise everybody."

What stood out most about Mary, in Michiel's view, was the unmistakable quality of heroism in her life and personality. "Not only is she brave and valiant, unlike other timid and spiritless women, but so courageous and resolute that neither in adversity nor peril did she ever even display or commit any act of cowardice or pusillanimity," he wrote. She kept "a wonderful grandeur and dignity" in all circumstances, and knew as well as any statesman in her service how to behave in order to maintain "the dignity of a sovereign." Now, nearly four years after her coronation, Mary still reminded observers of a constant flame burning amid a storm. "It may be said of her," Michiel claimed, "as Cardinal Pole says with truth, that in the darkness and obscurity of that kingdom she remained precisely like a feeble light buffeted by raging winds for its utter extinction, but always kept burning."

But if, as Michiel insisted, Mary's light still shone brightly in the world, it was fast becoming dimmed by her poor health and private griefs. Her old disease troubled her nearly constantly now, leading to depression and long periods of crying. To relieve this condition her doctors bled her frequently, "either from the foot or elsewhere," and she was always pale and emaciated from lack of blood. Her general health was poor, her teeth ached and she slept badly, though she worked on in spite of these problems and did not allow her sufferings to impair her public presence. Her anguish of mind, though, she could not keep hidden. Portraits of the queen painted toward the end of her reign show a gaunt, controlled woman of middle age, the pomegranate of Spain stitched into her brocaded sleeves, and around her neck her favorite jewel —the great diamond with the pendant pearl. Her face is still handsome, but the set of her lips in her thin cheeks suggests grim determination. She looks out with the frightening stare Michiel found so arresting, and her expression is one of haggard benevolence. Mary's controlled demeanor was maintained, these portraits imply, by an immense effort of will; behind her composure was a brittle sanity which might snap under the weight of her mounting sorrows.

Chief among these sorrows, Michiel believed, was her barrenness. It was impossible to overestimate the damage her fruitless pregnancy did her, he wrote. Without a child to succeed her every effort of her reign was futile. Even if she succeeded in rebuilding the churches and restoring the monasteries, and even if her religious policies purified the faith the entire process would be repudiated on her death unless she left behind her a Catholic heir. Yet far from encouraging her in the hope that she might yet bear a child, her courtiers and gentlewomen accepted her childlessness and withdrew their esteem accordingly. "No one believes in the possibility of her having progeny," Michiel wrote, "so that day by day she sees her authority and the respect induced by it diminish." And there were many other causes for grief. Plots against her life and against the government were uncovered more frequently now, and the people showed "a greater inclination and readiness for change than ever." The extraordinary affection her subjects had shown her early in the reign was swiftly being eroded. Her debts were huge, and her attempts to pay them by taxing her people only led to greater unrest. As a sovereign Mary faced the greatest challenge of her reign since the attempt of Dudley to seize the throne for Jane Grey.

Worse even than these adversities, Michiel believed, was Mary's painful realization that she was likely to live out her days deprived of the company of the man she passionately loved. According to the ambassador, Mary's feeling for her husband was one of "violent love"; "she may be said never to pass a day without anxiety" on Philip's account, and in his absence her one fear was that he might become seriously attached to another woman. She knew he had been unfaithful to her, but she believed his flirtations and seductions in Flanders had been no more than passing amusements. "If she does not hold the king chaste," Michiel wrote, "I at least know that she says she believes him free from love for any other woman." This at least was some consolation. But the longer Philip stayed away the more likely he was to fall deeply in love, and then she would be "truly miserable."

The tragedy of Mary's marriage was now apparent: she had sworn to adore and obey a man whose political responsibilities kept him all but totally separated from her, by whom she would have no children, and whose undivided love she was unlikely to keep for long. In this woeful state she was forced to watch "the eyes and hearts of the nation" turning more and more to the daughter of Anne Boleyn.

At twenty-three Elizabeth was a tall, good-looking young woman whose olive skin set off her lovely eyes and even features. Like Mary before her she was using her wits to survive in the midst of danger; she observed the Catholic rituals and claimed her observance was sincere, though Mary did not believe it. And even if Mary had been able to trust her half-sister's conversion there would still have been grounds for resentment. Mary had never believed Elizabeth to be legitimate, and was said to doubt whether she was Henry VIII's daughter at all. The realization that Elizabeth would in all likelihood come next to the throne seemed monstrously unjust, as if from beyond the grave Anne Boleyn was to enjoy an ultimate triumph after all. It was unspeakably odious to Mary, according to Michiel, "to see the illegitimate child of a criminal who was punished as a public strumpet on the point of inheriting the throne with better fortune than herself, whose descent is rightful, legitimate and regal."[3]

Philip's arrival temporarily drove these dark preoccupations from his wife's mind, though his presence was far from comforting. The "warmed-over honeymoon," as one diplomat described it, began badly. Mary had a severe cold and toothache, while Philip, who had been indisposed even before he left Brussels, was still recovering during his first days in England.[4] Mary had arranged a series of entertainments for her husband and his retinue—banquets, dances, and one "great masque of Almains, Pilgrims and Irishmen" to be staged at Whitehall on St. Mark's Day—but the festivities were marred by rivalries among the women and by the tense atmosphere at court. There was no disguising the true purpose of Philip's coming, and with very few exceptions the English did not intend to allow their nominal king to force them into his war. In a feeble effort to alleviate their mistrust some of the Spaniards tried to spread the story that Philip was only in England to restore good relations with Mary, and in particular to soothe her worries about his love affairs. No one believed this, however, and within days of Philip's coming libels appeared in the capital slandering the Spanish marriage. The old claim was revived that Philip's marriage to Mary was invalid because of his pre-contract with the Portuguese princess, and gossip about his romances was elaborated in every tavern. There were rumors too that Spanish troops would soon be landing on English shores, and when a proclamation appeared limiting the length of rapiers that could be worn in London the queen's subjects laughed at it and armed themselves to the teeth.

Philip's romances were indeed a sore point between the royal spouses, but far from trying to set Mary's mind at rest Philip brought with him to England the current object of his affections, his cousin the duchess of Lorraine. It was said that she was his mistress, and when Mary arranged the housing for Philip's party she was uneasy about where to put the duchess, finally settling her on the ground floor at Westminster, in an apartment overlooking the garden. The English sources are silent about the awkward relationship between the queen and the duchess. At the French court, though, stories about how Mary's jealousy got the better of her at dances and other entertainments, and how after two months of torment she forced the king's cousin to pack her trunks and leave, delighted Henri II and put the English queen in a pitiable light.[5]

Mary's domestic unhappiness did not keep her from getting on with the political business which had brought Philip to England. The power to move war and peace was of course entirely in her hands; the opinions of her councilors were, in the strictest sense, gratuitous. But in practice she needed their concurrence in order to wage war effectively, and in her campaign to gain that concurrence she was spurred, Noailles heard, by the most cogent of incentives. Unless she succeeded in swaying the Council as she had promised to do, Philip told Mary, he would never again return to her.

Mary opened her campaign by summoning the chief councilors—those designated as an inner or select Council—to her chamber. There, in Philip's presence, she made them a speech, beginning with the biblical arguments which compelled her to do her husband's will and going on to give a summary of European politics. The French menace was already on the point of driving Philip's forces out of Italy, she said; left unchecked, they would in time turn on England. Unless English troops and money were forthcoming, backed by a declaration of war, the Council would have a far worse crisis on its hands later on. A French informer who was present when Mary spoke told Noailles how impressive she was. Her arguments could not have been improved on for eloquence or subtle reasoning, he said, but the councilors were adamant. One of them, Mason, declared he would rather die than see England declare war, while others adopted the ominous view that "their intention and their duty was to have no respect either for king or for queen, but solely for the public good of the kingdom."[6]

It was obvious, as Philip wrote to Granvelle in mid-April, that he and Mary were encountering "a little more hardening" than they had expected. But Mary's determination was greater than her councilors' resistance. As Noailles remarked, she would force "not only men, but also the elements themselves, to consent to her will." When the Council made its negative response—written in Latin, so that Philip could read it—Mary angrily ordered the councilors to meet again and make a different answer "which would satisfy her and her husband." With each successive week they inched closer to a final compromise, offering more and more money and men but stopping short of agreeing to go to war with Philip.

In the end Mary used tactics her father would have approved. She talked loudly of dismissing all but a few of the Council members and then, when she had them off balance, brought each of them before her in private and threatened "some with death, some with the loss of their goods and estates, if they did not consent to the will of her husband."[7] Finally, following more deliberations and a new danger from the north where with French support Thomas Stafford and forty followers tried to raise a revolt against "the most devilish device of Mary, unrightful and unworthy queen of England," the Council gave in. On June 7 the declaration of war was published.

The following four weeks were the last period of happiness Mary was to know. Philip was pleased with her, and in high spirits about the coming battles. The duchess of Lorraine had left, and Mary had her husband's undivided attention—undivided, that is, save for the military preparations that absorbed both sovereigns for hours each day. Philip was occupied in planning how he would deploy his ten thousand footsoldiers and ten thousand cavalry, where he would put his sixty heavy cannon and his field artillery. Mary wrote out orders for the securing of the Scots border, oversaw the fitting out of the fleet, and, to raise additional money for Philip, released thousands of acres of crown property to be sold for cash. She expected to raise 800,000 crowns by this means, some of which would go to paying the English soldiers' baggage costs.[8] The time went by quickly, with the days divided between state business and hunting or hawking, and the long early summer nights in more work before vespers and compline. Both Mary and Philip, it was said, were as scrupulous as any religious in the observance of the canonical hours; now for a few weeks at least, they celebrated the services together.

Philip's delay in England had nothing whatever to do with Mary, of course. He was waiting for Ruy Gomez to return with men and money from Spain. On June 20 news came that the Spanish fleet had been sighted in the Channel. Ten days later Philip was ready to make his crossing. Mary went with him on his four-day journey from London to the coast, sleeping beside him in the rooms readied for them at Sittingbourne, Canterbury and Dover. Finally at three o'clock in the afternoon of July 6 they said their goodbyes, and Philip went on board the ship that was to carry him to Calais. Mary would never see him again.

A few days before war was declared in England a solitary figure came ashore at Boulogne, and rode swiftly eastward toward the French royal court. The rider was William Flower, Norroy King of Arms, and he carried a commission from Queen Mary to announce to Henri II that England and France were at war. The herald wore on his breast the escutcheon of England, but the folds of his long black cloak hid it from sight and it was as an anonymous traveler that he rode through the fields and villages between Boulogne and Rheims. The king was at Rheims, lodged in the abbey of St. Rémy, and when he heard that the herald had come he assembled his son the dauphin, the cardinals, dukes and other nobles and seated himself in their midst. The captain of the guard and two French heralds escorted the English king of arms into the hall, and he knelt before Henri, his coat of arms on his arm, to deliver his message.

The French king asked him in a loud voice by whom he had been sent and why. By the queen his mistress, Flower answered, and presented his commission. When it had been read aloud, Henri spoke again.

"Herald, I see that you have come to declare war on me on behalf of the queen of England. I accept the declaration, but I wish everyone to know that I have always observed toward her the good faith and amity which obtained between us." "Now that she picks so unjust a quarrel with me," he went on, "I hope that God will be pleased to grant me this grace, that she shall gain no more by it than her predecessors did when they attacked mine, or when they recently attacked me."

Henri wanted there to be no mistake about the real instigator of war between England and France. "I trust that God will show his might and justice toward him who is the cause of all the evil that lies at the root of this war," he added, making it clear that his magnanimous reception of the English herald was an acknowledgment of Mary's subordinate role in the Hapsburg quarrel.

"I act thus because the queen is a woman," he said irritably, "for if she were not I would employ other terms. But you will depart and leave my kingdom as quickly as you can."

The herald rode back the way he had come, wearing around his neck a gold chain worth two hundred crowns—a present from the French king. He was instructed to "bear witness," once he was back in England, "to the king's virtue and generosity," but in fact he took back intelligence about the military preparations of the enemy. The French, he told Mary and Philip once he returned, were lethargic and unfit for battle. From what he could see as he rode through the fields he judged the harvest to be scanty, especially near the border of the English pale where the troops would be massing. Overall the advantage lay with the king and queen's forces, the herald said, and his good news spurred the English captains to fresh activity. Philip, his strategy taking shape just as he had planned, set off for Flanders with "great hope of victory."

XLVIII

 My paynes who can expres,
Alas they are so stronge;
My dolor will not suffer strength
My lyfe for to prolonge.

Philip did not go into battle right away. After landing at Calais he made his way to Brussels, where he informed himself of the status of his forces in Italy and on the Flemish border. At Gualtiero some imperial soldiers who were "wasting their time in ravishing some women" were cut to pieces by the outraged townspeople of Borscello, but to the south of Rome Alva had won a victory over the papal forces at La Paliario, and the Italian campaign of the duke de Guise ended in futility. In the north Philip's commander the duke of Savoy was besieging St. Quentin. Toward the end of July Philip left Brussels for the border regions, along with Pembroke and his English fighting men. By the time the king and his English allies reached St. Quentin, however, most of the fighting was over. Savoy had taken the castle on August 10, overcoming a sizable relief force under the command of Montmorency, Constable of France. Thousands of footsoldiers and dozens of the most distinguished nobles of France, including the Constable himself, were taken prisoner. In two weeks the town itself was taken. Philip had won a major victory.

Mary pronounced the taking of St. Quentin "miraculous," and was said to be especially pleased that the siege was accomplished with so little loss of life. (She was not told that, once the official military surrender had been negotiated, the Swiss mercenaries in the imperial army burned the town to the ground and many of the residents with it.) This initial success was followed up by the seizure of Ham and Catelet, and in Italy, Alva and the pope came to terms at the end of September. As far as

Philip was concerned, the war was over, at least for the time being, and he ordered most of his troops to disband.

But Henri II was not satisfied. He was still at war with Mary, and he saw in the aftermath of the Hapsburg successes the ideal moment to launch a surprise assault on Calais. Recovery of Calais had always been the secret longing of the French king. With its outlying fortresses of Guines and Ham it was the last remnant of the Plantagenet empire on the continent. Throughout the centuries that Calais had been in English hands it had always been seen as impregnable. The high, turreted outer walls were double, and each wall was many feet thick. The siege engines of medieval warfare could not have breached them, even if an opposing army could have gotten into position for an assault. But this was virtually impossible, as the bulk of the town and surrounding walls arced out into the sea and the low-lying marshes at its back could be flooded by locks which formed part of the defense network. A land assault was clearly impractical, but the French believed the fortress might be taken by warships whose cannon could bombard it from the sea. The entrance into the harbor proper was guarded by the small fort of Risbank, situated on a slip of land at its outer edge. If the French could seize Risbank, their ships could sail practically up to the walls of Calais and, if the reports of their engineers proved true, breach them with their artillery.

Calais' vulnerability had been a matter of concern to Mary and her Council for some months. In May an extensive building program had been designed for the fortress, calling for new walls, including traverse walls "to stay the water," three additional bulwarks and a new gate. Two new sluices were to be dug, and ditches sunk around the perimeter of the walls.[1] Later in the summer, after Philip left, Mary requested the Deputy and Treasurer of Calais to send her a statement of the number of paid soldiers in the garrison, and corresponded with the commander, the earl of Pembroke, about the state of the defenses. Both Pembroke and his second in command, Wentworth, urged Mary to send five hundred more men to the region; it was never done, and the plans to strengthen the fortifications seem to have been laid aside, probably for lack of money to implement them.

Thus in December of 1557, as the French prepared to attack, Calais and its surrounding fortresses were ill equipped and undermanned. Calais itself had only half the number of men needed to defend its venerable ramparts, and Risbank was not only inadequately guarded but its food supplies were gone and its shore side so weak that an enemy could reportedly "come in a night to it." The winter weather too was on the side of the attackers, for the marshes of the Pale froze over and made the way easier for the approaching army of the duke de Guise as it took the first of the outworks upriver from Calais on New Years' Day.

The following day Guise's men began a bombardment of Risbank. The fortress was abandoned almost at once, the captain "jumping out of it through a breach the French had made" and putting himself at the mercy of the enemy.[2] At this point Wentworth—who was in command now that Pembroke was assisting Philip—should have summoned help from the nearest source, Philip's diminished army. But for a variety of reasons he did nothing more than request a few hundred men from Philip, trusting in some "artificial fire, which an engineer had asserted he would be able to use to great effect," to make up for the depleted ranks of his soldiers. He relied too on the country people who streamed into the town to escape the French. The men were little help, "absenting themselves in houses and secret places," but the women labored diligently, reinforcing the walls and digging defense works. In all likelihood Wentworth mistrusted Philip almost as much as he did the French, for in his letters to Mary he asked for massive aid and left no doubt of the desperate situation of the town.

Mary responded as quickly as she could, sending dozens of letters to the landowners of the southeastern counties ordering them to put their servants and tenants in arms and dispatch them to Dover. The admiral was instructed to ready his fastest ships to be sent to Calais, and the Warden of the Cinque Ports was commanded to provide mariners. If need be, Mary wrote to him, he could open any letters intended for the royal court that arrived from the besieged town or the war zone—"except the king's letters"—and adjust his preparations accordingly.[3] The Council too bestirred itself and considered the tactics of relieving Calais, finally hitting on a plan for communicating with the besieged garrison by means of letters shot over the walls with crossbows, sent in duplicate in case some were to "light on the tops of houses or other places where they may not be come by."

As these hurried efforts were being made in England Guise's ships were launching their first attack on Calais itself. The bombardment was under way before the captains realized that they had mistimed their assault. At high tide the ships in the harbor were dead even with the outer walls, but the attack began at low tide, when the cannon shot hit harmlessly five or six feet below them. At the same time Wentworth and his men were able to shoot down onto the decks of the French ships, and after a short time the attack was broken off. It was renewed two days later, however, and this time the tide was judged accurately. Within hours the French cannon opened a wide breach in the walls. The last line of defense for the English, the "artificial fire," failed to ignite—the engineer claimed that the French soldiers wet the powder with their dripping clothes as they entered the town. The fall of Calais was soon followed by the French capture of Guines and Ham, both of which were razed, and with their surrender the last foothold of the English on the continent was lost.

"We have felt great pain and anxiety on account of the fall of Calais," Philip wrote to the English Council ten days after news of the surrender reached the court, "greater indeed than we can express in words." Philip was heartened, though, to hear from Pole that Mary responded to the crisis by redoubling her efforts to send men and supplies across the Channel for an English counterattack. She put much of the blame for the loss on the unfortunate Wentworth, whose loyalty was much in doubt—he was officially charged with selling Calais to the French—and whose stupidity in failing to open the locks and flood the marshy hinterland at a crucial point in the siege had allowed the attackers clear access to the town. She accused Wentworth of "cowardice and want of spirit," to give way so easily when he stood within the walls of such an impregnable fortress; she reproached him with "standing in fear of his own shadow."[4] She was encouraged by Lord Grey's stalwart defense of Guines, however, and when he wrote her from the cell where the French kept him prisoner, in the top of a high tower in Suzain Castle, locked in with four locks and guarded by four archers day and night, she wrote back at some length. Grey had served her as well as Wentworth had served her ill, she said, and "exhorted him to be of good cheer." Mary's encouraging words had the effect of making Grey's plight worse, for as soon as his captors heard her herald read out her message, they promptly raised his ransom by ten thousand crowns.[5]

On the same day that Philip wrote to the Council expressing his grief over the loss of Calais he wrote to Pole to declare his joy over the news of the queen's pregnancy. Sometime in the fall of 1557 Mary had begun to believe, despite the odds against it, that she was expecting Philip's child. Because of the ridicule the announcement was certain to produce—and also because she wanted to be very certain in her own mind—Mary waited until December to inform her husband. Then, having "very sure signs" that this time there was no mistake, she let it be known that she expected to be delivered in March. The news, Philip told Pole, "went far to lighten the sorrow he had felt for the loss of Calais," and was "the one thing in the world he had most desired."[6]

For Mary the impending birth seems to have had overtones of finality. In March she made her will. "Foreseeing the great danger which by God's ordinance remain to all women in their travail of children," she wrote, she thought it good, "both for discharge of my conscience and continuance of good order within my realms and dominions," to declare her last will and testament. Mary's bequests reflected the people and things she valued most in life. First among these was the unborn child, the "heir, issue and fruit of her body" to whom she left her crown and all other "honors, castles, fortresses, manors, lands, tenements, prerogatives and hereditaments." Next was her lord, her "most dear and entirely beloved husband," to whom she bequeathed her "chiefest jewel," the love of her subjects, "to require the nobility of his heart" toward her. She also left Philip two enormous table diamonds, one her gift from Charles V and the other her wedding present from Philip himself, and with them the gold collar set with nine diamonds which Philip had given her on the Epiphany after their marriage and a very recent present from him, a ruby set in a gold ring. Monks and nuns were prominent on her list of bequests—the Carthusians of Sheen, the Observants of Greenwich and Southampton, the Benedictines of St. Bartholomew, the Brigittines of Sion and the "poor nuns of Langley." To Cardinal Pole she left a thousand pounds to serve as one of her executors, and charged him with continuing his work of rehabilitating the English church and taking care of the additional crown lands she ordered her executors to restore to the churchmen from whom her father and brother had taken them.

Katherine of Aragon was much honored in Mary's will. Besides the many masses to be said for her soul by the religious Mary supported, the royal executors were directed to exhume Katherine's body from its undistinguished resting place at Peterborough and bury it next to her daughter's. And, Mary added, she wanted "honorable tombs or monuments" made for them both, "for decent memory of us." About her father Mary was eloquent by her silence. The Protestants claimed later that Mary and Pole had secretly ordered Henry VIII's remains dug up and burned—a story too well documented to dismiss out of hand—but whether they did or not the late king was mentioned only briefly and impersonally in Mary's testament. Presumably he was to be included among the "other progenitors" besides Katherine whose souls were to be commemorated in prayer, but his name appeared only in connection with the debts remaining unpaid from his reign: Mary ordered them discharged.

To her household, as always, Mary was very generous. Immediately after her death two thousand pounds was to be distributed among her "poor servants that be ordinary," with special regard to those who had most need and had served her longest. Some thirty-four hundred pounds in personal benefactions were itemized, and the principal household officials were given two hundred pounds each. The queen meant to be generous, too, to many others of her subjects whom she would never see: the poor prisoners and the poor of London among whom a thousand pounds was to be distributed; the poor scholars of "Oxinford and Cambridge" who were to receive five hundred pounds; the sick in the hospital of the Savoy and all the royal creditors. If after her death there were to be found anyone she had "injured or done wrong"—"as to my remembrance willingly I have not," she added—they were to be paid or compensated for the injury. And finally, Mary ordered a new charitable institution to be established in her name, a hospital for soldiers. "Forasmuch as presently there is no house or hospital specially ordained and provided for the relief and help of poor and old soldiers," she wrote, "and namely of such as have been or shall be hurt or maimed in the wars and service of this realm, the which we think both honor, conscience and charity willeth should be provided for." Mary was thinking not only of the wounded from the Calais garrison and the few who escaped the butchery of Guines, but of the aging men who had fought for her against Wyatt, and of those now mustering at Dover to join her husband in the spring campaign.

It may have been at Philip's suggestion that Mary made her will. He was keeping a close watch on events in England in the early months of 1558 through his envoy the count of Feria. Feria arrived late in January, ostensibly to congratulate Mary on her pregnancy but more urgently to do all he could to persuade the queen and her Council to continue sending arms and money to the Hapsburg cause. The war, not the queen's dubious pregnancy, was the important thing, especially since in Feria's view Mary was only "making herself believe that she is with child, although she does not own up to it."[7] It was evident, though, that if Mary was not pregnant her swollen belly and amenorrhea, combined with her general ill health, were ominous signs. All things considered, Philip thought it prudent that she make her will.

In his letters to the king at Brussels Feria described the English court as a scene of confusion and bickering, with Mary imposing intermittent order on her quarrelsome councilors. The Council meetings were a chaos of personal insults and accusations. There were no clear factions any more, only disgruntled men embittered by the loss of Calais and disheartened by the lack of strong leadership. Paget, Arundel, Pembroke and the others who had once been most sympathetic to imperial interests—and who had been receiving handsome pensions from Philip until his recent bankruptcy—were now the most vocal in their opposition to Philip's pressure. "They do nothing but raise difficulties, whatever one proposes, and never find any remedy," Feria complained to his master. Mary did her best to restrain them long enough to get the work of government done, and the count commended her "spirit and good will," but by March the unceasing conflicts had become so impossible that she had to send a number of the Council members out to the shires to get rid of them while she tried to govern with the rest. By then Feria had lost all patience. "I am at my wits' end with these people here," he wrote, "as God shall be my witness, and I do not know what to do. Your Majesty must realise that from night to morning and morning to night they change everything they have decided, and it is impossible to make them see what a state they are in, although it is the worst any country has ever fallen into."[8]

The most acute problem was the financial extremity of the government. Late in February the situation became so desperate that Mary ordered all those charged with financial affairs to meet daily, and to report to Feria and Pole as soon as they could. Mary's finances had always been precarious. She inherited from her father and brother a depressed economy, plagued by alarming fluctuations in wages and prices, plunging employment levels and the visible miseries of ruined villages and vagabonds lining the high roads. The bad harvests of 1555 and 1556 had sharpened these hardships, and while local justices of the peace were given broad powers to intervene to prevent hoarding and ensure that the available food was distributed as equitably as possible, the numbers of beggars grew every year and the weekly collection of alms in each parish was not adequate to feed all those who were without bread. At court too expenditures exceeded income by more and more each year, and the loans taken by Mary's agents in Antwerp were left unpaid, their payment deadlines prolonged for months or years. As early as 1555 Mason had prayed that God would "put some good man in mind, whom the queen can be content to believe, to advise her to take the measure of her realm and to proportionate her receipts and expenses together." But no such man appeared, although Gresham consistently did Mary good service in the money markets of Flanders.[9] By the time Mason wrote Mary was considering recalling most of her ambassadors at foreign courts to save their cost, and ill-disposed foreigners at her court were remarking that her poverty was obvious even from the food on her table.

When Mary's financial officers made their report it was little more than an admission of disaster. Paget, who acted as spokesman, laced his remarks with recriminations, and admitted in effect that the best remedy he and his colleagues could imagine was to borrow £100,000 at Antwerp and try to raise another £50,000 from the merchants of London. These sums, Feria knew, would barely keep pace with the accumulating interest on current loans, let alone pay the vast cost of warfare. It cost nearly £15,000 a month to keep the fleet manned and afloat, and to provide each of the fourteen thousand sailors, gunners and soldiers with his pound of biscuit, two pots of beer and two pounds of beef a day.[10] Feria, exasperated by Paget's obstinacy and by the men around him who "all say that the country is rich and then add that they do not know how to raise the necessary money to defend it," told the councilors just what he thought of them and appealed to Mary.

But though she received him with her customary gravity and heard him out, Mary seemed preoccupied and bemused. She told Feria she would "continue to press them about the money" from Greenwich, where she was about to go, but would not consider putting off her change of residence to deal with the financial crisis. At Greenwich she would find solace amid the monks, still waiting and hoping for her labor pains to begin. She had begged Philip to come to England for her delivery, and he had given her some reason to hope that he might. If he came, he could handle Paget and the others; she was rapidly losing her inclination to wrestle with affairs of state. Overwhelmed by the complex role she was called upon to play, deferential to her husband yet sovereign within her own realm, forced to watch England's interests sacrificed to Philip's hazardous ventures abroad, Mary was giving in to her anxieties. She was slipping gradually into a world of her own.

And Pole, it seemed, was keeping her company. She had been governing without his vital aid for months. He was ill and vague in mind, and wandered through the court like a sleepwalker. "The cardinal is a dead man," Feria told Philip simply, and the tone of Pole's letters bore out Feria's judgment that he was no longer in full possession of himself. He wrote to other clerics and to the pope like an abstracted visionary, filling his letters with beatific sentiments and apocalyptic images of vindication for himself and his queen.

Pole was tormented by the thought that he had caused Mary a near-fatal sorrow. In June of 1557 the pope deprived Pole of his legatine authority in England and summoned him to Rome to appear before the tribunal of the Inquisition on a charge of heresy. Another man, Mary's one-time confessor William Peto, was appointed to take his place. Mary wrote to Paul IV protesting his action and asking him to "pardon her if she professed to know the men who are good for the government of her kingdom better than his Holiness," but his only response was visible exasperation. Pole was still archbishop of Canterbury, but in the eyes of the bishop of Rome he was a fugitive heretic.

Pole's loss of favor brought home to Mary the irreversible failure of her efforts to rebuild the Catholic church in England. She had once declared that her people's souls were worth more to her than ten kingdoms. But in the nearly five years that she had been queen she had not been able even to lay the foundations for the restoration of the church. Ruined churches and convents still blemished every town and every country landscape, and whatever spiritual rebuilding had been accomplished in the first years of Mary's reign had been swept away by the horror Catholics and Protestants alike felt at the grisly burnings that made the queen more hated every day. When Pole sent clerks to visit parishes in Lincoln and Canterbury in 1556 and 1557 they found neither the churches nor the clergy in a state of rehabilitation. Altars were still ruined, and many had no crosses; far too many parishes lacked candlesticks, vestments, service books and stoups for holy water. There were too few priests to serve these parishes, and too many of the existing priests were married or undereducated. Despite the laws that ordered attendance at mass and other observances the congregations Pole's clerks observed were very small, and the evidence of religious enthusiasm slight.[11]

Mary and Pole had been convinced from the outset that the physical destruction of the churches was an insurmountable barrier to a revival of Catholic piety, and most of their energies had gone to gathering the lost revenues that had supported the episcopal and monastic establishments in the early years of the century. But it proved to be all but impossible to trace income alienated for nearly a generation; after four years of Catholic rule the bishops had not even been able to submit accurate lists of what had once been owed. In the end both the church and the crown were too poor to accomplish more than token restoration of churches and monasteries, and attempts to regularize worship and doctrine met with much the same result.[12]

Neither Mary nor Pole should have expected to undo in a few years all the confusion, disillusionment and destruction brought into being by the two previous reigns. But as Mary watched the cadaverous figure of her archbishop of Canterbury pace the corridors of Greenwich she could not help but give in to defeat. The man who had absolved England from its heresy three and a half years earlier was now a stigmatized heretic himself, presiding over an unregenerate church.

In his distracted brain Pole could not bring himself to believe that Paul IV, his former friend, had turned against him. He wrote to the pope, begging him to say that he had only been testing Pole's loyalty, "as Christ is wont to place his dearest children in purgatory to try them." Even as he wrote he saw a vision of deliverance. He saw God sending his angels to stay the pope's hand from issuing the accusation of heresy. He saw Mary and Philip, "the Catholic Kings, and Defenders of the Faith," interceding for him, and a host of pious men, "coming like a legion of angels" to put themselves between the papal sword and Pole's head.[13] With these visions he comforted himself as his wasted body succumbed to the fevers that in time would carry him off.

XLIX

Farewell my pleasures past,
Welcum my present payne,
I fele my torments so increse
That lyfe cannot remayne.
Cease now the passing bell,
Rong is my doleful knell,
For the sound my deth doth tell;
Deth doth draw nye,
Sound my end dolefully,
For now I dye.

In the spring of 1558 Mary's sworn enemy John Knox shook his dour head over his Bible and muttered to himself about the sorry state of Protestantism in Europe. Apart from the few Lutheran principalities in the empire, Calvin's Geneva, and a handful of other towns, there were no Protestant bastions left. In France, Scotland, England, and the Netherlands—everywhere the doctrines of Luther and Calvin had won large followings—Protestant populations were being crushed by cruel rulers determined to root them out by fire and flail: Catherine de Médicis in France, Mary of Lorraine (mother of Mary Stuart, the future Mary Queen of Scots) in Scotland, Mary Tudor in England and, until recently, Charles V's sister Mary in the Netherlands. The more Knox pondered this situation from his refuge in Geneva, the more he became convinced that it was no accident that the sorry fortunes of Protestantism should coincide with an unprecedented concentration of power in the hands of women. That so many women were ruling over men, a condition condemned as unnatural in the Old and New Testaments and highly exceptional in recent European history, seemed a sure sign that the times were out of joint. It was up to godfearing men everywhere to denounce the plague of females before they utterly destroyed God's church.

Knox's *First Blast of the Trumpet Against the Monstrous Regiment of Women* was published anonymously in the late spring or early summer. It was the most thorough, the most uncompromising and the most venomous assault on female rulership yet published. "To promote a woman to bear rule, superiority, dominion or empire above any realm, nation, or city, is repugnant to nature, contumely to God, a thing most contrarious to his revealed will and approved ordinance, and finally it is the subversion of good order, of all equity and justice," Knox wrote. The incapacity of women was self-evident; they were, according to Knox's catalogue of imperfections, "weak, frail, impatient, feeble, foolish, inconstant, variable, cruel and lacking the spirit of counsel and regiment." If the stern patriarchs of antiquity were to be brought face to face with the female monarchs of the 1550s they would be so astonished "that they should judge the whole world to be transformed into Amazons," and would conclude that human society in its familiar order was coming to a disastrous end.

"For who can deny but it repugneth to nature, that the blind shall be appointed to lead and conduct such as do see?" Knox asked. "That the weak, the sick and impotent persons shall nourish and keep the whole and strong, and finally, that the foolish, mad and frenetic shall govern the discreet?" Whatever minimal competence women possess, compared to men "their sight is but blindness, their strength weakness, their counsel, foolishness, and judgment, frenzy."[1] The prevailing arrangement was clearly a political monstrosity; his treatise was intended to bring "this monstriferous empire of women" to an immediate end.

In his wholesale condemnation Knox did not discriminate among the women whose authority he deplored. He went out of his way, however, to denounce the two monarchs who had thwarted him personally. When the crown of Scotland was placed on the head of his nemesis Mary of Lorraine, he said, it was "as seemly a sight as to put a saddle upon the back of an unruly cow." Mary Tudor was even worse. To the Scotsman she was another Jezebel, Ahab's wicked wife who tried to annihilate the preachers of God's word and ended her life wretchedly, her corpse mutilated by dogs. Mary was England's "wicked Jezebel, who for our sins, contrary to nature and the manifest word of God, is suffered to reign over us in God's fury." Her accession to power was doubly objectionable in that she was a bastard and a vicious tyrant, "unworthy by reason of her bloody tyranny of the name of a woman." Mary surpassed even the worst vices of her sex; her crimes were so unutterable that even the base name of woman was too good for her.

Knox's attack was nothing short of treason, since he urged his readers to overthrow the women he condemned. In England the *First Blast of the Trumpet* was officially prohibited by royal proclamation. Copies of the treatise were to be burned on sight, and anyone failing to carry out this directive was subject to the death penalty. But despite the prohibition Knox's diatribe was read and reread by English men and women, and his indictment of Mary's "bloody tyranny" permanently affected public sentiment about the queen. And Knox was, in any case, only one of many writers vilifying Mary. In 1558 their pamphlets and treatises were reaching England in greater numbers than ever before, creating a new vocabulary of slander and robbing Mary of what peace of mind remained to her. They called her "a raging and mad woman," and nicknamed her "Traitorous Marie" and "Mischevious Marie." They ridiculed her authority and mocked her false pregnancy. They caricatured her piety as bigotry, her courage as ferocity, her devotion to her husband as a combination of slavery and uncontrollable lust. Cruelest of all, they jeered at her tragic marriage. Philip was gone for good, they wrote; his mistresses would keep him company from now on. He had nothing but contempt for his aging wife, and his subjects made her a laughing stock. Spaniards everywhere were wondering why he had married her in the first place, since she was clearly old enough to be his mother. "What shall the king do," they asked, "with such an old bitch?"[2]

Late in May a solicitous letter from Philip arrived at Greenwich. He was sorry he had not been able to join the queen as he had hoped, but he was glad to hear that she took the news "bravely." Philip thanked Pole for keeping his wife company and "cheering her loneliness," and referred him to Count Feria for further instructions.[3] The letter made no mention of Mary's pregnancy. It was now clear that her belly bore the distended outline of a fatal dropsy, and Philip's mind had already moved on to thoughts of her successor. He ordered Feria to visit Elizabeth on his behalf, to present his compliments, and to ingratiate himself with the men around her.[4]

Neither the queen nor Pole was in any condition to read Philip's letter. The archbishop was lost in the fitful dreams of a tertian fever, the queen "suffering from intermittent fever" and wayward mental states. Severe melancholia drove her to her rooms, where she lay as if in a deathlike stupor. In her hours of near-normal consciousness she bemoaned Philip's absence, the hatred she felt from her fickle subjects, and the loss of Calais. Charles V had once said of the Francophile Pope Paul III that, if his body were opened, three fleurs-de-lis would be found on his heart. Mary adapted the remark to herself. According to Foxe, who got the story at one remove from one of Mary's most intimate servants, the queen told this man and Susan Clarencieux during her last months of a secret sorrow, "the greatest wound that pierced her oppressed mind."

The two servants thought she meant Philip's infidelity, and told her "they feared she took thought for King Philip's departing from her."

"Not that only," Mary answered, "but when I am dead and opened, you shall find Calais lying in my heart."

In August Mary's fever was so grave that she was moved from Hampton Court to St. James. Her physicians and attendants were worried, because she was not ordinarily susceptible to fever, but to satisfy the Council the doctors tried to find some advantage in Mary's state. "Through this malady," they declared solemnly, "she will obtain relief from her habitual indisposition," meaning the complex of symptoms she suffered nearly every autumn. Mary did everything the physicians ordered, and took "the greatest care of herself," but even though her physical health fluctuated, sinking for a few days and then reviving in what had by now become a chronic pattern, waves of depression came over the queen with greater and greater frequency, and made her illness worse. "The truth is," one ambassador wrote, "that her malady is evidently incurable, and will end her life sooner or later, according to the increase or decrease of her mental anxieties, which harass her more than the disease, however dangerous it may be."

In October Mary was harassed by fresh griefs. Pole was dying, and news came that the two people who had been dearest to her since her mother's death, Charles V and his sister Mary, were dead. The queen had a relapse. Her doctors, headed by one "Mr. Cesar, Doctor in Physic," had to use all their skill to bring her back to lucidity. In her gratitude she ordered Dr. Cesar to be paid a hundred pounds, "by way of the queen's majesty's reward," but it was obvious even to Mary herself that she would not live much longer.[5] She wrote out a codicil to her will, adding the sad acknowledgment that there would be no "fruit of her body" to whom she could leave her crown and lands. At the same time she assured Susan Clarencieux's future by further gifts, and gave thought to the welfare of her servants and waiting women.[6] Her favorite Jane Dormer falling sick, Mary sent her one of her doctors and took great "care and regard" for her, "more like a mother or sister than her queen and mistress."[7] Jane's forthcoming wedding was a source of pleasure to Mary in her last weeks. After turning down many other suitors—Mary claimed that Jane "deserved a very good husband," and "knew not the man that was worthy of her"—she had finally found a man both she and the queen admired. He was none other than Philip's sometime envoy to England, the count of Feria, a "most perfect gentleman" who was said to be in "great favor" with the queen.[8] Mary insisted on giving the couple gifts and endowments worthy of her esteem, but she was too poor to provide them. At first she asked Jane to delay the marriage until Philip came back to England, and then, when she knew she was dying, she lamented that she would not live to see the ceremony.

Philip kept himself informed about the state of his wife's health through his envoys and informers and, at least until late September, through the letters Mary wrote him from time to time. When Mary's letters stopped, Philip worried. "She has not written to me for some days past," the king wrote on one occasion, "and I cannot help being anxious."[9] What worried him most, aside from the succession question, was that given her present vagueness of mind Mary might become the victim of swindlers. When a request came to his court from England asking his permission to export eight thousand corselets and an equal number of arquebuses and pikes, he worried about the purpose and destination of. the arms. The request was made "in the queen's name," but there was no confirming letter from Mary herself, and it was rumored that the entire enterprise was set afoot by "private individuals who intend to make money by selling these arms." Eventually the request was found to be a genuine order from the queen, and the arms were sent, but Philip remained on his guard "in order that there may be no fraud."[10]

When Philip received news of the queen's relapse in October he sent Feria back to England to represent him during her last days. Feria took with him a Portuguese physician, Lodovicus Nonnius, a man of wide reputation in imperial circles. Though Mary still enjoyed periods of rationality they were becoming fewer each day; many Londoners believed she was already dead. On November 4 she was still capable of advising her Council about what matters should be brought before Parliament, and urging her councilors to treat with Philip's peace commissioners—for he was negotiating a truce with the French—about the possible English recovery of Calais. But she was "both sick and very weak," and could not talk to them for very long. They prayed daily now for God to spare the queen, and gave orders that any subject who said she was dead should be set in the pillory.

Feria's mission involved far more than attendance at the bedside of the dying queen. Now that the accession of Mary's successor was only a few days or, at most, a few weeks away, the vexed problem of what to do about Elizabeth could no longer be left unsolved. Elizabeth had lived as a Catholic for the past five years, but those who judged her temperament accurately believed that once she was queen she would return England to some form of Protestantism. The changes she made in religion were likely to be paralleled by shifts in England's diplomatic alignment, as she was known to favor the French over the Spaniards. The only hopeful thing about Elizabeth Tudor, from the imperial point of view, was that she was unmarried; this meant that, if she could be given to a Spanish or Flemish husband, England need not be lost to Hapsburg interests on Mary's death. If Elizabeth could be married, say, to the duke of Savoy, he could be counted on to countermand her political preferences and to work closely with Philip in the conduct of European affairs.

Feria left Brussels with instructions "to try and dispose the queen to consent to Lady Elizabeth being married as her sister, and with the hope of succeeding to the crown."[11] It was not an easy assignment, for since her accession Mary had clung stubbornly to the belief that Elizabeth was not her sister, and could not bring herself to admit that the daughter of Anne Boleyn would soon be wearing her crown. The Council had already paved the way for Feria's persuasions, however. They had convinced Mary that she must either relent and acknowledge Elizabeth or leave the realm to the chaos of civil war. In the end Mary weakly agreed, and two of the Council members were dispatched to Hatfield to inform Elizabeth that she would soon be queen. At the same time Mary sent Jane Dormer to Hatfield to give Elizabeth her "rich and precious" jewels, and to ask her to promise three things: that she would uphold the Catholic faith, take care of Mary's servants, and pay her debts.

Philip's envoy made no headway with the hoped-for negotiations for Elizabeth's hand. Mary was in no condition to consider the merits of a Hapsburg match for her successor, and Elizabeth herself was scornful of the suggestion that she marry the duke of Savoy, telling Feria that she would be foolish to follow Mary's example and marry a foreigner. The more outlandish suggestion that, if she agreed to remain a Catholic, Philip himself might wish to marry her once he became a widower Elizabeth rejected out of hand. In Brussels, though, it was looked on as a certainty that when Mary died Philip would marry Elizabeth, and both the Flemish and the English courtiers were already transferring their attention to the red-haired princess who would soon be queen. The English were buying hundreds of yards of Antwerp silk in which to dress themselves for the coronation, and the Flemings talked of nothing but the king's forthcoming marriage.[12]

As the nobles, officials and household officers deserted St. James for Hatfield the queen grew weaker and weaker. She could no longer read the letter Feria had brought her from Philip; she could only ask that the count take him a ring as a sign of her undying love. She knew nothing of his proposal to Elizabeth, of course, but from her "much sighing," those around her believed she was dying of "thought and sorrow" more than from any physical disease. Once when she saw them grieving she tried to comfort them by describing the visions of heavenly joy that filled her dreams. "She told them what good dreams she had, seeing many little children like angels playing before her, singing pleasing notes, giving her more than earthly comfort." She went on to encourage them "ever to have the holy fear of God before their eyes," and to keep ever in mind that all human affairs were ordered by a single divine purpose. Whatever happened, she told the faithful servants gathered around her bedside, they should "have confidence that He would in mercy turn all to the best."

As she composed her own thoughts Mary recalled the prayer

she had written, "to be read at the hour of death." "O Lord Jesu! which art the health of all men living, and the everlasting life of them which die in faith," she prayed, "I, wretched sinner give and submit myself wholly unto thy most blessed will." "Willingly now I leave this frail and wicked flesh, in hope of the resurrection." She prayed for forgiveness, for mercy, and for the grace to endure the approach of her last hour with dignity, "that the weakness of my flesh be not overcome by the fear of death. Grant me, merciful Father," she concluded, "that when Death has shut up the eyes of my body, yet that the eyes of my soul may still behold and look upon thee; that when death hath taken away the use of my tongue and speech, yet that my heart may cry and say unto Thee *In manus tuas Domine, commendo spiritum meum*; that is, O Lord, into thy hands I give and commit my soul."[13]

More than forty years later, when Jane Dormer, duchess of Feria, was an old woman living in Spain, she wept as she told her biographer how Queen Mary died. "Being at the last point" and sick to death, Jane said, Mary nonetheless asked that mass be said in her chamber before dawn on the morning of November 17. Despite her extremity "she heard it with so good attention, zeal, and devotion, as she answered in every part with him that served the priest." The ceremony seemed to call forth what awareness remained to Mary, and her low, resonant voice was heard distinctly making the responses. "*Miserere nobis, miserere nobis. Dona nobis pacem.*" She lapsed then, Jane said, into what appeared to be a private meditation, from which she awoke to adore the host. Then, at the climax of the mass, she "closed her eyes and rendered her blessed soul to God." The last her mistress saw, Jane recounted, was "her Saviour and Redeemer," "no doubt to behold Him presently after in His glorious Body in heaven."[14]

Jane's description had all the pious drama of a saint's life, but according to other accounts there was nothing extraordinary about the queen's death. She gave up her life so peacefully that everyone but the attending doctor "thought her better, and that she would fain sleep." He alone realized that she had "made her passage," and that he had witnessed the fleeting transition between the reigns of Queen Mary and Queen Elizabeth.[15]

Across the river at Lambeth Pole received the news of Mary's death as he too prepared to die. This "final catastrophe" brought on his last paroxysms, and by seven o'clock that evening he too was dead.

Whatever sorrow Mary's subjects felt at her passing was soon overshadowed by their joyful welcoming of the new queen. Mary died between four and five in the morning; by midafternoon "all the churches in London did ring, and at night did make bonfires and set tables in the street, and did eat and drink and made merry for the new Queen

Elizabeth, Queen Mary's sister."[16] Elizabeth herself heard the news of Mary's death calmly, then fell on her knees and cried out, "This is the Lord's doing, and it is marvelous in our eyes."

Philip, writing to his sister in Spain (where, Knox would have heard with much headshaking, she was regent for her brother), seemed shaken by the deaths of his father, aunt and wife in so short a space of weeks. "You may imagine what a state I am in," he wrote. "It seems to me that everything is being taken from me at once." Of Mary he added "May God have received her in His glory! I felt a reasonable regret for her death. I shall miss her, even on this account." These few hasty sentences were doubtless sincere, but they were inserted in the middle of a long paragraph giving a detailed survey of the peace negotiations.[17] Even in dying Mary disturbed Philip's concentration on affairs of state only briefly, and without any lasting effect.

The corpse of the late queen lay in state at St. James' for more than three weeks while the mourning clothes and funeral accouterments were prepared. On December 12, when all was ready, her funeral cortege formed in the courtyard of the palace for the solemn procession to Westminster. A great company of mourners came first, under the standard of the falcon and the hart. Next in order were the hundreds of household servants in black gowns, walking two by two, the heralds riding up and down beside them to keep them in line. Then came the gentlemen mourners, under the banners of the white greyhound and falcon and of the arms of England, embroidered in gold. Immediately preceding the corpse were heralds bearing Mary's knightly ornaments—her helm, crest and mantle, her sword and coat armor. The coffin in its chariot was draped with a lifelike painted effigy. It showed Mary, dressed in her favorite color of crimson velvet, wearing her crown and carrying her scepter, her hands adorned with "many goodly rings on her fingers." The chief mourner, Mary's cousin Margaret Douglas, countess of Lennox, followed the chariot, and with her rode the gentlewomen of the court all in black robes that trailed over their horses' legs to the ground. The clerks of the royal chapel, the monks and the bishops brought up the rear.

The procession halted at the great door of Westminster Abbey, and the queen's coffin was carried inside. A hundred poor men in black gowns kept watch over her body all that night, holding long torches in their hands, and around them the soldiers of the royal guard stood with their staff torches. The next day the requiem mass was sung. The bishop of Winchester, conscious that he risked the severe disapproval of the woman who now ruled England, eulogized Mary in the warmest terms. He had been present at her death, he told his audience, and found her godliness and devotion so inspiring that he could not restrain his praise. "If angels were mortal, I would rather liken this her departure to the death of an angel, than of a mortal creature," he said, adding a list of the late queen's virtues and charitable deeds. "She was never unmindful or uncareful of her promise to her realm. She used singular mercy towards offenders. She used much pity and compassion towards the poor and oppressed. She used clemency among her nobles. She restored more noble houses decayed than ever did prince of this realm, or I pray God ever shall have the like occasion to do hereafter." The bishop said little about Mary's religious policies, but was eloquent in defense of her sincere faith. "I verily believe," he said, "the poorest creature in all this city feared not God more than she did."

When the eulogy was over the coffin was carried to Henry VII's chapel in the abbey, and placed in a grave on the north side. Her heart, "being severally inclosed in a coffin covered with velvet bound with silver," was separately interred. The household officers broke their staves and threw them into the grave, and as they did so the trumpets sounded to signal the beginning of the funeral banquet.

The chief mourners all went in to dinner, leaving the funeral trappings unguarded. In a few minutes the servants and hired mourners and the Londoners who had come to see the queen laid in her grave had torn down the banners and standards, the arms displayed around the altar and the hangings fastened to the walls. They scrambled and fought one another for scraps of cloth, "every man a piece that could catch it," until the embroidered cloths were in shreds and the queen's effigy pulled into a hundred pieces. The next day the bishop of Winchester was informed that, "for such offenses as he committed in his sermon at the funeral of the late queen," he was ordered to keep himself a prisoner in his own house during Queen Elizabeth's pleasure.

The Epitaphe upon the Death of the
Most Excellent and our late vertuous
Quene, Marie, deceased

Vayne is the blisse, and brittle is the glasse, of worldly wishèd welth;
The steppes unstayde, the life unsure, of lasting hopèd helth.
witnes (alas) may Marie be, late Quene of rare renowne,
whose body dead, her vertues live, and doth her fame resowne;
In whom suche golden giftes were grafte, of nature and of grace,
As when the tongue dyd ceasse to say, yet vertue spake in face.
what vertue is that was not founde within that worthy wight?
what vice is there that can be sayde wherin she had delight?
She never closde her eare to heare the rightous man distrest,
Nor never sparde her hande to helpe, wher wrong or power opprest.
when all was wracke, she was the porte from peryll unto ioye;
when all was spoyle, she sparèd all, she pitied to destroye.
As Princely was her birth, so Princely was her life,
Constante, courtise, modest, and mylde, a chast and chosen wife.
In greatest stormes she fearèd not, for God she made her shielde,
And all her care she cast on him, who forst her foes to yelde.
Her perfect life in all extremes her pacient hert dyd shoe,
For in this worlde she never founde but dolfull dayes and woe.[18]

Notes

ABBREVIATIONS

EETS — Early English Text Society

EHR — *English Historical Review*

L.P. — *Letters and Papers, Foreign and Domestic, of the Reign of Henry VIII*, ed. J. S. Brewer, R. H. Brodie and James Gairdner. 21 vols. London: Her Majesty's Stationery Office, 1862–1910.

Sp. Cal. — *Calendar of Letters, Despatches, and State Papers, relating to the Negotiations between England and Spain*, ed. Pascual de Gayangos et al. 13 vols. London: His, and Her Majesty's Stationery Office, 1867–1954.

Ven. Cal.— *Calendar of State Papers and Manuscripts, Relating to English Affairs, Existing in the Archives and Collections of Venice*, ed. Rawdon Brown and Allen B. Hinds. 38 vols. London: Longman & Co., 1864–1947.

References to *L.P.*, *Sp. Cal.*, *Ven. Cal.* and similar collections are to page numbers, not document numbers.

Chapter 1

1. Frederick Chamberlin, *The Private Character of Henry the Eighth* (New York, 1931), p. 129, facing p. 168.
2. *Ven. Cal.* II, 92.

Chapter II

1. *L.P.* I:i, 742.
2. Ibid., II:i, 435.
3. Rawdon Brown, ed. and trans., *Four Years at the Court of Henry VIII*, 2 vols. (London, 1854), I, 181.
4. Ibid., I, 182.
5. Ibid., I, 136 note 3.
6. J. S. Brewer, *The Reign of Henry VIII: from his Accession to the Death of Wolsey*, 2 vols. (London, 1884), I, 45.
7. Gladys Temperley, *Henry VII* (Boston and New York, 1914), pp. 207–8.
8. Ibid., 123.
9. Ibid., 55.
10. Chamberlin, p. 93.

Chapter III

1. Charles Wriothesley, *A Chronicle of England, during the Reigns of the Tudors*, ed. William Douglas Hamilton, 2 vols. (London, 1875–77), I, 10–11 and note.
2. John Caius, *A Boke or Counseill againste the Sweate*, folio 9, cited in Brewer, I, 238.
3. Peter Krivatsky, "Erasmus' Medical Milieu," *Bulletin of the History of Medicine*, XLVII (1973), 120–21.
4. *L.P.* II:ii, 1,473.
5. Ibid., 1,372.
6. Ibid., 1,376–77; Brown, II, 233–34.
7. Brown, II, 237.

Chapter IV

1. *L.P.* III:i, 37.
2. Ibid., II:ii, 1,547; III:i, 198.
3. *L.P.* II:ii, 1,108.
4. Frederick Madden, *Privy Purse Expenses of the Princess Mary* (London, 1831), p. xxix.
5. Ibid.
6. Quoted in H. Maynard Smith, *Pre-Reformation England* (London, 1938), p. 239.
7. John Brand, *Observations of Popular Antiquities*, arr. and rev. Henry Ellis, 3 vols. (London, 1813), II, 363.
8. Madden, p. xxxi.
9. *L.P.* III:ii, 1,098–99, 1,405ff.
10. *A Companion to Shakespeare Studies*, ed. Harley Granville-Barker and G. B. Harrison (Garden City, New York, 1960), p. 156.
11. Brown, I, 297–98 note.
12. Ibid., II, 163–64. This anecdote has been cited by Mary's biographers as proof of her precocious piety and obsession with the clergy, since she called

Memo "Priest, priest!" In fact, as the complete account of the incident shows clearly, it was his playing that delighted her and not his clerical status.

13. *Vives and the Renascence Education of Women*, ed. Foster Watson (New York and London, 1912), p. 96.

14. John E. Paul, *Catharine of Aragon and Her Friends* (London, 1966), p. 39.

15. *L.P.* III:ii, 629–30.

16. *Vives and the Renascence Education of Women*, p. 84 and passim.

17. Matthias A. Shaaber, *Some Forerunners of the Newspaper in England, 1472–1622* (Philadelphia, 1929), p. 147 and note.

18. *Vives and the Renascence Education of Women*, pp. 64–66.

19. Ibid., 96.

20. Temperley, p. 93.

21. *Vives and the Renascence Education of Women*, p. 10.

22. *Sp. Cal.* IV:ii, 737.

Chapter V

1. Sydney Anglo, *Spectacle Pageantry and Early Tudor Policy* (Oxford, 1969), pp. 172–73.

2. Smith, p. 35.

3. Brown, II, 17–18.

4. Ibid., II, 117.

5. Ibid., II, 88 note; Brewer, I, 113.

6. Brewer, I, 602.

7. Smith, p. 514.

8. Erwin Doernberg, *Henry VIII and Luther* (Stanford, California, 1967), p. 31.

9. *L.P.* III:ii, 719.

10. Robert Withington, *English Pageantry: An Historical Outline*, 2 vols. (Cambridge and London, 1918–20), I, 175–78.

11. Ibid., I, 97.

12. *L.P.* III:ii, 608–9, 613.

13. Paul, p. 55.

14. Madden, p. xxxii.

15. *L.P.* III:ii, 1,188.

Chapter VI

1. From a Garter manuscript, Sir H. Nares' Collections, folio MS p. 22, cited in Agnes Strickland, *Lives of the Queens of England*, 8 vols. (London, 1851), III, 514 note.

2. *Inventories of the Wardrobes, Plate, Chapel Stuff, etc., of Henry Fitzroy, Duke of Richmond*, ed. John Gough Nichols (London, 1854), p. xiv.

3. Brewer, II, 102–3.

4. Ibid.

5. *Inventories*, p. 19.

6. Ibid., pp. xlvii–xlviii.

7. Lord Ferrers, steward of Mary's Welsh household, referred to her Council as "the Prince's Council." *L.P.* IV:i:ii, 830.

8. A. F. Powell, *Henry VIII* (London, 1905; rev. ed. 1951), pp. 291–92.
9. *L.P.* IV:i:ii, 1,044–45.
10. Ibid., 709.
11. Ibid., 753.
12. Withington, I, 179.
13. Madden, p. xlii.
14. *L.P.* IV:ii, 1,093.
15. Ibid., 1,087.
16. Ibid., IV:i:ii, 830.
17. Ibid., 1,044.

Chapter VII

1. *L.P.* IV:ii, 1,075.
2. Anglo, p. 167.
3. Wriothesley, I, 107.
4. *L.P.* IV:i:ii, 1,001.
5. Ibid., 884.
6. Chamberlin, p. 148.
7. *L.P.* IV:i:ii, 864.
8. *Vives and the Renascence Education of Women*, pp. 102ff.
9. *L.P.* IV:ii, 1,157.
10. Ibid., 1,204–5, 1,238, 1,441.
11. Ibid., 1,271.
12. *L.P.* IV:i:ii, 634.
13. *Sp. Cal.* III:i, 82; J. M. Stone, *The History of Mary I Queen of England* (London, 1901), p. 27.
14. Quoted in Brewer, II, 152–53.
15. The foregoing has been drawn from three eyewitness accounts of the sack of Rome printed in Brewer, II, 116–27.

Chapter VIII

1. *L.P.* IV:ii, 1,638.
2. J. J. Scarisbrick, *Henry VIII* (Berkeley and Los Angeles, 1968), p. 151.
3. Wriothesley, I, 18 note.
4. *L.P.* IV:ii, 1,500–1.
5. *Inventories*, p. lvii.
6. *L.P.* IV:ii, 2,112.
7. *Sp. Cal.* IV:i, 96.
8. *L.P.* IV:ii, 2,113.

Chapter IX

1. *L.P.* V, 239.
2. *Sp. Cal.* IV:i, 351.
3. *L.P.* V, 136.
4. Ibid., 137.
5. *Sp. Cal.* IV:i, 351–52.
6. *L.P.* V, 110–11.

7. Ibid., 136.
8. Ibid., 591.
9. *Sp. Cal.* IV:i, 634.
10. *L.P.* IV:ii, 2,167.
11. Ibid., V, 239.
12. Ibid., 226–27.
13. Ibid., 683.
14. Ibid., 505, 438; *Sp. Cal.* IV:i, 773.
15. *L.P.* V, 505.
16. *Sp. Cal.* IV:i, 633.
17. *L.P.* V, 145.
18. Ibid., 101
19. Ibid., 210–11, 243.
20. Ibid., 753.
21. Ibid., 125.
22. *Sp. Cal.* IV: ii:i, 353–54.
23. *L.P.* V, 137.
24. Ibid., 161.
25. Quoted in Stone, p. 494.

Chapter X

1. *An English Garner: Tudor Tracts, 1532–1588* (Westminster, 1903), pp. 27–28. Descriptions of Anne's progress and coronation are taken from Wriothesley, I, 18ff., Withington, I, 180ff., Anglo, 258–59, and *L.P.* VI, 181–82, 250–51, 264–66, 276–78.
2. *Sp. Cal.* IV:ii:i, 487.
3. *L.P.* V, 288.
4. *Sp. Cal.* IV:ii:ii, 646, 688; William Chappell, *Old English Popular Music* (New York, 1855, reprint 1961), pp. 54–55.
5. *Sp. Cal.* IV:ii:ii, 646; Anglo, 259.
6. Ibid., 923.
7. Brewer, II, 173.
8. *Sp. Cal.* IV:ii:ii, 788.
9. Ibid., IV:ii:i, 584.
10. Ibid., IV:ii:ii, 693.
11. Ibid., 681.
12. Ibid., 645.
13. Ibid., 738.
14. Ibid., 646.
15. Ibid., 740.
16. Ibid., 1,058.
17. Strickland, III, 326–27.
18. Psalm 91: 5–7.
19. II Kings 6:16.

Chapter XI

1. *L.P.* VI, 418, 624, 584–89.
2. Ibid., 399–400.
3. Ibid., 655.
4. Ibid., 227.

5. Franklin Le Van Baumer, *The Early Tudor Theory of Kingship* (New Haven and London, 1940), p. 86.

6. *Sp. Cal.* IV:ii:ii, 822, 839.

7. Ibid., 839.

8. Ibid., 881–82.

9. *L.P.* VII, 8.

10. Ibid., 84.

11. Ibid., 69.

12. Ibid., 14–16.

13. Ibid., 214.

14. Ibid., 254.

15. Ibid., 127.

16. Ibid., 323.

17. Ibid., 634.

18. Ibid., 214.

19. *Sp. Cal.* V:i, 11.

Chapter XII

1. *L.P.* III:i, 508–9.

2. *L.P.* VIII, 76–77.

3. Ibid., 105.

4. Ibid., 1–2.

5. Ibid., 66.

6. Ibid., V, 90; VII, 463; Madden, liii–liv; *Sp. Cal.* IV:ii:ii, 724.

7. *L.P.* VII, 445.

8. Ibid., VIII, 172–73.

9. Ibid., VIII, 167.

10. *L.P.* VII, 463.

11. Ibid., 497.

12. *Sp. Cal.* V:i, 280.

13. *L.P.* VII, 463.

14. Paul Friedmann, *Anne Boleyn: A Chapter of English History 1527–1536*, 2 vols. (London, 1884), II, 50–51.

15. This list is taken from the works of the sixteenth-century surgeon Ambroise Paré, quoted in Ilza Veith, *Hysteria: the History of a Disease* (Chicago and London, 1965), pp. 116–17.

16. Veith, p. 118.

17. *L.P.* V, 169.

Chapter XIII

1. *L.P.* VIII, 251, 272.

2. Philip Hughes, *The Reformation in England*, 3 vols. (New York, 1951–54), I, 280.

3. *L.P.* VIII, 272.

4. Friedmann, II, 54.

5. Ibid., II, 82.

6. *L.P.* VII, 62.

7. *Sp. Cal.* V:i, 520.

8. *L.P.* VIII, 373.

Chapter XIV

1. *L.P.* VIII, 253.
2. Ibid., 210.
3. *Sp. Cal.* V:i, 410.
4. *L.P.* VIII, 103.
5. *Sp. Cal.* V:i, 433.
6. *L.P.* VIII, 194.
7. Ibid., 165.
8. Ibid., 370.
9. *Sp. Cal.* V:i, 573.
10. Ibid., 433; *L.P.* VIII, 169.
11. *Sp. Cal.* V:i, 519–20.
12. Ibid., 529.
13. Ibid., 465.
14. Ibid., 540.
15. *L.P.* IX, 230.
16. *Sp. Cal.* V:i, 559–60.
17. *L.P.* IX, 262, 288, 290.
18. *Ven. Cal.* V, 257–58.
19. *L.P.* X, 20–22.

Chapter XV

1. *Sp. Cal.* V:ii, 28.
2. *L.P.* VIII, 78–79.
3. *Ven. Cal.* V, 40.
4. *L.P.* X, 14.
5. Ibid., 104–6, 14–15.
6. Ibid., 27.
7. Ibid., 135.
8. Ibid., 67–70.
9. Ibid., 134.
10. Ibid., 103.
11. *Sp. Cal.* V:ii, 14.
12. *L.P.* X, 134.
13. Ibid., 116–17.
14. *Sp. Cal.* V:ii, 12–13; *L.P.* X, 69.
15. *L.P.* X, 315.
16. Ibid., 377–78.
17. Ibid., 378.
18. Ibid.
19. Ibid., 401.

Chapter XVI

1. *Sp. Cal.* V:ii, 124.
2. Ibid., 133.
3. Ibid., 107.
4. Wriothesley, I, 44.

5. Ibid., 51.
6. Ibid., 49.
7. *Sp. Cal.* V:ii, 139.
8. Wriothesley, I, 45.
9. *L.P.* X, 466–67.
10. Ibid., 422–24.
11. Ibid. XII:ii, 48, 341–42.
12. *Sp. Cal.* V:ii, 184.
13. *L.P.* X, 466–67.
14. *Sp. Cal.* V:ii, 183.

Chapter XVII

1. *L.P.* XIV:i, 81.
2. Ibid., XI, 26.
3. Ibid., X, 137–44.
4. Ibid., 144.
5. Ibid., XVI, 586.
6. *Sp. Cal.* V:ii, 195; Wriothesley, I, 51.
7. *Sp. Cal.* V:ii, 195.
8. *L.P.* XI, 136.
9. Ibid., 132.
10. *Sp. Cal.* V:ii, 199.
11. *L.P.* XI, 26.
12. Ibid., 54.
13. Ibid., 101.
14. Ibid., 65.

Chapter XVIII

1. *L.P.* XII:i, 579; Wriothesley, I, 64.
2. Quoted in Strickland, III, 13–14.
3. Madden, p. 43.
4. *L.P.* XII:ii, 319–20.
5. *L.P.* VII, 263–68.
6. Wriothesley, I, 65.
7. *L.P.* XII:i, 406.
8. Wriothesley, I, 59–60.
9. *L.P.* XI, 346.
10. Madden, p. 30.
11. *L.P.* XII:i, 292.
12. Ibid., XII:ii, 30.
13. Madden, pp. 44–45.
14. Ibid., 44.

Chapter XIX

1. *L.P.* XVI, 586.
2. Madden, p. clv.
3. Ibid., 176.

4. Ibid., 174ff.
5. Ibid., 178.
6. *Royal Letters*, ed. Wood, III, 17.
7. Madden, pp. 26, 31 and passim.
8. Ibid., 177.
9. Ibid., 211 and passim.
10. Ibid., cxxxiv.
11. Ibid., cxxxix-cxl.
12. *L.P.* XVI, 586.
13. Madden, p. 251.
14. Ibid., 30.
15. Ibid., 48 and passim.
16. *Sp. Cal.* V:ii, 198–99.
17. Ibid., 282–84.
18. *L.P.* XII:i, 307.
19. Ibid., XII:ii, 92.
20. *Sp. Cal.* V:ii, 284.
21. *L.P.* XII:i, 526.

Chapter XX

1. *A Relation . . . of the Island of England*, trans. Charlotte Augusta Sneyd (London, 1847), pp. 30–31, 83–84.
2. Wriothesley, I, 89–90 and note.
3. Ibid., 86 note.
4. *Sp. Cal.* VI:i, 25–26.
5. *L.P.* XIII:i, 26.
6. Ibid.
7. Ibid., 395–96.
8. Wriothesley, I, 115.
9. Ibid., 85.
10. *L.P.* XVI, 440.
11. Wriothesley, I, 73.
12. Ibid., 125.
13. *L.P.* XII:ii, 48.
14. Ibid., XIV:i, 18.
15. Ibid., XIII:ii, 269–70, 312–13, 318, 333; XIV:i, 15.
16. Ibid., XIII:ii, 318.
17. Ibid., XIV:i, 451–52.

Chapter XXI

1. *L.P.* XV, 389–91. There is no evidence that Henry ever referred to Anne as a "Flanders mare."
2. Ibid., 65.
3. *Sp. Cal.* VI:i, 408.
4. *L.P.* XVI, 217.
5. Ibid., 615–16.
6. Ibid., 618.

7. Ibid., 620; *Sp. Cal.* VI:i, 396.
8. *L.P.* XVI, 149, 217; *Sp. Cal.* VI:i, 309.
9. *L.P.* XVI, 637.
10. *Sp. Cal.* V:ii, 196.
11. *L.P.* XIV:ii, 257; XIII:ii, 69.
12. Ibid., XIV:i, 18, 41; XVI, 59.
13. Ibid., XVI, 115.
14. Ibid., XVII, 220–21.
15. Ibid., Addenda, I:ii, 443.
16. Ibid., XVII, 124, 140.
17. *Sp. Cal.* VI:i, 484, 506, 508.
18. *L.P.* XVII, 170.
19. Ibid., XVI, 552.
20. Ibid., 586.

Chapter XXII

1. *Sp. Cal.* VI:ii, 223, 138.
2. Ibid., 223, 190; *L.P.* XVII, 675.
3. *Sp. Cal.* VI:ii, 224; *L.P.* XVIII:i, 162.
4. *L.P.* XVIII:i, 1; *Sp. Cal.* VI:ii, 89.
5. *Sp. Cal.* VI:ii, 219.
6. *L.P.* XXI:i, 479.
7. Ibid., XXI:ii, 394ff.
8. Brewer, I, 233 and note.
9. Scarisbrick, pp. 485–86 and note.
10. Brewer, I, 233 and note.
11. *L.P.* XVIII:i, 483.
12. Ibid., XIX:i, 64, 189.
13. Ibid., XXI:ii, 175–76.
14. Madden, pp. 152, 220. Those of Mary's biographers who have assumed that she and her women did the embroidery themselves have overlooked the payment to Brellont.
15. *Sp. Cal.* VII, 109, 165.
16. *L.P.* XXI:i, 136, 169.
17. Wriothesley, I, 181.
18. *Ven. Cal.* VI:i, lviii–lix.
19. Patrick Fraser Tytler, *England Under the Reigns of Edward VI and Mary*, 2 vols. (London, 1839), I, 30.

Chapter XXIII

1. *L.P.* XIII:ii, 373.
2. Ibid., XXI:i, 282.
3. Ibid., 400.
4. Hughes, II, 25–29.
5. *Sp. Cal.* IX, 495–96.
6. Ibid., 101.
7. Ibid., 123.

Chapter XXIV

1. *Sp. Cal.* IX, 405.
2. Baumer, p. 104.
3. Quoted in Whitney R. D. Jones, *The Tudor Commonwealth 1529–1559* (London, 1970), p. 53. The foregoing is based in part on Jones' analysis of the multiple crises of Edward's reign.
4. Tytler, I, 188.
5. *Sp. Cal.* IX, 101.
6. Ibid., 298.
7. Quoted in Hughes, II, 170.
8. *Sp. Cal.* IX, 405.
9. Ibid., 350–51.
10. Ibid., 333.
11. Ibid., 336.
12. Ibid., 360–61.
13. *Calendar of State Papers, Domestic Series,* 2 vols. (London, 1856), I, 20; *Sp. Cal.* IX, 405–8.
14. *Sp. Cal.* IX, 444–47.
15. Ibid.

Chapter XXV

1. Tytler, I, 174.
2. *Sp. Cal.* IX, 459.
3. Ibid., 469–70.
4. Ibid.
5. Ibid., 469–70, 489–90.
6. Ibid., X, 6–7.
7. Ibid., 6.
8. Ibid., 43.
9. Viscount Dillon, "Barriers and Foot Combats," *Archaeological Journal,* LXI (1904), 304.
10. *Sp. Cal.* X, 9.
11. Henry Clifford, *The Life of Jane Dormer, Duchess of Feria* (London, 1887), pp. 62–63.
12. *Sp. Cal.* X, 144–45.
13. Ibid., IX, 99.
14. Ibid., X, 40–41.
15. Ibid., 68–69.
16. Ibid., 80–81.

Chapter XXVI

1. *Sp. Cal.* X, 97, 106, 116, 117.
2. Ibid., 80–86.
3. Ibid., 94.
4. What follows is taken from Dubois' own account of the rescue attempt, written a few days after it happened, "in full and as nearly as possible in the actual words spoken." *Sp. Cal.* X, 124–35.
5. Ibid., 126–27.

Chapter XXVII

1. *Sp. Cal.* X, 144–45.
2. Ibid., 152–53 and note.
3. *Literary Remains of Edward VI*, ed. J. G. Nichols, 2 vols. (London, 1857), II, 279.
4. *Sp. Cal.* X, 153.
5. Ibid., 145.
6. Tytler, I, 347.
7. *Sp. Cal.* X, 151–52.
8. Ibid., 207–8.
9. Clifford, pp. 61–62.
10. *Sp. Cal.* X, 9.
11. Ibid., 249.
12. Chapman, p. 200.
13. *Sp. Cal.* X, 209–10.
14. Ibid., 212.
15. Ibid., 215.
16. Ibid., 212–13.
17. Ibid., 258–60.

Chapter XXVIII

1. *Sp. Cal.* X, 257.
2. Ibid., 285.
3. Quoted in Jones, *Tudor Commonwealth*, p. 150.
4. *Sp. Cal.* X, 256–57 note.
5. Ibid., 347.
6. Andrews, pp. 127ff. From John Caius' book on the sweat of 1551.
7. Ibid., 357.
8. Ibid., 314.
9. Ibid., 248, 383.
10. What follows is taken from Rich's account of the interview, quoted in Strickland, III, 414–17, and from *Sp. Cal.* X, 358–60.
11. *The Accession of Queen Mary: being the Contemporary Narrative of Antonio de Guaras, a Spanish Merchant Resident in London*, ed. Richard Garnett (London, 1892), pp. 100–1.
12. *Sp. Cal.* X, 223.
13. Ibid., 8–9.
14. Ibid., 223.
15. Ibid., 384–85.
16. *Calendar of State Papers, Domestic*, I, 48.
17. *Sp. Cal.* X, 377.
18. Ibid., 379.
19. Ibid., XI, 40. The best brief description of the altering of the succession in the last days of Edward's reign is S. T. Bindoff, "A Kingdom at Stake, 1553," *History Today* (September 1953), pp. 642–48.
20. *Sp. Cal.* XI, 35.

Chapter XXIX

1. *Sp. Cal.* XI, 69.

2. Who the messenger was is unknown. According to one account, it was Mary's goldsmith; according to another, it was Nicholas Throckmorton. It is an intriguing mystery, but the fact that Mary was forewarned of her danger several days before Edward's death and that she had already decided to go north makes the identity of this anonymous "friend" less important than Mary's biographers have thought.

3. *The Accession of Queen Mary*, p. 89.

4. *Sp. Cal.* XI, 80; *The Diary of Henry Machyn, Citizen and Merchant-Taylor of London, from* A.D. *1550 to* A.D. *1563*, ed. John Gough Nichols (London, 1848), p. 35.

5. Machyn, p. 36.

6. *Sp. Cal.* XI, 94.

7. *The Accession of Queen Mary*, p. 91.

8. Ibid., 92.

9. Accounts of the rejoicing at Mary's proclamation are in *Sp. Cal.* XI, 108, 115; *Chronicle of Queen Jane and of Two Years of Queen Mary*, ed. John Gough Nichols (London, 1850), p. 11; *The Accession of Queen Mary*, p. 95.

10. *Sp. Cal.* XI, 112.

11. Ibid., 113.

12. Ibid., 114.

13. This account of Mary's entry into London follows Wriothesley, II, 92–95.

14. *Sp. Cal.* XI, 120.

Chapter XXX

1. Perlin's account of England in Mary's time, "A Description of England and Scotland," is in *The Antiquarian Repertory*, 4 vols. (London, 1775–84).

2. Machyn, p. 336 note.

3. *Calendar of State Papers, Foreign Series, of the Reign of Edward VI*, ed. William B. Turnbull (London, 1861), p. 55.

4. Percy Ernst Schramm, *A History of the English Coronation*, trans. Leopold G. Wickman Legg (Oxford, 1937), p. 57.

5. *L.P.* IV:i:ii, 267.

6. Tytler, II, 127.

7. *Ven. Cal.* VI:i, xxix.

8. Ibid., VI:i, 25, 95.

9. *Sp. Cal.* XIII, 248.

10. *Ven. Cal.* V, 533.

11. *Sp. Cal.* XI, 166.

12. *Ven. Cal.* V, 532.

13. *Sp. Cal.* XI, 373.

14. Helen Simpson, *The Spanish Marriage* (Edinburgh, 1933), p. 99.

Chapter XXXI

1. *Sp. Cal.* XI, 119–20.
2. Ibid., 183–86; *Antiquarian Repertory*, I, 227.
3. *Sp. Cal.* XI, 187.
4. Tytler, II, 244.
5. *Ven. Cal.* V, 384–85.
6. *Sp. Cal.* XI, 131.
7. *Acts of the Privy Council of England*, New Series, ed. John Roche Dasent, 32 vols. (London, 1890–1918), IV, 318.
8. *Sp. Cal.* XI, 169–70.
9. Ibid., 131.
10. Ibid., 188.
11. Cited in Philip Hughes, II, 195 note.
12. *Narratives of the Days of the Reformation*, ed. John Gough Nichols (Westminster, 1859), pp. 315–18.
13. Chappell, pp. 54–55.
14. *Chronicle of Queen Jane and of Two Years of Queen Mary*, p. 16.
15. Machyn, pp. 41, 332 note; Wriothesley, II, 97ff.
16. *Sp. Cal.* XI, 188, 172.
17. Ibid., 189.
18. Ibid., 132.
19. Ibid., 189.
20. Ibid., 215.

Chapter XXXII

1. Clifford, pp. 48–49.
2. *Sp. Cal.* XI, 262.
3. *Chronicle of Queen Jane and of Two Years of Queen Mary*, p. 27.
4. Ibid., p. 30.
5. This account of Mary's royal entry is taken from J. R. Planché, *Regal Records* (London, 1838), pp. 3–11; Anglo, pp. 319–22; and *Chronicle of Queen Jane and of Two Years of Queen Mary*, pp. 27–30.
6. *Sp. Cal.* XI, 259–60.
7. Ibid., 220.
8. The design of Mary's crown is given from a rare French print in Planché, p. 78.
9. *Sp. Cal.* XI, 262.
10. *Calendar of State Papers, Foreign Series, of the Reign of Mary, 1553–1558*, ed. William B. Turnbull (London, 1861), p. 18.
11. *Sp. Cal.* XI, 114.
12. Ibid., 241–42.
13. Ibid., 228.
14. Ibid., 431, 322, 114.
15. Ibid., 294.
16. Ibid., 165.

Chapter XXXIII

1. Tytler, II, 136ff.
2. *Sp. Cal.* XI, 225.
3. Ibid., 222–23.
4. William H. Prescott, *History of the Reign of Philip the Second, King of Spain*, ed. John Foster Kirk, 3 vols. (Philadelphia, 1883), II, 54–57.
5. *Sp. Cal.* X, 5 and note.
6. Tytler, II, 245.
7. *Sp. Cal.* II, 131–32.
8. Ibid., 206.
9. Prescott, *Philip The Second*, pp. 1, 85; *Sp. Cal.* XI, 177–78.
10. *Sp. Cal.* XI, 381.
11. Ibid., 391.
12. Ibid., 296–97.
13. Ibid., 228.
14. Ibid., 328.

Chapter XXXIV

1. René Aubert de Vertot, *Ambassades de Messieurs de Noailles en Angleterre*, 5 vols. (Leyden, 1763), II, 342.
2. Tytler, II, 260.
3. Ibid., 263.
4. Vertot, II, 142–48.
5. *Calendar of State Papers, Foreign, Reign of Mary*, pp. 16, 30–31.
6. *Documents Relating to the Revels at Court in the Time of King Edward VI and Queen Mary*, ed. Albert Feuillerat (Louvain and London, 1914), p. 289; Jones, *Tudor Commonwealth*, pp. 21–22.
7. *Sp. Cal.* XI, 357.
8. Stone, p. 263 note; *Sp. Cal.* XI, 367.
9. *Calendar of State Papers, Foreign, Reign of Mary*, p. 41.
10. Ibid., 17.
11. Ibid., 48.
12. *Sp. Cal.* XI, 392.
13. John Strype, *Ecclesiastical Memorials*, 7 vols. (Oxford, 1816), IV, 87–88.
14. *Sp. Cal.* XI, 363–65.
15. Ibid., 372.
16. Ibid., 307.

Chapter XXXV

1. *Sp. Cal.* XI, 300.
2. Ibid., 322–23.
3. Ibid., 292.
4. Clifford, p. 80.
5. *Sp. Cal.* XI, 393.
6. Ibid., 253.

7. Ibid., 252–53.

8. E. Harris Harbison, "French Intrigues at the Court of Queen Mary," *American Historical Review*, XLV (April 1940), 537ff.

9. *Sp. Cal.* XI, 388.

10. Ibid., XII, 5.

11. Ibid., XI, 403–7.

12. Ibid., XII, 28.

13. Wriothesley, II, 105.

14. *Sp. Cal.* XII, 17.

15. Ibid., XI, 439.

16. Ibid., XII, 54, 56.

17. *An English Garner*, pp. 218–22.

18. *Chronicle of Queen Jane and of Two Years of Queen Mary*, p. 39.

19. *Sp. Cal.* XII, 69.

20. *Ven. Cal.* V, 460; *Sp. Cal.* XII, 70.

21. *The Acts and Monuments of John Foxe*, ed. George Townsend and S. R. Cattley, 8 vols. (London, 1837–41), VI, 414.

Chapter XXXVI

1. *Chronicle of Queen Jane and of Two Years of Queen Mary*, pp. 43, 48.

2. *Narratives of the Days of the Reformation*, pp. 133ff.

3. Ibid., 133.

4. *Chronicle of Queen Jane and of Two Years of Queen Mary*, p. 52.

5. Robert Fabyan, *The New Chronicles of England and France* (London, 1911), 714; *Sp. Cal.* XII, 85.

6. Machyn, pp. 55–57; E. Harris Harbison, *Rival Ambassadors at the Court of Queen Mary* (Princeton and London, 1940), p. 138 note; Martin A. S. Hume, "The Visit of Philip II," *EHR*, VII (April 1892), 273.

7. *Calendar of State Papers, Foreign, Reign of Mary*, pp. 57, 59–60.

8. Ibid., 57.

9. D. M. Loades, *Two Tudor Conspiracies* (Cambridge, 1965), p. 91.

10. Tytler, II, 330; Vertot, III, 130.

11. Tytler, II, 303–4.

12. Ibid., 39.

13. Ibid., 198ff., 233.

14. Ibid., 15.

15. Ibid., 277.

16. Ibid., 220, 258–59, 261.

17. Ibid., 242.

18. Ibid., 14.

Chapter XXXVII

1. *Sp. Cal.* XII, 185.

2. Hume, "The Visit of Philip II," p. 261.

3. Ibid., 262.

4. Ibid., 264–65.

5. *Calendar of State Papers, Foreign, Reign of Mary*, p. 91.

6. Accounts of Philip's journey to England and his first few days there are in Vertot, III, 284, "John Elder's Letter" in *Chronicle of Queen Jane and of Two Years of Queen Mary*, pp. 136–40, and *Sp. Cal.* XIII, 7–9.

7. Prescott, *Philip The Second*, I, 105.

8. *Sp. Cal.* XIII, 2, 31.

9. Hume, "The Visit of Philip II," pp. 269–70.

Chapter XXXVIII

1. Hume, "The Visit of Philip II," p. 272.

2. *Sp. Cal.* XII, 45.

3. Ibid., XIII, 442.

4. Hume, "The Visit of Philip II," p. 273.

5. *Narratives of the Days of the Reformation*, p. 170 and note.

6. *Sp. Cal.* XIII, 11. Accounts of Philip and Mary's wedding and the banquet that followed it are in *Chronicle of Queen Jane and of Two Years of Queen Mary*, Appendix 10, pp. 141–44, Appendix 11, pp. 167–72, and *Sp. Cal.* XIII, 10–11.

7. *Sp. Cal.* XIII, 26.

8. Ibid., 28, 26.

9. Ibid., 6.

10. Ibid., 26.

11. Ibid., 63, 45–46.

12. Ibid., 6.

13. Ibid., 2.

14. Ibid., 30–31.

15. Ibid., 4.

Chapter XXXIX

1. *Sp. Cal.* XIII, 49–50.

2. Ibid., 51.

3. Ibid., 52.

4. Ibid., 38, 47.

5. *Ven. Cal.* V, 108–9, 382.

6. *Chronicle of Queen Jane and of Two Years of Queen Mary*, p. 159.

Chapter XL

1. Luke 1:30.

2. *The Acts and Monuments of John Foxe*, VI, 582–84.

3. Ibid., 584.

4. *Sp. Cal.* XIII, 86.

5. Ibid., 78; *Narratives of the Days of the Reformation*, p. 289 and note.

6. *Documents Relating to the Revels*, p. 292.

7. *Sp. Cal.* XIII, 119, 105.

8. Harbison, *Rival Ambassadors*, pp. 197–98.

9. *Ven. Cal.* V, 594.

10. *Sp. Cal.* XIII, 81.
11. Harbison, *Rival Ambassadors*, pp. 211–12.
12. Tytler, II, 455–56.
13. Ibid., 458.
14. *Sp. Cal.* XIII, 94.
15. *Acts of the Privy Council*, New Series, IV, 403.
16. *Sp. Cal.* XI, 253.
17. Tytler, II, 377; *Sp. Cal.* XIII, 46.
18. Wriothesley, II, 113.
19. Fabyan, p. 715.
20. *Sp. Cal.* XIII, 23.
21. Wriothesley, II, 117; Machyn, p. 65.
22. Tytler, II, 340–41; Wriothesley, II, 117–18.
23. *Calendar of State Papers, Foreign, Reign of Mary*, p. 105.
24. *The Acts and Monuments of John Foxe*, VI, 647–48, 658–59.

Chapter XLI

1. James Arthur Muller, *Stephen Gardiner and the Tudor Reaction* (New York, 1926), p. 268; Tytler, II, 366; *Sp. Cal.* XII, 200.
2. *Sp. Cal.* XIII, 64; Rex H. Pogson, "Reginald Pole and the Priorities of Government in Mary Tudor's Church," *The Historical Journal*, XVIII (March 1975), 10 and note.
3. D. M. Loades, "The Enforcement of Reaction, 1553–1558," *The Journal of Ecclesiastical Studies*, XVI (April 1965), 58 note.
4. *Sp. Cal.* XIII, 95.
5. *Ven. Cal.* VI:iii, Appendix, 1647.
6. *Bishop Burnet's History of the Reformation of the Church of England*, 6 vols. (London, 1820), IV, 354–55.
7. Loades, *Two Tudor Conspiracies*, p. 145 note.
8. *Sp. Cal.* XIII, 147.
9. *Documents Relating to the Revels*, pp. 166ff.
10. *Calendar of State Papers, Domestic*, I, 64; Wriothesley, II, 125.
11. Machyn, p. 78.
12. Ibid., p. 84.
13. *Ven. Cal.* VI:i, 32.
14. *Sp. Cal.* XIII, 166.
15. *Ven. Cal.* VI:i, 37.
16. Ibid., 50–51; Wriothesley, II, 127.
17. *Ven. Cal.* VI:i, 45.
18. Ibid., 57.
19. Ibid., 58.
20. Ibid., 60–61; Machyn, p. 86; Tytler, II, 470; *Calendar of State Papers, Foreign, Reign of Mary*, p. 165.

Chapter XLII

1. *The Acts and Monuments of John Foxe*, VII, 126.
2. *Ven. Cal.* VI:i, 76–77.
3. *Calendar of State Papers, Foreign, Reign of Mary*, p. 87.

4. Vertot, IV, 341–44.
5. Ibid., 225–27.
6. *Sp. Cal.* XIII, 102.
7. *Ven. Cal.* VI:ii, 1,060.
8. Ibid.
9. Chamberlin, p. 27.
10. *Ven. Cal.* VI:i, 72.
11. Vertot, IV, 341–43.
12. *Ven. Cal.* VI:i, 77.
13. *Sp. Cal.* XIII, 175.
14. *Ven. Cal.* VI:i, 77.
15. Ibid., 85; Machyn, p. 87; Wriothesley, II, 129.
16. Wriothesley, II, 128; *Ven. Cal.* VI:i, 85.
17. *Ven. Cal.* VI:i, 79.
18. Ibid., 80, 87.
19. Ibid., 148.
20. Ibid., 100.
21. Ibid., 84.
22. *Sp. Cal.* XIII, 207; *Ven. Cal.* VI:i, 112.
23. *Sp. Cal.* XIII, 222.
24. *Ven. Cal.* VI:i, 106.
25. Ibid., 93.
26. Ibid., 107, 99.
27. *Calendar of State Papers, Foreign, Reign of Mary*, pp. 383, 390; *Ven. Cal.* VI:i, 162.
28. *Ven. Cal.* VI:i, 83.
29. *Calendar of State Papers, Foreign, Reign of Mary*, pp. 173–74.
30. Ibid., pp. 172–73.
31. *Ven. Cal.* VI:i, 126.
32. Ibid., 126–27.
33. *Acts of the Privy Council*, New Series, V, 120.
34. *Ven. Cal.* VI:i, 144.
35. S. R. Maitland, *The Reformation in England* (London and New York, 1906), p. 113; Burnet, V, 357.
36. *Ven. Cal.* VI:i, 120.
37. Stone, p. 351, citing Sloane MS 1,583, f. 15.

Chapter XLIII

1. *Ven. Cal.* VI:i, 147–48.
2. Ibid., 229.
3. Stone, pp. 350–51, citing Sloane MS 1,583, f. 15.
4. *Ven. Cal.* VI:i, 180–81.
5. Ibid., 146, 162.
6. Ibid., 141.
7. *Sp. Cal.* XIII, 248.
8. *Ven. Cal.* VI:i, 174.
9. Ibid., 178–79.
10. Ibid., 173.
11. Ibid., 178.

12. Ibid., 177–80.
13. Ibid., 183, 186.
14. *Sp. Cal.* XIII, 238–39.
15. *Calendar of State Papers, Domestic,* I, 69; *Ven. Cal.* VI:i, 174.
16. *Ven. Cal.* VI:i, 239; H. F. M. Prescott, *A Spanish Tudor: The Life of "Bloody Mary."* (New York and London, 1940), p. 458.
17. *Ven. Cal.* VI:i, 190, 205.
18. Ibid., 213.
19. Ibid., 218, 197.
20. Ibid., 218, 215.
21. Ibid., 199, 214.
22. Ibid., 245.
23. Maitland, p. 55.
24. *Ven. Cal.* VI:i, 212.

Chapter XLIV

1. *Ven. Cal.* VI:i, 270.
2. Ibid., 303.
3. Ibid., 278.
4. Ibid., 281.
5. Ibid., 285.
6. Ibid., 294–97.
7. Ibid., 251.
8. Ibid., 356–57, 259.
9. Ibid., 411–12; Vertot, V, 342–43.
10. Wriothesley, II, 133; Machyn, p. 101.
11. Charles Read Baskervill, *The Elizabethan Jig* (Chicago, 1929), p. 44; *Calendar of State Papers, Domestic,* I, 82; Edmund Lodge, *Illustrations of British History,* 3 vols. (London, 1791), I, 212–13.
12. Shaaber, p. 202.
13. *Calendar of State Papers, Foreign, Reign of Mary,* p. 285.
14. Ibid., 222.
15. *Ven. Cal.* VI:i, 440.
16. Ibid., 377–78.
17. Madden, pp. 207–8.
18. *Ven. Cal.* VI:i, 398.
19. Ibid., 319.
20. *Calendar of State Papers, Foreign, Reign of Mary,* pp. 205–6.
21. Ibid., pp. 206–7.
22. *Ven. Cal.* VI:i, 374.
23. Ibid., 392.
24. Ibid., 410.

Chapter XLV

1. Stone, p. 356 note.
2. Clifford, p. 66.
3. Ibid., pp. 63–64.

4. Ibid., pp. 64–65.
5. *Calendar of State Papers, Foreign, Reign of Mary*, p. 251.
6. *Ven. Cal.* VI:i, 434–37.
7. Prescott, *A Spanish Tudor*, p. 393. The biblical origin of this view that wives ought to see in their husbands an image of Christ is St. Paul's admonition that husbands ought to love their wives as Christ loved his church.
8. *Sp. Cal.* XIII, 260.
9. *Ven. Cal.* VI:i, 376.
10. Ibid., 399.
11. Ibid., 444.
12. Ibid., 402.
13. Tytler, II, 483–86.
14. *Ven. Cal.* VI:i, 507 note.
15. Ibid., 371.
16. Prescott, *Philip The Second*, pp. 137–38.
17. *Ven. Cal.* VI:i, 495, 510.
18. *Calendar of State Papers, Domestic*, I, 77–78.
19. *Ven. Cal.* VI:i, 495.
20. *Sp. Cal.* XIII, 271.
21. *Ven. Cal.* VI:i, 558.
22. Ibid., 571.
23. Ibid.
24. Ibid., 578–79.

Chapter XLVI

1. *The Acts and Monuments of John Foxe*, VI, 611, 628.
2. *Ven. Cal.* VI:i, 386.
3. Shaaber, p. 49.
4. Hughes, II, 299–300 and notes; *Narratives of the Days of the Reformation*, p. 295.
5. Ibid., 269–70.
6. These statistics are taken from the careful research of Hughes, II, 259 and note, who took them from Foxe. Of course, Foxe gave few particulars about most of the Marian victims whose deaths he recorded, and his purpose in writing was to discredit Mary and her policies. His vast compilation, while it illuminates the history of Mary's reign, nevertheless obscures much. In the words of one modern commentator, Foxe's volumes "lie like a mountain range between ourselves and the facts of the Marian persecution."
7. Hughes, II, 275.
8. Ibid., 300.
9. *Ven. Cal.* VI:i, 363.
10. Machyn, pp. 101, 403.
11. *Ven. Cal.* VI:i, 409.
12. *Sp. Cal.* XIII, 276.
13. *Acts of the Privy Council*, New Series, V, 265.
14. *Calendar of State Papers, Foreign, Reign of Mary*, p. 231; *Ven. Cal.* VI:i, 620.
15. *Ven. Cal.* VI:ii, 1,061–63.
16. Ibid., 806.
17. Ibid., 748.

18. Ibid., 778.
19. *Calendar of State Papers, Foreign, Reign of Mary*, p. 278.
20. *Ven. Cal.* VI:ii, 868, 678–79.
21. Machyn, p. 124.

Chapter XLVII

1. *Sp. Cal.* XIII, xix.
2. Ibid.; *Ven. Cal.* VI:ii, 968.
3. *Ven. Cal.* VI:ii, 1,053–59.
4. Ibid., 1,008.
5. Ibid., 1,154.
6. Quoted in Harbison, *Rival Ambassadors*, p. 319.
7. Ibid., pp. 322ff.
8. *Ven. Cal.* VI:ii, 1,095, 1,208.

Chapter XLVIII

1. *Acts of the Privy Council*, New Series, VI, 91.
2. *Sp. Cal.* XIII, 330.
3. *Acts of the Privy Council*, New Series, VI, 235 and passim.
4. *Ven. Cal.* VI:iii, 1,445.
5. *Calendar of State Papers, Foreign, Reign of Mary*, p. 373; *Ven. Cal.* VI:iii, 1,446.
6. *Sp. Cal.* XIII, 340–41.
7. Ibid., 367.
8. Ibid., 366.
9. *Calendar of State Papers, Foreign, Reign of Mary*, p. 157.
10. *Sp. Cal.* XIII, 376–77.
11. Hughes, II, 236–39.
12. Rex H. Pogson, "Revival and Reform in Mary Tudor's Church: a Question of Money," *The Journal of Ecclesiastical History*, XXV (July 1974), 249–65 passim.
13. *Ven. Cal.* VI:iii, 1,482.

Chapter XLIX

1. John Knox, *The First Blast of the Trumpet against the Monstrous Regiment of Women*, ed. Edward Arber (London, 1878), pp. 11–12.
2. Madden, p. cxlv note.
3. *Sp. Cal.* XIII, 392–93.
4. Ibid., 392.
5. *Acts of the Privy Council*, New Series, VI, 122.
6. *Calendar of State Papers, Domestic*, I, 110.
7. Clifford, pp. 68–69.
8. *Ven. Cal.* VI:iii, 1,544.
9. *Sp. Cal.* XIII, 398.
10. Ibid., 399, 400.

11. *Ven. Cal.* VI:iii, 1,538.
12. Ibid., 1,549.
13. Strype, III, ii, 550.
14. Clifford, pp. 71–72.
15. *Ven. Cal.* VI:iii, 1,551, 1,556.
16. Machyn, p. 178.
17. *Sp. Cal.* XIII, 440.
18. *Old English Ballads*, ed. Hyder E. Rollins (Cambridge, 1920), pp. 23–24.

Select Bibliography

PRIMARY SOURCES

Acts of the Privy Council of England. New series, ed. John Roche Dasent. 32 vols. London: Her Majesty's Stationery Office, 1890–1918.

Awdeley, John. *The Fraternitye of Vacabondes,* ed. Edward Viles and F. J. Furnivall. London: EETS, 1869.

The Babees' Book: Medieval Manners for the Young. Done into Modern English from Dr. Furnivall's Texts by Edith Rickert. New York and London: Duffield and Co., Chatto and Windus, 1908.

Brown, Rawdon, ed. and trans. *Four Years at the Court of Henry VIII.* 2 vols. London: Smith, Elder & Co., 1854.

Calendar of Letters, Despatches, and State Papers, relating to the Negotiations between England and Spain, preserved in the Archives at Vienna, Simancas, Besançon and Brussels, ed. Pascual de Gayangos, G. A. Bergenroth, M. A. S. Hume, Royall Tyler, and Garrett Mattingly. 13 vols. London: His, and Her Majesty's Stationery Office, 1867–1954.

Calendar of State Papers, Domestic Series, of the Reigns of Edward VI, Mary, Elizabeth, 1547–1580, preserved in the State Paper Department of Her Majesty's Public Record Office, ed. Robert Lemon. 2 vols. London: Longman, Brown, Green, Longman and Roberts, 1856.

Calendar of State Papers, Foreign Series, of the Reign of Edward VI, 1547–1553, preserved in the State Paper Department of Her Majesty's Public Record Office, ed. William B. Turnbull. London: Longman, Green, Longman and Roberts, 1861.

Calendar of State Papers, Foreign Series, of the Reign of Mary, 1553–1558, preserved in the State Paper Department of Her Majesty's Public Record Office, ed. William B. Turnbull. London: Longman, Green, Longman and Roberts, 1861.

Calendar of State Papers and Manuscripts, Relating to English Affairs, Existing in the Archives and Collections of Venice, and in Other Libraries of Northern Italy, ed. Rawdon Brown and Allen B. Hinds. 38 vols. London: Longman and Co., 1864–1947.

Chronicle of the Grey Friars of London, ed. John Gough Nichols. London: Camden Society, 1852.

Chronicle of King Henry VIII of England, trans. and introduced by Martin A. S. Hume. London: George Bell and Sons, 1889.

Chronicle of Queen Jane and of Two Years of Queen Mary, and Especially of the Rebellion of Sir Thomas Wyatt, ed. John Gough Nichols. London: Camden Society, 1850.

Clifford, Henry. *The Life of Jane Dormer, Duchess of Feria*, transcribed by Canon E. E. Estcourt and ed. Rev. Joseph Stevenson. London: Burns and Oates, 1887.

The Diary of Henry Machyn, Citizen and Merchant-Taylor of London, from A.D. 1550 to A.D. 1563, ed. John Gough Nichols. London: Camden Society, 1848.

Documents Relating to the Revels at Court in the Time of King Edward VI and Queen Mary, ed. Albert Feuillerat. *Materialien zur Kunde des älteren Englischen Dramas*, Louvain and London, 1914.

The Elizabethan Home Discovered in Two Dialogues by Claudius Hollyband and Peter Erondell, ed. M. St. Clare Byrne. London: Frederick Etchells and Hugh Macdonald, 1925.

An English Garner: Tudor Tracts, 1532–1588, intro. by A. F. Pollard. Westminster: Archibald Constable, 1903.

Evans, Thomas. *Old Ballads, Historical and Narrative, With Some of Modern Date*, ed. R. H. Evans. 4 vols. London: W. Bulmer & Co., 1810.

Fabyan, Robert. *The New Chronicles of England and France, in two parts; named by himself the Concordance of History*. London: Rivington, 1911.

Foxe, John. *The Acts and Monuments of John Foxe*, ed. George Townsend and S. R. Cattley. 8 vols. London, 1837–41.

Guaras, Antonio de. *The Accession of Queen Mary: being the Contemporary Narrative of Antonio de Guaras, a Spanish Merchant Resident in London*, ed. with an intro., trans., notes and an appendix by Richard Garnett. London: Lawrence and Bullen, 1892.

Hall, Edward. *Chronicle; containing the History of England, during the Reign of Henry the Fourth, and the Succeeding Monarchs . . . in Which are Particularly described the Manners and Customs of those Periods*. London: J. Johnson, 1809.

Harington, John. *Nugae Antiquae: being a Miscellaneous Collection of Original Papers in Prose and Verse, written in the Reigns of Henry VIII, Queen Mary, Elizabeth, King James*, etc., ed. Rev. Henry Harington. 3 vols. London: J. Dodsley, 1779.

Holinshed, Raphael. *Holinshed's Chronicles of England, Scotland and Ireland*. 6 vols. London: J. Johnson, 1807.

Inventories of the Wardrobes, Plate, Chapel Stuff, etc., of Henry Fitzroy, Duke of Richmond, and of the Wardrobe Stuff at Baynard's Castle of Katherine, Princess Dowager, ed. John Gough Nichols. London: Camden Society, 1854.

Knox, John. *The First Blast of the Trumpet against the Monstrous Regiment of Women*, ed. Edward Arber. London: The English Scholars Library of Old and Modern Works, 1878.

Letters and Papers, Foreign and Domestic, of the Reign of Henry VIII, ed. J. S. Brewer, R. H. Brodie and James Gairdner. 21 vols. London: Her Majesty's Stationery Office, 1862–1910.

The Loseley Manuscripts, ed. Alfred John Kempe. London: John Murray, 1836.

Madden, Frederick. *Privy Purse Expenses of the Princess Mary, daughter of King Henry the Eighth, afterwards Queen Mary: with a Memoir of the Princess, and Notes*. London: William Pickering, 1831.

Malfatti, C. V. *Two Italian Accounts of Tudor England*. Barcelona: C. V. Malfatti, 1953.

Narratives of the Days of the Reformation, chiefly from the manuscripts of John Foxe the Martyrologist, ed. John Gough Nichols. Westminster: Camden Society, 1859.

The Northumberland Household Book, in *The Antiquarian Repertory: a Miscellany, intended to Preserve and Illustrate Several Valuable Remains of Old Times*. 4 vols. London: Francis Blyth, 1775–84.

Old English Ballads 1553–1625, ed. Hyder E. Rollins. Cambridge: Cambridge University Press, 1920.

Original Letters, Illustrative of English History; including Numerous Royal Letters. From Autographs in the British Museum. Notes and Illustrations by Henry Ellis. First series, 3 vols., second series, 4 vols., third series, 4 vols. London: Harding, Triphook and Lepard, 1825, 1827, 1846.

Papiers d'État du Cardinal de Granvelle, in *Collection de Documents Inédits sur l'Histoire de France*, première série: Histoire Politique. 9 vols. Paris: Imprimerie Royale, 1841–52.

Perlin, Stephen. "A Description of England and Scotland," in *The Antiquarian Repertory: a Miscellany, intended to Preserve and Illustrate Several Valuable Remains of Old Times*. 4 vols. London: Francis Blyth, 1775–84.

The Reign of Henry VII from Contemporary Sources, ed. A. F. Pollard. 3 vols. London: Longmans, Green and Co., 1913–14.

A Relation, or rather a True Account, of the Island of England; with sundry particulars of the customs of these people, and of the royal revenues under King Henry the Seventh, about the year 1500, trans. Charlotte Augusta Sneyd. London: Camden Society, 1847.

Rhodes, Hugh. *The boke of Nurture for men, servantes and children . . . very utyle and necessary unto all youth*. London: Thomas Petyt, 1545.

Rye, William Brenchley. *England as Seen by Foreigners in the Days of Elizabeth and James the First*. London: John Russell Smith, 1865.

Salter, Emma Gurney. *Tudor England through Venetian Eyes*. London: Williams and Norgate, 1930.

Scott, Sir Sibbald David. "'A Booke of Orders and Rules' of Anthony Viscount Montague in 1595." *Sussex Archaeological Collections, Relating to the History and Antiquities of the County*, VII (1854), 173–212.

Strype, John. *Ecclesiastical Memorials*. 3 vols. Oxford, 1820–40.

"Two Papers Relating to the Interview between Henry the Eighth of England, and Francis the First of France: Communicated by John Caley in a Letter to Henry Ellis." *Archaeologia: or Miscellaneous Tracts Relating to Antiquity*, XXI (1827), 175–91.

Vermigli, Pietro Martire (Peter Martyr). *The Common Places . . . of Peter Martyr, divided into foure principall parts*, trans. Anthonie Marten. London: Henrie Denham, 1583.

Vertot, René Aubert de. *Ambassades de Messieurs de Noailles en Angleterre*. 5 vols. Leyden, 1763.

Wriothesley, Charles. *A Chronicle of England, during the Reigns of the Tudors, from* A.D. *1485 to 1559,* ed. William Douglas Hamilton. 2 vols. London: Camden Society, New Series, 11, 1875–77.

SECONDARY SOURCES

Anglo, Sydney. *Spectacle Pageantry and Early Tudor Policy.* Oxford: The Clarendon Press, 1969.

The Antiquarian Repertory: a Miscellany, intended to Preserve and Illustrate Several Valuable Remains of Old Times. 4 vols. London: Francis Blyth, 1775–84.

Aydelotte, Frank. *Elizabethan Rogues and Vagabonds.* New York: Barnes and Noble, 1967.

Barker, Sir Ernest. *Traditions of Civility.* Cambridge: Cambridge University Press, 1948.

Baumer, Franklin Le Van. *The Early Tudor Theory of Kingship.* New Haven: Yale University Press and London: Oxford University Press, 1940.

Bayne, Diane Valerie. "The Instruction of a Christian Woman: Richard Hyrde and the Thomas More Circle." *Moreana,* XLV (February 1975), 5–15.

Behrens, Betty. "A Note on Henry VIII's Divorce Project of 1514." *Bulletin of the Institute of Historical Research,* XI, No. 33 (February 1934), 163–64.

Bindoff, S. T. "A Kingdom at Stake, 1553." *History Today,* September 1953, pp. 642–48.

Brand, John. *Observations of Popular Antiquities: Chiefly Illustrating the Origin of Our Vulgar Customs, Ceremonies, and Superstitions,* arr. and rev. Henry Ellis. 3 vols. London: F. C. and J. Rivington, 1813.

Brewer, J. S. *The Reign of Henry VIII: from his Accession to the Death of Wolsey,* ed. James Gairdner. 2 vols. London: John Murray, 1884.

Burnet, Gilbert. *Bishop Burnet's History of the Reformation of the Church of England.* 6 vols. London: Richard Priestley, 1820.

Byrne, Muriel St. Clare. *Elizabethan Life in Town and Country.* Rev. ed. London: Cox and Wyman, 1961.

Chamberlin, Frederick. *The Private Character of Henry the Eighth.* New York: Ives Washburn, 1931.

Chapman, Hester. *The Last Tudor King. A Study of Edward VI.* London: Jonathan Cape, 1958.

Childe-Pemberton, William S. *Elizabeth Blount and Henry the Eighth.* London: Eveleigh Nash, 1913.

Dickens, A. G. *The English Reformation.* London: B. T. Batsford, 1964.

Dillon, Viscount. "Barriers and Foot Combats." *Archaeological Journal,* LXI (1904), 276–308.

——. "Tilting in Tudor Times." *Archaeological Journal,* LV (1898), 296–339.

Doernberg, Erwin. *Henry VIII and Luther, an Account of their Personal Relations.* Stanford, California: Stanford University Press, 1967.

Elton, Geoffrey Rudolph. *England Under the Tudors.* London: Methuen, 1955.

——. *Policy and Police.* Cambridge: Cambridge University Press, 1972.

————. *The Tudor Revolution in Government: Administrative Changes in the Reign of Henry VIII*. Cambridge: Cambridge University Press, 1962.

Forneron, Henri. *Histoire de Philippe II*. 4 vols. Paris: Plon, 1881–82.

Friedmann, Paul. *Anne Boleyn: A Chapter of English History 1527–1536*. 2 vols. London: Macmillan, 1884.

Froude, J. A. *The Divorce of Catherine of Aragon*. New York: Charles Scribner's Sons, 1891.

Garrett, Christina Hallowell. *The Marian Exiles: A Study in the Origins of Elizabethan Puritanism*. Cambridge: Cambridge University Press, 1938.

Gould, J. D. *The Great Debasement: Currency and Economy in Mid-Tudor England*. Oxford: The Clarendon Press, 1970.

Haller, William. *The Elect Nation: the Meaning and Relevance of Foxe's Book of Martyrs*. New York and Evanston: Harper and Row, 1963.

Harbison, E. Harris. "French Intrigues at the Court of Queen Mary." *American Historical Review*, XLV, no. 3 (April 1940), 533–51.

————. *Rival Ambassadors at the Court of Queen Mary*. Princeton: Princeton University Press and London: Oxford University Press, 1940.

Harriss, G. L., and Penry Williams. "A Revolution in Tudor History?" *Past and Present*, XXV (July 1963), 3–58.

Hinds, Allen B. *The Making of the England of Elizabeth*. London: Rivington, Percival and Co., 1895.

Hughes, Philip. *The Reformation in England*. 3 vols. New York: Macmillan, 1951–54.

Hume, Martin A. S. "The Coming of Philip the Prudent," in *The Year After the Armada and Other Historical Studies*. London: T. Fisher Unwin, 1896.

————. "The Visit of Philip II." *English Historical Review*, VII, No. 26 (April 1892), 253–80.

Hurstfield, Joel, ed. *The Reformation Crisis*. London: Edward Arnold, 1965.

Jones, Paul Van Brunt. *The Household of a Tudor Nobleman*. Cedar Rapids, Iowa: The Torch Press, 1918.

Jones, Whitney R. D. *The Mid-Tudor Crisis 1539–1563*. London: Macmillan, 1973.

————. *The Tudor Commonwealth 1529–1559*. London: Athlone Press, 1970.

Levine, Mortimer. *Tudor England 1485–1603*. Cambridge: Cambridge University Press, 1968.

Loades, D. M. "The Enforcement of Reaction, 1553–1558." *The Journal of Ecclesiastical Studies*, XVI, No. 1 (April 1965), 54–66.

————. *Two Tudor Conspiracies*. Cambridge: Cambridge University Press, 1965.

Lodge, Edmund. *Illustrations of British History*. 3 vols. London: G. Nicol, 1791.

MacGregor, Geddes. *The Thundering Scot: A Portrait of John Knox*. London: Macmillan, 1958.

MacNalty, Sir Arthur S. *Henry VIII: a difficult patient*. London: Christopher Johnson, 1952.

Mackie, J. D. *The Earlier Tudors 1485–1558*. Oxford: The Clarendon Press, 1952.

Maitland, S. R. *The Reformation in England*. London and New York: John Lane, 1906.

Maltby, William S. *The Black Legend in England: the Development of anti-Spanish Sentiment, 1558–1660*. Durham, North Carolina: Duke University Press, 1971.

Marmion, John P. "Cardinal Pole in Recent Studies." *Recusant History*, XIII, No. 1 (April 1975), 56–61.

Mattingly, Garrett. *Catherine of Aragon*. Boston: Little, Brown, 1941.

Moreau, E. de. *Crise religieuse du XVIeme siècle. Histoire de l'Église*, XVI. Paris: Bloud et Gay, 1950.

Morrison, N. Brysson. *The Private Life of Henry VIII*. London: Robert Hale, 1964.

Mozley, J. F. *John Foxe and his Book*. London: Society for Promoting Christian Knowledge and New York: Macmillan, 1940.

Muller, James Arthur. *Stephen Gardiner and the Tudor Reaction*. New York: Macmillan, 1926.

Mumby, Frank Arthur. *The Youth of Henry VIII: a Narrative in Contemporary Letters*. London: Constable, 1913.

New Lights Thrown Upon the History of Mary Queen of England, Eldest Daughter of Henry VIII. Addressed to David Hume, esq., translated from the French. London: J. Wilkie, 1771.

Nichols, J. G. "Life of the Last Fitz-Alan, Earl of Arundel." *The Gentleman's Magazine*, 103:2 (1833), 10–18, 118–24, 209–15.

Oxley, James E. *The Reformation in Essex: to the Death of Mary*. Manchester: Manchester University Press, 1965.

Paul, John E. *Catherine of Aragon and Her Friends*. London: Burns and Oates, 1966.

Pinto, Lucille B. "The Folk Practice of Gynecology and Obstetrics in the Middle Ages." *Bulletin of the History of Medicine*, XLVII, No. 5 (September, October 1973), 513–23.

Planché, J. R. *Regal Records: or, A Chronicle of the Coronations of the Queens Regnant of England*. London: Chapman and Hall, 1838.

Pogson, Rex H. "Reginald Pole and the Priorities of Government in Mary Tudor's Church." *The Historical Journal*, XVIII, No. 1 (March 1975), 3–20.

———. "Revival and Reform in Mary Tudor's Church: a Question of Money." *The Journal of Ecclesiastical History*, XXV, No. 3 (July 1974), 249–65.

Pollard, A. F. *Henry VIII*. London: Longmans, Green and Co., 1905, new edition, 1951.

Powell, Chilton Latham. *English Domestic Relations, 1487–1653*. New York: Columbia University Press, 1917.

Prescott, H. F. M. *A Spanish Tudor: The Life of "Bloody Mary."* New York: Columbia University Press and London: Constable, 1940.

Prescott, William H. *History of the Reign of Philip the Second, King of Spain*, ed. John Foster Kirk. 3 vols. Philadelphia: Lippincott, 1883.

Ridley, Jaspar. *The Life and Times of Mary Tudor*. London: Weidenfeld and Nicolson, 1973.

Rogers, Katherine M. *The Troublesome Helpmate: a History of Misogyny in Literature*. Seattle and London: University of Washington Press, 1966.

Scarisbrick, J. J. *Henry VIII*. Berkeley and Los Angeles: University of California Press, 1968.

Schramm, Percy Ernst. *A History of the English Coronation*, trans. Leopold G. Wickman Legg. Oxford: The Clarendon Press, 1937.

Shaaber, Matthias A. *Some Forerunners of the Newspaper in England, 1472–1622*. Philadelphia: University of Pennsylvania Press, 1929.

Shaw, Henry. *Dresses and Decorations of the Middle Ages.* 2 vols. London: Bohn, 1858.

Simpson, Helen. *The Spanish Marriage.* Edinburgh: Peter Davies, 1933.

Smith, H. Maynard. *Pre-Reformation England.* London: Macmillan, 1938.

Stone, J. M. *The History of Mary I Queen of England.* London: Sands, 1901.

Strickland, Agnes. *Lives of the Queens of England.* 8 vols. London: Henry Colburn, 1851.

Temperley, Gladys. *Henry VII.* Boston and New York: Houghton Mifflin, and Cambridge: The Riverside Press, 1914.

Tytler, Patrick Fraser. *England Under the Reigns of Edward VI and Mary, with the Contemporary History of Europe, Illustrated in a Series of Original Letters Never Before Printed.* 2 vols. London: Richard Bentley, 1839.

Veith, Ilza. *Hysteria: the History of a Disease.* Chicago and London: University of Chicago Press, 1965.

Vives and the Renascence Education of Women, ed. Foster Watson. New York: Longmans, Green and London: Edward Arnold, 1912.

Waldman, Milton. *The Lady Mary: a biography of Mary Tudor, 1516–1558.* New York: Scribner's, 1972.

Wernham, Richard Bruce. *Before the Armada: the Growth of English Foreign Policy, 1485–1588.* London: Cape, 1966.

White, Beatrice. *Mary Tudor.* New York: Macmillan, 1935.

White, Helen C. *Social Criticism in Popular Religious Literature of the Sixteenth Century.* New York: Macmillan, 1944.

Wiesener, Louis. *La Jeunesse d'Elisabeth d'Angleterre 1533–1558.* Paris: Librairie Hachette, 1878.

Woodward, George William Otway. *The Dissolution of the Monasteries.* London: Blandford Press, 1966.

Index